Robin Hood
and
Other Outlaw Tales

Middle English Texts

General Editor

Russell A. Peck
University of Rochester

Associate Editor

Alan Lupack
University of Rochester

Advisory Board

Rita Copeland
University of Minnesota

Thomas G. Hahn
University of Rochester

Lisa Kiser
Ohio State University

Thomas Seiler
Western Michigan University

R. A. Shoaf
University of Florida

Bonnie Wheeler
Southern Methodist University

The Middle English Texts Series is designed for classroom use. Its goal is to make available to teachers and students texts which occupy an important place in the literary and cultural canon but which have not been readily available in student editions. The series does not include those authors such as Chaucer, Langland, the Pearl-poet, or Malory, whose English works are normally in print in good student editions. The focus is, instead, upon Middle English literature adjacent to those authors that teachers need in compiling the syllabuses they wish to teach. The editions maintain the linguistic integrity of the original work but within the parameters of modern reading conventions. The texts are printed in the modern alphabet and follow the practices of modern capitalization and punctuation. Manuscript abbreviations are expanded, and u/v and j/i spellings are regularized according to modern orthography. Hard words, difficult phrases, and unusual idioms are glossed on the page, either in the right margin or at the foot of the page. Textual and explanatory notes appear at the end of the text. The editions include short introductions on the history of the work, its merits and points of topical interest, and also include briefly annotated bibliographies.

Robin Hood
and
Other Outlaw Tales

Edited by
Stephen Knight and Thomas Ohlgren

with contributions by
Thomas E. Kelly
Russell A. Peck
Michael Swanton
Paul Whitfield White

Published for TEAMS
(The Consortium for the Teaching of the Middle Ages)
in Association with the University of Rochester

by

Medieval Institute Publications

WESTERN MICHIGAN UNIVERSITY

Kalamazoo, Michigan — 2000

Library of Congress Cataloging-in-Publication Data

Robin Hood and other outlaw tales / edited by Stephen Knight and Thomas Ohlgren ;
with contributions by Thomas E. Kelly ... [et al.].
     p. cm.
   "Published for TEAMS (the Consortium for the Teaching of the Middle Ages) in
Association with the University of Rochester."
   Includes bibliographical references.
   ISBN 1-58044-067-3 (pbk. : alk. paper)
     1. Robin Hood (Legendary character)--Literary collections. 2. English literature--
Middle English, 1100-1500. 3. Outlaws--England--Literary collections. 4. Middle
Ages--Literary collections. 5. English drama--To 1500. 6. Ballads, English. I.
Knight, Stephen. II. Ohlgren, Thomas H., 1941- III. Kelly, Thomas E. IV.
Consortium for the Teaching of the Middle Ages.

PR2125 .R63 2000
820.8'035106927--dc21

                                                                                    00-040115

Contents

Illustrations

The illustrations are taken mainly from Joseph Ritson, *Robin Hood: A Collection of all the Ancient Poems, Songs, and Ballads, now extant relative to that Celebrated English Outlaw.* 2 volumes (London: William Pickering, 1832; first published 1795), with wood engravings by Thomas and John Bewick; and John Mathew Gutch, *A Lytell Gest of Robin Hode with other Ancient & Modern Ballads and Songs Relating to this Celebrated Yeoman*, adorned with cuts by F. W. Fairholt. 2 volumes (London: Longman, Brown, Green, & Longmans, 1847). Volume I of Gutch includes at the end a second version of *The Lytell Geste* to which are added wood engravings by Bastin. Bastin mainly creates forest scenes beneath great oak trees.

Illustrations

Illustrations

Illustrations

Illustrations

Illustrations

Preface

"Many men speak of Robin Hood who never drew his bow": so runs the old proverb, suggesting both the popularity and the mystery of the Robin Hood tradition. A modern equivalent might be: "Many people know about Robin Hood but have never read the texts." This edition sets out to correct that situation by offering a full selection of the early Robin Hood materials and related texts, with glosses and notes so they can be read with ease and introductions that make clear the contexts and the interconnections of such a remarkable and remarkably little known body of material.

This volume offers a complete set of the early material on Robin Hood found in the chronicles, ballads, and popular plays from before 1600, a full text of Anthony Munday's *The Downfall of Robert, Earle of Huntington* (1598–99) and a selection from his *The Death of Robert, Earle of Huntington* (1598–99) as well as complete versions of the lengthy *A Gest of Robyn Hode* and its important analogues *Adam Bell* and *Gamelyn*. These texts can be understood in the light of major early versions of the outlaw tradition from contiguous cultures: Hereward, a genuine Anglo-Saxon freedom fighter just after the Norman Conquest, long before Robin Hood was cast in that mold; Fulk Fitzwarin, a noble outlaw of the late twelfth century who may well have provided a model for Robin the dispossessed Earl; Eustache, the rebellious cleric of a slightly later period who shares features with the outlaw hero.

From the later period of the broadside ballads and garlands this edition offers a full selection of both the best known Robin Hood ballads and also less familiar material. This indicates the range of the outlaw tradition and includes the lengthy *A True Tale of Robin Hood* (1632) in which Martin Parker summed up the tradition so far and influenced many a succeeding author.

In all of the English language texts, the editors have consulted the original sources and re-edited the texts, reporting any textual decisions of importance in the notes, along with any necessary explanatory material. The principle in editing texts has been conservative, and even the editorial emendations of the great ballad scholar F. J. Child have sometimes been rejected for the original readings, but at times minimal editorial intervention has been employed to create a readable ballad out of fragments, as in *The Death of Robin Hood*. The spelling of the original texts has been retained, though modern orthographic practices have been observed — the graphs *f, gh, th, u, v, z* are used in their modern forms, not their varying medieval versions, and modern punctuation has been employed throughout.

The editors would like to acknowledge a number of institutions for permission to print texts in their possession: The British Library, The Bodleian Library, Cambridge University Library, The National Library of Scotland, The National Trust (for *Gamelyn*), Trinity College Library, Cambridge. We are grateful to the Malone Society for permission to use Meagher's edited facsimiles as base texts for the Munday plays. Recognition should be made for funding support for this project provided by Purdue University, the University of Melbourne, the University of Wales, Cardiff, and the National Endowment for the Humanities, whose support sustained the final processes for preparing camera-ready copy.

Some portions of the volume are the result of collaborative effort. Thomas E. Kelly translated from Anglo-Norman the selections from *Eustache the Monk* and *Fouke le Fitz Waryn*; he also collaborated on the introductions to those sections. Andrew Kunka worked on an early draft of the Robin Hood in Performance section and collaborated on the introduction to the Munday plays. Russell A. Peck edited and wrote the notes to the Munday plays, and also contributed the edition of *Robin Hood and the Pedlars*. Cyrus Hoy provided a careful reading of the Munday plays and made several suggestions both on the texts and notes. Michael Swanton gave us permission to reprint his translation of *Hereward the Wake* and contributed the introduction. Paul Whitfield White edited and wrote the introductions and notes for *Robyn Hod and the Shryff off Notyngham* and *Robin Hood and the Friar* and *Robin Hood and the Potter*.

Personal thanks are due from Cardiff to the people who helped in preparation of this edition: Rosalind Field, Dawn Harrington, Alex Jones, Helen Phillips, Lucy Sussex, Norman Blake, and, especially, Thomas Hahn, who provided valuable comments on a draft of the ballad materials. At Purdue we are grateful to Margaret Moan Rowe, Thomas E. Kelly, Shaun Hughes, Ann Astell, and James Cruise. The following students in Medieval Studies at Purdue also contributed to this project at an early stage: Tracy Hagarty, Deb Hanna, Jenifer Ingraham, Jeff Kramer, and Christopher Leininger. A special part has been played in the production of this edition by colleagues who have provided their expertise: Arthur Freeman's comments on the Forresters manuscript have been invaluable; at the University of Rochester Thomas Hahn and Richard W. Kaeuper "field tested" the anthology in their classes on Robin Hood; Russell Peck dealt with many editorial and technical issues; Alan Lupack and Mara Amster gave the manuscript thoughtful critiques; and Jennifer Church worked extensively with the volume in early drafts and crafted it into its final form. At the Medieval Institute at Western Michigan University, Thomas Seiler saw the volume through the press.

With the support of this noble band of helpers, not to mention the magic of e-mail, the editors have found pleasure as well as labor in concentrating on their task of bringing the outlaw stories out of their fugitive lairs and, we hope, into the legitimate hands of readers and students around the world. No one enters Robin Hood's world without a demanding encounter with the hero, and we hope that our own editorial struggles with the texts and the spirited engagement that classes and teachers have with these materials will, as in the ballads, bring everyone to a final and festal celebration of the values to be found in *Robin Hood and Other Outlaw Tales*.

Stephen Knight
Thomas H. Ohlgren
1997

Robin Hood's Garland,

containing

His merry Exploits, and the several
Fights which he, Little John,
and Will Scarlett had upon
several occasions,

Some of them never before printed.

Entered according to order.

Printed for T. Coles, W. Vere, and J. Wright.
1670.

Robin Hood and Other Outlaw Tales

General Introduction

1. An Elusive, Enduring Hero

Six hundred years is a long time for a hero to endure. When in the 1370s William Langland mentioned the popularity of "rymes of Robyn Hode" (*Piers Plowman,* B V.395), he associated them with Sloth, but the energy of the hero and the stories have continued to the present; all the modern media constantly recreate the outlaw myth with all its direct, amusing, natural, romantic, and subliminally political vigor.

Only King Arthur of the medieval heroes has had such longevity, but there are striking differences. One is that where Arthur represents authority under some serious and ultimately tragic form of pressure, the Robin Hood tradition always presents, in many varied forms, resistance to authority — the two heroes in a real sense are the reflex of each other. But the differences between the outlaw tradition and that of Arthur are not only a matter of content. Where the noble adventures of the Round Table have often been enshrined in monumental prose and verse in many a prestigious genre, the stories of Robin Hood have always been more ephemeral — songs, short plays, proverbs, and place names; in our time, TV serials and films (some unmemorable) have been the media that have transmitted a tradition which is, like the outlaw himself, both fugitive and flexible, hard to pin down, whether in a sheriff's jail or under the ponderousness of canonical texts.

The hero and his myth are remarkably elusive: Chaucer once mentions "joly Robin" (*Troilus and Criseyde,* V.1174), probably a glimpse of the outlaw at a distance, but the author has weightier business in that poem; Shakespeare's *As You Like It* mentions in its first scene the forest myth, but clearly intends to separate itself from and also to outclass the popularity of Robin Hood on the Elizabethan stage. In *Ivanhoe* the hero has a limited part; Keats and Tennyson both wrote powerfully about the outlaw, but in minor parts of their work. Even today, when so much is edited, printed and reprinted, there is no anthology of the major Robin Hood texts readily available on the bookshop shelves. But against all that canonical marginality, almost every day a newspaper refers to the hero in a headline, and films, plays, pantomimes, and television productions continue to recreate this most volatile of heroes.

2. Outlaw Parallels

In terms of the literary and educational industry, as well as in thematic essence, Robin Hood remains an outlaw. Eric Hobsbawm, in his classic study *Bandits* (1985), takes him as the archetype of the social bandit, the man, and sometimes woman, thrown up by circumstances who becomes a focus of resistance to an imposed and oppressive authority. All around the world they occur, whether in reality or fiction: Brazil's Lampāio and Sicily's Salvatore Guiliano as well as the better-known Jesse James, Ned Kelly, and William Tell. But Robin Hood is not the only outlaw to emerge from medieval Britain, and several of the earlier versions may well have played a part in the development of his own tradition.

The late eleventh-century historical hero Hereward left a story well-known in Latin (*Gesta Herewardi*) and also in widespread references in English (*Anglo-Saxon Chronicle*, for instance). Composed in the mid-twelfth century (the sole surviving manuscript dates from the thirteenth century), three hundred years before the earliest datable Robin Hood text, *Hereward the Wake* prefigures a number of character types, settings, plot elements, and themes found in the later Robin Hood tradition. There is the hero himself, banished and outlawed at age eighteen, by King William I. After adventures in Cornwall, Ireland, and Flanders, he returns to England to avenge the murder of his brother and to reclaim his confiscated ancestral home. Like Robin Hood, he lives in the forest (chapters xix and xxvii); he forms a band of "fugitives, the condemned and disinherited" (chapter xvi); he wields a deadly bow (chapters xx and xxvii); he dons disguises to reconnoitre the enemy camp as a potter (chapter xxiv) and as a fisherman (chapter xxv); he engages in trickery, shoeing his horses backwards (chapter xxvii); he is captured and imprisoned but is rescued by his faithful companions (chapter xxxv); and, in the end, he receives the king's pardon and reclaims his estate (chapter xxxvi). Here then are the basic ingredients of the later Robin Hood tradition. There are differences — his noble status, his inheritance problems, and his blatant nationalism, and although these are lacking in the early ballads and plays they do crop up later in the Tudor period and beyond.

Another early outlaw tale is *Eustache the Monk*, which survives in a unique manuscript, dated 1284. Based on the life of a historical figure, Eustache the Monk (c. 1170–1217), the 2307-line story in Old French rhymed couplets recounts the adventures of the French nobleman who was unjustly outlawed and dispossessed of his lands by the Count of Boulogne. After his father is killed by a rival, Eustache leaves his religious order to seek justice from Count Rainald of Dammartin. When his champion loses a judicial trial by combat, Eustache's inheritance is seized by the count, forcing him to flee into the forest as an outlaw. To exact his revenge, Eustache, often in disguise, sallies out of the forest and harasses the count or his men

2

by robbing them of money or horses. A number of these activities closely resemble episodes in the Robin Hood ballads, strongly suggesting that they are sources rather than analogues. In addition to the capture and release of the Count of Boulogne, which closely parallels Robin's capture of the Sheriff of Nottingham in the *Gest*, we have another pair of episodes in which those who tell the truth are allowed to keep their money, while those who lie are robbed. This game of "truth or consequences" underlies two major scenes in the *Gest* involving Sir Richard at the Lee and the monk of St. Mary's Abbey in York. Other similarities include the stratagems of the trickster, the frequent use of disguise, and anti-clerical satire.

Another early outlaw who in some way influenced the Robin Hood tradition was Fouke le Fitz Waryn, grandson of Warin de Metz who settled on the Welsh borders after the Norman Conquest. The story in Anglo-Norman survives in a miscellany of some sixty works in Latin, French, and English, dated c. 1325–40. The prose romance is based on a thirteenth-century poetic version, now lost, and another version in Middle English is similarly lost. The first third of the ancestral romance (omitted in this edition) traces the history of the Fitz Waryn family from the Norman Conquest to the late twelfth century, and recounts the opportunistic marriages of Fouke's grandfather, Warin de Metz, and his father, Fouke le Brun, to two propertied heiresses, resulting in their lordship over Whittington and Ludlow. As the first part ends, the family loses control of both properties. The last two-thirds of the romance, which is included in English translation in this edition, covers the career of Fouke III, who after a four-year period (1200–03) of rebellion and outlawry, finally wins back his lands and titles. Of interest here is the outlaw narrative, consisting of the now familiar elements. After an argument with King John, who refuses to return his lands and titles, Fouke renounces his homage and leaves the court. When fifteen of the king's knights pursue Fouke and order him to return, he responds by killing fourteen, leaving one alive to report the incident (not unlike Robin's *Progess to Nottingham*). Fleeing to Brittany, Fouke is outlawed and stripped of his remaining lands. Returning to England, he hides in the forests, assembles a group of loyal knights, and plays a deadly game of hide and seek with the king's agents. Like Hereward and Eustache, Fouke and his second-in-command, John de Rampaigne, don various disguises — monk, merchant, collier — to avoid detection and to gather information. Three scenes in particular remind us of Robin Hood: like Little John in the *Gest*, Fouke's brother John waylays a caravan of merchants travelling through the forest and delivers them into Fouke's hands, and, as in *Eustache* and the *Gest*, there is a test of "truth or consequences"; in another episode, King John, like the sheriff in the *Gest*, is tricked into the forest, where he is captured and later released after swearing an oath; and finally, Fouke's brother William, after being severely wounded, begs his brother, as Little John begs Robin in the *Gest*, to kill him. To be

3

sure there are significant differences between *Fouke le Fitz Waryn* and Robin Hood, but the core of the outlaw narrative is substantially the same.

Although the careers of Eustache and Fouke, particularly the resistance to King John, sound familiar to film-goers, in fact these features were added to the original Robin Hood story. The hero of the early ballads, and indeed many of the later texts, was never dated in the time of King John. That was first suggested by John Major in a history of Britain published in 1521, and it seems to have been part of a general movement towards making Robin more respectable. If, like Fouke, he opposed a bad king as a dispossessed lord, then his resistance was in a real sense in support of the existing structures of authority — very different from the guerrilla tactics against forest laws and sheriff's rule which are found elsewhere in the medieval texts.

3. The Historical Robin Hood

All these analogous heroes, though, were historical figures, however much their stories became mythologized in the retelling. It remains an item of faith, or perhaps obsession, among many modern commentators that Robin Hood too was a real person, and they believe that enough careful attention to the records will produce a real Robin Hood who might, like the equally obscure King Arthur, be the real figure behind the myths — or legends, as such historians would want to call them. It is true (and usually ignored by the modern historians) that the earliest references to the hero all assume he was a real person amplified in story, an English Wallace, it might seem, especially because the earliest chroniclers who mention Robin are all Scottish. Part I of this edition shows how Wyntoun in the 1420s spoke of "waythemen," forest outlaws, who were "commendit gud" by the populace; and Bower a little later also understood them to be real outlaws who were also popular heroes; Major, even though he gentrified the hero, never displaced him into the realms of myth. Such an attitude was continued through the English commentators Grafton in the 1560s and Stow in the late sixteenth century, and the antiquarians joined in this process. Just as Camden found the cross that allegedly marked Arthur's grave at Glastonbury, so he wrote about the epitaph for Robin found at Kirklees and soon enough there was a stone-cut version to be seen and even a drawing of the grave (Holt, 1989, pp. 41–43). By 1600 there existed, preserved in a Sloane manuscript in the British Library, a prose *Life* of Robin Hood (discussed in Dobson and Taylor, 1976, pp. 286–87), and the first major edition of the ballads, by Joseph Ritson in 1795, was prefaced with a long "Life," with footnotes, references, and all the equipment of biography in the age of Boswell.

Far from being history, these accounts are a tissue of non-historical materials

4

straight from folklore or fiction. The Sloane *Life* is largely a reworking of some of the ballads, especially the lengthy fifteenth-century *Gest of Robyn Hode*. The epitaphs and illustrations of the grave show a distinctly literary inheritance, and the high point of Ritson's "Life" is his reprint of William Stukeley's genealogy of the hero which makes him descend from the nephew of William the Conqueror, and at the same time considers him a Saxon patriot. By contrast to this florid nonsense, the early chronicle references, though they know of the popular story, have a spare reference to the hero that, like the Welsh *Annals* in the case of Arthur, might be thought to imply authenticity. Though nothing in the texts can be traced to the thirteenth century, where the "real Robin Hood" historians would place him, there is some support for such an original date in that Wyntoun located his "waythemen" in 1283 and Bower put them back to the 1260s. Although there might well have been other reasons for that (to associate him in Wyntoun with Wallace and in Bower with Simon de Montfort) it does indicate their sense of the distant nature of the tradition.

That idea of antiquity and the prolific appearance of the name do not, however, suggest that there was one "original" Robin Hood, but that by then the name refers generally to someone who was in some way outside or against the law as it was being imposed. That interpretation is strongly suggested by evidence from another area, not considered by historians because it is neither individual nor criminal in orientation, but in fact providing by far the largest number of early references to the hero.

4. Plays and Games

If the existing references before 1600 are gathered (Knight, *Appendix,* 1994) one is struck by the remarkable number of plays and games of Robin Hood, up and down the country. From Exeter (1426–27) to Aberdeen (1438), from Norfolk (1441) to Wiltshire (1432), the length and breadth of Britain appears to have been populated with annual ritual activities focused on the hero. No scripts have certainly survived, though there are a few short plays (see pp. 269–95) that may derive from this widespread play and game tradition, focused on ritual-like activities that were non-literary like the many pageants and parades that still engage people's attention and emotions. There would be, in early summer, a procession, led by Robin, with people dressed in green and bearing forest symbols such as branches or garlands of leaves. They would go from one village to another, or one part of the town to another, and collect money, usually in return for some entertainment, for example, a short play featuring a fight and a rescue. The money would be used for the community, for mending the roads in one case, and although the church was involved in the events, it was effectively a civil activity involving the churchwardens rather than the priest.

There seems to have been real prestige involved in playing the hero, as people waited years for their turn and even handed down that right from father to son, hence the surname "Robinhood" found on some occasions.

None of this involves resistance to authority; the whole process is firmly within the law. Robin is the figurehead of a celebration of the combination of the natural and the communal. But if we are to believe the evidence of the very early texts, the pageants would present Robin's triumph against the hostile forces of law and order which came from a distance: the sheriff, the visiting forester like Guy of Gisborne, the oppressive abbot, but not the friendly grass-roots friar. With this fictional capacity for resistance, it is not surprising that on occasions Robin Hood became the actual as well as symbolic leader in carnivals that sometimes turned to riot at places as far apart as Wednesbury in the West Midlands (1497) and Scottish Edinburgh (1561). Even though gentrification was in full flow, in the seventeenth century this social-bandit capacity was well remembered and gave rise to the remarkable 1661 play *Robin Hood and His Crew of Souldiers,* in which the radical Robin Hood concedes defeat to the newly restored royalist authorities.

Two important conclusions arise from a study of the early plays and games. One is that they are so widely spread. As a hero of natural communality, Robin can emerge anywhere and even displace the existing carnival hero. In Aberdeen in 1508 he is described as replacing the previous ritual figure the Abbot of Bon Accord. The early references and tales have a much wider spread than modern Nottingham and its tourist industry would care to admit. For Wyntoun the outlaws are in Inglewood, near Carlisle, and also in Barnsdale. The *Gest* understands Barnsdale to be in Yorkshire, and that has been a common view through the ages, but there is also a Barnsdale in Rutland (between Nottingham and Rockingham), with many local references to the outlaw. Ballads and some prose stories make Robin active throughout the Midlands and the North of England, while place names and place associations locate Robin across most of Britain, with an apparent preponderance in the Southwest, the North Central Midlands, Yorkshire, and Lowland Scotland.

The other feature of interest arising from the plays and games is the clear sense that of all the genres in which the tradition appears, the original and in many ways the authentic genre is theater, here best called performance because of its deep informality. However long Robin Hood stories may become (and there are some three-decker novels) their essence is dramatic: an opening in the forest; a departure or meeting; an encounter in which Robin or one of the outlaws is in danger (often brought about by trickery or disguise as well as courage and skill); a harmonious ending, with either a feast or an agreement.

This structure is ideally suited to the stage. With exciting action and little dialogue, the combination of physical danger and spontaneous heroism in the Robin Hood stories has always been popular with actors and audiences. There is a remarkable consistency between the dynamic early playlets or ballads and the modern episode on TV; and there are many structural parallels between the composite ballads like the *Gest* or *A True Tale of Robin Hood* and the full-length epic film.

It may well be that the early ballads have the plays as their sources, rather than the other way round as literary scholars have usually thought. But the ballads soon asserted themselves as a natural genre for the myth, with their quick dramatic action and their effective use of poetic suggestion, whether violent or naturally beautiful in its form. Our good fortune is that these ballads flourished in a period when at least some were recorded, and so were preserved powerful versions of the early outlaw in his pre-gentrified form as the English social bandit.

5. Early Ballads

From before 1600 a small number of important ballads survive and some later texts can be confidently traced to that early period (for details see the separate introductions to each ballad in Early Ballads and Tales). The first ballads to survive are *Robin Hood and the Monk*, c. 1450, and *Robin Hood and the Potter*, c. 1500. Both quite full (longer than the later broadsides), they present a forest hero who outwits the forces of the town and the abbey, gaining money and property from the sheriff. Another version of the same structure is in *Robin Hood and Guy of Gisborne*. The Robin of these texts inhabits the forest with his band; when alone, an outlaw is at risk and needs cunning or heroics to survive, but both are available in plenty. These ballads are fiercer than the friendly Robin of later days — Guy of Gisborne, a monk, and the sheriff all die at the outlaw's hands, though the Potter story is less aggressive and the sheriff survives. Also, there is no charity as such: they rob the rich but give to themselves. Donations to the poor only emerge when Robin is a gentleman, able to afford such charity.

These ballads, and the early plays associated with them, outline a medieval social bandit in full vigor; that is also the basis of the *Gest*, which is a composite of a number of ballad stories and might well be termed a ballad epic. Its date is now thought to be somewhat later than the optimistic c. 1400 of earlier commentaries, and it represents, not unlike Malory's *Morte Darthur* in Caxton's hands, the intersection of popular manuscript materials and the new technology of printing. The *Gest* not only collects comic and violent ballad stories about the heroic forest band, it also adds a narrative about how they help a distressed knight and it does, accordingly, move Robin a little towards gentrification. He holds court in the forest consciously like King Arthur, and if he does not dole out money to the poor, at least he "dyde pore men moch god." That comment follows the tragic end of the story, unique until the later survival of the ballad about Robin's death and itself indicating the scope and weight of the story in the *Gest*.

Set as they are in forests close to towns, and resisting consistently what are felt to be the incursive forces represented by sheriff, abbot, and the urban market, these ballads clearly value the natural, the communal, and what is felt to be the organic against aspects of the new centralizing and legislating world. Ideals for these texts lie in the forest, always glimpsed at the beginning and end, in the community that the outlaws form and negotiate as free parties, and in physical strength, skill, and a cheerful cunning that resembles the folkloric art of the trickster. The context is not irreligious — Robin especially has a devotion to Mary, rather than the established church. Nor is it absolutely revolutionary: the king himself is honored and obeyed, if sometimes eluded. But the outlaws do represent clear aspects of resistance and dissidence, and many notes are struck in common with Langland's direct satire and the ironic critiques of Chaucer.

The audience has been a matter of speculation. Some have thought it was close to the discontented peasantry who were central to the 1381 revolt (Hilton, 1976); another view saw the ballads as a set of general complaints from the lower gentry (Holt, 1989). Neither party has accounted for the lack of agrarian and tenurial issues, apart from the unusual episode of the knight in the *Gest*. Another commentator has seen the dynamic of the ballads in the struggle for power in towns themselves and the forest as a fantasy land of freedom (Tardif, 1983). As a result of these debates there now seems general agreement that the audience was not single, that it represented the social mobility of the late Middle Ages, and the myth was diffused across a wide variety of social groupings who were alive to the dangers of increasingly central authority, whether over town, village, or forest (Coss, 1985). Dobson and Taylor have accepted Holt's concept of a "lower gentry" audience, but add: "It seems likely, therefore, that the earliest 'rhymes' of Robin Hood were disseminated not simply through the great households, but also through the medium of fairs where minstrels played to popular audiences" (1995, p. 40).

Robin Hood poems were not the only medieval texts to deal with outlaws in the forest, and Early Ballads and Tales also provides several analogues. *Robyn and Gandelyn* is a mysterious short ballad, or perhaps lyric, which may be close to both the mythic and the tragic heart of the tradition. *Adam Bell* is a northern parallel telling of three heroes from the Carlisle region in a long and strong story, somewhat simpler in its resolution than the *Gest*; though it was very popular in the broadside period, it is a poem without the flexibility and openness to interpretation that has kept alive the Robin Hood tradition. Equally monologic is the heroic romance of *Gamelyn,* depicting a rough-hewn distressed gentleman from the late fourteenth

8

century, who becomes an outlaw chief as a means of regaining his patrimony. The story is both colloquial and concerned with property and is notable partly for being broadly parallel to the knightly section of the *Gest* and also for generating a hero who in later stories actually joins Robin Hood (see *Robin Hood and Will Scarlet*).

These analogues also share with the early Robin Hood texts the same sense that, although they are written down, they are close to oral performance. Rhyme is rarely perfect throughout, and half rhyme is very common. The absence of rhyme in three stanzas in *Robin Hood and the Potter*, lines 93–96, 191–94, 249–52, is probably due to imperfect copying, though the rhyme elsewhere in this ballad is quite erratic. Occasionally the stanza form changes, and not because the scribe or printer has misplaced a line or two: there are numerous six-line stanzas and at least one apparently genuine stanza of five lines (*Adam Bell*, lines 293–97) and one of seven (*Robin Hood and the Potter*, lines 219–25).

With these parallels and on this strong base of a few precious early texts, the tradition of Robin Hood narratives develops. The two manuscript ballads were not printed in the seventeenth century, though *Robin Hood and the Butcher,* a reworking of the *Potter*, reprinted in Ritson (II, 27–32), is a popular broadside and garland text. The few surviving early ballads must represent only a part, probably a small part, of the widespread material referred to by the chroniclers. In a number of cases it is possible to see that ballads surviving later must have had forms at least as early as the sixteenth century, often because they were mentioned or pillaged in the process of gentrification, which, historically speaking, varies the social bandit structure of the early ballads before that tradition continues and develops in printed form in broadside and garland.

6. The Distressed Gentleman

The sixteenth-century chroniclers are the first to give Robin Hood a raised social position and a historical setting which permits his resistance to authority to seem a form of noble behavior in both moral and social terms. This may be in part because Robin was in actuality being dignified: Hall's *Chronicle* tells of two occasions when Henry VIII entered the tradition, once in 1510 when he and his friends played outlaws to excite the ladies, and then in 1515 when a formal Robin Hood pageant entertained the court as it was, very appropriately, passing up Shooters Hill (Knight, 1994, pp. 109–10).

The literary gentrification process took off in the 1590s when the booming London theater, hungry for new subjects, adapted the popular dramatic materials long associated with the hero. At first Robin was just used marginally as a filler in Peele's

Edward I, where one scene is a Robin Hood play game, or as a defining alterity as in Greene's *George a Greene,* where Robin Hood, the possible rebel, plays second fiddle to George, loyal to both king and town (Nelson, 1973). It was Anthony Munday, friend of Stow the historian, who conceived of the dramatic value of gentrification and told a tragedy of Robin which established the main features of the newly ennobled outlaw. His land is taken, just like that of King Richard and (as in the *Gest*), his reinstallation at court is only the prologue to his betrayal and death.

Full-blown tragedy of a sometimes ponderous kind suits Munday's somber theme, although the comic and tricksterish spirit survives through the presence of John Skelton, presented as waggish poet to Henry VIII and playing both the interlocutor and Friar Tuck. There are two striking features: the presence of Marian, the forest name for Matilda Fitzwater, Robin's consort; now that he is ennobled he needs a lady to provide heirs, while the social bandit is almost always partnerless. If she is in the cast we almost always have a gentrified story, at least until modern times. More surprising is the fact that Prince John is not consistently the villain: Robin's enemies, and the king's, are the corrupt medieval Catholic clergy. Prince John is more like an amiable nuisance, a low-life Laertes to Robin's Hamlet, lecherous but inept, at least until he destroys Marian in *The Death.*

Munday's reconstruction of the myth had many effects. It was dissipated through Martin Parker's *A True Tale of Robin Hood*; it influenced Ben Jonson's ambitious but sadly uncompleted masque *The Sad Shepherd*; and it even, by emulation, drove Shakespeare, writer for a rival company, to produce his own forest outlaw story in *As You Like It.* Most importantly, Munday inspired, directly or indirectly, the metamorphosis by which the story has been reduced in political tension and become an all purpose myth, in that Robin in many later stories, other than the ballads, is more or less a gentleman, never really one of the common people and never at all opposing true hierarchy. That diminution — or perhaps emasculation — of the social-bandit story no doubt has made it seem more acceptable in the context of commercial productions such as the pantomimes and musicals of the nineteenth century and the major films of this century. But before deploring such mercantile conservatism it should be remembered that the village Robin Hood of the plays and games was always capable of being fully involved with the orderly processes of conservative society and only in certain conflicted contexts developed his radical potential.

If gentrification brought the Robin Hood story out of the forests of popular dissent into the halls of settled and conservative society, this did not do much for the story in artistic terms: Munday's play is the best of them (apart from Jonson's splendid fragment), and the dire ballad operas of the eighteenth century, just like Tennyson's *The Foresters* and the feeble Georgian playlets of the early twentieth century, are testimonies to what happens when an art form lacks an inner thematic and political tension. Gentrification was a powerful current, but until the nineteenth century it was not found in the mass forms of the tradition. Indeed, one of the main weaknesses of early gentrification texts was that they hardly used any of the traditional and vigorous stories, and so their plots are without the demotic energy and the mythic dimension that derived from the popular forest hero. But that lack of interaction worked both ways: without any major contamination from the distressed gentleman, the popular forms of the ballad in print remained generally true to the medieval image of the hero and his saga.

7. Broadsides, Garlands, and the Mass-Market Outlaw

Of the thirty-eight ballads collected in the 1882–89 edition of Child's great *English and Scottish Popular Ballads*, thirty-six appear in the printed tradition of the seventeenth and eighteenth century. This early collection of ballads provided a great source for Robin Hood material. His tradition is the most popular of all the broadside themes: there were plenty of miraculous births, horrid murders, and sea monsters, but they all describe different events and people. The name and fame of Robin Hood are the strongest single focus in the whole wealth of popular singing and reading matter that was sold through the streets of London and sent up and down the country by cart, coach, and hawkers on foot.

The partially autonomous nature of the printed ballads is indicated by the fact that there is relatively little continuity between the late medieval Robin Hood ballads and the staple diet of the seventeenth and eighteenth centuries. Of the early ballads in this anthology, none appeared in broadside or garland form. This is partly a matter of length: the *Gest* and *Adam Bell* are printed texts, but far too long to make into a one-page broadside, or to fit into a garland. *Robin Hood and the Monk*, *Robin Hood and Guy of Gisborne*, and *Robin Hood and the Potter* would also, at more than two hundred lines, have been too long. It may be that their medieval themes did not suit the newly urbanized audience; the only one that does appear in print is the town-oriented *Robin Hood and the Potter* in a shortened and adapted form as *Robin Hood and the Butcher*.

Though the form and topics of the broadside and garland ballads differ from the earliest group of Robin Hood texts, the themes of the later ballads show many connections with the medieval period. The largest thematic grouping of Robin Hood's ballads is basically very simple in plot, telling of an encounter between one or more of the outlaws and some stranger. Quite often it is just a fight, which they all enjoy — as in the revealingly entitled *Robin Hood's Delight* (Ritson II, 120–25). Sometimes after the fight the opponent joins the band. Little John, Will Scarlet,

Friar Tuck, and even Maid Marian become forest outlaws in this way. And Robin never does conspicuously well in the fight: he is sometimes beaten, occasionally humiliated, but usually manages to scrape a draw. His physical quality is not his main power (though he is almost always the best at the skill of archery); his most valued quality is that of a natural leader. The conflicts over leadership and the arguments of the early ballads have been forgotten: Robin's fame is enough for anyone to join his band, and the "Robin Hood meets his match" conflict turns into communality.

Another notable category is the "prequel," ballads which seem to have been constructed to explain some feature of the tradition. Examples appear to be *Robin Hood and Little John,* which explains how the powerful outlaw joined the existing band: this cannot be ancient because it contradicts the fact that he and Robin alone are mentioned from the very start by the chroniclers. Similarly, ballads tell how Allin a Dale, Will Scarlet, and Marian herself joined the band. Robin's own prequel is given in the early *Robin Hood's Progress to Nottingham,* which tells how he was provoked into becoming an outlaw.

A few ballads rework the anti-clerical feeling of the old days, and Protestant England obviously enjoys robbing a bishop. But the previous skepticism about kings and the definite hatred of sheriffs is almost completely absent in those days of centralized power. Parker's *A True Tale* ends with a very interesting and sometimes uneasy set of reflections of the need to contain outlawry these days. A small number of ballads seem to preserve quite ancient themes: *The Death of Robin Hood* has some aura of magic and mystery to it, especially in the fragmentary version preserved in Bishop Percy's manuscript, dated at 1650 or just before. *Robin Hood's Progress to Nottingham* has a ferocity only found in the very early manuscript ballads, as the young Robin shoots down the foresters who mistreat him, and *Robin Hood's Fishing* has economic and social concerns that seem like a maritime update of *Robin Hood and the Potter.* But if those texts look backwards, some ballads are definitely in a newer mode: *Robin Hood and Maid Marian* is for the most part gentrified in theme and tone (with some popular elements), and there is a somewhat inactive and literary mood visible in *Robin Hood and the Golden Arrow.*

Somewhere between old plain style and courtly degeneration lies the style and approach of the professional balladeers. The texts that have clearly been through their hands have the internal rhyme in the third line, giving a pattern-like effect quite foreign to the earlier ballads, often supported by a repeated refrain which implies that singing was the expected medium of delivery. This seems to have been a development: the early texts often lack refrains, and Bronson reports that there were remarkably few tunes attached to Robin Hood ballads (1966, III, 13–14). The language of the broadsides also in some cases moves away from the direct and lucid language of the early ballads towards the cant and catchphrases of the contemporary stage and journalism, as in *Robin Hood and Little John* or, briefly, *Robin Hood and*

General Introduction

Maid Marian.

Many of the ballads appeared in single-sheet broadside, with strong, even crude, woodcuts at the top of the page. Convenience often superseded art: one woodcut might do for more than one ballad from the same workshop, and sometimes the text was trimmed to fit the sheets. These sold for a halfpenny or a penny, and fortunately for us both Samuel Pepys and Antony Wood were compulsive collectors. Others came later into the safe hands of Francis Douce. Alongside this wealth in the ancient libraries can also be found a physically smaller, yet in its time a more up-market Robin Hood source, which is the garland. Named because it was felt to be an intertwined series of poems honoring the hero, the garlands were a printer's marketing strategy, a kind of Robin Hood omnibus of its day. The early ones just collect twelve or sixteen ballads, and sometimes the same printer will add more in a second edition. But in the eighteenth century they are more likely to have full-page wood engravings and even a lengthy introduction purporting to link these together into a "Life," so suggesting an audience more intellectually ambitious than those who just wanted a broadside text to sing to a well known tune.

Some of the ballads have many versions, such as *Robin Hood Rescues Three Young Men;* others, like *Robin Hood and Maid Marian,* survive in single priceless copies. This was not a gentrified market. In garland form, the ballads went on appearing well into the nineteenth century, especially in the provinces. They overlap the sophisticated novels and liberal romanticism of the reshaped Robin Hood, just as they go back to crabbed manuscripts of the Middle Ages. If it is one of the enigmas of the Robin Hood tradition that we know so little about the language and action of the play game, a compensating richness lies in the wealth of our knowledge about the seventeenth- and eighteenth-century popular ballad tradition, firing as it does its broadsides of pithy outlaw poetry and wearing its garlands of heroic vitality.

In 1993 a new source appeared, and the British Library acquired a manuscript containing nothing but twenty-two Robin Hood ballads. In a pamphlet published by Bernard Quaritch, the bookseller that acquired the manuscript, Arthur Freeman suggested that the date of the handwriting is 1640–70 (1993, p. 5); the British Library experts propose 1650–74, with a preference for the later part of the period. Freeman argued that all the texts preceded those of Child and so should have editorial priority. His dating would make this speculative: the later date makes it fairly unlikely. In any case, collation suggests that a number of the texts are less than authoritative: full details can be found in *Robin Hood: The Forresters Manuscript* (Knight, 1998), but a summary of the main textual issues is appropriate to justify the present volume's treatment of the manuscript.

Some ballads are pastiches of existing texts: *Robin Hood and the Bride* is a weak version of *Robin Hood and Allin a Dale*, and *Robin Hood and the Old Wife* is a variant of *Robin Hood and the Bishop*, with the sheriff playing the hostile role. It is conceivable that this was the original, linking to the sheriff's role in the short plays, and that the *Bishop* version is a post-reformation redirection of hostility. But the frequency of pastiche among the early texts in this manuscript makes this an insecure hypothesis. *Robin Hood and the Sherriffe* is a skillful combination of the Little John and sheriff episode in the *Gest* with *Robin Hood's Golden Prize*, a compilation that cannot have been ancient, since the ballad is clearly fairly late. In a similar maneuver *Robin Hood and the King* links the king-in-disguise scene in the *Gest* to the end of Parker's *A True Tale*. If these ballads are suspect because of innovation, others are too faithful to have prime status. The last four ballads in the manuscript appear to be copied from a version of the 1670 garland, and several other ballads appear to be lightly edited versions of existing broadsides.

But in two cases the manuscript has valuable texts, and accordingly they are used in this edition. *Robin Hood and Queen Catherin* is in Child's best text a jerky and sometimes incoherent story (the outlaws' aliases are thoroughly obscure) and his version of *Robin Hood's Fishing* is unclear in the final naval action. Both of these ballads seem to have been clumsily cut to fit a broadside sheet, and the Forresters manuscript has better texts. It also has a version of *Robin Hood's Progress to Nottingham* (called *Robin Hood and the Forresters*, the first in the source, which provides it its name) that has some better readings than Child's best, but in a manuscript with so much editing and such skilled pastiching it seems bad practice to use a text at best marginally superior. In the case of the other two, the existing texts are so deficient that the Forresters text is worth publishing even if it is edited; this does not in fact appear to be the case as in every instance its good readings and passages appear to be behind the awkwardness of the existing broadsides and it may well be that the manuscript compiler had access to the sources used by the printers of the broadsides themselves. Other interesting Forresters texts are not used here because they seem derived from the texts found in Child. Though the Forresters manuscript has a full and lucid version of *Robin Hood Rescues Three Young Men*, this seems to be an editorialized expansion of the existing texts, and is not employed as copy text in this edition. Similarly, the lengthy version of *Robin Hood and the Pinder of Wakefield*, which Freeman (p. 7) feels to be an important and "entirely new text," seems to be a literary composition showing knowledge of the play *George a Greene* (c. 1592), with some influence from the prose history of the *Pinner* which was in print by 1632, though the only existing copy is from 1706. As this ballad seems "entirely new" in the sense of having a rather late and literary character, it seems preferable to continue to use the text printed by Child from a Wood broadside, which appears to derive from a version that pre-exists Greene's play: a very similar text to this is also in the Forresters manuscript (only the Pinder has two ballads, the longer one being numbered in the text as 10b).

It remains unclear what were the compiler's intentions. The manuscript looks in some ways like a hand-written garland, and the relation of the final texts to the 1670 garland suggests the link. Yet the first part of the manuscript seems to avoid deliberately the well known versions, which professional garlandeers used, and has rather a set of unique and in some cases, it would seem, nonce-created texts. That suggests someone who is both a connoisseur and a practitioner of the ballads, more in the mold of Sir Walter Scott than the compiler of the Percy manuscript, but whatever speculations are possible about the production of the Forresters manuscript, in this context its importance is that it has some valuable texts for printing or at least collation, and also offers important evidence for the renewed interest in the English outlaw in the early part of the Restoration period, as also seen in the 1661 play, the contemporary *Life*, the 1663 garland, and the number of broadsides that come from this period and so parallel the activity of the Forresters manuscript.

8. Towards the Modern Robin Hood

By the end of the eighteenth century the Robin Hood tradition was in many ways a museum piece. Gentrification had run into the sands of ballad opera, a sub-genre notable for puerile humor and, despite its bourgeois context, servile aristocratism. The early ballads themselves had been excavated first by Thomas Percy (though he only reprinted *Robin Hood and Guy of Gisborne* of the six in his manuscript) and then in 1795 by Joseph Ritson. But much as Ritson admired Robin, it was for reasons without a future: he admired what he saw as a radical spirit, but that view would not survive the widespread revulsion from the French Revolution, and his feeling that here lay the English version of noble savagery would soon be swamped by the more genteel rusticity of the lake poets. And yet, despite those ill-fated positions, from the combination of the gentrified idea (which even Ritson accepted as a principle) and from the newly disseminated ancient stories there arose a conception of the hero and his story, which, by including some crucially new ideas and structures, was able to reinvigorate for the modern world those patterns of critique and dissidence with which the early tradition was thoroughly imbued (Hanawalt, 1992, pp. 168–71).

It is true that in 1818 Scott marginalized Robin Hood in his *Ivanhoe*. But Scott's illiterate yeoman Locksley is a formidable figure, firmly involved with the concept of nationalism: he is, more convincingly than Ivanhoe, in essence an English hero. This idea was both developed and more fully focused on Robin Hood by Thomas Love Peacock in his *Maid Marian*, and although this was the least read of Peacock's novellas, in its stage musical version it was the most widely known element of his

15

work through the nineteenth century. The combination of Scott's imagination and Peacock's lucidity made very powerful and widely accepted the idea of Robin Hood as a national and anti-French hero, representing an Englishness that was both ancient and strongly independent, a powerful mythic figure on which to found the developing edifice of national identity.

While Scott's nationalism has a decidedly conservative edge, Peacock brought a liberal politics that appealed to many throughout the nineteenth century, and that was given value by Peacock's characteristically cool enlightenment tone. This model of the hero could be accepted by the reform movement in English politics. But the hero was to have wider appeal, both to those who were conservative and those who were more interested in the personal than the political. A generically new, but fully compatible, emotive range of themes was combined with the Scott-Peacock modernized structure to make a potent new combination through what may be the single most crucial intervention in the renovation of the myth.

In one quickly written poem, *Robin Hood* (1818), John Keats shaped, in response to his friend John Hamilton Reynolds' sonnets, Robin the romantic forest dweller, an image of an England less urban, more attractive to the feelings than what was increasingly being felt to be a degraded present (Knight, 1994, pp. 159–66). When Keats wrote "Honour to bold Robin Hood / Sleeping in the underwood," he shaped for many to imitate in poetry, fiction, drama, even pantomime, the essence of greenwood nostalgia. That anti-urban displaced patriotism was enormously attractive to people, and it newly empowered Robin Hood, especially when around the turn of the twentieth century a new syllabus for English was being constructed, heavily coded with nationalism. Robin Hood flourished anew in editions, plays, and reprints firmly in the junior school curriculum — not only in England, but also in America, largely through Howard Pyle's brilliant renovation and illustration of the stories (1883) and through the powerful impact of Augustin Daly's production in America in 1892, with Arthur Sullivan's music, of Tennyson's *The Foresters*.

National, nostalgic, at once both liberal and conservative through the combination of radical action and distressed gentleman status, this new Robin Hood had world-wide appeal: he was the exciting but acceptable outlaw compensating for early forms of urban anomie. The lack of sexual intrigue in the story made it, unlike the Arthur or Tristan myth, highly suitable for schools and early screens, while at the same time the heavy coding of sexuality in the story, from splitting the arrow to the forest world of a hunter, not to mention the form-fitting green tights and the conspicuous handsomeness of actors from Errol Flynn (1938) to Patrick Bergin (1991), meant that the whole myth took on new life in the dynamic world of visual fiction. Five Robin Hood films were made before 1914, and when in 1922 Douglas Fairbanks was persuaded that he would not seem like a plodding Englishman in the part, Allan

Dwan's sub-D. W. Griffith *Robin Hood* stormed the world of cinema, made Fairbanks a very rich man, and stimulated many later versions — more than sixty in all to the present (Harty, 2000, p. 88), ranging from the classic Hollywood polish of the 1938 Warner's version through many a plodding pastiche, with cowboy ponies or damp woodlands, depending which side of the Atlantic they were made, to the modern exotica of Mel Brooks' *Robin Hood: Men in Tights* (1993), reminiscent of the sixteenth-century friar play in its banal gagging, and the social subversion, if not quite social banditry, of the BBC's late 1980s TV series *Maid Marian,* in the new genre of feminist farce.

9. Bold Robin Hood

The vigor of a cultural tradition can be identified by the way it can be parodied, ironized, clumsily repeated, and journalistically dissipated, yet never somehow lose its inner core of credibility and evaluative significance. Like George Washington or Florence Nightingale, like Sherlock Holmes or Miss Marple, Robin Hood stands for something that is still widely recognized and valued, in spite of the lame and stagey children's anthologies that still appear, and in spite of the stiff rehashings of the myth that recurrently plod across the cinema screen.

To some it is a matter of myth in its most mysterious kind. The editor of the *Dictionary of National Biography* no doubt surprised his readers when, in that age of biographical historicism, he wrote a long entry on Robin Hood proclaiming him to be a mythic figure; when Michael Curtiz made Errol Flynn's cheerful outlaws hide in a tree and make it come to green and surging life, he was touching the same recurrent supernatural element in the hero which seems to persist in spite of all that historicists and dull rewriters of the story can do to extinguish it.

There may be more technically accountable ways to describe that unquenchability of the hero: his story is so simple, so concentrated — just an idea of freedom, and fighting, and the quest for natural and egalitarian harmony — that it can take forms suitable to any period and any audience. Like the much disguised and always elusive hero, the tradition itself glides through the forests of our culture, always ready to appear when there are injustices to discuss, always armed with deadly arrows of humor, vitality, directness, perhaps still tipped with a little magic.

During six hundred years to our knowledge, and no doubt many more that remain out of sight, the tradition of Robin Hood has spoken without the complications of high culture — the self-gratifying sonorities of novel and opera remain inherently foreign to the tradition — but has spoken with a light, trenchant, suggestive, and persuasive voice. The existence of an outlaw always implies there is something wrong with the law. The idea of legal inadequacy has changed enormously over time, from the constraints imposed by abbots, foresters, sheriffs, and even kings to the modern bogeymen of international oppression, inadequate families, patriarchy, and business irresponsibility. Whatever the perceived inadequacies of authority through the ages, the figure of Robin Hood has always been available to make them his target. No doubt the polymorphic outlaw will take more shapes in time to come: Rocket Robin Hood on American television and the ecological hero of a recent London production may point the way ahead. There remains something compelling about the image of the calm, witty, well-armed man standing in the forest and about to move suddenly into decisive action in support of true law. It seems possible to predict with confidence that, as his earliest chronicler said, the archetype of the outlaw will continue, in whatever forms he may materialize, to be "commendit gud."

Select Bibliography

Bronson, Bertrand. *The Traditional Tunes of the Child Ballads*. 4 vols. Princeton: Princeton University Press, 1959–72.

Carpenter, Kevin, ed. *Robin Hood: The Many Faces of that Celebrated Outlaw*. Aldenburg: Bibliotheks- und Informationssystem der Universität, 1995.

Child, F. J., ed. *English and Scottish Popular Ballads*. 5 vols. Boston: Houghton Mifflin and Company, 1882–98; rpt. New York: Dover, 1965.

Coss, Peter. "Aspects of Cultural Diffusion in Medieval England: The Early Romances, Local Society and Robin Hood." *Past and Present* 108 (1985), 35–79.

Dobson, R. B., and J. Taylor, eds. *Rymes of Robin Hood: An Introduction to the English Outlaw*. Pittsburgh: Pittsburgh University Press, 1976; London: Heinemann, 1976.

———. "'Rymes of Robin Hood': The Early Ballads and the *Gest*." In Carpenter, pp. 35–44.

Freeman, Arthur. *Robin Hood: The "Forresters" Manuscript*. [London]: Bernard Quaritch, 1993.

Hahn, Thomas, ed. *Robin Hood in Popular Culture: Violence, Transgression, and Justice*. Woodbridge, Suffolk, and Rochester, NY: D. S. Brewer, 2000.

Hanawalt, Barbara A. "Ballads and Bandits: Fourteenth-Century Outlaw and the Robin Hood Poems." In *Chaucer's England: Literature in Historical Context*. Minneapolis: University of Minnesota Press, 1992. Pp. 154–75.

Harty, Kevin. "Robin Hood on Film: Moving Beyond a Swashbuckling Stereotype." In Hahn (2000). Pp. 87–100.

Hilton, R. H. "The Origins of Robin Hood." *Past and Present* 14 (1958), 30–44; rpt. in R. Hilton, ed. *Peasants, Knights and Heretics: Studies in Medieval Social History*. Cambridge: Cambridge University Press, 1976. Pp. 221–35.

Hobsbawm, Eric. *Bandits*. Second ed. London: Pelican, 1985.

Holt, J. C. *Robin Hood*. London: Thames and Hudson, 1982. Second ed. 1989. [Chap. VI.]

———. "Robin Hood: The Origins of the Legend." In Carpenter (1995). Pp. 27–34.

Knight, Stephen. *Robin Hood: A Complete Study of the English Outlaw*. Oxford: Blackwell, 1994.

———, ed. *Robin Hood, The Forresters Manuscript, British Library Additional MS 71158*. Cambridge: D. S. Brewer, 1998.

———, ed. *Robin Hood: Anthology of Scholarship and Criticism*. Woodbridge, Suffolk: D. S. Brewer: 1999.

Nelson, Malcolm A. *The Robin Hood Tradition in the English Renaissance*. Salzburg Studies in English Literature, English Drama 14. Salzburg: Institut für Englische Sprache und Literatur, Universität Salzburg, 1973.

Percy, Thomas, ed. *Reliques of Ancient English Poetry*. 3 vols. London: J. Dodsley, 1765.

Potter, Lois, ed. *Playing Robin Hood: The Legend as Performance in Five Centuries*. Newark: University of Delaware Press, 1998.

Pyle, Howard. *The Merry Adventures of Robin Hood of Great Renown in Nottinghamshire*. New York: Scribner, 1883.

Ritson, Joseph. *Robin Hood: A Collection of All the Ancient Poems, Songs, and Ballads Now Extant Relative to that Celebrated English Outlaw. To Which are Prefixed Historical Anecdotes of His Life*. London: Pickering, 1795; rpt. in 2 vols., 1832.

Singman, Jeffrey L. *Robin Hood: The Shaping of the Legend*. Westport, CT, Greenwood Press, 1998.

Tardif, Richard. "The 'Mistery' of Robin Hood: A New Social Context for the Texts." In *Words and Worlds: Studies in the Social Role of Verbal Culture*. Ed. Stephen Knight and Soumyen Mukherjee. Sydney: Association for Studies in Society and Culture, 1983. Pp. 130–45.

The Chroniclers' Robin Hood

Introduction

Best known for his stirring adventures, Robin Hood is also an object of study by archivists and historians, seeking traces of a real Robin Hood who might, like the equally elusive King Arthur, be the real figure behind the myths — or legends, as such historians would want to call them. In 1852 Joseph Hunter found a man called Robin Hood who was actually a valet to King Edward II in the north of England and assumed that he lay behind some of the story of the *Gest*. But there was no sign that the king's valet was ever thought of as an outlaw. More recently archivists have found other traces of criminals known to the medieval legal authorities as Hood, R.

The earliest contender is one Robert Hod, described as a fugitive, who is mentioned in the York assizes record of 1226: his goods were being confiscated because he owed money to St. Peter's of York (Owen, 1936). The debt is not unlike that of Sir Richard in the *Gest* and certainly consistent with the fierce hostility toward abbeys and rich churchmen through the whole myth. A slightly later reference speaks of William Le Fevre, son of a smith, who was indicted at Reading for larceny in 1261 (Crook, 1984). Nothing very surprising about that, except that in the following year there is another reference to him, and now he is called William Robehod, as if that surname has become appropriate to his condition as a fugitive from justice.

The fact that Robin Hood's name was interpreted in that way in legal circles is clear from a record from Tutbury, Staffordshire for 1439, which says that a certain Piers Venables, of nearby Aston,

> gadered and assembled unto hym many misdoers beynge of his clothinge and, in manere of insurrection, wente into the wodes in that contre, like as it hadde be Robyn Hode and his meyne. (Child, 1965, III, 41)

Historians have liked to trace through these references a personalized and historicized process; they feel there must have been a certain Robin Hood who started the legend and others were identified with him: their arguments have been recently summarized by Bellamy (1985, chs. 1 and 2). The question is which was in fact the first reference: which was this notionally real Robin Hood? Only a few years before the miscreant of York comes a legal record of a man called Robert Hood, servant to the Abbot of Cirencester, who killed a man called Ralph between 1213 and 1216 (Holt, 1982, p. 54). And in 1354 in the forest of Rockingham, Northampton-shire, a man gave his name as Robin Hood when he was arrested for a forest offence.

The obvious interpretation, unpleasing as it may be to literal-minded historians, is that "Robin Hood" means fugitive from (probably unfair) justice, that like "Santa Claus" it is a name for a role, a mask to be worn in appropriate circumstances (Knight, 1994, pp. 14–15). What the legal references tell us most is not who was the real Robin Hood but how many versions there were and what the circumstances might have been to cause the intriguing changes that the tradition underwent in its quasi-historical forms as well as in its frankly fictional ballads and plays.

This is a message that comes through the references found in a series of chronicles in the late Middle Ages which have something to say about the outlaw. The relevant excerpts will each be printed here with a note about the author and his context, and what he might have understood as the meaning of the outlaw and his activities.

Select Bibliography

Texts

Andrew of Wyntoun. *The Orygynale Cronykil of Scotland*. Ed. David Laing. 3 vols. Edinburgh: Edmonton and Douglas, 1872–79.

——. *The Original Chronicle of Andrew of Wyntoun printed on parallel pages from the Cottonian and Wemyss MSS, with the variants of the other texts*. Ed. F. J. Amours. 6 vols. Edinburgh: Printed for the Scottish Text Society by W. Blackwood and Sons, 1903–14.

Bower, Walter. *Continuation of Fordun's Scotichronicon*. Ed. T. Hearne. Oxford: Sheldonian Theatre, 1722.

Dobson, R. B., and J. Taylor, eds. *Rymes of Robin Hood: An Introduction to the English Outlaw*. Pittsburgh: Pittsburgh University Press, 1976; London: Heinemann, 1976.

Grafton, Richard. *A Chronicle At Large and meere History of the affayres of England; and Kings of the Same*. London: Tottle and Toye, 1568–69. Rpt. London: J. Johnson, 1809.

Introduction

Major, John. *A History of Greater Britain As Well England and Scotland*. Trans. and ed. Archibald Constable. Scottish History Society. Vol. 10. Edinburgh: University Press, 1892.

Commentary and Criticism

Bellamy, John C. *Robin Hood: An Historical Inquiry*. London: Croom Helm, 1985.

Child, F. J. *English and Scottish Popular Ballads*. 5 vols. Boston: Houghton Mifflin and Company, 1882–98; rpt. New York: Dover, 1965.

Crook, David. "Some Further Evidence Concerning the Dating of the Origins of Robin Hood." *English Historical Review* 99 (1984), 530–34.

Holt, J. C. *Robin Hood*. Second ed. London: Thames and Hudson, 1989.

Hunter, Joseph. "The Great Hero of the Ancient Minstrely of English: Robin Hood, his period, real character etc. investigated." *Critical and Historical Tracts* IV. London: Smith, 1852. Pp. 28–38.

Knight, Stephen. *Robin Hood: A Complete Study of the English Outlaw*. Oxford: Blackwell, 1994.

Owen, L. V. D. "Robin Hood in the Light of Research." *The Times, Trade and Engineering Supplement* 38, no. 864 (1936), xxix.

Spence, Lewis. "Robin Hood in Scotland." *Chambers Journal* 18 (1928), 94–96.

The Chroniclers' Robin Hood

From Andrew of Wyntoun's *Orygynale Chronicle* (c. 1420)

[The *Orygynale Chronicle* was compiled for Andrew of Wyntoun's patron Sir John of Wemyss in the 1420s in Scotland. Andrew was an Augustinian canon of St. Sers Inch, a religious house set on an island in Loch Leven, and a daughter house of the great St. Andrew's priory. The chronicle is strongly pro-Scottish in tone, especially severe on the malpractices of Edward I in his war against the Scots and his treatment of the national hero William Wallace. In the period of these wars, under the year 1283, Andrew mentions two forest outlaws (*waythmen,* i.e., men who lie in wait) from the long turbulent area of the borders. They operated, it seems, both just south of the border near Carlisle in Inglewood (meaning *English Wood*), and much further south in England in Barnsdale. Andrew's apparent approval of their efforts and his report of the common praise of them is no doubt related to the fact that they were enemies of the English crown and its officers. After the battles of Dunbar (1296) and Falkirk (1298) William Wallace and the Scots took to the forests themselves, and many later people saw resemblances between Robin Hood and the Scottish nationalist outlaw (Spence, 1928).

The reference to Barnsdale is surprising, as it is far to the south, but it has been argued that this may refer to the forest of Barnsdale in Rutland, not that in Yorkshire where the *Gest of Robyn Hode* is set. In the Middle Ages the royal forest of Barnsdale in Rutland was owned by the Earl of Huntington, and this title was closely connected to the royal house of Scotland (Knight, 1994, p. 31). Internal evidence suggests this fact came to Wyntoun's notice: the language of the reference is rather oddly amplified, and it may be that there was an earlier popular jingle which ran:

> *Litil Iohun and Robert Hude Waythmen war in Ingilwode.*

It may be that Andrew's discovery, through royal contacts, of the Barnsdale Robin Hood might have led him to recast the couplet into the slightly awkward four lines he offers.]

Litil Iohun and Robert Hude
Waythmen war commendit gud;   *Forest outlaws; praised*
In Ingilwode and Bernnysdaile
Thai oyssit al this tyme thar trawale.   *practiced; labor*

The Chroniclers' Robin Hood

From Walter Bower's *Continuation* of John of Fordun's *Scotichronicon* (c. 1440)

[In the 1440s Bower, like Andrew of Wyntoun, a canon of St. Andrew's Priory and eventually Abbot of Incholm (a religious house on an island in the Firth of Forth near Edinburgh) was reworking the chronicle written in Latin some twenty years before by John of Fordun. As well as bringing it up to date he inserted passages, including a lengthy comment on Robin Hood and Little John.

Under the year 1266 he described Robin as a *famosus siccarius* (a well-known cutthroat), a more severe account than Wyntoun's *waythmen* who were *commendit gud*. He also seems critical when he says that "the foolish people are so inordinately fond of celebrating [him] in tragedy and comedy" (trans. Dobson and Taylor, 1976, p. 5). It is interesting to speculate what he meant. The terms do not necessarily refer to drama at this time. Presumably "comedy" refers to the ballads where Robin triumphs, like *Robin Hood and the Monk*, recorded very soon after this. But what does he mean by "tragedies?" The only tragic event in the Robin Hood tradition is the hero's death, and this must imply that by Bower's time the death story is well known. The *Gest*, probably in its present shape by about the mid-fifteenth century, clearly knows of this tradition, which is itself recorded in a mid seventeenth-century ballad, as well as Munday's plays of 1598–99.

Bower places the outlaw in the context of Simon de Montfort's rebellion against Henry III, and refers to Robin as fighting among the "disinherited," the name given to the dissidents led by Simon. This change of date from Wyntoun — which Bower must have known — has the effect of removing the resemblance to Wallace, and Bower is in general much less pro-Scottish than Wyntoun. It also linked Robin Hood with what was eventually to be one of the central fables of English liberalism: in the nineteenth century Simon de Montfort was thought of as the founder of parliament, through forcing a consultative process on the king in the "Provisions of Oxford" in 1258. Popular political culture revived the link that Bower had imagined: G. P. R. James's *Forest Days* (1843) is a rather effective historical novel about Robin the proto-parliamentarian.

Like Langland, Bower testifies to the widespread popularity of the outlaw myth in the mouths of the "foolish people," but he then gives, in Latin prose, a priceless typical version of a Robin Hood story, and it turns out to be one where the church is itself supported by the outlaw. Bower's Latin is quite difficult, not meant for public consumption; it is a message to the learned and perhaps something of a covert sharing of officially disapproved stories. Robin, deep in the forest, celebrates Mass and refuses to be disturbed by the marauding "viscount" or sheriff; he finishes his Mass and then routs the enemy — the motif of a hero mixing devotion and casualness survives in the myth of Drake playing bowls as the Armada approached.

Robin's devotion to the Mass is found in *Robin Hood and the Monk*; the nervousness of some of his followers is found again in Martin Parker's *A True Tale of Robin Hood*, and the sheriff's failed excursion to the woods is a frequent feature of the tradition, early and late. But Bower's story is focussed to make Robin a hero of the church, and the fact that he transfers plunder to the church and always supports Mass-attendance conveys a polemical tone suited to Bower's own religious context.]

Then arose the famous murderer, Robert Hood, as well as Little John, together with their accomplices from among the disinherited, whom the foolish populace are so inordinately fond of celebrating both in tragedies and comedies, and about whom they are delighted to hear the jesters and minstrels sing above all other ballads. About whom also certain praiseworthy things are told, as appears in this — that when once in Barnsdale, avoiding the anger of the king and the threats of the prince, he was according to his custom most devoutly hearing Mass and had no wish on any account to interrupt the service — on a certain day, when he was hearing Mass, having been discovered in that very secluded place in the woods when the Mass was taking place by a certain sheriff (*viscount*) and servant of the king, who had very often lain in wait for him previously, there came to him those who had found this out from their men to suggest that he should make every effort to flee. This, on account of his reverence for the sacrament in which he was then devoutly involved, he completely refused to do. But, the rest of his men trembling through fear of death, Robert, trusting in the one so great whom he worshipped, with the few who then bravely remained with him, confronted his enemies and easily overcame them, and enriched by the spoils he took from them and their ransom, ever afterward singled out the servants of the church and the Masses to be held in greater respect, bearing in mind what is commonly said: "God harkens to him who hears Mass frequently."

(Latin text, Child, III, 41; trans. A. I. Jones.)

From John Major's *Historia Majoris Britanniae* (1521)

[John Major was a Scottish historian and intellectual who, unlike Wyntoun and Bower, worked outside the country; he spent many years at the University of Paris, where he became well enough known to be mentioned ironically in Rabelais's *Gargantua* as the author of a treatise on black puddings. He returned to teach at the University of Glasgow in about 1500 but he had apparently already completed his *Historia Majoris Britanniae* (*History of Greater Britain*, though, oddly, it also translates as *Major's History of Britain*). Written in a newly humanist Latin, rather than Bower's old fashioned style, this also has much less Scottish sympathies than his predecessors: he cuts the discussion of Edward I's ruelty and sees him as less of a real threat to Scotland than did his predecessors — and also his followers, Hector Boece and David Buchanan.

In addition to reducing the pro-Scottish element of other Scottish historians, Major also relocates the Robin Hood story into the late twelfth century, the much more distant time of King John. This is the first time that the outlaw is linked with the period of King Richard. In later hands this was to re-shape Robin's resistance to authority itself as an act of a noble conservatism, since bad King John could be attacked and true kingship defended at the same time. This does not appear to be Major's motif: his redating of the story in the period of John is probably due to the influence of the story of *Fouke le Fitz Waryn*, a noble outlaw and enemy of bad authority from that period.

Major's "exceptionally influential eulogy" of Robin (Dobson and Taylor, 1976, p. 5) presents him as a bold but moral hero, only killing in self-defense, a protector of women and the poor. This suggests that Major was familiar with the *Gest* and its presentation of the outlaw, and that accords with the idea that he was not only a humane robber but also a "chief." The Latin word was *dux*, which just means "leader," but can also, as "duke," have aristocratic implications. In this way, while not decisively creating the distressed gentleman who is to be the new "renaissance Robin Hood," Major established the basis for that figure by removing the Scottish — or anti-English — point of view, moralizing his deeds, elevating his character to the edge of gentrification and, perhaps the most important thing, removing any trace of Bower's hero of Catholicism.]

About this time it was, as I conceive, that there flourished those most famous robbers Robert Hood, an Englishman, and Little John, who lay in wait in the woods, but spoiled of their goods those only that were wealthy. They took the life of no man, unless he either attacked them or offered resistance in defence of his property. Robert supported by his plundering one hundred bowmen, ready fighters every one, with whom four hundred of the strongest would not dare to engage in combat. The feats of this Robert are told in song all over Britain. He would allow no woman to suffer injustice, nor would he spoil the poor, but rather enriched them from the plunder taken from the abbots. The robberies of this man I condemn, but of all robbers he was the humanest and the chief. (1892, pp. 156–67)

From Richard Grafton's *Chronicle at Large* (1569)

[Richard Grafton was a printer and scholar whose very influential history summarized Major's version and moved on to give an account which both carried a good deal more detail than had previously been provided and also firmly gentrified the hero. This is the first chronicle which deliberately includes material from the ballads, though the earlier chroniclers were clearly aware of the popular tradition. Nevertheless, Grafton presents Robin as a real figure and does not mention Little John: gentrification and elevation of the hero develop together.

This obviously provided a structure for Martin Parker's quasi-biographical *A True Tale of Robin Hood*, and Grafton himself claims authenticity in several ways. The king's price on Robin's head, says Grafton, is to be confirmed "by the recordes in the Exchequer." In the same spirit of verification, the story ends by insisting that Robin's gravestone and memorial cross are available for inspection, and it also claims ancient authenticity on the basis of using as source "an olde and auncient Pamphlet." None of this evidence has survived, and probably never existed. The gravestone was later described and drawn (Holt, 1989, p. 43), but it looks suspiciously like an artist's impression of Grafton's remarks.

No "auncient Pamphlet" has survived which tells Grafton's story of an earl — or perhaps a soldierly man who became an earl — who was disgraced through wastefulness and so became a leader of an outlaw band and an enemy to the king. This sounds more like Fouke than Robin the yeoman, and *Fouke le Fitz Waryn* is a possible distant source. The second part of Grafton's story, where Robin is hunted by the king and betrayed by the Prioress, is not found in any previous text, though the *Gest* does touch on these events to some degree.

Grafton certainly consulted sources: his priory is called Bircklies probably because he misread a capital *K* (printed or written) in the familiar name Kirklees. It remains conceivable that there was a lost story combining the yeoman outlaw with an aristocrat fallen from grace, but it is more likely that for the "pamphlet" he has in mind the well known *Gest*, perhaps the equally widely distributed *Gamelyn*, and that the references to grave, cross and records are based on contemporary hearsay.

Partly through this aura of credibility, Grafton's popularization of a now firmly gentrified hero set the tone for the gentlemanly outlaw who was to appear in play and song and, in some sense, to be absorbed into the mainstream right through into gallant Sir Robin of modern Hollywood. After summarizing Major, Grafton strikes out on his own]:

But in an olde and auncient Pamphlet I finde this written of the sayd Robert Hood. This man (sayth he) discended of a nobel parentage: or rather beyng of a base stocke and linage, was for his manhoode and chivalry advaunced to the noble dignité of an Erle. Excellyng principally in Archery, or shootyng, his manly courage agreeyng therunto: But afterwardes he so prodigally exceeded in charges and expences, that he fell into great debt, by reason wherof, so many actions and sutes were commenced against him, wherunto he aunswered not, that by order of lawe he was outlawed, and then for a lewde shift, as his last refuge, gathered together a companye of Roysters and Cutters, and practised robberyes and spoylyng of the kynges subjects, and occupied and frequentede the Forestes or wilde Countries. The which beyng certefyed to the King, and he beyng greatly offended therewith, caused his proclamation to be made that whosoever would bryng him quicke or dead, the king would geve him a great summe of money, as by the recordes in the Exchequer is to be seene: But of this promise, no man enjoyed any benefite. For the sayd Robert Hood, beyng afterwardes troubled with sicknesse, came to a certein Nonry in Yorkshire called Bircklies, where desirying to be let blood, he was betrayed and bled to deth. After whose death the Prioresse of the same place caused him to be buried by the high way side, where he had used to rob and spoyle those that passed that way. And upon his grave the sayde Prioresse did lay a very fayre stone, wherin the names of Robert Hood, William of Goldesborough and others were graven. And the cause why she buryed him there was for that the common passengers and travailers knowyng and seeyng him there buryed, might more safely and without feare take their jorneys that way, which they durst not do in the life of the sayd outlawes. And at eyther end of the sayde Tombe was erected a crosse of stone, which is to be seene there at this present (1569, pp. 84–85).

Robin Hood and the Monk

Introduction

Robin Hood and the Monk is preserved in Cambridge University manuscript Ff.5.48. The manuscript is damaged by stains and hard to read and was, it seems, not known to Percy or Ritson, unlike all the other major Robin Hood ballads. It was first printed and given this title by Robert Jamieson in his *Popular Ballads and Songs* of 1806 (II, 54–72). The edition itself was quite heavily edited and erroneous, and a better text appeared in C. H. Hartshorne's *Ancient Metrical Tales* in 1829. Nevertheless, Sir Frederick Madden wrote, in a slip preserved in his copy in the British Library, that this was "the worst edited text" he had come across, and he re-collated the whole edition; his version of this ballad then appeared in an appendix in the second edition of Ritson's *Robin Hood* in 1832 as *Robin Hood and the Monk*. Although this title, like that of other early ballads, only refers to the initial enemy, not the sheriff who is the ultimate threat, it still seems better than "A Tale of Robin Hood" used by Hartshorne and Gutch.

The Cambridge manuscript (here called *a*) is written in a "very clear cursive hand" (Dobson and Taylor, 1976, p. 115) and dated some time after 1450. The reference in line 331 to *oure cumly kyng* (also found in the *Gest*, see note on line 1412) has been taken as referring to the notably handsome Edward IV, which would date the ballad in this form as after 1461; this is by no means impossible, but the phrase was certainly used of Edward III, and the errors in copying could well suggest an earlier text that had been transmitted several times. There is also a single manuscript leaf preserved in *The Bagford Ballads* in the Printed Books collection in the British Library (here called *b*) which also appears to be of the later fifteenth century, and although *a* is obviously the only source for the poem as a whole, it is held in this edition that *b* provides a few preferred readings.

The date is important. Though some have thought the *Gest* is earlier, it is at base a literary compilation, and so *Robin Hood and the Monk* is the oldest extant example of the "rymes of Robin Hood" referred to by Langland in the 1370s, implied by Andrew of Wyntoun in the 1420s, and both described and exemplified by Walter Bower in the 1440s. Bower's Latin summary of a Robin Hood story is the nearest contemporary to this ballad as a narrative, and the two texts share a sense of Robin's deep religious faith as well as suspicion and hostility towards royal officials: both also lack the lighthearted tone that is found in *Robin Hood and the Potter* and the *Gest*, and that characterizes most of the later tradition.

Although no direct sources have been proposed, Robin's devotion to the Virgin may provide a clue. In spite of the obvious dangers, Robin is determined to attend Mass in Nottingham "With the myght of mylde Marye" (line 28). After angrily separating from Little John, he goes on to town alone and prays "to God and myld Mary / To bryng hym out save agayn" (lines 69–70). Once in town he enters "Seynt Mary chirch" and "knelyd down before the rode" (lines 71–72). Arousing the suspicions of a "gret-hedid munke," he is captured by the sheriff and cast into prison. Having learned that Robin has been captured, Little John rallies the spirits of the outlaws by reassuring them that since Robin has "servyd Oure Lady many a day . . . No wyckud deth shal he dye" (lines 133–36). Little John then promises that with the "myght of mylde Mary" he will take care of the treacherous monk and rescue Robin. While Child notes Robin's devotion to the Virgin (III, 96), he does not cite a "miracle of the Virgin" as a potential source. The episodes just summarized closely resemble a type of miracle known as the "knight and the Virgin," of which seven examples were printed by Wynkyn de Worde in the late fifteenth century *The Myracles of Oure Lady*. Two of these short prose miracles (numbers four and six in Peter Whiteford's edition) relate how two knights, captured and imprisoned by their enemies, are delivered out of prison by the intercession of the Virgin.

In spite of its early existence, *Robin Hood and the Monk* did not have a strong influence on the following centuries, though perhaps it inspired the *Gest*'s account of robbing a "fat-heded monke" (line 364). There were no broadside versions of this ballad and it is absent from the many garlands of the seventeenth and eighteenth centuries, but this story of Robin's arrest in Nottingham and his rescue by Little John and Much has been accepted by all readers as a classic.

Child welcomed *Robin Hood and the Monk* as "very perfection in its kind" (III, 95) and Dobson and Taylor assert that it has "held pride of place as the most distinguished and artistically accomplished of all the Robin Hood ballads" (1976, p. 113). This view appears to stem in part from a sense of antiquity (Child prints it next but one after the *Gest* — *Robin Hood and Guy of Gisborne* intervenes, see p. 168 on its dating), but clearly also from his idea of its originary excellence, especially his admiration of the arresting opening stanzas. This high valuation is tolerant of the fact that the ballad clearly lacks some material: commentators all agree that a substantial passage is missing after line 120, and that this has been caused by the loss of a leaf in the original of this manuscript. The lacuna in the manuscript, like the pages torn from Percy's Folio manuscript, may itself have appeared attractively *Gothick* in its antique incompletion.

A dissenting voice on the ballad is that of Holt, who calls it "a blood and thunder adventure" and feels that after the return to Sherwood "the remnant of the tale is crude moral comment": overall it is "a shallow tale, but one well and crisply told" (1989, pp. 28–30). More literary-minded commentators usually agree with Gray that this is "an excellent piece of vivid narrative" and, however it was delivered, would be a "splendid performance" (1984, p. 13). In terms of the recurrent motifs found in the outlaw myth, this ballad offers an excellent example of the natural setting which has an implied value, a full statement of the danger of conflict within the band and the consequent dangers of isolation, a strongly developed representation of Robin's devotion to our lady, the hostility between the outlaws and the established church, a brief statement of the dangers of the town (reduced by the loss of material), a mission in disguise (John and Much), the involvement of the king, the frustration of the sheriff, the re-forming of the outlaw band, the establishment of the true values held by the band and their recognition by the king (John's fidelity in particular).

These central motifs, also found in the *Gest* in one form or another and recurrent right through the tradition down to the present, find brisk and memorable realization in *Robin Hood and the Monk*, giving it a stronger social meaning than Child or Dobson and Taylor appreciate, and a much weightier sub-text than Holt envisages. But Holt's point about melodrama has its force. Though the sheriff is not killed in this ballad (as he is in the *Gest* and in *Robin Hood and Guy of Gisborne*), the jailer is summarily executed in line 278. This is very like (including some verbal echoes) the rescue of William of Cloudeslye in *Adam Bell*, and also like the rescue of Johnie Armstrong in the border ballad of that name. Jailers, as Child remarks a little ironically, receive short shrift in these narratives (III, 95, footnote). But here even brusquer treatment appears when John and Much catch up with the Monk who has (legally enough) caused the arrest of Robin Hood. After a preliminary sequence of pretence, claiming they too are victims of an outlaw, with ferocious vengeance they simply pull down and kill not only the monk but also his boy, a potential witness. This savagery accords with the killing of Guy and the Sheriff in *Robin Hood and Guy of Gisborne* and of the sheriff towards the end of the *Gest* — yet they were established villains. There is a casualness about the monk's killing that may seem unsettling, especially when the sheriff is merely humiliated, not killed in the same ballad. This "blood and thunder" element is also found in *Robin Hood and Guy of Gisborne* and in *Robin Hood's Progress to Nottingham* and may be traced to the social bandit tradition.

Against such ferocity, though, is set the innately valuable natural world "in feyre foreste" and "under the grene wode tre," realized in two stanzas of a "fine lyrical introduction" (Gray, 1984, p. 11). The forest setting seems a state of harmony to which the outlaws return after urban disruptions. But just as violence enters this Edenic world, the communal calm of the outlaw band is disrupted by conflict, and the argument between John and Robin is the most fully worked out instance of this important theme in the tradition, which here is finally resolved in a specific debate over who should lead the band.

Their dispute focusses, as it tends to do elsewhere, on gambling. As in trades where coin is exchanged for goods (potter or butcher for example), and as with carrying large amounts of money through the forest, the exchange of money through a contest seems to be a threat to harmony in the world of the Robin Hood ballads. This little noted but insistent feature supports the idea of a "natural" economy under threat by some early form of cash nexus.

In social terms, Robin here, as in other early texts, is clearly himself a yeoman, whose leadership of the band is by consent. That is tested and reaffirmed in this ballad, so constructing a dream of yeomanly community and self-protection, a set of values that mesh with the realization of a fully natural world, where towns, cash, letters, royal seals and the institutions of religion and commerce are all to be judged as threatening and, in fiction at least, can be successfully confronted. This appears to relate to the question of audience, discussed in the General Introduction, pp. 7–8.

Robin Hood and the Monk has a consistent and well-managed rhyming pattern, based on the abcb stanza, with an unusually small number of poor rhymes (38/40, 48/50, 56/8, 300/302, 332/4) and only rare variation of the rhyme scheme to abab (13–16, 151–54 and, by repetition, 39–42, 315–18). If the rhyming is at a high standard, the diction is somewhat less vigorous than some commentators suggest: cliché or near cliché can be found at 14, 30, 67, 186 and the weak line *The* [or *For*] *sothe as I you say* is found no less than six times at 108, 188, 236, 248, 260, 308.

Simple and often direct as it is, the style of *Robin Hood and the Monk* emphasizes the ballad's power, poetic and thematic. Gray draws attention to what he calls the "open ending" of this ballad (1984, p. 17), that is the way in which the king admires the values of the foresters, without either incorporating them (as in *Adam Bell*) or ensuring their defeat (as in *A True Tale of Robin Hood*). This earliest of the surviving ballads, with its fine opening, its speed and directness, its condensed and highly suggestive plot moving between the forest retreat and the threatening outside world, presents in strong form the social challenge of the outlaw myth that has, in various reconstructions, survived to the present.

Select Bibliography

Texts

Cambridge University Manuscript Ff 5.48.

Manuscript leaf in *The Bagford Ballads*, British Library Printed Books Collection C40.m.9–11.

Child, F. J., ed. *English and Scottish Popular Ballads*. 5 vol. Rpt. New York: Dover, 1995. Vol. III, no. 119. Pp. 94–101.

Dobson, R. J., and J. Taylor, eds. *Rymes of Robin Hood*. London: Heinemann, 1976. Pp. 113–22.

Gutch, J. M., ed. *A Lytelle Gest of Robin Hood with other Auncient and Modern Ballads and Songs Relating to the Celebrated Yeoman*. 2 vols. London: Longman, 1847. Vol. II, 1–20. [Titled "A Tale of Robin Hood."]

Hartshorne, C. H., ed. *Ancient Metrical Tales*. London: Pickering, 1829. Pp. 179–97. [Titled "A Tale of Robin Hood." One copy in British Library includes re-collation by Sir Frederick Madden.]

Jamieson, Robert, ed. *Popular Ballads and Songs, From Traditions, Manuscripts, and Scarce Editions with Translations of Similar Pieces from the Ancient Danish Language, and a Few Originals by the Editor*. 2 vols. Edinburgh: Constable, 1806. Vol. II, pp. 54–72.

Ritson, Joseph, ed. *Robin Hood: A Collection of All the Ancient Poems, Songs and Ballads Relative to the Celebrated English Outlaw*. 2 vols. Second edition. London: Pickering, 1832. Appendix VIII, 221–36.

Whiteford, Peter, ed. *The Myracles of Oure Lady*. Middle English Texts 23. Heidelberg: Carl Winter, 1990. [Includes miracles of a knight and the Virgin.]

Commentary and Criticism

Child, F. J., pp. 94–96.

Dobson, R. J., and J. Taylor, pp. 113–15.

Gray, Douglas. "The Robin Hood Ballads." *Poetica* 18 (1984), 1–39.

Holt, J. C. *Robin Hood*. Second ed. London: Thames and Hudson, 1989.

Robin Hood and the Monk

In somer, when the shawes be sheyne,   *woods are bright*
And leves be large and long,
Hit is full mery in feyre foreste   *fair*
To here the foulys song,   *hear; birds'*

5   To se the dere draw to the dale,   *deer*
And leve the hilles hee,   *high*
And shadow hem in the leves grene,   *shelter themselves*
Under the grene wode tre.

Hit befel on Whitson
10 Erly in a May mornyng,
The son up feyre can shyne,   *did*
And the briddis mery can syng.

"This is a mery mornyng," seid Litull John,
"Be Hym that dyed on tre;   *By Christ; Cross*
15 A more mery man then I am one   *than*
Lyves not in Cristianté.   *Christendom*

"Pluk up thi hert, my dere mayster,"
Litull John can sey,
"And thynk hit is a full fayre tyme
20 In a mornyng of May."

"Ye, on thyng greves me," seid Robyn,   *one*
"And does my hert mych woo: *woe*
That I may not no solem day
To mas nor matyns goo.   *Mass nor Matins*

25 "Hit is a fourtnet and more," seid he,   *It's been a fortnight*
"Syn I my Savyour see;   *Since I've been to Mass*

37

To day wil I to Notyngham," seid Robyn,
"With the myght of mylde Marye."   *Virgin Mary*

Than spake Moche, the mylner sun,   *miller's son*
30 Ever more wel hym betyde!   *May good happen to him!*
"Take twelve of thi wyght yemen,   *strong yeomen*
Well weppynd, be thi side.   *Well armed*
Such on wolde thi selfe slon,   *He who would kill you*
That twelve dar not abyde."   *Would not dare face those twelve*

35 "Of all my mery men," seid Robyn,
"Be my feith I wil non have,   *By*
But Litull John shall beyre my bow,   *carry*
Til that me list to drawe."   *Until I choose to shoot*

"Thou shall beyre thin own," seid Litull Jon,
40 "Maister, and I wyl beyre myne,
And we well shete a peny," seid Litull Jon,   *shoot arrows for a penny wager*
"Under the grene wode lyne."   *linden trees*

"I wil not shete a peny," seyd Robyn Hode,
"In feith, Litull John, with the,
45 But ever for on as thou shetis," seide Robyn,
"In feith I holde the thre."   *I bet you three pennies (for one)*

Thus shet thei forth, these yemen too,   *two*
Bothe at buske and brome,   *bush and shrub*
Til Litull John wan of his maister
50 Five shillings to hose and shone.   *for socks and shoes*

A ferly strife fel them betwene,   *great argument*
As they went bi the wey;
Litull John seid he had won five shillings,
And Robyn Hode seid schortly nay.   *abruptly*

55 With that Robyn Hode lyed Litul Jon,   *called Little John a liar*
And smote hym with his hande;   *struck*
Litul Jon waxed wroth therwith,   *grew angry*
And pulled out his bright bronde.   *sword*

Robin Hood and the Monk

60	"Were thou not my maister," seid Litull John,	
	"Thou shuldis by hit ful sore;	*pay for it sorely*
	Get the a man wher thou wille,	
	For thou getis me no more."	
	Then Robyn goes to Notyngham,	
	Hym selfe mornyng allone,	*grieving*
65	And Litull John to mery Scherwode,	
	The pathes he knew ilkone.	*every one*
	Whan Robyn came to Notyngham,	
	Sertenly withouten layn,	*Certainly; lie*
	He prayed to God and myld Mary	
70	To bryng hym out save agayn.	*safe*
	He gos in to Seynt Mary chirch,	
	And knelyd down before the Rode;	*Cross*
	Alle that ever were the church within	
	Beheld wel Robyn Hode.	
75	Beside hym stod a gret-hedid munke,	*large-headed*
	I pray to God woo he be!	*woe*
	Ful sone he knew gode Robyn,	
	As sone as he hym se.	
	Out at the durre he ran,	*door*
80	Ful sone and anon;	*At once*
	Alle the gatis of Notyngham	*gates*
	He made to be sparred everychon.	*barred*
	"Rise up," he seid, "thou prowde schereff,	
	Buske the and make the bowne;	*Hurry yourself; yourself ready*
85	I have spyed the kynggis felon,	*(see note)*
	For sothe he is in this town.	*truly*
	"I have spyed the false felon,	
	As he stondis at his masse;	
	Hit is long of the," seide the munke,	*It's your fault*
90	"And ever he fro us passe.	*If; escapes*

"This traytur name is Robyn Hode,
Under the grene wode lynde;   *linden trees*
He robbyt me onys of a hundred pound,   *once*
Hit shalle never out of my mynde."

95   Up then rose this prowde schereff,
And radly made hym yare;   *quickly made himself ready*
Many was the moder son
To the kyrk with hym can fare.   *church; did go*

In at the durres thei throly thrast,   *doors they strenuously pressed*
100   With staves ful gode wone;   *with plenty of staves*
"Alas, alas!" seid Robyn Hode,
"Now mysse I Litull John."

But Robyn toke out a too-hond sworde,   *two-handed sword*
That hangit down be his kne;
105   Ther as the schereff and his men stode thyckust,   *thickest*
Thedurwarde wolde he.   *Thitherward*

Thryes thorow at them he ran then,   *Thrice through*
For sothe as I yow sey,   *Truly*
And woundyt mony a moder son,
110   And twelve he slew that day.

His sworde upon the schireff hed   *sheriff's head*
Sertanly he brake in too;   *two*
"The smyth that the made," seid Robyn,   *thee (the sword)*
"I pray to God wyrke hym woo!   *woe*

115   "For now am I weppynlesse," seid Robyn,   *weaponless*
"Alasse! agayn my wyll;
But if I may fle these traytors fro,   *Unless*
I wot thei wil me kyll."   *know*

Robyn in to her churche ran,   *their (see note)*
120   Thro out hem everilkon,   *each one*
....

Robin Hood and the Monk

Sum fel in swonyng as thei were dede,   *swooning*
And lay stil as any stone;
Non of theym were in her mynde   *kept their heads*
But only Litull Jon.

125   "Let be your rule," seid Litull Jon,   *wailing*
"For His luf that dyed on tre,   *Christ's love*
Ye that shulde be dughty men;   *doughty*
Het is gret shame to se.

"Oure maister has bene hard bystode   *beset*
130   And yet scapyd away;   *escaped*
Pluk up your hertis, and leve this mone,   *hearts; lament*
And harkyn what I shal say.   *listen to*

"He has servyd Oure Lady many a day,
And yet wil, securly;   *surely*
135   Therfor I trust in hir specialy
No wyckud deth shal he dye.

"Therfor be glad," seid Litul John,
"And let this mournyng be;
And I shal be the munkis gyde,   *take care of the monk*
140   With the myght of mylde Mary,
And I mete hym," seid Litul John   *If*
"We will go but we too.

"Loke that ye kepe wel owre tristil-tre,   *trysting or meeting tree*
Under the levys smale,
145   And spare non of this venyson,
That gose in thys vale."

Forthe then went these yemen too,   *two*
Litul John and Moche on fere,   *together*
And lokid on Moch emys hows;   *Much's uncle's house*
150   The hye way lay full nere.

Litul John stode at a wyndow in the mornyng,
And lokid forth at a stage;   *from an upper room*

41

He was war wher the munke came ridyng,
And with hym a litul page.

155 "Be my feith," seid Litul John to Moch,
"I can the tel tithyngus gode;   *tell you good tidings*
I se wher the munke cumys rydyng,
I know hym be his wyde hode."

They went in to the way, these yemen bothe,
160 As curtes men and hende;   *Like courteous and gracious men*
Thei spyrred tithyngus at the munke,   *asked news*
As they hade bene his frende.

"Fro whens come ye?" seid Litull Jon,
"Tel us tithyngus, I yow pray,
165 Of a false owtlay,
Was takyn yisterday.

"He robbyt me and my felowes bothe
Of twenti marke in serten;
If that false owtlay be takyn,
170 For sothe we wolde be fayn."   *glad*

"So did he me," seid the munke,
Of a hundred pound and more;
I layde furst hande hym apon,
Ye may thonke me therfore."

175 "I pray God thanke you," seid Litull John,
"And we wil when we may;
We wil go with you, with your leve,
And bryng yow on your way.

"For Robyn Hode hase many a wilde felow,
180 I tell you in certen;
If thei wist ye rode this way,   *knew*
In feith ye shulde be slayn."

Robin Hood and the Monk

As thei went talking be the way,
The munke and Litull John,
185 John toke the munkis horse be the hede,
Ful sone and anon.   *At once*

Johne toke the munkis horse be the hed,
For sothe as I yow say;
So did Much the litull page,
190 For he shulde not scape away.   *escape*

Be the golett of the hode   *throat-piece*
John pulled the munke down;
John was nothyng of hym agast,   *afraid*
He lete hym falle on his crown.

195 Litull John was so agrevyd,
And drew owt his swerde in hye;   *in haste*
The munke saw he shulde be ded,
Lowd mercy can he crye.

"He was my maister," seid Litull John,
200 "That thou hase browght in bale;   *harm*
Shalle thou never cum at oure kyng,
For to telle hym tale."

John smote of the munkis hed,   *struck off*
No longer wolde he dwell;   *wait*
205 So did Moch the litull page,
For ferd lest he wolde tell.   *fear*

Ther thei beryed hem bothe,   *buried*
In nouther mosse nor lyng,   *neither bog nor heath*
And Litull John and Much in fere   *together*
210 Bare the letturs to oure kyng.

Litull John cam in unto the kyng
He knelid down upon his kne:
"God yow save, my lege lorde,
Jhesus yow save and se!   *watch over*

43

215   "God yow save, my lege kyng!"   *lord*
        To speke John was full bolde;
        He gaf hym the letturs in his hand,
        The kyng did hit unfold.

        The kyng red the letturs anon,   *immediately*
220   And seid, "So mot I the,   *So may I thrive*
        Ther was never yoman in mery Inglond
        I longut so sore to se.   *longed*

        "Wher is the munke that these shuld have brought?"
        Oure kyng can say.
225   "Be my trouth," seid Litull John,
        "He dyed after the way."   *along*

        The kyng gaf Moch and Litul Jon
        Twenti pound in sertan,
        And made theim yemen of the crown,
230   And bade theim go agayn.

        He gaf John the seel in hand,
        The scheref for to bere,
        To bryng Robyn hym to,
        And no man do hym dere.   *harm*

235   John toke his leve at oure kyng,
        The sothe as I yow say;
        The next way to Notyngham   *nearest*
        To take he yede the way.   *went*

        Whan John came to Notyngham
240   The gatis were sparred ychon;   *all barred*
        John callid up the porter,
        He answerid sone anon.   *at once*

        "What is the cause," seid Litul Jon,
        "Thou sparris the gates so fast?"
245   "Because of Robyn Hode," seid porter,
        "In depe prison is cast.

"John and Moch and Wyll Scathlok,
For sothe as I yow say,
Thei slew oure men upon oure wallis,
250 And sawten us every day."   *assault*

Litull John spyrred after the schereff,   *asked*
And sone he hym fonde;
He oppyned the kyngus privé seell,   *king's privy seal*
And gaf hym in his honde.

255 Whan the scheref saw the kyngus seell,
He did of his hode anon: *He took off his hood*
"Wher is the munke that bare the letturs?"
He seid to Litull John.

"He is so fayn of hym," seid Litul John,   *[The king] is so pleased with him*
260 "For sothe as I yow say,
He has made hym abot of Westmynster,
A lorde of that abbay."

The scheref made John gode chere,
And gaf hym wyne of the best;
265 At nyght thei went to her bedde,   *their*
And every man to his rest.

When the scheref was on slepe,
Dronken of wyne and ale,
Litul John and Moch for sothe
270 Toke the way unto the gale.   *jail*

Litul John callid up the jayler,
And bade hym rise anon;
He seyd Robyn Hode had brokyn the prison,
And out of hit was gon.

275 The porter rose anon sertan,
As sone as he herd John calle;
Litul John was redy with a swerd,
And bare hym throw to the walle.   *stabbed*

"Now wil I be jayler," seid Litul John,
280   And toke the keyes in honde;
He toke the way to Robyn Hode,
And sone he hym unbonde.

He gaf hym a gode swerd in his hond,
His hed ther with to kepe,   *protect*
285   And ther as the wallis were lowyst
Anon down can thei lepe.   *did*

Be that the cok began to crow,
The day began to spryng;
The scheref fond the jaylier ded,
290   The comyn bell made he ryng.   *town bell*

He made a crye thoroout al the town,   *proclamation*
Wheder he be yoman or knave,
That cowthe bryng hym Robyn Hode,   *could*
His warison he shuld have.   *reward*

295   "For I dar never," seid the scheref,
"Cum before oure kyng;
For if I do, I wot serten   *I know for certain*
For sothe he wil me heng."   *hang*

The scheref made to seke Notyngham,   *search*
300   Bothe be strete and styne,   *alleys*
And Robyn was in mery Scherwode,
As light as lef on lynde.   *carefree; tree*

Then bespake gode Litull John,
To Robyn Hode can he say,
305   "I have done the a gode turne for an ill,
Quit me whan thou may.   *Repay*

"I have done the a gode turne," seid Litull John,
"For sothe as I the say;
I have brought the under the grene-wode lyne;
310   Fare wel, and have gode day."

"Nay, be my trouth," seid Robyn,
"So shall hit never be;
I make the maister," seid Robyn,
"Of alle my men and me."

315 "Nay, be my trouth," seid Litull John,
"So shalle hit never be;
But lat me be a felow," seid Litull John,
"No noder kepe I be."   *Nothing else do I care to be*

Thus John gate Robyn Hod out of prison,
320 Sertan withoutyn layn;   *lie*
Whan his men saw hym hol and sounde,
For sothe they were full fayne.   *glad*

They filled in wyne and made hem glad,
Under the levys smale,
325 And yete pastes of venyson,   *ate pasties*
That gode was with ale.

Than worde came to oure kyng
How Robyn Hode was gon,
And how the scheref of Notyngham
330 Durst never loke hym upon.

Then bespake oure cumly kyng,   *handsome*
In an angur hye:
"Litull John hase begyled the schereff,
In faith so hase he me.

335 "Litul John has begyled us bothe,
And that full wel I se;
Or ellis the schereff of Notyngham
Hye hongut shulde he be.   *High hanged*

"I made hem yemen of the crowne,
340 And gaf hem fee with my hond;   *money*
I gaf hem grith," seid oure kyng,   *pardon*
"Thorowout all mery Inglond.

"I gaf theym grith," then seid oure kyng;   *security*
"I say, so mot I the,   *so may I prosper*
345   For sothe soch a yeman as he is on
In all Inglond ar not thre.

"He is trew to his maister," seid oure kyng;
"I sey, be swete Seynt John,
He lovys better Robyn Hode
350   Then he dose us ychon.   *Than; each of us*

"Robyn Hode is ever bond to hym,   *obligated*
Bothe in strete and stalle;   *stable*
Speke no more of this mater," seid oure kyng,
"But John has begyled us alle."

355   Thus endys the talkyng of the munke
And Robyn Hode I wysse;   *to be sure*
God, that is ever a crowned kyng,
Bryng us alle to His blisse!

Notes

1   *somer*. The season is said in lines 9–10 to be Whitsuntide in May. Whitsun usually falls in late May, by which time many wild flowers are in bloom (hence the name "White" Sunday). Although many commentators link Robin Hood plays and games with May Day, the earliest references make it clear that late May, and so early summer, is the time when Robin Hood rituals occurred (Knight, 1994, pp. 103–04). Although the *reverdie* or "regreening" theme is associated with spring as in the opening of the *Canterbury Tales*, that actually refers to late spring, when April is largely over: and poems other than the Robin Hood ballads celebrate early summer, like the lyric "Summer is ycumen in."

    shawes. The early Robin Hood ballads locate the outlaws in the opening stanzas in a green forest setting, as if this is the validating context for their action.

9   *Whitson*. Jamieson read "Whitsontyde" and Madden accepted Hartshorne's "Whitsontide" in his re-collation of the manuscript against Hartshorne's edition. Child agreed, but said the last four letters were "no longer legible." However, there is no sign in the manuscript, including under ultra-violet light, that they were ever present.

13   In the early ballads, Robin Hood's *meyné* or company consists of three named characters, Little John, Much the Miller's son, and William Scarlock or Scathelock (both names imply Will is good at effecting violent entry), plus a group of unnamed *wight yemen*, ranging in number from twelve to one hundred and forty. Little John is second in command, a major character in his own right.

14   The oath *Be Hym that dyed on tre* is both an asseveration and a line-filler, often used to provide one of the *b* rhymes in a four-line stanza rhyming *abcb*. For another example see line 126 and, with the same rhyme scheme, the *Gest*, lines 405, 439, 1227, 1363.

21   *Ye*. Dobson and Taylor emend the manuscript to *yea*, but *ye* is a possible form for a positive response, modern *yes*, and the emendation is unnecessary.

24   Matins is the first of the canonical hours of the day. It was originally sung soon after midnight, but "matins with lauds" came to be the office associated with daybreak, which is the sense here.

25   *he*. MS: *h*. The vowel has become invisible.

29   Much the Miller's son is one of Robin's three named companions in early ballads, where he is a more forceful and less youthful figure than in recent films. When Robin announces his intention to attend Mass in Nottingham, Much advises him to be cautious and to take twelve yeomen with him for protection — similar advice is given Robin by Little John in *Robin Hood and Guy of Gisborne* and by Will in *Robin Hood's Fishing* and *The Death of Robin Hood*. The hero's rash isolation appears to invite danger.

      This line begins a six-line stanza, of the kind identified in this edition in *Robin Hood and the Potter* at lines 208 and 254, and elsewhere; see the discussion in the General Introduction, p. 7 and the note on lines 141–44 below.

30   *betyde*. The last four letters are very hard to decipher, but this seems the most likely reading.

42   MS: *lyne*. Parallel usages indicate this refers to the forest trees, not the "line" of the forest; see line 92 where the spelling *lynde* makes it clearer that the reference is to trees, probably trees in general, not specifically the lime-trees indicated by the word.

51   The argument between Robin and Little John begins in line 37, when Robin orders John to carry his bow, and he refuses. The theme of internal strife which threatens the solidarity of the outlaw band also occurs in the *Gest*, where Little John becomes angry for no clear reason (line 442) and also in *Robin Hood and Guy of Gisborne*, where John orders Robin to wait under a tree while he interrogates the mysterious stranger: Robin loses his temper and threatens John. They separate, Little John is captured, and eventually rescued by Robin, the reverse of events here.

61   MS: *wille*. Only the first *w* is now legible. Hartshorne and Madden, and Child, both read it as the grammatically correct *wilt*, but the space suggests four letters rather than three: *thou wille* could either be read as a very precise subjunctive or as a loose usage and is accepted here.

72   MS: *knelyd*. Child prints *kneled*, presumably a minor error.

75   When Robin goes to St Mary's church in Nottingham (the city church, very close to the market he visits as a potter), he is recognised by a *gret-hedid* monk, whom Robin has robbed of one hundred pounds. The scene is reminiscent of the episode in the *Gest* when Robin steals eight hundred pounds from a *fat-heded* monk (line 364), who is the cellarer of St Mary's Abbey, York.

83–86   By reporting to the sheriff the presence of Robin Hood in the church, the monk has violated the ancient privilege of sanctuary. The betrayal is particularly heinous because Robin was attending mass when he was discovered. As the following excerpt makes clear, even felons were protected by sanctuary: "There are some felons who, when they are liable to arrest, flee to a church or some other sacred place, whence they must not be drawn or thrust forth, lest laymen who draw them forth incur sentence of excommunication or clergy who thrust them forth incur the taint of irregularity by their rash act. For it has been enacted that the English church shall have its rights and franchises unimpaired and also that the peace of the church and the land shall be preserved inviolate and that equal justice shall be dispensed to all men alike" (Harry Rothwell, ed., *English Historical Documents 1189–1327*, vol. III [London: Eyre & Spottiswoode, 1968], p. 567).

In describing Robin Hood to the sheriff, the monk uses the term *kynggis felon* "king's felon." In English law there were two types of legal proceedings or pleas: criminal and civil. Criminal offenses "appertain to the crown of the lord king," while civil charges "fall within the jurisdiction of the sheriffs of shires." Criminal charges included "tending to the death of the king, or the moving of a sedition against his person or his realm or in his army" and "a breach of the king's peace: homicide, arson, robbery, rape, falsifying . . . ." Civil actions were handled in shire courts and dealt with questions of status and dower, breach of fine, performance of homage, debts owed by lay persons, and the right of freehold and ownership (David C. Douglas and George W. Greenaway, eds., *English Historical Documents 1042–1189*, vol. II [London: Eyre & Spottiswoode, 1968], pp. 462–63).

85   The phrase *the kynggis felon* indicates that Robin Hood has been proclaimed outlaw, and so can be be captured at will; the monk also has a personal grievance, see lines 77–78 and 171–74.

95 MS: *schereff*. Child prints "shereff," presumably in error.

103 *too-hond*. The first part of the word is very hard to read, but does seem much the same as the clearer *too* in line 142. Robin and his men often fight with swords; the bow was not a hand-to-hand weapon, and military archers usually carried a sword for close fighting.

107 MS: *thorow at*. Child emends to *thorowout,* but the original makes sense — Robin runs both through and at them, much as William of Clowdeslye does, see *Adam Bell*, line 142.

   The last word in this line is hard to read; indeed there may not have been a word there at all. Hartshorne, Madden and Dobson, and Taylor leave *then* out; if, as seems likely, *thorow at* is trisyllabic, the meter does not require another word. Child printed *then*; the enigmatic marks could as easily be read as *wel*, but that would strain the sense improbably. On the assumption that a word did exist here, it seems best to accept Child's reading as being either correct or a probable emendation.

108 There is another word before *For sothe*. Hartshorne printed *Then*, and Madden apparently agreed. Dobson and Taylor (1976, p. 117) guess at *As*, but under ultra-violet light it appears to be *Ffor*. It can hardly mean *Four*, as a rhetorical *correctio* of *Thryes* in the previous line; this is a familiar, if weak, line, and presumably the second *for* must be an error.

112 The motif of the broken sword is a common theme in epic and heroic literature. In the *Aeneid* (Book XII, lines 969–82) Turnus's sword shatters on Aeneas's armor; in Prudentius's *Psychomachia*, Ira's sword breaks as she strikes the helmet of Patientia (v. 145); in *Beowulf*, the hero's sword *Naegling,* breaks in the fight with the dragon (line 2680); and in Malory's *Le Morte Darthur*, Balin's sword "burst in sunder" when it was struck by King Pellam's weapon. There is no sense here that Robin should be fighting with a bow rather than a sword: he and his fellow often fight with swords in the early ballads. The bow is seen primarily as a weapon for hunting or displaying skill.

119 This line is very hard to read. Child offers: *Robin in the churche ran*, which makes sense though as Dobson and Taylor note, it might be expected he would run out of the church (1976, p. 117). Madden thought it read *Robyn in to the churche ran* (he was correcting Hartshorne's error *Robyns men*). Under ultra-

violet light the manuscript appears to read *Robin in to . . . churche ran*; the short word before *churche* does not begin with *t* but may start with *h*. It could be *her,* which might refer to Our Lady or perhaps the *hem* of the next line; the action may suggest he is seeking sanctuary. But the reading is very indistinct, and in any case what follows is absent.

120   There is a gap in the narrative here, between the bottom of the verso of one leaf and the top of the recto of the next; in the interim we would have been told how Robin is captured and how the outlaws hear of it (probably through a boy carrying the message). Evidently a single leaf has been lost, carrying probably 48 lines (24 to the page is the average in this poem). As the poem continues the scene has changed to Sherwood where news of this disaster has just arrived, and all but Little John are deeply upset.

141–42   *"And I mete hym," seid Litul John*
"We will go but we too.

Child prints these two lines in reverse order (presumably an error) as if they are lines 2 and 3 of a damaged stanza (there is no gap in the MS). Dobson and Taylor accept this, and complete the stanza with some ingenuity:

Then spake Much the mylner son
"We will go but we too."
"And I mete hym," seid Litul John,
"I truste to wyrke hym woo." (1976, p. 118)

Lucid as this might be, it is highly suppositious, and the two lines are still in the wrong order. In fact the two lines, if printed in their manuscript order, make good sense as the end of a six-line stanza, albeit one where the rhyme is weak (*be, Mary,* and *too,* though if the last were its variant form *twey* this would be a better, though still imperfect, rhyme). This sort of uneven stanza is by no means uncommon in this and other poems, and it seems better to leave the MS just as it is. The sense of the two lines is that John and the Monk will have a one-to-one encounter. See the similar usage in *Robin Hood and the Potter,* line 61: *Togeder then went thes to yemen.*

155   MS: *my.* Inserted above line by scribe.

165   This is a very short line: to fill it out Child adds *callid Robin Hode*. But the drama of the short line and the resultant multiple rhyme is rather effective and here has been retained; Hartshorne and Madden accepted it as such. Jamieson filled out with *we wold feyn here*.

171   MS: *me*. Inserted above line by scribe.

195   MS: *so*. Child emends to *sore*, but this is not needed: *so* can act as a general intensive in Middle as in Modern English.

197   MS: *The*. Child has *This*, perhaps an error rather than an unnecessary emendation.

198   *can*. Dobson and Taylor note that *can* has the force of *gan*, which they translate as *began* (1976, p. 118). But it is used here and elsewhere as a past auxiliary, parallel to *did*.

207   MS: *hym*. An error for the plural *hem*.

211   This line is missing in the text but is easily reconstructed as here, though Child leaves it blank; Hartshorne does not leave a gap, treating this as a three line stanza.

229   MS: *theim*. The *i* is very indistinct, but as it is a little clearer in the following line, it seems best to accept Child's reading of the MS here. Madden's collations correct Hartshorne to *theim* in line 229 but not in line 230.

245   Child inserts *the* before *porter*, but this is not necessary in the sometimes condensed style of the ballads. Jamieson included *the*, so did Hartshorne, and Madden either accepted this as editing or did not notice it in his collation.

246   Prison conditions in the time of Edward II (1307–27) could be brutal. In an excerpt from the *Life of Edward the Second*, the Monk of Malmesbury describes the treatment meted out to one who would not plead: "The prisoner shall sit on the cold, bare floor, dressed only in the thinnest of shirts, and pressed with as great a weight of iron as his wretched body can bear. His food shall be a little rotten bread, and his drink cloudy and stinking water. The day on which he eats he shall not drink, and the day on which he has drunk he shall not taste bread. Only superhuman strength survives this punishment beyond the fifth or sixth

day" (Harry Rothwell, ed., *English Historical Documents 1189–1327*, [New York: Oxford University Press, 1975], III, 566–67).

249   MS: *oure*. Whereas Child prints the first possessive as *oure* and the second as *our*, it is clear that the second is also *oure*.

270   MS: *the* (first instance). It might seem more idiomatic if this were a plural possessive (*took their way*), but *the way* is a common idiom (see line 237 and, with slightly different reference, line 225). In any case the plural would be *her*, so this can hardly be a scribal shortening.

    MS: *gale*. Child's *jale* may be an emendation, but he does not note the fact.

273   MS: *the*. This is the first of several readings taken here from the fragmentary *b* manuscript; Child merely reports them as variants to *a*, but in several cases they seem sharper and probably original and, unless apparently erroneous, will be preferred, as here.

278   MS *b*: *throw to*. A more dramatic reading from *b*; *a* just has *to*.

279   MS *b*: *jayler*. Where *a* repeats *porter*, *b* has a sharper variation.

280   MS *b*: *toke*. Fragment *b* has the past tense and narration, where *a* has the present tense *take* and, presumably, continues John's direct speech. There is little between them, and the repetition of *toke* in the next line might seem against *b* apart from its other qualities hereabouts, but there seems little reason to prefer *a* here.

284   MS *b*: *ther with to kepe*. The *a* reading *with for to keepe* seems clumsy against this *b* reading.

285   MS *b*: *wallis were*. The *a* reading *walle was* seems vaguer than *b* here.

300   MS: *stye*. This reading (only in *a*: *b* lacks these lines) makes a poor rhyme with *lynde* and to use the easily lost plural *styne* makes them closer.

305   MS *b*: *ill*. The *b* is metrically better than *a*'s "evyll."

306   MS b: *me*. This is a better reading than *a*'s *Quyte the* (though *acquit yourself* does make sense).

308   MS b: *the*. The *a* reading *yow* is less likely as the pronoun John would use at this point, both because they are friends and because they have been quarrelling; in the next line both texts use *the*.

309   MS b: *the*. This is metrically better than *a*'s reading, which lacks *the*.

311   Here and in line 313 the *b* version has simply "Robyn," which seems better suited to this personal exchange, than the full name, as in *a* and printed by Child.

314   A word is crossed out before *me*; it appears to be *and* written again accidentally, but the *d* is not finished.

331   MS: *oure cumly kyng*. The phrase occurs six times in the *Gest*. See note to line 1412; he is identified there as Edward, but it is not clear which one of that name.

358   MS: *alle*. The manuscript appears to read this, not Child's *all*.

The scribe has written *Amen* at the end.

Robin Hood and the Potter

Introduction

The ballad survives only in one manuscript, Cambridge E.e.4.35, a collection of popular and moral poems dated around 1500. It is written in what Dobson and Taylor call "a clear bastard hand" (1976, p. 123) and the text is complete, though at line 271 a line appears to be missing through scribal error. Child thought there were other gaps, but if a six-line stanza is acceptable (as is found elsewhere), and since there is no break in the sense, all the other gaps he identified disappear except that before line 224, and that too may be the result of an irregular stanza.

Like the other early manuscript ballad, *Robin Hood and the Monk*, *Robin Hood and the Potter* plays no part in the popular printed tradition, though *Robin Hood and the Butcher*, based closely on this ballad, is in both Pepys's and Wood's collections and also in the earliest surviving garlands of 1663 and 1670. Although this Potter version was not reprinted until Ritson's edition of 1795, which gave it its present name (as in other early ballads, the title focusses on the first action, before the encounter with the sheriff is developed from it), the story was clearly well known, since Copland's edition of the *Gest* (c. 1560) also prints two short plays, one of which is a dramatized encounter with a potter that begins like the ballad.

The relation between the play and the ballad has been misunderstood. Child said the play was "founded on" the ballad (III, 108) and this is also the conclusion come to by Steadman, as is suggested by the title of his essay on "The Dramatization of the Robin Hood Ballads" (1919); the same view has been proffered by Simeone (1951, p. 266) and Nelson (1973, pp. 47–51). Ritson's comment is somewhat subtler, saying the play "seems allusive to the same story" (1795, p. 60). In fact the plays and ballads are generically different treatments of the same themes, covering the issues central to the myth to different degrees and in genre-appropriate ways (Knight, 1994, pp. 112–13). The Potter play has a quite different narrative from the parallel ballad; it shapes a vivid dramatic action which, as in most of the early plays, leads up to a good rousing fight as finale.

The events and structure of the ballad are a good deal more complex. There are three sections, here represented as fitts, as suggested by the language of the texts (see lines 119–20, 237). Fitt 1 occurs in the greenwood, and is basically a "Robin Hood meets his match" sequence. Fitt 2 transfers the action to Nottingham, with Robin in disguise. He encounters the sheriff, and this is fleshed out with an archery competition, as found in the *Gest* and in the later ballad *Robin Hood's Golden Prize*. Fitt 3 sees the return to the greenwood, where the sheriff is surprised and the outlaws gather about Robin at the sound of his horn.

Among these familiar events are a set of themes central to the myth. Major features are: Robin is a yeoman among yeomen; recurrent suspicion of the towns and its activities; Robin's innate skill at archery; the full and free ethics of the forest. These mesh fully with the values found in other early texts, a fact which seems to contradict Holt's view that this is a "tale very dependent on comic situations" (1989, p. 34), but *Robin Hood and the Potter* also adds some other themes. The generosity and honesty characteristic of Robin in other early texts are here interwoven with more obvious aspects of the trickster: this is, as Dobson and Taylor note, "more deliberately light-hearted" than parallel texts (1976, p. 124), and the humor of the outlaws, the wry responses of Robin and the ironic tricking of the Sheriff are all stressed and realized with buoyant humor: presumably it is this element that Holt downgrades as "trite" (1989, p. 34).

This text makes specific the suspicion of towns and business practices touched on elsewhere, as when in the *Gest* Little John refuses to measure cloth like a draper, or when Robin returns the knight's repayment to honor them both. Robin is a comically bad marketeer, and the canny folk of Nottingham throng to buy his pots (*Robin Hood and the Butcher* relishes this motif): Robin's largesse is continued when he pays the potter with reckless generosity for his whole cartload at the end. Throughout the ballad the world of mercantile values is mocked and dismissed.

With the same sense of excess, Robin smashes the feeble townsmen's bows offered to him by the sheriff, trounces professional marksmen and thoroughly trivializes the threat of the sheriff — who is found much more deadly in other texts, where his own death is a reflex of that threatening personality. The conflict with the sheriff is also, it seems, fought in part on the terrain of masculinity: *Robin Hood and the Potter* is the only early text which shows Robin in relation with any woman (except the Virgin Mary and the treacherous Prioress). The text seems deliberately to insinuate that the sheriff's wife is more than a little interested in the powerful potter. When they first meet she speaks more respectfully than might be expected, addressing the quasi-potter as "sir" and by the end of the ballad she compares this enigmatic masculine figure favorably to her mocked husband: Holt saw in this contact "a distant distorted echo of courtly love" (1989, p. 126).

These thematic features might well be held to compensate in their complexity for what has been seen as a relative simplicity in style. Dobson and Taylor find this "a much less skilful work of literary composition" than other early texts (1976, p. 124) and Ritson went so far as to say "the writing is evidently that of a vulgar and illiterate person" (1795, p. 60). There is a fairly limited use of cliché and line filler (lines 30, 52, 54, 62, 102, 122, 166, 226, 252, 275, 314), but the rhyme pattern is decidedly irregular, exhibiting various departures from the standard *abcb*: either incomplete rhyme (114/6, 134/6, 193/5, 201/3, 234/6, 254/6, 282/4), rhyme varied to *abac* (33–36, 53–56, 77–80, 101–04, 117–20, 200–03, 245–48), varied to *abcc* (85–88), or even *abbc* (89–92, 168–71, 293–96?), at times a lack of rhyme altogether (93–96, 191–94, 249–52) and the last of these variants, full rhyme *abab* (1–4, 37–40, 57–60, 137–40, 176–79, 208–11, 214–17, 225–28, 233–36, 259–62; because of the possibility of half rhyme being acceptable, some of the *abac* and *abcb* cases could be taken as *abab*).

Less than polished as the ballad certainly is in terms of style, it also has, as Dobson and Taylor remark a "direct form of address" (1976, p. 124). It uses dialogue more than other early Robin Hood ballads (55% of the lines, as against 45% in *Robin Hood and the Monk* and 50% in *Robin Hood and Guy of Gisborne*, the other two dialogue-heavy texts). In keeping with that it is notable for a rapid change of viewpoint, especially in the opening greenwood sequence. This dramatic yet simple quality has led to the connection of the ballad to the minstrel style, that is a rather casual technique based on direct communication and emotive effects, assumed to indicate a popular context. But it is notable that this technically simple ballad has some complexities. Though Robin Hood is firmly a yeoman, he is also, as in *Robin Hood and the Monk*, noted for his quality of being *corteys and free*, the latter adjective having both its senses of lordly generosity and yeomanly independence. The tone and impact of the ballad may well show more art than has sometimes been assumed: its plot is quick-moving and highly effective, its tone vigorous and direct, with a strong and well-maintained level of irony. Gray, in connection with these elements, sees aspects of the fabliau behind the ballad (1984, p. 18).

These subtleties may also be thematic. At the beginning and end the ballad asserts the elusive value of *god yemanrey*, and it may well be that this text, like other early Robin Hood ballads, is something of an exploration and realization of just what these values might be. As with other newly formed genres, they may relate to new social formations: Tardif has argued for the importance of disaffected craftsmen in the formation of the Robin Hood genres (1983, pp. 131–32). This ballad appears to develop some values consistent with this thesis, promulgating ideas of a newly identified social stratum, neither serf nor lord, interested in communal values and threatened by a new world of towns and laws imposed from a distance. For them the youthful, witty, brave, and cunning hero, representing and leading his band of near equals, is a good deal more than trite, and his mythic values come strongly through a text whose literary surface is simple and, therefore, capable of wide diffusion.

Select Bibliography

Texts

Cambridge University MS E.e.4.35.

Child, F. J., ed. *English and Scottish Popular Ballads*. 5 vols. Boston: Houghton Mifflin and Company, 1882–98; rpt. New York: Dover, 1965. Vol. III, no. 121.

Dobson, R. B., and J. Taylor. *Rymes of Robin Hood*. London: Heinemann, 1976. Pp. 123–32.

Gutch, J. M., ed. *A Lyttele Gest of Robin Hood with other Auncient and Modern Ballads and Songs Relating to the Celebrated Yeoman.* 2 vols. London: Longman, 1847. Vol. II, 21–35.

Ritson, Joseph, ed. *Robin Hood: A Collection of All the Ancient Poems, Songs and Ballads Now Extant Relative to the Celebrated English Outlaw.* 2 vols. London: Egerton and Johnson, 1795. Rpt. London: William Pickering, 1832. Vol. 1, 81–96.

Commentary and Criticism

Child, F. J, pp. 108–09.

Dobson, R.B., and J. Taylor, pp. 123–25.

Gray, Douglas. "The Robin Hood Poems." *Poetica* 18 (1984), 1–39.

Holt, J. C. *Robin Hood*. Second ed. London: Thames and Hudson, 1989.

Knight, Stephen. *Robin Hood: A Complete Study of the English Outlaw*. Oxford: Blackwell, 1994.

Nelson, Malcolm A. *The Robin Hood Tradition in the English Renaissance*. Salzburg Studies in English Literature, English Drama 14. Salzburg: Institut für Englische Sprache und Literatur, Universität Salzburg, 1973.

Simeone, W. E. "The May Games and the Robin Hood Legend." *Journal of American Folklore* 64 (1951), 265–74.

Steadman, J. M., Jr. "The Dramatization of the Robin Hood Ballads." *Modern Philology* 17 (1919), 9–23.

Tardif, Richard. "The 'Mistery' of Robin Hood: A New Social Context for the Texts." In *Words and Worlds: Studies in the Social Role of Verbal Culture*. Eds. Stephen Knight and S. N. Mukherjee. Sydney: Sydney Association for Studies in Society and Culture, 1983.

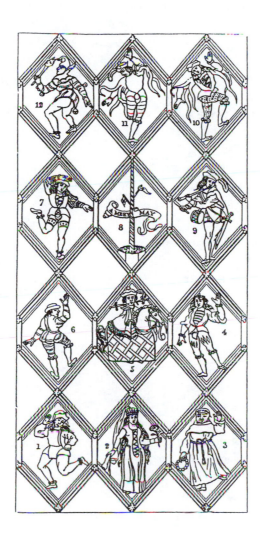

Robin Hood and the Potter

Fitt 1

In schomer, when the leves spryng,	*summer*
The bloschoms on every bowe,	*blossoms*
So merey doyt the berdys syng	*merry do*
Yn wodys merey now.	*completely joyful*

5	Herkens, god yemen,	*Listen*
	Comley, corteys, and god,	*Fair, well-bred, and good*
	On of the best that yever bare bowe,	*One; ever bore*
	Hes name was Roben Hode.	

	Roben Hood was the yemans name,	
10	That was boyt corteys and fre;	*both courteous and generous*
	For the loffe of owre ladey,	*love of our lady (Virgin Mary)*
	All wemen werschepyd he.	*honored*

	Bot as the god yeman stod on a day,	*But*
	Among hes mery maney,	*his merry band of men*
15	He was ware of a prowd potter,	*aware*
	Cam dryfyng owyr the leye.	*Came hastening over the open land*

	"Yonder comet a prod potter," seyde Roben,	*comes a proud*
	"That long hayt hantyd this wey;	*has regularly passed*
	He was never so corteys a man	*courteous*
20	On peney of pawage to pay."	*One penny of road-toll to pay*

	"Y met hem bot at Wentbreg," seyde Lytyll John,	*Wentbridge*
	"And therefore yeffell mot he the!	*evil may he thrive (damn him)!*
	Seche thre strokes he me gafe,	*Such; gave*
	Yet by my seydys cleffe they.	*The blows are still splitting my sides*

25	"Y ley forty shillings," seyde Lytyll John,	*I wager*
	"To pay het thes same day,	*it*
	Ther ys nat a man among hus all	*us*
	A wed schall make hem leye."	*Who can force him to make a payment*

	"Here ys forty shillings," seyde Roben,	
30	"More, and thow dar say,	*if you dare gamble (it)*
	That Y schall make that prowde potter,	*I shall*
	A wed to me schall he ley."	*He shall make me a payment*

	There thes money they leyde,	*laid down*
	They toke het a yeman to kepe;	*gave it to*
35	Roben beffore the potter he breyde,	*jumped*
	And bad hem stond stell.	*ordered him to stand still*

	Handys apon hes hors he leyde,	*upon*
	And bad the potter stonde foll stell;	*absolutely still*
	The potter schorteley to hem seyde,	*briefly*
40	"Felow, what ys they well?"	*what is thy will*

	"All thes thre yer, and more, potter," he seyde,	
	"Thow hast hantyd thes wey,	*regularly passed*
	Yet were tow never so cortys a man	*were you never*
	On peney of pavage to pay."	*One; road-toll*

45	"What ys they name," seyde the potter,	
	"For pavage thow aske of me?"	
	"Roben Hod ys mey name,	
	A wed schall thow leffe me."	*A payment you shall leave me*

	"Wed well y non leffe," seyde the potter,	*I will not leave a payment*
50	"Nor pavag well Y non pay;	*Nor will I pay a toll*
	Awey they honde fro mey hors!	*from my*
	Y well the tene eyls, be mey fay."	*I will do thee evil otherwise, by my faith*

	The potter to hes cart he went,	
	He was not to seke;	*did not hide*
55	A god to-hande staffe therowt he hent,	*good two-handed; took out*
	Beffore Roben he leppyd.	*Before; leaped*

Roben howt with a swerd bent, *pulled out a sword*
A bokeler en hes honde; *buckler*
The potter to Roben he went,
60 And seyde, "Felow, let mey hors go."

Togeder then went thes to yemen, *these two*
Het was a god seyt to se; *good sight*
Thereof low Robyn hes men, *Robin's men laughed*
There they stod onder a tre. *Where*

65 Leytell John to hes felow he seyde,
"Yend potter well steffeley stonde": *That; will staunchly stand*
The potter, with an acward stroke, *with a back-handed stroke*
Smot the bokeler owt of hes honde. *Struck*

And ar Roben meyt get het agen *before; might get it*
70 Hes bokeler at hes fette, *feet*
The potter yn the neke hem toke, *hit him on the neck*
To the gronde sone he yede. *at once he fell*

That saw Roben hes men, *Robin's men saw that*
As they stod onder a bow; *bough [of a tree]*
75 "Let us helpe owre master," seyde Lytell John,
"Yonder potter," seyde he, "els well hem slo." *will him slay*

Thes wight yemen with a breyde, *These strong; rush*
To thes master they cam. *this*
Leytell John to hes master seyde, *his*
80 "Ho haet the wager won? *Who has*

"Schall Y haffe yowre forty shillings," seyde Lytl John, *Will I have*
"Or ye, master, schall haffe myne?"
"Yeff they were a hundred," seyde Roben, *If*
"Y feythe, they ben all theyne." *In faith, they are*

85 "Het ys fol leytell cortesey," seyde the potter, *It is very discourteous*
"As I hafe harde weyse men saye, *heard*
Yeffe a pore yeman com drywyng over the way, *If; driving*
To let hem of hes gorney." *hinder him; journey*

Robin Hood and the Potter

	"Be mey trowet, thow seys soyt," seyde Roben,	*By my faith; speak truth*
90	"Thow seys god yemenrey;	*You speak good yeomanry*
	And thow dreyffe forthe yevery day,	*If thou go forth*
	Thow schalt never be let for me."	*be delayed*

	"Y well prey the, god potter,	*I will ask thee*
	A felischepe well thow haffe?	*Will you have a fellowship*
95	Geffe me they clothyng, and thow schalt	*Give*
	hafe myne;	
	Y well go to Notynggam."	

	"Y grant thereto," seyde the potter,	
	"Thow schalt feynde me a felow gode;	
	Bot thow can sell mey pottys well,	*Unless*
100	Com ayen as thow yede."	*went*

	"Nay, be mey trowt," seyde Roben,	*truth*
	"And then Y bescro mey hede,	*beshrew (curse) myself*
	Yeffe Y bryng eney pottys ayen,	*If*
	And eney weyffe well hem chepe."	*If any wife will buy them*

105	Than spake Leytell John,	
	And all hes felowhes heynd,	*friendly fellows*
	"Master, be well ware of the screffe	*wary; sheriff*
	of Notynggam,	
	For he ys leytell howr frende."	*little our friend*

	"Thorow the helpe of Howr Ladey,	*With; Our Lady*
110	Felowhes, let me alone.	
	Heyt war howte!" seyde Roben,	*Gee up!*
	"To Notynggam well Y gon."	*will I go*

	Robyn went to Notynggam,	
	Thes pottys for to sell;	
115	The potter abode with Robens men,	*stayed*
	There he fered not eylle.	*fared well*

| | Tho Roben droffe on hes wey, | *hastened* |
| | So merey ower the londe: | |

65

Her es more, and affter ys to saye,
120 The best ys beheynde.   *is yet to come*

Fitt 2

When Roben cam to Notynggam,
The soyt yef Y scholde saye,   *If I were to tell the truth*
He set op hes hors anon,   *stabled*
And gaffe hem hotys and haye.   *gave him oats and hay*

125 Yn the medys of the towne,   *In the midst*
There he schowed hes ware;   *showed his wares*
"Pottys! pottys!" he gan crey foll sone, *began to shout at once*
"Haffe hansell for the mare!" *Have a present the more you buy*

Foll effen agenest the screffeys gate *Right against; sheriff's*
130 Schowed he hes chaffare;   *merchandise*
Weyffes and wedowes abowt hem drow, *Wives; drew about him*
And chepyd fast of hes ware.   *quickly purchased*

Yet "Pottys, gret chepe!" creyed Robyn, *great bargain!*
"Y loffe yeffell thes to stonde." *I hate to leave these standing*
135 And all that say hem sell   *saw him selling*
Seyde he had be no potter long. *he had not been a potter long*

The pottys that were worthe pens feyffe, *five pence*
He solde tham for pens thre;
Preveley seyde man and weyffe, *Privately; woman*
140 "Ywnder potter schall never the." *Yonder; prosper*

Thos Roben solde foll fast,
Tell he had pottys bot feyffe;   *Till; five*
Op he hem toke of hes car, *He took them up from his cart*
And sende hem to the screffeys weyfe. *wife*

145 Thereof sche was foll fayne,   *very happy*
"Gereamarsey," seyde sche, "sir, than, *Thank you*

Robin Hood and the Potter

When ye com to thes contré ayen,   *these parts again*
Y schall bey of the pottys, so mo Y the."   *buy from you; as I may prosper*

"Ye schall haffe of the best," seyde Roben,
150 And sware be the Treneyté.   *Trinity*
Foll corteysley sche gan hem call,   *With full courtesy; him*
"Com deyne with the screfe and me."   *Come dine; sheriff*

"God amarsey," seyde Roben,   *God thank you*
"Yowre bedyng schall be doyn."   *bidding; done*
155 A mayden yn the pottys gan bere,   *bore the pots in*
Roben and the screffe weyffe folowed anon.   *at once*

Whan Roben yn to the hall cam,
The screffe sone he met;   *sheriff at once*
The potter cowed of corteysey,   *understood courtesy*
160 And sone the screffe he gret.   *greeted*

"Lo, ser, what thes potter hayt geffe yow and me,   *Look sir; has given*
Feyffe pottys smalle and grete!"   *Five*
"He ys foll wellcom," seyd the screffe,   *very*
"Let os was, and to mete."   *Let's wash and [go] to food*

165 As they sat at her methe,   *their food*
With a nobell chere,   *noble cheer*
To of the screffes men gan speke   *Two; began to*
Of a gret wager,

Of a schotyng, was god and feyne,   *Of a shooting match; fine*
170 Was made the tother daye,   *other*
Of forty shillings, the soyt to saye,   *the truth to tell*
Who scholde thes wager gayne.   *win*

Styll than sat thes prowde potter,   *Silent*
Thos than thowt he,   *Thus; thought*
175 As Y am a trow Cerstyn man,   *true Christian*
Thes schotyng well Y se.   *will I see*

	Whan they had fared of the best,	*dined*
	With bred and ale and weyne,	*wine*
	To the bottys the made them prest,	*targets they hurried*
180	With bowes and boltys foll feyne.	*arrows*
	The screffes men schot foll fast,	*shot very quickly*
	As archares that weren prowe,	*archers; skillful*
	There cam non ner ney the marke	*nearer the mark*
	Bey halffe a god archares bowe.	*By half the length of*
185	Stell then stod the prowde potter,	*Still*
	Thos than seyde he:	*Thus*
	"And Y had a bow, be the Rode,	*If; by Christ's Cross*
	On schot scholde yow se."	*One shot you would see*
	"Thow schall haffe a bow," seyde the screffe,	
190	"The best that thow well cheys of thre;	*will choose*
	Thou semyst a stalward and a stronge,	*seem*
	Asay schall thow be."	*Tested*
	The screffe commandyd a yeman that stod hem bey	
	After bowhes to weynde;	*To go for bows*
195	The best bow that the yeman browthe	*brought*
	Roben set on a stryng.	*fitted a string*
	"Now schall Y wet and thow be god,	*know if you are any good*
	And polle het op to they nere."	*pull it up to your ear*
	"So god me helpe," seyde the prowde potter,	
200	"Thys ys bot ryght weke gere."	*but very feeble tackle*
	To a quequer Roben went,	*quiver*
	A god bolt owthe he toke;	*good arrow he took out*
	So ney on to the marke he went,	*near to the mark*
	He fayled not a fothe.	*didn't miss by a foot*
205	All they schot a bowthe agen,	*a round again*
	The screffes men and he;	
	Off the marke he welde not fayle,	*would not miss*
	He cleffed the preke on thre.	*cleft; peg into three pieces*

	The screffes men thowt gret schame	*thought (i.e., felt) great shame*
210	The potter the mastry wan;	*won the contest*
	The screffe lowe and made god game,	*laughed*
	And seyde, "Potter, thow art a man.	
	Thow art worthey to bere a bowe	
	Yn what plas that thow goe."	*In whatever place*

	"Yn mey cart Y haffe a bow,	*my*
215	For soyt," he seyde, "and that a godde;	*In truth; it's a good one*
	Yn mey cart ys the bow	
	That gaffe me Robyn Hode."	*Robin Hood gave me*

	"Knowest thow Robyn Hode?" seyde the screffe,	
220	"Potter, Y prey the tell thow me."	
	"A hundred torne Y haffe schot with hem,	*bouts*
	Under hes tortyll-tre."	*trysting tree*
	"Y had lever nar a hundred ponde," seyde the screffe,	*rather than have*
	And sware be the Trinity,	
225	"That the fals outelawe stod be me."	

	"And ye well do afftyr mey red," seyde the potter,	*If you will follow my counsel*
	"And boldeley go with me,	*boldly*
	And to morow, or we het bred,	*before we eat*
	Roben Hode well we se."	

	"Y well queyt the," kod the screffe,	*I will reward thee, said*
230	"And swere be God of meythe."	*almighty*
	Schetyng thay left, and hom they went,	*They stopped shooting*
	Her soper was reddy deythe.	*Their supper was prepared*

Fitt 3

	Upon the morrow, when het was day,	*it*
235	He boskyd hem forthe to reyde;	*He got himself ready to ride*
	The potter hes cart forthe gan ray,	*began to make ready his cart*
	And wolde not leffe beheynde.	*leave (it) behind*

He toke leffe of the screffys wyffe,   *took leave*
And thankyd her of all thyng:
240   "Dam, for mey loffe and ye well thys were,   *if you will wear this*
Y geffe yow here a golde ryng."

"Gramarsey," seyde the weyffe,   *Many thanks*
"Sir, God eylde het the."   *God reward you for it*
The screffes hart was never so leythe,   *light*
245   The feyre foreyst to se.

And when he cam yn to the foreyst,
Under the leffes grene,
Berdys there sange on bowhes prest,   *Birds sang freely on boughs there*
Het was gret goy to se.   *great joy*

250   "Here het ys merey to be," seyde Roben,   *To be here is merry*
"For a man that had hawt to spende;   *who had anything to spend*
Be mey horne ye schall awet   *By my horn you shall discover*
Yeff Roben Hode be here."

Roben set hes horne to hes mowthe,
255   And blow a blast that was foll god;
That herde hes men that there stode,   *heard his*
Fer downe yn the wodde.
"I her mey master blow," seyde Leytell John,
They ran as thay were wode.   *crazy*

260   Whan thay to thar master cam,
Leytell John wold not spare;   *hold back*
"Master, how haffe yow fare yn Notynggam?   *how did you fare*
How haffe yow solde yowre ware?"   *did you sell*

"Ye, be mey trowthe, Leytyll John,   *Little*
265   Loke thow take no care;
Y haffe browt the screffe of Notynggam,   *brought*
For all howre chaffare."   *As a result of our business*

"He ys foll wellcom," seyde Lytyll John,   *very*
"Thes tydyng ys foll godde."   *news*

270   The screffe had lever nar a hundred ponde   *rather than*
           He had never seen Roben Hode.

           "Had I west that befforen,   *Had I known that before*
           At Notynggam when we were,
           Thow scholde not com yn feyre forest
275   Of all thes thowsande eyre."   *years*

           "That wot Y well," seyde Roben,   *I know that well*
           "Y thanke God that ye be here;
           Thereffore schall ye leffe yowre hors with hos,   *leave; us*
           And all yowre hother gere."   *your other gear*

280   "That fend I Godys forbod," kod the screffe,   *May God forbid that, said*
           "So to lese mey godde."   *So to lose my goods*
           "Hether ye cam on hors foll hey,   *Hither you came high upon a horse*
           And hom schall ye go on fote;
           And gret well they weyffe at home,   *greet; your wife*
285   The woman ys foll godde.

           "Y schall her sende a wheyt palffrey,   *white palfrey*
           Het hambellet as the weynde,   *It trots; wind*
           Nere for the loffe of yowre weyffe,   *Were it not*
           Off more sorow scholde yow seyng."   *you should sing*

290   Thes parted Robyn Hode and the screffe;   *Thus*
           To Notynggam he toke the waye;
           Hes weyffe feyre welcomed hem hom,
           And to hem gan sche saye:

           "Seyr, how haffe yow fared yn grene foreyst?   *how did you fare*
295   Haffe ye browt Roben hom?"   *brought*
           "Dam, the deyell spede hem, bothe bodey and bon;   *Lady, the devil take him*
           Y haffe hade a foll gret skorne.   *full great harm*

           "Of all the god that Y haffe lade to grene wod,   *Of all the property I had taken*
           He hayt take het fro me;   *has taken it from me*
300   All bot thes feyre palffrey,   *All but this*
           That he hayt sende to the."   *has*

With that sche toke op a lowde lawhyng,   *let out a loud laugh*
And swhare be Hem that deyed on tre,   *swore by*
"Now haffe yow payed for all the pottys
305   That Roben gaffe to me.

"Now ye be com hom to Notynggam.
Ye schall haffe god ynowe."   *plenty of property*
Now speke we of Roben Hode,
And of the pottyr ondyr the grene bowhe.   *under*

310   "Potter, what was they pottys worthe
To Notynggam that Y ledde with me?"   *that I took with me*
"They wer worthe to nobellys," seyde he,   *two nobles*
"So mot Y treyffe or the;   *So may I thrive or prosper*
So cowde Y had for tham,   *So [much] could I have had*
315   And Y had be there."   *If I had been there*

"Thow schalt hafe ten ponde," seyde Roben,   *pounds*
"Of money feyre and fre;
And yever whan thow comest to grene wod,   *always*
Wellcom, potter, to me."

320   Thes partyd Robyn, the screffe, and the potter,   *Thus*
Ondernethe the grene wod tre;
God haffe mersey on Roben Hodys solle,   *soul*
And saffe all god yemanrey!

4	MS: *merey now*. This is not "merry now," which has little meaning, but is a spelling variant of *merey ynow*, a familiar phrase in this context which means "completely joyful"; *enough* in Middle English means "as much as is appropriate."
6	MS: *cortessey*. Child emends to the required adjective *corteys*.
12	MS: *werschep ye*. Child emends both tense and pronoun to *werschepyd he*; both changes seem necessary.
16	MS: *lefe*. An easy error for *leye* (see line 28). Child spells it *ley*, but the simplification of spelling is not necessary.
21	Wentbridge is a small town on the River Went near the Yorkshire Barnsdale; see note on the *Gest*, lines 69–70, for a discussion of locations.
24	MS: *Yet they cleffe by my seydes*. The scribe has clearly misremembered the order of the elements of the line and so lost the rhyme. Child reorders the line to *Yet by my seydys cleffe they*, that is "The blows are still splitting my sides," and this is accepted.
27	MS: *hys*. Emended by Child to *hus*; the error was presumably influenced by *ys* earlier in the line.
28	MS: *hem leffe*. The same misreading as in line 16 has again lost the rhyme. The sense is the same here: to leave a pledge or to lay a pledge. Child emends *leffe* to *ley* to preserve the rhyme, and this is accepted, though as in 16 the spelling *leye* is preferred.
41	MS: *he seyde*. The final attribution to a speaker makes the line very long, but there are similar lines elsewhere, especially in this ballad (lines 81, 222, 225) and the *Gest* (lines 310, 442, 630, 758). There seems no good reason to omit *he seyde*.

65   MS: *ffelow he*. Child makes this *ffelowhes,* interpreting the *he* as part of the noun, and adding *s* because John seems to be addressing more than one companion. There is not much space between the *w* and the *h*, but more than is usual in a continuous word, and *he* must be the pronoun. Dobson and Taylor treat it as such, but also accept Child's notion of a plural audience, and read *ffelows he seyde*. But the singular idiom is common, and emendation is not necessary.

The line begins with a large capital *L,* presumably because it is at the top of a new page in the MS.

67   MS: *a caward stroke*. Child emends to *acward*, meaning "backhand." Though *caward* makes sense as " a cowardly blow," it is unlikely, in view of the rest of the ballad, that the Potter would be represented as cowardly. Child's emendation is accepted, and it is also assumed that in misreading *acward* as *caward* the scribe also changed *an* to *a*. Robin himself defeats Guy with "an awkward stroke" (see *Robin Hood and Guy of Gisborne*, line 159).

76   MS: *hels*. Child emends to *els*.

MS: *sclo*. Child emends to *slo*: this scribe has a tendency to add an unnecessary *c* after *s*. Compare line 233.

77   MS: *Thes went yemen*. Child inverts the two words to *yemen went*, but the verb *cam* follows in the next line. It is more likely that the scribe has miswritten *wight*, a very familiar word in this context; this would also maintain the rhythm better than Child's emendation.

78   *thes*. Child emends unnecessarily to *ther*, but *thes* is simply a form of "this," as in line 77. See also *hes* in line 79, which means "his."

87   MS: *over*. Child reads *on*, but the manuscript clearly has *ou* with an abbreviation mark.

100   MS: *yede*. Child emends to *yode* to improve the rhyme, but although rhymes in general in this ballad are better than in the *Gest,* this is unnecessary.

103   MS: *eney*. Child reads *eny*, presumably a minor error.

109–12   Child reorders these lines, as he feels they do not make sense in the existing order: he prints:

> "Heyt war howte!" seyde Roben,
> "Ffelowhes, let me alone;
> Thorow the helpe of Howr Ladey
> To Notynggam well y gon."

As Dobson and Taylor note (1976, p. 127), the re-arrangement seems "hardly necessary." Although the stanza's first two lines are rather condensed, it does make sense overall, and is printed here as in the manuscript. In the first line of the stanza Robin appeals to Mary to help against the sheriff, and so (line two) feels his fellows can allow him to go alone; then in line three he stirs up his horse to head off to (line four) Nottingham.

113–16   This stanza is wrongly located in the text after line 96 — presumably the scribe's eye has skipped from Nottingham in line 96 to Nottingham in line 113. The fact that the stanza begins a new page may have facilitated the error.

121   The language suggests this is an obvious place to begin a new fitt, as Ritson does (1795, p. 64); Child's text has an extra space here (though not at line 234, here taken as the start of Fitt 3). The MS does not mark a new fitt in either place.

143   MS: *car*. Child reads *care*, feeling there is an abbreviated *e*; but if so (and it is not clear) this would be an erroneous spelling of this word for *cart*. Dobson and Taylor print *car* (1976, p. 128).

146   As Child reports, after *sche* there is a "character" in the manuscript, which he expands to *ser* and also relocates after *Gereamarsey*. Here it is expanded as *sir*. Dobson and Taylor reject this and merely print a stray apostrophe after *sche* (1976, p. 231). However the abbreviation is clear and is also used in line 243. Child presumably moves it (*with than*) to improve the rhyme, but in the light of the uncertain rhymes found in this ballad, there seems insufficient reason to move it: the later usage in line 243 has the same structure, separating *sir* from *Gereamarsey*, and the line is printed here as it stands. It might seem unusual for a sheriff's wife to address a potter she has just met as "sir," though less so in line 243, after he has given her a gold ring. Perhaps the implication is that Robin from the start is identified by the wife as more than a mere potter, leading to the slight sexual rapport suggested between them later on.

148 MS: *the* (first instance). Child emends to *they* (=thy), but it would be a strangely intimate (or perhaps rude) thing for a sheriff's wife to say to a tradesman — especially when she has just called him *sir*. There is no need for any personal pronoun.

MS: *of the*. Crossed out after *pottys*.

151 *sche*. MS: *he*.

161 As with line 65, a large initial *L* starts the line, presumably because it begins a new page.

164 *to*. MS: *to to*. Child emends to *go to*, but it is more likely that the Middle English idiom "let us to meat" is used, and "to" has been accidentally repeated.

When the sheriff suggests that they wash their hands before eating the meal, he is following a custom of "civilized" behavior that originated in the banquet hall of the medieval court. Since food was served in communal bowls, diners picked it out with their hands; hence, the need for clean hands. As Norbert Elias observes, in *The Civilizing Process: The History of Manners* (New York: Urizen Books, 1978), table manners were adopted by the bourgeois during the fourteenth and fifteenth centuries (p. 62). This display of "courtly" manners is paralleled by the sheriff's wife calling Robin "sir" and by Robin's gifts to her of five pots, a gold ring, and a white palfrey. For other hand-washing references, see line 125 and line 922 in the *Gest* and line 527 in *Adam Bell*.

169 *schotyng*. Since English armies recruited their archers from rural levies and city militias, the populace was required to own bows and arrows and to practice archery. In the *Statute of Winchester* of 1285, Edward I "commanded that every man have in his house arms for keeping the peace" and be "sworn to arms according to the amount of his lands and of his chattels." All men having land worth between 40 and 100 shillings a year were required to own a sword, bow and arrows, and a knife (Harry Rothwell, ed., *English Historical Documents 1189–1327*, vol. III [New York: Oxford University Press, 1975], 461–62). In a royal writ, dated 1363, King Edward III ordered all the sheriffs in England to proclaim "that everyone in the shire, on festival days when he has holiday, shall learn and exercise himself in the art of archery, and use for his games bows and arrows, or crossbolts or bolts" (Alec R. Myers, ed., *English Historical Documents 1327–1485* [New York: Oxford University Press, 1969], IV, 1182). To encourage practice and to identify expert marksmen, municipal and shire competitions

were routinely held. In addition to the match in *Robin Hood and the Potter*, there are four other competitions described in the *Gest* (578–89, 1130–81, 1586–1614) and in *Adam Bell* (612–51). More informal archery matches include the games of *plucke buffet* (*Gest*, 1690–1705) and *shete a peny* (*Robin Hood and the Monk*, 41–50). For a detailed treatment of the history of archery, including a chapter on Robin Hood, see Jim Bradbury, *The Medieval Archer* (Woodbridge: The Boydell Press, 1985).

170   MS: *the tho ther*. Child prints as *the thother*, which Dobson and Taylor accept (1976, p. 129), but this is not a dialectical variant but an error: emend to *the tother*.

172   MS: *wen*. The rhyme has been lost, and the original was probably *gayne*, with the half-rhyme common in this ballad.

179   MS: *pottys*. Presumably this reading was influenced by the trade Robin has assumed, but it cannot make sense. Child's emendation to *bottys*, that is "butts," is sensible.

180   MS: *bolt yt*: *boltys*.

182   MS: *goode*. Child accepts this as the final word in the line, with a consequent failure to rhyme; however, this is so common a cliché (often as *ful goode*) that a scribe has obviously slipped into it and spoiled the rhyme: the rarer word *prowe* provides a good rhyme and is accepted here. The equally familiar *good ynow*, which would rhyme, would be metrically very clumsy.

198   In his note Child speculates whether *thow* should be inserted after *And*, but he does not print this, and it is unnecessary.

The long bow was very hard to pull to its full extent; the sheriff thinks this will test whether the "potter" is really a bowman. In fact the sheriff's bows are too weak for Robin's mighty arm: this sense of his special strength underlies the well-known proverb "Many men speak of Robin Hood who never bent his bow."

205   MS: *a bowthe*. As in the *Gest*, Child treats this like an adverb, modern *about*, meaning *in turn*. But the MS does separate the *a* from *bowthe* (as is noted by Child at the end of his collations). This is more likely, here and elsewhere, to be a noun phrase, meaning "a round (of a contest)," from which the sense "in turn" develops.

213 There is disturbance in this passage through to line 224. Lines 213–14 are, most unusually, a couplet, with the same rhyme as the following stanza. Line 217 unemended lacks a rhyme in the MS; there may be a line missing after line 223. These problems can be made to disappear by a tissue of emending and reordering; however the policy here has been to print as much of the existing text as possible and show how it does in fact make sense, though metrically unusual.

218 MS: *That Robyn gaff me.* This is metrically poor and has lost the rhyme. As this stanza appears, apart from this problem, coherent, it would seem the scribe has remembered the line the wrong way round because it is a little strained for rhyme, as in Child's convincing emendation to *That gaffe me Robyn Hode.*

225 Child feels a line is missing in the manuscript before this line (though no gap occurs) and he leaves a blank. But there is no gap in the sense, and the rhyme runs on from the previous stanza (as emended). This may well be a rare seven-line stanza (see General Introduction, p. 9), perhaps produced as a scribe tried to rework a passage damaged in the original. The text is left as it stands.

226 MS: *the B* crossed out after *seyde.*

230 MS: *well*, not *wel* as Child has it.

231 *meythe.* MS: *meythey.*

233 *soper.* MS: *scoper.*

247 MS: *Yonder.* Child accepts this reading but it does not make sense unless it is seen as a strange spelling of *Under*: that would make a very familiar statement in the outlaw ballads, and emendation seems appropriate.

252 *ye.* MS: *he.* Child emends to "I." Dobson and Taylor read "he" with "I" in brackets as a possible emendation. But the obvious reading, easily misread as "he," is *ye.*

258–59 Child treats these lines as if they are the first and last of a fragmentary stanza, but in fact they fit easily as the end of a six line stanza. They do however start a new page, with a large capital *I.*

264 *Leytyll.* MS: *I leyty.* Child's emendation.

270   Note the ironic repetition from line 223, when the sheriff thought meeting Robin Hood worth £100.

272–73   The manuscript has the line *He had west that befforen* after line 269, so lacking a rhyme for line 268. Child, assuming the scribe has jumped from *He had* in line 270 to *Had I* in line 271, has reconstructed the lost line and this fine piece of editing is accepted.

275   After *thes* is a canceled abbreviation for five hundred.

280–81   Child regards these two lines as the beginning of a fragmentary stanza, but in fact they fit as the start of a six-line stanza, with, as is common in the four-line stanza, the speaker changing after two lines.

286   Before this stanza the text includes the lines:

> *Y schall her sende a wheyt palffrey*
> *That ambellet be mey ffey*

           As Child notes, the scribe mistook the rhyme and started the stanza again, so the lines should be dropped.

297   After *hade*, *haffe* is crossed out.

308   The manuscript repeats line 305 after this line, an "eyeskip" error.

309   MS: *bowhes*. This is a more common version of this familiar statement, but the rhyme calls for emendation to the singular, as found in Child.

312   MS: *to nobellys*. Two nobles was thirteen shillings and four pence (i.e., two thirds of a pound), quite a large sum. The ten pounds Robin provides would have been something like a year's wages.

314   Child inserts *haffe* before *had* presumably on grammatical grounds, but *cowde Y had* is idiomatic Middle English and is retained.

315   MS: *be there*. Child inverts the words to *there be* for a better rhyme, but this is not necessary.

323   After this line the original scribe has added *Expleycyt Robyn Hode*.

A Gest of Robyn Hode

Introduction

The "most substantial and most ambitious" of the early Robin Hood texts (Gray, 1984, p. 22) was first recorded in printed form early in the first half of the sixteenth century, and its popularity is shown by the existence of "a dozen printed editions of the sixteenth and seventeenth centuries" (Fowler, 1980, p. 1769). There is no manuscript version, and the best text is a set of substantial fragments (formerly called the Lettersnijder edition), printed by Jan van Doesbroch in Antwerp around 1510, here called *a* (Fowler, 1980, p. 1769) and now in the National Library of Scotland, Edinburgh. The other early edition was by Wynkyn de Worde, which may have been in print before the Antwerp text. This was used as a basis by Ritson and Gutch, but Child and Dobson and Taylor used "Lettersnijder" and filled it out from Wynkyn, here called *b*. This choice appears correct, as Wynkyn has more errors and seems less close to their exemplar than the Antwerp text. Child consulted several other early fragments, some from a text printed by Richard Pynson about 1530 and some in the Douce collection (Bodleian Library, Oxford). These four texts are referred to in the notes as "early texts," while the popular edition by William Copland of about 1560 and its successor by Edward White (later sixteenth century) are referred to as "later texts" which sometimes cast light on how the earlier material was understood. The text printed here is derived from a new collation of the two earliest sources, Antwerp and Wynkyn, while consulting the early fragments and later editions for possible correction of the earlier sources (see notes for details of the sources used when the *a* text is not followed).

The date of the *Gest* is not clear; the often repeated idea of an origin about 1400 or even earlier is almost certainly wrong. When Child said there were "a number of Middle English forms" in the poem he meant linguistic forms, and he suggested they "may have been relics" of the ballads from which the poem was then held to be based, or, he went on, the poem itself "may have been put together as early as 1400, or before" (III, 40). This is a good deal more cautious than Gutch's confident statement that the poem dated "from the time of Chaucer or before" (1847, I, vii), which Child was implicitly criticizing. Nevertheless his words have been taken as confirmation of 1400 as a base date for the *Gest*, perhaps because of its resemblance in length and style to *Gamelyn* (undoubtedly of the Chaucerian period), and no doubt in part through a desire to find antiquity in the popular myth.

Various improbabilities are involved in the idea of an early date for the *Gest*. It would mean that this compilation had survived from half a century before the earliest of its components (*Robin Hood and the Monk*) and for a century before any others. It would also mean that a long text on this popular subject survived without trace in manuscript for a century and, when printed, was still in an unvaried and undamaged form. As Fowler comments, the poem "is unlikely to have had a long life before finding its way into print" (1980, p. 1769). These considerations as well as some linguistic evidence on the survival of Child's "Middle English forms" (see Knight, 1994, pp. 47–48) suggest a date in the mid-fifteenth century. Holt has recently suggested c. 1450 to be a "safer date" than 1400 (1995, p. 30).

If the date of the text itself is less than certain, equally obscure is the date of the events within it. Historians have often felt its legal, social, and military structures belong to the thirteenth century (Maddicott, 1978; for a summary discussion see Holt, 1989, pp. 75–81), but this overlooks the atemporal character of medieval narrative (Malory's text deals with trial by battle in quite ancient forms, not to mention its fantasies of feudality). Similarly fictional is the setting: the *Gest* operates in the Yorkshire Barnsdale, very clearly specified as such (see note to lines 69–70), and yet Little John can hurry from Nottingham, fifty miles distant, to rejoin his companions in less than a day: apparently they are in Sherwood, but that name is not used in the *Gest*. Child argues (III, 51) that two separate ballad cycles have been condensed, but the Robin Hood geography is usually general, even vague, in this way and the apparent problem is only created by the unusually specific reference to the Yorkshire Barnsdale in this text.

The audience of the poem has been a matter of dispute in recent years. Earlier commentators did not concern themselves with such mundane issues, assuming either that ballads served some antique organic community now lost in the mists of time, or that the author communicated directly to the present through what Child called, in an unusually vague moment, "the ballad-muse" (III, 42). A more historically attuned approach led to greater specificity: Rodney Hilton in particular argued strongly for a continuity between the Robin Hood ballads including the *Gest* and the dissident forces typified in the so-called Peasants' Revolt of 1381 (1958). This was supported by Maurice Keen in the first edition of his book on *The Outlaws of Medieval Legend* (1961). J. C. Holt attacked that generally radical affiliation in an article by asserting, with some reason, that rural and peasant issues are nowhere found within the texts, and proposing that the dissident audience was in fact the lower gentry, their hangers-on and higher servitors (1960). Dobson and Taylor largely accept this, but still claim that Robin Hood is "a yeoman hero for a yeoman audience" (1976, p. 34). Keen later agreed (1976). Holt returns to the issue in his book, devoting a whole chapter to very full detail intended to prove the essentially conservative character of the audience and the texts, which are held to embody the anxiety of the lesser land-owning gentry and their affiliations (1989, pp. 109–58). This argument seems open to Holt's own techniques of rejection through lack of internal evidence, in that only the knight in the *Gest* has tenurial problems on his mind and the rest of the characters resist all kinds of service, unless to Robin Hood.

Recent arguments have sophisticated Hilton's original argument about the texts as providing for an audience interested in some form of political resistance. Peter Coss (1985) rests his case on the concept of "cultural diffusion" and Richard Tardif (1983) explored the mediation of contemporary conflict by relating the strains of the texts to urban problems, seeing the greenwood as a place of imagined freedom for displaced craftsmen. That, unlike the peasant or lower gentry argument, certainly meshes with the bookish character of the texts — in manuscript and printed form long before other ballads, and in their earliest occurrences not often obviously connected with tunes.

The audience remains unclear, but commentators seem now agreed that it was probably mixed. The story of the *Gest* links Robin and his varied band with a knight, a cook, and the king. Fictions of social harmony can hardly reach further, and they appear to be newly focused versions (focused in a more class-conscious and wide-ranging way) of the images of natural community that were at the core of the older Robin Hood plays and games. Audiences, like the politics and the themes of the ballads, appear to be flexible and multiple.

The only major source suggested for the *Gest* is the Robin Hood ballads themselves, and scholars have often pointed out how the rescue of the knight from Nottingham has resemblances to *Robin Hood and the Monk*, how John tricks the sheriff much as Robin does in *Robin Hood and the Potter*, and the final stanzas relate to *The Death of Robin Hood* in some way — although that is a later ballad, no one has agreed with D. C. Fowler that it was itself inspired by these stanzas in the *Gest* (1968, pp. 79–80). William Clawson (1909, pp. 125–27) provided a schema of how twelve ballads had been gathered into the *Gest*, but the argument was weakened by the fact that only four reasonably close contacts with existing ballads can be found; these links are explored in detail by Dobson and Taylor (1976, pp. 74–78). However, there are as many parallels, as noted by Child (III, 43), between episodes in the story and the outlaw legends of Fulk Fitzwarin and Eustace the Monk.

In addition to the ballad sources, Clawson convincingly demonstrates that a "miracle of the Virgin" must account for the lengthy episode of the impoverished knight, Sir Richard of the Lee, who offers the Virgin as his surety for the loan of four hundred pounds from Robin Hood (1909, pp. 25–41). While no exact source has been located, two Middle English versions of *The Merchant's Surety*, dating c. 1390 and c. 1450, provide some similarities in plot and diction: both the knight and the merchant Theodorus love the Virgin; both are impoverished (due to different circumstances); both are required to pledge security for a loan; both offer the Virgin as their *borowe/borwe*; and both swear that they will repay the loan on a certain day. While these parallels are suggestive, there are major differences, particularly the ways in which the two loans are repaid. To explain these differences, Clawson suggests that the *Gest* poet drew his ending from an *exemplum* in which "the person [Robin] to whom the money is due takes it from a monk [the high cellarer of St. Mary's abbey] whom he regards as the earthly representative of the saint or deity [the Virgin] and as the instrument of the return of the loan" (p. 26). While elements of a "miracle" are certainly present, the positing of an unknown *exemplum* is not very convincing. If there is a lost source, it may be related to another group of miracles of the "knight and Virgin" type, seven prose examples of which were printed by Wynkyn de Worde in the late fifteenth-century *The Myracles of Oure Lady*. Here are enough similiarities to suggest that the *Gest* poet was familiar with this sub-genre. The eighth miracle in Peter Whiteford's edition describes: "How a knyght fyll to poverte, & by the devyll was made ryche, & by the merytes of his wyfe was, by our Lady, restored agayn to good and vertuouse lyvyng" (p. 49). Of interest too is the twenty-seventh miracle, which opens with the sentence: "In a wood was a certayn theef that robbed men & kylled them that came by" (p. 61). For additional parallels, see the Introduction to *Robin Hood and the Monk*.

The construction of the *Gest* has been considered by some to be clumsy and artificial (Holt, 1989 p. 17), while others have regarded it more favorably, ranging from Clawson's very general praise of its "admirable artistic skill" (1909, p. 128) to Gray's more measured sense that the text has "excellent scenes," that "the construction has been neatly done" and that "the 'loose ends' that have been noticed would not be as obvious in oral performance (of whatever kind) as they are to a reader of the printed page" (1984, p. 23).

As has often been observed, the overall structure is triune — "a three-ply web" as Child calls it (III, 50). Fitts 1 and 2 deal with the impoverished knight who is lent money by Robin to regain his lands from the rapacious church; in the later part of Fitt 4 the same knight returns to repay Robin. In the "interlaced" episode, Fitt 3 and the first part of Fitt 4, Little John, whom Robin has sent to serve and help the knight, is sought as a servitor by the sheriff: he leaves the sheriff's house disgruntled by his poor treatment, brings with him the Cook, and then traps the sheriff into entering the forest and losing his possessions. The second part of the *Gest* starts in Fitt 5 with the Sheriff's archery contest and trap, after which the outlaws take refuge with the knight of Fitt 1. He is then, Fitt 6, kidnapped by the sheriff and rescued by the outlaws, who kill the sheriff. As Dobson and Taylor note, the *Gest* is "not so much a single unified work as a weaving together of various tales" (1995, p. 37).

These stories, interwoven as they are, involve adventures coming to and spreading out from Robin's forest base, much as knightly adventures do in Arthur's court, and the text seems aware of the connection, presenting as it does Robin's desire to have an adventure before he can feast, in a deliberate reference — perhaps, as Child suggests, a "humorous imitation" III, 51. Arthurian stories climax with royal praise for the hero, and this is also the case here, but for that to happen the king has to come to the forest; Fitts 7 and 8 offer a version of the well known "King and Subject" theme in which the King in disguise meets, then in some way conflicts with, one of his subjects, and the result is honor both to the king's flexibility and also the subject's deep-seated loyalty. In the *Gest* King Edward meets, engages with, and at least symbolically joins the forest outlaws. But, different from *Adam Bell*, his offer for Robin to join his court is not successful, and the poem ends with Robin's return to the greenwood, unhappy with the inactive and expensive nature of court life. The last stanzas, more a palinode than a climax, sketch in the story of Robin's death. Like other heroes he is betrayed by someone close to him and leaves a shrine and a noble memory.

Those like Holt who find this episodic structure clumsy appear to be thinking of the neatly motive-oriented procedure of the conventional novel rather than the more open and situation-oriented pattern of medieval narrative: the poem's episodic structure actually operates very well to focus and dramatize its presentation of major points, such as the angry frustration of the abbot, the delayed fidelity of the knight, the sheriff's discomforting, the royal revelation. These set-pieces dramatize in almost ritual form the interplay of values within the text and construct a level of complexity different from, and in some senses reaching further than, the novel's concern with humanist individuality.

In terms of poetic form, the text is not complex, but has its own modes of persuasive force. The rhyme is generally steadier than in parallels like *Robin Hood and the Potter* and *Adam Bell*. Weak or half rhymes are few — 35 in all, of which 12 could be resolved by a dialectal variant. Only one stanza rhymes *abab* (lines 45–48), and one other does so by repetition (lines 101–04). Unlike the other early ballads, unduly long lines are very rare (lines 537 and 631) and weak lines are a good deal rarer than in the parallels — about 35 in the whole poem, with a curious clustering of them around line 1200, in the rescue of Sir Richard sequence (was a casually rhymed ballad perhaps being re-used?). The most striking feature of the rhyme scheme is the common retention of the rhyme sound from one stanza to another, in effect creating an eight line stanza. In fairly simple diction like that of this poem, the number of rhymes available is not enormous and so this repetition must sometimes occur by sheer chance, but over ten percent of the stanzas contribute to this *laisse-*

like effect, so emphasizing the lyrical or performance quality of a text normally thought to be somewhat prosaic.

Equally unpoetic, in terms of usual expectation, is the diction and the type of imagery offered. The language is limited in vocabulary and range, and most striking of all, there are very few images or even descriptions in the whole poem. But what might seem uninspired and unimaginative from a Shakespearean viewpoint can also have a curious potency. Gray speaks of the "constant repetition of stereotypical value words" in the poem (1984, p. 25) and a set of strong and generalized positions is created through recurrent evaluative descriptions. The sheriff is consistently *proude* (23 times), the knight is recurrently described as *gentyll* (19 times), while Robin and sometimes his men are *gode* (17 times), though the men are also manly, *wight* (7 times) and occasionally *mery* (3 cases). Robin is only once *curteys* and *gentyll*, suggesting limits to his social aspirations and those of the poem (a point against Holt's interpretation of audience). Interestingly, he is once given the sheriff's epithet *prowde*, right at the beginning of the poem when his component values are being established. Another, perhaps more casually, shared adjective is *dere* — used once of Mary, God, and Robin as Little John's master.

These terms lay out, almost allegorically, the forces at work: bureaucratic pride versus a yeoman goodness which supports enfeebled gentility. The stereotypical adjectives very noticeably cluster twice, first when Robin lays down his rules for engagement with the world (lines 3–24) and then again when he finally returns to the forest (lines 1777–96). Framing the narrative as they do, these evaluative summaries construct a striking social triangle of the proud, the genteel, and the good, with the *wight* power of the outlaws resolving the conflict in the favor of the last two.

Some have felt the text also benefits from an ironic touch. Both Child and Gray find the Arthur references light-hearted (III, 51; 1984, pp. 26–27), and Gray also sees irony in the play on Mary as a faithful guarantor, as well as more direct comedy in Little John's buffoonish cloth measuring (lines 290–97) and his cartoon-like adventures both against and with the sheriff's cook (1984, pp. 27–29). Irony is certainly one of the poem's weapons, especially in the humiliation of abbott and sheriff, yet Robin as a trickster seems more fully figured in other texts (*Robin Hood and the Curtal Friar* and *Robin Hood and Allin a Dale*, for example), and the overall tone of the poem seems earnest, relieved occasionally by some sardonic irony, not unlike other texts of this kind, from *Gamelyn* to *Chevy Chase*.

Bessinger described the poem as "class conscious" and "anti-ecclesiastical" like other major late medieval texts from the pens of Chaucer, Langland and Gower (1974, p. 364). Its relation with the ballads often tends to obscure that weighty and valid connection. The poem certainly has a strong and recurrent satirical force; Kaeuper said it was "a running commentary on the corrupt power of the sheriff in local society, and it provides a visit by a corrupt chief justice from Westminster as well" (1988, pp. 335–36). But the *Gest* is not only a social commentary; as Keen, a historian who has strongly elucidated the political aspect of the poem, has observed, it also has a "wide variation of mood" (1961, p. 116), and this mobile character is both part of its quality and a sign of its direct relation to the multivalent outlaw myth. The poem is at times almost mystical in its creation of the greenwood and its value, at other times a knockabout comic morality. In that variety it shares the dual thrust of the local and ritual Robin Hood plays. But it also expresses in some detail a sense of the wrongs imposed by the alienated authorities of church, town, and state, and in that sense it connects with fully developed strains of the period and the tensions basic to the outlaw myth.

In terms of the Robin Hood texts, the *Gest* does not raise any themes which are not touched elsewhere, but it raises them at length, in coherent relation with each other, and with a confident narrative and poetic technique. Child, in his characteristic mode, both scholarly and appreciative, remarked that the *Gest* at one point appeared to be deploying a theme found in *Fulk Fitzwarin* and other outlaw analogues: but, he added, "the story is incomparably better here than elsewhere" (III, 53). Gray speaks persuasively of the effectiveness of the poem in its performative context, and also of its capacity to touch the mythic potential of the Robin Hood tradition (1984, p. 38). Different from the ballads as it is, the *Gest* is nevertheless not unfaithful to their tradition or their style, in both form and content. While its elaborated narrative and interlocking events must in some sense lack the pared-down mystery of the sparer and starker of the ballads, the *Gest* gives full weight to just what makes this elusive hero so *gode*. The author of the *Gest* shares with that other fifteenth-century compiler, Sir Thomas Malory, the ability to combine and develop materials of high potency and complexity into a generically new whole of great future impact, which manages to convey and even enhance the source materials' innate values and power.

Select Bibliography

Texts

Child, F. J., ed. *The English and Scottish Popular Ballads*. 5 vols. Rpt. New York: Dover, 1965. Vol. III, no. 117.

Dobson, R. B., and J. Taylor. *Rymes of Robyn Hode*. London: Heinemann, 1976. Pp. 71–112.

A Gest of Robyn Hode

Fragments of an early printed version, perhaps by Wynkyn de Worde, of the *Gest*. [Now in the Douce Collection, Bodleian Library, Oxford.]

A Gest of Robyn Hode ("Lettersnijder" edn.). Antwerp: Van Doesbroch, c. 1510. [Now in National Library of Scotland.]

Gutch, J. M., ed. *A Lytelle Gest of Robin Hood and other Auncient and Modern Ballads and Songs Relating to the Celebrated Yeoman.* 2 vols. London: Longman, 1847. I, 139–219.

A Lytell Geste of Robyn Hode. London: Wynkyn de Worde, ?1506–10. [Now in Cambridge University Library.]

A Mery Geste of Robyn Hoode. London: Copland, c. 1560. [Now in the British Library.]

A Merry Iest of Robin Hood. London: Edward White, late sixteenth century. [Now in the Bodleian Library, another copy in the British Library.]

Phillips, Helen, ed. *The Awntyrs off Arthure at the Terne Wathelyne: A Northern Middle English Romance set in Inglewood Forest.* Lancaster Modern Spelling Texts. Vol. 1. Lancaster: University of Lancaster, 1988.

Ritson, Joseph, ed. *Robin Hood, A Collection of All the Ancient Poems, Songs, and Ballads Now extant Relative to the Celebrated English Outlaw.* 2 vols. London: Egerton and Johnson, 1795. I, 1–80.

Whiteford, Peter, ed. *The Myracles of Oure Lady.* Middle English Texts 23. Heidelberg: Carl Winter, 1990. [Includes a miracle of a knight and the Virgin (no. 8), and a miracle of "a certayne thefe" (no. 27).]

Commentary and Criticism

Bellamy, John. *Crime and Public Order in England in the Later Middle Ages.* London: Routledge, 1973.

——. *Robin Hood: An Historical Inquiry.* London: Croom Helm, 1985.

Bessenger, J. B., Jr. "The *Gest of Robin Hood* Revisited." In *The Learned and the Lewed: Studies in Chaucer and Medieval Literature*. Ed. Larry D. Benson. Cambridge: Harvard University Press, 1974. Pp. 355–69.

Carpenter, Kevin. *Robin Hood: The Many Faces of that Celebrated English Outlaw*. Oldenburg: Bibliotheks- und Enformationssystem der Universität Oldenburg, 1995

Child, F. J., pp. 39–56.

Clawson, William H. *The Gest of Robin Hood*. Toronto: University of Toronto Library, 1909.

Coss, Peter R. "Aspects of Cultural Diffusion in Medieval England: The Early Romances, Local Society and Robin Hood." *Past and Present* 108 (1985), 35–79.

Dobson, R. B., and J. Taylor. " 'Rhymes of Robin Hood': The Early Ballads and the *Gest*." In Carpenter, 1995. Pp. 35–44. See also Dobson and Taylor (1976), especially pp. 71–79.

Fowler, D. C. *A Literary History of the Popular Ballad*. Durham: Duke University Press, 1968.

———. "The Ballads." In *The Manual of Writings of Middle English, 1050–1550*, new series. Ed. A. E. Hartung. Vol. 6. New Haven, CT: The Connecticut Academy of Arts and Sciences, 1980. Pp. 1753–1808.

Gray, Douglas. "The Robin Hood Poems." *Poetica* 18 (1984), 1–39.

Hilton, Rodney. "The Origins of Robin Hood." *Past and Present* 14 (1958), 30–44; rpt. in R. Hilton, ed. *Peasants, Knights and Heretics*. Cambridge: University Press, 1976. Pp. 221–35.

Hoffman, Dean A. " 'With the Shot Y Wyll / Alle Thy Lustes to Full-Fyl': Archery as Symbol in the Early Ballads of Robin Hood." *Neuphilologische Mitteilungen* 86 (1985), 494–505.

Holt, J. C. "The Origins and Audience of the Ballads of Robin Hood." *Past and Present* 18 (1960), 89–110; rpt. in Hilton, pp. 236–57.

———. *Robin Hood*. Second ed. London: Thames and Hudson, 1989.

———. "Robin Hood: The Origins of the Legend." In Carpenter, 1995. Pp. 27–34.

Hunter, Joseph. "The Great Hero of Ancient Minstrelsy of England: Robin Hood, his Period, Real Character, etc. Investigated." *Critical and Historical Tracts* 4 (London: Smith, 1852), 28–38.

Ikegami, Masa. "The Language and Date of 'A Gest of Robyn Hode.' " *Neuphilologische Mitteilungen* 96 (1995), 271–81.

Kaeuper, Richard W. *War, Justice and Public Order*. Oxford: Clarendon Press, 1988.

Keen, Maurice. *The Outlaws of Medieval Legend*. London: Routledge, 1961. [The second edition of 1977 reprints the previous book with no new material, although a preface indicates Keen's new position on audience.]

———. "Robin Hood: Peasant or Gentleman?" *Past and Present* 19 (1961), 7–15. Rpt. in Hilton, 1976, see above. Pp. 258–66. [With a short afterword indicating that he now agrees with Holt on audience.]

Maddicott, J. R. "The Birth and Setting of the Ballads of Robin Hood." *English Historical Review* 93 (1978), 276–99.

Ohlgren, Thomas H. "Edwardus Redivivus in A Gest of Robyn Hode." *Journal of English and Germanic Philology* 99 (2000), 1–29.

———. "The 'Marchaunt' of Sherwood: Mercantile Ideology in A Gest of Robin Hood." In Hahn (2000), pp. 175–90.

Parker, David. "Popular Protest in 'A Gest of Robyn Hode.' " *Modern Language Quarterly* 32 (1971), 3–20.

Powicke, M. *Military Obligation in Medieval England*. Oxford: Clarendon Press, 1962.

Tardif, Richard. "The 'Mistery' of Robin Hood: A New Social Context for the Texts." In *Worlds and Words: Studies in the Social Role of Verbal Culture*. Eds. Stephen Knight and S. N. Mukherjee. Sydney: Sydney Association for Studies in Society and Culture, 1983. Pp. 130–45.

A Gest of Robyn Hode

The First Fytte

Lythe and listin, gentilmen,   *Attend*
That be of frebore blode;   *freeborn blood*
I shall you tel of a gode yeman,
His name was Robyn Hode.

5   Robyn was a prude outlaw,   *proud*
      Whyles he walked on grounde:
      So curteyse an outlawe as he was one
      Was nevere non founde.

      Robyn stode in Bernesdale,   *stood*
10   And lenyd hym to a tre,   *leaned against*
      And bi hym stode Litell Johnn,
      A gode yeman was he.

      And alsoo dyd gode Scarlok,
      And Much, the millers son:
15   There was none ynch of his bodi
      But it was worth a grome.   *man*

      Than bespake Lytell Johnn   *spoke*
      All untoo Robyn Hode:
      "Maister, and ye wolde dyne betyme   *if you would dine early*
20   It wolde doo you moche gode."   *much*

      Than bespake hym gode Robyn:
      "To dyne have I noo lust,   *desire*
      Till that I have som bolde baron,
      Or som unkouth gest.   *strange visitor*

25   "Here shal come a lord or sire
    That may pay for the best,
    Or som knyght or squyer,   *squire*
    That dwelleth here bi west."

    A gode maner than had Robyn;   *custom*
30   In londe where that he were,
    Every day or he wold dyne   *before*
    Thre messis wolde he here.   *masses; hear*

    The one in the worship of the Fader,
    And another of the Holy Gost,
35   The thirde of Our dere Lady,   *Virgin Mary*
    That he loved allther moste.   *the most of all*

    Robyn loved Oure dere Lady:
    For dout of dydly synne,   *fear; of deadly sin*
    Wolde he never do compani harme
40   That any woman was in.

    "Maistar," than sayde Lytil Johnn,
    "And we our borde shal sprede,   *If; table*
    Tell us wheder that we shal go,   *where*
    And what life that we shall lede.

45   "Where we shall take, where we shall leve,
    Where we shall abide behynde;
    Where we shall robbe, where we shal reve,   *despoil*
    Where we shall bete and bynde."   *beat and tie up*

    "Therof no force," than sayde Robyn,   *no matter*
50   "We shall do well inowe;   *enough*
    But loke ye do no husbonde harme,   *small farmer*
    That tilleth with his ploughe.

    "No more ye shall no gode yeman
    That walketh by grene wode shawe,   *thicket*
55   Ne no knyght ne no squyer
    That wol be a gode felawe.   *companion*

"These bisshoppes and these archebisshoppes,
Ye shall them bete and bynde;
The hye sherif of Notyingham,   *high*
60   Hym holde ye in your mynde."

"This worde shalbe holde," sayde Lytell Johnn,   *kept*
"And this lesson we shall lere;   *learn*
It is fer dayes, God sende us a gest,   *far on in the day; guest*
That we were at oure dynere!"

65   "Take thy gode bowe in thy honde," sayde Robyn;
"Late Much wende with the: *Let; go; thee*
And so shal Willyam Scarlok,
And no man abyde with me.

"And walke up to the Saylis,   *(see note)*
70   And so to Watlinge Strete,
And wayte after some unkuth gest,   *look for; unknown*
Up chaunce ye may them mete.   *Upon, by*

"Be he erle, or ani baron,   *earl*
Abbot, or ani knyght,
75   Bringhe hym to lodge to me;   *with*
His dyner shall be dight."   *ready*

They wente up to the Saylis,
These yeman all thre;
They loked est, they loke weest;
80   They myght no man see.

But as they loked in to Bernysdale,
Bi a derne strete,   *secret way*
Than came a knyght ridinghe,
Full sone they gan hym mete.   *At once; did meet him*

85   All dreri was his semblaunce,   *sad; appearance*
And lytell was his pryde;
His one fote in the styrop stode,   *stirrup*
That othere wavyd beside.

His hode hanged in his iyn two; *hood; eyes*
90 He rode in symple aray, *array (clothing)*
A soriar man than he was one *sadder*
Rode never in somer day.

Litell Johnn was full curteyes,
And sette hym on his kne: *went down*
95 "Welcom be ye, gentyll knyght,
Welcom ar ye to me.

"Welcom be thou to grene wode,
Hende knyght and fre; *Courteous; noble*
My maister hath abiden you fastinge, *awaited you without food*
100 Syr, al these oures thre." *hours*

"Who is thy maister?" sayde the knyght;
Johnn sayde, "Robyn Hode."
"He is gode yoman," sayde the knyght,
"Of hym I have herde moche gode.

105 "I graunte," he sayde, "with you to wende,
My bretherne, all in fere; *in company*
My purpos was to have dyned to day
At Blith or Dancastere."

Furth than went this gentyl knight,
110 With a carefull chere; *sorrowful expression*
The teris oute of his iyen ran, *tears; eyes*
And fell downe by his lere. *face*

They brought hym to the lodge door, *hut door*
Whan Robyn hym gan see,
115 Full curtesly dyd of his hode *took off*
And sette hym on his knee. *kneeled down*

"Welcome, sir knight," than sayde Robyn,
"Welcome art thou to me;
I have abyden you fastinge, sir,
120 All these ouris thre." *hours*

Than answered the gentyll knight,
With wordes fayre and fre:
"God the save, goode Robyn,   *thee*
And all thy fayre meyné."   *company*

125 They wasshed togeder and wyped bothe,   *dried (their hands)*
And sette to theyr dynere;   *dinner*
Brede and wyne they had right ynoughe,   *in plenty*
And noumbles of the dere.   *organ meats (sweetbreads)*

Swannes and fessauntes they had full gode,   *pheasants*
130 And foules of the ryvere;   *birds; river-bank*
There fayled none so litell a birde   *lacked*
That ever was bred on bryre.   *branch*

"Do gladly, sir knight," sayde Robyn;   *Eat well*
"Gramarcy, sir," sayde he,   *Grant mercy, thank you*
135 "Such a dinere had I nat
Of all these wekys thre.   *weeks*

"If I come ageyne, Robyn,
Here by thys contré,
As gode a dyner I shall the make   *thee*
140 As that thou haest made to me."

"Gramarcy, knyght," sayde Robyn,
"My dyner whan that I it have;
I was never so gredy, bi dere worthy God,   *hungry*
My dyner for to crave.

145 "But pay or ye wende," sayde Robyn;   *before you go*
"Me thynketh it is gode ryght;
It was never the maner, by dere worthi God,   *custom*
A yoman to pay for a knyght."

"I have nought in my coffers," saide the knyght,   *money chest*
150 "That I may profer for shame."
"Litell Johnn, go loke," sayde Robyn,
"Ne let nat for no blame.   *delay*

94

"Tel me truth," than saide Robyn,
"So God have parte of the."   *protect*
155 "I have no more but ten shelynges," sayde the knyght,   *shillings*
"So God have part of me."

"If thou hast no more," sayde Robyn,
"I woll nat one peny,
And yf thou have nede of any more,
160 More shall I lend the.

"Go nowe furth, Littell Johnn,
The truth tell thou me:
If there be no more but ten shelinges,
No peny that I se."   *(see note)*

165 Lyttell Johnn sprede downe hys mantell
Full fayre upon the grounde,
And there he fonde in the knyghtes cofer   *money chest*
But even halfe pounde.   *ten shillings*

Littell Johnn let it lye full styll,   *alone*
170 And went to hys maysteer lowe.   *master, i.e., Robin*
"What tidynges Johnn?" sayde Robyn;   *news*
"Sir, the knyght is true inowe."   *enough*

"Fyll of the best wine," sayde Robyn,
"The knyght shall begynne;
175 Moche wonder thinketh me   *Much*
Thy clothynge is so thin.   *threadbare*

"Tell me one worde," sayde Robyn,
"And counsel shal it be:
I trowe thou warte made a knyght of force,   *by compulsion (see note)*
180 Or ellys of yemanry.   *else*

"Or ellys thou hast bene a sori husbande,   *miserable*
And lyved in stroke and stryfe,   *conflict and strife*
An okerer or ellis a lechoure," sayde Robyn,   *usurer; lecher*
"Wyth wronge hast led thy lyfe."

185   "I am none of those," sayde the knyght,
       "By God that made me;
       An hundred wynter here before
       Myn auncetres knyghtes have be.   *ancestors*

       "But oft it hath befal, Robyn,
190   A man hath be disgrate,   *disgraced (deprived of status)*
       But God that sitteth in heven above   *Unless*
       May amende his state.

       "Withyn this two yere, Robyne," he sayde,
       "My neghbours well it wende,   *knew*
195   Foure hundred pounde of gode money
       Ful well than myght I spende.

       "Nowe have I no gode," saide the knyght,   *possessions*
       "God hath shaped such an ende,
       But my chyldren and my wyfe,
200   Tyll God yt may amende."

       "In what maner," than sayde Robyn,
       "Hast thou lorne thy rychesse?"   *lost*
       "For my greate foly," he sayde,
       "And for my kyndnesse.   *kindness*

205   "I hade a sone, forsoth, Robyn,
       That shulde have ben myn ayre,   *heir*
       Whanne he was twenty wynter olde,
       In felde wolde just full fayre.   *joust*

       "He slewe a knyght of Lancaster,
210   And a squyer bolde;
       For to save hym in his ryght
       My godes beth sette and solde.   *goods*

       "My londes beth sette to wedde, Robyn,   *pledged as security*
       Untyll a certayn day,
215   To a ryche abbot here besyde
       Of Seynt Mari Abbey."

"What is the som?" sayde Robyn;   *sum*
"Trouth than tell thou me."
"Sir," he sayde, "foure hundred pounde;
220 The abbot told it to me."   *counted*

"Nowe and thou lese thy lond," sayde Robyn, *lose*
"What woll fall of the?"
"Hastely I wol me buske," sayde the knyght, *hurry*
"Over the salte see,

225 "And se where Criste was quyke and dede, *alive*
On the mount of Calveré;
Fare wel, frende, and have gode day;
It may no better be."

Teris fell out of hys iyen two;   *Tears; eyes*
230 He wolde have gone hys way.
"Farewel, frende, and have gode day;
I ne have no more to pay."

"Where be thy frendes?" sayde Robyn.
"Syr, never one wol me knowe:
235 While I was ryche ynowe at home
Great boste than wolde they blowe.   *boast; spread*

"And nowe they renne away fro me,   *run*
As bestis on a rowe;
They take no more hede of me   *notice*
240 Thanne they had me never sawe."

For ruthe thanne wept Litell Johnn,   *pity*
Scarlok and Muche in fere;   *together*
"Fyl of the best wyne," sayde Robyn, *Fill your cups with*
"For here is a symple chere.   *hospitality*

245 "Hast thou any frende," sayde Robyn,
"Thy borowe that wolde be?"   *security (guarantee)*
"I have none," than sayde the knyght,
"But God that dyed on tree."   *Except; the Cross*

"Do away thy japis," than sayde Robyn,   *jokes*
250   "Thereof wol I right none;
Wenest thou I wolde have God to borowe,   *Think you*
Peter, Poule, or Johnn?

"Nay, by Hym that me made,
And shope both sonne and mone,   *created*
255   Fynde me a better borowe," sayde Robyn,   *security*
"Or money getest thou none."

"I have none other," sayde the knyght,
"The sothe for to say,
But yf yt be Our dere Lady;   *Unless*
260   She fayled me never or thys day."   *failed; before*

"By dere worthy God," sayde Robyn,
"To seche all Englonde thorowe,
Yet fonde I never to my pay   *pleasure*
A moche better borowe.   *security*

265   "Come nowe furth, Litell Johnn.
And go to my tresouré,
And bringe me foure hundred pound,
And loke well tolde it be."   *counted*

Furth than went Litell Johnn,
270   And Scarlok went before;
He tolde oute foure hundred pounde   *counted*
By eightene and two score.   *twenty twenties*

"Is thys well tolde?" sayde litell Much;
Johnn sayde, "What greveth the?
275   It is almus to helpe a gentyll knyght,   *alms, charity*
That is fal in poverté.   *fallen*

"Master," than sayde Lityll John,
"His clothinge is full thynne;
Ye must gyve the knight a lyveray,   *livery (suit of clothing)*
280   To lappe his body therin.   *wrap*

98

"For ye have scarlet and grene, mayster,
And many a riche aray;   *clothing*
Ther is no marchaunt in mery Englond
So ryche, I dare well say."

285 "Take hym thre yerdes of every colour,   *Give*
And loke well mete that it be."   *measured*
Lytell Johnn toke none other mesure
But his bowe-tree,   *bow-stave*

And at every handfull that he met   *measured*
290 He leped footes three.   *added*
"What devylles drapar," sayid litell Muche,   *draper (a dealer in cloth)*
"Thynkest thou for to be?"

Scarlok stode full stil and loughe,   *laughed*
And sayd, "By God Almyght,
295 Johnn may gyve hym gode mesure,
For it costeth hym but lyght."   *little*

"Mayster," than said Litell Johnn
To gentill Robyn Hode,
"Ye must give the knight a hors,
300 To lede home this gode."   *carry; goods*

"Take hym a gray coursar," sayde Robyn,   *Give; courser (swift horse)*
"And a saydle newe;   *saddle*
He is Oure Ladye's messangere;
God graunt that he be true."

305 "And a gode palfray," sayde lytell Much,   *saddle horse*
"To mayntene hym in his right."
"And a peyre of botes," sayde Scarlock,   *boots*
"For he is a gentyll knight."

"What shalt thou gyve hym, Litell John?" said Robyn.
310 "Sir, a peyre of gilt sporis clene,   *shining spurs*
To pray, for all this company,
God bringe hym oute of tene."   *sorrow*

"Whan shal mi day be," said the knight,   *repayment day*
"Sir, and your wyll be?"   *if*
315   "This day twelve moneth," saide Robyn,
"Under this grene-wode tre.

"It were greate shame," sayde Robyn,
"A knight alone to ryde,
Withoute squyre, yoman, or page,
320   To walke by his syde.

"I shall the lende Litell John, my man,   *thee*
For he shalbe thy knave;   *servant*
In a yemans stede he may the stande,   *place; serve thee*
If thou greate nede have."

The Seconde Fytte

325   Now is the knight gone on his way:
This game hym thought full gode;
Whanne he loked on Bernesdale
He blessyd Robyn Hode.

And whanne he thought on Bernysdale,
330   On Scarlok, Much, and Johnn,
He blyssyd them for the best company
That ever he in come.   *came*

Then spake that gentyll knyght,
To Lytel Johan gan he saye,
335   "To-morrowe I must to Yorke toune,
To Saynt Mary abbay.

"And to the abbot of that place
Foure hondred pounde I must pay;
And but I be there upon this nyght
340   My londe is lost for ay."   *forever*

100

A Gest of Robyn Hode

The abbot sayd to his covent,   *convent, body of monks*
There he stode on grounde,   *Where*
"This day twelfe moneth came there a knyght
And borrowed foure hondred pounde.

345   "He borrowed foure hondred pounde,
Upon all his londe fre;
But he come this ylke day   *Unless; same*
Dysheryte shall he be."   *Disinherited*

"It is full erely," sayd the pryoure,   *prior (monk ranking under the abbot)*
350   "The day is not yet ferre gone;
I had lever to pay an hondred pounde,   *would rather*
And lay downe anone.   *(see note)*

"The knyght is ferre beyonde the see,
In Englonde ryght,   *England's cause*
355   And suffreth honger and colde,
And many a sory nyght.

"It were grete pyté," said the pryoure,
"So to have his londe;
And ye be so lyght of your consyence,   *easy*
360   Ye do to hym moch wronge."

"Thou arte ever in my berde," sayd the abbot,   *in my way*
"By God and Saynt Rychere."
With that cam in a fat-heded monke,
The heygh selerer.   *cellarmaster (chief steward)*

365   "He is dede or hanged," sayd the monke,
"By God that bought me dere,   *redeemed me at a high price*
And we shall have to spende in this place
Foure hondred pounde by yere."

The abbot and the hy selerer
370   Sterte forthe full bolde,   *Leaped*
The justyce of Englonde   *chief justice*
The abbot there dyde holde.   *control*

The hye justyce and many mo
Had take in to theyr honde
375 Holy all the knyghtes det,   *Wholly*
To put that knyght to wronge.   *humiliate*

They demed the knyght wonder sore,   *judged; severely*
The abbot and his meyné: *company*
"But he come this ylke day   *But if (Unless); same*
380 Dysheryte shall he be."

"He wyll not come yet," sayd the justyce,
"I dare well undertake."   *swear*
But in sorowe tyme for them all   *as a disappointment*
The knyght came to the gate.

385 Than bespake that gentyll knyght
Untyll his meyné: *To*
"Now put on your symple wedes   *clothing*
That ye brought fro the see."   *from overseas*

They put on their symple wedes,
390 They came to the gates anone;
The porter was redy hymselfe,
And welcomed them everychone.   *everyone*

"Welcome, syr knyght," sayd the porter,
"My lorde to mete is he,   *at dinner*
395 And so is many a gentyll man,
For the love of the."

The porter swore a full grete othe,
"By God that made me,
Here be the best coressed hors   *bodied (built)*
400 That ever yet sawe I me.

"Lede them in to the stable," he sayd,
"That eased myght they be."
"They shall not come therin," sayd the knyght,
"By God that dyed on a tre."

102

405 Lordes were to mete isette   *seated at dinner*
    In that abbotes hall;
    The knyght went forth and kneled downe,
    And salued them grete and small.   *greeted*

    "Do gladly, syr abbot," sayd the knyght,
410 "I am come to holde my day."
    The fyrst word the abbot spake,
    "Hast thou brought my pay?"

    "Not one peny," sayd the knyght,
    "By God that maked me."
415 "Thou art a shrewed dettour," sayd the abbot; *cursed*
    "Syr justyce, drynke to me.

    "What doost thou here," sayd the abbot,
    "But thou haddest brought thy pay?"   *Unless*
    "For God," than sayd the knyght,
420 "To pray of a lenger daye."   *To beg for*

    "Thy daye is broke," sayd the justyce,   *You missed your appointed payment*
    "Londe getest thou none."
    "Now, good syr justyce, be my frende,
    And fende me of my fone!"   *defend me from my enemies*

425 "I am holde with the abbot," sayd the justyce, *retained by*
    "Both with cloth and fee."
    "Now, good syr sheryf, be my frende!"
    "Nay, for God," sayd he.

    "Now, good syr abbot, be my frende,
430 For thy curteysé,
    And holde my londes in thy honde
    Tyll I have made the gree!   *paid my debt to you*

    "And I wyll be thy true servaunte,
    And trewely serve the,
435 Tyl ye have foure hondred pounde
    Of money good and free."

The abbot sware a full grete othe,
"By God that dyed on a tree,
Get the londe where thou may,   *thee*
440   For thou getest none of me."

"By dere worthy God," then sayd the knyght,
"That all this worlde wrought,
But I have my londe agayne,   *Unless*
Full dere it shall be bought.   *Someone will suffer for it*

445   "God, that was of a mayden borne,
Leve us well to spede!   *Grant; to succeed*
For it is good to assay a frende   *try out*
Or that a man have need."   *Before*

The abbot lothely on hym gan loke,   *with hatred*
450   And vylaynesly hym gan call: *vilely*
"Out," he sayd, "thou false knyght,
Spede the out of my hall!"   *Hurry*

"Thou lyest," then sayd the gentyll knyght,
"Abbot, in thy hall;
455   False knyght was I never,
By God that made us all."

Up then stode that gentyll knyght,
To the abbot sayd he,
"To suffre a knyght to knele so longe,
460   Thou canst no curteysye.   *You know no good manners*

"In joustes and in tournement
Full ferre than have I be,   *far*
And put my selfe as ferre in press   *in as great danger*
As ony that ever I se."   *any*

465   "What wyll ye gyve more," sayd the justice,
"And the knyght shall make a releyse?   *If; release his claim*
And elles dare I safly swere   *confidently*
Ye holde never your londe in pees."   *peace*

"An hondred pounde," sayd the abbot;
470   The justice sayd, "Gyve hym two."
"Nay, be God," sayd the knyght,
"Yit gete ye it not so."   *Yet*

"Though ye wolde gyve a thousand more,
Yet were ye never the nere;   *no nearer success*
475   Shall there never be myn heyre   *heir*
Abbot, justice, ne frere."

He stert hym to a borde anone,   *table*
Tyll a table rounde,
And there shoke oute of a bagge
480   Even four hundred pound.   *Exactly*

"Have here thi golde, sir abbot," saide the knight,
"Which that thou lentest me;
Had thou ben curtes at my comynge,   *courteous*
Rewarded shuldest thou have be."

485   The abbot sat styll, and ete no more,
For all his ryall fare;   *royal food*
He cast his hede on his shulder,
And fast began to stare.   *fixedly*

"Take me my golde agayne," saide the abbot,   *Give*
490   "Sir justice, that I toke the."
"Not a peni," said the justice,
"Bi God that dyed on tree."

"Sir abbot and ye men of lawe,
Now have I holde my daye;
495   Now shall I have my londe agayne,
For ought that you can saye."

The knyght stert out of the dore,
Awaye was all his care,
And on he put his good clothynge,
500   The other he lefte there.

He wente hym forth full mery syngynge,   *singing*
As men have tolde in tale;
His lady met hym at the gate,
At home in Verysdale.

505   "Welcome, my lorde," sayd his lady;
"Syr, lost is all your good?"   *possessions*
"Be mery, dame," sayd the knyght,
"And pray for Robyn Hode,

"That ever his soule be in blysse:
510   He holpe me out of tene;   *trouble*
Ne had be his kyndenesse,
Beggers had we bene.

"The abbot and I accorded ben,   *are in agreement*
He is served of his pay;
515   The god yoman lent it me,
As I cam by the way."

This knight than dwelled fayre at home,
The sothe for to saye.
Tyll he had gete four hundred pound,
520   Al redy for to pay.

He purveyed him an hundred bowes,   *provided*
The strynges well ydyght,   *fitted*
An hundred shefe of arowes gode,
The hedys burneshed full bryght;   *points*

525   And every arowe an elle longe,   *ell (45 inches)*
With pecok wel idyght,   *peacock (feathers); fitted*
Inocked all with whyte silver;   *Grooved at the end (see note)*
It was a semely syght.   *fine*

He purveyed hym an hundreth men,
530   Well harnessed in that stede.
And hym selfe in that same sete,
And clothed in whyte and rede.

He bare a launsgay in his honde,   *light lance*
And a man ledde his male,   *carried his trunk*
535   And reden with a lyght songe   *rode*
Unto Bernsydale.

But at Wentbrydge ther was a wrastelyng,
And there taryed was he,   *delayed*
And there was all the best yemen
540   Of all the west countree.

A full fayre game there was up set,
A whyte bulle up i-pyght,   *placed*
A grete courser, with sadle and brydil,
With golde burnyssht full bryght.

545   A payre of gloves, a rede golde rynge,
A pype of wyne, in fay;   *cask; in truth*
What man that bereth hym best i-wys   *indeed*
The pryce shall bere away.   *prize*

There was a yoman in that place,
550   And best worthy was he,
And for he was ferre and frembde bested,   *(see note)*
Slayne he shulde have be.

The knight had ruthe of this yoman,   *pity*
In place where he stode;
555   He sayde that yoman shulde have no harme,
For love of Robyn Hode.

The knyght presed in to the place,
An hundreth folowed hym in fere,   *together*
With bowes bent and arowes sharpe,
560   For to shende that companye.   *destroy*

They shulderd all and made hym rome,   *gathered together; made room for him*
To wete what he wolde say;   *know*
He toke the yeman bi the hande,
And gave hym al the play.   *made him champion*

565	He gave hym fyve marke for his wyne,	*mark, two-thirds of a pound*
	There it lay on the molde,	*ground*
	And bad it shulde be set a broche,	*tapped and set running*
	Drynke who so wolde.	

	Thus longe taried this gentyll knyght,	
570	Tyll that play was done;	*game, sport*
	So longe abode Robyn fastinge,	
	Thre houres after the none.	*noon*

The Thirde Fytte

	Lyth and lystyn, gentilmen,	
	All that nowe be here,	
575	Of Litell Johnn, that was the knightes man,	*servant*
	Goode myrth ye shall here.	*hear*

	It was upon a mery day	
	That yonge men wolde go shete,	*shooting*
	Lytell Johnn fet his bowe anone,	*fetched; at once*
580	And sayde he wolde them mete.	

	Thre tymes Litell Johnn shet aboute,	
	And alwey he slet the wande:	*split the stick stuck in the ground*
	The proude sherif of Notingham	
	By the markes can stande.	*Stood by the targets*

585	The sherif swore a full greate othe:	
	"By Hym that dyede on a tre,	
	This man is the best arschere	*archer*
	That ever yet sawe I me.	

	"Say me nowe, wight yonge man,	*brave (strong)*
590	What is nowe thy name?	
	In what countré were thou borne,	*region*
	And where is thy wonynge wane?"	*dwelling place*

A Gest of Robyn Hode

      "In Holdernes, sir, I was borne,   *(in east Yorkshire)*
      Iwys al of my dame;   *mother*
595   Men cal me Reynolde Grenelef
      Whan I am at hame."

      "Sey me, Reynolde Grenelefe,
      Wolde thou dwell with me?
      And every yere I woll the gyve
600   Twenty marke to thy fee."

      "I have a maister," sayde Litell Johnn,
      "A curteys knight is he;
      May ye leve gete of hym,   *permission*
      The better may it be."

605   The sherif gate Litell John   *got*
      Twelve monethes of the knight;
      Therefore he gave him right anone   *at once*
      A gode hors and a wight.   *A good strong horse*

      Nowe is Litell John the sherifes man
610   God lende us well to spede!   *May God grant us to succeed!*
      But alwey thought Lytell John
      To quyte hym wele his mede.   *To pay him his just desert*

      "Nowe so God me helpe," sayde Litell John,
      "And by my true leutye,   *fidelity*
615   I shall be the worst servaunt to hym
      That ever yet had he."

      It fell upon a Wednesday
      The sherif on huntynge was gone,
      And Litel John lay in his bed,
620   And was foriete at home.   *forgotten (left)*

      Therefore he was fastinge   *without food*
      Til it was past the none.
      "God sir stuarde, I pray to the,   *keeper of the hall*
      Gyve me my dynere," saide Litell John.

625 "It is longe for Grenelefe
Fastinge thus for to be;
Therfor I pray the, sir stuarde,
Mi dyner gif thou me."

"Shalt thou never ete ne drynke," saide the stuarde,
630 "Tyll my lorde be come to towne."
"I make myn avowe to God," saide Litell John,
"I had lever to crake thy crowne."   *I would rather*

The boteler was full uncurteys,   *butler*
There he stode on flore;
635 He start to the botery
And shet fast the dore.

Lytell Johnn gave the boteler suche a tap   *blow*
His backe were nere in two;
Though he lived an hundred ier,   *years*
640 The wors shuld he go.   *walk*

He sporned the dore with his fote,   *kicked*
It went open wel and fyne,
And there he made large lyveray,   *took a big helping*
Bothe of ale and of wyne.

645 "Sith ye wol nat dyne," sayde Litell John,
"I shall gyve you to drinke,
And though ye lyve an hundred wynter,
On Lytel Johnn ye shall thinke."

Litell John ete, and Litel John drank,
650 The while that he wolde;
The sherife had in his kechyn a coke,   *cook*
A stoute man and a bolde.

"I make myn avowe to God," saide the coke,
"Thou arte a shrewde hynde   *cursed servant*
655 In ani hous for to dwel,
For to aske thus to dyne."

	And there he lent Litell John	*gave*
	God strokis thre;	*Good*
	"I make myn avowe to God," sayde Lytell John,	
660	"These strokis lyked well me.	

	"Thou arte a bolde man and hardy,	
	And so thinketh me;	
	And or I pas fro this place	*before*
	Assayed better shalt thou be."	*Tested*

665	Lytell Johnn drew a ful gode sworde,	
	The coke toke another in hande;	
	They thought no thynge for to fle,	*They didn't think of fleeing*
	But stifly for to stande.	*unyielding*

	There they faught sore togedere	
670	Two myle way and well more;	*The time it takes to walk two miles*
	Myght neyther other harme done,	
	The mountnaunce of an owre.	*For the period of an hour*

	"I make myn avowe to God," sayde Litell Johnn,	
	"And by my true lewté,	*loyalty*
675	Thou art one of the best swordemen	
	That ever yit sawe I me.	

	"Cowdest thou shote as well in a bowe,	*Could*
	To grene wode thou shuldest with me,	
	And two times in the yere thy clothinge	
680	Chaunged shulde be,	

	"And every yere of Robyn Hode	*from*
	Twenty merke to thy fe."	*as thy fee*
	"Put up thy swerde," saide the coke,	
	"And felowes woll we be."	

685	Thanne he fet to Lytell Johnn,	*fetched*
	The nowmbles of a do,	*sweetbreads of a doe*
	Gode brede, and full gode wyne;	
	They ete and drank theretoo.	

690

And when they had dronkyn well,
Theyre trouthes togeder they plight,
That they wolde be with Robyn
That ylke same nyght.   *very*

They dyd them to the tresoure hows,   *went; treasure-house*
As fast as they myght gone;
695   The lokkes, that were of full gode stele,   *locks; steel*
They brake them everichone.   *everyone*

They toke away the silver vessell,
And all that thei might get;
Pecis, masars, ne sponis,   *Dishes, drinking cups, nor spoons*
700   Wolde thei not forget.

Also they toke the gode pens,   *pence*
Three hundred pounde and more,
And did them streyte to Robyn Hode,   *went straight*
Under the grene wode hore.   *ancient wood*

705   "God the save, my dere mayster,
And Criste the save and se!"   *watch over thee*
And thanne sayde Robyn to Litell Johnn,
"Welcome myght thou be.

"Also be that fayre yeman   *is (welcome)*
710   Thou bryngest there with the;
What tydynges fro Notyngham?   *news*
Lytill Johnn, tell thou me."

"Well the gretith the proude sheryf,   *greets thee*
And sende the here by me
715   His coke and his silver vessell,
And thre hundred pounde and thre."

"I make myne avowe to God," sayde Robyn,
"And to the Trenyté,   *Trinity*
It was never by his gode wyll   *(the sheriff's) good will*
720   This gode is come to me."   *These possessions*

Lytyll Johnn there hym bethought
On a shrewde wyle;   *crafty trick*
Fyve myle in the forest he ran;
Hym happed all his wyll.   *All his wish came to pass*

725   Than he met the proude sheref,
      Huntynge with houndes and horne;
      Lytell Johnn coude of curtesye,   *knew about*
      And knelyd hym beforne.

      "God the save, my dere mayster,
730   And Criste the save and se!"   *watch over you*
      "Reynolde Grenelefe," sayde the shyref,
      "Where hast thou nowe be?"

      "I have be in this forest;
      A fayre syght can I se;
735   It was one of the fayrest syghtes
      That ever yet sawe I me.

      "Yonder I sawe a ryght fayre harte,   *male deer*
      His coloure is of grene;
      Seven score of dere upon a herde
740   Be with hym all bydene.   *together*

      "Their tyndes are so sharpe, maister,   *antlers*
      Of sexty, and well mo,
      That I durst not shote for drede,
      Lest they wolde me slo."   *slay*

745   "I make myn avowe to God," sayde the shyref,
      "That syght wolde I fayne se."   *gladly*
      "Buske you thyderwarde, mi dere mayster,   *Hasten*
      Anone, and wende with me."   *go*

      The sherif rode, and Litell Johnn
750   Of fote he was full smerte,   *nimble*
      And whane they came before Robyn,
      "Lo, sir, here is the mayster-herte."

113

Still stode the proude sherief,
A sory man was he;

755 "Wo the worthe, Raynolde Grenelefe,
Thou hast betrayed nowe me."

"I make myn avowe to God," sayde Litell Johnn,
"Mayster, ye be to blame;
I was mysserved of my dynere   *badly provided with*

760 Whan I was with you at home."

Sone he was to souper sette,
And served well with silver white,
And whan the sherif sawe his vessell,
For sorowe he myght nat ete.

765 "Make glad chere," sayde Robyn Hode,
"Sherif, for charité,
And for the love of Litill Johnn
Thy lyfe I graunt to the."

Whan they had souped well,
770 The day was al gone;
Robyn commaunded Litell Johnn
To drawe of his hosen and his shone,   *To take off; shoes*

His kirtell, and his cote of pie,   *tunic; parti-colored cloak*
That was fured well and fine,
775 And toke hym a grene mantel,   *gave*
To lap his body therin.   *To wrap*

Robyn commaundyd his wight yonge men,
Under the grene wode tree,
They shulde lye in that same sute,   *(dressed) the same*
780 That the sherif myght them see.

All nyght lay the proude sherif
In his breche and in his schert;   *breeches; shirt*
No wonder it was, in grene wode,
Though his sydes gan to smerte.   *hurt*

A Gest of Robyn Hode

785   "Make glade chere," sayde Robyn Hode,
      "Sheref, for charité,
      For this is our ordre iwys,
      Under the grene wode tree."

   "This is harder order," sayde the sherief,
790   "Than any ankir or frere;   *anchorite (religious hermit)*
      For all the golde in mery Englonde
      I wolde nat longe dwell her."   *here*

   "All this twelve monthes," sayde Robyn,
      "Thou shalt dwell with me;
795   I shall the teche, proude sherif,
      An outlawe for to be."

   "Or I be here another nyght," sayde the sherif,   *Before*
      "Robyn, nowe pray I the,
      Smythe of mijn hede rather to-morowe,   *Strike off my head*
800   And I forgyve it the.

   "Lat me go," than sayde the sherif,
      "For saynte charité,
      And I woll be thy best frende
      That ever yet had ye."

805   "Thou shalt swere me an othe," sayde Robyn,   *oath*
      "On my bright bronde: *sword*
      Shalt thou never awayte me scathe,   *plot me harm*
      By water ne by lande.

   "And if thou fynde any of my men,
810   By nyght or day,
      Upon thyn othe thou shalt swere
      To helpe them that thou may."   *as far as*

   Now hathe the sherif sworne his othe,
      And home he began to gone;
815   He was as full of grene wode
      As ever was hepe of stone.   *hip (fruit) with stone*

115

The Fourth Fytte

The sherif dwelled in Notingham
He was fayne he was agone,   *glad*
And Robyn and his mery men
820   Went to wode anone.   *at once*

"Go we to dyner," sayde Littell Johnn;
Robyn Hode sayde, "Nay,
For I drede Our Lady be wroth with me,   *angry*
For she sent me nat my pay."

825   "Have no doute, maister," sayde Litell Johnn,
"Yet is nat the sonne at rest;
For I dare say, and savely swere,   *safely*
The knight is true and truste."

"Take thy bowe in thy hande," sayde Robyn,
830   "Late Much wende with the,   *go*
And so shal Wyllyam Scarlok,
And no man abyde with me.

"And walke up under the Sayles,
And to Watlynge-strete,
835   And wayte after such unketh gest;   *look for; unknown*
Up-chaunce ye may them mete.   *By chance*

"Whether he be messengere,
Or a man that myrthes can,   *minstrel who entertains*
Of my good he shall have some,
840   Yf he be a pore man."

Forth then stert Lytel Johan,
Half in tray and tene,   *anger and annoyance*
And gyrde hym with a full good swerde,
Under a mantel of grene.

116

845 They went up to the Sayles,
  These yemen all thre;
  They loked est, they loked west,
  They myght no man se.

  But as they loked in Bernysdale,
850 By the hye waye,
  Than were they ware of two blacke monkes,   *Benedictine monks*
  Eche on a good palferay.

  Then bespake Lytell Johan,
  To Much he gan say,
855 "I dare lay my lyfe to wedde,   *as a pledge*
  The monkes have brought our pay.

  "Make glad chere," sayd Lytell Johan,
  "And drese our bowes of ewe,   *make ready*
  And loke your hertes be seker and sad,   *sure and steadfast*
860 Your strynges trusty and trewe.

  "The monke hath two and fifty   *fifty-two men*
  And seven somers full stronge;   *sumpters (pack horses)*
  There rydeth no bysshop in this londe
  So ryally, I understond.   *royally*

865 "Brethern," sayd Lytell Johan,
  "Here are no more but we thre;
  But we brynge them to dyner,   *Unless*
  Our mayster dare we not se.

  "Bende your bowes," sayd Lytell Johan,
870 "Make all yon prese to stonde;   *that crowd stop*
  The formost monke, his lyfe and his deth,
  Is closed in my honde.   *contained*

  "Abyde, chorle monke," sayd Lytell Johan,   *churl (crude, low-born)*
  "No ferther that thou gone;   *go*
875 Yf thou doost, by dere worthy God,
  Thy deth is in my honde.

"And evyll thryfte on thy hede," sayd Litell Johan,   *evil luck*
"Ryght under thy hattes bonde,   *hat-band*
For thou hast made our mayster wroth,   *angry*
880   He is fastynge so longe."

"Who is your mayster?" sayd the monke;
Lytell Johan sayd, "Robyn Hode."
"He is a stronge thefe," sayd the monke,
"Of hym herd I never good."

885   "Thou lyest," than sayd Lytell Johan,
"And that shall rewe the;   *make you sorry*
He is a yeman of the forest,
To dyne he hath bode the."   *bidden (commanded)*

Much was redy with a bolte,   *arrow*
890   Redly and anone;   *Quickly and at once*
He set the monke to-fore the brest,   *aimed at; before*
To the grounde that he can gone.   *So that he dismounted*

Of two and fyfty wyght yonge yemen
There abode not one,
895   Saf a lytell page and a grome,   *Except; groom*
To lede the somers with Lytel Johan.   *pack horses*

They brought the monke to the lodge dore,
Whether he were loth or lefe,   *Whether he liked it or not*
For to speke with Robyn Hode,
900   Maugré in theyr tethe.   *In spite of them*

Robyn dyde adowne his hode,   *lowered his hood*
The monke whan that he se;   *saw*
The monke was not so curteyse,
His hode then let he be.   *left in place*

905   "He is a chorle, mayster, by dere worthy God,"
Than sayd Lytell Johan.
"Thereof no force," sayd Robyn,   *no matter*
"For curteysy can he none.   *knows*

"How many men," sayd Robyn,
910 "Had this monke, Johan?"
"Fyfty and two whan that we met,
But many of them be gone."

"Let blowe a horne," sayd Robyn,
"That felaushyp may us knowe."
915 Seven score of wyght yemen
Came pryckynge on a rowe.   *hurrying*

And everych of them a good mantell   *loose, sleeveless coat*
Of scarlet and of raye,   *striped cloth*
All they came to good Robyn,
920 To wyte what he wolde say.   *know*

They made the monke to wasshe and wype,
And syt at his denere,
Robyn Hode and Lytell Johan
They served him both in fere.   *in company*

925 "Do gladly, monke," sayd Robyn.   *Eat with pleasure*
"Gramercy, syr," sayd he.   *Thank you*
"Where is your abbay, whan ye are at home,
And who is your avowé?"   *patron*

"Saynt Mary abbay," sayd the monke,
930 "Though I be symple here."   *humble*
"In what offyce?" sayd Robyn,
"Syr, the hye selerer."   *chief steward*

"Ye be the more welcome," sayd Robyn,
"So ever mote I the.   *So may I always prosper*
935 Fyll of the best wyne," sayd Robyn,
"This monke shall drynke to me.

"But I have grete mervayle," sayd Robyn,
"Of all this longe day,
I drede Our Lady be wroth with me,
940 She sent me not my pay."

"Have no doute, mayster," sayd Lytell Johan,
"Ye have no nede, I saye;
This monke it hath brought, I dare well swere,
For he is of her abbay."

945   "And she was a borowe," sayd Robyn,   *security*
"Betwene a knyght and me,
Of a lytell money that I hym lent,
Under the grene wode tree.

"And yf thou hast that sylver i-brought,
950   I pray the let me se,
And I shall helpe the eftsones,   *in return*
Yf thou have nede to me."

The monke swore a full grete othe,
With a sory chere,   *miserable countenance*
955   "Of the borowehode thou spekest to me,   *security*
Herde I never ere."

"I make myn avowe to God," sayd Robyn,
"Monke, thou art to blame,
For God is holde a ryghtwys man,
960   And so is His dame.

"Thou toldest with thyn owne tonge,
Thou may not say nay,
How thou arte her servaunt,
And servest her every day.

965   "And thou art made her messengere,
My money for to pay;
Therfore I cun the more thanke   *may thank thee more*
Thou arte come at thy day.

"What is in your cofers?" sayd Robyn,
970   "Trewe than tell thou me."
"Syr," he sayd, "twenty marke,
Al so mote I the."   *As I may prosper*

"Yf there be no more," sayd Robyn,
"I wyll not one peny;
975   Yf thou hast myster of ony more,   *need*
Syr, more I shall lende to the.

"And yf I fynde more," sayd Robyn,
"Iwys thou shalte it for gone,   *forgo*
For of thy spendynge sylver, monke,   *traveling expenses*
980   Thereof wyll I ryght none.

"Go nowe forthe, Lytell Johan,
And the trouth tell thou me;
If there be no more but twenty marke,
No peny that I se."

985   Lytell Johan spred his mantell downe,
As he had done before,
And he tolde out of the monkes male   *traveling chest*
Eyght hundred pounde and more.

Lytell Johan let it lye full styll,
990   And went to his mayster in hast.
"Syr," he sayd, "the monke is trewe ynowe,
Our Lady hath doubled your cast."   *doubled your throw (the knight's loan)*

"I make myn avowe to God," sayd Robyn,
"Monke, what tolde I the?
995   Our Lady is the trewest woman
That ever yet founde I me.

"By dere worthy God," sayd Robyn,
"To seche all Englond thorowe,
Yet founde I never to my pay
1000   A moche better borowe.

"Fyll of the best wyne, and do hym drynke," sayd Robyn,
"And grete well thy lady hende,   *greet; gracious*
And yf she have nede to Robyn Hode,
A frende she shall hym fynde.

121

1005   "And yf she nedeth ony more sylver,
        Come thou agayne to me,
        And, by this token she hath me sent,
        She shall have such thre."   *three times the amount*

        The monke was goynge to London-ward,
1010   There to holde grete mote,   *meeting*
        The knyght that rode so hye on hors,
        To brynge hym under fote.

        "Whether be ye away?" sayd Robyn.   *Where are you going?*
        "Syr, to maners in this londe,   *Sir [i.e., Robyn]; manors*
1015   Too reken with our reves,   *To deal with our bailifs*
        That have done moch wronge."

        "Come now forth, Lytell Johan,
        And harken to my tale;
        A better yeman I knowe none,
1020   To seke a monkes male.   *search; baggage*

        "How moch is in yonder other corser?" sayd Robyn,   *horse*
        "The soth must we see."   *truth*
        "By Our Lady," than sayd the monke,
        "That were no curteysye,

1025   "To bydde a man to dyner,   *ask*
        And syth hym bete and bynde."   *afterwards*
        "It is our olde maner," sayd Robyn,
        "To leve but lytell behynde."   *To waste little*

        The monke toke the hors with spore,   *spurred his horse*
1030   No lenger wolde he abyde:
        "Aske to drynke," than sayd Robyn,   *Ask permission*
        "Or that ye forther ryde."   *Before*

        "Nay, for God," than sayd the monke,
        "Me reweth I cam so nere;
1035   For better chepe I myght have dyned   *more cheaply*
        In Blythe or in Dankestere."

"Grete well your abbot," sayd Robyn,
"And your pryour, I you pray,
And byd hym send me such a monke
1040   To dyner every day."

Now lete we that monke be styll,
And speke we of that knyght:
Yet he came to holde his day,
Whyle that it was lyght.

1045   He dyde him streyt to Bernysdale,   *took himself*
Under the grene wode tre,
And he founde there Robyn Hode,
And all the mery meyné.   *company*

The knyght lyght doune of his good palfray;   *dismounted*
1050   Robyn whan he gan see,
So curteysly he dyde adoune his hode,
And set hym on his knee.

"God the save, Robyn Hode,
And all this company."
1055   "Welcome be thou, gentyll knyght,
And ryght welcome to me."

Than bespake hym Robyn Hode,
To that knyght so fre:
"What nede dryveth the to grene wode?,
1060   I praye the, syr knyght, tell me.

"And welcome be thou, gentyll knyght,
Why hast thou be so longe?"
"For the abbot and the hye justyce
Wolde have had my londe."

1065   "Hast thou thy londe agayne?" sayd Robyn;
"Treuth than tell thou me."
"Ye, for God," sayd the knyght,
"And that thanke I God and the.

"But take not a grefe, that I have be so longe;   *Don't be offended*
1070 I came by a wrastelynge,
And there I holpe a pore yeman,
With wronge was put behynde."   *downgraded*

"Nay, for God," sayd Robyn,
"Syr knyght, that thanke I the;
1075 What man that helpeth a good yeman,
His frende than wyll I be."

"Have here foure hondred pounde," than sayd the knyght,
"The whiche ye lent to me,
And here is also twenty marke
1080 For your curteysy."

"Nay, for God," than sayd Robyn,
"Thou broke it well for ay,   *enjoy it forever*
For Our Lady, by her selerer,   *wine steward*
Hath sent to me my pay.

1085 "And yf I toke it i-twyse,   *twice*
A shame it were to me,
But trewely, gentyll knyght,
Welcom arte thou to me."

Whan Robyn had tolde his tale,
1090 He leugh and had good chere: *laughed*
"By my trouthe," then sayd the knyght,
"Your money is redy here."   *available*

"Broke it well," sayd Robyn,   *Enjoy it*
"Thou gentyll knyght so fre,   *generous*
1095 And welcome be thou, gentyll knyght,
Under my trystell-tre.   *meeting tree*

"But what shall these bowes do?" sayd Robyn,
"And these arowes ifedred fre?"   *finely feathered*
"By God," than sayd the knyght,
1100 "A pore present to the."

124

"Come now forth, Lytell Johan,
And go to my treasuré,
And brynge me there foure hondred pounde;
The monke over-tolde it me.   *over-paid*

1105 "Have here foure hondred pounde,
Thou gentyll knyght and trewe,
And bye hors and harnes good,
And gylte thy spores all newe.   *gild*

"And yf thou fayle ony spendynge,   *lack*
1110 Com to Robyn Hode,
And by my trouth thou shalt none fayle,
The whyles I have any good.   *while*

"And broke well thy foure hondred pound,   *enjoy*
Whiche I lent to the,
1115 And make thy selfe no more so bare,
By the counsell of me."

Thus than holpe hym good Robyn,
The knyght all of his care:
God, that syt in heven hye,
1120 Graunte us well to fare!

The Fyfth Fytte

Now hath the knyght his leve i-take,
And wente hym on his way;
Robyn Hode and his mery men
Dwelled styll full many a day.   *quietly*

1125 Lyth and lysten, gentil men,
And herken what I shall say,
How the proud sheryfe of Notyngham
Dyde crye a full fayre play,

That all the best archers of the north
1130 Sholde come upon a day,
And that shoteth allther best   *best of all*
The game shall bere away.

He that shoteth allther best,   *Whoever; best of all*
Furthest, fayre and lowe,
1135 At a payre of fynly buttes,   *fine butts*
Under the grene wode shawe,   *thicket*

A ryght good arowe he shall have,
The shaft of sylver whyte,
The hede and the feders of ryche rede golde,
1140 In Englond is none lyke.

This than herde good Robyn,
Under his trystell-tre:
"Make you redy, ye wyght yonge men;
That shotynge wyll I se.

1145 "Buske you, my mery yonge men,   *Hurry*
Ye shall go with me,
And I wyll wete the shryves fayth,   *test*
Trewe and yf he be."

Whan they had theyr bowes i-bent,
1150 Theyr takles fedred fre,   *finely feathered arrows*
Seven score of wyght yonge men
Stode by Robyns kne.

Whan they cam to Notyngham,
The buttes were fayre and longe,
1155 Many was the bolde archere
That shot with bowes stronge.

"There shall but syx shote with me;
The other shal kepe my hede,   *protect my head*
And stande with good bowes bent,
1160 That I be not desceyved."

The fourth outlawe his bowe gan bende,
And that was Robyn Hode,
And that behelde the proud sheryfe,
All by the but he stode.

1165   Thryes Robyn shot a bout,   *a match*
       And alway he slist the wand,   *slit*
       And so dyde good Gylberte
       Wyth the Whyte Hande.

       Lytell Johan and good Scatheloke
1170   Were archers good and fre;
       Lytell Much and good Reynolde,
       The worste wolde they not be.

       Whan they had shot a boute,
       These archours fayre and good,
1175   Evermore was the best,
       For soth, Robyn Hode.

       Hym was delyvered the good arowe,   *He was given*
       For best worthy was he;
       He toke the yeft so curteysly,   *prize (gift)*
1180   To grene wode wolde he.

       They cryed out on Robyn Hode,   *demanded the arrest of*
       And grete hornes gan they blowe:
       "Wo worth the, treason!" sayd Robyn,   *Misery come to you!*
       "Full evyl thou art to knowe.

1185   "And wo be thou! thou proude sheryf,
       Thus gladdynge thy gest;   *pleasing thy guest*
       Other wyse thou behote me   *promised*
       In yonder wylde forest.

       "But had I the in grene wode,
1190   Under my trystell-tre,
       Thou sholdest leve me a better wedde   *pledge*
       Than thy trewe lewté."   *sworn trust*

Full many a bowe there was bent,
And arowes let they glyde;
1195   Many a kyrtell there was rent,   *knee-length tunic*
And hurt many a syde.

The outlawes shot was so stronge   *barrage of shooting*
That no man myght them dryve,
And the proud sheryfes men,
1200   They fled away full blyve.   *quickly*

Robyn sawe the busshement to-broke,   *ambush*
In grene wode he wolde have be;
Many an arowe there was shot
Amonge that company.

1205   Lytell Johan was hurte full sore,
With an arowe in his kne,
That he myght neyther go nor ryde;
It was full grete pyté.

"Mayster," then sayd Lytell Johan,
1210   "If ever thou lovest me,
And for that ylke Lordes love   *same*
That dyed upon a tre,

"And for the medes of my servyce,   *rewards*
That I have served the,
1215   Lete never the proude sheryf
Alyve now fynde me.

"But take out thy browne swerde,   *blood-stained*
And smyte all of my hede,
And gyve me woundes depe and wyde,
1220   No lyfe on me be lefte."

"I wolde not that," sayd Robyn,
"Johan, that thou were slawe,   *slain*
For all the golde in mery Englonde,
Though it lay now on a rawe."   *in a row*

A Gest of Robyn Hode

1225   "God forbede," sayd Lytell Much,
        "That dyed on a tre,
        That thou sholdest, Lytell Johan,
        Parte our company."   *Leave*

        Up he toke hym on his backe,
1230   And bare hym well a myle;
        Many a tyme he layd hym downe,
        And shot another whyle.

        Then was there a fayre castell,   *castle*
        A lytell within the wode;
1235   Double-dyched it was about,
        And walled, by the Rode.   *by the Cross*

        And there dwelled that gentyll knyght,
        Syr Rychard at the Lee,
        That Robyn had lent his good,   *given his property*
1240   Under the grene wode tree.

        In he toke good Robyn,
        And all his company:
        "Welcome be thou, Robyn Hode,
        Welcome arte thou to me,

1245   "And moche I thanke the of thy confort,
        And of thy curteysye,
        And of thy grete kyndenesse,
        Under the grene wode tre.

        "I love no man in all this worlde
1250   So much as I do the;
        For all the proud sheryf of Notyngham,   *Despite*
        Ryght here shalt thou be.

        "Shyt the gates, and drawe the brydge,   *Shut*
        And let no man come in,
1255   And arme you well, and make you redy,
        And to the walles ye wynne.   *make your way*

"For one thynge, Robyn, I the behote;   *promise*
I swere by Saynt Quyntyne,   *Quentin*
These forty dayes thou wonnest with me,   *dwell*
1260   To soupe, ete, and dyne."

Bordes were layde, and clothes were spredde,
Redely and anone;
Robyn Hode and his mery men
To mete can they gone.

The Sixth Fytte

1265   Lythe and lysten, gentylmen,
And herkyn to your songe,
Howe the proude shyref of Notyngham,
And men of armys stronge

Full fast cam to the hye shyref,
1270   The contré up to route,   *To raise the countryside*
And they besette the knyghtes castell,   *besieged*
The walles all aboute.

The proude shyref loude gan crye,
And sayde, "Thou traytour knight,
1275   Thou kepest here the kynges enemys,
Agaynst the lawe and right."

"Syr, I wyll avowe that I have done,   *openly acknowledge what*
The dedys that here be dyght,   *done*
Upon all the landes that I have,
1280   As I am a trewe knyght.

"Wende furth, sirs, on your way,   *Go forth*
And do no more to me
Tyll ye wyt oure kynges wille,   *know*
What he wyll say to the."

1285   The shyref thus had his answere,
    Without any lesynge;   *lying*
    Furth he yede to London towne,   *went*
    All for to tel our kinge.

    Ther he telde him of that knight,
1290   And eke of Robyn Hode,
    And also of the bolde archars,
    That were soo noble and gode.

    "He wyll avowe that he hath done,
    To mayntene the outlawes stronge;
1295   He wyll be lorde, and set you at nought,
    In all the northe londe."

    "I wyl be at Notyngham," saide our kynge,
    "Within this fourteenyght,   *fortnight (14 days)*
    And take I wyll Robyn Hode,
1300   And so I wyll that knight.

    "Go nowe home, shyref," sayde our kynge,
    "And do as I byd the,
    And ordeyn gode archers ynowe,   *organize; enough (i.e., many)*
    Of all the wyde contré."   *From*

1305   The shyref had his leve i-take,
    And went hym on his way,
    And Robyn Hode to grene wode,
    Upon a certen day.

    And Lytel John was hole of the arowe   *whole (i.e., healed)*
1310   That shot was in his kne,
    And dyd hym streyght to Robyn Hode,
    Under the grene wode tree.

    Robyn Hode walked in the forest,
    Under the levys grene;
1315   The proude shyref of Notyngham
    Thereof he had grete tene.   *vexation*

The shyref there fayled of Robyn Hode,   *missed*
He myght not have his pray;   *prey, quarry*
Than he awayted this gentyll knight,   *watched for*
1320 Bothe by nyght and day.

Ever he wayted the gentyll knyght,
Syr Richarde at the Lee,
As he went on haukynge by the ryver-syde,
And lete haukes flee.

1325 Toke he there this gentyll knight,
With men of armys stronge,
And led hym to Notyngham warde,   *toward Nottingham*
Bounde bothe fote and hande.

The sheref sware a full grete othe,
1330 Bi Hym that dyed on Rode,   *the Cross*
He had lever than an hundred pound   *would rather*
That he had Robyn Hode.

This harde the knyghtes wyfe,   *heard*
A fayr lady and a free;
1335 She set hir on a gode palfrey,
To grene wode anone rode she.

Whanne she cam in the forest,
Under the grene wode tree,
Fonde she there Robyn Hode,
1340 And al his fayre mené.   *company*

"God the save, gode Robyn,
And all thy company;
For Our dere Ladyes sake,
A bone graunte thou me.   *boon, favor*

1345 "Late never my wedded lorde   *Let*
Shamefully slayne be;
He is fast bowne to Notingham warde,
For the love of the."   *Because he supported you*

Anone than saide goode Robyn
1350 To that lady so fre,
"What man hath your lorde take?"
"The proude shirife," than sayd she.

"The shirife hatt hym take," she sayd,
"For soth as I the say;
1355 He is nat yet thre myles
Passed on his way."

Up than sterte gode Robyn,
As man that had ben wode:
"Buske you, my mery men,
1360 For Hym that dyed on Rode.

"And he that this sorowe forsaketh,
By hym that dyed on tre,
Shall he never in grene wode
No lenger dwel with me."

1365 Sone there were gode bowes bent,
Mo than seven score;
Hedge ne dyche spared they none
That was them before.

"I make myn avowe to God," sayde Robyn,
1370 "The sherif wolde I fayne see,
And if I may hym take,
I-quyte shall it be."

And whan they came to Notingham,
They walked in the strete,
1375 And with the proude sherif iwys
Sone can they mete.

"Abyde, thou proude sherif," he sayde,
"Abyde, and speke with me;
Of some tidinges of oure kinge
1380 I wolde fayne here of the.

At once

furious
Hurry
the Cross

this sad case

Revenged

"This seven yere, by dere worthy God,
Ne yede I this fast on fote;   *went*
I make myn avowe to God, thou proude sherif,
It is nat for thy gode."

1385   Robyn bent a full goode bowe,
An arrowe he drowe at wyll;
He hit so the proude sherife
Upon the grounde he lay full still.

And or he myght up aryse,   *before*
1390   On his fete to stonde,
He smote of the sherifs hede   *off*
With his bright bronde.

"Lye thou there, thou proude sherife,
Evyll mote thou cheve!   *Badly may you end!*
1395   There myght no man to the truste   *trust in you*
The whyles thou were a lyve."

His men drewe out theyr bryght swerdes,
That were so sharpe and kene,
And layde on the sheryves men,
1400   And dryved them downe bydene.   *forthwith*

Robyn stert to that knyght,   *leapt*
And cut a two his bonde,   *in two*
And toke hym in his hand a bowe,
And bad hym by hym stonde.   *bade*

1405   "Leve thy hors the behynde,
And lerne for to renne;   *run*
Thou shalt with me to grene wode,
Through myre, mosse, and fenne.   *mire, moss, and fen*

"Thou shalt with me to grene wode,
1410   Without ony leasynge,   *lying*
Tyll that I have gete us grace
Of Edwarde, our comly kynge."   *handsome*

A Gest of Robyn Hode

The Seventh Fytte

The kynge came to Notynghame,
With knyghtes in grete araye, *in great force*
1415 For to take that gentyll knyght
And Robyn Hode, and yf he may.

He asked men of that countré
After Robyn Hode,
And after that gentyll knyght,
1420 That was so bolde and stout.

Whan they had tolde hym the case
Our kyng understode ther tale,
And seased in his honde *seized*
The knyghtes londes all.

1425 All the compasse of Lancasshyre *Through the whole*
He went both ferre and nere,
Tyll he came to Plomton Parke; *missed*
He faylyd many of his dere.

There our kynge was wont to se
1430 Herdes many one,
He coud unneth fynde one dere, *scarcely*
That bare ony good horne.

The kynge was wonder wroth withall,
And swore by the Trynyté,
1435 "I wolde I had Robyn Hode,
With eyen I myght hym se.

"And he that wolde smyte of the knyghtes hede, *cut off*
And brynge it to me,
He shall have the knyghtes londes,
1440 Syr Rycharde at the Le.

"I gyve it hym with my charter,
And sele it my honde,   *seal*
To have and holde for ever more,
In al mery Englonde."

1445   Than bespake a fayre olde knyght,
That was treue in his fay: *true in his faith*
"A, my leege lorde the kynge,   *liege (feudal superior)*
One worde I shall you say.

"There is no man in this countré
1450   May have the knyghtes londes,
Whyle Robyn Hode may ryde or gone,
And bere a bowe in his hondes,

"That he ne shall lese his hede,
That is the best ball in his hode:
1455   Give it no man, my lorde the kynge,
That ye wyll any good."

Half a yere dwelled our comly kynge
In Notyngham, and well more;
Coude he not here of Robyn Hode,
1460   In what countré that he were.

But alwey went good Robyn
By halke and eke by hyll,   *hiding place*
And alway slewe the kynges dere,
And welt them at his wyll.   *used*

1465   Than bespake a proude fostere,   *forester*
That stode by our kynges kne:
"Yf ye wyll se good Robyn,
Ye must do after me.   *according to*

"Take fyve of the best knyghtes
1470   That be in your lede,   *group*
And walke downe by yon abbay,
And gete you monkes wede.   *garment or habit*

136

A Gest of Robyn Hode

"And I wyll be your bedesman,   *religious guide*
And lede you the way,
1475   And or ye come to Notyngham.   *before*
Myn hede then dare I lay   *wager*

"That ye shall mete with good Robyn,
On lyve yf that he be;
Or ye come to Notyngham,   *Before*
1480   With eyen ye shall hym se."

Full hastly our kynge was dyght,   *clothed*
So were his knyghtes fyve,
Everych of them in monkes wede,
And hasted them thyder blyve.   *quickly*

1485   Our kynge was grete above his cole,   *cowl (a monk's hood worn round the neck)*
A brode hat on his crowne,   *top of head*
Ryght as he were abbot-lyke,
They rode up into the towne.

Styf botes our kynge had on,
1490   Forsoth as I you say;
He rode syngynge to grene wode,   *singing*
The covent was clothed in graye.   *group of "monks"*

His male-hors and his grete somers   *baggage horse; pack horses*
Folowed our kynge behynde,
1495   Tyll they came to grene wode,
A myle under the lynde.   *woods*

There they met with good Robyn,
Stondynge on the waye,
And so dyde many a bolde archere,
1500   For soth as I you say.

Robyn toke the kynges hors,
Hastely in that stede,   *place*
And sayd, "Syr abbot, by your leve,
A whyle ye must abyde.

137

1505 "We be yemen of this foreste,
Under the grene wode tre;
We lyve by our kynges dere,
Under the grene wode tre.

"And ye have chyrches and rentes both,
1510 And gold full grete plenté;
Gyve us some of your spendynge,
For saynt charyté."

Than bespake our cumly kynge,
Anone than sayd he:
1515 "I brought no more to grene wode
But forty pounde with me.

"I have layne at Notyngham   *stayed*
This fourtynyght with our kynge,   *fortnight (14 days)*
And spent I have full moche good,
1520 On many a grete lordynge.

"And I have but forty pounde,
No more than have I me;
But yf I had an hondred pounde,
I vouch it halfe on the."   *promise half to thee*

1525 Robyn toke the forty pounde,
And departed it in two partye; *divided it into two parts*
Halfendell he gave his mery men,   *Half*
And bad them mery to be.

Full curteysly Robyn gan say;
1530 "Syr, have this for your spendyng;
We shall mete another day."
"Gramercy," than sayd our kynge.

"But well the greteth Edwarde, our kynge,
And sent to the his seale,   *sends*
1535 And byddeth the com to Notyngham,
Both to mete and mele."   *food and meat*

A Gest of Robyn Hode

He toke out the brode targe,   *shield (see note)*
And sone he lete hym se;   *at once*
Robyn coud his courteysy,   *knew his manners*
1540   And set hym on his kne.

"I love no man in all the worlde
So well as I do my kynge;
Welcome is my lordes seale;
And, monke, for thy tydynge,   *tidings, news*

1545   "Syr abbot, for thy tydynges,
To day thou shalt dyne with me,
For the love of my kynge,
Under my trystell-tre."

Forth he lad our comly kynge,
1550   Full fayre by the honde;
Many a dere there was slayne,
And full fast dyghtande.   *prepared*

Robyn toke a full grete horne,
And loude he gan blowe;
1555   Seven score of wyght yonge men
Came redy on a rowe.

All they kneled on theyr kne,
Full fayre before Robyn;
The kynge sayd hym selfe untyll,   *to himself*
1560   And swore by Saynt Austyn,   *St. Augustine*

"Here is a wonder semely syght;
Me thynketh, by Goddes pyne,   *pain*
His men are more at his byddynge
Then my men be at myn."

1565   Full hastly was theyr dyner idyght,   *prepared*
And therto gan they gone;
They served our kynge with al theyr myght,
Both Robyn and Lytell Johan.

139

Anone before our kynge was set
1570 The fatte venyson,
The good whyte brede, the good rede wyne,
And therto the fyne ale and browne.

"Make good chere," said Robyn,
"Abbot, for charyté,
1575 And for this ylke tydynge,
Blyssed mote thou be.   *may*

"Now shalte thou se what lyfe we lede,
Or thou hens wende;   *Before you go away*
Than thou may enfourme our kynge,
1580 Whan ye togyder lende."   *dwell*

Up they sterte all in hast,   *haste*
Theyr bowes were smartly bent;
Our kynge was never so sore agast,
He wende to have be shente.   *He thought he would be killed*

1585 Two yerdes there were up set,   *rods*
Thereto gan they gange;   *they began to go*
By fyfty pase, our kynge sayd,
The merkes were to longe.

On every syde a rose-garlonde,   *a small target*
1590 They shot under the lyne;   *trees*
"Who so fayleth of the rose-garlonde," sayd Robyn,   *misses*
"His takyll he shall tyne,   *forfeit his arrows (or gear)*

"And yelde it to his mayster,
Be it never so fyne;
1595 For no man wyll I spare,
So drynke I ale or wyne:

"And bere a buffet on his hede,   *blow (cuff)*
Iwys ryght all bare."
And all that fell in Robyns lote,   *fell to Robin (to strike)*
1600 He smote them wonder sare.   *struck; sorely*

140

A Gest of Robyn Hode

Twyse Robyn shot a boute,   *Twice*
And ever he cleved the wande,   *split*
And so dyde good Gylberte
With the Whyte Hande.

1605   Lytell Johan and good Scathelocke,
For nothynge wolde they spare;
When they fayled of the garlonde,
Robyn smote them full sore.

At the last shot that Robyn shot,
1610   For all his frendes fare,   *success*
Yet he fayled of the garlonde,   *missed the target*
Thre fyngers and mare.   *By more than three fingers' width*

Than bespake good Gylberte,
And thus he gan say:
1615   "Mayster," he sayd, "your takyll is lost,
Stande forth and take your pay."   *punishment*

"If it be so," sayd Robyn,
"That may no better be,
Syr abbot, I delyver the myn arowe,
1620   I pray the, syr, serve thou me."

"It falleth not for myn ordre," sayd our kynge,
"Robyn, by thy leve,   *permission*
For to smyte no good yeman,
For doute I sholde hym greve."   *fear*

1625   "Smyte on boldely," sayd Robyn,
"I give the large leve."   *full permission*
Anone our kynge, with that worde,
He folde up his sleve,   *folded*

And sych a buffet he gave Robyn,
1630   To grounde he yede full nere:
"I make myn avowe to God," sayd Robyn,
"Thou arte a stalworthe frere.   *stalwart (strong) brother*

141

"There is pith in thyn arme," sayd Robyn,   *force*
"I trowe thou canst well shete."   *I warrant; shoot*
1635   Thus our kynge and Robyn Hode
Togeder gan they mete.

Robyn behelde our comly kynge
Wystly in the face,   *Intently*
So dyde Syr Rycharde at the Le,
1640   And kneled downe in that place.

And so dyde all the wylde outlawes,
Whan they see them knele:
"My lorde the kynge of Englonde,
Now I knowe you well."

1645   "Mercy then, Robyn," sayd our kynge,
"Under your trystyll-tre,
Of thy goodnesse and thy grace,
For my men and me!"

"Yes, for God," sayd Robyn,
1650   "And also God me save,
I aske mercy, my lorde the kynge,
And for my men I crave."

"Yes, for God," than sayd our kynge,
"And therto sent I me,   *I assent*
1655   With that thou leve the grene wode,   *Provided*
And all thy company,

"And come home, syr, to my courte,
And there dwell with me."
"I make myn avowe to God," sayd Robyn,
1660   "And ryght so shall it be.

"I wyll come to your courte,
Your servyse for to se,
And brynge with me of my men
Seven score and thre.

1665   "But me lyke well your servyse,   *Unless; pleases me*
        I come agayne full soone,
        And shote at the donne dere,   *brown*
        As I am wonte to done."   *accustomed*

The Eighth Fytte

        "Haste thou ony grene cloth," sayd our kynge,
1670   "That thou wylte sell nowe to me?"
        "Ye, for God," sayd Robyn,
        "Thyrty yerdes and thre."

        "Robyn," sayd our kynge,
        "Now pray I the,
1675   Sell me some of that cloth,
        To me and my meyné."   *company*

        "Yes, for God," then sayd Robyn,
        "Or elles I were a fole: *fool*
        Another day ye wyll me clothe,
1680   I trowe, ayenst the Yole."   *for Christmas*

        The kynge kest of his cole then,   *cast off his cowl*
        A grene garment he dyde on,
        And every knyght had so, iwys,
        Another hode full sone.

1685   Whan they were clothed in Lyncolne grene,
        They keste away theyr graye:
        "Now we shall to Notyngham,"
        All thus our kynge gan say.

        Theyr bowes bente, and forth they went,
1690   Shotynge all in fere,   *together*
        Towarde the towne of Notyngham,
        Outlawes as they were.   *as if*

Our kynge and Robyn rode togyder,
For soth as I you say,
1695 And they shote plucke buffet,
As they went by the way.

And many a buffet our kynge wan   *received*
Of Robyn Hode that day,
And nothynge spared good Robyn
1700 Our kynge in his pay.   *payment (of buffets)*

"So God me helpe," sayd our kynge,
"Thy game is nought to lere;   *not (hard) to learn*
I sholde not get a shote of the,
Though I shote all this yere."

1705 All the people of Notyngham
They stode and behelde;
They sawe nothynge but mantels of grene
That covered all the felde.

Than every man to other gan say,
1710 "I drede our kynge be slone: *slain*
Come Robyn Hode to the towne, iwys
On lyve he lefte never one."   *Alive*

Full hastly they began to fle,
Both yemen and knaves,
1715 And olde wyves that myght evyll goo,   *hardly walk*
They hypped on theyr staves.   *hopped on their crutches*

The kynge loughe full fast,   *laughed very much*
And commaunded theym agayne;   *gave them orders*
When they se our comly kynge,   *saw*
1720 I wys they were full fayne.   *pleased*

They ete and dranke and made them glad,
And sange with notes hye;
Than bespake our comly kynge
To Syr Rycharde at the Lee.

1725 He gave hym there his londe agayne,
     A good man he bad hym be;
     Robyn thanked our comly kynge,
     And set hym on his kne.   *kneeled down*

     Had Robyn dwelled in the kynges courte
1730 But twelve monethes and thre,   *Only*
     That he had spent an hondred pounde,
     And all his mennes fe.   *payment*

     In every place where Robyn came
     Ever more he layde downe,   *paid out*
1735 Both for knyghtes and for squyres,
     To gete hym grete renowne.

     By than the yere was all agone
     He had no man but twayne,
     Lytell Johan and good Scathelocke,
1740 With hym all for to gone.

     Robyn sawe yonge men shote
     Full ferre upon a day;   *far*
     "Alas!" than sayd good Robyn,
     "My welthe is went away.   *wealth*

1745 "Somtyme I was an archere good,
     A styffe and eke a stronge;   *hardy*
     I was comted the best archere   *reckoned*
     That was in mery Englonde.

     "Alas!" then sayd good Robyn,
1750 "Alas and well a woo!
     Yf I dwele lenger with the kynge,
     Sorowe wyll me sloo."   *slay*

     Forth than went Robyn Hode
     Tyll he came to our kynge:
1755 "My lorde the kynge of Englonde,
     Graunte me myn askynge.

"I made a chapell in Bernysdale,
That semely is to se,
It is of Mary Magdaleyne,
1760   And thereto wolde I be.

"I myght never in this seven nyght
No tyme to slepe ne wynke,
Nother all these seven dayes   *Neither*
Nother ete ne drynke.

1765   "Me longeth sore to Bernysdale,
I may not be therfro;
Barefote and wolwarde I have hyght   *with wool next the skin; vowed*
Thyder for to go."

"Yf it be so," than sayd our kynge,
1770   "It may no better be,
Seven nyght I gyve the leve,
No lengre, to dwell fro me."

"Gramercy, lorde," then sayd Robyn,
And set hym on his kne;
1775   He toke his leve courteysly,
To grene wode then went he.

Whan he came to grene wode,
In a mery mornynge,
There he herde the notes small   *delicate*
1780   Of byrdes mery syngynge.

"It is ferre gone," sayd Robyn,   *long ago*
"That I was last here;
Me lyste a lytell for to shote   *It pleases me*
At the donne dere."   *brown*

1785   Robyn slewe a full grete harte,
His horne than gan he blow,
That all the outlawes of that forest
That horne coud they knowe,   *they recognized*

146

And gadred them togyder,
1790 In a lytell throwe;   *while*
Seven score of wyght yonge men
Came redy on a rowe.

And fayre dyde of theyr hodes,
And set them on theyr kne:
1795 "Welcome," they sayd, "our mayster,
Under this grene wode tre."

Robyn dwelled in grene wode,
Twenty yere and two;
For all drede of Edwarde our kynge,
1800 Agayne wolde he not goo.

Yet he was begyled, iwys,
Through a wycked woman,
The pryoresse of Kyrkely,
That nye was of hys kynne,   *near; kin*

1805 For the love of a knyght,
Syr Roger of Donkesly,
That was her owne speciall;   *favorite*
Full evyll mote they the!   *prosper*

They toke togyder theyr counsell
1810 Robyn Hode for to sle,   *slay*
And how they myght best do that dede,
His banis for to be.   *murderers*

Than bespake good Robyn,
In place where as he stode,
1815 "To morow I muste to Kyrkely,
Craftely to be leten blode."   *Skillfully*

Syr Roger of Donkestere,
By the pryoresse he lay,
And there they betrayed good Robyn Hode,
1820 Through theyr false playe.

147

Cryst have mercy on his soule,
That dyded on the Rode!
For he was a good outlawe,
And dyde pore men moch god.

Cross

Notes

3   *yeman* denotes a broad social rank below knights and squires, ranging from a
       small landowning farmer to an attendant, servant, or lesser official in a royal or
       noble household (Middle English *yoman*, perhaps contraction of *yongman*); for
       the relevance of the term to the audience of the Robin Hood materials, see
       General Introduction, pp. 9–11.

5   *outlaw*. A person excluded from legal protection and rights (Old English *utlaga*,
       from Old Norse *utlagi*). Although the term "outlaw" was applied to anyone who
       had committed a serious crime — robbery, murder, or rape, the term had a more
       limited meaning in medieval law. The sentence of outlawry was reserved for
       those criminals who refused to appear for trial in court: "They become outlaws
       when, having been lawfully summoned, they do not appear, and are awaited and
       even sought for throughout the lawful and appointed terms, and yet they do not
       present themselves for trial" (David C. Douglas and George W. Greenaway,
       eds., *English Historical Documents 1042–1189*, [London: Eyre & Spottiswoode,
       1968], II, 552). Given the harsh punishments that awaited the convicted felon
       — blinding, loss of limb, or castration — it is not surprising that many fled to
       the forest or abroad to escape judgment.

6–7   Apart from *as he was one* these lines are missing in *a*, the "Lettersnijder" text,
       and as with other gaps in this source are provided from *b*, Wynkyn de Worde's
       edition.

9   *Bernesdale* or *Bernysdale* are medieval spellings of Barnesdale. This has long
       been identified as a tract of land in the West Riding of Yorkshire: the most
       recent discussion is by Holt (1989, pp. 83–87). As he notes, however, "there was
       no forest or chase," and he speculates that the three major locations of the
       myth — Barnsdale, Sherwood Forest, and Nottingham — "are all confounded."
       More recently Knight (1994, pp. 29–32) has identified another ancient
       Barnsdale in Rutland, being a royal forest with other Robin Hood references
       nearby and even some association with the Earls of Huntingdon before that link
       was made in literary form in the late sixteenth century. The *Gest*, however,

clearly links Barnsdale with named places in Yorkshire, see lines 69–70. It does not mention Sherwood Forest in Nottinghamshire, but does set part of the story in Nottingham, see note to line 59.

24   *gest*. Like King Arthur in *Sir Gawain and the Green Knight* and many other romances, Robin Hood refuses to eat "until something strange and wonderful happens, until he is provided with an appropriately distinguished or unusual guest" (Dobson and Taylor, 1976, p. 32). Though the word *Gest* in the title of the poem refers to an event or deed (from Latin *res gestae*, "things done," as used in the French epic *Chansons de geste*), this context clearly uses the other word *gest*, meaning "guest," see lines 63–64, 835.

25   This line is missing in all the sources, and Child leaves it blank. It is supplied here on the model of similar passages in early ballads, though it is conceivable that, as the rhymes are the same in the two stanzas, it might have originally been an irregular seven-line stanza.

27   Child inserts *som* again before *squyer*, presumably on metrical grounds; it appears in the later texts, but is not necessary.

35   Robin here reveals his special devotion to the Virgin Mary. The Marian cult is of course one of the major features of Roman Catholicism, and it reached its apogee in Western Europe in the eleventh and twelfth centuries. Robin's devotion to the Virgin, and to all women (lines 39–40), has an ironic poignancy when we recall that he is murdered by a religious woman, the prioress of Kyrkely priory. The allusion to the Virgin is also significant because a "miracle of the Virgin" underlies one of the central episodes in the *Gest* — Robin's loan of four hundred pounds to Sir Richard. See the Introduction and note to line 255.

57   Robin's outlawry is directed primarily at civil and ecclesiastical oppression and corruption. While he is a devoted Christian (see lines 31–37), he targets local officials and religious orders for abusing their authority and for usury, the lending of money at an exorbitant or illegal rate of interest; for a summary see Dobson and Taylor, 1976, pp. 30–31.

59   The Sheriff of Nottingham is Robin Hood's traditional adversary. The *Gest* does not explain why the Sheriff of one county, Nottinghamshire, would be interested in the activities of an outlaw living and operating in another county; the same

occurs in *Robin Hood and Guy of Gisborne*. This is presumably the result of different ballads being meshed into one longer story. On the variation of place, see Dobson and Taylor, 1976, pp. 14–15 and, for the real activities of such sheriffs, see Bellamy, 1985, Chap. 4.

69–70   These place-names set Robin Hood's activities firmly in the area of the Yorkshire Barnsdale. The Roman Road to the north (in this text erroneously called Watling Street, actually named Ermine Street, and later the Great North Road and the A1) runs north from Barnsdale Bar, crossing the River Went at Wentbridge. *The Saylis* has been identified by Dobson and Taylor as a plot of ground overlooking the highway on the northern edge of Barnsdale (1976, pp. 22–23); see also Holt, 1989, pp. 83–85.

To counteract the prevalence of highway robbery, Edward I sponsored special measures in the *Statute of Winchester* (A.D. 1285): "It is likewise commanded that the highways from market towns to other market towns be widened where there are woods or hedges or ditches, so that there may be no ditch, underwood or bushes where one could hide with evil intent within two hundred feet of the road on one side or the other, provided that this statute extends not to oaks or to large trees so long as it is clear underneath" (Harry Rothwell, ed., *English Historical Documents 1189–1327*, [New York: Oxford University Press, 1975], III, 461).

79   *loke*. Child emends to "loked" for consistency of tense, but all the early sources have this dramatic present, which is retained here.

83   The knight is identified with the knight rescued by the outlaws from Nottingham and named as Sir Richard at the Lee (lines 1239–41). He comes from *Verysdale* (line 504), which is probably the hamlet of Lee in Wyresdale in Lancashire (see Child III, 50; Holt, 1989, p. 100).

103   Child inserts *a* before *gode yoman*, but the text is idiomatic Middle English as it stands.

108   Blyth and Doncaster are located on the main road south of the Barnsdale region.

113   *lodge* refers to a temporary shelter in a forest, usually used for hunting.

125   For the cultural significance of hand washing before a meal, see the note to line 164 of *Robin Hood and the Potter*. See also line 921 in the *Gest*, and line 527 in *Adam Bell*.

128   *noumbles*. Organ meats such as liver, heart, and kidney, but also, in early usage, particularly for venison, loin cuts. See OED.

145   The source has *wened*, meaning "thought." Child emends to *wende* for sense, and this is accepted.

148   Child reads, with the source, *knyhht*, but this is probably a printer's error.

164   This unusual statement is repeated in line 984, and is not varied by any of the early texts. It presumably means "No peny (of that) I will have."

168   Child inserts *a* before *pounde,* but this does not seem required either for sense or meter.

170   Child inserts *full* before *lowe*: this is in some other early texts, but seems unnecessary, especially with *full styll* in the previous line.

177   Child inserts *one* before *worde*, as is usual in this collocation; it is found in other early texts and seems necessary for both sense and meter.

179   *knyght of force* refers to the practice of "distraint of arms," that is "requiring military tenants who held £20 *per annum* to receive knighthoods or pay a compensation, begun under Henry III, as early as 1224, and continued by Edward I" (Child III, 51). In a Parliamentary writ, dated 1278, Edward I ordered all sheriffs in England "to distrain [compel] without delay all those of your bailiwick who have lands worth twenty pounds a year, or one whole knight's fee worth twenty pounds a year, and hold of us in chief and ought to be knights but are not, to receive from us before Christmas or on that feast the arms of a knight" (Harry Rothwell, ed., *English Historical Documents 1189–1327* [New York: Oxford University Press, 1975], III, 413).

180   *Or ellys of yemanry* refers to the requirement for people owning less than a pound or 20 shillings to provide yeoman such as archers for royal forces (Powicke, 1962, p. 197).

204   Child inserts medial *e* in *kyndnesse*, presumably for metrical reasons, but this is not necessary.

212–13   In both lines Child prints *both* as in the earliest text and some later ones; the *b* text has *beth* in 213. It seems that *both* makes no sense in 213, and has been introduced into 212 by the juxtaposition of the doublet *sette and solde*. This text emends to *beth* in each line.

217   In order to provide bail for his son, who has killed a knight in a joust, Sir Richard has pledged his lands as security for a loan of 400 pounds from the abbot of St Mary's Abbey in York. The loan is due, but the knight has only ten shillings, and as a result he stands to lose his pledged property.

255   When Robin asks for security (*borowe*) for the loan of four hundred pounds, the knight replies that he has none other than *Our dere Lady*, which, because of his devotion to the Virgin, Robin readily accepts. Sagacious as usual, Child (III, 51–52) cites two parallels: one from the *Legenda aurea* in which a knight robs travellers, and the other from a Latin miracle of the Virgin in which a Christian borrows money from a Jewish money-lender and pledges the Virgin as his security. While the first example is a little remote — it is the knight in the *Gest* who is waylaid by robbers — the miracle of the Virgin is much more promising. When we consider (apparently unknown to Child) that the miracle entitled *The Merchant's Surety* exists in two Middle English versions dating from c. 1390 and c. 1450, the probability of influence is greatly increased. Although there are significant differences between the version in the *Gest* and the Middle English miracle, the opening plot elements and language are strikingly close: both the knight and the merchant love the Virgin; both are impoverished (due to differing circumstances); both are asked to pledge security for a loan; both offer the Virgin as their *borowe/borwe*; in both it is proclaimed that the Virgin will never *fayle*; both swear that they will repay the loans on a certain day; and, finally, Little John and the Jew make sure that the money is *wel tolde/wel itold*. For the text of *The Merchant's Surety*, see pp. 44–49 in Beverly Boyd, *The Middle English Miracles of the Virgin* (San Marino, California: The Huntington Library, 1964). Another edition is in Carl Horstmann, ed., *The Minor Poems of the Vernon MS*, Early English Text Society, o.s. 98 (London: Kegan Paul, Trench, Trübner & Co., 1892), 157–61.

273   The source reads *Much*, but other texts call him *litill Much* here, as does the source at lines 291 and 305. Conceivably this name came from confusion with

"litill John," but the adjective seems to improve the meter before "Much" in these instances and is accepted here.

279   Robin Hood on several occasions provides "livery" for those he protects. This is more than clothing: "livery and maintenance" were ways of building up a band of retainers, and it was frequently regarded as a crime if a man did not have the right to do that (Bellamy, 1973, especially pp. 8–9). Thus giving livery in an honest cause is another of Robin Hood's "good" crimes.

281   *scarlet and grene.* While the text is in no doubt about these colors, and both are used of the outlaws' clothing in early ballads, it seems likely that the line was originally *scarlet in graine*, that is a particularly good form of scarlet dye. But that is no reason to emend. It is, however, a sign that green was not the original color of the outlaws' clothing, but one of the accreted details of the myth.

289–90   Here appears a minor instance of the "bad tradesman" motif, especially clear in *Robin Hood and the Potter.*

332   The *a* text is deficient from this point until line 473 and *b* is followed.

334   The spelling of *Litell John* changes to *Lytel Johan* as the *b* text is taken up as the source.

335   Some thirty miles north of Barnsdale, York, a fine walled city with a 2000-year history, is the location of the powerful St. Mary's Abbey, where the knight must repay his 400 pounds or lose his land.

345   The text has a line missing, and Child sensibly repeats the line that ends the previous stanza — a repetition which may have caused the omission in the first place. Such repetitions for emphasis are not uncommon in early ballads.

351–52   The meaning of the lines seems obscure, but there are no signs of editing in the early texts to suggest miscomprehension. Presumably the Prior means "(If it were me) I would rather pay the hundred pounds right away."

353–54   The Prior seems to have knowledge of the knight's military activities *ferre beyonde the see* in England's cause. In line 388 the knight confirms that he has just returned from abroad with his *meyné* or company of soldiers.

354   Child inserts *is his* into this line, which in the text reads simply *In Englonde ryght*. The *b* text reads *In Englonde he is right* and the later *f* and *g*, like Child, have *is his right*. This suggest different ways of editing an original line reading simply *In Englonde ryght*, acceptable Middle English for *In England's cause*, which makes better sense both grammatically and in terms of the support the Prior is here giving the knight. There seems no ground for changing the original.

362   *Saynt Rychere*. The source reads *Richard* but the rhyme clearly requires *Rychere*. It is not fully clear which saint is referred to. In a note on *Gamelyn*, line 137 (which reads *Rychere*), Skeat states that, among a number of minor St. Richards, this one, popular in outlaw oaths, is the thirteenth century St. Richard of Chichester, who was "a pattern of brotherly love" (1884, pp. 38–39). Rhyme itself seems sufficient reason to emend to *Rychere*.

371   *justyce*. Child inserts *hye*; the expanded title is also found in some other early texts, but there seems little need for the emendation in terms either of sense or meter.

388   The knight speaks as if he and his company have (as the Prior suspected in line 353) been abroad, perhaps on a military campaign or crusade. This was not indicated earlier, and seems contradicted by his apparent plans to go on crusade (lines 223–28). He was traveling south when he met the outlaws, see lines 107–08. The uncertainty may arise from combining different ballads.

389   With a line missing in all the texts, Child inserts a repetition from line 387, which seems sensible.

416   *Syr justyce*. The justice, or professional lawyer, is the agent of a powerful lord — the abbot in this case. Justices were an important part of the county court system, performing a variety of functions: "pleaders, attorneys, seignorial bailiffs, and seneschals, as well as occasionally filling royal positions such as undersheriff, sheriff, and county clerk" (Robert C. Palmer, *The County Courts of Medieval England 1150–1350*. Princeton: Princeton University Press, 1982, p. 89). When the lawyer says he is *holde with the abbot . . . Both with cloth and fee*, he is revealing that he has been hired by the abbey to render legal services for a fee or annual annuity (Palmer, pp. 95–96).

425 Referring to the justice's being *holde with the abbot*, Kaeuper notes that "in the first half of the fourteenth century the practice by which lords retained the king's justices was more prevalent than it had been earlier or would be again" (1988, p. 180).

426 The phrase *cloth and fee* echoes the Latin formula *cum robis et foedis*, used to designate payment of legal services with both money and gifts of clothing. The abbot had retained the chief justice in order to help him bankrupt the knight. According to Child (III, 52) the practice of giving and receiving robes for such purposes was considered a conspiracy in the legal code of King Edward I, 1305–06; in another statute of King Edward III, dated 1346, justices were required to swear that they would accept robes and fees only from the king.

450 *call*: the rhyme word is missing in Child's source (*b* here) but is in other early texts and needs inserting.

465 The abbot is seeking to gain the land by "purchas," that is, by cash sale, not by inheritance. At lines 471–76 the knight resists this; it was an increasingly common form of land transfer in the period, and is at the basis of the conflict in *Gamelyn* (see note to line 14).

473 The *a* text is available from this line until 831, with a gap at 532–44.

484 Child notes "the knight would have given something for the use of the four hundred pounds had the abbot been civil, though under no obligation to pay interest" (III, 52).

489 The abbot, having failed to gain the land, asks the justice to repay his retainer, intended to facilitate this process.

493 The *a* text has only *Sir . . . n of lawe* and then has a gap until line 507; the text is supplied from *b*.

504 *Verysdale*. See note to line 83.

527 The nock is a small v-shaped cut in the end of an arrow to fit the string. This cut can split, and a horn or metal cap prevents this. Silver would be unusually lavish.

530–31   The *a* text is damaged in the second half of these two lines and then has a gap until line 545. The text is supplied from *b*.

537   *at Wentbrydge*. Child reads, with the earliest text, *But as he went at a brydge*: this is obviously an attempt to edit by a compositor who did not know Wentbridge (this is its first mention in the poem). Child includes this necessary emendation as a possible reading in his textual note, III, 79.

Wrestling was not, by the fourteenth century, considered an aristocratic sport. In the portrait of the Miller in the General Prologue to *The Canterbury Tales*, Chaucer observes of this "churl" that "at wrastlynge he wolde have alwey the ram" (line 548). In Chaucer's Tale of Sir Thopas — a burlesque of the popular romances and ballads of the day — the effeminate hero engages in both wrestling and archery. In *Gamelyn* the hero only wrestles when he has been effectively disinherited.

548   The prize for an ordinary wrestling match was a ram: in this contest, however, the victor wins a bull, a saddled horse, a pair of gloves, a gold ring, and a cask of wine. This may suggest an "art" or literary context for the *Gest*.

551   *ferre and frembde bested*. This appears to mean "set far (from home) and as a stranger." Dobson and Taylor translate as "And because he was a stranger and in the predicament of being a foreigner" (1976, p. 89).

558   *in fere*. Child emends the phrase to *free* for the sake of the rhyme, but this is very vague in meaning compared with *in fere*, and rhymes in the *Gest* are frequently imprecise.

582   Shooting at sticks stuck in the ground was the hardest challenge for any archer in the ballads; Little John split the stick each time.

588   *sawe I me*. Child adds *me* to the line to improve the rhyme; this is found in *b*, but later texts edit differently *That ever I did see*. Child follows the same practice in line 675 where there is a little more support in the early texts for *I me* at the end of the line. The resultant expression seems unusual — a reflexive use of *see* — but it is found in lines 400 and 736, so the emendation is accepted.

624   While it might seem tempting to emend the source to *Gyve me my dynere sone*, so improving both the rhyme and the meter, long lines and imprecise rhymes

are common in the *Gest,* and the text is best left unemended.

628   *Mi dyner gif thou me.* Though Child accepts the source *Mi dyner gif me;* this very short line is filled out uniformly with *thou* in other early texts and it seems more probable that *thou* was lost in a compositor's error rather than different texts hit on the same amplification, simple though it is.

650   *The while that he wolde.* This is how Child emends the source's *The while he wole* for both meter and rhyme. Other early texts insert *that* after *while,* which is accepted here on metrical grounds, but none has the past tense in *wolde.* Yet *wole* and *bolde* would make a very poor rhyme, and the loss of *d* is very easy: Child's reading is accepted.

675   *sawe I me.* Child's addition of *me* for rhyme is accepted; see note to line 588 for discussion.

701   Child inserts *they,* with other early texts, and though this is not grammatically essential, it seems a sensible emendation.

704   *hore.* Hoar or gray, due to the absence of foliage or because of the gray lichen that attaches itself to aged tree trunks.

714   Child emends *sende* to *sendeth* to keep the tense consistent with the previous line, but this is not necessary in Middle English.

731   Child prints the source's *shryef,* but though this is a conceivable condensation of *shire-reeve,* it is most likely a compositor's error and is emended to *shyref.*

738   As line 752 reveals, the green hart, with his herd of seven score deer, is an ironic reference (perhaps subliminally mythic) to Robin Hood, the *mayster-herte* and his men.

775   *toke.* Child emends the source's *to* to *toke,* with other early texts. This is not absolutely necessary grammatically, but *to him* would be a somewhat strained reading, and Child's emendation is accepted.

803   *thy best.* Child emends the source to *the beste,* presumably on grounds of sense and meter, but this seems unnecessary.

810   Child inserts *by* before *day*, as do some early texts, presumably on metrical grounds, but this is not necessary.

822–24 Robin is waiting to be repaid the four hundred pounds loaned to the knight, Sir Richard. This is the one year anniversary of their agreement in line 315. Commercial interests have invaded the greenwood: Robin is acting like the avaricious abbot of St. Mary's and the Jewish money-lender in *The Merchant's Surety* (see note to line 255). The knight is late because he stopped to help the yeoman at the wrestling match. See also the note to line 939.

832   The *a* text is not available until line 1255, and *b* is followed.

835   *such unketh gest.* The source's reading does make sense, if with some awkwardness — "Look for the kind of unknown guest (we seek)." Other early texts read more simply "some strange." In printing *some unketh* Child uncharacteristically produces a hybrid reading that no one can have had and which can hardly have been an error for *such unketh.* In the absence of any obvious emendation, the earliest source is retained here, as it does make sense.

842   See line 51 of *Robin Hood and the Monk* for a fuller instance of Little John's anger: it is clear there that Robin's commands have annoyed him.

849   *they.* The source has *he*, presumably an error, as the plural pronoun of line 848 is used again in line 851. Child's emendation is accepted.

856   The source has *That*, which Child accepts and then inserts *these* afterwards to make sense, as do some early texts. But the more probable error is to have misread initial *The* as an abbreviated *That*, and this change is made here. *The monkes have brought our pay* introduces a recurrent ironic joke, that the robbery of the monks is a repayment, sanctioned by Mary, of the money lent to the knight. The joke recurs in *Robin Hood's Golden Prize*, lines 57–58.

858   *b* reads *frese*, which Child prints, but in his collation suggests *leese*, meaning "let loose" or *drese* meaning "get ready." The latter seems much more likely, fitting well with 860.

861   Child inserts *men* at the end of the line, but the noun is not needed and is not in the earliest texts.

159

870   The syntax is colloquial: John instructs the outlaws to stop the crowd of travellers, and picks the leading monk as his own target.

921   For the custom of hand washing, see the note to line 164 of *Robin Hood and the Potter*. Other references occur in line 125 of the *Gest* and line 527 in *Adam Bell*.

930   *here. there* might seem a more obvious word in terms of sense, but there is no support for it in the early texts.

939   Again Robin is preoccupied with being repaid his loan to the knight. The emphasis on *pay, money, borowe, cofers, marke, peny, sylver, male, pounde*, and *doubled your cast* permeates the scene that follows, and casts Robin in the role of a concerned money-lender.

960   The source has *ame*, but this is clearly an error for *dame* and needs emending; Child records the error as *name*.

984   See also line 164 for this idiom.

988   The source only has *eight*, but *hundred*, easily lost as the Roman numeral *c*, is obviously needed, and Child emends accordingly.

991   An ironic moment: the monk's fidelity depends on the outlaw's pretending to assume that Mary has meant him to carry money to Robin.

1012   The abbot is attempting to use a legal means to overturn the knight's victory in lines 493–96.

1018   *tale* is ironic: they have listened to the monk's *tale* in the previous stanza.

1048   The source reads *they mery meyne*: Child emends a notional *thy* to *his*, but the error is more probably based on an original reading of *the*, which is adopted here.

1069   This very long line is even longer in most sources, which insert *sayd the knyght* after *grefe*: Child accepts this. There are a number of long lines that identify a speaker (see note to line 41 of *Robin Hood and the Potter*), but they begin speeches. The knight has already been identified as the speaker and so *sayd the knyght* can be omitted here.

1083   *selerer*. Child inserts *hye* before the noun; this is found in later texts, but seems unnecessary; see the similar insertion before *justyce* in line 371.

1127   Here and in several later instances (lines 1163, 1199, 1251) Child adds *e* to *proud,* presumably on metrical grounds; although the spelling *proude* does appear in the text, this and the other instances of the emendation seem unnecessary.

1131   Child inserts *he* after *And*; this is not in the other early texts (though two late ones have *they*) and does not seem needed, *that* here having full pronominal, not simply relative force.

1135   *buttes*. Mounds or other prominences (usually artificial) marking the limits of a shooting range.

1158   Child inserts *ve* into *hede*, so the older form of the word (from OE *heafod*) can rhyme with *desceyved*. Rhyme is at times so imprecise in the *Gest* that the emendation appears unnecessary and no early texts seem to find it difficult: perhaps they read *desceyved* as having three syllables and so rhyming with *hede* perfectly, but see also note to line 1218.

1165   *a bout*. Child spells *about* and treats it like an adverb, but, as in *Robin Hood and the Potter* (see note to line 205) the source separates the letters into article and noun, and this makes sense in the action.

1166   Child emends the source's *they* to *he*, and while *they* could be taken to make sense, rather vaguely, and was accepted by some early texts, the change seems justified and has support in the other early texts.

1167   Gylberte with the White Hand seems to be Robin's near equal in the tournament, and this may be a version of the "shoot-off" which will in Scott lead to splitting the arrow (*Ivanhoe*, ch. 13), where Locksley's opponent is Hubert. But, as in line 1604, Gylberte is again mentioned in the same formulaic way, and this time the competition is in the forest, among the archers. He does not appear elsewhere.

1171   In line 595 *Reynolde* is the alias of Little John; here he is depicted as a separate character. Child prints in his Introduction to the *Gest* a ballad telling how Reynold joined the outlaws (III, 54). There was a *Reynoldyn* in the comic list of outlaw names found in the Wiltshire parliamentary rolls as early as 1432; a late fifteenth-century poem speaks of "how Reynall and Robin Hode runnen at the gleve," and in 1502 Robert Fabyan's *Chronicle* speaks of a criminal arrested about Midsummer "which had renued many of Robin Hodes pageantes, which named himself Granelef" (for these references see Knight, 1994, Appendix, pp. 264–68). With such evidence of a Reynold Greenleaf as one of the extended band, the question is why Little John took on his name? Was there perhaps a ballad of how Reynold served the Sheriff, which was absorbed by the compiler of the *Gest*?

1181   The populace are, it seems, raising the hue and cry against Robin Hood, and in that case the town constables had to make an arrest (Bellamy, 1973, p. 93). See note to line 1713.

1210   *lovest.* Child inserts *d*, apparently so *lovedest* can retain the consistency of a past tense; but by line 1216 John is speaking in the present and the emendation seems unnecessary.

1218   Child does not insert *f* into *hede* for the purpose of a better rhyme with *lefte,* though most later texts emend the line to create a good rhyme. The earliest texts seem to overlook the problem, so emendation seems unnecessary. See also line 1158, where the problem likewise occurs; there Child does amend to *hefte.*

1245   Child inserts *I* after *moche*, as do the later texts, and this seems required.

1254   *a* is available again until line 1395.

1258   St. Quentin is, according to the *Oxford Dictionary of Saints*, a martyr who "preached at Amiens where the probably fictitious prefect Rictiovarus arrested and interrogated him, finally killing him by a series of fearsome tortures." Perhaps it is fitting that Sir Richard swear by St. Quentin that he will protect Robin Hood and thus save him from the sort of arrest and torture that the saint suffered.

1297   The source reads *wyl* not *wil* as Child has it.

1317   The source reads *fayles* which would be a sharp change of tense; all but the two earliest sources vary it, and Child's emendation to *fayled* is accepted.

1323   Hawking is an aristocratic pastime, and the knight would not be fully armed; there is a supposition of the sheriff's improper behavior in his capture.

1324   Child inserts *his* before *haukes*, apparently on metrical grounds; the earliest text lacks *his*, and the emendation seems unnecessary.

1352–53 These two lines are left blank by Child. Copland offers *"The proude shiriffe,"* *then sayd she*, which completes well the stanza 1349–52, but he then offers two new and weak lines in place of 1354–56: "He is not yet passed thre myles, / You may them overtake." It seems best to produce a new line as 1353 based on repetition (see line 345).

1392   Child inserts *e* on the end of *bright*, presumably on metrical grounds, but this seems unnecessary.

1395   The *a* text is not available for the rest of the poem and *b* is followed.

1402   The source has *hoode* which does not make sense, unless the knight had a hood over his head — but at line 1328 the knight was merely said to be bound. None of the other early texts seem to see any problem, but Child's emendation to *bonde* is accepted.

1412   Three Edwards reigned in succession from 1272 to 1377: Edward I, 1272–1307; Edward II, 1307–27; Edward III, 1327–77. Joseph Hunter noted that Edward II had in 1324 a "valet de chambre" with the name of Robin Hood, though there was no indication that he had been in trouble with the law (pp. 35–38). Holt discusses the connection with some scepticism, but also feels that some of the events in the seventh and eighth fitts had a basis in historical fact (1989, pp. 155–56). He notes that after Edward II's execution of Thomas, Earl of Lancaster, in 1322, the earl's supporters committed wide-spread acts of vengeance, including the pillaging of the king's deer in the royal forests, and that as in the *Gest*, Edward II himself travelled to the area to investigate these disturbances. Knight has suggested that Edward IV, who may best fit the description *our comly kynge* (also in lines 1457, 1513, 1549, 1637, 1727), is referred to, as his period of rule (1461–83) is not inconsistent with the argument that the *Gest* is composed much later than has usually been thought (1994, pp. 46–48). We may, however, be on firmer ground in now identifying the king in fitts seven and eight as Edward III, because Laurence Minot refers to him as *Edward, oure cumly king* in line 1 of *Poem IV*, which was composed

163

about 1339 to commemorate Edward III's invasion of France at the beginning of the Hundred Years War (Richard Osberg, ed., *The Poems of Laurence Minot, 1333–1352*, Kalamazoo: Medieval Institute Publications, 1996).

1425   The source reads *the passe of Lancashire* which makes no sense. Some of the later texts read *compasse*, which is very unlikely to be an editorial emendation because of its inherent complexity, and is probably the original reading.

1427   Ritson, relying on Camden's *Britannia,* suggested Plompton Park was "upon the banks of the Penterill in Cumberland" (1795, p. xxv), and Child (III, 54–55) agreed, though noting that Hunter, "citing no authority" said it was part of the forest of Knaresborough in Yorkshire. Dobson and Taylor follow Hunter, though they include "possibly" in their note (1976, p. 105) and locate it in the West Riding of Yorkshire. Holt (1989, p. 101) argues for Plumpton Wood in Lancaster, near the king's demesne wood of Myerscough. However, it seems clear that the reference is to part of Inglewood Forest near Carlisle, providing an interesting connection with Andrew of Wyntoun's early location of Robin and Little John there. In her edition of *The Awntyrs of Arthur,* Helen Phillips notes that "Plumptoun Laund . . . was an area of grassland within the forest (walled in between 1332–35), within which was Plumpton Hay, a fenced park" (1988, p. 8). Plumpton is mentioned again in *Robin Hood's Fishing*, lines 65 and 71, possibly there a reference to the *Gest* as Dobson and Taylor suggest (1976, p. 181).

1429   Forest law. Royal laws regulating the use of forests can be traced back to the legal codes of Ine (A.D. 688–94), Alfred (871–99), and Cnut (1020–23). In the latter, "everyone is to avoid trespassing on my hunting, wherever I wish to have it preserved, on pain of full fine" (Dorothy Whitelock, ed., *English Historical Documents c. 500–1042* [London: Eyre & Spottiswoode, 1955], I, 430). After the Norman Conquest, William the Conqueror "gathered the woods and hunting preserves of the Saxon kings into a jurisdiction under the forest law he brought from Normandy and added new forests to that core" (Charles R. Young, *The Royal Forests of Medieval England*. Philadelphia: University of Pennsylvania Press, 1979, p. 150). It is estimated that one-fourth of the area of England was designated royal forest, including entire shires (Huntingdonshire). In his "Coronation Charter," dated 1100, William's youngest son, Henry I, reminded the kingdom that "I have retained the forests in my own hands as my father did before me" (David C. Douglas and George Greenaway, eds., *English Historical Documents 1042–1189* [London: Eyre & Spottiswoode, 1968], II, 402). King

A Gest of Robyn Hode

Stephen made a similar claim in 1136 (Douglas and Greenaway, eds., *English Historical Documents 1042–1189*, vol. II, 403). In the *Assize of the Forest* (1184), Henry II set forth the first piece of legislation devoted exclusively to the royal forest. It begins by forbidding "that anyone shall transgress against him in regard to his hunting-rights or his forests in any respect." If anyone is convicted of offending his forests, "he wills that full justice be exacted from the offender." To oversee the protection of the forests, the king instructed the sheriff in each shire to appoint twelve knights to guard his venison (red deer, fallow deer, and roe deer) and vert (wood). Baronial discontent with forest law reached its peak in the years leading up to *Magna Carta* (1215). In the "Articles of the Barons," the barons demanded that King John amend the "wicked customs connected with forests and with foresters and warrens and sheriffs and river-banks . . ." (Harry Rothwell, ed., *English Historical Documents 1189–1327* [New York: Oxford University Press, 1975], III, 314). These calls for reform appeared in *Magna Carta* itself (p. 321), were later omitted (p. 331), and were reissued in expanded form in *The Charter of the Forest* in 1217 (p. 337). Item ten reads: "No one shall henceforth lose life or limb because of our venison" (p. 339). And item fifteen: "All who . . . have been outlawed for a forest offence only shall be released from their outlawry without legal proceedings . . ." (p. 340). But the harsh penalties continued. In the *Statute of Winchester* of 1275, Edward I ordered that if anyone is convicted of wrongdoing in the parks or preserves, the plaintiff "shall be awarded appropriate and heavy damages according to the nature of the offense and three years imprisonment." If the accused cannot pay the fine, "he shall abjure the realm," and, if he takes flight and ignores the lawful inquest, "let him be outlawed" (p. 403).

1442   *my honde*. Child inserts *with* before this phrase; this does appear in the later texts but is not needed: *my honde* is an idiomatic Middle English instrumental phrase.

1454   *ball in his hode*. The phrase refers to the head, and appears to have an ironic, even macabre, reference to games in which the ball was originally a human head.

1473   The sources all have *ledesman*, which, influenced by *lede* in line 1474, misses the play on a religious disguise continued in *bedesman*.

165

1481   *hastly*. Child spells *hastely*, presumably for metrical reasons, but this is not necessary; the same occurs in lines 1565 and 1713.

1506   The second and fourth lines of this stanza are identical in the earlier texts. Child thought this was an error and supplied a new fourth line (*Other shyft have not wee*). But such repetitions are not uncommon in this kind of text, and this statement before the king is a suitable occasion for such an emphatic celebration of the greenwood ethos.

1512   *saynt*. Child adds an *e*, presumably for metrical reasons, but this is not necessary.

1524   *I vouch it halfe on the*. The source's reading makes good sense: the "abbot" says he would split his money with the outlaws, and Robin acts accordingly. Child's emendation to *I wolde vouch it safe on the*, while intelligent, is unnecessary.

1534   The king, in disguise, presents his royal image in the form of a seal, which is both in itself revered and the instrument of recognition. The sense of the power of the king's presence and gaze is realized in the story.

1537   *targe*. According to the OED this is "a name applied in the reigns of the first three Edwards to the King's private or privy seal (perhaps bearing a shield as its device)."

1645   In a little-noted correction in a later volume (V, 297), Child inserts *to* before *our kynge* and repunctuates to change speakers: now Robin asks mercy from the king. This is the reading of Copland and White, the later texts. It is also necessary to change *your* to *this* so the king does not seem to possess the *trystyll-tre*. It seems much more likely that the early source is correct and that the king-abbot is still theatrically playing his part — to which Robin responds by asking mercy in turn. Dobson and Taylor retain the original reading, as here.

✗ 1663   The idea of Robin holding an alternative lordship, with his own retinue, is clear.

1666   *come*. Child inserts *wyll* before the verb, but although this is the construction in line 1661 it is only in the later texts here, and is not needed.

1668   The gap between fitts is not as clear as that in earlier instances. Previous fitts have definite breaks, although fitts five, six, and seven are all rather short. This break appears to have been inserted editorially.

1681–82   The king adopts Robin's green livery in place of religious black. This acknowledges forest values, at least in play. Hall records Henry VIII and his courtiers dressing in green to pay a surprise visit to the queen and her ladies (Knight, 1994, pp. 105–10).

1683   *had so, iwys.* Child emends to "also i-wys." This appears credible, but a sharper sense is produced if the error is assumed to be in the next line with *had* repeated from line 1683 instead of *hod* ("hood"). The point of the passage is that the king's men are changing their black cowls for green hoods and Child's emendation obscures this. So line 1683 is retained as in the original and in line 1684 *had* is emended to *hode*.

1689   *Theyr bowes bente, and.* For no clear reason Child accepts the later texts' apparent editing of the source to *They bente theyr bowes*: this loses the condensed force of the original as well as its sprightly internal rhyme.

1695   *plucke buffet.* According to Dobson and Taylor (1976, p. 110), "An archery competition with the forfeit of receiving a 'pluck' or knock for missing the target." Here this seems to have been extended to receiving a blow for losing a bout and so seems a euphemism of more violent encounters with the bow. See Introduction to *Robyn and Gandelyn*, p. 228. Child notes that *plucke-buffet* is played in the romance of *Richard Coer de Lion* and in *The Turke and Gowin* (III, 55).

1713   Compare the action of *Robin Hood's Progress to Nottingham* (p. 507), which also shows townspeople in fear of the outlaw. *Adam Bell* has a similar scene, where the townspeople capture the hero William of Cloudesley, lines 141–48. This, like the hue and cry in line 1181, seems a sharp form of opposition between forest and urban values, and suggests a stronger sociopolitical conflict than the usual notion of Robin Hood as a universal hero.

1731   *he had spent.* The source only has *spent* and Child inserts *he had*, which is found in the later texts. While in many cases they seem to amplify a condensed Middle English usage, here their addition appears required.

1742   *Full ferre.* Child accepts the reading *Full fayre* which is in a Douce fragment and the later texts, but it makes better sense to accept the earlier reading: Robin is

167

impressed by the distance these young men can shoot.

1747 Child prints *compted* as an emendation of the source's *commytted*; the logic of his emendation is correct, but the original must have been *comted*, which gives rise both to *committed* and, in the later texts, *commended*.

1767 To walk barefoot with wool next to the skin implies penance rather than poverty. Robin is suggesting to the king a pilgrimage to the chapel in Barnsdale, but also implies his rejection of the luxuries of court life.

1795 Child inserts *dere* from a Douce fragment, but it seems unnecessary: though "my master dear" is a common enough phrase in general, there is little sentiment of this kind in the *Gest*.

1803 *Kyrkely*. The place of Robin's death is known either as Kirklee (Church Lee) or Kirklees/Kyrklyes (see *The Death of Robin Hood*, where it is for the most part Kirkly and Churchlee and also Kirklys and Churchlees). There was a priory of this name near Wakefield in West Yorkshire; for a discussion of the location, see Dobson and Taylor, 1976, pp. 19–20. Child emends the source's *Kyrkely* to *Kyrkesly* at line 1803 and kept it as *Kyrkesly* at line 1815. The reverse is necessary: it appears that he was for once mistaken about a fact, as he refers to the site in his Introduction as "Kyrkesly or Kirklees" (III, 50).

1806 *Syr Roger* is presumably the same figure as Red Roger, Robin Hood's assailant in one version of *The Death of Robin Hood*, see line 97; he is referred to in the Sloane *Life*, which presumably draws on the *Gest* here as elsewhere.

Donkesly. Line 1817 refers to Doncaster. *Donkesly* could perhaps be an erroneous compound of Doncaster and Kirklees.

168

Robin Hood and Guy of Gisborne

Introduction

Robin Hood and Guy of Gisborne only survives in the folio manuscript acquired by Thomas Percy (British Library Add MSS 27879), which is dated in the mid seventeenth century and clearly is a collection of pre-existing materials; this is the only one of the six Robin Hood ballads in the manuscript that Percy printed in his *Reliques* of 1765. He gave it the title used here, though in other more recent versions of the title Robin's opponent is called Sir Guy. This honorific is used frequently in the text, but Percy may have omitted it, as Child does, from the ballad's title because the text states that he and Robin are both yeoman (line 87), and so the knightly title seems anomalous, though Percy did add a note that "Sir" was used outside the knightly class (1765, p. 86). He edited the manuscript version considerably for meter and comprehension, though in his fourth edition he reinstated some of the original readings; Ritson also edited the text fairly heavily for his 1795 collection.

Child prints this text first after the *Gest*, presumably because of the evident antiquity of the story: *Sir Guy* is mentioned in Dunbar's poem *Of Sir Thomas Norry*, to be dated by the early sixteenth century, but before that a similar plot is told in a play found in a manuscript written about 1475 (see pp. 281–84 in this edition). Because Child assumed the plays were based on ballads, this might have led him to assume a date for the ballad even earlier than *Robin Hood and the Monk*, hence his ordering of the texts. This assumption would seem questionable: although the difference between play and ballad is not so great in this instance as in that of the Potter story, it still seems that they are generic variants of the same theme, and one cannot be placed before the other. But the ballad may well date from the fifteenth century in something very much like its present form, and as Fowler remarks it "may well be one of the earliest of all the Robin Hood ballads" (1980, p. 1782).

In making his judgment on date, Child might have been influenced by Percy's comment that this ballad bore "marks of much greater antiquity than any of the common popular songs on this subject" (1765, p. 124), though *Robin Hood and the Monk* was apparently unknown to Percy. Child's early location of the ballad may also be influenced by what seem to be quite ancient motifs in the ballad, notably Guy's horse-hide and head, which seems more like a ritual costume than a disguise, and also by what Dobson and Taylor call the ballad's "exceptionally violent tone" (1976,

169

p. 141). When Robin defaces this enemy's head and places it on his bow's end, both ritual and savagery seem to be invoked. The importance of the "mythic" Robin Hood is a matter for debate, but if that interpretation has any force, this ballad is one of its locations. The idea of a conflict between a true and a false forester (who has some resonances of the devil in Chaucer's *Friar's Tale*), the hero's unflinching ferocity against his enemies, his understanding of their rituals (including his appropriation of their own ritual costume), his capacity to be polymorphous — at the end, both false Guy and a quasi-priest — his insistence on facing this enemy himself even at the expense of his own *fellowship*, these are all elements which create a slightly different Robin (also found in the equally fierce *Robin Hood's Progress to Nottingham*), more emphatic, more inspired, more like the mythic international hero than the inherently human friend to many found in other early texts.

The ballad is set in the Yorkshire Barnsdale area (line 181) and Gisborne, wherever precisely it may be, is in the same region (see note to line 138). This makes it seem odd that the outlaw's major enemy is the Sheriff of Nottingham. Though sheriffs did have some duty to pursue felons outside their precincts, this is too far for credibility, and this ballad, early though its origins are, must represent to some extent a conflation — oral or literary — of the differently located Robin Hood myths, a process taken further in the *Gest*. In the suggestion that the sheriff has employed Sir Guy (lines 99–100 and 187–90), we may well see a conscious articulation of two separate enemies, and at least one element of rationalization within this emotively intense text.

The power of this ballad also derives from its speed and its capacity to exploit the elisions and emphases of the ballad form. Though these qualities have been noted — Dobson and Taylor speak of its "concisely dramatic qualities" (1976, p. 141) — the extent of the significance of these features has not been fully appreciated by most commentators, more meshed in the tradition of realist humanism than aware of what Gray calls "the inherently expressionist form" of ballads (1984, p. 16). One example of this misinterpretation is the problem allegedly caused by the fact that Robin, having argued with John and set off on his own, cannot know that John has been seized by the sheriff — and yet goes straight to rescue him. Child thinks this shows "considerable derangement of the story" (III, 90), and Dobson and Taylor agree (1976, pp. 140–41). Yet this sort of instinctive certainty is just what empowers the hero of romance: he is led to his heroic encounter by fortune and self-confidence. Narrative elisions of this dramatic kind are common enough throughout the ballads — *Sir Patrick Spens* being a famous example.

A more striking example of this failure to "read" the genre of the poem lies in the assumption by commentators that there is a substantial sequence missing in the early stanzas. While it is evident that *Robin Hood and the Monk* has lost a leaf (and so about 48 lines) after line 120, and the Percy Folio has some pages torn in half, there is in fact no need to assume, as rationalists requiring the comfort of a blow-by-blow narrative have done, that there is anything missing between lines 6 and 7 of *Robin Hood and Guy of Gisborne*. Rapid moving the text certainly is — but then John says in line 13 that *sweavens are swift*, and the ballads characteristically slip very quickly into their action, often giving the impression that the audiences knew quite well who these people were and what they did, so that fussier introductions would be superfluous; compare the opening of *Robin Hood and the Monk*, which has a very cursory introduction to the characters; *Adam Bell* is another case.

In terms of style this ballad is not unlike *Robin Hood and the Monk*: it has a relatively consistent metrical pattern and a recurrent abcb rhyme (with one six-line stanza, lines 21–27), occasional use of the abab pattern (lines 26–30, 35–38, 43–46, 59–62), and relatively few poor rhymes (lines 6/8, 36/8, 48/50, 88/90, 100/02, 112/14). Compared with *Robin Hood and the Potter* the language of the ballad is in general sure-footed, lacking the element of line-filler and cliché common to the popular ballad as it develops. This vigorous language emphasizes the effect of the pace and rapid variation of the narrative, the poetic drive which is the central instrument of this fierce and powerful ballad, creating powerfully its dramatic story and deepening the thematic impact of its "mysterious story" (Holt, 1989, p. 30).

In a number of ways it summarizes major themes that are to work strongly in the myth right through to the present. The argument between Little John and Robin that makes them separate leaves them both vulnerable: in this respect the poem is a partner piece to *Robin Hood and the Monk*. Robin's opponent is a personal enemy, with a vengeful, almost diabolic character, and his humiliation and destruction are an essential part of the story. The whole encounter has elements of natural myth about it, suggested rather than expressed. The final triumph is dependent not only on courage and fidelity among the outlaws but also on some supreme piece of trickery that stamps their spirit as well as their success on the story. This ballad also creates vividly the essential agon versus the villain. In nineteenth-century tradition the name of Sir Guy had just the right ring for a melodramatic villain, but the mixture of menace and mystery borne by Robin Hood's central opponent is originally and splendidly created in this strong ballad, which, by combining a dramatic fight with a bold rescue, remains at the core of the whole myth.

Select Bibliography

Texts

Child, F. J. *The English and Scottish Popular Ballads.* 5 vol. (1882–98). Rpt. New York: Dover, 1965. Vol. III, no. 118.

Dobson, R. B., and J. Taylor. *Rymes of Robyn Hood.* London: Heinemann, 1976.

Gutch, J. M. *A Litell Gest of Robin Hood with other Auncient and Modern Ballads and Songs Relating to the Celebrated Yeoman.* London: Longman, 1847. Vol. II, 68–83.

Thomas Percy's Folio Manuscript (c. 1640–50).

Percy, Thomas, ed. *Reliques of Ancient English Poetry.* 3 vols. London: J. Dodsley, 1765.

Ritson, Joseph, ed. *Robin Hood, A Collection of All the Auncient Poems, Songs and Ballads Now Extant Relative to the Celebrated English Outlaw.* 2 vols. London: Egerton and Johnson, 1795; rpt. 1832. I, 114–25.

Commentary and Criticism

Bellamy, John C. *Robin Hood: An Historical Inquiry.* London: Croom Helm, 1985.

Child, F. J., pp. 89–91.

Dobson, R. B., and J. Taylor., pp. 140–41.

Fowler, D. C. "Ballads." In *The Manual of Writings in Middle English 1050–1550*, new series. Ed. A. E. Hartung. New Haven, Connecticut: Academy of Arts and Sciences, 1980. Pp. 1753–1808.

Gray, Douglas. "The Robin Hood Ballads." *Poetica* 18 (1984), 1–39.

Holt, J. C. *Robin Hood.* Second ed. London: Thames and Hudson, 1989.

Robin Hood and Guy of Gisborne

When shawes beene sheene and shradds full fayre,[1]
And leeves both large and longe,
Itt is merry, walking in the fayre forrest,
To heare the small birds singe.

5 The woodweele sang, and wold not cease,   *woodwall (golden oriole)*
Amongst the leaves a lyne.   *in a row*
"And it is by two wight yeoman,   *sturdy*
By deare God, that I meane.

"Me thought they did mee beate and binde,
10 And tooke my bow mee froe;   *from me*
If I bee Robin a-live in this lande,
Ile be wrocken on both them towe."   *revenged; two*

"Sweavens are swift, master," quoth John,   *Dreams*
"As the wind that blowes ore a hill,   *over*
15 For if itt be never soe lowde this night,   *loud*
To-morrow it may be still."

"Buske yee, bowne yee, my merry men all,   *Prepare you, get ready*
For John shall goe with mee,
For Ile goe seeke yond wight yeomen
20 In greenwood where the bee."   *they*

The cast on their gowne of greene,   *They put on*
A shooting gone are they,
Untill they came to the merry greenwood,
Where they had gladdest bee;

---

[1] *When woods are bright, and branches full fair*

173

25 There were the ware of wight yeoman,   *they were aware*
    His body leaned to a tree.   *against a tree*

    A sword and a dagger he wore by his side,
    Had beene many a mans bane,   *murderer*
    And he was cladd in his capull-hyde,   *horse-hide*
30 Topp and tayle and mayne.

    "Stand you still, master," quoth Litle John,
    "Under this trusty tree,   *trysting tree*
    And I will goe to yond wight yeoman,
    To know his meaning trulye."

35 "A, John, by me thou setts noe store,
    And thats a farley thinge;   *amazing*
    How offt send I my men beffore,
    And tarry myselfe behinde?

    "It is noe cunning a knave to ken,   *takes no skill to know a knave*
40 And a man but heare him speake;   *If*
    And itt were not for bursting of my bowe,   *damaging*
    John, I wold thy head breake."

    But often words they breeden bale;   *cause anger*
    That parted Robin and John;
45 John is gone to Barnsdale,
    The gates he knowes eche one.   *ways*

    And when hee came to Barnesdale,
    Great heavinesse there hee hadd;
    He found two of his owne fellowes
50 Were slaine both in a slade,   *forest glade*

    And Scarlett a foote flyinge was,   *on foot*
    Over stockes and stone,   *stumps*
    For the sheriffe with seven score men
    Fast after him is gone.

174

55   "Yett one shoote Ile shoote," sayes Litle John,   *shot I'll shoot*
       "With Crist his might and mayne;
       Ile make yond fellow that flyes soe fast
       To be both glad and faine."   *happy*

       John bent up a good yeiwe bow,   *yew*
60   And fetteled him to shoote;   *prepared*
       The bow was made of a tender boughe,
       And fell downe to his foote.

       "Woe worth thee, wicked wood," sayd Litle John,   *Misery come to you*
       "That ere thou grew on a tree!
65   For this day thou art my bale,   *trouble*
       My boote when thou shold bee!"   *help*

       This shoote it was but looselye shott,   *inaccurately*
       The arrowe flew in vaine,
       And it mett one of the sheriffes men;
70   Good William a Trent was slaine.

       It had beene better for William a Trent
       To hange upon a gallowe
       Then for to lye in the greenwoode,
       There slaine with an arrowe.

75   And it is sayd, when men be mett,
       Six can doe more then three:
       And they have tane Litle John,   *taken*
       And bound him fast to a tree.   *firmly*

       "Thou shalt be drawen by dale and downe,"   *dragged by a horse*
           quoth the sheriffe,
80   "And hanged hye on a hill."
       "But thou may fayle," quoth Litle John,
       "If itt be Christs owne will."

       Let us leave talking of Litle John,
       For hee is bound fast to a tree,

85   And talke of Guy and Robin Hood,
      In the green woode where they bee.

      How these two yeomen together they mett,
      Under the leaves of lyne,   *lime (trees in general)*
      To see what marchandise they made   *business*
90   Even at that same time.

      "Good morrow, good fellow," quoth Sir Guy;
      "Good morrow, good felow," quoth hee,
      "Methinkes by this bow thou beares in thy hand,
      A good archer thou seems to be."

95   "I am wilfull of my way," quoth Sir Guye,   *uncertain*
      "And of my morning tyde."   *time*
      "Ile lead thee through the wood," quoth Robin,
      "Good felow, Ile be thy guide."

      "I seeke an outlaw," quoth Sir Guye,
100   "Men call him Robin Hood;
      I had rather meet with him upon a day,
      Then forty pound of golde."

      "If you tow mett, itt wold be seene whether were better   *If you two met; which*
      Afore yee did part awaye;
105   Let us some other pastime find,
      Good fellow, I thee pray.

      "Let us some other masteryes make,   *competitive feats of skill*
      And wee will walke in the woods even;
      Wee may chance meet with Robin Hoode
110   Att some unsett steven."   *unexpected occasion*

      They cutt them downe the summer shroggs   *bushes*
      Which grew both under a bryar,
      And sett them three score rood in twinn,   *330 yards apart*
      To shoote the prickes full neare.

115   "Leade on, good fellow," sayd Sir Guye,
       "Lead on, I doe bidd thee."
       "Nay, by my faith," quoth Robin Hood,
       "The leader thou shalt bee."

       The first good shoot that Robin ledd
120   Did not shoote an inch the pricke froe;   *center of the target*
       Guy was an archer good enoughe,
       But he cold neere shoote soe.

       The second shoote Sir Guy shott,
       He shott within the garlande;   *ring suspended on stick*
125   But Robin Hoode shott it better than hee,
       For he clove the good pricke-wande.   *stick that holds up ring*

       "Gods blessing on thy heart!" says Guye,
       "Goode fellow, thy shooting is goode,
       For an thy hart be as good as thy hands,   *if; heart*
130   Thou were better then Robin Hood.

       "Tell me thy name, good fellow," quoth Guy,
       "Under the leaves of lyne."
       "Nay, by my faith," quoth good Robin,
       "Till thou have told me thine."

135   "I dwell by dale and downe," quoth Guye,
       "And I have done many a curst turne;   *cursed deed*
       And he that calles me by my right name
       Calles me Guye of good Gysborne."

       "My dwelling is in the wood," sayes Robin,
140   "By thee I set right nought;
       My name is Robin Hood of Barnesdale,
       A fellow thou has long sought."

       He that had neither beene a kithe nor kin   *friends or relatives*
       Might have seene a full fayre sight,
145   To see how together these yeomen went,
       With blades both browne and bright.   *bloodstained*

To have seene how these yeomen together fought,
Two howers of a summers day; *hours*
Itt was neither Guy nor Robin Hood
150 That fettled them to flye away. *prepared*

Robin was reachles on a roote, *careless*
And stumbled at that tyde,
And Guy was quicke and nimble with-all,
And hitt him ore the left side. *on*

155 "Ah, deere Lady!" sayd Robin Hoode, *Virgin Mary*
"Thou art both mother and may! *maiden*
I thinke it was never mans destinye
To dye before his day."

Robin thought on Our Lady deere,
160 And soone leapt up againe,
And thus he came with an awkwarde stroke; *backhanded*
Good Sir Guy hee has slayne.

He tooke Sir Guys head by the hayre, *hair*
And sticked itt on his bowes end:
165 "Thou hast beene traytor all thy liffe,
Which thing must have an ende."

Robin pulled forth an Irish kniffe,
And nicked Sir Guy in the face,
That hee was never on a woman borne
170 Cold tell who Sir Guye was. *Could*

Saies, "Lye there, lye there, good Sir Guye,
And with me be not wrothe; *angry*
If thou have had the worse stroakes at my hand,
Thou shalt have the better cloathe."

175 Robin did his gowne of greene, *took off*
On Sir Guye it throwe; *Threw it over Guy's body*
And hee put on that capull-hyde, *horse-hide*
That cladd him topp to toe.

"The bowe, the arrowes, and litle horne,
180 And with me now Ile beare;
For now I will goe to Barnsdale,
To see how my men doe fare."

Robin sett Guyes horne to his mouth,
A lowd blast in it he did blow;
185 That beheard the sheriffe of Nottingham,
As he leaned under a lowe.   *stood; hill*

"Hearken! hearken!" sayd the sheriffe,
"I heard noe tydings but good,
For yonder I heare Sir Guyes horne blowe,
190 For he hath slaine Robin Hoode.

"For yonder I heare Sir Guyes horne blow,
Itt blowes soe well in tyde,   *time*
For yonder comes that wight yeoman,
Cladd in his capull-hyde.

195 "Come hither, thou good Sir Guy,
Aske of mee what thou wilt have."
"Ile none of thy gold," sayes Robin Hood,
"Nor Ile none of itt have.

"But now I have slaine the master," he sayd,
200 "Let me goe strike the knave;   *servant (i.e., Little John)*
This is all the reward I aske,
Nor noe other will I have."

"Thou art a madman," said the shiriffe,
"Thou sholdest have had a knights fee;   *fief (land-holding)*
205 Seeing thy asking bee soe badd,
Well granted it shall be."

But Litle John heard his master speake,
Well he knew that was his steven;   *voice*
"Now shall I be loset," quoth Litle Iohn, *set loose*
210 "With Christs might in heaven."

But Robin hee hyed him towards Litle John,   *hastened*
Hee thought hee wold loose him belive;   *at once*
The sheriffe and all his companye
Fast after him did drive.

215   "Stand abacke! stand abacke!" sayd Robin;
      "Why draw you mee soe neere?
      Itt was never the use in our countrye
      One's shrift another shold heere."   *confession*

      But Robin pulled forth an Irysh kniffe,
220   And losed John hand and foote,
      And gave him Sir Guyes bow in his hand,
      And bade it be his boote.   *benefit*

      But John tooke Guyes bow in his hand
      His arrowes were rawstye by the roote;   *rusty with blood at their tips*
225   The sherriffe saw Litle John draw a bow
      And fettle him to shoote.   *prepare*

      Towards his house in Nottingam
      He fled full fast away,
      And soe did all his companye,
230   Not one behind did stay.

      But he cold neither soe fast goe,   *could*
      Nor away soe fast runn,
      But Litle John, with an arrow broade,
      Did cleave his heart in twinn.   *twain*

1	MS: *shales*. Child emends to *shawes*, a word frequently used to set the early summer scene for a Robin Hood ballad. It is not an obvious error for a scribe to make, but no other likely emendation offers itself.

1   MS: *shales*. Child emends to *shawes*, a word frequently used to set the early summer scene for a Robin Hood ballad. It is not an obvious error for a scribe to make, but no other likely emendation offers itself.

4   MS: *singe*. Child emends to *songe* for the sake of rhyme, but this seems unnecessary in the context of the fairly relaxed practices of ballad rhyming.

5   MS: *woodweete*. Child emends to *woodweele*, the woodwall or golden oriole; this may have become confused with bird names like godwit and peewit.

7   Editors have felt that although there is no break in the manuscript a substantial piece of narrative is missing. They feel that in the missing stanzas Robin has introduced and described a bad dream. Child locates the gap after line 8, and Dobson and Taylor agree. However, the reason they can reconstruct the notionally missing lines is that (unlike the case in *Robin Hood and the Monk* after line 120) there is no information missing from the poem. In view of the characteristic "leaping and lingering" style of ballads, and the way in which many Robin Hood adventures begin very rapidly after a short nature introduction, there seems in fact no reason other than the fixed ideas of realist-minded scholars to assume a gap here. The text works as it stands in the manuscript.

13   Little John tries to reassure Robin that since dreams are fleeting they do not need to be taken seriously. Dream lore is a popular theme in Middle English poetry; see Chaucer's Nun's Priest's Tale, lines 2907–3156; *The House of Fame*, 1–52; and *The Romaunt of the Rose*, lines 1–20. Like Pertelote in the Nun's Priest's Tale, Little John is giving Robin bad advice.

21   This is a six-line stanza, which can also be identified in several other early texts, e.g., *Adam Bell*, lines 358–63, *Robin Hood and the Potter*, lines 208–13, 254–59, 280–85, *Robin Hood and the Monk*, lines 137–42, as well as several stanzas in the short *Robin and Gandeleyn*.

25   Child inserts *a* between *of* and *wight*, but these early ballads are often very clipped in their utterance (as in line 28), and there is no convincing case for the emendation.

32   *trusty tree*. Presumably a corruption of the phrase "trystyng tree." It also appears as "trystyll" (trestle or platform) tree — presumably suitable for speeches or even hangings. The three notions of *tryst*, *trust*, and *trestle* all embody central concepts of the outlaw band, with its meetings, fidelity, and occasional addresses by the leader.

45   *Barnsdale*. Child emends to *Barnesdale*, but this seems a freely varying spelling at this time.

49   Child omits *owne*.

59   *yeiwe*. Child reads the manuscript, damaged here, as *veiwe* and so, with less certainty, do Dobson and Taylor (1976, p. 142). Under ultra-violet light the word appears to be, as might be expected, *yeiwe*.

70   Dobson and Taylor comment "The confusion of sense in this stanza makes it probable that the text hereabouts is corrupt" (1976, p. 142); it is not clear what they mean by confusion. The action seems straightforward: because John's bow breaks, his inaccurate (and so "vaine," yet still fatal) shot misses the sheriff and hits one of his men.

76   Child reports this line as mostly illegible, but ultra violet light supports his hypothetical reading.

79   This is a long line; Percy remarks that *quoth the sheriff* has probably been added to clarify matters (*Reliques*, 1765, p. 80), yet these opening lines of speech with a speaker added recur in the ballads (see *Gest*, lines 309, 441, 629, 757, 1001, *Potter*, lines 21, 41, 81, 222, 226), and there seem no good grounds to emend; see line 103 below.

88   *lyne*. The lime tree is a linden, a tree that is particularly fragrant when in bloom. The term is used often for trees in general, however.

91   Guy speaks the first line and Robin the next three.

103   Guy pretends to be another forester, who also seeks Robin Hood; Little John uses the same maneuver in *Robin Hood and the Monk*, lines 162–82.

109   MS: *mee*. Ritson, Gutch, and Child emend to *meet*.

129   MS: *on*: *an*, meaning "if" seems a probable emendation.

138   *Gysborne*. Child says that "Gisburne is in the West Riding of Yorkshire, on the borders of Lancashire, seven miles from Clitheroe" (III, 91), but Bellamy suggests that Guy is connected with the village of "Guisborough in the North Riding (known in the middle ages as Giseburne)" (1985, pp. 34–35).

151   MS: *reachles*. Child emends to *reacheles*, presumably on metrical grounds, but this is unnecessary.

161   Percy emends to "backward," but "acward" meaning "back-handed," here spelled *awkwarde*, is common in Middle English.

167   *Irish kniffe*. Presumably a form of hunting knife.

175–76   MS: *Robin did on his gowne of green, / On Syr Guye hee did it throwe*. This does not make sense. Child emends *on* in line 175 to *off*, but this is still very awkward. It is better to assume that having inserted *on* erroneously in line 175 (because of the collocation with *did* in the context of clothing), the scribe then tried to patch line 176 by adding "hee did it." If these notional insertions are omitted, the text has the characteristically condensed tone of the early ballad.

181   MS: *Barnsdale*. As in line 45, Child inserts *e* unnecessarily.

193   *wight*. The MS has "wighty," which Child accepts, but this is probably a confusion of the true reading *wight* and "mighty."

205   Child inserts *hath* before MS *beene*. The manuscript reading is certainly unacceptable, but a better emendation would be *bee*, which a scribe could easily misread as a plural.

218   *shrift*. Robin continues the suggestion that he is to kill Little John and momentarily plays the priest, who hears the dying man's last words, as well as the executioner.

234   Percy euphemized the action by changing the line to "He shott him into the 'backe'-syde."

The Tale of Gamelyn

Introduction

The Tale of Gamelyn survives in twenty-five early manuscripts, yet this is not a sign that it was popular. The poem was added to one version of *The Canterbury Tales* (known as the *cd* group of manuscripts) where it follows the unfinished Cook's Tale, often with a spurious link to make it his second tale. The *cd* connection with *Gamelyn* began very early (Manly and Rickert, 1940, II, 170–72), and it may have been generated at a stage when Chaucer himself had included *Gamelyn* among his papers, with the intention of rewriting it for a suitable character. Nevertheless, there is, as Laura Hibberd stated (1924, p. 156), no sign that Chaucer's own hand was involved in the transmission of the text.

Skeat edited the poem separately in 1884 and included it in an appendix to his *The Complete Works of Geoffrey Chaucer*, relying on what he thought was the best manuscript, Harley 7334. A more recent edition by N. Daniel (in a University of Chicago Ph.D. dissertation, 1967) was based on the Corpus MS. Editorial work on *The Canterbury Tales* has shown these two manuscripts to be unreliable. In the case of the Petworth manuscript of *Gamelyn*, collation shows it to offer the best readings in many instances and only rarely to be in need of emendation: in this version *Gamelyn* on a significant number of occasions seems a better poem: *e.g.*, lines 2–4 which have shorter first half-lines and more attack, especially than Skeat's text; or lines 616–57 where, as Gamelyn and Adam meet the outlaws, the language is a little sharper and the prosody somewhat tighter than in the manuscripts previously used as a base for the published text.

If the source of the text itself is both intriguing and enigmatic, the origin of its content remains obscure. Skeat (1884, p. vii) favored an Anglo-French original as with *Havelock*, but no contender has emerged. Prideaux (1886) felt that the story of *Fulk Fitzwarin* was close to this text, but there is little or no identity of incident. Commentators have linked *Gamelyn* to other robust stories involving physical heroism: W. F. Schirmer felt there was a category of *germanischen romanzen* embracing this text, *King Horn, Havelock,* and *Athelstan* (Mehl, 1968, p. 269, n.17). But unlike these other heroes, Gamelyn has no royal status, and a more thematically oriented connection was made by Ramsey in identifying this poem, *Athelstan, Raoul of Cambrai, Fouke le Fitz Waryn*, and *The Song of Lewes* as "rebel romances" (1983,

p. 93).

This concept has generic implications. Skeat called *Gamelyn* "the older and longer kind of ballad" (1884, p. vii), while others have, like Ramsey, preferred to think of it as a rough and ready romance. Kaeuper (1983, p. 51) refers approvingly to Schmidt and Jacobs' broad definition of the romance (1980, I, 1–7). Pearsall's influential essay on "The Development of Middle English Romance," while not referring to *Gamelyn*, did assert the existence of a category of "epic romance" (1965, p. 111). However, the lack of any kind of aristocratic connection or dealing with women does make *Gamelyn* a difficult member of even such a limited romantic category, and it is tempting to think of the poem, like the *Gest*, *Adam Bell*, and long battle ballads of the sixteenth century such as *Chevy Chase* or *The Battle of Otterburn,* as best described by the term used by Child of the *Gest*, "popular epic" (III, 49).

Some commentators have seen an originary force in historical reality, noting like Sands (1966, p. 155) or detailing like Kaeuper (1983) and Scattergood (1994) the many resemblances to medieval legal practices and conflicts. That might, however, better be seen as a strong contextual feature of a story which, as Dunn notes, is known in folklore as the maltreatment of the youngest child (1967, p. 32) and which appears in romance proper as the *fair unknown*, but in this version deals with inheritance problems of a distinctly fourteenth-century kind.

The date of the poem has not been reconsidered carefully in recent years. Though Lindner offered the thirteenth century (1879, pp. 112–13), Skeat placed it about 1340, feeling its events and legal structures were basically of the late thirteenth and early fourteenth century. That would be a very early date for a secular and satirical English poem of this kind, and later commentators have inched it forward — about the middle of the fourteenth century for the historians Keen (1961, p. 78) and Holt (1989, p. 71), and for Dunn 1350–70 (1967, p. 32). Since the text may have been transmitted no more than once to the source of the surviving manuscripts (judging from the coherence of the existing versions), this period would seem likely, with a preference for the later part of it.

The dialect has always been identified as North Midlands, but Dunn was more precise, nominating the North East Midlands, even perhaps Nottinghamshire (1967, p. 32), which need not imply that the forest in which Gamelyn becomes an outlaw is Sherwood. In fact, the small but noticeable number of words of Scandinavian origin (including *Litheth*, the first word of the whole poem) suggests an origin in a more Danelaw-oriented part of the region, such as Lincolnshire or, perhaps better because less northerly in dialect, Leicestershire, the scene of the notorious outlaw activities of the Folvilles and others much cited in the context of the poem (see Kaeuper [1983, pp. 54–57] and Scattergood [1994, pp. 170–74]). The text itself has no place names, and Gamelyn's family name of Boundys just signifies a boundary of some kind.

Audience has, as with many poems of this kind, remained a problem. Dunn felt it was enough to speak of "the common people" (1967, p. 32) who liked this rough-hewn form, while Holt thought (1989, p. 72) that in this and other respects the text was "more sophisticated" than the *Gest* which he located among the lower gentry and their affiliates. Both views have some force and the error may be to seek one social level to which the text belongs. It appears to invoke a multiple social response in that it brings together the interests of dispossessed landholders in Gamelyn himself, the falsely accused, like the king of the outlaws, upper servitors like Adam who have to decide whom to serve, and the bondsmen who resist the pressures imposed by Gamelyn's vicious eldest brother. This range of interests and audience members spreads out from a composite focal audience described by Kaeuper as an amorphous social level of minor landowners, lesser knights and retainers — those who might at most hobnob with the prior of a nearby religious house or know the sheriff, but whose horizons are essentially local (1983, p. 53).

Barron comments (1987, p. 84) that the text, not unlike fabliau, has a double form, offering Gamelyn both as a "strong arm champion of bourgeois values" and also, pleasing a higher social stratum, as a parody of the middle class as "strong, crude and inherently stupid"; the concept refers to and sophisticates a position suggested in Menkin's article on "Comic Irony and the Sense of Two Audiences in *The Tale of Gamelyn*" (1969). Kaeuper has seen these two elements as being connected: "No doubt the tale was meant to amuse and entertain (admittedly with a very dark variety of humor), but perhaps we can hear echoes of the 'fierce' mocking laughter which Owst detected in the literature of satire and complaint" (1988, p. 336).

The poem's style has been seen as direct rather than subtle, though it is often treated sympathetically. Skeat said the poem worked well if read slowly (1884, p. xxvi), and Sands recommended it be "read aloud" for best effect (1966, p. 156). Skeat noted "the variableness of the metre" (1884, p. xxiii), which is not as simple as Sands suggests in calling it a "seven stress affair" (1966, p. 156). That implies a line of four stresses before and three after the caesura which, as the poem is in couplets, could be taken as a version of ballad meter. But both the actual state of the meter and the frequency of four line syntax units (longer than a ballad stanza) refute this possibility. Skeat noted that many first half lines have three stresses, and this is more visible in the sparer, less scribally inflated, style of the Petworth manuscript, where three stresses before and two after the caesura is the norm, with a number of unstressed or half stressed syllables frequently added, and the occasional "heavy" line. This makes the meter not unlike that found in alliterative poetry, and there is a recurrence, though no regularity, of alliterative phrasing in the poem. In view of its early date and apparently uncourtly audience, this compromise between alliteration and rhyme is not a surprising metrical pattern.

186

The Tale of Gamelyn

The rhymes tend to be quite accurate, and there is less of the *laisse*-like continued rhyme than is to be seen in the *Gest*; when compared with other rhyming poems of the period it is notable how few of the rhymes fall on polysyllabic and French-derived words: only nine according to Lindner's statistics, with another five on the name Gamelyn (1879, pp. 101–06). Equally the "rhyme-breaking" characteristic of Chaucer, where syntax crosses rhyme units, is almost unknown in *Gamelyn*, which tends to march steadily on with two and four line statements, all squarely mapped onto rhyme.

A similarly plain effect is created by the unadorned diction of the poem, and the frequent use of fillers and semi-proverbial statements of the *also mot I thryve* and *soth for to telle* kind. Some thirty of these occur. They, like the quite common "awkward verbal repetitions" (Scattergood, 1994, p. 160), are elements of a style that most commentators have felt to be at least in part oral: clarity and communication are the central elements of the style.

Yet these features can have an effect capable of some subtlety in a context of dynamic meaning. In the opening sequence, as Sir Johan of Boundys lies on his death bed, the text keeps repeating how he lay increasingly *stille* and *syke*. At the same time the poem keeps returning, as he does, to the question of his lands. In performance the passage has considerable power: as the man grows weaker, his lands become mobile, more and more a matter of obsession for him and, as it transpires, others. The identity of landowner and land, the difficult dissolution of that bond and the crucial nature of its re-formation, these issues central to the period and the land-holding classes lie behind the emphatic language of this highly effective opening passage.

If repetition of language can have such a marked effect, the use of imagery — a rare feature — can also strike deep. In general this effect is highly stylized and proverbial, of the *as a wilde lyoun* or *stille as stoon* kind. But in the central fight scene (lines 489–540), where Gamelyn and Adam wreak their revenge on the clerical visitors, a heavy irony frames their violent acts with a quasi-religious signification: Gamelyn sprays them with a *spire*, that is both a club and an asperge; he makes *orders* of them in new ways. As Bennett and Gray remark, the poem can have "a touch of the grimmer humour" (1986, p. 163) found in heroic poetry.

A third range of stylistic vigor is found in the text when a point is emphasized with a strongly colloquial image which also has the force of collective wisdom and so provides generalized support for the hero and his values. When *four and twenty yonge men* form a posse to arrest Gamelyn and Adam after their onslaught on the clergy (line 549), the heroes treat the threat lightly and Adam says they will so welcome the sheriff's men:

That some of hem shal make her beddes in the fenne. (line 584)

The *yonge men* are defeated and some flee. Adam invites them back for *right good wyne drynk*, but one refuses for fear of a specially physical kind of hangover:

It wolde make a mannys brayn to lyen on his hode. (line 594)

Hearing the sheriff is on his way, Gamelyn and Adam leave for the forest, and so the sheriff finds in the house *nyst but non aye* (line 606). The vigorous sequence of colloquial, folkloric images roots the resistance made by Gamelyn and Adam deep in popular discourse, linguistically sustaining the sense that the ordinary people and enduring values are very much on their side.

In terms of structure the poem has quite complex resources within an apparently plain and effective exterior: a "well-told story" (Dunn, 1967, p. 32) is a characteristic description. This, oddly, is not really the case, or not at least in terms of classic realism. The narrative is in fact shot through with incoherences and improbabilities. Why did Gamelyn take so many years to grasp his sorry position — it appears to be sixteen (see line 356)? Why did his brother suddenly lock him out when he went to the wrestling; and how did his brother find safety in the *solar* (line 349 — not the *cellere* as in other texts, including Harley 7334 and Corpus)? Why, on earth, did Adam not set Gamelyn free as soon as they became allies, rather than wait for a public brawl? What precisely makes Gamelyn at the end suddenly return to court to rescue Ote rather than remain free? And what, most of all, leads Gamelyn to give up his quest for his own lands and accept from Ote the position of heir which had been unacceptable when offered by his brother?

It is possible to imagine answers, or at least discussions, relating to these points, but the text does not consider them as important. Rather than a coherent novel-like sequence of action and reaction, the text in fact arranges a series of dramatic encounters, much like the melodramatic surges of action and rhetoric in romance. Adam does not free Gamelyn early simply to generate a splendid brawl with the clerics. Gamelyn returns to court so he can break the judge's arm and then hang the whole jury — to dry in the wind, in another of the poem's brusquely colloquial images, grim irony again.

If the structure in this way prepares high moments of ethical melodrama, the theme is accordingly directed towards such highly flavored moments of violent frustration of the forces of evil. Most commentators have found the poem strong meat, along a scale ranging from Keen's identification of "simple rumbustious energy" (1961, p. 8) to Scattergood's sense of "barbarism" (1994, p. 160). But, as Bennett and Gray point out, there is a purpose to the violence. This is a poem of "rough justice" (1986, p. 163), and Crane remarks that "corruption runs deep in the world of *Gamelyn*, that, to resolve his claim, Gamelyn must move beyond his unsuccessful verbal pleas and the unsupportable local institutions to a direct physical attack on the suborned royal jury" (1986, p. 73).

But whereas most commentators have related Gamelyn's rugged sense of equity to the real processes of medieval law (Kaeuper provides the fullest account, 1983), there is a strong fictional and ideological structure of ethics at the heart of the poem. The disinherited younger son is a common figure in the Middle Ages, generated according to Georges Duby by changes of inheritance practice in the eleventh century (1977). In romance this figure will win both a lady and a land with his prowess and his courtesy. Gamelyn's social standing is less aristocratic, his trajectory less fantastic, and women play no part at all. And whereas the fair unknown will reveal his birth, like Sir Gareth or Lybeaus Desconus, and all will fall into his lap, Gamelyn's late birth, inscribed in his name ("old man's son") is the problem from the beginning. In this moderately realistic context, the author derives a resolution for this "male Cinderella" story (on this see Wittig, 1978, especially Chapter 5, "Speculations and Conclusions," pp. 179–90) not from the fantastic resources of romance but from another uncomfortable reality of medieval life, the outlaws who challenged settled law through the period. Nevertheless they too are romanticized, being as Keen notes (1961, pp. 92–93) somewhat genteel in their forest mode, and also having their leader conveniently removed for Gamelyn's benefit.

Though stripped of his true familial base, with this new *meyné*, Gamelyn is able to exercise lordship and rescue the true elder brother Sir Ote from the corrupt legal hands of the false elder brother Sir Johan. Family is reconstituted with outlaw help, just as the knight's world is rectified in the *Gest*. Then, however, follows a remarkable shift in the story, largely unnoticed by commentators. In this new familial context, both Gamelyn and the story go quietly. With good lordship in place, the younger son's problems are managed without the partition of inheritance that the wise men at the beginning tried to avoid. Old Sir Johan's wishes never come true. For all his heroism and violence, Gamelyn fits back into the family when it is purged of its "shrewed," that is diabolic, bad leader: primogeniture is recuperated and all in the family is again well.

Not only does the text arrive at this consoling conclusion by a series of melodramatic and violent events; these actions also reveal the sub-textual operations of a structure of social and ethical forces that in fact define the ideology of the text. Gamelyn is attended by four categories of value, and it is only at the end that all are benevolent to him and fully at his service: they are strength, family, honor, and law. Through the action he negotiates with these forces as one or the other is either taken from him or made hostile to him. At first a child without strength, having lost his familial role with the death of his father, Gamelyn has no honor and, through his elder brother, law is turned against him. Steadily he regains control over each component of value — though some, like law, are highly elusive. It is only at the very end, when he and Ote reform their family, when he is honored by the king and made an agent of a true law, that his tremendous strength and strong support are no longer agents of social and narrative disruption but belong to and reinforce traditional society.

It is, as Keen noted with some disappointment (1961, p. 93), finally a quite conservative story. As Barron remarks of the author, "his remedy is a change of personnel, not system" (1987, p. 84). Only the church is resisted systematically — or rather its religious orders. Here, as in Langland and Chaucer there is no hostility to parish priests. Hatred of regular clergy and deep knowledge of the ways of the law are the underpinning instrumentalities of *Gamelyn* as a poem, and resistance to wrongful authority is as fully realized here as anywhere in the turbulent literature of the period.

But there remains a distance between this text and those where the outlaw life is central to the theme rather than, as here, merely instrumental to the resolution. Of the gentry rather than a yeoman, seeking land rather than occupying the potent spaces of the forest, without trickster characteristics or being close to natural imagery, Gamelyn is very different from Robin Hood, and his text survives from a period when it seems that the Robin Hood ballads were still entirely oral in medium. There is something gentrified about Gamelyn, thuggish though he might be, whereas the more socially elusive medieval Robin is never clearly tied to a class faction and its ideology.

The power of the myth of the greenwood outlaw worked dialectically with the Gamelyn tradition. At two points, Gamelyn walks in the forest, as Robin does at the start of many a ballad (lines 767 and 783–84). The possibilities of connection were not missed. It seems that Gamelyn's character was attracted towards the Robin Hood saga; *Robyn and Gandelyn* may well be an early example of that process; *Robin Hood and Will Scarlet* certainly is, but at a much later date when such literary rationalization is commonplace. The two traditions interwove thoroughly in the undergrowth of the nineteenth century novel, when the Gamwells of Gamwell Hall provided ample subplot to fill out the three volumes required of a novel, and for which the spare suggestive encounters of the Robin Hood ballads were distinctly unaccommodating (Pierce Egan's *Robin Hood and Little John, or The Merry Men of Sherwood Forest* of 1840 is the classic example). And popular culture did not forget the link: in the Warner Brothers *Adventures of Robin Hood* starring Errol Flynn (Curtiz, 1938), Robin's close friend, resplendent in scarlet, is named Will a Gamwell. A more elusive interface between the two traditions was in the hands of a more culturally elevated artist. The Robin Hood mini-craze of the 1590s theatre eventually produced in 1600 the ludicrous disguise comedy *Looke Aboute You*, notable mostly for the stage direction "Enter Robin Hood in Lady Faukenbridge's nightgown, a turban on his head." The Admiral's Men did good business with this nonsense, building on their triumph with Munday's two Robin Hood plays of 1598–99. The Chamberlain's Men's house writer, William Shakespeare, appears to have responded immediately with that Italianate outlaw play, *As You Like It,* relying on the elaborations Thomas Lodge had imposed on *Gamelyn* in his deeply gentrified and highly euphuized version entitled *Rosalynde* (1590).

Gamelyn has both original force and elusive interrelations with other outlaw texts, even acting as a ghostly link between the works of Chaucer and Shakespeare. Its survival depends on its presence, at some stage, among Chaucer's papers, and it is intriguing to think that he saw something worth his embellishing touch — as he had in a raw fabliau for the Miller or in Boccaccio's cold amatorial enigma for the Franklin. Some have thought it would have been the Yeoman's tale for its forest connections (Skeat, 1884, p. xv, was firm on the point; see also de Lange, 1935, p. 36) and Dunn improbably suggested the Franklin because he was a rural magistrate (1967, p. 32), but Chaucer deals by displaced projections, and it may well be that the reference to Gamelyn refusing to cook for his brother and wielding the pestle as a weapon (lines 92 and 128) was the link through which he intended to develop the propertied dreams of Roger, his tough London scullion.

Speculations aside, it was only that Chaucerian connection which preserved *Gamelyn.* It is, as Keen says "the first outlaw legend which has survived in the English language" (1961, p. 88), an important link in the chain that just survives between the early distressed gentleman sagas of Eustace and Fulk and the plainer English heroes of forest resistance like Robin Hood and Adam Bell. This is a poem whose robust and direct qualities have always been visible, and whose subtleties have largely been overlooked on behalf of its simpler status as historical and legal corroboration. But as the author says *Lithes and listeneth and harkeneth aright*, and in the allusions and elisions of the text there will be heard something more literary, more imaginative, more resonant through time and the outlaw tradition.

Select Bibliography

Texts

Manuscripts: *Gamelyn* is found in twenty-five of the manuscripts of the *Canterbury Tales*, in the *c* and *d* families. It has been edited twice from the manuscript:

Daniel, Neil, ed. *The Tale of Gamelyn: A New Edition*. Indiana University Ph.D., 1967 [from the Corpus manuscript].

Manly, John M., and Edith Rickert. *The Text of the Canterbury Tales Studied on the Basis of All Known Manuscripts*. 8 vols. Chicago: University of Chicago Press, 1940.

Skeat, W. W., ed. *The Tale of Gamelyn*. Oxford: Clarendon Press, 1884 (from Harley 7334).

Gamelyn also appears in two anthologies:

French, W. A., and C. B. Hales, eds. *Middle English Metrical Romances*. New York: Prentice-Hall, 1930. I, 207–35. [Text based on Harley 7334 as printed in Furnivall's edition in the Chaucer Society Publications, vol. 73.]

Sands, Donald B., ed. *Middle English Verse Romances*. New York: Holt Rinehart, 1966. Pp. 154–81. [Combines features of Skeat's and French and Hale's editions.]

Commentary and Criticism

Barron, W. R. J. *Medieval English Romances*. London: Longman, 1987.

Bennett, J. A. W., and D. Gray. *Middle English Literature*. Oxford: Clarendon, 1986.

Crane, Susan. *Insular Romance*. Berkeley: University of California Press, 1986.

Duby, Georges. "Youth in Medieval Society." In *The Chivalrous Society*. Trans. C. Postan. London: Arnold, 1977. Pp. 112–22.

Dunn, C. W. "Romances Derived from English Legend." In *Manual of Writings in Middle English, 1050–1500*. Vol. 1. *Romances*. Ed. J. B. Severs. New Haven: The Connecticut Academy of Arts and Sciences, 1967. Pp. 17–37.

Hibberd, Laura. *Medieval Romance in England*. New York: Oxford University Press, 1924.

Hoffman, Dean A. " 'After Bale Cometh Boote': Narrative Symmetry in the Tale of Gamelyn." *Studia Neophilologica* 60 (1988), 159–66.

The Tale of Gamelyn

Holt, J. C. *Robin Hood*. Second ed. London: Thames and Hudson, 1989.

Kaeuper, Richard. "An Historian's Reading of *The Tale of Gamelyn*." *Medium Ævum* 52 (1983), 51–62.

——. *War, Justice, and Public Order*. Oxford: Clarendon Press, 1988.

Keen, Maurice. *The Outlaws of Medieval Legend*. London: Routledge, 1961.

Lange, Joost de. *The Relation and Development of English and Icelandic Outlaw Traditions*. Haarlem: Willink, 1935.

Lindner, F. "The Tale of Gamelyn." *Englische Studien* 2 (1879), 94–114, 321–43.

Mehl, Dieter. *The Middle English Romances of the Thirteenth and Fourteenth Centuries*. London: Routledge, 1968.

Menkin, Edward Z. "Comic Irony and the Sense of Two Audiences in *The Tale of Gamelyn*." *Thoth* 10 (1969), 41–53.

Pearsall, D. A. "The Development of Middle English Romance." *Medieval Studies* 27 (1965), 91–116.

Prideaux, W. F. "Who Was Robin Hood?" *Notes and Queries*, 7th Series, II (1886), 421–24.

Ramsey, Lee C. *Chivalric Romances*. Bloomington: Indiana University Press, 1983.

Scattergood, John. "*The Tale of Gamelyn*: The Noble Robber as Provincial Hero." In *Readings in Medieval English Romance*. Ed. Carol M. Meale. Cambridge: Brewer, 1994. Pp. 159–94.

Schmidt, A. V. C., and Nicolas Jacobs. *Medieval English Romances*. London: Hodder and Stoughton, 1980.

Shannon, Jr., Edgar F. "Mediaeval Law in *The Tale of Gamelyn*." *Speculum* 28 (1951), 458–64.

Wittig, Susan. *Stylistic and Narrative Structures in the Middle English Romances*. Austin: University of Texas Press, 1978.

The Tale of Gamelyn

Fitt 1

Lithes and listneth and harkeneth aright,	*List and listen and harken closely*
And ye shul here of a doughty knyght;	*hear; brave*
Sire John of Boundes was his name,	
He coude of norture and of mochel game.	*He knew about breeding and sport*
5 Thre sones the knyght had and with his body he wan,	*begot*
The eldest was a moche schrewe and sone bygan.	*wicked rascal; [to show it]*
His brether loved wel her fader and of hym were agast,	*brothers; their*
The eldest deserved his faders curs and had it atte last.	
The good knight his fadere lyved so yore,	*long*
10 That deth was comen hym to and handled hym ful sore.	*tormented him bitterly*
The good knyght cared sore sik ther he lay,	*where*
How his children shuld lyven after his day.	
He had bene wide where but non husbonde he was,	*far and wide; farmer*
Al the londe that he had it was purchas.	
15 Fayn he wold it were dressed amonge hem alle,	*Eagerly; divided; them*
That eche of hem had his parte as it myght falle.	
Thoo sente he in to contrey after wise knyghtes	*Then; the shire*
To helpen delen his londes and dressen hem to-rightes.	*divide; evenly divide*
He sent hem word by letters thei shul hie blyve,	*quickly hasten*
20 If thei wolle speke with hym whilst he was alyve.	*alive*

Whan the knyghtes harden sik that he lay,	*When; heard*
Had thei no rest neither nyght ne day,	
Til thei come to hym ther he lay stille	
On his dethes bedde to abide goddys wille.	
25 Than seide the good knyght seke ther he lay,	
"Lordes, I you warne for soth, without nay,	*truly, without denial*
I may no lenger lyven here in this stounde;	*time*
For thorgh goddis wille deth droueth me to grounde."	*draws*
Ther nas noon of hem alle that herd hym aright,	
30 That thei ne had routh of that ilk knyght,	*pity; same*

194

And seide, "Sir, for goddes love   dismay you nought;
God may don boote of bale   that is now ywrought."   *remedy of evil*
Than speke the good knyght   sik ther he lay,
"Boote of bale God may sende   I wote it is no nay;   *I know there is no denying it*
35   But I beseche you knyghtes   for the love of me,
Goth and dresseth my londes   amonge my sones thre.   *divide*
And for the love of God   deleth not amyss,
And forgeteth not Gamelyne   my yonge sone that is.
Taketh hede to that oon   as wel as to that other;
40   Seelde ye seen eny hier   helpen his brother."   *Seldom you see any heir*

Thoo lete thei the knyght lyen   that was not in hele,   *health*
And wenten into counselle   his londes for to dele;   *divide*
For to delen hem alle to on   that was her thought.   *their intent*
And for Gamelyn was yongest   he shuld have nought.   *nothing*
45   All the londe that ther was   thei dalten it in two,
And lete Gamelyne the yonge   without londe goo,
And eche of hem seide   to other ful loude,
His bretheren myght yeve him londe   whan he good cowde.   *give*
And whan thei had deled   the londe at her wille,   *divided; their*
50   They commen to the knyght   ther he lay stille,
And tolde him anoon   how thei had wrought;   *done*
And the knight ther he lay   liked it right nought.

Than seide the knyght,   "Be Seint Martyne,
For al that ye han done   yit is the londe myne;
55   For Goddis love, neighbours   stondeth alle stille,   *delay all action*
And I wil delen my londe   after myn owne wille.
John, myne eldest sone   shal have plowes fyve,   *(see note)*
That was my faders heritage   whan he was alyve;
And my myddelest sone   fyve plowes of londe,
60   That I halpe forto gete   with my right honde;
And al myn other purchace   of londes and ledes   *tenants*
That I biquethe Gamelyne   and alle my good stedes.   *horses*
And I biseche you, good men   that lawe conne of londe,   *understand*
For Gamelynes love   that my quest stonde."   *bequest*
65   Thus dalt the knyght   his londe by his day,
Right on his deth bed   sik ther he lay;

195

And sone afterward   he lay stoon stille,
And deide whan tyme come   as it was Cristes wille.   *died*

Anoon as he was dede   and under gras grave,   *As soon as*
70   Sone the elder brother   giled the yonge knave;   *beguiled; boy*
He toke into his honde   his londe and his lede,   *tenants*
And Gamelyne him selven   to clothe and to fede.
He clothed him and fedde him   evell and eke wroth,   *badly and also ill*
And lete his londes forfare   and his houses bothe,   *go to ruin*
75   His parkes and his wodes   and did no thing welle;
And sithen he it abought   on his owne felle.   *after; paid for; skin*
So longe was Gamelyne   in his brothers halle,
For the strengest, of good will   they douted hym alle;   *of their own accord; feared*
Ther was noon therinne   neither yonge ne olde,
80   That wolde wroth Gamelyne   were he never so bolde.   *anger*

Gamelyne stood on a day   in his brotheres yerde,
And byganne with his hond   to handel his berde;
He thought on his landes   that lay unsowe,   *unsown*
And his fare okes   that doune were ydrawe;   *pulled down*
85   His parkes were broken   and his deer reved;   *broken into; stolen*
Of alle his good stedes   noon was hym byleved;   *left*
His hous were unhilled   and ful evell dight;   *unroofed; repaired*
Tho thought Gamelyne   it went not aright.   *Then*

Afterward come his brother   walking thare,
90   And seide to Gamelyne,   "Is our mete yare?"   *food ready*
Tho wrathed him Gamelyne   and swore by Goddys boke,   *angered*
"Thow schalt go bake thi self   I wil not be thi coke!"
"What? brother Gamelyne   howe answerst thou nowe?
Thou spekest nevere such a worde   as thou dost nowe."
95   "By feithe," seide Gamelyne   "now me thenketh nede;   *it seems to me necessary*
Of al the harmes that I have   I toke never yit hede.   *I never took notice*
My parkes bene broken   and my dere reved,   *stolen*
Of myn armes ne my stedes   nought is byleved;   *weapons and horses; left*
Alle that my fader me byquathe   al goth to shame,
100   And therfor have thou Goddes curs   brother be thi name!"

The Tale of Gamelyn

	Than spake his brother that rape was and rees,	*who was quick to anger*
	"Stond stille, gadlynge and holde thi pees;	*churl (lowborn, bastard)*
	Thou shalt be fayn to have thi mete and thi wede;	*clothing*
	What spekest thow, gadelinge of londe or of lede?"	*fool; tenants*
105	Than seide Gamelyne, the child so yinge,	*young*
	"Cristes curs mote he have that me clepeth gadelinge!	*may; calls*
	I am no wors gadeling ne no wors wight,	*fellow*
	But born of a lady and gete of a knyght."	*begotten*
	Ne dorst he not to Gamelyn never a foot goo,	
110	But cleped to hym his men and seide to hem thoo,	
	"Goth and beteth this boye and reveth hym his witte,	*beat; rob*
	And lat him lerne another tyme to answere me bette."	*better*
	Than seide the childe yonge Gamelyne,	
	"Cristes curs mote thou have brother art thou myne!	
115	And if I shal algates be beten anoon,	*must in any case*
	Cristes curs mote thou have but thou be that oon!"	*(see note)*
	And anon his brother in that grete hete	*anger*
	Made his men to fette staves Gamelyn to bete.	*fetch*
	Whan every of hem had a staf ynomen,	*everyone; taken*
120	Gamelyn was werre whan he segh hem comen;	*aware; saw*
	Whan Gamelyne segh hem comen he loked overall,	
	And was ware of a pestel stode under the wall;	*club-shaped grinder*
	Gamelyn was light and thider gan he lepe,	*he leapt*
	And droof alle his brotheres men right sone on an hepe	*drove; heap*
125	And loked as a wilde lyon and leide on good wone;	*a good number*
	And whan his brother segh that he byganne to gon;	*saw*
	He fley up into a loft and shette the door fast;	*flew up; shut*
	Thus Gamelyn with his pestel made hem al agast.	*terrified them all*
	Some for Gamelyns love and some for eye,	*for awe (of him)*
130	Alle they droughen hem to halves whan he gan to pleye.	*sides; fight*
	"What now!" seyde Gamelyne, "evel mot ye the!	*may ye prosper ill!*
	Wil ye bygynne contecte and so sone flee?"	*combat*
	Gamelyn sought his brother whider he was flowe,	*fled*
	And seghe where he loked out a wyndowe.	
135	"Brother," sayde Gamelyne "com a litel nere,	
	And I wil teche thee a play at the bokelere."	*buckler (small round shield)*
	His brother him answerde and seide by Seint Richere,	

197

"The while that pestel is in thine honde   I wil come no nere;
Brother, I will make thi pees   I swer by Cristes oore;   *peace; grace*
140   Cast away the pestel   and wrethe the no more."   *anger yourself*
"I most nede," seide Gamelyn,   "wreth me at onys,   *once*
For thou wold make thi men   to breke my bonys,
Ne had I hadde mayn   and myght in myn armes,   *If I had not had power*
To han hem fro me   thei wold have done me harmes."
145   "Gamelyn," seide his brother,   "be thou not wroth,   *angry*
For to sene the han harme   me were right loth;   *loath*
I ne did it not, brother,   but for a fondinge,   *except for a test*
For to loken wher thou art stronge   and art so yenge."   *see whether*
"Come adoune than to me   and graunt me my bone   *request*
150   Of oon thing I wil the axe   and we shal saught sone."   *be reconciled*

Doune than come his brother   that fikel was and felle,   *was deceitful and cruel*
And was swith sore afeerd   of the pestelle.   *very much*
He seide, "Brother Gamelyn   axe me thi bone,   *ask; request*
And loke thou me blame   but I it graunte sone."
155   Than seide Gamelyn,   "Brother, iwys,   *indeed*
And we shul be at one   thou most graunte me this: *If; reconciled*
Alle that my fader me byquath   whilst he was alyve,   *bequeathed*
Thow most do me it have   if we shul not strive."
"That shalt thou have, Gamelyn   I swere be Cristes oore!   *grace*
160   Al that thi fadere the byquathe,   though thou wolde have more;
Thy londe that lith ley   wel it shal be sawe,   *untilled; sown*
And thine houses reised up   that bene leide ful lawe."   *raised*
Thus seide the knyght   to Gamelyn with mouthe,
And thought on falsnes   as he wel couthe.   *knew how to*
165   The knyght thought on tresoun   and Gamelyn on noon,
And wente and kissed his brother   and whan thei were at oon   *reconciled*
Alas, yonge Gamelyne   no thinge he ne wist   *knew*
With such false tresoun   his brother him kist!

Fitt 2

Lytheneth, and listeneth,   and holdeth your tonge,
170   And ye shul here talking   of Gamelyn the yonge.
Ther was there bisiden   cride a wrastelinge,   *announced a wrestling match*

And therfore ther was sette a ramme and a ringe; *[the usual prizes]*
And Gamelyn was in wille to wende therto, *desirous to go*
Forto preven his myght what he coude doo.
175 "Brothere," seide Gamelyn, "by Seint Richere,
Thow most lene me tonyght a litel coursere *lend; swift horse*
That is fresshe for the spore on forto ride; *eager*
I moste on an erande a litel here beside."
"By god!" seide his brothere, "of stedes in my stalle
180 Goo and chese the the best spare noon of hem alle *choose*
Of stedes and of coursers that stoden hem byside;
And telle me, good brother, whider thou wilt ride."
"Here beside, brother, is cried a wrastelinge,
And therfore shal be sette a ram and a ringe;
185 Moche worschip it were brother to us alle, *honor*
Might I the ram and the ringe bringe home to this halle."
A stede ther was sadeled smertly and skete; *quickly and swiftly*
Gamelyn did a peire spores fast on his fete. *put on*
He sette his foote in the stirop the stede he bistrode,
190 And towardes the wrastelinge the yonge childe rode. *squire*

Whan Gamelyn the yonge was riden out atte gate,
The fals knyght his brother loked yit after thate,
And bysought Jesu Crist that is hevene kinge,
He myghte breke his necke in the wrastelinge.
195 As sone as Gamelyn come ther the place was,
He lighte doune of his stede and stood on the gras, *dismounted*
And ther he herde a frankeleyn "weiloway" singe, *woe is me!*
And bygonne bitterly his hondes forto wringe.
"Good man," seide Gamelyn, "whi mast thou this fare? *make; behavior*
200 Is ther no man that may you helpen out of care?" *grief*
"Allas!" seide this frankeleyn, "that ever was I bore!
For twey stalworth sones I wene that I have lore; *two; know; lost*
A champion is in the place that hath wrought me sorowe,
For he hath sclayn my two sones but if God hem borowe. *slain; pledge*
205 I will yeve ten pound by Jesu Christ! and more, *give*
With the nones I fonde a man wolde handel hym sore."
"Good man," seide Gamelyn, "wilt thou wele doon,
Holde my hors the whiles my man drowe of my shoon, *shoes*
And helpe my man to kepe my clothes and my stede,

210	And I wil to place gon to loke if I may spede."	*win*
	"By God!" seide the frankleyn, "it shal be doon;	
	I wil myself be thi man to drowe of thi shoon,	*pull off; shoes*
	And wende thou into place, Jesu Crist the spede,	*you*
	And drede not of thi clothes ne of thi good stede."	

215	Barefoot and ungirt Gamelyn inne came,	
	Alle that were in the place hede of him nam,	*took heed of him*
	Howe he durst aventure him to doon his myght	
	That was so doghty a champion in wrasteling and in fight.	
	Up stert the champioun rapely anon,	*quickly and at once*
220	And toward yonge Gamelyn byganne to gon,	
	And seide, "Who is thi fadere and who is thi sire?	
	For sothe thou art a grete fool that thou come hire!"	
	Gamelyn answerde the champioun tho,	
	"Thowe knewe wel my fadere while he myght goo,	
225	The whiles he was alyve, by seynt Martyn!	
	Sir John of Boundes was his name, and I am Gamelyne."	

	"Felawe," sayde the champion, "so mot I thrive,	*may*
	I knewe wel thi fadere the whiles he was alyve;	
	And thi silf, Gamelyn, I wil that thou it here,	
230	While thou were a yonge boy a moche shrewe thou were."	*mischievous fellow*
	Than seide Gamelyn and swore by Cristes ore,	*grace*
	"Now I am older wexe thou shalt finde me a more!"	*grown; greater (rogue)*
	"By God!" seide the champion, "welcome mote thou be!	*may*
	Come thow onys in myn honde thou shalt nevere the."	*once; thrive*

235	It was wel within the nyght and the mone shone,	
	Whan Gamelyn and the champioun togider gon gone.	
	The champion cast turnes to Gamelyne that was prest,	*holds; ready*
	And Gamelyn stode and bad hym doon his best.	
	Than seide Gamelyn to the champioun,	
240	"Thowe art fast aboute to bringe me adoun;	*very eager*
	Now I have proved mony tornes of thine,	*withstood*
	Thow most," he seide, "oon or two of myne."	
	Gamelyn to the champioun yede smertely anoon,	*went*
	Of all the turnes that he couthe he shewed him but oon,	*knew*
245	And cast him on the lift side that thre ribbes to-brake,	*threw; crushed*

200

And therto his owne arme   that yaf a grete crake.   *gave; crack*
Than seide Gamelyn   smertly anon,
"Shal it bi hold for a cast   or ellis for non?"   *considered; throw*
"By God!" seide the champion,   "whedere it be,
250   He that cometh ones in thi honde   shal he never the!"   *prosper*

Than seide the frankeleyn   that had the sones there,
"Blessed be thou, Gamelyn,   that ever thou bore were!"   *born*
The frankleyn seide to the champioun   on hym stode hym noon eye,
"This is yonge Gamelyne   that taught the this pleye."   *you*
255   Agein answerd the champioun   that liketh no thing wel,   *who was displeased*
"He is alther maister   and his pley is right felle;   *of all; cruel*
Sithen I wrasteled first   it is goon yore,   *a long time*
But I was nevere in my lif   handeled so sore."

Gamelyn stode in the place   anon without serk,   *shirt*
260   And seide, "Yif ther be moo   lat hem come to werk;
The champion that pyned him   to worch sore,
It semeth by his countenance   that he wil no more."   *demeanor; wishes*
Gamelyn in the place   stode stille as stone,
For to abide wrastelinge   but ther come none;
265   Ther was noon with Gamelyn   that wold wrastel more,
For he handeled the champioun   so wonderly sore.   *hard*

Two gentile men   that yemed the place,   *had charge of*
Come to Gamelyn   God yeve him goode grace!   *give*
And seide to him,   "Do on thi hosen and thi shoon,   *Put on*
270   For soth at this tyme   this fare is doon."   *this fair is over*
And than seide Gamelyn,   "So mot I wel fare,
I have not yete halvendele   sold my ware."   *by half*
Thoo seide the champioun,   "So broke I my swere,   *idiom: as I use my neck*
He is a fool that therof bieth   thou selleth it so dere."
275   Tho seide the frankeleyne   that was in moche care,
"Felawe," he saide,   "whi lackest thou this ware?   *blame*
By seynt Jame of Gales   that mony man hath sought,
Yit is it to good chepe   that thou hast bought."   *merchandise*
Thoo that wardeynes were   of that wrastelinge   *Those; umpires*
280   Come and brought Gamelyn   the ramme and the rynge,

201

And Gamelyn bithought him   it was a faire thinge,
And wente with moche joye   home in the mornynge.

His brother see wher he came   with the grete route,   *company*
And bad shitt the gate   and holde hym withoute.   *ordered to be shut*
285 The porter of his lord   was soor agaast,   *afraid*
And stert anoon to the gate   and lokked it fast.   *closed it quickly*

Fitt 3

Now lithenes and listneth   both yonge and olde,   *harken*
And ye schul here gamen   of Gamelyn the bolde.   *sport*
Gamelyn come to the gate   forto have come inne,
290 And it was shette faste   with a stronge pynne;   *shut*
Than seide Gamelyn,   "Porter, undo the yate,   *gate*
For good menys sones   stonden ther ate."
Than answerd the porter   and swore by Goddys berd,   *by God's beard*
"Thow ne shalt, Gamelyne,   come into this yerde."   *yard*
295 "Thow lixt," seide Gamelyne,   "so broke I my chyne!"   *lie; as I may use my chin*
He smote the wikett with his foote   and breke awaie the pyne.   *latch*
The porter seie thoo   it myght no better be,   *saw then*
He sette foote on erth   and bygan to flee.
"By my feye," seide Gamelyn,   "that travaile is ylore,   *that effort is lost*
300 For I am of fote as light as thou   if thou haddest it swore."[1]
Gamelyn overtoke the porter   and his tene wrake,   *anger avenged*
And girt him in the nek   that the boon to-brake,   *struck*
And toke hym by that oon arme   and threwe hym in a welle,
Seven fadme it was depe   as I have herde telle.   *fathoms (i.e., 42 feet deep)*

305 Whan Gamelyn the yonge   thus had plaied his playe,
Alle that in the yerde were   drowen hem awaye;
Thei dredden him ful sore   for werk that he wrought,   *feared*
And for the faire company   that he thider brought.
Gamelyn yede to the gate   and lete it up wide;   *went*
310 He lete inne alle   that gone wolde or ride,

---

[1] *For I am as light of foot as you, even if you swore it to the contrary*

And seide, "Ye be welcome   without eny greve,   *trouble*
For we wil be maisters here   and axe no man leve.   *permission*
Yusterday I lefte,"   seide yonge Gamelyne,
"In my brothers seler   fyve tonne of wyne;   *cellar; barrels of wine*
315   I wil not this company   partyn atwynne,   *part from each other*
And ye wil done after me   while sope is therinne;   *If; any mouthful of liquid*
And if my brother gruche   or make foule chere,   *complain*
Either for spence of mete and drink   that we spende here,   *cost*
I am oure catour   and bere oure alther purs,   *caterer; dearest purse*
320   He shal have for his grucchinge   Seint Maries curs.   *grumbling*
My brother is a nigon,   I swere be Cristes oore,   *niggard (miser); honor*
And we wil spende largely   that he hath spared yore;
And who that make grucchinge   that we here dwelle,
He shal to the porter   into the drowe-welle."   *drawing well*

325   Seven daies and seven nyghtes   Gamelyn helde his feest,   *feast*
With moche solace   was ther noon cheest;   *merriment; quarreling*
In a litel torret   his brother lay steke,   *turret; hidden*
And see hem waast his good   and dorst no worde speke.   *saw; waste*
Erly on a mornynge   on the eight day,
330   The gestes come to Gamelyn   and wolde gone her way.   *and would depart*
"Lordes," seide Gamelyn,   "will ye so hie?   *hurry off*
Al the wyne is not yit dronke   so brouke I myn ye."   *if I thus can use my eye*
Gamelyn in his herte   was ful woo,
Whan his gestes toke her leve   fro hym for to go;
335   He wolde thei had dwelled lenger   and thei seide nay,
But bytaught Gamelyn,   "God and good day."
Thus made Gamelyn his feest   and brought wel to ende,
And after his gestes   toke leve to wende.   *afterward; asked permission to leave*

Fitt 4

Lithen and listen   and holde your tunge,
340   And ye shal here game   of Gamelyn the yonge;   *sport*
Harkeneth, lordingges   and listeneth aright,
Whan alle gestis were goon   how Gamelyn was dight.   *treated*
Alle the while that Gamelyn   held his mangerye,   *feast*
His brothere thought on hym be wroke   with his trecherye.   *to be avenged*

203

345	Whan Gamylyns gestes were riden and goon,	
	Gamelyn stood anon allone frend had he noon;	
	Tho aftere felle sone within a litel stounde,	*happened; time*
	Gamelyn was taken and ful hard ybounde.	
	Forth come the fals knyght out of the solere,	*solar (upper room)*
350	To Gamelyn his brother he yede ful nere,	*went very close*
	And saide to Gamelyn, "Who made the so bold	
	For to stroien the stoor of myn household?"	*waste the supplies*
	"Brother," seide Gamelyn, "wreth the right nought,	*anger you*
	For it is many day gon sith it was bought;	*since it was paid for*
355	For, brother, thou hast had by Seint Richere,	*Richard*
	Of fiftene plowes of londe this sixtene yere,	
	And of alle the beestes thou hast forth bredde,	
	That my fader me byquath on his dethes bedde;	
	Of al this sixtene yere I yeve the the prowe,	*profit*
360	For the mete and the drink that we han spended nowe."	
	Than seide the fals knyght (evel mote he thee!)	*may he have ill luck!*
	"Harken, brothere Gamelyn what I wil yeve the;	
	For of my body, brother, here geten have I none,	*children*
	I wil make the myn here I swere by Seint John."	*heir*
365	"Par fay!" seide Gamelyn "and if it so be,	*"By my faith!"*
	And thou thenk as thou seist God yeelde it the!"	*reward*
	Nothinge wiste Gamelyn of his brother gile;	*knew; guile*
	Therfore he hym bygiled in a litel while.	
	"Gamelyn," seyde he, "oon thing I the telle;	
370	Thoo thou threwe my porter in the drowe-welle,	*When*
	I swore in that wrethe and in that grete moote,	*anger; hostile assembly*
	That thou shuldest be bounde bothe honde and fote;	
	This most be fulfilled my men to dote,	*trick*
	For to holden myn avowe as I the bihote."	*vow as I promised you*
375	"Brother," seide Gamelyn, "as mote I thee!	*as I may prosper*
	Thou shalt not be forswore for the love of me."	
	Tho maden thei Gamelyn to sitte and not stonde,	
	To thei had hym bounde both fote and honde.	*Until*
	The fals knyght his brother of Gamelyn was agast,	*frightened*
380	And sente efter fetters to fetter hym fast.	*fetters; shackle*
	His brother made lesingges on him ther he stode,	*told lies about*

204

And tolde hem that commen inne   that Gamelyn was wode.   *insane*
Gamelyn stode to a post   bounden in the halle,
Thoo that commen inne   loked on hym alle.   *Those who*
385 Ever stode Gamelyn   even upright!   *straight*
But mete and drink had he noon   neither day ne nyght.
Than seide Gamelyn,   "Brother, be myn hals,   *neck*
Now have I aspied   thou art a party fals;   *discovered; partly*
Had I wist the tresoun   that thou hast yfounde,   *known; invented*
390 I wold have yeve strokes   or I had be bounde!"   *given blows; before*

Gamelyn stode bounde   stille as eny stone;
Two daies and two nyghtes   mete had he none.   *food*
Than seide Gamelyn   that stood ybounde stronge,
"Adam Spencere me thenketh   I faste to longe;
395 Adam Spencere   now I biseche the,
For the moche love   my fadere loved the,   *great*
If thou may come to the keys   lese me out of bonde,   *release; bonds*
And I wil part with the   of my free londe."   *divide*
Than seide Adam   that was the spencere,   *officer in charge of provisions*
400 "I have served thi brother   this sixtene yere,
Yif I lete the gone   out of his boure,   *chamber*
He wold saye afterwardes   I were a traitour."
"Adam," seide Gamelyn,   "so brouke I myn hals!   *as I use my neck!*
Thow schalt finde my brother   at the last fals;   *false*
405 Therfore brother Adam   lose me out of bondes,   *free*
And I wil parte with the   of my free londes."
"Up such forward,"   seide Adam, "ywis,   *Upon that agreement; certainly*
I wil do therto   al that in me is."
"Adam," seide Gamelyn,   "as mote I the,   *as I hope to thrive*
410 I wil holde the covenaunt   and thou wil me."   *if thou will do also with me*

Anoon as Adams lord   to bed was goon,   *As soon as*
Adam toke the kayes   and lete Gamelyn out anoon;
He unlocked Gamelyn   both hondes and fete,
In hope of avauncement   that he hym byhete.   *advancement; promised*
415 Than seide Gamelyn,   "Thonked be Goddis sonde!   *God's Providence*
Nowe I am lose   both fote and honde;
Had I nowe eten   and dronken aright,
Ther is noon in this hous   shuld bynde me this nyght."

Adam toke Gamelyn   as stille as eny stone,
420 And ladde him into the spence   raply anon,   *pantry; quickly*
And sette him to sopere   right in a privey styde,   *secret place*
He bad him do gladly   and so he dide.

Anoon as Gamelyn   had eten wel and fyne,   *finely*
And therto y-dronken wel   of the rede wyne,
425 "Adam," seide Gamelyn,   "what is nowe thi rede?   *advice*
Or I go to my brother   and gerd of his heed?"   *Shall I go; strike off*
"Gamelyn," seide Adam,   "it shal not be so.
I can teche the a rede   that is worth the twoo.   *plan; that's worth two (of yours)*
I wote wel for soth   that this is no nay,   *know; denying*
430 We shul have a mangerye   right on Sonday;   *banquet*
Abbotes and priours   mony here shul be,
And other men of holy chirch   as I telle the;
Thou shal stonde up by the post   as thou were bounde fast,   *as if; tightly*
And I shal leve hem unloke   that away thou may hem cast.
435 Whan that thei han eten   and wasshen her handes,   *washed*
Thow shalt biseche hem alle   to bringe the oute of bondes;   *beseech*
And if thei willen borowe the   that were good game,   *go bail for you*
Than were thou out of prisoun   and out of blame;
And if ecche of hem   saye to us nay,
440 I shal do another   I swere by this day!   *I shall try another course*
Thow shalt have a good staf   and I wil have another,
And Cristes curs haf that on   that failleth that other!"

"Ye for God," seide Gamelyn,   "I say it for me,
If I faille on my side   evel mot I thee!
445 If we shul algate   assoile hem of her synne,   *absolve*
Warne me, brother Adam,   whan we shul bygynne."
"Gamelyn," seid Adam,   "by Seinte Charité,
I wil warne the biforn   whan it shal be;
Whan I winke on the   loke for to gone,   *wink at you*
450 And caste away thi fetters   and come to me anone."
"Adam," seide Gamelyn,   "blessed be thi bonys!
That is a good counseill   yeven for the nonys;   *given for the occasion*
Yif thei warne the me   to bringe out of bendes,   *forbid you; bonds*
I wil sette good strokes   right on her lendes."   *loins*

455	Whan the Sonday was comen and folk to the feest,	
	Faire thei were welcomed both leest and mest;	*both high and low*
	And ever as thei at the haldore come inne,	*hall door*
	They casten her yen on yonge Gamelyn.	*their eyes*
	The fals knyght his brother ful of trecherye,	
460	Al the gestes that ther were at the mangerye,	*at the banquet*
	Of Gamelyn his brother he tolde hem with mouthe	
	Al the harme and the shame that he telle couthe.	*could*
	Whan they were yserved of messes two or thre,	*courses*
	Than seide Gamelyn, "How serve ye me?	
465	It is not wel served by God that alle made!	
	That I sitte fastinge and other men make glade."	*fasting (i.e., starving)*

	The fals knyght his brother ther as he stode,	
	Told to all the gestes that Gamelyn was wode;	*insane*
	And Gamelyn stode stille and answerde nought,	
470	But Adames wordes he helde in his thought.	
	Thoo Gamelyn gan speke doolfully withalle	*dolefully indeed*
	To the grete lordes that seton in the halle:	
	"Lordes," he seide, "for Cristes passioun,	
	Helpe to bringe Gamelyn out of prisoun."	
475	Than seide an abbot, sorowe on his cheke,	
	"He shal have Cristes curs and Seinte Maries eke,	*also*
	That the out of prison beggeth or borowe,	
	And ever worth him wel that doth the moche sorowe."	*(see note)*
	After that abbot than speke another,	
480	"I wold thine hede were of though thou were my brother!	*head were cut off*
	Alle that the borowe foule mot hem falle!"	*(see note)*
	Thus thei seiden alle that were in the halle.	

	Than seide a priour, evel mote he threve!	
	"It is grete sorwe and care boy that thou art alyve."	*alive*
485	"Ow!" seide Gamelyn, "so brouke I my bone!	*so profits my petition!*
	Now have I spied that frendes have I none	*discovered*
	Cursed mote he worth both flesshe and blood,	*Cursed may he be*
	That ever doth priour or abbot eny good!"	*may do*

	Adam the spencere took up the clothe,	
490	And loked on Gamelyn and segh that he was wrothe;	*saw; angry*

	Adam on the pantry litel he thought,	*did not think at all*
	And two good staves to the halle door he brought,	*cudgels*
	Adam loked on Gamelyn and he was warre anoon,	*aware at once*
	And cast away the fetters and bygan to goon;	*move*
495	Whan he come to Adam he took that on staf,	*one*
	And bygan to worch and good strokes yaf.	*work; gave*
	Gamelyn come into the halle and the spencer bothe,	
	And loked hem aboute as thei hadden be wrothe;	*as if; angry*
	Gamelyn spreyeth holy watere with an oken spire,	*(see note)*
500	That some that stode upright felle in the fire.	
	Ther was no lewe man that in the halle stode,	*ignorant (i.e., layman)*
	That wolde do Gamelyn enything but goode,	
	But stoden bisides and lete hem both wirche,	*aside; work*
	For thei had no rewthe of men of holy chirche;	*pity*
505	Abbot or priour, monk or chanoun,	*canon*
	That Gamelyn overtoke anoon they yeden doun	*fell*
	Ther was noon of alle that with his staf mette,	
	That he ne made hem overthrowe to quyte hem his dette.	*paid them*

	"Gamelyn," seide Adam, "for Seinte Charité,	
510	Pay good lyveré for the love of me,	*pay a liberal allowance (of blows)*
	And I wil kepe the door so ever here I masse!	*guard; as sure as I hear Mass*
	Er they bene assoilled ther shal non passe."	*Before they have been absolved*
	"Doute the not," seide Gamelyn, "whil we ben ifere,	*Fear you not; together*
	Kepe thow wel the door and I wil wirche here;	*work*
515	Bystere the, good Adam, and lete none fle,	*Stir thyself*
	And we shul telle largely how mony that ther be."	*count fully*
	"Gamelyn," seide Adam, "do hem but goode;	*do them only good*
	Thei bene men of holy churche drowe of hem no blode	
	Save wel the crownes and do hem no harmes,	*Respect their tonsures*
520	But breke both her legges and sithen her armes."	*then their*

	Thus Gamelyn and Adam wroughte ryght faste,	*worked*
	And pleide with the monkes and made hem agaste.	
	Thidere thei come ridinge joly with swaynes,	*servants*
	And home ayein thei were ladde in cartes and waynes.	*farm wagons*
525	Tho thei hadden al ydo than seide a grey frere,	*friar*
	"Allas! sire abbot what did we nowe here?	
	Whan that we comen hidere it was a colde rede,	*bad advice*

Us had be bet at home   with water and breed."   *better off*
While Gamelyn made orders   of monke and frere,
530 Evere stood his brother   and made foule chere;   *acted distraught*
Gamelyn up with his staf   that he wel knewe,
And girt him in the nek   that he overthrewe;   *struck; fell down*
A litel above the girdel   the rigge-boon he barst;   *waist; backbone he broke*
And sette him in the fetters   theras he sat arst.   *shackles; where he sat before*
535 "Sitte ther, brother," seide Gamelyn,
"For to colen thi body   as I did myn."   *cool*
As swith as thei had wroken hem   on her foon,   *soon; avenged themselves; foes*
Thei asked water   and wasshen anon,   *asked for; washed*
What some for her love   and some for her awe,   *because of fear*
540 Alle the servantes served hem   on the beste lawe.   *manner*
The sherreve was thennes   but fyve myle,   *thence; only*
And alle was tolde him   in a lytel while,
Howe Gamelyn and Adam   had ydo a sorye rees,   *made a grievous attack*
Boundon and wounded men   ayeinst the kingges pees;   *against the king's peace*
545 Tho bygan sone   strif for to wake,   *Then; at once*
And the shereff about   Gamelyn forto take.   *went about*

Fitt 5

Now lithen and listen   so God geve you good fyne!   *ending*
And ye shul here good game   of yonge Gamelyne.
Four and twenty yonge men   that helde hem ful bolde,   *considered themselves*
550 Come to the shiref   and seide that thei wolde
Gamelyn and Adam   fette by her fay;   *fetch; their faith*
The sheref gave hem leve   soth for to say;   *permission*
Thei hiden fast   wold thei not lynne,   *hurried; tarry*
To thei come to the gate   there Gamelyn was inne.   *Until; where*
555 They knocked on the gate   the porter was nyghe,   *close at hand*
And loked out atte an hool   as man that was scleghe.   *cautious*
The porter hadde bihold hem   a litel while,
He loved wel Gamelyn   and was dradde of gyle,   *fearful of guile*
And lete the wikett   stonde ful stille,   *small door or window; fastened up*
560 And asked hem without   what was her wille.
For all the grete company   speke but oon,
"Undo the gate, porter   and lat us in goon."

Than seide the porter,   "So brouke I my chyn,
Ye shul saie youre erand   er ye come inne."

565   "Sey to Gamelyn and Adam   if theire wil be,   *if it be their will*
       We wil speke with hem   two wordes or thre."
       "Felawe," seide the porter,   "stonde ther stille,
       And I wil wende to Gamelyn   to wete his wille."   *go; know*
       Inne went the porter   to Gamelyn anoon,
570   And saide, "Sir, I warne you   here ben comen youre foon;   *foes*
       The shireves men   bene at the gate,
       Forto take you both   ye shul not scape."   *escape*
       "Porter," seide Gamelyn,   "so mote I the!   *as I may thrive*
       I wil alowe thi wordes   whan I my tyme se.   *praise; see a chance*
575   Go ageyn to the gate   and dwelle with hem a while,   *dally*
       And thou shalt se   right sone porter, a gile."   *trick*

       "Adam," seide Gamelyn,   "hast the to goon;   *get ready to go*
       We han foo men mony   and frendes never oon;   *many foes; not one*
       It bene the shireves men   that hider bene comen,
580   Thei ben swore togidere   that we shal be nomen."   *taken*
       "Gamelyn," seide Adam,   "hye the right blyve,   *hasten you quickly*
       And if I faile the this day   evel mot I thrive!
       And we shul so welcome   the shyreves men,
       That some of hem shal make   her beddes in the fenne."   *them; fen (mud)*
585   At a postern gate   Gamelyn out went,   *rear gate*
       And a good cartstaf   in his hondes hent;   *tongue or shaft of a cart; seized*
       Adam hent sone   another grete staff
       For to helpen Gamelyne   and good strokes yaf.   *gave*
       Adam felled tweyn   and Gamelyn thre,   *knocked down two*
590   The other sette fete on erthe   and bygan to flee.   *others*
       "What," seide Adam,   "so evere here I masse!
       I have right good wyne,   drynk er ye passe!"
       "Nay, by God!" seide thei,   "thi drink is not goode,
       It wolde make a mannys brayn   to lyen on his hode."   *(see note)*

595   Gamelyn stode stille   and loked hym aboute,
       And seide "The shyref cometh   with a grete route."   *company*
       "Adam," seyde Gamelyn   "what bene now thi redes?   *suggestions*
       Here cometh the sheref   and wil have our hedes."

Adam seide to Gamelyn,   "My rede is now this,

600 Abide we no lenger   lest we fare amys: *badly*

I rede we to wode gon   er we be founde,   *before*

Better is ther louse   than in the toune bounde."   *free*

Adam toke by the honde   yonge Gamelyn;

And every of hem dronk   a draught of wyn,   *each*

605 And after token her cours   and wenten her way;

Tho fonde the scherreve   nyst but non aye.   *Then; nest; eggs*

The shirrive light doune   and went into halle,   *dismounted from his horse*

And fonde the lord fetred   faste withalle.

The shirreve unfetred hym   right sone anoon,

610 And sente aftere a leche   to hele his rigge boon.   *doctor; backbone*

Lat we now the fals knyght   lye in hys care,   *grief*

And talke we of Gamelyn   and of his fare.   *fortune*

Gamelyn into the wode   stalked stille,   *walked cautiously*

And Adam Spensere   liked right ille;   *was not pleased*

Adam swore to Gamelyn,   "By Seint Richere,

615 Now I see it is mery   to be a spencere,

Yit lever me were   kayes to bere,   *I would rather; keys*

Than walken in this wilde wode   my clothes to tere."

"Adam," seide Gamelyn,   "dismay the right nought;   *don't be alarmed*

Mony good mannys child   in care is brought."   *sorrow*

620 As thei stode talkinge   bothen in fere,   *together*

Adam herd talking of men   and right nyghe hem thei were.   *near them*

Tho Gamelyn under wode   loked aright,

Sevene score of yonge men   he seye wel ydight;   *well armed*

Alle satte at the mete   compas aboute.   *food; in a circle*

625 "Adam," seide Gamelyn,   "now have I no doute,   *fear*

Aftere bale cometh bote   thorgh Goddis myght;   *after evil comes good*

Me think of mete and drynk   I have a sight."

Adam loked thoo   under wode bough,

And whan he segh mete   was glad ynogh;   *saw*

630 For he hoped to God   to have his dele,   *share*

And he was sore alonged   after a mele.   *sorely longing for*

As he seide that worde   the mayster outlawe

Saugh Adam and Gamelyn   under the wode shawe.   *thicket in the woods*

"Yonge men," seide the maistere,   "by the good Rode,   *Cross*

635 I am ware of gestes God send us goode;   *aware of guests*
   Yond ben twoo yonge men wel ydight,   *Yonder; well armed*
   And parenture ther ben mo whoso loked right.   *perhaps*
   Ariseth up, yonge men and fette hem to me;   *fetch them*
   It is good that we weten what men thei be."   *know*
640 Up ther sterten sevene from the dynere,
   And metten with Gamelyn and Adam Spencere.
   Whan thei were nyghe hem than seide that oon,
   "Yeeldeth up, yonge men your bowes and your floon." *arrows*
   Than seide Gamelyn that yong was of elde,   *age*
645 "Moche sorwe mote thei have that to you hem yelde!
   I curs noon other but right mysilve;
   Thoo ye fette to you fyve than be ye twelve!"   *(see note)*
   Whan they harde by his word that myght was in his arme,
   Ther was noon of hem that wolde do hym harme,
650 But seide to Gamelyn myldely and stille,
   "Cometh afore our maister and seith to hym your wille."
   "Yong men," seide Gamelyn, "be your lewté,   *loyalty*
   What man is youre maister that ye with be?"
   Alle thei answerd without lesing,   *lying*
655 "Our maister is crowned of outlawe king."
   "Adam," seide Gamelyn, "go we in Cristes name;
   He may neither mete ne drink warne us for shame. *refuse*
   If that he be hende and come of gentil blood,   *courteous*
   He wil yeve us mete and drink and do us som gode."
660 "By Seint Jame!" seide Adam, "what harme that I gete, *whatever*
   I wil aventure me that I had mete."   *food*

   Gamelyn and Adam went forth in fere,   *together*
   And thei grette the maister that thei fond there.   *greeted*
   Than seide the maister king of outlawes,
665 "What seche ye, yonge men, under the wode shawes?"
   Gamelyn answerde the king with his croune,
   "He most nedes walk in feeld that may not in toune.
   Sire, we walk not here no harme to doo,
   But yif we mete a deer to shete therto,   *shoot*
670 As men that bene hungry and mow no mete fynde, *may no food find*
   And bene harde bystad under wode lynde." *beset; in the forest*
   Of Gamelyns wordes the maister had reuthe,   *pity*

	And seide, "Ye shul have ynow have God my trouth!"	*enough*
675	He bad hem sitte doun for to take rest;	
	And bad hem ete and drink and that of the best.	
	As they eten and dronken wel and fyne,	
	Than seide on to another, "This is Gamelyne."	
	Tho was the maistere outlaw into counseile nome,	*Then; taken*
680	And tolde howe it was Gamelyn that thider was come.	
	Anon as he herd how it was byfalle,	*happened*
	He made him maister under hym over hem alle.	
	Withinne the thridde weke hym come tydinge,	*third week; tidings came to him*
	To the maistere outlawe that was her kinge,	*who was their king*
685	That he shuld come home his pees was made;	
	And of that good tydinge he was ful glade.	
	Thoo seide he to his yonge men soth forto telle,	
	"Me bene comen tydinges I may no lenger dwelle."	*tarry*
	Tho was Gamelyn anoon withoute taryinge,	*delay*
690	Made maister outlawe and crowned her kinge.	*their*
	Whan Gamelyn was crowned king of outlawes,	
	And walked had a while under the wode shawes,	
	The fals knyght his brother was sherif and sire,	
	And lete his brother endite for hate and for ire.	*had; indicted*
695	Thoo were his boond men sory and no thing glade,	*serfs*
	Whan Gamelyn her lord wolfeshede was made;	*(see note)*
	And sente out of his men wher thei might hym fynde,	*wherever*
	For to go seke Gamelyne under the wode lynde,	
	To telle hym tydinge the wynde was wente,	*changed*
700	And al his good reved and al his men shente.	*robbed; badly treated*
	Whan thei had hym founden on knees thei hem setten,	
	And adoune with here hodes and her lord gretten;	*drew down their hoods*
	"Sire, wreth you not for the good Rode,	*Cross*
	For we han brought you tyddyngges but thei be not gode.	
705	Now is thi brother sherreve and hath the bayly,	*power (of the sheriff)*
	And hath endited the and wolfesheed doth the crye."	
	"Allas!" seide Gamelyn, "that ever I was so sclak	*careless*
	That I ne had broke his nek whan I his rigge brak!	
	Goth, greteth wel myn husbondes and wif,	*the people of my estates*
710	I wil be at the nexte shyre have God my lif!"	*(see note)*
	Gamelyn come redy to the nexte shire,	

And ther was his brother   both lord and sire.

Gamelyn boldely come into   the mote halle,   *hall of justice*

And putte adoun his hode   amonge tho lordes alle;

715   "God save you, lordinggs   that here be!

But broke bak sherreve   evel mote thou thee!   *broken-back*

Whi hast thou don me   that shame and vilenye,

For to lat endite me   and wolfeshede do me crye?"

Thoo thoghte the fals knyght   forto bene awreke,   *Then; avenged*

720   And lette Gamelyn   most he no thinge speke;   *hindered; not allowed to speak*

Might ther be no grace   but Gamelyn atte last   *mercy*

Was cast in prison   and fettred faste.

Gamelyn hath a brothere   that highte Sir Ote,   *was called*

Als good an knyght and hende   as might gon on foote.   *As; courteous*

725   Anoon yede a massager   to that good knyght   *went*

And tolde him altogidere   how Gamelyn was dight.   *treated*

Anoon whan Sire Ote herd   howe Gamelyn was dight,

He was right sory   and no thing light,   *not at all happy*

And lete sadel a stede   and the way name,   *had saddled; took*

730   And to his tweyne bretheren   right sone he came.   *two*

"Sire," seide Sire Ote   to the sherreve thoo,

"We bene but three bretheren   shul we never be mo;   *more*

And thou hast prisoned   the best of us alle;

Such another brother   evel mote hym byfalle!"

735   "Sire Ote," seide the fals knyght,   "lat be thi cors;   *curse*

By God, for thi wordes   he shal fare the wors;   *because of; worse*

To the kingges prisoun   he is ynome,   *taken*

And ther he shal abide   to the justice come."   *until*

"Par de!" seide Sir Ote,   "better it shal be;   *"By God!"*

740   I bid hym to maynprise   that thou graunte me   *I demand bail for him*

To the next sitting   of delyveraunce,   *legal hearing*

And lat than Gamelyn   stonde to his chaunce."

"Brother, in such a forward   I take him to the;   *agreement; commit*

And by thine fader soule   that the bigate and me,

745   But he be redy   whan the justice sitte,   *Unless*

Thou shalt bere the juggement   for al thi grete witte."

"I graunte wel," seide Sir Ote,   "that it so be.

Lat delyver him anoon   and take hym to me."   *Have him freed; give*

	Tho was Gamelyn delyvered to Sire Ote, his brother;	
750	And that nyght dwelled the oon with the other.	
	On the morowe seide Gamelyn to Sire Ote the hende,	*courteous*
	"Brother," he seide, "I mote forsoth from you wende	*go*
	To loke howe my yonge men leden her liff,	*see; lead their*
	Whedere thei lyven in joie or ellis in striff."	
755	"By God" seyde Sire Ote, "that is a colde rede,	*bad plan*
	Nowe I se that alle the carke schal fal on my hede;	*responsibility*
	For whan the justice sitte and thou be not yfounde,	
	I shal anoon be take and in thi stede ibounde."	*taken; place*
	"Brother," seide Gamelyn, "dismay you nought,	
760	For by saint Jame in Gales that mony men hath sought,	*Galicia, Spain*
	Yif that God almyghty holde my lif and witte,	*maintain*
	I wil be redy whan the justice sitte."	
	Than seide Sir Ote to Gamelyn, "God shilde the fro shame;	*shield*
	Come whan thou seest tyme and bringe us out of blame."	

Fitt 6

	Litheneth and listeneth and holde you stille,	
765	And ye shul here how Gamelyn had al his wille.	
	Gamelyn went under the wode-ris,	*forest branches*
	And fonde ther pleying yenge men of pris.	*worth*
	Tho was yonge Gamelyn right glad ynoughe,	
770	Whan he fonde his men under wode boughe.	
	Gamelyn and his men talkeden in fere,	*together*
	And thei hadde good game her maister to here;	*their; hear*
	His men tolde him of aventures that they had founde,	
	And Gamelyn tolde hem agein howe he was fast bounde.	
775	While Gamelyn was outlawe had he no cors;	*curse (public criticism)*
	There was no man that for him ferde the wors,	
	But abbots and priours, monk and chanoun;	*Except*
	On hem left he nought whan he myghte hem nome.	*take*
	While Gamelyn and his men made merthes ryve,	*abundant joy*
780	The fals knyght his brother evel mot he thryve!	*evil may he thrive!*
	For he was fast aboute both day and other,	*very busy*
	For to hiren the quest to hongen his brother.	*bribe; inquest*

Gamelyn stode on a day   and byheeld

The wodes and the shawes   and the wild feeld,   *groves*

785 He thoughte on his brothere   how he hym byhette   *promised*

That he wolde be redy   whan the justice sette;   *sits*

He thought wel he wold   without delay,

Come tofore the justice   to kepen his day,   *appointment*

And saide to his yonge men,   "Dighteth you yare,   *Make yourself ready*

790 For whan the justice   sitte we most be thare,

For I am under borowe   til that I come,   *bail*

And my brother for me   to prison shal be nome."   *taken*

"By Seint Jame!" seide his yonge men,   "and thou rede therto,   *advise*

Ordeyn how it shal be   and it shal be do."   *done*

795 While Gamelyn was comyng   ther the justice satte,

The fals knyght his brother   forgate he not that,

To hire the men of the quest   to hangen his brother;   *bribe; inquest*

Thoughe thei had not that oon   thei wolde have that other

Tho come Gamelyn   from under the wode-ris,

800 And brought with hym   yonge men of pris   *excellence*

"I see wel," seide Gamelyn,   "the justice is sette;

Go aforn, Adam,   and loke how it spette."   *before; what is happening*

Adam went into the halle   and loked al aboute,

He segh there stonde lordes   grete and stoute,   *bold*

805 And Sir Ote his brother   fetred ful fast;

Thoo went Adam out of halle   as he were agast.   *as if he were terrified*

Adam seide to Gamelyn   and to his felawes alle,

"Sir Ote stont fetered   in the mote halle."

"Yonge men," seide Gamelyn,   "this ye heeren alle:

810 Sir Ote stont fetered   in the mote halle.

If God geve us grace   well forto doo,   *to succeed*

He shal it abigge   that it broughte therto."   *pay for*

Than seide Adam   that lockes had hore,   *who had gray hair*

"Cristes curs mote he have   that hym bonde so sore!

815 And thou wilt, Gamelyn,   do after my rede,   *If; plan*

Ther is noon in the halle   shal bere awey his hede."

"Adam," seide Gamelyn,   "we wil not do soo,

We wil slee the giltif   and lat the other go.   *others*

I wil into the halle   and with the justice speke;

820 Of hem that bene giltif   I wil ben awreke.   *avenged*

216

Lat no skape at the door   take, yonge men, yeme;   *escape, take . . . heed*
For I wil be justice this day   domes to deme.   *to hand down verdicts*
God spede me this day   at my newe werk!
Adam, com with me   for thou shalt be my clerk."
825   His men answereden hym   and bad don his best,
"And if thou to us have nede   thou shalt finde us prest;   *ready*
We wil stonde with the   while that we may dure;   *endure*
And but we worchen manly   pay us none hure."   *Unless; wages*
"Yonge men," seid Gamelyn,   "so mot I wel the!   *thrive*
830   A trusty maister   ye shal fynde me."

Right there the justice   satte in the halle,
Inne went Gamelyn   amonges hem alle.
Gamelyn lete unfetter   his brother out of bende.   *had unfettered; bonds*
Than seide Sire Ote   his brother that was hende,   *courteous*
835   "Thow haddest almost, Gamelyn,   dwelled to longe,   *waited*
For the quest is out on me   that I shulde honge."   *verdict*
"Brother," seide Gamelyn,   "so God yeve me good rest!
This day shul thei be honged   that ben on the quest;   *inquest*
And the justice both   that is the juge man,   *judge*
840   And the sherreve also   thorgh hym it bigan.
Than seide Gamelyn   to the justise,
"Now is thi power don,   the most nedes rise;   *finished, you must*
Thow hast yeven domes   that bene evel dight,   *verdicts; unjustly given*
I will sitten in thi sete   and dressen hem aright."   *arrange them correctly*
845   The justice satte stille   and roos not anon;
And Gamelyn cleved   his chekebon;   *broke*
Gamelyn toke him in his armes   and no more spake,
But threwe hym over the barre   and his arme brake.   *railing*
Dorst noon to Gamelyn   seie but goode,
850   Forfeerd of the company   that without stoode.   *Terrified*

Gamelyn sette him doun   in the justise sete,
And Sire Ote his brother by him   and Adam at his fete.
Whan Gamelyn was sette   in the justise stede,   *place*
Herken of a bourde   that Gamelyn dede.   *Listen; jest*
855   He lete fetter the justise   and his fals brother,   *had fettered*
And did hem com to the barre   that on with that other.   *made; bar of justice*
Whan Gamelyn had thus ydon   had he no rest,

217

Til he had enquered who was on his quest *found out; jury*
Forto demen his brother Sir Ote for to honge;
860   Er he wist what thei were hym thought ful longe. *Until he knew who*
But as sone as Gamelyn wist where thei were,
He did hem everechon fetter in fere, *had; fettered together*
And bringgen hem to the barre and setten in rewe; *row*
"By my feith!" seide the justise, "the sherrive is a shrewe!"
865   Than seide Gamelyn to the justise,
"Thou hast yove domes of the worst assise; *given judgments; worst court of law*
And the twelve sesoures that weren on the quest, *jurors*
Thei shul be honged this day so have I good rest!"
Than seide the sheref to yonge Gamelyn,
870   "Lord, I crie thee mercie brother art thou myn."
"Therfor," seide Gamelyn, "have thou Cristes curs,
For and thow were maister I shuld have wors." *if*

For to make shorte tale and not to longe,
He ordeyned hym a quest of his men stronge;
875   The justice and the shirreve both honged hie, *high*
To weyven with the ropes and the winde drye; *To swing on*
And the twelve sisours (sorwe have that rekke!) *misery to anyone who cares!*
Alle thei were honged fast by the nekke.
Thus endeth the fals knyght with his trecherye,
880   That ever had lad his lif in falsenesse and folye.
He was honged by the nek and not by the purs,
That was the mede that he had for his faders curs. *reward*

Sire Ote was eldest and Gamelyn was yenge, *young*
Wenten to her frendes and passed to the kinge;
885   Thei maden pees with the king of the best sise. *assize*
The king loved wel Sir Ote and made hym justise.
And after, the king made Gamelyn in est and in west,
The cheef justice of his free forest;
Alle his wight yonge men the king foryaf her gilt, *bold*
890   And sithen in good office the king hath hem pilt, *after; put*
Thus wane Gamelyn his land and his lede, *won (back); tenants*
And wreke him on his enemyes and quytte hem her mede; *avenged; reward*
And Sire Ote his brother made him his heire,
And sithen wedded Gamelyn a wif good and faire;

The Tale of Gamelyn

895   They lyved togidere   the while that Crist wolde,
And sithen was Gamelyn   graven under molde.   *buried under earth*
And so shull we alle   may ther no man fle:
God bring us to that joye   that ever shal be!

Notes

For discussion of textual issues in *Gamelyn* see Stephen Knight, " 'herkeneth aright': Reading *Gamelyn* for Text Not Context." In *Tradition and Transformation in Medieval Romance*. Ed. Rosalind Field. Cambridge: D. S. Brewer, 1999. Pp. 15–28.

1   Fitt titles and numbers are not marked in the Petworth manuscript, but spaces in the manuscript and the formulaic *Lithes and listeneth* opening (and its variants) make it clear where a new fitt begins; there are six.

3   The name appears to be spelt in the manuscript *Bonndes*, but in line 348 *ybounde* is written in just the same way, and this should be taken as a sign of the ambiguity possible in these minim-based letters (in much the same way *Arveragus* in Chaucer's Franklin's Tale appears to be spelt *Ameragus* throughout the excellent Hengwrt manuscript).

     The name should mean *of the boundaries* or *of the borders*, which is not very informative, especially since it is obscure where this story is set.

14   Sir John's land was held in *purchas* or *fee simple* as he had gathered it in his lifetime, not inherited it. Though line 58 refers to a portion he had inherited from his father, it was not all entailed to the eldest son, and the father could divide it among the three sons, though this was itself against the contemporary practice of primogeniture; hence the reaction of the advisers in line 43.

38   The name Gamelyn is held to mean *son of the old man*, from OE *gamol*, old man. According to line 356 Gamelyn has been oppressed by his brother for sixteen years before he comes to manhood. This would suggest he is very young as the poem starts, adding point to Sir John's description of him in this line as *my yonge sone*.

42   Before *londes* the letters *hon* are crossed out.

45   It seems that the advisers decide to split the land into two as a compromise between Sir John's proposal for a tripartite division and their own preference for keeping it all together.

53   St. Martin of Tours was a Roman cavalry officer in fourth-century France who became a highly influential Christian leader; he is an appropriate person for a

knight to swear by, perhaps especially as Sir John divides his possessions, since he was famous for parting his cloak with a beggar.

56 Sir John speaks his own dying will, to divide the property into three. This takes effect, though the eldest brother subverts it.

57 A ploughland was the amount of land that could be worked throughout the year by eight oxen, so this is a handsome bequest.

82 Gamelyn handles his beard in a sign that he has come to maturity; this is also a sign of thoughtfulness.

90 The eldest brother is obviously treating Gamelyn as a kitchen servant, a frequent feature of this "male Cinderella" story; cf. the placement of Sir Gareth in King Arthur's kitchen in Malory's *Tale of Sir Gareth*.

92 Gamelyn uses the impolite second person singular to express his feelings, and so outrages his brother: they were evidently not on the level of intimacy which would have made the *thou* form natural.

102 *gadlynge* is a rude term for a youth, which may also imply illegitimacy. This is how Gamelyn takes it in line 108.

116 Sands notes (1966, p. 160) that Gamelyn means "Unless you be the one (that is, dare to be the one to beat me)."

122 A pestle could, in a large kitchen, be a sizeable club; Gamelyn, being treated like a servant, has no conventional weapons at hand.

127 The *loft* where the brother takes refuge would be a floor above the shared hall; there would probably be a ladder that could be drawn up. This is almost certainly the same place as the *solere* where he takes refuge later (line 349) and possibly also the *torret* (line 327).

130 MS *thei* is corrected by the scribe to *he*.

137 Skeat suggested (1884, pp. 38–39) that this refers to St. Richard of Chichester (also mentioned, it seems, in the *Gest,* line 362), and seen as a "pattern of brotherly love"; the saint is invoked again in line 614.

146   The letter *w* is deleted before *me*.

165   MS: *anon*. This reading is unique to Petworth and is most unlikely to be
       original: to make sense of it would require dropping *And* at the start of the next
       line. It is better to assume the scribe has misread the quite precise *on noon*,
       found in the other MSS and parallel to *on tresoun* earlier in the line.

197   A franklin ranks below a knight, so Gamelyn shows his nobility by helping him.
       There is some resemblance hereabouts to the action in the *Gest* when the knight
       helps a yeoman at a rural sport festival, lines 536–67. Some feel the franklin's
       sons are dead (Scattergood, 1994, p. 160), but this is a version of the knightly
       rescue of those oppressed by an ogre. At line 204 the franklin fears he has lost
       his sons *but if God hem borowe*, and at 251, after Gamelyn has defeated the
       champion, the franklin has his sons again. There is some resemblance to the
       uncompleted story of the knight's son in the *Gest* (lines 105–12).

230   If Gamelyn was very young when his father died (see note to line 38), how did
       the champion know of him in this way? There seems an inconsistency in the
       chronology.

251   The MS has *thre* crossed out before *there*.

267   MS: *that* is inserted above the line. The word is absent in most MSS, but a few
       amplify to *there were that*. Only Petworth has the single relative pronoun as an
       afterthought, which suggests that it might have been an editor's insertion in its
       exemplar.

272   By saying "I have not sold half my goods," Gamelyn uses a mercantile metaphor
       to suggest "I have hardly started yet." The champion and the franklin continue
       in the same metaphor in lines 274 and 276.

273   The verb *broke* or *brouke* (line 332) means use or enjoy, and in company with
       a part of the body makes a bland oath like "As I live and breathe" (also see
       lines 295, 563).

277   The shrine of St. James the Apostle was at Santiago di Compostela in Galicia,
       North-Western Spain, a major focus of medieval pilgrimage. Skeat felt this line
       (repeated at line 760) derived from *A Poem on the Times of Edward II*, which

had some other verbal similarities to *Gamelyn* (1884, pp. xii–iii), but the connections are all very general and, like this line, in common usage.

296   MS has *a* corrected by the scribe before *smote*.

319   *catour*. The word means *caterer*, but the scribe writes it with a capital *C*; this may be influenced by the classical figure Cato, but the abbreviation for *our* is also very clear, so this is probably an instance of the casual capitalization characteristic of medieval manuscripts.

327   *torret*. See the note on *loft*, line 127.

333   MS: *a* is corrected by the scribe before *was*.

336   *God and good day* was a familiar farewell.

364   The eldest brother, having appropriated the property that their father willed to Gamelyn on his death-bed, now offers to make Gamelyn his heir, and Gamelyn apparently accepts.

369   MS: *Gamelyn seyde*. It is necessary to insert *he* after *seyde*: the Petworth scribe has not realized that a speech begins with *Gamelyn*, but most of the MSS have *seyde he*.

392   *Two* (the first of its occurrences in this line). MS: *Tho*.

404   *my*. MS: *thy*.

407   Adam transfers loyalty to Gamelyn not blindly, but with a due sense of return from such an action. Some have felt this is mean-minded of Adam, but it rather represents the processes of "bastard feudalism" at work, and there is no suggestion in the poem that Adam is anything other than a true supporter of Gamelyn.

426   *his*. MS: *his his*.

445   Gamelyn speaks ironically: "If we shall anyway absolve them of their sin," i.e., "take vengeance." The priestly metaphor is recurrent in this scene, see lines 499, 512, 519, 529.

447   The reference is either generally to "holy love" or specifically to St. Charity, reputed to be the daughter of St. Sophia, whose other daughters were St. Faith and St. Hope.

453   The MS has *me the*, but, as *the* is the object of the first verb *warne* and *me* is the object of the second verb *bringe*, syntactic logic requires that they appear in the reverse order, and the text is so emended.

        MS: *bondes*. The rhyme requires *bendes*, which is in most other manuscripts.

460   *gestes*. MS: *gettes*.

478   "But may they always prosper, who cause you much grief" — a positively phrased form of curse on Gamelyn.

481   "All who give you security, may evil befall them" — the reverse of the wish in line 478.

499   *spreyeth*. MS: *spreyneth*. Most MSS have some form of *spreyneth* or *sprengeth*, which Skeat translates as "sprinkle" (1884, p. 43). It seems most likely that the original read *spreyeth*, but the religious irony of the passage was not picked up by an early scribe who, assuming a nasal abbreviation, wrote *spreyneth* in the spirit of physical combat. In an attempt to restore the irony perceived because a spire can be a club, or an asperge for sprinkling holy water, scribal emendation to *spreyngeth* occurred.

520   *armes*. MS: *arnes*.

528   *bet*. MS: *bet haue be*. Most MSS have *better* and all of them lack *haue be*. This seems the one instance where Petworth is more wordy than other MSS, and it seems necessary to emend on these grounds.

529   Religious irony continues: Gamelyn is giving the holy men "orders" in the form of attention to their tonsures, with his own forceful way of laying on of hands.

533   MS: *brast*. This is linguistically acceptable, but can be emended to *barst* to improve the rhyme.

563   *So brouke I my chyn.* "As I may use my chin": a vague form of oath like "As I live and breathe."

594   An idiom to describe a bad hangover.

605   *her.* MS: *he.*

606   *Tho.* MS: *To.*

647   Gamelyn says, "If you brought five with you, you would be twelve," mocking the comfort they are (foolishly) taking in numbers.

655   Skeat feels this "evidently refers to an English outlaw, such as Robin Hood" (1884, p. 45).

661   "I will venture so I might have food" — ironic understatement by Adam.

696   The MS has *ca'd* before *made.* Most other MSS have *cried and made,* which makes for a long line. It may be the Petworth scribe was here reading an emended manuscript, and started to write an excised *ca'd and* or *called and.* There seems no reason to follow the other MSS, and *ca'd* is omitted.

      A man was pronounced "wolfshead" to indicate that as an outlaw his life was worth no more than a wolf's: anyone could hunt him. His land was also forfeited, in this case to his elder brother, who is also the sheriff, so confirming his appropriation of Gamelyn's property.

699   Harley 7334 and some MSS influenced by it read *To telle hym tydinges how the wynde was wente,* a characteristic scribal inflation against the condensed clarity of the Petworth line.

704   *tyddyngges.* MS reads *tyddyngge,* though a small final flourish may suggest a plural abbreviation.

709   Daniel notes that *wif* is an uninflected plural (1967, p. 140) and refers to the wives of the *husbondes,* that is, farmers, householders, stewards and so on. Several manuscripts emended to *both husbonde and wif* to clarify that Gamelyn is not being described as married at this point; he will marry in the last lines of the poem.

710   *nexte shyre*. The next county where his brother has jurisdiction.

724   *foote*. MS: *fotte*.

735   MS: *cours*, with the *u* subpuncted for correction.

775   *had he no cors* means that like Robin Hood he was universally popular.

777   Gamelyn was especially feared by clerics in orders. This feature is shared with the Robin Hood tradition, but also with Chaucer, Langland, and other contemporary satirists, who, like the author of *Gamelyn*, have no criticism of parish priests, but much of the "regular" clergy.

782   The eldest brother is now bribing the jurors to bring in a result favorable to him: this was a common corrupt practice in the period.

784   This line, like 799–800, and perhaps 767–68, seems a reference to the traditional greenwood opening of the Robin Hood ballads, particularly in the use of the word *shawes*.

800   *men*. MS: *mon*.

807–10   These lines are the most striking example in the poem of the "awkward verbal repetition" (Scattergood, 1994, p. 160) which apparently relates to oral performance. Some manuscripts drop lines 807–08, but they clearly belong to the poem in its original form.

853   *stede*. MS has *sete* which has been erroneously carried on from line 851. The logical reading in this collocation, which also gives good rhyme, is *stede*.

864   *sherrive*. MS: *sherrve*.

875   *shirreve*. MS: *sirreve*.

889   Gamelyn has won his *land and his lede* (line 891) through the king's generosity, not through the fulfilment of his father's will. That he becomes Sir Ote's heir in line 893 (as he became their brother's in line 364) seems another way of avoiding the implications of the planned breach of primogeniture. For a discussion see Introduction, p. 185.

Robyn and Gandelyn

Introduction

This poem is preserved only in the Sloane MS 2593, a neatly written repository of lyrics and carols, thought by Gray to be "probably a song book, although there is no music" (1984, p. 12), and dated around 1450. However, it does not automatically challenge *Robin Hood and the Monk* for the status of the earliest extant Robin Hood text. There must be serious doubt to what extent, as Child says, "the Robin in this ballad is Robin Hood" (III, 12), and he prints it among the parallel outlaw tales, between *Johnie Cock* and *Adam Bell*. Ritson did not print it with the Robin Hood poems but in *Ancient Songs* (1790) under the title *Robyn Lyth* (see note to line 1). Dobson and Taylor remark that "by no stretch of the imagination can the 'Robin' of this lyric be properly identified with the Robin Hood of the other ballads" (1976, p. 256).

Yet whereas *Johnie Cock* and *Adam Bell* provide analogues to the major outlaw myth, this poem has clear continuities with some features of the Robin Hood saga. This is not so much a matter of the title — Robin is a common enough name for a young man, whether a lover or a trickster, and the "Robin and Marion" French song cycle and the Robin Goodfellow tradition present figures who are clearly not the same as Robin Hood. But two other names in this poem connect with the tradition of the English outlaw.

Gandelyn is often assumed to be linked with Gamelyn. Skeat in his edition of that poem states the name "is a mere corruption of Gamelyn" (1884, p. ix). He is speaking of the poem which is itself a distant analogue of the Robin Hood tradition, but in a later ballad, *Robin Hood and Will Scarlet*, a character with a name close to Gamelyn, Will Gamwell, joins Robin's band, and a number of the nineteenth-century expansions of the myth (notably Pierce Egan's novel of 1840) develop this aspect of the story. It may well be, of course, that making Will Gamwell Robin Hood's gentry cousin is only a way of rationalizing the existence of the early poem telling the outlaw-linked adventure of the knightly Gamelyn, but the early existence of *Robyn and Gandelyn* suggests that there had been at least some connection between the two names well before the narrative exploitation of their similarity in the later ballad.

The other name that seems to point towards Robin Hood is that of Wrennock. It has been suggested that when John Major and other sixteenth-century writers recast the outlaw tradition as that of a distressed nobleman in the period of bad King John, they had in mind the model of *Fouke le Fitz Waryn*. One of Fouke's worst enemies was a Welshman called Morris of Powys whose son went by the name of Wrennoc: the similarities have been outlined in some detail by Prideaux (1886).

There are many resonances throughout the Robin Hood tradition of the events in this poem: two outlaws are in the woods looking for game; they are attacked and Robin is bested; the other outlaw avenges him with courage and skill. That is not in the ballads a fatal encounter for Robin and rarely for his enemies, but *Robin Hood and the Monk*, one of the versions of *The Death of Robin Hood*, and, to some extent, *Robin Hood and Guy of Gisborne* have resemblances with this kind of fatal duel, while the "Robin Hood meets with his match" ballads euphemize this forest encounter, as in another way does the exchange of blows that in the *Gest* and *The King's Disguise and Friendship with Robin Hood* has become reduced to *pluck buffet*, where the blow is a result of winning at archery, and so is a distant version of the fatal duel seen here.

In form the poem is closer to a narrative lyric than an extended ballad, as is suggested by its presence in a lyrical anthology. This formal character is constructed not so much by the existence of a refrain (not an uncommon feature in the Robin Hood ballads) but by the brevity of the poem, the simplicity of its diction, as well as by the suggestive, incomplete nature of the action which is a good deal more gnomic than even the more "expressionist" ballads, like *Robin Hood and Guy of Gisborne*.

The manuscript has no division into stanzas, but Child's lay-out seems convincing; it includes no less than three six-line stanzas, verified by the rhyme pattern, and the rhymes, as is usual in lyrics, are almost all good ("ale/knawe" in the last stanza seems the only half-rhyme) and consistently on an abcb pattern (lines 45 and 47 are repetition, not an additional *a* rhyme). The diction, again as usual in the lyric, avoids redundancy and cliché, though there is a good deal of measured and rhetorical repetition as in lines 9 and 13, 27–28, 25 and 31, 39 and 41, 46 and 50, 48 and 52, 63–66, and 68–71.

Gray calls this poem "mysterious and eerie" (1984, p. 12), and there are other lyrics of that primarily suggestive kind, such as the *Corpus Christi Carol* and, with some verbal resonance, *Adam lay yboundyn*. In a similar context, Rosalind Field has suggested to the editor that the "unblemished" deer (line 17) may be supernatural, and killing them may be taboo, as with the kine of Helios in *The Odyssey*. Nevertheless, mystery is not the poem's only direction: the emergent themes of honest outlaws under threat, of unflinching loyalty, and of both plenitude and threat in the forest all look towards the concerns of the Robin Hood myth rather than to any other medieval corpus of material.

Robyn and Gandelyn

Select Bibliography

Texts

Sloane Manuscript 2593 (in British Library).

Child, F. J., ed. *The English and Scottish Popular Ballads*. 5 vols. 1882–98. Rpt. New York: Dover, 1965. Vol. III, no. 115.

Dobson, R. J., and J. Taylor., eds. *Rymes of Robin Hood*. London: Heinemann, 1976. Pp. 255–57.

Gutch, J. M., ed. *A Lytelle Gest of Robin Hood with other Auncient and Modern Ballads and Songs Relating to the Celebrated Yeoman*. 2 vols. London: Longman, 1847. Vol. II, 35–39.

Ritson, Joseph, ed. *Ancient Songs from the Time of King Henry the Third to the Revolution*. London: J. Johnson, 1790. Pp. 48–51. [Ritson titles the poem "Robin Lyth" and includes it as the first in class II, songs "Comprehending the Reigns of Henry IV, Henry V, and Henry VI."]

Commentary and Criticism

Child, F. J., pp. 12–13.

Dobson, R. J., and J. Taylor, pp. 255–56.

Egan, Piers, the Younger. *Robin Hood and Little John, or The Merry Men of Sherwood Forest*. London: Forster and Hextall, 1840.

Gray, Douglas. "The Robin Hood Poems." *Poetica* 18 (1984), 1–39.

Prideaux, W. F. "Who Was Robin Hood?" *Notes and Queries*, 7th Series, II (1886), 421–24.

Skeat, W. W., ed. *The Tale of Gamelyn*. Oxford: Clarendon Press, 1884.

Robyn and Gandelyn

Robynn lyth in grene wode bowndyn.   *bound (in a shroud)*

I herde a carpyng of a clerk,   *singing; learned person*
Al at yone wodes ende,   *yonder*
Of gode Robyn and Gandeleyn;
5   Was ther non other gynge.   *company*

Stronge thevys wer tho chylderin non,   *those youths*
But bowmen gode and hende;   *skillful; honorable*
He wentyn to wode to getyn hem fleych,   *They; flesh (meat)*
If God wold it hem sende.

10 Al day wentyn tho chylderin too,   *two*
And fleych fowndyn he non,   *meat they found none*
Til it were ageyn evyn;   *toward evening*
The chylderin wolde gon hom.

Half an honderid of fat falyf der   *fallow deer*
15 He comyn ayon,   *They came upon*
And alle he wern fayr and fat inow,   *enough*
But markyd was ther non;   *blemished*
"Be dere God," seyde gode Robyn,
"Here of we shul have on."   *shall have one*

20 Robyn bent his joly bowe,
Ther in he set a flo;   *arrow*
The fattest der of alle
The herte he clef a to.   *cleaved in two*

He hadde not the der iflawe,   *flayed*
25 Ne half out of the hyde,
There cam a schrewde arwe out of the west,   *devilish arrow*
That felde Robertes pryde.   *struck down*

230

Robyn and Gandelyn

Gandeleyn lokyd hym est and west,
Be every syde:
30 "Hoo hat myn mayster slayin?   *Who has*
Ho hat don this dede?
Shal I never out of grene wode go
Til I se sydis blede."

Gandeleyn lokyd hym est and lokyd west,   *gazed*
35 And sowt under the sunne;   *stared*
He saw a lytil boy
He clepyn Wrennok of Donne.   *They call*

A good bowe in his hond,
A brod arwe ther ine,
40 And fowre and twenty goode arwys,   *twenty four*
Trusyd in a thrumme: *Tied; bundle*
"Be war the, war the, Gandeleyn,
Her of thu shalt han summe.

"Be war the, war the, Gandeleyn,
45 Hir of thu gyst plenté."   *will get plenty*
"Ever on for an other," seyde Gandeleyn;
"Mysaunter have he shal fle.   *Misfortune may he have who flees*

"Wher-at shal oure marke be?"   *Where*
Seyde Gandeleyn.
50 "Everyche at otheris herte,"   *Each at the other's heart*
Seyde Wrennok ageyn.

"Ho shal yeve the ferste schote?"   *Who*
Seyde Gandeleyn:
"And I shul geve the on be-forn."   *the first one*
55 Seyd Wrennok ageyn.

Wrennok schette a ful good schote,   *shot*
And he schet not to hye;
Throw the samclothis of his bryk,   *apron; breeches*
It towchyd neyther thye.   *thigh*

60   "Now hast thou govyn me on beforn,"   *given me one first*
    Al thus to Wrennok seyde he,
    "And throw the myght of our Lady
    A bettere I shal yeve the."   *A better [shot] I shall give thee*

    Gandeleyn bent his goode bowe,
65   And set ther in a flo;   *arrow*
    He schet throw his grene certyl,   *He shot through his green kirtle*
    His herte he clef on too.   *cleft in two*

    "Now shalt thu never yelpe, Wrennok,   *boast*
    At ale ne at wyn,
70   That thu hast slawe goode Robyn,   *slain*
    And his knave Gandeleyn.   *servant*

    "Now shalt thu never yelpe, Wrennok,
    At wyn ne at ale,
    That thu hast slawe goode Robyn,
75   And Gandeleyn his knawe."   *servant*

    Robyn lyeth in grene wode bowndyn.

Notes

1   This refrain line apparently refers to Robin's burial in a shroud as a result of the action of this poem; an analogue is the refrain of *Adam lay ybounden*. The line is usually printed as line 5, but actually begins the text in the MS.

     Robynn lyth was read by Ritson (1790, p. 48) as the name of one of the characters, and made the title of the poem, but it is clearly a subject and verb.

4   *Gandeleyn*. The name is close to Gamelyn (Skeat feels it is descended from it, 1884, p. ix). Gutch remarked that Gandalin is a name found in the Old Spanish romance *Amadis de Gaul* (1847, II, 36).

5   MS: *gynge*. Child emends to *thynge*, presumably on grounds of sense, but as Dobson and Taylor suggest (1976, p. 256), *gynge* meaning "gang" or "company" makes sharper sense.

13   MS: *wolde*. The final *e* is almost completely lost by the clippping of the page.

18   *Robyn* has probably been clipped from the edge of the MS: it seems necessary and is supplied.

20   MS: *went*. Child emends to *bent*, the verb regularly used in this collocation.

27   *Robertes*. I.e., Robin's. The balladeer uses the outlaw's more formal name when speaking of his pride.

33   *Til*. MS: *ti*.

     Child inserts *his* before *sydis*, but this seems unnecessary and is not accepted by Dobson and Taylor (1976, p. 256).

45   MS: *Hir*. Child emends to *Her*, but this is unnecessary.

54   MS *ȝewe* is corrected to *ȝeue* by the scribe, and so Child's emendation to this is not necessary.

55   MS: *seyd*. Child adds a final *e,* presumably for meter, but this is unnecessary and is omitted by Dobson and Taylor (1976, p. 257).

58   Child and Dobson and Taylor read the MS as *sanchothis* but the first *h* is overwritten to make it more like an *l.* The reading *sanclothis* should be emended to *samclothis*, a "semigarment" formed by the loose cloth hanging down from a pair of breeches between the legs; the *MED* refers to this instance of the word.

62   MS: *thu*. Child emends to *the*.

74   MS: *sw* is crossed out before *slawe*.

75   *Gandeleyn*. MS: *Gandelyyn*.

      MS: *knawe*. Child emends to *knave* which seems sensible, but does damage the rhyme. An unaffricated bilabial, as is possible in *knawe*, would give a better rhyme with *ale* in line 73.

Adam Bell, Clim of the Clough, and William of Cloudesley

Introduction

This extended outlaw narrative was popular in the sixteenth and seventeenth centuries: five different printed versions are known, and there were many reprints of the later editions. But the existence of a saga about these three forester heroes of Cumberland appears to go back almost as far as that of Robin Hood himself. A 1432 Parliament Roll for Wiltshire adds to a list of local members, presumably in a spirit of satire, a sequence of outlaw names — Robin Hood, Little John, Much, Scathelock and Reynold are there, but, remarkably in so southern an area, the list is led by "Adam Belle, Clim O'Cluw, Willyam Cloudesle." Presumably the first named is also the Allan Bell mentioned as a fine archer in Dunbar's poem *Of Sir Thomas Norrey*, datable to the early sixteenth century at the latest.

It was under the name of Adam Bell that the poem was entered in the Stationers' Register in 1557–58, indicating it was a mainstream text by then, and this is confirmed by reference to the poem by Shakespeare, *Much Ado* I.1 — to Adam; Jonson, *The Alchemist,* Act I — to Clim; and Davenant, *The Long Vacation in London* (see Dobson and Taylor, 1976, p. 259). This popularity led to a late and feeble second part of the ballad being produced, it seems, as early as 1586; in that year a "new" ballad with this title was claimed to exist, which could hardly be credible if it was the same as the one already printed at least four times, including the imprint by the well-known William Copland. This was added to Part I in the Percy Folio. The similarity to Robin Hood was no doubt part of the reason for the original ballad's success, and this also led to another piece of opportunism, a ballad which combined their stories, *Robin Hood's Birth, Breeding, Valour and Marriage.*

Copland's text of the mid-sixteenth century is the earliest full version (*C*) and provides the basis for modern editions. As Child showed, there are some earlier fragments which offer good readings when they are available: *A*, from John Byddel's press from about 1536, provides only lines 452–506 and 642–80. Another fragment, *B*, may have been printed by Wynkyn de Worde, and at least a little earlier than Byddell's; it offers some valuable readings from lines 211–446. These three are referred to in the notes as "earlier texts." Two "later texts" sometimes referred to are both printed by James Roberts in the very early seventeenth century; there is also a version in the Percy Folio which appears to have been copied from a text of the Roberts type, and has no value for textual purposes.

235

In its own terms *Adam Bell* has many virtues. Gray described it as an "excellent long ballad" (1984, p. 11), and Dobson and Taylor found it "the most dramatically exciting of all English outlaw ballads" (1976, p. 258). Some of these qualities resemble patterns found in the Robin Hood myth. *Adam Bell* is lucidly constructed in three discrete fitts (not unlike *Robin Hood and the Potter* and, if it were all available, *Robin Hood and the Monk*). As in those ballads, the first fitt sees one of the outlaws enter the town and encounter danger; in the second fitt there follows an exciting rescue not unlike that in the *Gest* or *Robin Hood and the Monk*; in the last fitt the outlaw heroes are forgiven by the king, despite the damage they have caused, as happens in the *Gest* and is implicit in *Robin Hood and the Monk*.

Other motifs that are shared with *Robin Hood and the Monk* (and more generally with other texts) are the brisk but vivid nature opening (there seem to be verbal echoes with *Robin Hood and the Monk*: the latter seems likely to be the source, as it is sharper-focussed in both language and imagery); a fellow outlaw's advice to avoid the town, which is ignored; the harsh treatment of the jailer; the use of a messenger; the hostile role of sheriff and justice; the use of a royal seal for entry into the town (forged in *Adam Bell*, stolen in *Robin Hood and the Monk*); the king's eventual and somewhat reluctant approval.

But *Adam Bell* also has a range of original features of some importance. Whereas the Robin Hood texts explore pressures felt by outlawed men with no visible family, and *Gamelyn* deals with a disinherited younger son, *Adam Bell* concentrates on another type of distressed male, the husband and father separated from his family. While the social bandit, in Hobsbawm's definition, will be without dependants unless, like Jesse James, he was a historical figure actually in that situation, William of Cloudeslye, very much the hero of the ballad, is impelled to return to Carlisle to see his wife and children, and though after his rescue they play little part in the action, they are still included in the royal resolution at the end, when fatherhood is again central in the apple-splitting scene. The connection continues, as William's son is the focus of the sequel.

This stress on familial structures may also be related to the emphasis put on the role of women as well as the wife. William is betrayed by an "old wyfe" who has lived long in his house, and he and his outlaw colleagues are redeemed, from a position of great risk, by the generous queen who calls up a favor given her by the king at their wedding. Theorists of gender relations might well see in the three women who attend William a triad of wife, crone, and queen, projections of the male imagination (or anxiety) when dealing with the female. That feature is almost invisible in the rest of the outlaw ballads unless the Virgin Mary, the Prioress of Kirkleys, Queen Katherine, and the shadowy future figure of Maid Marian were variously invoked to represent this triune form of the feminine.

Adam Bell, Clim of the Clough, and William of Cloudesley

Another notable feature of this ballad is the fully resolved nature of its ending. Most Robin Hood ballads end with the outlaw band returning to the stasis that was disturbed by the original incursion into the greenwood of a stranger, or concluding with a renewed delicate balance where the hostile forces are still implicitly alive. Some have a tragic ending: the *Gest*, *The Death of Robin Hood*, *A True Tale of Robin Hood*; and a few later and gentrified ones have a blissfully resolved sense of future security. It is this last unproblematically happy ending that *Adam Bell* provides, which seems strange in an early, violent, and quite realistic ballad. The end has none of what Gray calls the "open" quality of the last part of *Robin Hood and the Monk* (1984, p. 17), where the king's ironic appreciation of the outlaws' loyalty (John's tough fidelity in particular) both threatens and validates their state of independence. At the end of *Adam Bell* William is a court gentleman, his colleagues are yeomen, William's wife a queen's gentlewoman, and promises of advancement are even made to William's son. Medieval literature usually brings such court happiness to rapid misery, but here all that follows is an equally neat verbal resolution, tying up the theme of archery with that of salvation, wishing for all good archers that *of heven they may never mysse* (line 683).

Redolent of heroic simplicity rather than the more uneasy world of the usual outlaw ballads, this ending does of course follow on from this ballad's single element most unlike Robin Hood adventures, the climactic moment where William proves his skill and his nerve — and perhaps his inherently unparental character — by shooting an apple from his son's head. At long distance, with a difficult and deadly weapon (the heavier broad arrow, not the light "bearing arrow" with which he has previously shown his skill) William performs a feat that, as Child shows at some length (III, 16–22), is a recurrent motif in international heroic story, not merely the *pièce de resistance* of William Tell. One scholar localizes this event; the closest version of the story, known as early as Wright's commentary as "a Northern story" (1846, II, 208), might, Holt suggests, belong to the Carlisle region through its close contact with Norse culture (1989, p. 71). That may well be so: it is also one of the elements by which this long ballad is stagey in a way avoided by most of the Robin Hood ballads, whose dramatic interchanges are those of immediate street theater, direct fights, simple disguises, rather than this lengthy, masque-like sequence of activity, more elaborate than the recurrent but usually brief archery contest.

A similar level of elaboration is embodied in the narrative methodology of the ballad, though as it is a feature that realism has handed down as "natural," commentators fail to observe it as a specific technique. *Adam Bell* is very notable for a narrative which moves briskly and neatly stanza by stanza: each quatrain brings a new event, a new explanation of the way it derives from the previous events. The narrative of *Adam Bell* tends to explain everything: the sequence where Adam and Clim trick their way into Carlisle has an almost positivist note in the way it gives all relevant details and actions (e.g., the porter cannot read and so is tricked by the forged seals, line 220). The mimesis is insistently realistic and rationalized, even when, or perhaps especially when, the narrative is improbable (as in the carefully outlined apple-shooting episode). The overall tone is lucid, steady, metronomic narrative, most unlike the mildly mysterious stop-start movement of the popular and lyric ballad, and much more like the measured tread of the sixteenth-century historicist poems *Chevy Chase* or *The Battle of Otterburn*, and indeed not in this respect unlike the *Gest* itself, in this as in its compilation status a somewhat bookish text. However, to recognize the unusually realistic mode of the poem does not necessarily lead to a narrow historicism like Joseph Hunter's notion (1845, p. 245) that Adam Bell really existed. Child is more generously dismissive in this case than in dealing with Hunter's equally positivist approach to the *Gest* (III, 21–22), while Dobson and Taylor simply call Hunter's arguments "extraordinarily unconvincing" (1976, p. 260, n.2).

In terms of stylistic character *Adam Bell* is of limited interest. Its vocabulary is unremarkable either for imaginative variety or meaningless repetition. There are not many poor rhymes (lines 74/6, 78/80, 122/4, 154/6, 210/2, 226/8 stress, 246/8, 278/80, 445/7, 453/5, 593/5, 609/11, 673/5) and in terms of stanza form, as in many other ballads, the author appears to have been happy with *abab* when it came to hand easily (lines 109–12, 129–32, 161–64, 452–55, 464–67, 468–71, 492–95, 536–39, 564–67, 632–35, 636–39, 640–63). There seems to be a trace of grouping here, especially in the stanzas relating the apple-splitting episode. In the exciting sequence when William is rescued from Carlisle, the author appears to have adopted the *abab* stanza as his basic mode (see lines 205–387, and especially 314–87) and he appears to have got so much into the swing of full rhyming that he produced a five-line stanza in the process (lines 293–97).

In these ways, in terms of style, action, and temperament, the ballad of *Adam Bell* is a little less pointed and vivid than the earlier Robin Hood ballads; and yet in comparison with the feebly literary late-seventeenth-century broadsides, it seems to have in full measure the robust and daring directness of the true outlaw ballad. Adam, Clim, and William are indeed examples of the "good yeomen" archetype, realizing both the sturdy values and anxious projections of the other early outlaw texts. It is both a measure of the inherent quality of the story and of the massive pull of the major outlaw myth, that their story has become so closely linked to the tradition of Robin Hood himself.

Select Bibliography

Texts

Fragments of a copy. London: Byddell, c. 1536, in Cambridge University Library. [Referred to as *A* in notes.]

Fragment of a copy, perhaps by Wynkyn de Worde and therefore earlier than above. [Referred to as *B* in notes.]

Adambel, Clym of the cloughe, and Wyllyam of cloudesle. London: Copland, c. 1550–60. [Referred to as *C* in notes.]

Adam Bell, Clim of the Clough, and William of Cloudesle. London: Roberts, c. 1605.

Child, F. J., ed. *English and Scottish Popular Ballads*. 5 vol. 1882–98; rpt. New York: Dover, 1965. Vol. III, no. 116.

Dobson, R. J., and J. Taylor. *Rymes of Robin Hood*. London: Heinemann, 1976. Pp. 258–73.

Thomas Percy's folio manuscript, Add. MSS 27879, British Library.

Percy, Thomas, ed. *Reliques of English Poetry*. 3 vols. London: J. Dodsley, 1765. I, 129–60.

Ritson, Joseph. *Pieces of Ancient Popular Poetry*. London: C. Clark for T. and J. Egerton, 1791. Pp. 1–30.

Commentary and Criticism

Child, F. J., pp. 14–22.

Dobson, R. J., and J. Taylor, pp. 258–60.

Gray, Douglas. "The Robin Hood Ballads." *Poetica* 18 (1984), 1–39.

Hobsbawm, E. J. *Bandits*. Second ed. London: Penguin, 1985.

Early Ballads and Tales

Holt, J. C. *Robin Hood*. Second ed. London: Thames and Hudson, 1989.

Hunter, Joseph. *New Illustrations of the Life, Studies, and Writings of Shakespeare*. 2 vols. London: Nichols, 1845. I, 245–47.

Wright, Thomas. "On The Popular Cycle of the Robin Hood Ballads." In *Essays on Subjects connected with the Literature, Popular superstition, and History of England in the Middle Ages*. 2 vols. London: J. R. Smith, 1846. Pp. 164–211.

Adam Bell, Clim of the Clough, and William of Cloudesley

Fitt 1

Mery it was in grene forest,
Amonge the leves grene,
Where that men walke both east and west,
Wyth bowes and arrowes kene,

5   To ryse the dere out of theyr denne;   *to rouse; deer; den*
Suche sightes as hath ofte bene sene,
As by the yemen of the north countrey,
By them it is as I meane.

The one of them hight Adam Bel,   *was called*
10   The other Clym of the Clough,
The thyrd was William of Cloudesly,
An archer good ynough.   *completely good*

They were outlawed for venyson,   *venison (i.e., poaching deer)*
These thre yemen everechone;   *everyone*
15   They swore them brethen upon a day,   *brothers*
To Englysshe wood for to gone.   *Inglewood Forest*

Now lith and lysten, gentylmen,   *attend and listen*
And that of myrthes loveth to here: *entertainments; hear*
Two of them were single men,
20   The third had a wedded fere.   *wife*

Wyllyam was the wedded man,
Muche more then was hys care:
He sayde to hys brethen upon a day,
To Carelel he would fare,   *Carlisle*

25 For to speke with fayre Alse hys wife,   *Alice*
   And with hys chyldren thre:
   "By my trouth," sayde Adam Bel,
   "Not by the counsell of me.

   "For if ye go to Caerlel, brother,
30 And from thys wylde wode wende,
   If the justice mai you take,
   Your lyfe were at an ende."   *would be*

   "If that I come not to morowe, brother,
   By pryme to you agayne,   *first hour of the day (sunrise)*
35 Truste not els but that I am take,
   Or else that I am slayne."

   He toke hys leave of hys brethen two,
   And to Carlel he is gone;
   There he knocked at hys owne wyndowe,
40 Shortlye and anone.   *Quickly and at once*

   "Wher be you, fayre Alyce my wyfe,
   And my chyldren three?
   Lyghtly let in thyne husbande,   *Quickly*
   Wyllyam of Cloudeslé."

45 "Alas!" then sayde fayre Alyce,
   And syghed wonderous sore,
   "Thys place hath ben besette for you *besieged because of*
   Thys halfe yere and more."

   "Now am I here," sayde Cloudeslé,
50 "I woulde that I in were;
   Now feche us meate and drynke ynoughe,
   And let us make good chere."

   She feched him meat and drynke plenty,
   Lyke a true wedded wyfe,
55 And pleased hym with that she had,
   Whome she loved as her lyfe.

Adam Bell, Clim of the Clough, and William of Cloudesley

There lay an old wyfe in that place,   *woman*
A lytle besyde the fyre,
Whych Wyllyam had found, of cherytye,   *provided for; charity*
60   More then seven yere.

Up she rose, and walked full styll,   *quietly*
Evel mote she spede therefoore!   *may she fare*
For she had not set no fote on ground
In seven yere before.

65   She went unto the justice hall,
As fast as she could hye: *go*
"Thys nyght is come unto thys town
Wyllyam of Cloudeslé."

Thereof the justice was full fayne,   *pleased*
70   And so was the shirife also:
"Thou shalt not travaile hether, dame, for nought;   *come hither*
Thy meed thou shalt have or thou go."   *reward; before*

They gave to her a ryght good goune,   *gown*
Of scarlat it was, as I heard saye;
75   She toke the gyft, and home she wente,
And couched her doune agayne.

They rysed the towne of mery Carlel,   *aroused*
In all the hast that they can,   *haste*
And came thronging to Wyllyames house,
80   As fast they might gone.

Theyr they besette that good yeman,
Round about on every syde;
Wyllyam hearde great noyse of folkes,
That heytherward hyed.   *Who hurried there*

85   Alyce opened a shot wyndow,   *window with shutters*
And loked all about;
She was ware of the justice and the shrife bothe,
Wyth a full great route.   *crowd*

  "Alas! treason," cryed Alyce,
90 "Ever wo may thou be!
  Go into my chambre, my husband," she sayd,
  "Swete Wyllyam of Cloudeslé."

  He toke hys sweard and hys bucler,   *buckler (small shield)*
  Hys bow and hys chyldren thre,
95 And wente into hys strongest chamber,
  Where he thought surest to be.   *safest*

  Fayre Alice folowed him as a lover true,
  With a pollaxe in her hande: *ax with long handle*
  "He shalbe deade that here commeth in
100 Thys dore, whyle I may stand."

  Cloudeslé bent a wel good bowe,
  That was of trusty tre,
  He smot the justice on the brest,
  That hys arrowe brest in thre.   *burst*

105 "God's curse on his hartt," saide William,
  "Thys day thy cote dyd on;   *coat put on*
  If it had ben no better than myne,
  It had gone nere thy bone."

  "Yelde the, Cloudeslé," sayd the justise,   *thee*
110 "And thy bowe and thy arrowes the fro."
  "Gods curse on hys hart," sayde fair Alice,
  "That my husband councelleth so."

  "Set fyre on the house," saide the sherife,
  "Syth it wyll no better be,
115 And brenne we therin William," he saide,
  "Hys wyfe and chyldren thre."

  They fyred the house in many a place,   *set fire to*
  The fyre flew upon hye;
  "Alas!" than cryed fayr Alice,
120 "I se we shall here dy."   *die*

Adam Bell, Clim of the Clough, and William of Cloudesley

William openyd hys backe wyndow,
That was in hys chambre on hye,
And wyth shetes let hys wyfe downe,   *sheets*
And hys chyldren thre.

125   "Have here my treasure," sayde William,
"My wyfe and my chyldren thre;
For Christes love do them no harme,
But wreke you all on me."

Wyllyam shot so wonderous well,
130   Tyll hys arrowes were all go,
And the fyre so fast upon hym fell,
That hys bow stryng brent in two.   *burned*

The spercles brent and fell hym on,   *embers*
Good Wyllyam of Cloudeslé;
135   But than was he a wofull man and sayde,
"Thys is a cowardes death to me.

"Lever I had," sayde Wyllyam,   *I'd rather*
"With my sworde in the route to renne,   *run*
Then here among myne ennemyes wode   *furious*
140   Thus cruelly to bren."   *burn*

He toke hys sweard and hys buckler,
And among them all he ran;
Where the people were most in prece,   *in a crowd*
He smot downe many a man.

145   There myght no man stand hys stroke,   *withstand*
So fersly on them he ran;   *fiercely*
Then they threw wyndowes and dores on him,
And so toke that good yeman.

There they hym bounde both hand and fote,
150   And in depe dongeon hym cast;
"Now, Cloudeslé," sayde the hye justice,
"Thou shalt be hanged in hast."

"One vow shal I make," sayde the sherife,
"A payre of new galowes shall I for the make,
155   And al the gates of Caerlel shalbe shutte,
There shall no man come in therat.

"Then shall not helpe Clim of the Cloughe,
Nor yet Adam Bell,
Though they came with a thousand mo,
160   Nor all the devils in hell."

Early in the mornyng the justice uprose,
To the gates fast gan he gon,   *began he to go*
And commaunded to be shut full cloce   *closed tightly*
Lightlie everychone.   *Quickly every one*

165   Then went he to the market-place,
As fast as he coulde hye;
A payre of new gallous there dyd he up set,   *gallows*
Besyde the pyllory.   *pillory*

A lytle boy stod them amonge,
170   And asked what meaned that gallow-tre;
They sayde, "To hange a good yeaman,
Called Wyllyam of Cloudeslé."

That lytle boye was the towne swyne-heard,   *swineherd*
And kept there Alyce swyne;   *Alice's pigs*
175   Full oft he had sene Cloudeslé in the wodde,
And geven hym there to dyne.   *given him food*

He went out of a creves in the wall,   *crevice*
And lightly to the woode dyd gone;
There met he with these wyght yonge men,
180   Shortly and anone.

"Alas!" then sayde that lytle boye,
"Ye tary here all to longe;
Cloudeslé is taken and dampned to death,   *condemned*
All readye for to honge."

185   "Alas!" then sayde good Adam Bell,
    "That ever we see thys daye!
    He myght her with us have dwelled,
    So ofte as we dyd him praye.   *pleaded*

    "He myght have taryed in grene foreste,   *tarried*
190   Under the shadowes sheene,   *lovely*
    And have kepte both hym and us in reste,
    Out of trouble and teene."   *harm*

    Adam bent a ryght good bow,
    A great hart sone had he slayne;   *at once*
195   "Take that, chylde," he sayde, "to thy dynner,
    And bryng me myne arrowe agayne."

    "Now go we hence," sayed these wight yong men,   *strong*
    "Tary we no lenger here;
    We shall hym borowe, by Gods grace,   *ransom*
200   Though we bye it full dere."   *pay for it dearly*

    To Caerlel went these good yemen,
    In a mery mornyng of Maye:
    Her is a fyt of Cloudesli,
    And another is for to saye.

Fitt 2

205   And when they came to mery Caerlell,
    In a fayre mornyng tyde,   *morning time*
    They founde the gates shut them untyll,   *against them*
    Round about on every syde.

    "Alas!" than sayd good Adam Bell,
210   "That ever we were made men!
    These gates be shyt so wonderly well,
    That we may not come herein."

Than spake Clymme of the Cloughe:
"With a wyle we wyll us in brynge;   *deceitful stratagem*
215   Let us say we be messengers,
Streyght comen from oure kynge."

Adam sayd, "I have a lettre wryten wele,   *written*
Now let us wysely werke;   *cunningly*
We wyll say we have the kynges seale,
220   I holde the porter no clerke."   *think; unable to read*

Than Adam Bell bete on the gate,   *beat*
With strokes greate and stronge;
The porter herde such a noyse therate,
And to the gate he thronge.   *hastened*

225   "Who is there nowe," sayde the porter,
"That maketh all this knockynge?"
"We be messengers," sayd Clymme of the Clough,
"Be come ryght frome our kynge."

"We have a letter," sayd Adam Bell,
230   "To the justyce we must it brynge
Let us in oure message to do,
That we were agayne to our kyng."   *So we can return*

"Here cometh none in," sayd the porter,
"By Hym that dyed on a tre,   *By Christ who was crucified*
235   Tyll a false thefe be hanged,
Called Wyllyam of Cloudeslé."

Than spake that good yeman, Clym of the Cloughe,
And swore by Mary fre,   *the gracious Virgin Mary*
"If that we stande long wythout,
240   Lyke a thefe hanged shalt thou be.

"Lo! here we have the kynges seale;
What, lordane, arte thou wode?"   *fool; mad*
The porter had wende it had been so,   *thought*
And lyghtly dyd of hys hode.   *quickly took off his hood*

245 "Welcome be my lordes seale," sayd he,
　　　"For that shall ye come in."
　　　He opened the gate ryght shortly,
　　　An evyl openynge for hym!

　　　"Now are we in," sayde Adam Bell,
250 "Wherof we are full fayne;　　　　　　　　　*glad*
　　　But Cryst knoweth that herowed hell,　　　*who harrowed Hell*
　　　How we shall come oute agayne."

　　　"Had we the keys," sayd Clym of the Clowgh,
　　　"Ryght well than sholde we spede;　　　　　*prosper*
255 Than myght we come out well ynough,
　　　Whan we se tyme and nede."

　　　They called the porter to a councell,
　　　And wronge hys necke in two,　　　　　　　*wrung*
　　　And kest hym in a depe dongeon,　　　　　　*cast*
260 And toke the keys hym fro.

　　　"Now am I porter," sayd Adam Bell;
　　　"Se, broder, the keys have we here;
　　　The worste porter to mery Carlell,
　　　That ye had this hondreth yere.

265 "Now wyll we oure bowes bende,
　　　Into the towne wyll we go,
　　　For to delyver our dere broder,
　　　Where he lyeth in care and wo."

　　　Then they bent theyr good yew bowes,
270 And loked theyr stringes were round;　　　　*properly aligned*
　　　The market-place of mery Carlyll,
　　　They beset in that stounde.　　　　　　　　*moment*

　　　And as they loked them besyde,
　　　A payre of newe galowes there they se,
275 And the justyce, with a quest of swerers,　　*inquest of jurors*
　　　That had juged Clowdyslé there hanged to be.　*judged*

And Clowdyslé hymselfe lay redy in a carte,
Fast bounde bothe fote and hande,
And a strong rope aboute his necke,
280   All redy for to be hangde.

The justyce called to hym a ladde;   *lad*
Clowdysles clothes sholde he have,
To take the mesure of that good yoman,
And therafter to make his grave.

285   "I have sene as greate a merveyll," sayd Clowdyslé,
"As bytwene this and pryme,
He that maketh thys grave for me,
Hymselfe may lye therin."

"Thou spekest proudely," sayd the justyce,
290   "I shall hange the with my hande."
Full well that herde his bretheren two,
There styll as they dyd stande.

Than Clowdyslé cast hys eyen asyde,
And sawe hys bretheren stande,
295   At a corner of the market place,
With theyr good bowes bent in theyr hand,
Redy the justyce for to chase.

"I se good comforte," sayd Clowdyslé,
"Yet hope I well to fare;
300   If I myght have my handes at wyll,   *free*
Ryght lytell wolde I care."

Than bespake good Adam Bell,
To Clymme of the Clowgh so fre;
"Broder, see ye marke the justyce well;
305   Lo yonder ye may him se.

"And at the sheryf shote I wyll,
Strongly with an arowe kene."

A better shotte in mery Carlyll,
Thys seven yere was not sene.

310	They loused theyr arowes bothe at ones,	*released*
	Of no man had they drede;	
	The one hyt the justyce, the other the sheryf,	
	That bothe theyr sydes gan blede.	

	All men voyded that them stode nye,	*moved away*
315	Whan the justyce fell to the grounde,	
	And the sheryf fell nyghe hym by;	
	Eyther had his dethes wounde.	

	All the citezens fast gan fle,	*did*
	They durste no lenger abyde;	*dared*
320	There lyghtly they loused Clowdyslé,	*quickly; freed*
	Where he with ropes lay tyde.	*tied*

	Wyllyam sterte to an offycer of the towne,	*rushed*
	Hys axe out his hande he wronge;	*wrenched*
	On eche syde he smote them downe,	*struck*
325	Hym thought he had taryed to longe.	

Wyllyam sayd to his bretheren two,
"Thys daye let us togyder lyve and deye;
If ever you have nede as I have nowe,
The same shall ye fynde by me."

330	They shyt so well in that tyde,	*shot; time*
	For theyr strynges were of sylke full sure,	*silk*
	That they kepte the stretes on every syde;	*held*
	That batayll dyd longe endure.	

They fought togyder as bretheren true,
335 Lyke hardy men and bolde;
Many a man to the grounde they threwe,
And made many an herte colde.

But whan theyr arowes were all gone,
Men presyd on them full fast;
340   They drewe theyr swerdes than anone,
And theyr bowes from them caste.

They wente lyghtly on theyr waye,   *quickly*
With swerdes and buckelers rounde,
By that it was the myddes of the daye,
345   They had made many a wounde.

There was many an oute-horne in Carlyll blowen,   *(see note)*
And the belles backwarde dyd they rynge;   *(see note)*
Many a woman sayd "Alas,"
And many theyr handes dyd wrynge.

350   The mayre of Carlyll forth come was,   *mayor*
And with hym a full grete route;   *crowd*
These thre yomen dredde hym full sore,
For theyr lyves stode in doubt.

The mayre came armed a full greate pace,   *speedily*
355   With a pollaxe in hys hande;
Many a stronge man with hym was,
There in that stoure to stande.   *contest*

The mayre smote at Clowdyslé with his byll,   *ax or halberd*
His buckeler he brast in two;
360   Full many a yoman with grete yll,   *harm*
"Alas, treason!" they cryed for wo.
"Kepe we the gates fast," they bad,   *ordered*
"That these traytours theroute not go."

But all for nought was that they wrought,
365   For so fast they downe were layde
Tyll they all thre, that so manfully fought,
Were goten without at a brayde.   *outside in a rush*

"Have here your keys," sayd Adam Bell,
"Myne offyce I here forsake;

370   Yf ye do by my councell,
       A newe porter ye make."

       He threwe the keys there at theyr hedes,
       And bad them evyll to thryve,
       And all that letteth ony good yoman   *hinder*
375   To come and comforte his wyve.

       Thus be these good yomen gone to the wode,
       As lyght as lefe on lynde;   *linden, tree*
       They laughe and be mery in theyr mode,
       Theyr enemyes were farre behynde.

380   Whan they came to Inglyswode,
       Under theyr trysty-tre,   *meeting tree*
       There they founde bowes full gode,
       And arowes greate plenté.

       "So helpe me God," sayd Adam Bell,
385   And Clymme of the Clowgh so fre,
       "I wolde we were nowe in mery Carlell,
       Before that fayre meyné."   *company*

       They set them downe and made good chere,
       And eate and dranke full well:
390   Here is a fytte of these wyght yonge men,
       And another I shall you tell.

Fitt 3

       As they sat in Inglyswode,
       Under theyr trysty-tre,
       Them thought they herde a woman wepe,
395   But her they myght not se.

       Sore syghed there fayre Alyce, and sayd,
       "Alas that ever I se this daye!

For now is my dere husbonde slayne,
Alas and welawaye!

400   "Myght I have spoken wyth hys dere bretheren,
With eyther of them twayne,
To shew to them what him befell
My herte were out of payne."

Clowdyslé walked a lytell besyde,
405   And loked under the grene wodde lynde;   *tree*
He was ware of his wyfe and his chyldren,   *children*
Full wo in herte and mynde.

"Welcome, wyfe," than sayd Wyllyam,
"Unto this trysty-tre;
410   I had wende yesterdaye, by swete Saint John,   *thought*
Thou sholde me never have se."

"Now wele is me," she sayd, "that ye be here,   *it is good for me*
My herte is out of wo."
"Dame," he sayd, "be mery and glad,
415   And thanke my bretheren two."

"Here of to speke," sayd Adam Bell,
"I wys it is no bote;   *Truly it is no use*
The meat that we must supp withall,
It runneth yet fast on fote."

420   Then went they down into a launde,   *clearing*
These noble archares all thre,
Eche of them slewe a harte of grece,   *fat hart*
The best they coude there se.

"Have here the best, Alyce my wyfe,"
425   Sayde Wyllyam of Clowdyslé,
"By cause ye so boldely stode me by,
Whan I was slayne full nye."

Than they wente to theyr souper,
Wyth suche mete as they had,
430   And thanked God of theyr fortune;
They were bothe mery and glad.

And whan they had souped well,   *supped*
Certayne withouten leace,   *lying*
Clowdyslé sayde, "We wyll to oure kynge,
435   To get us a chartre of peace."   *letter of pardon*

"Alyce shal be at sojournynge,   *temporarily stay*
In a nunry here besyde;
My tow sonnes shall with her go,   *two*
And ther they shall abyde.

440   "Myne eldest sone shall go with me,
For hym have I no care,   *anxiety*
And he shall breng you worde agayne
How that we do fare."

Thus be these wight men to London gone,
445   As fast as they maye hye,
Tyll they came to the kynges palays,
There they woulde nedes be.

And whan they came to the kynges courte,
Unto the pallace gate,
450   Of no man wold they aske leve,
But boldly went in therat.

They preced prestly into the hall,   *rushed quickly*
Of no man had they dreade;
The porter came after and dyd them call,
455   And with them began to chyde.

The ussher sayd, "Yemen, what wolde ye have?
I praye you tell me;
Ye myght thus make offycers shent: *disgraced*
Good syrs, of whens be ye?"

460   "Syr, we be outlawes of the forest,
       Certayne withouten leace,   *without falsehood*
       And hyther we be come to our kynge,
       To get us a charter of peace."

       And whan they came before our kynge,
465   As it was the lawe of the lande,
       They kneled downe without lettynge,   *delay*
       And eche helde up his hande.

       They sayd, "Lorde, we beseche you here,
       That ye wyll graunte us grace,
470   For we have slayne your fatte falowe dere,
       In many a sondry place."

       "What is your names?" than sayd our kynge,
       "Anone that you tell me."   *At once*
       They sayd, "Adam Bell, Clym of the Clough,
475   And Wylliam of Clowdeslé."

       "Be ye those theves," than sayd our kynge,
       "That men have tolde of to me?
       Here to God I make a vowe,
       Ye shall be hanged all thre.

480   "Ye shall be deed without mercy,
       As I am kynge of this lande."
       He commanded his officers everichone
       Fast on them to lay hand.

       There they toke these good yemen,
485   And arested them all thre:
       "So may I thryve," sayd Adam Bell,
       "Thys game lyketh not me.

       "But, good lord, we beseche you nowe,
       That ye wyll graunte us grace,
490   In so moche as we be to you commen;
       Or elles that we may fro you passe,

"With suche weapons as we have here,
Tyll we be out of your place;
And yf we lyve this hondred yere,
495   We wyll aske you no grace."

"Ye speke proudly," sayd the kynge,
"Ye shall be hanged all thre."
"That were great pity," sayd the quene,
"If any grace myght be.

500   "My lorde, whan I came fyrst in to this lande,
To be your wedded wyfe,
The first bone that I wolde aske,   *boon*
Ye wolde graunte me belyfe.   *immediately*

"And I asked you never none tyll nowe,
505   Therfore, good lorde, graunte it me."
"Nowe aske it, madame," sayd the kynge,
"And graunted shall it be."

"Than, good lorde, I you beseche,
The yemen graunte you me."
510   "Madame, ye myght have asked a bone
That sholde have ben worthe them thre.

"Ye myght have asked towres and townes,
Parkes and forestes plentie."
"None so pleasaunt to mi pay," she said,   *liking*
515   "Nor none so lefe to me."   *dear*

"Madame, sith it is your desyre,
Your askyng graunted shalbe;
But I had lever have geven you   *rather*
Good market-townes thre."

520   The quene was a glad woman,
And sayd, "Lord, gramarcy;   *thank you*
I dare undertake for them
That true men shall they be.

"But, good lord, speke som mery word,
525 That they comfort may se."
"I graunt you grace," then said our king,
"Wasshe, felos, and to meate go ye."

They had not setten but a whyle,
Certayne without lesynge,   *without lying*
530 There came messengers out of the north,
With letters to our kyng.

And whan they came before the kynge,
The kneled downe upon theyr kne,
And sayd, "Lord, your offycers grete you wel,
535 Of Caerlel in the north cuntré."   *country*

"How fare my justice," sayd the kyng,
"And my sherife also?"
"Syr, they be slayne, without leasynge,   *lying*
And many an officer mo."

540 "Who hath them slayne?" sayd the kyng,
"Anone thou tell me."
"Adam Bel, and Clime of the Clough,
And Wyllyam of Cloudeslé."

"Alas for rewth!" then sayd our kynge,
545 "My hart is wonderous sore;
I had lever than a thousand pounde
I had knowne of thys before.

"For I have y-graunted them grace,
And that forthynketh me;   *grieves me*
550 But had I knowne all thys before,
They had ben hanged all thre."

The kyng opened the letter anone,
Hymselfe he red it tho,   *then*
And founde how these thre outlawes had slaine,
555 Thre hundred men and mo.

Fyrst the justice and the sheryfe,
And the mayre of Caerlel towne;
Of all the constables and catchipolles   *officers of the sheriff*
Alyve were left not one.   *Alive*

560   The baylyes and the bedyls both,   *bailiffs and beadles*
And the sergeauntes of the law,
And forty fosters of the fe   *foresters of the estate*
These outlawes had y-slaw,   *slain*

And broken his parks, and slaine his dere;
565   Over all they chose the best;
So perelous outlawes as they were
Walked not by easte nor west.

When the kynge this letter had red,
In hys harte he syghed sore;
570   "Take up the table," anone he bad,
"For I may eate no more."

The kyng called hys best archars,
To the buttes with hym to go;
"I wyll se these felowes shote," he sayd,
575   "That in the north have wrought this wo."

The kynges bowmen busked them blyve,   *prepared themselves at once*
And the quenes archers also,
So dyd these thre wyght yemen,
Wyth them they thought to go.

580   There twyse or thryse they shote about,
For to assay theyr hande;
There was no shote these thre yemen shot
That any prycke might them stand.   *target*

Then spake Wyllyam of Cloudeslé:
585   "By God that for me dyed,
I hold hym never no good archar
That shuteth at buttes so wyde."

"Wher at?" then sayd our kyng,
"I pray thee tell me."
590   "At suche a but, syr," he sayd,
"As men use in my countree."

Wyllyam wente into a fyeld,
And his to brothren with him;
There they set up to hasell roddes,   *two hazel sticks*
595   Twenty score paces betwene.

"I hold him an archar," said Cloudeslé,
"That yonder wande cleveth in two."
"Here is none suche," sayd the kyng,
"Nor none that can do so."

600   "I shall assaye, syr," sayd Cloudeslé,   *try*
"Or that I farther go."   *Before*
Cloudeslé, with a bearyng arow,   *flight arrow (see note)*
Clave the wand in to.   *Cleft*

"Thou art the best archer," then said the king,
605   "Forsothe that ever I se."
"And yet for your love," sayd Wylliam,
"I wyll do more maystry."   *show more skill*

"I have a sonne is seven yere olde,
He is to me full deare;
610   I wyll hym tye to a stake,
All shall se that be here,

"And lay an apple upon hys head,
And go syxe score paces hym fro,
And I my selfe, with a brode arow,
615   Shall cleve the apple in two."

"Now hast the," then sayd the kyng;
"By Him that dyed on a tre,
But yf thou do not as thou hest sayde,
Hanged shalt thou be.

260

620   "And thou touche his head or gowne,
         In syght that men may se,
         By all the sayntes that be in heaven,
         I shall hange you all thre."

         "That I have promised," said William,
625   "I wyl it never forsake."
         And there even before the kynge,
         In the earth he drove a stake,

         And bound therto his eldest sonne,
         And bad hym stande styll therat,
630   And turned the childes face fro him,
         Because he shuld not sterte.   *flinch*

         An apple upon his head he set,
         And then his bowe he bent;
         Syxe score paces they were outmet,   *120 paces were measured out*
635   And thether Cloudeslé went.

         There he drew out a fayr brode arrowe,
         Hys bowe was great and lange;
         He set that arrowe in his bowe,
         That was both styffe and stronge.

640   He prayed the people that was there
         That they would styll stande;
         "For he that shooteth for such a wager,
         Behoveth a stedfast hand."   *Requires*

         Muche people prayed for Cloudeslé,
645   That hys lyfe saved myght be,
         And whan he made hym redy to shote,
         There was many a wepynge eye.

         Thus Clowdeslé clefte the apple in two,
         That many a man it se;
650   "Over Goddes forbode," sayd the kynge,   *May God forbid*
         "That thou sholdest shote at me!"

"I gyve the eighteen pens a daye,
And my bowe shalte thou bere,
And over all the north countree
655   I make the chefe rydere."   *ranger*

"And I gyve the twelve pens a day," sayd the quene,
"By God and by my faye;
Come fetche thy payment whan thou wylt,
No man shall say the naye.

660   "Wyllyam, I make the gentylman   *thee*
Of clothynge and of fee,
And thy two brethren yemen of my chambre,
For they are so semely to se.

"Your sone, for he is tendre of age,
665   Of my wyne seller shall he be,   *In my wine cellar*
And whan he commeth to mannes state,
Better avaunced shall he be.

"And, Wylliam, brynge me your wyfe," sayd the quene;
Me longeth sore here to se;
670   She shall be my chefe gentylwoman,
And governe my nursery."

The yemen thanked them full courteysly,
And sayd, "To Rome streyght wyll we wende,
Of all the synnes that we have done
675   To be assoyled of his hand."   *absolved; [the pope's]*

So forthe be gone these good yemen,
As fast as they myght hye,
And after came and dwelled with the kynge,
And dyed good men all thre.

680   Thus endeth the lyves of these good yemen,
God sende them eternall blysse,
And all that with hande-bowe shoteth,
That of heven they may never mysse!

Notes

Abbreviations: A = John Byddell (c. 1536); B = Wynkyn de Worde (c. 1510); C = Copland (c. 1550).

7   *the*. Child emends to *thre* as the outlaws are consistently mentioned as a threesome, but while this makes sense it does not seem necessary.

16   *Englysshe wood*. Child prints the name without a gap, presumably on the model of Inglewood, the usual name for this forest. It is mentioned in the first quasi-historical reference to Robin Hood and Little John, that is, in the chronicle by Andrew of Wyntoun written in the 1420s; it is also a forest of adventure in *The Awntyrs of Arthur*, a fifteenth-century alliterative poem. However, little is made of the forest as a location in this ballad.

50   The source reads "In woulde," and while a construction could begin this way, it is more likely that "In" is an error for "I," as Child emends.

74   *saye*. Child emends to *sayne* for the sake of the rhyme, which seems unnecessary.

80   Child inserts *as* (not in any of the sources) after *fast,* but this is an acceptable Middle English condensed idiom and the emendation is not necessary.

84   Child inserts *they* (not in any of the sources) before *hyed,* presumably on metrical grounds, but this is not necessary.

95   *hys*. A: *hy.*

99   *commeth*. Not *cometh,* as Child has it.

132   *bow*. A: *bo.*

133   *spercles* is an unusual version of "sparks," here apparently meaning "embers."

174   *there*. Child emends to *fayre* and Dobson and Taylor (1976, p. 264) add *fayre* to *there*. There seems no ground for either of these versions.

191   *reste*. A: *reate*. Child spells it as *reaste* as if the *s* has dropped out, rather than being mis-set by *A*, which is more likely.

204   Child leaves a gap here, but does not insert a fitt marker. He does the same at each later fitt break.

211   At this point Child begins to use the source he calls *B*, a fragmentary print which does appear to have some good readings, but is not here always accepted, as *C* seems in several instances better.

227   Child's source *B* provides *two* before *messengers*, but *C* seems to have the sharper line and is accepted here.

228   *come ryght*. This is the *C* reading, where the *B* fragment has *comen streyght* which, like *two* in the previous line, seems the sort of expansion and banalization that comes with a later text.

241   Child prints *got* from *B* after *have;* this (as in line 228) seems a weaker reading and is here not accepted.

249   Child follows *B* in reading *Now we are in* (though *Now* is from *C*, as *B* here is cropped). However, the *C* reading *Now are we in* is better Middle English, inverting subject and verb after an initial conjunction or adverbial. Therefore *C* is accepted.

250   Child prints *Therof,* but in fact *C*, from which he draws the initial letter (*B* is still cropped), has *Wherof*.

268   *lyeth* is Child's reading, which is accepted; it is presumably an emendation of *C* which reads *lyveth* (*B* lacks lines 268–70), an inappropriate term for being in captivity compared with the familiar collocation with *lie*: see line 277, where William *lay* in a cart.

270   This action is a preparation for shooting seriously; if the bow strings are twisted, not running straight between the two ends of the bow, the arrow may veer off course.

275   *swerers*. *B*'s reading is clearly much better than *C* and the rest with the meaningless *squyeres*: the *swerers*, or jurors, formed the jury.

285   *Clowdyslé*, not as Child has it *Clowdeslye*.

293   This is a five-line stanza, presumably because the author added a rhyming line, thinking *market place* ended the second, not third line. This casts some light on the irregularities found elsewhere, when it does not always seem that a line is missing when a stanza is deficient.

301–30   Child is again using *B* and providing the opening words from *C* as the *B* leaf is cropped in these lines.

346   *an oute-horne*. Skeat suggested this should be emended to *a noute-horne*, that is, a horn which was sounded at need *(noute)*. Child accepted this, but it is clear (as Dobson and Taylor note, 1976, p. 267) that an "out horn" was sounded to bring every body *out* in the streets, and the text can stand.

347   A peal of bells is rung "backward," that is, out of their usual order, for an alarm.

353   *For theyr lyves stode in doubt*. The more elaborate *C* version *For of theyr lyves they stode in great doubt* appears derived from *B*, and the *C* editor or compositor has personalized the idiom "to stand in doubt." Therefore, Child's *B* reading is accepted here.

360   *yll*, from *B*, seems a better reading than *C*'s *evyll*: *yll* implies an injury, but *evyll* is less well focussed.

394   The *B* fragment here lacks the word *wepe* at the end of the line, but although this is an elaboration, the line seems so much weaker without it that it is accepted.

402   Child feels there is a line missing, and employs one found in a later print. This is accepted here, though it is curious that, as in a number of other cases where the regular four-line-stanza pattern seems disrupted, the rhyme scheme is related to a line in the previous stanza. Could this in fact be an irregular seven-line stanza? While this is conceivable, it seems simpler to print, following Child, the extra line.

406　The *B* fragment only has *chyldre* but although this, a version of *childer*, is an acceptable plural for *child*, the text is cropped hereabouts: the final *n*, found in *C*, has probably been lost, and is printed here. However, *B* is unlikely to have had room for *thre* before clipping, and this is omitted as a *C* filler.

452　At this point Child adopts the *A* fragment as a basis of his text, and this is followed here; it is distinctly earlier than Copland's *C* text and has some good readings.

455　Child finds *chyde* invisible and adds it from a later text, but it is in fact just readable.

480　*deed*. Child emends the spelling to *dead*, but *deed* is perfectly acceptable as a spelling.

512　*A* reads *toures and towne* and while this might seem a sensible reading, the king does shortly refer to *townes* being on offer (line 519), so Child's plural emendation seems sensible.

525　*C* reads *they comfort* not *comfort they* as Child has it.

527　For the cultural significance of hand washing before a meal, see the note to line 164 of *Robin Hood and the Potter*. See also lines 125 and 921 in the *Gest*.

536　*fare*. Child emends to *fareth*, but in fact the subject is plural, being both *justice* and, in the next line, *sherife*.

546　*than*. MS: *an*. Emended by Child to *than*, as is found in later texts and seems essential.

576　With the *C* text Child reads *buske* but this would make a very dramatic historic present, not supported by anything else in context, and it seems the later texts are right to use a past tense *busked*.

594　This describes the hardest test of shooting; elsewhere (see *Gest*, lines 1165–66, 1600–01) archers aimed simply at peeled wands set in the ground. Sometimes the wands carried circular targets, like wreaths, but even then to split the wands was the greatest skill.

602   *a bearyng arow*, as Dobson and Taylor note (1976, p. 271), is the opposite of a "broad arrow," and is designed for distance rather than causing damage; it is also called a "flight arrow." When William uses a "broad" or heavy arrow to split the apple (line 614) the range of 120 paces makes the feat all the more remarkable.

637   *lange*. Child emends to *longe* for rhyme, but this is unnecessary in the context of the relaxed practices of ballad rhyming.

642   The *A* fragment is used by Child as the basis of his text until the end of the text, see note to line 452.

673   The *A* text alone says *To Rome streyght wyll we wende,* and Dobson and Taylor suggest that the fact that it is torn after this point is a result of this Catholic statement (1976, p. 273). However, if sectarian feeling had interfered with the text, it would be probable that the Catholic statement would be destroyed, and casual damage is a more likely reason for the missing lines. Sectarianism is, however, evident in the fact that all the post-reformation texts read *To some bishop we will wende.*

Robyn Hod and the Shryff off Notyngham

Introduction

Notwithstanding his important role in ballads and prose fiction, Robin Hood would have been best known in communities throughout fifteenth- and sixteenth-century Britain as the subject of a wide range of theatrical and quasi-theatrical entertainments. Most took the form of ceremonial games, dances, pageants, processions, and other mimetic events of popular culture of which we only get a fleeting glimpse in surviving civic and ecclesiastical records. Revels featuring the legendary outlaw appear to have surged in growth towards the close of the fifteenth century and remained popular from the royal court to the rural village green throughout the following century (Lancashire, p. xxvi). Indeed, it is not exaggerating to say that Robin Hood plays and games were *the* most popular form of secular dramatic entertainment in provincial England for most of the sixteenth century (for records of performance, see Lancashire, index under "Robin Hood"). This is generally unrecognized by both literary and theatrical historians, many of whom assume that the Tudor Reformation quickly put an end to such popular pastimes — it did not (White, p. 163). But there are other reasons for overlooking Robin Hood spectacles: few Robin Hood play scripts survive (folk plays were rarely written down and published) and only in the past few years have archivists and provincial historians (many working on the Records of Early English Drama project) begun to document in a systematic way records of theatrical entertainment in early modern England.

Although the first record of a Robin Hood play is from Exeter in 1426–27 (Lancashire, p. 134), the earliest extant play text, a twenty-one line dramatic fragment from East Anglia known as *Robyn Hod and the Shryff off Notyngham*, is dated half-a-century later. The text is written on one side of a single sheet of paper, now housed in Trinity College Library, Cambridge; the other side of the page, in a hand thought to be from the same period, contains accounts of money received by one John Sterndalle in 1475–76 (Dobson and Taylor, p. 203). Scholars connect the manuscript to Sir John Paston, who, in a letter of April 1473, complains that his horse-keeper W. Wood has "goon into Bernysdale" (i.e., left his service). Paston further remarks that "I have kepyd hym thys iij. yer to pleye Seynt Jorge and Robyn Hod and the Shryff off Notyngham" (Gairdner, p. 185). It would appear, therefore, that this script is of a Robin Hood play sponsored by the household of this well-to-do Norwich gentleman and performed by his servants in the early 1470s.

As the transcription of the manuscript version, which lacks speaker rubrics, scene divisions, and stage directions, makes clear, the text is more of "a scenario or mnemonic providing a framework for improvisation" than a finished script (Wiles, p. 37). While there are certainly ambiguities in the text, the settings, speakers, and actions, especially in the first scene, are relatively easy to follow, which suggests that the script may be complete as it stands. The mentions of the *lynde* in line 3 and the *prysone* in line 20 indicate that there are two fictional settings: the greenwood and a prison. We say "fictional" because the staging conventions of the time required little more than a spacious outdoor playing area — perhaps a field near the Paston household, where archery, wrestling, and stone-throwing competitions could take place freely. The dialogue, much of it in direct address, often mentions the addressee's name: *Syr Sheryffe* (line 1), *Robyn Hode* (line 5), *Syr Knyght* (line 15), indicating a cast of three actors for the scene, possibly others if Robin's men appear when summoned (line 17). Likewise, the simple active verbs identify most of the actions and act as stage directions: *caste the stone* (line 11), *blowe myn horne* (line 17), and *off I smyte* (line 22). The second scene, however, is much less clear in speaker identity and action, although it is reasonable to conclude that it requires seven or more actors to play two unnamed outlaws, Friar Tuck, the Sheriff, his deputies, and Robin Hood.

The minimal dialogue and the active verbs underscore the real appeal of the play — improvisational action. What is important here is robust activity: an archery match, stone throwing, tossing the pole ("caber" in Scotland), wrestling, and vigorous sword fighting. "The dialogue," as David Wiles observes, "serves simply to punctuate the action" (pp. 31, 37). The various sporting competitions are akin to those performed in May games, of which, in many communities, Robin Hood plays formed an important part (see Introduction to *Robyn Hood and the Friar* and *Robyn Hood and the Potter*, pp. 281–84), and the climactic hero-combat of the first scene and the melee at the end of the second recall two other types of folk drama popular in the fifteenth century, the St. George play and the Hock Tuesday play. Not surprisingly, Paston's servant/player, Wood, excelled in the St. George play as well (see Mills, pp. 136–37).

As mentioned above, the plot of the first scene is relatively straightforward. An unidentified knight offers to capture Robin Hood, and the sheriff agrees, offering to pay him *golde and fee*. The sheriff apparently withdraws, while the knight confronts Robin under a tree and challenges him to an archery contest. The shooting match proceeds, and Robin wins when he splits the target. Next the pair compete at stone casting, pole throwing, and wrestling. Robin wins one fall, while the knight wins the other. After being thrown, Robin curses the knight and blows his horn to summon help from his companions. Robin then challenges the knight to a sword fight to the death, and Robin kills the knight and cuts off his head, placing the severed head in his hood. Robin then dons the knight's attire, and the first scene ends. As David Mills remarks, a good part of the play's impact derives "from the comic social inversion of the knight's defeat, and a further part from the recognition and dramatic frustration of the 'death-resurrection-triumph' pattern of hero-combat plays. The knight's death here is final, followed by his functional beheading (to prevent identification?)" (Mills, p. 136).

The second scene begins when two unidentified outlaws greet each other, one telling the other that Robin and some of his men have been captured by the sheriff. (This revelation does not follow logically from what has happened at the end of the first scene, when Robin kills the bounty-hunting knight and dons his clothing. In order for the second scene to make sense, Robin has to have been identified and captured by the sheriff; so something is missing here.) The two outlaws then agree to *sette on foote* (line 29) in order to find and kill the sheriff. On route to town, they see Friar Tuck drawing his bow; he is single-handedly fighting the sheriff and his men. The three of them are suddenly surrounded and ordered to yield. One of the outlaws (Little John?), addressing Friar Tuck, exclaims that they have been captured and bound. As the three outlaws are taken to the gates of the prison, the sheriff orders the *fals outlawe* (line 37), presumably Robin Hood who is inside, to come out to face his execution. As the gates are opened for the *thevys* to go in — and this is conjectural — Robin and the men inside jump the sheriff and his men, rescue the three outlaws outside, and escape. This reading resolves the problem, as created by Wiles and others, of having Robin, still in disguise as the knight, show up to rescue his men and throw the sheriff in prison. While Wiles's reading gives the play ironic closure — the "jailer jailed" — it ignores the fact that Robin has been taken prisoner in lines 27–28.

Much of the critical commentary has attempted to link the play to the ballad *Robin Hood and Guy of Gisborne*. While there are similarities — the sheriff hires a bounty-hunter to kill Robin, Robin and the antagonist engage in a shooting match and a sword fight, Robin decapitates his enemy and blows a horn, and Robin frees Little John from the sheriff — the major differences suggest instead that the play and the ballad share a common but distant source.

Two other points are worth noting. First, the references to Frere Tuke in lines 31 and 36 of the play are significant because they mark the first appearance of the outlaw ecclesiastic in literature. The early ballads — *Robin Hood and the Monk*, *Robin Hood and the Potter*, and the *Gest* — feature Robin, Little John, Much, and Will, but not Friar Tuck. In *Robin Hood and the Monk*, Robin is forced to go to Nottingham to attend mass because he has no chaplain in Sherwood. Like Maid Marian, Friar

271

Tuck enters the legend relatively late and from a source different from the early ballads. One theory identifies Friar Tuck as the criminal alias of a historical outlaw, Robert Stafford, chaplain of Lindfield, Sussex, who was charged in 1417 with a variety of serious offenses, including poaching, robbery, and murder (Holt, 1989, 58–59). Another theory connects Friar Tuck to the morris dances, in which a friar is paired with a "girlfriend," popularly identified as Maid Marian. The morris dance, however, is a late medieval, if not a Tudor, development, and, hence, too late to have influenced the 1475 play (Knight, 1994, p. 104). A third theory, not mentioned by previous commentators, is that Friar Tuck is somehow related to another historical outlaw, Eustache the Monk (c. 1170–1217), who is the subject of a thirteenth-century French romance, *Li Romans de Witasse le Moine*. After his father was murdered, Eustache left the abbey of Saint Samer and demanded justice from the count of Boulogne. When Eustache's champion loses the judicial duel, his lands and titles are confiscated by the count. Eustache escapes and disguises himself as a monk, calling himself Witasse le Moine. Using a variety of other disguises and tricks, Eustache exacts his revenge on the count by harrying his men and stealing his property. Eustache was not unknown in England, where for a time he supported the cause of King John against the French. Switching sides, he was killed by the English in a naval battle at Sandwich in 1217. In *The Lost Literature of Medieval England* (London: Methuen, 1970), R. M. Wilson observes that the stories of Eustache were well-known in England (p. 117). Among other accounts, now lost, two fourteenth-century chroniclers, John of Canterbury and William of Guisborough, recounted his adventures.

Of further significance is that the play, like contemporary ballads and commentary through to the mid-sixteenth century, emphasizes Robin Hood as a "figure of anarchy rather than of justice" (Mills, p. 133) who is openly defiant of constituted authority. Not surprisingly, some government officials perceived the plays as politically subversive. Around 1540, Richard Morrison, an advisor to Henry VIII, condemned "the lewdenes and ribawdry that there is opened to the people, disobedience also to your [i.e., the King's] officers, is tought, whilest these good bloodes go about to take from the shiref of Notyngham one that for offendyng the lawes should have suffered execution" (text in Anglo; see p. 179). Critics in the past have explained the inversion of authority in the plays as a civic-and-church sponsored "safety-valve" to release pent-up frustrations of the common people, and indeed at least one contemporary reported that the mock fighting was a useful form of military exercise for the citizenry preparing for invasion and war (Child, III, 45). Nevertheless some recent scholarship has connected seasonal festivity involving Robin Hood to popular resistance and even peasant rebellions (Billington, p. 1). Certainly there are instances of social disorder, even riots, occasioned by Robin Hood games, but surviving records are either ambiguous about the cause of disorder or indicate that the riots, or threatened riots, arose from prohibitions against the popular revels (Lancashire, p. 91). Moreover, studies undertaken by Peter Greenfield and James Stokes demonstrate that in the majority of cases in provincial towns of England, "Robin Hood games and king-ales function as charitable fund-raisers, authorized by and organized by local officials — usually the churchwardens — and usually culminating in a communal feast," and that they are "anything but spontaneous expressions of popular resistance to authority" (Greenfield, p. 2; Stokes).

The text of the dramatic fragment is presented in two versions: an exact transcription of the manuscript, retaining the spellings and punctuation, and a conjectural reconstruction of the fragment in two scenes.

Select Bibliography

Manuscript

Trinity College Library, Cambridge, R.2.64 (fragment).

Editions

Child, F. J., ed. *English and Scottish Popular Ballads*. 5 vols. Boston: Houghton Mifflin and Company, 1882–98; rpt. New York: Dover, 1965. Vol III, 90–91.

Dobson, R. B., and J. Taylor, eds. *Rymes of Robin Hode: An Introduction to the English Outlaw*. London: William Heinemann, 1976. Pp. 203–07.

Greg, W. W., ed. "Robin Hood and the Sheriff of Nottingham, A Dramatic Fragment." *Collections Part II*. The Malone Society. Vol. 1. Oxford, 1908. Pp. 120–24.

Manly, J. M., ed. *Specimens of the Pre-Shakespearean Drama*, I. Boston: Ginn and Company, 1897. Pp. 279–81.

Wiles, David. *The Early Plays of Robin Hood*. Cambridge: D. S. Brewer, 1981.

Commentary and Criticism

Anglo, Sydney. "An Early Tudor Programme for Plays and Other Demonstrations against the Pope." *Journal of the Warburg and Courtauld Institutes* 20 (1957), 176–79.

Plays: Robin Hood in Performance

Billington, Sandra. *Mock Kings in Medieval Society and Renaissance Drama*. Oxford: Clarendon, 1992. P. 1.

Chambers, E. K. *The English Folk-Play*. Oxford, 1933.

———. *The Medieval Stage*, I. Oxford: Clarendon Press, 1953. Pp. 160–81.

Child, F. J., ed. *English And Scottish Popular Ballads*. 5 vols. Boston: Houghton Mifflin and Company, 1882–98; rpt. New York: Dover, 1965.

Dobson, R. B., and J. Taylor, eds. *Rymes of Robyn Hood: An Introduction to the English Outlaw*. London: William Heinemann, 1976.

Gairdner, James, ed. *The Paston Letters A.D. 1422–1509*. New York: AMS Press, 1965.

Greenfield, Peter. "The Carnivalesque in the King Ales and Robin Hood Games of Southern England." Unpublished paper presented at S. I. T. M., August 3, 1995.

Holt, J. C. *Robin Hood*. London: Thames and Hudson, 1982. Second ed. 1989.

Knight, Stephen. *Robin Hood: A Complete Study of the English Outlaw*. Oxford: Blackwell, 1994.

Lancashire, Ian. *Dramatic Texts and Records of Britain: A Chronological Topography to 1558*. Toronto: University of Toronto Press, 1984.

MacLean, Sally-Beth. "King Games and Robin Hood: Play and Profit at Kingston upon Thames." *Research Opportunities in Renaissance Drama* 29 (1986–87), 85–93.

Mills, David. "Drama and Folk-Ritual." *The Revels History of Drama in English, Volume I: Medieval Drama*. London: Methuen, 1983. Pp. 122–51.

Stokes, James. "Robin Hood and the Churchwardens in Yeovil." *Medieval and Renaissance Drama in England* 3 (1986), 4.

White, Paul Whitfield. *Theatre and Reformation: Protestantism, Patronage, and Playing in Tudor England*. Cambridge: Cambridge University Press, 1993.

Wiles, David. *The Early Plays of Robin Hood*. Cambridge: D. S. Brewer, 1981.

Wilson, R. M. *The Lost Literature of Medieval England*. London: Methuen, 1970.

Robyn Hod and the Shryff off Notyngham

I. Manuscript Version

Transcribed from Cambridge, Trinity College MS R.2.64 (fragment), c. 1475

Syr sheryffe for thy sake   Robyn hode wull y take.
I wyll the gyffe golde and fee   This be heste þᵘ holde me.
Robyn hode ffayre and fre   vndre this lynde shote we.
with the shote y wyll   Alle thy lustes to full fyll.
5   Have at the pryke.   And y cleue the styke.
late vs caste the stone   I grūnte well be seynt Iohn.
late vs caste the exaltre   have a foote be fore the.
syr knyght ye haue a falle.   And I the Robyn qwyte shall
Owte on the I blowe myn horne.   hit ware better be vn borne.
10   lat vs fyght at ottraunce   he that fleth god gyfe hym myschaunce.
Now I haue the maystry here   off I smyte this sory swyre
This knyghtys clothis wolle I were   And in my hode his hede woll bere.
welle mete felowe myn   What herst þᵘ of gode Robyn
Robin hode and his menye   wᵗ the sheryffe takyn be.
15   sette on foote wᵗ gode wyll   And the sheryffe wull we kyll
Be holde wele ffrere tuke   howe he dothe his bowe pluke
3eld yow syrs to the sheryffe.   Or elles shall yoʳ bowes clyffe.
Now we be bownden alle in same   ffrere [T]uke þis is no game.
Co[m]e þᵘ forth þᵘ fals outlawe .   Þᵘ shall [be] hangyde and y drawe.
20   Now allas what shall we doo   we [m]oste to the prysone goo
Opy[n] the yatis [faste] anon   An[d la]te theis thevys ynne gon

II. Reconstruction of the dramatic fragment in two scenes with designated speakers.

Scene One

[*The scene is set in the forest.*]

Knight	Syr Sheryffe, for thy sake		
	Robyn Hode wull Y take.		
Sheriff	I wyll the gyffe golde and fee	*give you*	
	This beheste thou holde me.	*promise*	

[*The Sheriff exits, and Robin Hood enters.*]

5	*Knight*	Robyn Hode, ffayre and fre,	
		Undre this lynde shote we.	*tree*
	Robin Hood	With the shote Y wyll	
		Alle thy lustes to full-fyll.	*desires*
	Knight	Have at the pryke.	*target or bull's eye*
10	*Robin Hood*	And Y cleve the styke.	*stick*

[*They shoot at the target, and Robin wins.*]

Robin Hood	Late us caste the stone.	*throw*
Knight	I graunte well, be Seynt John.	

[*They throw stones.*]

Robin Hood	Late us caste the exaltre.	*axle-tree, cart axle*

[*They toss the wooden axle.*]

Knight	Have a foote before the.	*Half a foot*

[*They wrestle, and Robin throws the knight.*]

15	*Robin Hood*	Syr Knyght, ye have a falle.	
	Knight	And I the, Robyn, qwyte shall.	*pay back*

[*They wrestle again, and the Knight throws Robin.*]

Robin Hood	Owte on the, I blowe myn horne.	*A curse on thee*

[*Robin blows his horn to summon help.*]

	Knight	Hit ware better be un-borne.	
	Robin Hood	Lat us fyght at ottraunce.	*to the death*
20		He that fleth, God gyfe hym myschaunce.	

[*They sword fight, and Robin wins.*]

| Robin Hood | Now I have the maystry here, | |
| | Off I smyte this sory swyre. | *neck* |

[*Robin decapitates the knight.*]

| Robin Hood | This knyghtys clothis wolle I were | |
| | And in my hode his hede woll bere. | |

[*Robin dresses in the knight's clothing, and places his head in his hood.*]

Scene Two

[*Robin Hood is in prison with several of his men.*]

| | Outlaw #1 | Welle mete, felowe myn. | |
| 25 | | What herest thou of gode Robyn? | |

| | Outlaw #2 | Robyn Hode and his menye | *company* |
| | | With the Sheryffe takyn be. | |

| | Outlaw #1 | Sette on foote with gode wyll, | |
| 30 | | And the Sheryffe wull we kyll. | |

| | Outlaw #2 | Beholde wele Frere Tuke | |
| | | Howe he dothe his bowe pluke. | *draw back the string* |

[*Friar Tuck is presumably attacking the Sheriff single-handedly.*]

| | Sheriff | Yeld yow, syrs, to the Sheryffe, | *Yield* |
| | | Or elles shall your bowes clyffe. | *crack* |

[*The three outlaws are captured, and taken to the prison gates.*]

| | Outlaw #1? | Now we be bownden alle in same. | *bound* |
| 35 | | Frere Tuke, this is no game. | |

[*The Sheriff opens the gates and orders Robin Hood to come out.*]

| | Sheriff | Come thou forth, thou fals outlawe. | |
| | | Thou shall be hangyde and y-drawe. | |

| | Outlaw #1? | Nowe allas, what shall we doo? | |
| 40 | | We moste to the prysone goo. | |

| | Sheriff | Opyn the gatis faste anon, | |
| | | And late theis thevys ynne gon. | |

[*As the gates are opened, Robin and the other outlaws presumably attack the Sheriff and escape.*]

Notes

I. Manuscript version

1   The final *e* in *hode* consists of a point.

2   MS: *þ* "thorn" with a superior letter *u = thou*.

3   *ffayre*. Orthographic double f = capital F.

        lynde. The final *e* is a point.

6   *grūnte = graunte*. As indicated by the horizontal line, the medial *a* has been omitted.

14   MS: *w* with superior *t = with*.

17   MS: *ʒeld = Yeld*.

18   Two vertical tears in the sheet disturb some of the letters in the last four lines.

        The *T* of *Tuck* is missing, but easily reconstructed.

19   The *m* of *come* and the auxiliary verb *be* are missing. A later hand has added the missing letters.

20   The end of the word *Now* is missing, but it can be easily reconstructed from the same word in line 18. The second tear disturbs the initial letter of *moste*, and Greg's reconstruction is accepted (p. 121).

21   This line is damaged by two tears and a smudge. The last letter of the first word is easily determined by context. The fourth word is badly smudged, but the initial letters *fa* can just be discerned. The MED (vol. E–F, p. 413) lists *faste anon* as meaning "quickly, instantly, or immediately," so this is the likely

278

reading. The second tear obscures the ending of one word and the beginning of another; we accept Greg's emendation: *An[d la]te*.

II. Reconstruction of the dramatic fragment

1   In line 15 Robin addresses the bounty-hunter as *Syr Knyght*. By contrast, in *Robin Hood and Guy of Gisborne*, the putative source, the antagonist is a *wight yeoman* (line 19).

3   *golde and fee*. In feudal law, a fee is "an estate in land, held on condition of homage and service to a superior lord" (OED). In *Robin Hood and Guy of Gisborne* (line 204), the sheriff offers Robin, disguised in Gisborne's horse-hides, a *knights fee*.

6   *lynde*. The linden tree (*tilia europaea*), but in ME poetry any kind of tree (OED). The presence of a tree indicates a forest setting.

5–10   The sequence of speakers and their actions in these lines is unclear. In lines 5–6 the knight challenges Robin to a shooting match, and in 7–8 Robin agrees to satisfy the knight's desire. If line 9 is assigned to the knight, then Robin would be the winner when he splits the bull's eye in line 10. However, if line 9 is a continuation of Robin's response, then line 10 should be assigned to the knight, who then would be the winner of the match. There is precedent for Robin losing a shooting match: in lines 47–50 of *Robin Hood and the Monk*, Robin loses the game of *shete a peny* to Little John. Robin also loses the shooting game of *plucke buffet* to King Richard in the *Gest* (lines 1609–12).

10   *styke*. A stick or wand stuck in the ground in front of the *pryke* or bull's-eye, see *Adam Bell*, lines 580–603.

13   *exaltre* = axle-tree. A beam of wood used as the axle of a cart (OED).

14   On wrestling, see note to line 548 of the *Gest*.

22   In *Robin Hood and Guy of Gisborne* (lines 167–70), Robin not only decapitates Guy but literally "defaces" him.

279

23 In *Robin Hood and Guy of Gisborne*, Guy is dressed in *capull-hyde* or horse hides, and Robin exchanges clothing with him after he kills him (lines 175–78).

24 *in my hode his hede*. This grotesque act may be related to the expression *best ball in his hode* in line 1454 of the *Gest*.

25 Based on parallels with *Robin Hood and Guy of Gisborne*, Little John and Will Scarlock are identified as the speakers.

Robin Hood and the Friar and Robin Hood and the Potter

Introduction

The survival of *Robin Hood and the Friar* and *Robin Hood and the Potter*, our next earliest play script following the fragment of c. 1475, is due to printer William Copland's decision to append it to his edition of *A Mery Geste of Robyn Hoode and of Hys Lyfe*, dated somewhere between 1549 and 1569, but most likely printed in 1560 when he entered a Robin Hood play in the Stationers' Register. There are no extant manuscript versions. The appended text preserves two dramatic pieces: lines 1–122 in this edition contain the well-known account of Robin's initial confrontation with Friar Tuck, in which physical and verbal sparring of the two is followed by the cleric carrying Robin on his back through a stream before dropping him into the water. After further fighting Robin seeks help from his men and then offers Friar Tuck gold and "a lady" (a precursor to Maid Marian as bawd?) in exchange for service. Lines 123–203 recount a second example of "Robin meets his match," this time with a potter who refuses to pay road-toll, for which Robin breaks his pots and engages in a fencing duel.

Unlike *Robyn Hod and the Shryff off Notyngham*, which is linked with a particular gentleman's household in late fifteenth-century East Anglia, no specific auspices can be found for this drama, although Copland's introductory remark that it is "verye proper to be played in Maye Games" suggests that the two dramatic pieces were typical of the numerous Robin Hood plays sponsored by parishes and civic organizations all across Britain throughout the Tudor era. The lengthy festive season for May games often extended from May 1 through Whitsuntide (a holy day celebrated seven weeks after Easter) when towns and villages chose a May King and Queen (or Lord and Lady) to preside over various festivities, including dances around the Maypole, nights sleeping in the greenwood, sporting contests (e.g., wrestling and archery) and processions around town and to neighboring villages, often for the purpose of raising money for poor relief and church maintenance.

By the end of the fifteenth century, many villages and towns renamed their May king (also known as Summer Lord, Lord of Misrule, Abbot of Bon Accord) Robin Hood, and followed suit by calling the May Queen Maid Marian and their attendants, Friar Tuck, Little John, and the rest of the merry band of outlaws bearing pipes, tabors, and drums. In some towns the change of title is very deliberate and can be precisely dated, as in Aberdeen, Scotland, where an order of 17 November 1508 formally announces that the traditional procession through town will be led by "Robert huyd and litile Iohn" formally known as "Abbot and priour of Bonacord" (Mills, p. 135). E. K. Chambers and others speculate that Robin and Marian entered the May game via the old French *pasteurella* popularized in England by French minstrels (*Medieval Stage*, I, 160–81). This lyric poem is about a shepherdess called Marion who rejects the advances of a knight out of fidelity to another lover named Robe. However, this alone is not an adequate explanation. The already legendary home-grown hero's associations with nature and the forest, with physical prowess, generosity, camaraderie, as well as the subversive spirit of summer games themselves, made him the perfect choice as the fictional persona of the Summer Lord. Moreover, Robin Hood, Maid Marian, and their colorful entourage of outlaws gave an added theatrical dimension to the May revels. As David Mills asserts, "identification by costume was essential," indicated in the churchwarden's accounts of Kingston-on-Thames, 1507–29, which show "regular expenditure on the costumes and appurtenances ('banner,' 'cote,' 'gloves and shoes') of 'Robyn Hode,'" and other dress items displaying Maid Marian as the May Queen and the Friar as one of the morris dancers (Mills, p. 135). This is not to suggest that communities dispensed with the traditional generic role of the Summer Lord. At Wells in May 1607, for example, the "Lord of the May" led a procession which included Robin Hood and his men as one of ten such groups of characters (Lancashire, p. 280). By the latter part of the sixteenth century, the May-game Marian developed her own separate persona as a figure of sexual license, frequently presented as a conspicuously cross-dressed male, as illustrated in an anti-Marprelate play of the 1580s where Martin appears on stage as the "Maide marian," possibly to satirize puritan opposition to boys playing female roles (see Chambers, *Elizabethan Stage*, IV, 231).

Contemporary records indicate that civic and parish sponsored Robin Hood plays, like most of the other May games, took place outdoors, and indeed the first sequence involving Friar Tuck may have been performed next to a river or stream, for the dialogue has the Friar, with Robin on his back, wading into water before Robin is dropped in (Blackstone, pp. 6–7). A body of water, however, is not necessary for the action to be effective, and since local actors often took their productions to neighboring towns, little if any scenery and only a few properties (e.g., clubs and staves, a horn, and perhaps some musical instruments) would be expected. If the two dramatic pieces are performed together, a minimum of seven actors are required. Since one of the characters is "a lady," six men and one woman may have participated, but considering Tudor conventions of acting and of the depiction of Maide Marian at the time (noted above), the female character was likely impersonated by a cross-dressed male. An intriguing feature of *Robin Hood and the Friar* is the evident requirement of three dogs who accompany Friar Tuck when he enters ("these dogs all three"). Animals, in fact, were not infrequent participants in productions of the time (see White, p. 120 and p. 221 n. 67). However, whereas in the ballad version of the play the Friar's dogs fight Robin's men, in the play (where this might have been too dangerous to stage) they are replaced by the Friar's own men (albeit with canine names like Cut and Bause) who fight with staves and clubs (see Blackstone, p. 4).

The relationships of the two dramatic texts to their narrative and visual sources are problematic. The first play antedates its corresponding ballad, *Robin Hood and the Curtal Friar*, by at least one hundred years. A late medieval ballad probably existed because a fighting friar appears in the Paston fragment of c. 1475. The play's anti-fraternal satire recall's Chaucer's depiction of Frere Huberd, who was himself strong "as a champioun," and yet it is also representative of Protestant ballads and plays of the mid-sixteenth century in which the boasting, lecherous, and merrymaking mendicant is widely featured and often conflated with the comic Vice (see, for example, John Bale's anti-Catholic plays). It's worth noting that Francis Child omitted the eight-line bawdy speech of the Friar near the end in his truncated version of the play, and by so doing destroyed the continuing anti-clerical satire and carnivalesque atmosphere of the May games in which social conventions were mocked or inverted. The Friar's remark *Here is an huckle duckle/An inch above the buckle* (lines 115–16) suggests he may have sported an artificial phallus to signify sexual virility like that of comic figures in the folk drama (for example, Robin Goodfellow appeared with horns, goat-feet and a phallus [see White, pp. 31–32 and fig. 4]). Child's omission also deprives the play of the dramatic resolution inherent in the dance in which Friar Tuck joins with "the lady." A stained glass window in Betley Hall, Staffordshire, pictures Friar Tuck participating in a morris dance with a lady who appears to be Maide Marian, but whether the play's female figure is Marian is questionable, even if she does suggest the licentious Marian of the May games (see Blackstone, p. 13 and fig. 3). In the case of the second play text, the ballad, *Robin Hood and the Potter*, antedates the play by about sixty years. We may be witnessing, as Dobson and Taylor claim, the "transformation from recited tale to dramatic version" (p. 215). Two pairs of lines are virtually identical:

ballad:	Ne was never so corteys a man	
	On peney of pawage to pay	(lines 19–20)
play:	Yet was he never so curteyse a potter	
	As one peny passage to paye	(lines 132–33)
ballad:	Yend potter well steffeley stonde	(line 66)
play:	And I wyll styfly by you stande	(line 199)

However, if the play were a dramatized version of the first fitt of the ballad, one would expect to find many more borrowings, such as the amount of the bet — *forty shillings* versus *twenty pound* in the play. Also, Jack the potter's boy is not found in the ballad. If the play script was adapted from the longer and more complex ballad, one would also expect a minor character to be omitted rather than added. There is no question that the play is based upon the story of the potter, but it is probably not the exact one that survives.

Select Bibliography

Early Printed Texts

Copland, William. *A Mery Geste of Robyn Hoode and of Hys Lyfe*. Printed at Three Cranes Wharf, London, c. 1560. British Library copy, press-mark C.21.C.63.

White, Edward. *A Merry Jest of Robin Hood*. Printed at London, c. 1590. Bodleian Library copy, 2.3 Art, Seld.

Editions

Blackstone, Mary A., ed. *Robin Hood and the Friar*. PLS Performance Text 3. Toronto: Poculi Ludique Societas, 1981.

Dobson, R. B., and J. Taylor, eds. *Rymes of Robyn Hood: An Introduction to the English Outlaw*. London: William Heinemann, 1976.

Farmer, John S., ed. *Robin Hood c. 1561–9*. Amersham: Tudor Facsimile Texts 102, 1914.

Greg, W. W., ed. "A Play of Robin Hood for May-games from the Edition by William Copland, c. 1560." *Collections Part II*. The Malone Society. Oxford, 1908.

Manly, John Matthews, ed. *Specimens of the Pre-Shakspearean Drama*. 2 vols. Boston: Ginn and Company, 1897. I, 281–88.

Robin Hood and the Friar and Robin Hood and the Potter

Commentary and Criticism

Blackstone, Mary A., pp. 1–24.

Chambers, E. K. *The Elizabethan Stage*. 4 vols. Oxford: Clarendon, 1923.

——. *The Medieval Stage*, 2 vols. Oxford: Clarendon, 1903.

Dobson, R. B., and J. Taylor, pp. 210–14, 216–19.

Jones, William Powell. *The Pasteurella: A Study of the Origins and Tradition of a Lyric Type*. Cambridge, MA: Harvard University Press, 1931.

Knight, Stephen. *Robin Hood: A Complete Study of the English Outlaw*. Oxford: Blackwell, 1994. Pp. 100–01.

Lancashire, Ian. *Dramatic Texts and Records of Britain: A Chronological Topography to 1558*. Toronto: University of Toronto Press, 1984.

Mills, David. "Drama and Folk-Ritual." In *The Revels History of Drama in English, Volume I: Medieval Drama*. London: Methuen, 1983. Pp. 122–51.

Wiles, David. *The Early Plays of Robin Hood*. Cambridge: D. S. Brewer, 1981. Pp. 39–40.

White, Paul Whitfield. *Theatre and Reformation: Protestantism, Patronage, and Playing in Tudor England*. Cambridge: Cambridge University Press, 1993.

Robin Hood and the Friar and Robin Hood and the Potter

Source: William Copland's *A Mery Geste of Robyn Hoode and of Hys Lyfe*
(British Library copy, press mark C.21.C.63)

Here beginnethe the Playe
of Robyn Hoode, verye
proper to be played
in Maye Games

[*Enter Robin Hood and his men.*]

Robyn Hode	Now stand ye forth my mery men all,		
	And harke what I shall say;		*listen*
	Of an adventure I shal you tell,		
	The which befell this other day.		
5	As I went by the hygh way,		
	With a stoute frere I met,		
	And a quarter staffe in his hande.		*a thick pole*
	Lyghtely to me he lept,		*Quickly*
	And styll he bade me stande.		
10	There were strypes two or three,		*blows*
	But I cannot tell who had the worse;		
	But well I wote the horeson lepte within me		*son of a whore*
	And fro me he toke my purse.		
	Is there any of my mery men all		
15	That to that frere wyll go,		
	And bryng him to me forth withall,		
	Whether he wyll or no?		
Lytell John	Yes, mayster, I make God avowe,		
	To that frere wyll I go,		
	And bryng him to you,		
20	Whether he wyl or no.		

[*Exit Robin Hood and his men. Enter Friar Tuck with three dogs.*]

Fryer Tucke	Deus hic! Deus hic! God be here!		*God be here!*
	Is not this a holy worde for a frere?		

286

		God save all this company!	
		But am not I a jolly fryer?	
25		For I can shote both farre and nere,	
		And handle the sworde and buckler,	*small round shield*
		And this quarter staffe also.	
		If I mete with a gentylman or yeman,	
		I am not afrayde to loke hym upon,	
30		Nor boldly with him to carpe;	*talk*
		If he speake any wordes to me,	
		He shall have strypes two or thre,	*blows with the staff*
		That shal make his body smarte.	
		But, maister, to shew you the matter	
35		Wherfore and why I am come hither,	
		In fayth I wyl not spare,	
		I am come to seke a good yeman,	
		In Barnisdale men sai is his habitacion.	
		His name is Robyn Hode,	
40		And if that he be better man than I,	
		His servaunt wyll I be, and serve him truely;	
		But if that I be better man than he,	
		By my truth my knave shall he be,	*male servant*
		And lead these dogges all three.	

[*Enter Robin Hood seizing the friar by the throat.*]

45	**Robyn Hode**	Yelde the, fryer, in thy long cote.	*Yield*
	Fryer Tucke	I beshrew thy hart, knave, thou hurtest my throt.	*curse*
	Robyn Hode	I trowe, fryer, thou beginnest to dote:	*believe; act foolishly*
		Who made the so malapert and so bolde	*impudent*
		To come into this forest here	
50		Amonge my falowe dere?	*yellow-brown deer*

[*Friar Tuck shakes off Robin Hood.*]

	Fryer Tucke	Go louse the, ragged knave.	*delouse yourself*
		If thou make mani wordes,	
		I wil geve the on the eare,	*hit*
		Though I be but a poore fryer.	
55		To seke Robyn Hode I am com here,	
		And to him my hart to breke.	*reveal my intentions*
	Robyn Hode	Thou lousy frer, what wouldest thou with hym?	
		He never loved fryer nor none of freiers kyn.	

	Fryer Tucke	Avaunt, ye ragged knave!	*Go away; base rogue*
60		Or ye shall have on the skynne.	*be hit*
	Robyn Hode	Of all the men in the morning thou art the worst,	
		To mete with the I have no lust;	*desire*
		For he that meteth a frere or a fox in the morning,	
		To spede ell that day he standeth in jeoperdy.	*To prosper badly*
65		Therefore I had lever mete with the devil of hell,	*rather*
		Fryer, I tell the as I thinke,	
		Then mete with a fryer or a fox	
		In a mornyng, or I drynke.	*before I drink*
	Fryer Tucke	Avaunt, thou ragged knave, this is but a mock!	*Go away*
70		If you make mani words, you shal have a knock.	
	Robyn Hode	Harke, frere, what I say here;	
		Over this water thou shalt me bere;	
		The brydge is borne away.	
	Fryer Tucke	To say naye I wyll not;	
75		To let the of thine oth it were great pitie and sin;	
		But upon a fryers backe and have even in.	
	Robyn Hode	Nay, have over.	

     [Robin Hood climbs on the Friar's back.]

	Fryer Tucke	Now am I, frere, within, and, thou, Robin, without,	
		To lay the here I have no great doubt.	

     [Friar Tuck throws Robin Hood.]

80		Now art thou, Robyn, without, and I, frere, within,	
		Lye ther, knave; chose whether thou wilte sinke or swym.	
	Robyn Hode	Why, thou lowsy frere, what hast thou doon?	
	Fryer Tucke	Mary, set a knave over the shone.	*put a fool in your shoes*
	Robyn Hode	Therfore thou abye.	*shall suffer the consequences*
85	*Fryer Tucke*	Why, wylt thou fyght a plucke?	*bout with clubs*
	Robyn Hode	And God send me good lucke.	
	Fryer Tucke	Than have a stroke for Fryer Tucke.	

     [They fight.]

	Robyn Hode	Holde thy hande, frere, and here me speke.

	Fryer Tucke	Saye on, ragged knave,	
90		Me semeth ye begyn to swete.	*It seems to me*

Robyn Hode	In this forest I have a hounde,	
	I wyl not give him for an hundreth pound:	
	Geve me leve my horne to blowe,	
	That my hounde may knowe.	

95	*Fryer Tucke*	Blowe on, ragged knave, without any doubte,	
		Untyll bothe thyne eyes starte out.	*bulge*

[*Robin Hood blows his horn; his men enter.*]

Here be a sorte of ragged knaves come in,
Clothed all in Kendale grene,
And to the they take their way nowe.

100	*Robyn Hode*	Peradventure they do so.	*Perhaps*

Fryer Tucke	I gave the leve to blowe at thy wyll;	*permission*
	Now give me leve to whistell my fyll.	

Robyn Hode	Whystell, frere, evyl mote thou fare!	*may*
	Untyll bothe thyne eyes starte.	

[*The Friar whistles.*]

105	*Fryer Tucke*	Now Cut and Bause!
		Breng forth the clubbes and staves,
		And downe with those ragged knaves.

[*They all fight.*]

	Robyn Hode	How sayest thou, frere, wylt thou be my man,
		To do me the best servyse thou can?
110		Thou shalt have both golde and fee.
		And also here is a lady free:

[*Enter the Lady.*]

	I wyll geve her unto the,	
	And her chapplayn I the make	*chaplain*
	To serve her for my sake.	

115	*Fryer Tucke*	Here is an huckle duckle,	
		An inch above the buckle.	
		She is a trul of trust,	*trollop or prostitute*
		To serve a frier at his lust,	
		A prycker, a prauncer, a terer of shetes,	*A rider; a tearer of sheets*

120	A wagger of ballockes when other men slepes.	*testicles*
	Go home, ye knaves, and lay crabbes in the fyre,	*iron trivets*
	For my lady and I wil daunce in the myre,	*soft mud*
	For veri pure joye.	

[*A dance.*]

*   *   *   *   *   *   *   *   *   *

Robyn Hode Lysten to me my mery men all
125 And harke what I shall say
Of an adventure I shall you tell
That befell this othere daye.
With a proude potter I met;
And a rose garlande on his head,
130 The floures of it shone marvaylous freshe.
This seven yere and more he hath used this waye,
Yet was he never so curteyse a potter
As one peny passage to paye.   *toll*
Is there any of my mery men all
135 That dare be so bolde
To make the potter paie passage either silver or golde?

Lytell John Not I, master, for twenty pound redy tolde.
For there is not among us al one
That dare medle with that potter man for man.
140 I felt his handes not long agone,
But I had lever have ben here by the.   *rather*
Therfore I knowe what he is;
Mete hem when ye wil or mete him whan ye shal
He is as propre a man as ever you medle withal.   *good*

145 **Robyn Hode** I wil lai with the, Litel John, twenty pound so read,   *bet; red*
If I wyth that potter mete
I wil make him pay passage, maugré his head.   *against his will*

Lytell John I consente therto, so eate I bread;
If he pay passage, maugré his head,
150 Twenti pound shall ye have of me for your mede.   *reward*

[*Robin's men leave. Enter Jack the potter's boy.*]

Jacke Out alas that ever I sawe this day!
For I am clene out of my waye
From Notygham towne.

		If I hye me not the faster,	*hurry*
155		Or I come there the market wel be done.	*Before*

| **Robyn Hode** | Let me se, are the pottes hole and sounde? |

[*Robin throws a pot to the ground.*]

| **Jacke** | Yea, meister, but they will not breake the ground. |

	Robyn Hode	I wil them breke for the cuckold thi maister's sake;
		And if they will breake the grounde,
160		Thou shalt have thre pence for a pound.

[*Robin breaks more pots.*]

Jacke	Out alas! What have ye done?
	If my maister come, he will breke your crown.

[*The potter enters.*]

	The Potter	Why, thou horeson, art thou here yet?	*bastard*
		Thou shouldest have bene at market.	

	Jacke	I met with Robin Hode, a good yeman;
165		He hath broken my pottes,
		And called you kuckolde by your name.

	The Potter	Thou mayst be a gentylman, so God me save,	
		But thou semest a noughty knave.	*naughty*
170		Thou callest me cuckolde by my name,	
		And I swere by God and Saynt John,	
		Wyfe had I never none:	
		This cannot I denye.	
		But if thou be a good felowe,	
175		I wil sel mi horse, mi harneis, pottes and paniers to,
		Thou shalt have the one halfe, and I wil have the other.
		If thou be not so content,	
		Thou shalt have stripes, if thou were my brother.	

	Robyn Hode	Harke, potter, what I shall say;
180		This seven yere and more thou hast used this way,
		Yet were thou never curteous to me
		As one penny passage to paye.

| **The Potter** | Why should I paye passage to thee? |

	Robyn Hode	For I am Robyn Hode, chiefe governoure
185		Under the grene woode tree.

The Potter	This seven yere have I used this way up and downe,	
	Yet payed I passage to no man;	
	Nor now I wyl not beginne, to do the worst thou can.	

Robyn Hode Passage shalt thou pai, here under the grene wode tre,
190   Or els thou shalt leve a wedded with me.   *forfeit*

The Potter If thou be a good felowe, as men do the call,
                 Laye awaye thy bowe,
                 And take thy sword and buckeler in thy hande,
                 And se what shall befall.

195   *Robyn Hode* Lyttle John, where art thou?

Lyttell John Here, mayster, I make God avowe.
                 I told you, mayster, so God me save,
                 That you should fynde the potter a knave.
                 Holde your buckeler [fast in your hand],
200   And I wyll styfly by you stande,
                 Ready for to fyghte;
                 Be the knave never so stoute,
                 I shall rappe him on the snoute,
                 And put hym to flyghte.

              [A fight follows, and the text ends.]

          Thus endeth the play of Robyn Hode

Imprinted at London upon the Crane wharf by Wyllyam Copland

Notes

21   *Deus hic!* The Friar's knowledge of Latin is questionable. The phrase is probably a corruption of *Haec dicit Dominus Deus* ("Thus saith the Lord God") from the *Roman Missal.* It's the same phrase that Chaucer's friar uses in the Summoner's Tale, line 1770, as the friar approaches the ailing Thomas (glossed in Benson's edition as "God be here!" as does our author). Mary A. Blackstone (p. 28) suggests that the actor's saying of *hic* could be accompanied by hiccups, an auditory pun and that the Friar makes the sign of the cross. In the early Elizabethan context, the Friar's speech and gesturing were familiar instances of anti-Catholic satire. The earliest citation for *hicket,* an early form of "hiccup," is dated 1544 in the OED.

22   This line has been partially cropped, but it is still legible.

34   MS: *maister.* Dobson and Taylor emend to *maisters.*

44   *these dogges all three.* See Introduction, above.

58   Robin's dislike of clergy is also evident in *Robin Hood and the Monk*, where he is betrayed by a *gret-hedid munke*, and in the *Gest*, where he orders Little John to *bete and bynde* bishops and archbishops.

63–64   Mary A. Blackstone (p. 31) detects the presence of a proverb in these lines, but the one she cites from *Proverbs, Sentences, and Proverbial Phrases From English Writings Mainly Before 1500*, Bartlett J. Whiting, ed. (Cambridge: Harvard University Press, 1968), is not very close: *Two Friars and a fox make three shrews* (p. 214). The actual meaning of the proverb is: if you meet a friar or fox in the morning before you eat or drink, you will have bad luck the rest of the day. See Vincent S. Lean, *Lean's Collectanea*, Volume II, Part I (Bristol: J. W. Arrowsmith, 1903), p. 193.

72   See the Introduction for a discussion of the presence or absence of water in the original staging.

293

82   MS: *donee*. Dobson and Taylor emend to *doon*.

92   MS: *an hundreth*. Dobson and Taylor emend to *a hundred*.

98   *Kendale grene*. Fabric manufactured in Kendal, Westmorland.

105   *Cut and Bause*. These sound suspiciously like dogs' names (possibly those referred to in line 44), and while dogs might bring forth the clubs and staves of line 106, it is unlikely that they would fight with them! *Cut* and *Bause*, therefore, are probably the Friar's "men."

111   Dobson and Taylor (1989, p. 214, n. 1) identify the "lady free" with the Maid Marian of the May morris dances, but Stephen Knight (1994, p. 102) notes that the lady is not named in the play and Marian in the morris is never called "Maid."

114   *To serve her for my sake*. As the lines below make clear, the friar's "service" has unmistakable erotic meaning.

115–16 Mary A. Blackstone (p. 37) observes that *huckle duckle* is "a phrase of unclear meaning probably invented to rhyme with *buckle* and convey bawdy innuendo." According to the OED, *huckle* means "hip" or "hip-bone," and "the complete phrase may describe the extent of his physical excitement." For the possible use of a phallus, see Introduction.

119   MS: *sheses*. White's edition (c. 1590) has *shetes*, which we accept.

122   *My lady and I wil daunce*. This likely calls for a morris dance involving all the players; see Introduction.

123   Because the rhyme *fyre / myre* in lines 121–22 indicates a complete couplet, we have added the phrase *for veri pure joye* as a separate short line.

        Following this line, and without a break in the text, is the speaker designation, *Robyn Hode*, as if the play *Robin Hood and the Friar* were continuing at this point. Line 124 clearly indicates — *Lysten to me my mery men all* — that we have the beginning of a second play, which editors call *Robin Hood and the Friar*. While Child and Dobson and Taylor separate the two plays, we have respected the authority, flawed as it is, of Copland's text.

124   Dobson and Taylor add *me*, and this is accepted.

126   The line, which is cropped at the top of the page, is supplied by Dobson and Taylor from Edward White's edition of c. 1590 (Oxford, Bodleian Library Art. Seld. Z.3).

144   MS: *medle*. Dobson and Taylor emend to *medled*.

145   MS: *xx*: *twenty*.

152   The line, which is at the top of the page, is partially cropped.

169   MS: *noughty*. Dobson and Taylor emend to *naughty*.

171   MS: *saynt*. Dobson and Taylor emend to *seynt*.

176   The line, which is at the top of the page, is partially cropped.

182   MS: *penny*. Dobson and Taylor have *peny*.

199   The line, which is at the top of the last page, is partially cropped. Dobson and Taylor supply the missing half line from the White edition, and this is accepted. Manly supplies "The rest is wanting" (p. 288).

Introduction to the Munday Plays

In these two plays Robin Hood appears in the prestigious panoply of Elizabethan historical tragedy. Anthony Munday should have most of the credit. Philip Henslowe's diary records that he paid Munday the substantial sum of £5 for a Robin Hood play in February 1598. Both the diary note and internal evidence indicate that this was to be a single work — line 2229 predicts "Robins Tragedie" at the end of the current play. However, plans were changed, probably because there was too much material for one play, and *The Death* is attributed by Henslowe to both Munday and Henry Chettle. As Chettle was also paid 10/- for "the mending of The First Part of Robart Hoode" on 25 November 1598, it is likely that Chettle revamped Munday's over-long play draft, providing an end for *The Downfall*, moving the death of the hero into the second play, and, probably in conjunction with Munday, completing it with an extensive sequence about Prince John's designs on Matilda and her own tragic and honorable death. This material was drawn largely from Michael Drayton's poem "Matilda the faire and chaste daughter of the Lord R. Fitzwater," which Munday had already used in *The Downfall*. The likelihood of joint authorship could account for the patchwork quality of various portions of both plays. Some of the overlaps and repetitions could be due to the compositor, who might have been working from multiple copies, including acting scripts.

Produced by the Admiral's Men in 1599 and kept in their repertoire for some time, the two plays were clearly successful. The company offered as a follow-up *Looke About You*, which makes the gentrified hero central to a disguise-obsessed farce in King Richard's days, and it is presumably no accident that the house author for the rival Chamberlain's Men, one W. Shakespeare, produced in 1602 his own outlaw play *As You Like It*, with a casual reference to Robin Hood in the first act.

In creating this high-theater Robin Hood, Munday fulfilled the trend towards gentrification that had been clear in the chroniclers Major and Grafton (see The Choniclers' Robin Hood). Yet if it was simple for a chronicler to recast the hero as a gentleman, to provide enough material for a full play was another matter — and it may well be that Munday's inventive energies in this respect were excessive, so generating the need for Chettle's play-doctoring. Munday takes an approach different from several contemporaries who had included the outlaw in plays, though not creating a Robin Hood play as such. George Peele's *Edward I* (1593) contains one scene where the Welsh rebels play a Robin Hood disguising game; Richard Greene

296

almost certainly wrote *George a Greene* (by 1592), in which Robin plays second fiddle to the heroic Pinder of Wakefield: these plays are discussed fully by M. A. Nelson (1973). The writers were adapting popular traditions for the stage as so many others did in the period, and this was presumably also the case in the lost plays *Robin Hood and Little John* (1594) and *Robin Hood's Penn'orths* (1600).

Munday, however, made a decision not to rely on the wide range of popular Robin Hood material that must have been available to him. It would have been easy to adapt the action of the *Gest* to the period of Richard I, as many novels and films have done in the modern period, and Copland's well-known edition of the *Gest* (c. 1560) had two robust plays at the end featuring Robin, his friends, and enemies. Munday, however, sought a higher tone in setting and content, and made very little use of the popular tradition. In scene vii he clearly uses the theme of the ballad *Robin Hood Rescues Three Young Men*; the Prior of York and Sir Doncaster come at some remove from the *Gest* and there may well be reference to Robin's orders to the outlaws in the *Gest* when Little John administers the Sherwood Articles of behavior (*Downfall*, lines 1329–59); the hostility between Little John and the sheriff may also derive from the *Gest*; and there is a review of Robin Hood related characters and places in *Downfall* lines 1279–89, which includes ballad material but also presents apparently new ideas and unusually specific reference to villages in the Sherwood area.

These links with the earlier popular material are of little weight, and Munday's principal resource is to take Major's idea about a distressed gentleman in the period of King Richard and Prince John and flesh it out with new plot and contemporary aristocratic concerns. The enemies here are not the threatening local sheriff or voracious provincial clerics, as in the ballads and the *Gest*. The politics of the play, like so many other historical dramas of the period, operate across the complex quadrilateral of crown, clergy, barons and bureaucrats, a force field which is evidently late sixteenth century in its reference. Prince John himself is not the villain that in more personalized modern dramas he has become: hot-tempered though he is, having taken power he is easily dislodged and in fact takes to the forest himself, fights a "joining the band" duel with the friar, and plays the role of Marian's somewhat over-enthusiastic admirer.

Robert, Earl of Huntington, is in the tense opening scenes betrayed by his uncle the Prior of York and by his own steward, Warman, conceived initially as a Judas figure. For renaissance aristocrats like those who owned the play-companies, living on lands taken from the Catholic church and fearful of the unreliability of those they had to trust, Munday could hardly find a more gratifying pair of villains. In accordance with this socially conservative reconstruction of the myth, Munday's own career was that of a semi-official agent of the state. His activities hovered between fact-finding missions and outright espionage, and his literary work was consistently close to the interests of the powerful and wealthy: he was a writer of political essays, a well-known balladeer, a highly successful translator of romances, and a writer of city pageants, one of which was another Robin Hood drama, a masque called *Metropolis Coronata, The Triumphs of Ancient Drapery or Rich Cloathing in England* (1615), in which both author and outlaw praise to the point of servility the drapers for whom it was written. (Munday's father, it should be noted, had been a draper.)

But Munday was an artist as well as a political author, and he made the elegant decision to set the play itself at the court of Henry VIII. That monarch had himself been involved in Robin Hood activities, as Hall's chronicle reports (Knight, 1994, pp. 109–10) and he — father to Elizabeth I — is the ultimate validator of this play. In the opening scene and elsewhere through the play, John Skelton, who will play Tuck, debates with Sir John Eltham, a typical new-age diplomat who plays Little John, concerning the nature of the play. Eltham remarks (lines 2210–13) that he sees none of the traditional elements; Skelton who, for all his intellectual power (he was Henry's tutor), was remembered as a popular comedian, states firmly (as Friar) that the king himself has approved this new material and plot (lines 2219–20), and so Skelton presides over the rejection of popular material he himself by tradition represents, in favor of the appropriation into nobility of the material and the hero. (See also lines 2787 ff.)

In dramatic terms the play suffers from this decision, as did the eighteenth-century ballad operas that palely followed it: almost all the exciting action of the myth has gone because judged too vulgar; the only fight that occurs is between Prince John and the friar; the final recognition and re-establishment scene beloved of stage and screen is here simply that of Robin, not the returning King; the forest is never seen as a world of freedom and possible resistance, just as a site of aristocratic shame: Robin's "downfall" is his degradation from noble status and having to take to the woods. In terms of action, the fighting outlaw has become as passive as King Arthur at his most nobly inactive. At times the set pieces almost make up for this — Robin's fine speech about making the woods into a surrogate stately home (lines 1366–81) has reverberated through to Tennyson's *The Foresters*, and in *The Death* the hero's funeral scene, mournful as it must be, still has real dramatic power, especially in its musical context (lines 848–59).

There remain some signs of haste and incomplete editing, even after Chettle "mended" *The Downfall*. Matilda is called Marian too early (perhaps a sign that Munday discovered Michael Drayton's poem after he had begun his work); her father is at first Lacy and then Fitzwater; the Earl of Leicester is either two unrationalized characters or a villain who becomes suddenly loyal without explanation of the change (see note to *The Downfall*, line 782, for further discussion). These are no doubt slips in drafting or the result of inconsistently recording performance versions: less easily explicable is the origin of the hero's title. Munday is the first to name him Earl of Huntington, as he spells it, or as the town and former county are now spelled, Huntingdon. One suggestion that has been offered, without much confidence, is that a wordplay on "hunting" is the key. Bevington linked the name with the puritan Earl of the earlier sixteenth century, and also argued that the play had a strongly puritan anti-church and aristocracy theme (1968, pp. 295–96). Neither case seems convincing. It is conceivable that Munday derived the name from the existence of such an earl in the time of King Richard: the well-informed historian John Stow was a friend of Munday's, and it seems likely that he might have had a hand in the ideas for the play, including this name (Knight, 1994, p. 131).

Rarely performed, the two "big" Robin Hood plays have an importance in the tradition and an impact that surpasses their limited artistic standing. The semi-gentrified ballads and lives of Robin Hood created in the seventeenth and eighteenth century derived, directly or indirectly, from these plays. They created the authorizing narrative of gentrification and much as the 1938 Warner Brothers film makes film-makers remember that Robin Hood is a theme that can always make money, so the Munday-Chettle plays gave status to the myth that both stimulated more adaptations — like Ben Jonson's tantalizingly unfinished *The Sad Shepherd* — and also assisted the perseverance of the popular tradition both in association with and sometimes in resistance to the newly dignified dramatic hero.

Select Bibliography

Black-Letter Editions

The Downfall of Robert, Earle of Huntington, Afterward Called Robin Hood of merrie Sherwodde: with his love to chaste Matilda, the Lord Fitzwaters daughter, afterwardes his faire Maide Marian. London: William Leake, 1601. 4°. [Ten copies of this printing are known to have survived.]

The Death of Robert, Earle of Hvntington. Otherwise Called Robin Hood of merrie Sherwodde: with the lamentable Tragedie of chaste Matilda, his faire maid Marian, poysoned at Dunmowe by King Iohn. London: William Leake, 1601. 4°. [Fourteen copies of this printing are known to have survived.]

Modern Editions

Collier, John Payne, ed. *Five Old Plays, Forming a Supplement to the Collections of Dodsley and Others*. Illustrated with notes by Collier. London: Septimus Prowett, 1828. Rpt. London: W. Pickering, 1883. [Collier's edition modernizes the text and emends it somewhat facilely, though many of his emendations are adopted by Meagher (1980). Dodsley's *A Selection of Old Plays* was published in 12 volumes (1825–27). Collier's contribution is sometimes referred to as Vol. 13. Collier used British Library pressmark 161.k.70 and C.34.d.18 as his base texts for the two Munday plays.]

Hazlitt, W. Carew, ed. *A Selection of Old English Plays, originally published by Robert Dodsley in the year 1744*. Vol. 8. London: Reeves and Turner, 1874. [Based on Collier, with additional notes, introduction and a number of emendations and additions, especially in stage directions. *The Downfall*, pp. 93–207; *The Death*, pp. 209–327.]

The Downfall of Robert, Earl of Huntingdon. By Anthony Munday. Issued for subscribers by John S. Farmer. Amersham: Tudor Facsimile Texts, 1913. [Unpaginated. Based on the "only known edition, 1601." Farmer used BL.161.k.70 for his facsimile, a copy that Meagher calls "slightly defective" (1965, p. viii). Farmer notes that the play was first staged in 1598–99.]

The Death of Robert, Earl of Huntingdon. By Anthony Munday in collaboration with Henry Chettle. Issued for subscribers by John S. Farmer. Amersham: Tudor Facsimile Texts, 1913. [Farmer uses BL press-mark C.34.D.18 of Leake's 1601 edition as his copy text. He suggests Chettle as a collaborator; but see Meagher (1980, pp. 96–107) on the minor role Chettle may have had.]

Meagher, John Carney, ed. *The Downfall of Robert Earl of Huntingdon by Anthony Munday, 1601*. The Malone Society Reprints. Oxford: Oxford University Press, 1964 (1965). [Based on a collation of the ten extant copies of Leake. Includes textual introduction.]

——. *The Death of Robert Earl of Huntingdon by Anthony Munday, 1601*. The Malone Society Reprints. Oxford: Oxford University Press, 1965 (1967). [Based on the fourteen extant copies of Leake's 1601 edition. With textual introduction.]

——. *The Huntingdon Plays: A Critical Edition of The Downfall and The Death of Robert, Earl of Huntingdon*. A Garland Series: Renaissance Drama: A Collection of

Critical Editions. New York: Garland Publishing Inc., 1980. [A photocopy of Meagher's typescript. Introduction, pp. 7–117; Commentary, pp. 462–582. Excellent discussion of the history and critical issues of the texts. The scholarship is extensive, both in terms of Renaissance drama and Robin Hood materials. A number of typographical errors survive uncorrected. Originally, this was Meagher's University of London dissertation, 1961.]

Dobson, R. B., and J. Taylor, eds. *Rymes of Robin Hood: An Introduction to the English Outlaw.* London: Heinemann, 1976. [Excerpts from both plays, with Introduction and Notes. Pp. 220–30.]

Scholarship, Commentary, and Related Texts

Bevington, David. *Tudor Drama and Politics.* Cambridge: Harvard University Press, 1968.

Byrne, M. St. C. "Bibliographical Clues in Collaborate Plays." *Library: Transactions of the Bibliographical Society*, 13 (1932), 21–48. [Presents arguments for co-authorship of *The Death* by Anthony Munday and Henry Chettle, based on stylistic analysis. See especially pp. 43–48. In the main refuted by Meagher (1980), pp. 73, 76–77, 96–107.]

Drayton, Michael. *The Legend of Matilda. The faire and chaste Daughter of the Lord Robert Fitzwater, The True Glorie of the Noble House of Sussex.* 1594. *Newly corrected and augmented and reprinted with The Tragicall Legend of Robert, Duke of Normandy, surnamed Short-Thigh, eldest sonne to William the Conquerer. With the Legend of Matilda the chast, daughter to the Lord Robert Fitzwater, poysoned by King Iohn.* London: Ia. Roberts for N. L., 1596. In *The Works of Michael Drayton*, ed. J. William Hebel. 4 vols. Oxford: Shakespeare Head Press, 1931. Vol. I, 209–46. [The principal source for about two-thirds of *The Death*.]

Henslowe, Philip. *Diary.* Edited with supplementary material, introduction, and notes by R. A. Foakes and R. T. Rickert. Cambridge: Cambridge University Press, 1961. [Entries on the 1598 production of Munday's *Robin Hood* and on moneys paid to Henry Chettle for revision and licensing of the second part of *Robin Hood*. Eight entries in all. Fols. 44–52.]

Robin Hood Plays

Holt, J. C. *Robin Hood: Revised and Enlarged Edition*. London: Thames and Hudson, 1989.

Knight, Stephen. *Robin Hood: A Complete Study of the English Outlaw*. Oxford: Blackwell, 1994.

Meagher, John Carney. See Introduction and Commentary to the Garland Critical Edition, cited above.

Nelson, Michael A. *The Robin Hood Tradition in the English Renaissance*. Elizabethan Studies 14. Salzburg: Salzburg Studies in English Literature, 1973.

Seccombe, Thomas. "Anthony Munday." *Dictionary of National Biography* (London: Smith, Elder, and Co., 1909) 13, 1187–94.

Singman, Jeffrey, L. "Munday's Unruly Earl." In *Playing Robin Hood: The Legend as Performance in Five Centuries*. Ed. L. Potter. Newark: University of Delaware Press, 1998. Pp. 63–76.

Spivack, Bernard. *Shakespeare and the Allegory of Evil: The History of a Metaphor in Relation to his Major Villains*. New York: Columbia University Press, 1958. Pp. 362–64. [Draws parallels between Doncaster and Iago.]

Thorndike, A. H. "The Relation of *As You Like It* to Robin Hood Plays." *Journal of English and Germanic Philology* 4 (1902), 59–69. [Suggests several borrowings by Shakespeare from Munday's plays.]

The Downfall of Robert, Earle of Huntington

by Anthony Munday

List of Characters

in the order of their appearance

Sir John Eltham
Skelton
Little Tracy
Sir Thomas Mantle   } Characters of
Clown   the Induction.
The other Players, the
   characters of the dumbshow

Gilbert de Hood, Prior of York and uncle to
   Robert, Earl of Huntingdon.
Justice Warman, Steward to Robert, Earl of
   Huntingdon; later Sheriff of Notingham.
Robert Hood, Robert Earle of Huntingdon.
Little John, his Servant.
Marian, his betrothed (after line 781, Matilda,
   daughter of Lord Fitzwater).
Eleanor, the Queen Mother.
Lord Sentloe
Sir Hugh Lacy   } Conspirators against
Sir Gilbert Broghton   the Earl of Huntingdon.
Mistress Warman.
Prince John.
The Bishop of Ely.
Much, the Miller's Son, a clown.
A Messenger from Ely.
Simon, Earl of Leicester (after line 781, Lord
   Salisbury).

Lord Lacy, brother of Sir Hugh and father of
   Marian (after line 781, Lord Fitzwater).
A Boy, servant to Sir Hugh Lacy.
Lord Chester.
Friar Tuck.
Ralph, Warman's man.
Scarlet.
Scathlock.
First Collier.
Second Collier.
Widow Scarlet, mother of Scarlet and
   Scathlock.
Sir Doncaster of Hothersfield.
Jinny, daughter of the Widow Scarlet.
A Servant of the Prior.
Another servant, messenger from York.
A Herald.
Earl of Leicester.
Richmond.
Warman's Cousin.
Jailer of Notingham.
Mistress Thomson.
King Richard.
Sheriff's men, Sir Doncaster's ruffians,
   Leicester's drum and ancient, soldiers,
   officers, attendants, Jailer's dog.

Robin Hood Plays

[*Scene i*]

[*Enter Sir John Eltam, and knocke at Skeltons doore.*

	Eltham	Howe, maister Skelton? What, at studie hard?	
		[*Opens the doore.*	
5	**Skelton**	Welcome and wisht for, honest Sir John Eltham.	
		I have sent twice, and either time	
		He mist that went to seeke you.	*missed*
	Eltham	So full well hee might.	
		These two howers it pleas'd his Majesty	*hours*
10		To use my service in survaying mappes	
		Sent over from the good King Ferdinand,	
		That to the Indies, at Sebastians sute,	
		Hath lately sent a Spanish Colonie.	
	Skelton	Then twill trouble you, after your great affairs,	
15		To take the paine that I intended to intreat you to	
		About rehearsall of your promis'd play.	
	Eltham	Nay master Skelton, for the King himselfe,	
		As wee were parting, bid mee take great heede	
		Wee faile not of our day; therefore I pray	
20		Sende for the rest that now we may rehearse.	
	Skelton	O they are readie all, and drest to play.	*dressed*
		What part play you?	
	Eltham	Why I play Little John	
		And came on purpose with this greene sute.	*suit*
25	**Skelton**	Holla my masters, Little John is come.	

[*At every doore all the Players runne out, some crying "where? where?" Others welcome Sir John; among others the boyes and Clowne.*

	Skelton	Faith little Tracy you are somewhat forward:	
30		What, our Maid Marian leaping like a lad?	

The Downfall of Robert, Earle of Huntington

If you remember, Robin is your love:
Sir Thomas Mantle yonder, not Sir John.

Clown   But master, Sir John is my fellowe, for I am
Much, the Millers sonne. Am I not?

35   **Skelton**   I know yee are, sir,
And gentlemen, since you are thus prepar'd,
Goe in and bring your dumbe scene on the stage,
And I, as Prologue, purpose to expresse
The ground whereon our historie is laied.

40   [*Exeunt; manet Skelton.*   remains

[*Trumpets sounde; enter first king Richard, with drum
and Auncient, giving Ely a purse and scepter, his mother,*   Ensign
*and brother John, Chester, Lester, Lacie, others at the
kings appointment doing reverence. The king goes in;*   direction
45   *presently Ely ascends the chaire; Chester, John, and the
Queene part displeasantly. Enter Robert, Earle of Huntington, leading Marian; followes him Warman, and, after
Warman, the Prior, Warman ever flattering and making
curtsie, taking gifts of the Prior behinde, and his master*
50   *before. Prince John enters, and offereth to take Marian.
Queene Elinor enters, offering to pull Robin from her,
but they infolde each other and sit downe within the
curteines; Warman with the Prior, Sir Hugh Lacy, Lord
Sentloe, & Sir Gilbert Broghton folde hands, and drawing*
55   *the curteins, all but the Prior enter and are kindely received by Robin Hoode. The curteins are againe shut.*

Skelton   Sir John, once more, bid your dumbe shewes come in,
That as they passe I may explane them all.

[*Enter King Richard with drumme and scepter, and Ensigne,*
60   *giving Ely a purse; his mother and brother John,
Chester, Lester, Lacie, others at the Kings appointment,
doing reverence. The King goes in.*

Richard calde Cor de Lyon takes his leave,   *Lion-hearted*
Like the Lords Champion, gainst the Pagan foes
65   That spoyle Judea and rich Palestine.
The rule of England and his princely seate
He leaves with Ely, then Lord Chancellor,
To whom the mother Queene, her sonne, Prince John,
Chester, and all the Peeres are sworne.

70   [*Exit Richard cum militibus.*   *with soldiers*

305

[*Ely ascends the chaire; Chester, John and the Queene part displeasantly.*   *hostilely*

Now reverend Ely, like the deputie
Of Gods greate deputie, ascends the throne,
75   Which the Queene mother, and ambitious John
Repining at, rais'd many mutinies;
And how they ended you anone shall heare.

[*Exeunt omnes.*   *All exit*

[*Enter Robert, Earle of Huntington, leading Marian; fol-
80   lowes him Warman, and after Warman the Prior, Warman ever flattering and making curtsie, taking gifts
of the Prior behinde, and his master before. Prince
John enters, offereth to take Marian. Queene Elinor
enters, offering to pull Robin from her; but they in-
85   folde each other, and sit downe within the curteines.*

This youth that leads yon virgin by the hand
(As doth the Sunne, the morning richly clad)
Is our Earle Robert, or your Robin Hoode,
That in those daies was Earle of Huntington.
90   The ill fac't miser, brib'd in either hand,   *faced*
Is Warman, once the Steward of his house,
Who Judas-like betraies his liberall Lord   *generous*
Into the hands of that relentlesse Prior,
Calde Gilbert Hoode, uncle to Huntington.
95   Those two that seeke to part these lovely friends
Are Elenor the Queene and John the Prince;
She loves Earle Robert, he Maide Marian,
But vainely: for their deare affect is such,
As only death can sunder their true loves.
100   Long had they lov'd, and now it is agreed
This day they must be troth-plight, after wed.   *betrothed*
At Huntingtons faire house a feast is helde,
But envie turnes it to a house of teares.
For those false guestes, conspiring with the Prior,
105   To whome Earle Robert greatly is in debt,
Meane at the banquet to betray the Earle,
Unto a heavie writ of outlawry.
The manner and escape you all shall see.

Eltham   Which all, good Skelton?

110   **Skelton**   Why, all these lookers on,

306

Whom, if wee please, the King will sure be pleas'd,
Looke to your entrance, get you in Sir John.   [*Exit Sir John.*
My shift is long, for I play Frier Tucke,   *robe*
Wherein if Skelton have but any lucke

115   Heele thanke his hearers oft, with many a ducke.   *He'll; bow*
For many talk of Robin Hood that never shot in his bowe,
But Skelton writes of Robin Hood what he doth truly knowe.
    Therefore, I pray yee,
    Contentedly stay yee

120   And take no offending,
    But sit to the ending.
    Likewise I desire,
    Yea would not admire,   *wonder about*
    My rime so I shift.

125   For this is my drift,   *intention*
    So mought I well thrive,   *must*
    To make yee all blithe: *glad*
    But if ye once frowne,
    Poore Skelton goes downe,

130   His labour and cost,
    He thinketh all lost,
    In tumbling of bookes   *reading books*
    Of Mary goe lookes.
    The Sheriffe with staves,

135   With catchpoles and knaves,   *law officers (see note)*
    Are comming, I see,
    High time tis for mee
    To leave off my babble
    And fond ribble rabble.   *babble*

140   Therefore with this curtsie
    A while I will leave yee.   [*Exit.*

[*Scene ii*]

[*Enter, as it were in haste, the Prior of Yorke, the*
Sheriffe, Justice Warman, steward to Robin Hoode.

Prior   Here master Warman, there's a hundred crowns,
145   For your good will and furtherance in this.

Warman	I thanke you my Lord Prior, I must away
	To shunne suspicion, but be resolute,
	And wee will take him, have no doubt of it.
Prior	But is Lord Sentloe and the other come?
150	*Warman*	Lord Sentloe, Sir Hugh Lacie, and Sir Gilbert Broghton
	Are there and, as they promist you last night,
	Will helpe to take him, when the Sheriffe comes. [*Exit Warman.*
Prior	A while farewell, and thankes to them and you.
	Come master Sheriffe, the outlawry is proclam'd;
155		Sende therefore quickly for more companie,
	And at the backe gate wee will enter in.
Sheriff	Wee shall have much adoe I am afraide.
Prior	No, they are very merry at a feast,
	A feast, where Marian, daughter to Lord Lacy,
160		Is troth-plighted to wastfull Huntington.
	And at the feast are my especiall friends,
	Whom hee suspectes not: come weele have him, man, *we'll*
	And for your paines, here is a hundred markes. *Exeunt.*
Sheriff	I thanke your Lordshippe, weele be diligent.

[*Scene iii*]

165

[*Enter Robin Hoode, Little John following him — the one Earle of Huntington, the other his servant, Robin having his napkin on his shoulder, as if hee were sodainly raised from dinner.*]

| *Robin* | As I am outlawed from my fame and state, |
170 | | Be this day outlawed from the name of daies: |
| | Day lucklesse, outlawe lawlesse, both accurst. |

[*Flings away his napkin, hat, and sitteth downe.*]

| *Lit. John* | Doe not forget your honourable state, |
| | Nor the true noblesse of your worthy house. |
175 | *Robin* | Doe not perswade mee; vaine as vanitie |
| | Are all thy comforts — I am comfortlesse. |
| *Lit. John* | Heare mee my Lord. |

Robin	What shall I heare thee say?	
	Alreadie hast thou saide too much to heare.	
180	Alreadie hast thou stabd mee with thy tongue,	
	And the wide wound with words will not be clos'd.	
	Am I not outlawed, by the Prior of Yorke,	
	Proclaim'd in court, in citie, and in towne,	
	A lawlesse person? This thy tongue reports:	
185	And therefore seeke not to make smooth my griefe:	
	For the rough storme thy windie words hath rais'd	
	Will not be calm'd till I in grave be laied.	

Lit. John Have patience yet.

Robin Yea, now indeede thou speakest.
190 Patience hath power to beare a greater crosse
Then honours spoyle, or any earthly losse.   *Than*

Lit. John Doe so my Lord.

Robin I, now I would beginne;   *Indeed*
But see, another Scene of griefe comes in.

195   [*Enter Marian.*

Marian Why is my Lord so sad? Wherefore so soone,   *early*
So sodainely arose yee from the boorde?   *table*
Alas my Robin, what distempering griefe
Drinkes up the roseat colour of thy cheekes?   *red*
200 Why art thou silent? Answere mee my love.

Robin Let him, let him, let him make thee as sad.
Hee hath a tongue can banish thee from joy,
And chase thy crimson colour from thy cheekes.
Why speakest thou not? I pray thee Little John,
205 Let the short story of my long distresse
Be uttered in a word. What mean'st thou to protract?
Wilt thou not speake? Then Marian list to mee.
This day thou wert a maide, and now a spowse,
Anone (poore soule) a widdowe thou must bee:
210 Thy Robin is an outlawe, Marian,
His goods and landes must be extended on,   *seized*
Himselfe exilde from thee, thou kept from him,

            [*She sinkes in his armes.*

		By the long distance of unnumbred miles.
215		Faint'st thou at this? Speake to mee Marian,
		My olde love newely met, parte not so soone;
		Wee have a little time to tarry yet.

Marian If but a little time, let mee not stay,
Part wee today, then will I dye today.

220 **Lit. John** For shame my Lord, with courage of a man,
Bridle this over-greeving passion,
Or else dissemble it, to comfort her.

Robin I like thy counsell. Marian, cleare these clouds,
And with the sunny beames of thy bright eyes,
225 Drinke up these mistes of sorrowe that arise.

Marian How can I joy, when thou art banished?

Robin I tell thee love, my griefe is counterfaite,
And I abruptly from the table rose,
The banquet being almost at an ende,
230 Onely to drive confused and sad thoughts
Into the mindes of the invited guestes.
For, gentle love, at greate or nuptiall feastes,
With Comicke sportes, or Tragicke stately plaies,
Wee use to recreate the feasted guestes,
235 Which I am sure our kinsfolke doe expect.

Marian Of this what then? This seemes of no effect.

Robin Why thus of this, as Little John can tell,
I had bespoken quaint Comedians:
But greate John, John the Prince, my lieges brother,
240 My rivall, Marian, he that crost our love,
Hath crost mee in this jest, and at the court,   *entertainment*
Imploies the Players, should have made us sport;
This was the tydings brought by Little John,
That first disturbd mee and begot this thought
245 Of sodaine rysing, which by this I know
Hath with amazement, troubled all our guestes:
Goe in, good love; thou as the Chorus shalt
Expresse the meaning of my silent griefe,
Which is no more but this: I only meane
250 (The more to honour our right noble friends)
Myselfe in person to present some Sceanes

		Of tragick matter, or perchance of mirth,	
		Even such as first shall jumpe with my conceipt.	*agree with my idea*

	Marian	May I be bolde thou hast the worst exprest?	
255	**Lit. John**	Faire mistresse, all is true my Lord hath said.	
	Robin	It is, it is.	

	Marian	Speake not so hollow then;	
		So sigh and sadly speake true sorrowing men.	*truly*

	Robin	Beleeve mee love, beleeve mee (I beseech)	
260		My first Scene tragick is, therefore tragicke speech,	
		And accents, fitting wofull action, I strive to get.	
		I pray thee sweete goe in, and with thy sight,	
		Appease the many doubts that may arise.	
		That done, be thou their usher, bring them to this place,	
265		And thou shalt see mee with a loftie verse,	
		Bewitch the hearers eares and tempt their eyes	
		To gaze upon the action that I use.	*wonder*

	Marian	If it be but a play, Ile play my part:	
		But sure some earnest griefe affrights my heart.	

	Lit. John	Let mee intreate yee, Madam, not to feare,	
270		For by the honestie of Little John,	
		Its but a tragicke Scene we have in hand,	
		Only to fit the humour of the Queene,	
		Who is the chiefest at your troth-plight feast.	

275	**Marian**	Then will I fetch her Highnesse and the rest.	[*Exit Marian.*

	Robin	I, that same jealous Queene, whose doting age	*Aye*
		Envies the choyce of my faire Marian,	
		She hath a hande in this.	

	Lit. John	Well, what of that?	
280		Now must your honour leave these mourning tunes,	
		And thus by my areede you shall provide;	*advice*
		Your plate and jewels Ile straight packe up,	
		And toward Notingham convey them hence,	
		At Rowford, Sowtham, Wortley, Hothersfield.	
285		Of all your cattell, mony shall be made,	*property*
		And I at Mansfield will attend your comming,	
		Where weele determine, which waie's best to take.	*we'll*

Robin	Well be it so, a Gods name let it be;	
	And if I can, Marian shall come with mee.	
Lit. John	Else care will kill her; therefore if you please,	
	At th'utmost corner of the garden wall,	
	Soone in the evening waite for Marian,	
	And as I goe Ile tell her of the place,	
	Your horses at the Bell shall readie bee,	
	I meane Belsavage, whence as citizens	
	That meant to ride for pleasure some small way,	
	You shall set foorth.	
Robin	Be it as thou dost say.	
	Farewell a while.	
	In spight of griefe, thy love compels mee smile,	
	But now our audience comes, wee must looke sad.	

290
295

300

> [*Enter Queene Elinor, Marian, Sentloe, Lacie, Brogh-ton, Warman, Robins stewarde. As they meete, John whispers with Marian.*

305

> [*Exit John.*

Queene	How now my Lord of Huntington?	
	The mistresse of your love, faire Marian,	
	Tels us your sodaine rising from the banquet	
	Was but a humor, which you meane to purge,	
	In some high Tragicke lines, or Comick jests.	
Robin	Sit down faire Queen (the Prologues part is plaid,	
	Marian hath tolde yee, what I bad her tell);	
	Sit downe Lord Sentloe, cosin Lacy sit,	
	Sir Gilbert Broghton, yea, and Warman sit;	
	Though you my steward be, yet for your gathering wit,	*self-assurance*
	I give you place, sit downe, sit downe I say,	

310

315

> [*Sets them all downe.*

Gods pittie sit; it must, it must be so:
For you will sit, when I shall stande I knowe.
And, Marian, you may sit among the rest,
I pray yee doe, or else rise, stand apart;
These helps shall be beholders of my smart.   *hired helpers*
You that with ruthlesse eyes my sorrowes see,
And came prepar'd to feast at my sad fall,
Whose envie, greedinesse, and jealousie

320

325

Afforde mee sorrowe endlesse, comfort small,
Knowe what you knewe before, what you ordaind
To crosse the spousall banquet of my love,
That I am outlawed by the Prior of Yorke,

330   My traiterous uncle, and your trothlesse friend.
Smile you Queene Elinor? laugh'st thou Lord Sentloe?
Lacy look'st thou so blithe at my lament?
Broghton a smooth browe graceth your sterne face:
And you are merry Warman at my mone.   *grief*

335   The Queene except, I doe you all defie.
You are a sort of fawning sycophants,   *group*
That while the sunshine of my greatnesse dur'd,
Reveld out all my day for your delights,   *Celebrated*
And now yee see the blacke night of my woe

340   Oreshade the beautie of my smiling good,   *Overshadow*
You to my griefe adde griefe, and are agreed
With that false Prior, to reprive my joyes   *delay*
From execution of all happinesse.

Warman   Your honour thinks not ill of mee, I hope.

345   **Robin**   Judas speakes first, with "Master, is it I?"
No, my false Steward, your accounts are true.
You have dishonoured mee, I worship you.   *honored*
You from a paltry pen and inkhorne clarke,
Bearing a buckram satchell at your belt,

350   Unto a Justice place I did preferre,   *elevate*
Where you unjustly have my tenants rackt,   *charged excessive rents*
Wasted my treasure and increast your store.
Your sire contented with a cottage poore,
Your mastershippe hath halles and mansions built,

355   Yet are you innocent, as cleare from guilt,
As is the ravenous mastife that hath spilt
The bloode of a whole flocke, yet slily comes
And couches in his kennell with smeard chaps.   *mouth*
Out of my house, for yet my house it is,

360   And followe him yee catchpole bribed groomes;
For neither are ye Lords, nor Gentlemen,
That will be hired to wrong a Nobleman.
For hir'd yee were last night, I knowe it I,
To be my guests, my faithlesse guestes this day,

365   That your kinde hoste you trothlesse might betray: *falsely*

But hence, and helpe the Sheriffe at the doore,
Your worst attempt; fell traitors, as you bee,
Avoide, or I will execute yee all,
Ere any execution come at mee,   [*Runne away.*
370   They ran away, so ends the tragedie.
Marian, by Little John, my minde you know,
If you will, doe: if not, why, be it so.   [*Offers to goe in.*

Queene   No words to me Earle Robert ere you goe?

Robin   O to your Highnesse? Yes, adieu proud Queene;
375   Had not you bene, thus poore I had not beene.   [*Exit.*

Queene   Thou wrongst mee Robert, Earle of Huntington,
And were it not for pittie of this maide,
I would revenge the words that thou hast saied.

Marian   Adde not, faire Queene, distresse unto distresse;
380   But if you can, for pittie make his lesse.

Queene   I can and will forget deserving hate,
And give him comfort in this wofull state.
Marian, I knowe Earle Roberts whole desire
Is to have thee with him from hence away;
385   And though I loved him dearely to this day,
Yet since I see hee dearlier loveth thee,
Thou shalt have all the furtherance I may.
Tell mee, faire girle, and see thou truly tell,
Whether this night, tomorrowe, or next day,
390   There be no pointment for to meete thy love.

Marian   There is, this night there is, I will not lie,
And be it disappointed, I shall die.   *unmet*

Queene   Alas poore soule, my sonne, Prince John my son,
With severall troupes hath circuited the court,
395   This house, the citie, that thou canst not scape.

Marian   I will away with death, though he be grim,
If they deny mee to goe hence with him.

Queene   Marian, thou shalt go with him clad in my attire,
And for a shift, Ile put thy garments on,   *disguise (stratagem)*
400   It is not mee, my sonne John doth desire;
But Marian it is thee he doteth on.

314

When thou and I are come into the field,
Or any other place where Robin staies,
Mee in thy clothes, the ambush will beset,
405   Thee in my roabes they dare not once approach:
So while with mee a reasoning they stay,
At pleasure thou with him maist ride away.

Marian   I am beholding to your Majesty,
And of this plot will sende my Robin worde.

410   Queene   Nay, never trouble him, least it breede suspect: *suspicion*
But get thee in, and shift of thy attire,   *take off*
My roabe is loose, and it will soone be off,
Goe gentle Marian, I will followe thee,
And from betrayers hands will set thee free.

415   Marian   I thanke your Highnesse, [*Aside*] but I will not trust ye,
My Robert shall have knowledge of this shift: *deception*
For I conceive alreadie your deepe drift.   [*Exit.*   *intention*

Queene   Now shall I have my will of Huntington,
Who taking mee this night for Marian,
420   Will harry mee away in steade of her: *drag*
For hee dares not stand trifling to conferre:
Faith, prettie Marian, I shal meete with you,   *be even with*
And with your lovely sweete heart Robert too:
For when wee come unto a baiting place,   *resting*
425   If with like love my love hee doe not grace,
Of treason capitall I will accuse him,
For traiterous forcing me out of the court,
And guerdon his disdaine with guiltie death,   *reward*
That of a Princes love so lightly weighes.   [*Exit.*

[**Scene iv**]

430   [*Enter Little John, fighting with the Sheriffe and his men,*
Warman perswading him.

Lit. John   Warman, stand off, tit tattle, tel not me what ye can do:
The goods I say are mine, and I say true.

Warman   I say the Sheriffe must see them ere they goe.

435   Lit. John   You say so Warman; Little John saies no.

	Sheriff	I say I must for I am the kings Shrieve.	*Sheriff*
	Lit. John	Your must is false, your office I beleeve.	
	Watch	Downe with him, downe with him.	
440	Lit. John	Ye barke at me like curres, but I will downe With twentie stand-and-who-goe-theres of you, If yee stand long tempting my patience. Why, master Shrive, thinke you mee a foole? What justice is there you should search my trunkes, Or stay my goods, for that my master owes?	
445	Sheriff	Here's Justice Warman, steward to your Lord, Suspectes some coyne, some jewels, or some plate That longs unto your Lord, are in your trunkes, And the extent is out for all his goods: Therefore wee ought to see none be convaid.	*writ of seizure*
450	Warman	True, Litle John, I am the sorier.	
455	Lit. John	A plague upon ye else, how sore ye weepe? Why, say thou, upstart, that there were some helpe, Some little little helpe in this distresse, To aide our Lord and master comfortlesse; Is it thy part, thou screenfac't snotty nose, To hinder him that gave thee all thou hast?	*two-faced*

[*Enter Justice Warmans wife, odly attyred.*

	Wife	Who's that husband? You, you, means he you?	
	Warman	I, ber Lady is it, I thanke him.	*by our Lady*
460	Wife	A, ye kneve you, Gods pittie hisband, why dis not your worshippe sende the kneve to Newgate?	*knave; doesn't*
	Lit. John	Well master Sheriffe, shall I passe or no?	
	Sheriff	Not without search.	
465	Lit. John	Then here the casket stands, Any that dares unto it set their hands, Let him beginne.	
	Wife	Doe hisband, you are a Majestie, y'warrant ther's olde knacks, cheins, and other toyes.	*Magistrate* *things*
	Lit. John	But not for you, good Madam beetle browes.	*shaggy*

316

470	*Wife*	Out upon him. By my truly master Justice, and ye	*if you*
		doe not clap him up, I will sue a bill of remorse, and ne-	
		ver come betweene a pere of sheetes with yee. Such a	
		kneve as this, downe with him I pray.	

[Set upon him. He knockes some downe.

475	*Wife*	A good Lord, come not neere good hisband, only
		charge him; charge him. A good God; helpe, helpe.

*[Enter Prince John, the Bishoppe of Ely, the Prior of
Yorke, with others. All stay.*

	Pr. John	What tumult have wee here? Who doth resist
480		The kings writs with such obstinate contempt?
	Wife	This knave.
	Warman	This rebell.
	Pr. John	How now Little John,
		Have you no more discretion than you shewe?
485	*Ely*	Lay holde, and clappe the traitor by the heeles.
	Lit. John	I am no traitor, my good Lord of Ely,
		First heare mee, then commit me if you please.
	Pr. John	Speake and be briefe.
	Lit. John	Heere is a little boxe,
490		Containing all my gettings twentie yeare;
		Which is mine owne, and no mans but mine owne.
		This they would rifle, this I doe defend,
		And about this we only doe contend.
	Pr. John	You doe the fellow wrong: his goods are his;
495		You only must extend upon the Earles.
	Prior	That was my Lord; but nowe is Robert Hood,
		A simple yeoman as his servants were.

	Wife	Backe with that legge, my Lord Prior:	*curtsey*
		There be some that were his servantes thinke foule	
500		scorne to be cald yeomen.	

	Prior	I cry your worshippe mercy, mistresse Warman.
		The squire your husband was his servant once.
	Lit. John	A scurvie squire, with reverence of these Lords.

317

	Wife	Doo's he not speake treason, prey.	*[I] pray*
505	*Ely*	Sirra, yea are too saucie; get you hence.	
	Warman	But heare mee first, my Lords, with patience. This scoffing carelesse fellowe, Little John, Hath loaden hence a horse, twixt him and Much, A silly rude knave, Much the millers sonne.	

510   *[Enter Much, clowne.*

	Much	I am here to answere for myselfe, and have ta- ken you in two lies at once. First, Much is no knave, neither was it a horse Little John and I loded, but a little curtaile, of some five handfuls high, sib to the Apes	*small horse*
515		onely beast at Parish garden.	
	Lit. John	But master Warman, you have loded carts And turnd my Lords goods to your proper use. Who ever hath the right, you doe the wrong, And are . . .	*personal*
520	*Wife*	What is hee kneve?	
	Lit. John	Unworthy to be named a man.	
	Much	And Ile be sworne for his wife,	
	Wife	I, so thou maist Nich.	*Much*
	Much	That shee sets newe markes of all my olde ladies	
525		linnen (God rest her soule) and my young Lord never had them since.	
	Wife	Out, out, I tooke him them but to whiting, as God mende mee.	*for bleaching*
	Ely	Leave off this idle talke. Get yee both hence.	
530	*Lit. John*	I thanke your honours. Wee are not in love with being here; wee must seeke service that are master- lesse.	*[Exeunt Much, John.*
	Ely	Lord Prior of Yorke, here's your commission. You are best make speede, least in his country houses,	
535		By his appointment, all his heards be solde.	*livestock*
	Prior	I thanke your Honour, taking humble leave.	*[Exit.*

	Ely	And master Warman, here's your Patent seald,	
		For the high Sheriffewick of Notingham:	
		Except the King our master doe repeale	
540		This gift of ours.	
	Pr. John	Let him the while possesse it.	
	Ely	A Gods name, let him; he hath my good will.	[*Exit.*
	Pr. John	Well Warman, this proude Priest I can not brooke.	*i.e., Ely*
		But to our other matter, send thy wife away.	
545	**Warman**	Goe in good wife, the Prince with mee hath	
		private conference.	
	Wife	By my troth yee will anger mee: now yee have	
		the Paterne, yee should call mee nothing but mistresse	*Patent*
		Sheriffe: for I tell you I stand upon my replications.	*reputation*
550		[*Exit.*	
	Pr. John	Thinkest thou that Marian meanes	
		To scape this evening hence with Robin Hoode?	
	[**Warman**]	The horse boy tolde mee so, and here he comes,	*(see note)*
		Disguised like a citizen me thinkes.	
555	[**Pr. John**]	Warman, lets in. Ile fit him presently;	*let us go in*
		Only for Marian am I now his enemie.	[*Exeunt.*

[*Scene v*]

[*Enter Robin like a citizen.*

	Robin	Earle John and Warman, two good friends of mine:
		I thinke they knewe mee not, or if they did
560		I care not what can followe. I am sure
		The sharpest ende is death, and that will come.
		But what of death or sorrowe doe I dreame?
		My Marian, my faire life, my beautious love,
		Is comming, to give comfort to my griefe,
565		And the sly Queene, intending to deceive,
		Hath taught us how we should her sleights receive. [*Enter John.*
		But who is this? Gods pittie, here's Prince John.
		We shall have some good rule with him anone.

	Pr. John	God even, sir; this cleare evening should portend
570		Some frost I thinke. How judge you honest friend?
	Robin	I am not weatherwise; but it may be,
		Wee shall have hard frost. For true charitie,
		Good dealing, faithfull friendshippe, honestie,
		Are chil-colde, deade with colde.
575	**Pr. John**	O good sir, stay.
		That frost hath lasted many a bitter day.
		Knowe yee no frozen hearts that are belov'd?
	Robin	Love is a flame, a fire, that being mov'd,
		Still brighter growes; but say, are you belov'd?

580   **Pr. John** I would be, if I be not; but passe that.   *never mind*
                      Are ye a dweller in this citie, pray?

        Robin   I am, and for a gentlewoman stay,
                      That rides some foure or five mile in great haste.

                      [*Enter Queene, Marian.*]

585   **Pr. John** I see your labour, sir, is not in waste.
                      For here come two: are either of these yours?

        Robin   Both are, one must.   *must be*

        Pr. John Which doe you most respect?   *prefer*

        Robin   The youngest and the fairest I reject.

590   **Pr. John** [*Aside*] Robin, Ile try you whether yee say true.

        Robin   [*Aside*] As you with mee, so John Ile jeast with you.

        Queene   Marian, let me goe first to Robin Hood,
                      And I will tell him what wee doe intend.

        Marian   Doe what your Highnesse please. Your will is mine.

595   **Pr. John** My mother is with gentle Marian;
                      O it doth grieve her to be left behinde.

        Queene   Shall we away my Robin, least the Queene
                      Betray our purpose? Sweete, let us away.
                      I have great will to goe, no heart to stay.

600   **Robin**   Away with thee? No! Get thee farre away
                      From mee foule Marian, faire though thou be nam'd,

For thy bewitching eyes have raised stormes,
That have my name and noblesse ever sham'd.

Prince John, my deare friend once, is now, for thee,   *because of you*
605   Become an unrelenting enemie,

Pr. John   But Ile relent, and love thee, if thou leave her.

Robin   And Elinor, my soveraignes mother Queene,
That yet retaines true passion in her breast,
Stands mourning yonder. Hence, I thee detest.
610   I will submit mee to her Majestie.
Greate Princesse, if you will but ride with mee,
A little of my way, I will expresse
My folly past, and humble pardon beg.

Marian   I grant, Earle Robert, and I thanke thee too.

615   **Queene**   She's not the Queene, sweete Robin, it is I.

Robin   Hence sorceresse, thy beauty I defie.
If thou have any love at all to mee,
Bestowe it on Prince John: he loveth thee.

               [*Exeunt Robin, Marian.*

620   **Pr. John**   And I will love thee Robin, for this deede,
And helpe thee too, in thy distressefull neede.

Queene   Wilt thou not stay nor speake, proud Huntington?
Ay mee, some whirlwinde hurries them away.

Pr. John   Follow him not, faire love, that from thee flies:
625   But flie to him that gladly followes thee.
Wilt thou not, girle? Turnst thou away from mee?

Queene   Nay, we shall have it then,
If my queint sonne, his mother gin to court.   *strange; takes*

Pr. John   Wilt thou not speake, faire Marian, to Prince John,
630   That loves thee well?

Queene   Good sir, I know you doe.

Pr. John   That can maintaine thee?

Queene   I, I know you can: *Aye*
But hitherto I have maintained you.

635   **Pr. John**   My princely mother?

	Queene	I, my princely sonne.	*Aye*
	Pr. John	Is Marian then gone hence with Huntington?	
	Queene	I, she is gone, ill may they either thrive.	*Aye*
	Pr. John	Mother, they must goe whom the divell drives.	*devil*
640		For your sharpe furie, and infernall rage,	
		Your scorne of mee, your spite to Marian,	
		Your over-doting love to Huntington,	
		Hath crost yourselfe, and mee it hath undone.	
	Queene	I, in mine owne deceipt, have met deceipt.	
645		In briefe, the manner thus I will repeate;	
		I knewe, with malice that the Prior of Yorke	
		Pursu'd Earle Robert; and I furdred it,	*furthered*
		Though God can tell, for love of Huntington.	
		For thus I thought, when he was in extreames,	
650		Neede, and my love would winne some good regarde	
		From him to mee, if I reliev'd his want.	
		To this end came I to the mock-spouse feast;	
		To this end made I change for Marians weede,	*clothes*
		That me, for her, Earle Robert should receive.	
655		But now I see they both of them agreed,	
		In my deceipt, I might myselfe deceive.	
		Come in with mee, come in and meditate	
		How to turne love, to never changing hate. [*Exit.*	
	Pr. John	In by yourselfe; I passe not for your spels.	*care not*
660		Of youth and beautie still you are the foe.	
		The curse of Rosamond rests on your head,	
		Faire Rose confounded by your cankers hate.	*cankerous*
		O that she were not as to mee she is,	
		A mother, whom by nature I must love,	
665		Then would I tell her shee were too too base,	
		To dote thus on a banisht carelesse groome:	
		Then should I tell her that shee were too fond,	
		To thrust faire Marian to an exiles hand.	
		[*Enter a messenger from Ely.*	
670	**Messenger**	My Lord, my Lord of Ely sends for you,	
		About important businesse of the state.	
	Pr. John	Tell the proude prelate I am not dispos'd,	
		Nor in estate to come at his commaunde.	*of rank*

[Smite him, hee bleedes.

675		Be gon with that, or tarry and take this.
		Zwouns, are yee listning for an after-arrant? *[Exit Messenger. (see note)*
		Ile followe, with revengefull murdrous hate,
		The banisht, beggerd, bankrout Huntington. *bankrupt*

[Enter Simon, Earle of Leicester.

680	*Leicester*	How now, Prince John? Bodie of mee, I muse *wonder*
		What mad moodes tosse yee, in this busie time,
		To wound the messenger that Ely sent,
		By our consents? Yfaith yee did not well.

	Pr. John	Leyster, I meant it Ely, not his man:
685		His servants heade but bleedes; hee headlesse shall
		From all the issues of his traitor necke,
		Poure streames of bloode, till he be bloodlesse left.
		By earth it shall, by heaven it shall be so,
		Leister, it shall though all the world say no.

690	*Leicester*	It shall, it shall, but how shall it be done?
		Not with a stormie tempest of sharpe words,
		But slowe, still speaches, and effecting deedes.
		Here comes olde Lacy and his brother Hugh.
		One is our friend, the other is not true.

| 695 | | *[Enter Lord Lacy, Sir Hugh, and his boy.* |

	Lacy	Hence trechor as thou art! By Gods blest mother *traitor*
		Ile lop thy legges off, though thou be my brother,
		If with thy flatring tongue thou seeke to hide
		Thy traiterous purpose. Ah poore Huntington,
700		How in one houre have villaines thee undone?

	Hugh	If you will not beleeve what I have sworne,
		Conceipt your worst. My Lord of Ely knowes *Imagine*
		That what I say is true.

| | *Lacy* | Still facest thou? *dissemble* |
| 705 | | Drawe boy, and quickly see that thou defende thee. |

	Leicester	Patience, Lord Lacy, get you gon, Sir Hugh,
		Provoke him not, for he hath tolde you true.
		You knowe it, that I knowe the Prior of Yorke,
		Together with my good Lord Chauncellor,

710		Corrupted you, Lord Sentloe, Broghton, Warman,
		To feast with Robert on his day of fall.
	Hugh	They lie that say it; I defie yee all.
	Pr. John	Now by the Roode thou lyest. Warman himselfe,
		That creeping Judas, joyed, and tolde it mee.
715	*Lacy*	Let mee, my Lords, revenge me of this wretch,
		By whome my daughter and her love were lost.
	Pr. John	For her, let mee revenge with bitter cost.
		Shall Sir Hugh Lacy and his fellowes buy
		Faire Marians losse, lost by their treachery.
720		And thus I pay it.

Cross appears in the right margin beside lines 712–713.

[*Stabs him. He falles; boy runnes in.*

	Leicester	Sure paiment, John.
	Lacy	There let the villane lie.
		For this, olde Lacie honours thee, Prince John;
725		One trecherous soule, is sent to answere wrong.

[*Enter Ely, Chester, officers, Hugh Lacies boy.*

	Boy	Here, here, my Lord,
		Looke where my master lies.
	Ely	What murdrous hand hath kild this gentle knight,
730		Good Sir Hugh Lacy, steward of my lands?
	Pr. John	Ely, he died by this princely hand.
	Ely	Unprincely deed. Death asketh death you know.
		Arrest him officers.
	Pr. John	O sir, Ile obey; you will take baile, I hope.
735	*Chester*	Tis more, sir, than hee may.
	Leicester	Chester, he may by lawe, and therefore shall.
	Ely	Who are his baile?
	Leicester	I.
	Lacy	And I.
740	*Ely*	You are confederates.
	Pr. John	Holy Lord, you lye.

conspirators appears in the right margin beside line 740.

	Chester	Be reverent, Prince John; my Lord of Ely,	
		You knowe, is Regent for his Majestie.	
	Pr. John	But here are letters from his Majesty,	
745		Sent out of Joppa, in the holy land,	*Haifa*
		To you, to these, to mee, to all the State,	
		Containing a repeale of that large graunt,	
		And free authoritie to take the seale,	
		Into the hands of three Lords temporall,	
750		And the Lord Archbishoppe of Roan, he sent,	
		And hee shall yielde it, or as Lacy lies,	
		Desertfully, for pride and treason stabd,	
		He shall ere long lye. Those that intend as I	
		Followe this steely ensigne, lift on high.	

755   *[Lifts up his drawne sword:*
       Exit, cum Lester and Lacy.   *with*

	Ely	A thousand thousand ensignes of sharpe steele,	
		And feathered arrowes, from the bowe of death,	
		Against proud John, wrongd Ely will imploy.	
760		My Lord of Chester, let mee have your aide,	
		To lay the pride of haute usurping John.	*proud*
	Chester	Some other course than warre let us bethinke.	
		If it may be, let not uncivill broiles,	
		Our civill hands defile.	
765	**Ely**	God knowes that I,	
		For quiet of the realme, would ought forbeare.	
		But give mee leave, my noble Lord, to feare,	
		When one I dearely lov'd is murdered	
		Under the colour of a little wrong	
770		Done to the wastfull Earle of Huntington,	
		Whom John, I knowe, doth hate unto the death,	
		Only for love he beares to Lacies daughter.	
	Chester	My Lord, its plaine this quarrel is but pickt	
		For an inducement to a greater ill;	
775		But wee will call the Counsell of Estate,	
		At which the mother Queene shall present be.	
		Thither by summons shall Prince John be cald,	
		Lester, and Lacy, who, it seemes,	
		Favour some factious purpose of the Prince.	

780	**Ely**	You have advised well, my Lord of Chester; And as you counsell, so doe I conclude.	[*Exeunt.*

[*Scene vi*]

[*Enter Robin Hoode, Matilda [i.e., Marian], at one doore; Little John,
and Much the millers sonne at another doore.*]

785	**Much**	Luck I beseech thee, Marry and amen, Blessing betide hem, it be them indeede, Ah my good Lord, for and my little Ladie.	*Mary* *them, if it be* *and also*
	Robin	What? Much and John, well met in this ill time.	
	Lit. John	In this good time my Lord; for being met, The world shall not depart us till wee die.	
790	**Matilda**	Saist thou mee so, John? As I am true maide, If I live long, well shall thy love be paide.	
	Much	Well, there be on us, simple though wee stand here, have as much love in hem as Little John.	*them*
795	**Matilda**	Much, I confesse thou lovest mee very much, And I will more reward it than with words.	
	Much	Nay I know that, but wee millers children love the cogge a little, and the faire speaking.	*(see note)*
800	**Robin**	And is it possible that Warmans spite Should stretch so farre, that he doth hunt the lives, Of bonnie Scarlet, and his brother Scathlock.	
	Much	O, I, sir. Warman came but yesterday to take charge of the Jaile at Notingham, and this day he saies he will hang the two outlawes. He meanes to set them at libertie.	*indeed*
805	**Matilda**	Such libertie God send the pievish wretch In his most neede.	*mischievous*
	Robin	Now by my honours hope, Yet buried in the lowe dust of disgrace, He is too blame. Say John, where must they die?	
810	**Lit. John**	Yonders their mothers house, and here the tree, Whereon (poore men) they must foregoe their lives.	

326

		And yonder comes a lazie, lozell Frier	*worthless*
		That is appointed for their confessor,	
		Who, when we brought your monie to their mothers,	
815		Was wishing her to patience for their deaths.	

[*Enter Frier Tucke, and Ralphe, Warmans man.*

	Ralph	I am timorous, sir, that the prigioners are passed	
		from the Jaile.	
	Frier	Soft, sirra, by my order I protest,	*religious order*
820		Ye are too forward; tis no game, no jeast	
		We goe about.	
	Robin	Matilda, walke afore,	
		To widowe Scarlets house. Looke where it stands.	
		Much, man your Ladie; Little John and I	
825		Will come unto you thither presently.	
	Much	Come Madame, my Lord has pointed the pro-	
		perer man to goe before yee.	
	Matilda	Be carefull, Robin, in this time of feare.	

[*Exit Much, Matilda.*

830	**Frier**	Now by the reliques of the holy Masse,	
		A prettie girle, a very bonny lasse.	
	Robin	Frier, how like you her?	
	Frier	Mary, by my hoode,	
		I like her well, and wish her nought but good.	
835	**Ralph**	Yee protract, master Frier. I obsecrate ye with	*delay; beseech*
		all curtesie, omitting complement, you would vouch,	*formality*
		or deigne to proceede.	
	Frier	Deigne, vouch, protract, complement, obsecrate?	
		Why, good man tricks, who taught you thus to prate?	*chatter*
840		Your name, your name, were you never christned?	
	Ralph	My nomination Radulfe is or Ralph;	
		Vulgars corruptly use to call mee Rafe.	
	Frier	O foule corruption of base palliardize,	*lewdness (see note)*
		When idiots witlesse travell to be wise.	*labor*
845		Age barbarous, times impious, men vitious,	

Able to upraise,
Men deade many daies,
That wonted to praise,
The Rimes and the laies
850   Of Poets Laureate,
Whose verse did decorate,
And their lines lustrate   *illustrate*
Both Prince and Potentate.
These from their graves,
855   See asses and knaves,
Base idiot slaves,
With boastings and braves,   *exhibitions*
Offer to upstie,   *fly up*
To the heavens hie,   *high*
860   With vaine foolery,
And rude ribaldry.
Some of them write
Of beastly delight,
Suffering their lines,
865   To flatter these times,
With Pandarisme base,   *obsequious sycophancy*
And lust doe uncase,
From the placket to the pappe: *pudendum; nipple*
God send them ill happe.
870   Some like quaint pedants,
Good wits true recreants,
Yee cannot beseech
From pure Priscian speech.   *grammatically strict*
Divers as nice,
875   Like this odde vice,
Are wordmakers daily.
Others in curtsie
When ever they meete yee,
With newe fashions greete yee,
880   Chaunging each congee,   *bow*
Sometime beneath knee,
With, good sir, pardon mee,
And much more foolerie,
Paltry, and foppry,
885   Dissembling knavery,

> Hands sometime kissing,
> But honestie missing.
> God give no blessing
> To such base counterfaiting.

890	*Lit. John*	Stoppe, master Skelton; whither will you runne?
	Frier	Gods pittie, Sir John Eltam, Little John,
		I had forgotte myselfe; but to our play.
		Come, good man fashions, let us goe our way,
		Unto this hanging businesse. Would, for mee,
895		Some rescue, or repreeve might set them free.

[Exeunt Frier, Ralph.

	Robin	Heardst thou not, Little John, the Friers speach,
		Wishing for rescue, or a quicke repreeve?
	Lit. John	He seemes like a good fellowe, my good Lord.
900	*Robin*	He's a good fellowe, John, upon my word.
		Lend mee thy horne, and get thee in to Much,
		And when I blowe this horne, come both and helpe mee.
	Lit. John	Take heed my Lord: the villane Warman knows you,
		And ten to one, he hath a writ against you.
905	*Robin*	Fear not; below the bridge a poore blind man doth dwell,
		With him I will change my habit, and disguise,
		Only be readie when I call for yee,
		For I will save their lives, if it may bee.
	Lit. John	I will doe what you would immediatly. *[Exeunt.*

[Scene vii]

910		*[Enter Warman, Scarlet, and Scathlock bounde, Frier*
		Tuck as their confessor, Officers with halberts.
	Warman	Master Frier, be briefe, delay no time.
		Scarlet and Scathlock, never hope for life.
		Here is the place of execution,
915		And you must answere lawe for what is done.
	Scarlet	Well, if there be no remedie, we must,
		Though it ill seemeth, Warman, thou shouldst bee
		So bloodie to pursue our lives thus cruellie.

	Scathlock	Our mother sav'd thee from the gallowes, Warman;
920		His father did preferre thee to thy Lord. *get advancement for*
		One mother had wee both, and both our fathers,
		To thee and to thy father, were kinde friends.

Scathlock Our mother sav'd thee from the gallowes, Warman;
920 His father did preferre thee to thy Lord.   *get advancement for*
One mother had wee both, and both our fathers,
To thee and to thy father, were kinde friends.

Frier Good fellowes, here you see his kindnesse ends.
What he was once, hee doth not now consider.
925 You must consider of your many sinnes;
This day, in death, your happinesse beginnes.

Scarlock If you account it happinesse, good Frier,
To beare us companie, I you desire.
The more the merrier, wee are honest men.

930 Warman Ye were first outlaws, then ye prooved theeves,
And now all carelessely yee scoffe at death.
Both of your fathers were good honest men;
Your mother lives, their widowe, in good fame.
But you are scapethrifts, unthrifts, villanes, knaves, *spendthrifts, wastrels*
935 And, as yee liv'd by shifts, shall die with shame.

Scathlock Warman, good words, for all your bitter deeds.
Ill speach, to wretched men, is more than needs.

[*Enter Raphe, running.*

Ralph Sir, retire yee, for it hath thus succeeded, the car-
940 nifex, or executor, riding on an ill curtall, hath tituba-
ted or stumbled, and is now cripplefied, with broken or
fracted tibiards, and sending you tidings of successe, saith,
yourselfe must be his deputie.

Warman Ill luck! But, sirra, you shall serve the turne.
945 The cords that binde them, you shall hang them in.

Ralph How are you, sir, of mee opiniated? Not to possesse
your seneschalship, or sherivaltie, not to be Earle of
Notingham, will Ralph be nominated by the base scan-
dalous vociferation of a hangman.

950 [*Enter Robin Hoode, like an old man.*

Robin Where is the shrieve, kinde friends? I you beseech,
With his good worshippe, let mee have some speech.

Frier Here is the Sheriffe, father, this is hee.

Robin Frier, good alms, and many blessings thank thee.

955		Sir, you are welcome to this troublous sheere.	
		Of this daies execution did I heare.	
		Scarlet and Scathlocke murdered my young sonne,	
		Mee have they robd, and helplessely undoone.	
		Revenge I would, but I am olde and dry:	
960		Wherefore, sweete master, for saint charitie,	
		Since they are bound, deliver them to mee,	
		That for my sons blood I reveng'd may bee.	

	Scarlet	This old man lies, we nere did him such wrong.	*never*

	Robin	I doe not lie, you wote it too too well;	*know*
965		The deede was such, as you may shame to tell.	
		But I with all intreats might not prevaile	
		With your sterne stubborne mindes, bent all to blood.	
		Shall I have such revenge then, master Sheriffe,	
		That with my sonnes losse, may suffice myselfe?	

970   *[Robin whispers with them.*

Warman   Doe, father, what thou wilt, for they must die.

Frier   I never heard them toucht with bloode till now.

Warman   Notorious villanes, and they made their brags,
               The Earle of Huntington would save their lives;
975   But hee is downe the winde, as all such shall,
               That revell, wast and spende, and take no care.

Robin   My horne once winded, Ile unbinde my belt,
               Whereat the swords and bucklers are fast tied.

Scathlock   Thankes to your Honour. Father, we confesse,
980   And, were our armes unbounde, we would upheave
               Our sinfull hands with sorrowing hearts to heaven.

Robin   I will unbinde you, with the Sheriffes leave.

Warman   Doe. Helpe him Ralphe; go to them, master Frier.

Robin   And as yee blew your horns, at my sons death,
985   So will I sound your knell, with my best breath.

                [Sound his horne.

And here's a blade, that hangeth at my belt,
Shall make ye feele in death, what my sonne felt.

              [Enter Little John, Much, Scarlet, and Scathlock. Fight: the
990   *Frier, making as if he helpt the Sheriffe, knockes downe*

his men, crying, "Keepe the kings peace."

Ralph O they must be hangd, father.

Robin Thy master and thyselfe supply their roomes.
Warman, approach mee not, tempt not my wrath.
995   For if thou doe, thou diest remedilesse.

Warman It is the outlawed Earle of Huntington;
Downe with him Frier. Oh, thou dost mistake.
Fly Ralph, wee die else; let us raise the shire.

[Sheriffe runnes away, and his men.

1000 **Frier** Farewell Earle Robert, as I am true frier,
I had rather be thy clarke, then serve the Prior.   *[Exit Frier.*

Robin A jolly fellowe, Scarlet, knowest thou him?

Scarlet Hee is of Yorke, and of Saint Maries Cloister.
There where your greedie uncle is Lord Prior.

1005 **Much** O murren on ye, have you two scap't hanging?   *plague*
Harke yee, my Lord, these two fellowes kept at Barns-
dale seaven yeare, to my knowledge, and no man.

Robin Here is no biding masters. Get yee in;   *waiting*
Take a short blessing at your mothers hands.
1010   Much, beare them companie, make Matilda merry.
John and myselfe will followe presently. *[Exeunt Much, Scarlet, Scath.*
John, on a sodaine thus I am resolv'd,
To keepe in Sherewodde, till the Kings returne,   *wait*
And being outlawed, leade an outlawes life.
1015   Seaven yeares these brethren, being yeomens sons,
Lived and scap't the malice of their foes.
How thinkest thou, Little John, of my intent?

Lit. John I like your Honours purpose exceeding well.

Robin Nay, no more honour, I pray thee Little John.
1020   Henceforth I will be called Robin Hoode,
Matilda shall be my Maid Marian.
Come, John, friends all, for now beginnes the game,
And after our deserts, so growe our fame.   *[Exeunt.*   *according to*

The Downfall of Robert, Earle of Huntington

[Scene viii]

[*Enter Prince John and his Lords, with souldiers.*

1025	**Pr. John**	Now is this comet shot into the sea,	
		Or lies like slime, upon the sullen earth.	
		Come, he is deade, else should we heare of him.	*i.e., Ely*
	Salsbury	I knowe not what to thinke herein, my Lord.	
	Fitzwater	Ely is not the man I tooke him for,	
1030		I am afraide wee shall have worse than hee.	
	Pr. John	Why, good Fitzwater, whence doth spring your fear?	
	Fitzwater	Him, for his pride, we justly have supprest;	
		But prouder climers are about to rise.	
	Salsbury	Name them, Fitzwater; know you any such?	
1035	**Pr. John**	Fitzwater meanes not any thing, I know;	
		For if he did, his tongue would tell his heart.	
	Fitzwater	An argument of my free heart, my Lord,	
		That lets the worlde be witnesse of my thought.	
		When I was taught, true dealing kept the schoole;	
1040		Deeds were sworne partners with protesting words.	
		We said and did, these say and never meane.	
		This upstart protestation of no proofe,	
		This, I beseech you, sir, accept my love;	
		Commaund mee, use mee, O you are too blame	
1045		That doe neglect my everlasting zeale,	
		My deare, my kinde affect, when God can tell,	
		A sodaine puffe of winde, a lightning flash,	
		A bubble on the streame doth longer dure,	
		Than doth the purpose of their promise bide.	
1050		A shame upon this peevish apish age,	*ape-like*
		These crouching hypocrite dissembling times.	
		Well, well, God rid the patrones of these crimes,	
		Out of this land. I have an inward feare,	
		This ill, well-seeming sinne will be bought deare.	
1055	**Salsbury**	My Lord Fitzwater is inspir'd I thinke.	
	Pr. John	I, with some divell; let the olde foole dote.	

[*Enter Queene Mother, Chester, Sheriffe, Kent souldiers.*

333

	Queene	From the pursuing of the hatefull Priest,
1060		And bootlesse search of Ely are wee come.
	Pr. John	And welcome is your sacred Majestie.
		And, Chester, welcome too, against your will.
	Chester	Unwilling men come not without constraint,
		But uncompeld comes Chester to this place,
1065		Telling thee, John, that thou art much too blame
		To chase hence Ely, Chauncelor to the King,
		To set thy footesteppes on the cloath of state,
		And seate thy body in thy brothers throne.
	Salsbury	Who should succeede the brother, but the brother?
1070	Chester	If one were deade, one should succeede the other.
	Queene	My sonne is king, my son then ought to raigne.
	Fitzwater	One sonne is king, the State allows not twaine.
	Salsbury	The subjects many yeares the king have mist.
	Chester	But subjects must not chuse what king they list.
1075	Queene	Richard hath conquered kingdomes in the East.
	Fitzwater	A signe hee will not loose this in the West.
	Salsbury	By Salsburies honour, I will follow John.
	Chester	So Chester will, to shunne commotion.
	Queene	Why? John shall be but Richards deputie.
1080	Fitzwater	To that, Fitzwater gladly doth agree.
		And looke to't Lady, minde King Richards love:
		As you will answer't, doe the King no wrong.
	Queene	Well said old conscience; you keep still one song.
	Pr. John	In your contentious humours, noble Lords,
1085		Peeres, and upholders of the English State,
		John silent stoode, as one that did awaite
		What sentence yee determind for my life.
		But since you are agreed that I shall beare
		The weightie burthen of this kingdomes state,
1090		Till the returne of Richard, our dread king,
		I doe accept the charge, and thanke you all,
		That think me worthie of so great a place.

The Downfall of Robert, Earle of Huntington

	All	Wee all confirme you Richards deputie.	
	Salsbury	Now shall I plague proud Chester.	
1095	**Queene**	Sit you sure, Fitzwater.	
	Chester	For peace, I yield to wrong.	
	Pr. John	Now olde man, for your daughter.	
	Fitzwater	To see wrong rule, my eyes run streams of water.	

[*A noyse within.*

1100   [*Enter a Collier, crying a monster.*

	Collier	A monster, a monster! Bring her out Robin, a monster, a monster!	
	Salsbury	Peace gaping fellowe. Knowest thou where thou art?	*bawling*
	Collier	Why? I am in Kent, within a mile of Dover.	
1105		Sbloud, where I am, peace, and a gaping fellow?	*God's blood*
		For all your dagger, wert not for your ging,	*crew (gang)*
		I would knocke my whipstocke on your addle head.	
		Come out with the monster, Robin.	
	Within	I come, I come, help mee she scrats.	*scratches*
1110	**Collier**	Ile gee her the lash; come out yee bearded witch.	*give*

[*Bring forth Ely, with a yarde in his hand, and lin-
nen cloath, drest like a woman.*

	Ely	Good fellowes let mee goe, there's gold to drinke.
		I am a man, though in a womans weedes.
1115		Yonders Prince John, I pray yee let mee goe.
	Queene	What rude companions have we yonder Salsbury?
	1 Coll.	Shall we take his money?
	2 Coll.	No, no; this is the thiefe that robd master
		Mighels, and came in like a woman in labour, I war-
1120		rant yee.
	Salsbury	Who have yee here, honest colliers?
	2 Coll.	A monster, a monster! A woman with a bearde,
		a man in a petticote! A monster, a monster!
	Salsbury	What my good Lord of Ely, is it you?
1125		Ely is taken; here's the Chauncelor.

335

1 Coll.	Pray God wee be not hangd for this tricke?	
Queene	What my good Lord?	
Ely	I, I, ambitious Ladie.	*Aye*
Pr. John	Who, my Lord Chauncelour?	
1130 *Ely*	I, you proud usurper.	
Salsbury	What, is your surplesse turned to a smock?	
Ely	Peace, Salibury, thou changing weathercocke.	
Chester	Alas, my Lord, I grieve to see this sight.	
Ely	Chester, it will be day for this darke night.	

1135 *Fitzwater*	Ely, thou wert the foe to Huntington:
	Robin, thou knewest, was my adopted sonne:
	O Ely, thou to him wert too too cruell,
	With him fled hence Matilda, my faire jewell.
	For their wrong, Ely, and thy hautie pride,
1140	I helpt Earle John; but now I see thee lowe,
	At thy distresse, my heart is full of woe.

Queene	Needes must I see Fitzwaters overthrowe.
	John, I affect him not; he loves not thee.
	Remoove him John, least thou remooved bee.

1145 *Pr. John*	Mother, let mee alone. By one and one,	*leave it to me*
	I will not leave one, that envies our good.	
	My Lord of Salsbury, give these honest colliers,	
	For taking Ely, each a hundred markes.	

Salsbury	Come fellowes, goe with mee.
1150 *1 Coll.*	Thanke yee faith; farewell, monster.

       [*Exeunt Salsbury, Colliers.*

Pr. John	Sheriffe of Kent, take Ely to your charge,
	From Shreeve to Shreeve, send him to Notingham
	Where Warman, by our Patent, is high Shreeve.
1155	There as a traitor, let him be close kept,
	And to his triall wee will follow straight.

Ely	A traitor, John?
Pr. John	Doe not expostulate.
	You at your trial shal have time to prate. [*Exeunt cum Ely.*

1160	*Fitzwater*	God for thy pittie, what a time is here?
	Pr. John	Right gratious mother, wold yourself and Chester
		Would but withdrawe you for a little space,
		While I conferre with my good Lord Fitzwater.
	Queene	My Lord of Chester, will you walke aside?
1165	*Chester*	Whether your Highnesse please, thither I wil.

Whither

        [*Exeunt Chester, Queene.*

	Pr. John	Souldiers, attend the person of our mother. [*Exeunt.*
		Noble Fitzwater, now wee are alone,
		What oft I have desir'd, I will intreate,
1170		Touching Matilda, fled with Huntington.
	Fitzwater	Of her what wold you touch? Touching her flight,
		She is fledde hence with Robert, her true knight.
	Pr. John	Robert is outlawed, and Matilda free.
		Why through his fault should she exiled be?
1175		She is your comfort, all your ages blisse.
		Why should your age, so great a comfort misse?
		She is all Englands beautie, all her pride.
		In forren lands, why should that beautie bide?
		Call her againe Fitzwater, call againe
1180		Guiltlesse Matilda, beauties souveraigne.
	Fitzwater	I graunt, Prince John, Matilda was my joy,
		And the faire sunne, that kept old winters frost
		From griping deade the marrowe of my bones.
		And she is gone, yet where she is, God wote,
1185		Aged Fitzwater truly guesseth not.
		But where she is, there is kinde Huntington;
		With my faire daughter, is my noble sonne.
		If he may never be recald againe,
		To call Matilda backe it is in vaine.
1190	*Pr. John*	Living with him, she lives in vitious state,
		For Huntington is excommunicate.
		And till his debts be paid, by Romes decree,
		It is agreed, absolv'd he can not be.
		And that can never be. So never wife,
1195		But in a loath'd adult'rous beggers life,

sinful

337

Must faire Matilda live? This you may amend
And winne Prince John, your ever during friend.

Fitzwater As how, as how?

Pr. John Cal her from him; bring her to Englands court,
1200 Where, like faire Phoebe, she may sit as Queene,
Over the sacred honourable maids
That doe attend the royall Queene, my mother.
There shall shee live a Princes Cynthia,
And John will be her true Endimion.

1205 **Fitzwater** By this construction, she should be the Moone,
And you would be the man within the Moone.

Pr. John A pleasant exposition, good Fitzwater:
But if it fell so out that I fell in,
You of my full joyes should be chiefe partaker.

1210 **Fitzwater** John, I defie thee. By my honours hope,
I will not beare this base indignitie.
Take to thy tooles. Thinkst thou a noble man   *Draw your sword*
Will be a Pandar to his proper childe?
For what intendst thou else? Seeing I knowe,
1215 Earle Clepstowes daughter is thy married wife.
Come, if thou be a right Plantaginet,
Drawe and defende thee. Oh our Ladie helpe
True English Lords, from such a tyrant Lord.
What, doest thou thinke I jeast? Nay by the Roode,
1220 Ile loose my life, or purge thy lustfull bloode.

Pr. John What my olde Ruffian, lye at your warde?   *en garde*
Have at your froward bosome, olde Fitzwater.

> [*Fight: John falles. Enter Queene, Chester, Salsbury*
> *hastily.*

1225 **Fitzwater** O that thou werte not Royal Richards brother,
Thou shouldst here die in presence of thy mother.

> [*John rises. All compasse Fitzwater; Fitzwater chafes.*

What, is he up? Nay Lords, then give us leave.

Chester What meanes this rage Fitzwater?

1230 **Queene** Lay hands upon the Bedlam, traitrous wretch.   *crazy man*

Pr. John Nay, hale him hence, and heare you old Fitzwater;

| | See that you stay not five daies in the Realme, |
| | For if you doe, you die remedilesse. |

| *Fitzwater* | Speak Lords. Do you confirme what he hath said? |

| 1235 | *All* | He is our Prince, and he must be obaid. |

| *Fitzwater* | Harken, Earle John, but one word will I say. |

| *Pr. John* | I will not heare thee, neither will I stay. |
| | Thou knowest thy time.   [*Exit.* |

| *Fitzwater* | Will not your Highnesse heare? |

| 1240 | *Queene* | No, thy Matilda robd mee of my deare.   [*Exit.* |

| *Fitzwater* | I aided thee in battell, Salsbury. |

| *Salsbury* | Prince John is moov'd; I dare not stay with thee.   [*Exit Salsbury.* |

| *Fitzwater* | Gainst thee and Ely, Chester, was I foe? |
| | And dost thou stay to aggravate my woe? |

1245	*Chester*	No, good Fitzwater, Chester doth lament
	Thy wrong, thy sodaine banishment.
	Whence grue the quarrell twixt the Prince and thee?

Fitzwater	Chester, the divell tempted old Fitzwater,
	To be a Pandar to his only daughter,
1250		And my great heart, impatient, forst my hand,
	In my true honours right, to chalenge him.
	Alas the while, wrong will not be reproov'd.

| *Chester* | Farewell, Fitzwater. Wheresoere thou bee, |
| | By letters, I beseech thee, send to mee.   [*Exit.* |

1255	*Fitzwater*	Chester, I will, I will.
	Heavens turne to good this woe, this wrong, this ill.
	[*Exit.*

[*Scene ix*]

[*Enter Scathlocke and Scarlet, winding their hornes at severall doores. To them enter Robin Hoode, Matilda*
1260 *all in greene, Scathlockes mother, Much, Little John, all the men with bowes and arrowes.*]

| *Robin* | Widowe, I wish thee homeward now to wend, |

339

		Least Warmans malice worke thee any wrong.	*Lest*
	Widow	Master I will, and mickle good attend	*much*
1265		On thee, thy love, and all these yeomen strong.	
	Matilda	Forget not, widowe, what you promise mee.	
	Much	O I, mistresse, for Gods sake lets have Jinny.	*Oh yes*
	Widow	You shall have Jinny sent you with all speede.	
		Sonnes farewell, and by your mothers reede,	*counsel*
1270		Love well your master: blessing ever fall	
		On him, your mistresse, and these yeomen tall. [*Exit.*	*brave*
	Much	God be with you, mother; have much minde I	
		pray on Much, your sonne, and your daughter Jinny.	
	Robin	Wind once more, jolly huntsmen, all your horns,	
1275		Whose shrill sound, with the ecchoing wods assist,	
		Shall ring a sad knell for the fearefull deere,	
		Before our feathered shafts, deaths winged darts,	
		Bring sodaine summons for their fatall ends.	
	Scarlet	Its ful seaven years since we were outlawed first,	
1280		And wealthy Sherewood was our heritage.	
		For all those yeares we raigned uncontrolde,	
		From Barnsdale shrogs to Notinghams red cliffes;	*thickets (undergrowth)*
		At Blithe and Tickhill were we welcome guests.	
		Good George a Greene at Bradford was our friend,	
1285		And wanton Wakefields Pinner lov'd us well.	
		At Barnsley dwels a Potter tough and strong,	
		That never brookt we brethren should have wrong.	
		The Nunnes of Farnsfield, pretty nunnes they bee,	
		Gave napkins, shirts, and bands to him and mee.	
1290		Bateman of Kendall, gave us Kendall greene,	
		And Sharpe of Leedes, sharpe arrowes for us made:	
		At Rotheram dwelt our bowyer, God him blisse.	*bow maker; bless*
		Jackson he hight; his bowes did never misse.	*was called*
		This for our good, our scathe let Scathlocke tell,	*peril*
1295		In merry Mansfield, how it once befell.	
	Scathlock	In merry Mansfield, on a wrestling day,	
		Prizes there were, and yeomen came to play.	
		My brother Scarlet and myselfe were twaine.	
		Many resisted, but it was in vaine,	

1300		For of them all we wonne the mastery,	
		And the gilt wreathes were given to him and mee.	
		There by Sir Doncaster of Hethersfield,	
		Wee were bewraid, beset, and forst to yield,	*betrayed*
		And so borne bound, from thence to Notingham,	
1305		Where we lay doom'd to death, till Warman came.	

	Robin	Of that enough. What cheere, my dearest love?

	Much	O good cheare anone, sir, she shall have venson	*venison*
		her bellyfull.	

	Matilda	Matilda is as joyfull of thy good,
1310		As joy can make her. How fares Robin Hood?

	Robin	Well, my Matilda, and if thou agree,
		Nothing but mirth shall waite on thee and mee.

	Marian	O God, how full of perfect mirth were I,
		To see thy griefe turnd to true jollitie!

1315	*Robin*	Give me thy hand; now Gods curse on me light,
		If I forsake not griefe, in griefes despight.
		Much, make a cry, and yeomen stand yee round.
		I charge yee never more let woefull sound
		Be heard among yee; but what ever fall,
1320		Laugh griefe to scorne; and so make sorrowes small.
		Much, make a cry, and loudly, Little John.

	Much	O God, O God, helpe, helpe, helpe! I am un-
		doone, I am undoone.

	Lit. John	Why how now, Much? Peace, peace, you roaring
1325		slave.

	Much	My master bid mee cry, and I will cry till hee
		bid me leave. Helpe, helpe, helpe: I, mary, will I.

	Robin	Peace, Much; reade on the Articles good John.

	Lit. John	First, no man must presume to call our master,
1330		By name of Earle, Lord, Baron, Knight, or Squire,
		But simply by the name of Robin Hoode.

	Robin	Say, yeomen, to this order will ye yielde?

	All	We yield to serve our master Robin Hoode.

341

	Lit. John	Next tis agreed (if thereto shee agree)
1335		That faire Matilda henceforth change her name,
		And while it is the chance of Robin Hoode,
		To live in Sherewodde a poore outlawes life,
		She, by Maid Marians name, be only cald.

| | **Matilda** | I am contented; reade on, Little John, |
| 1340 | | Henceforth let me be nam'd Maid Marian. |

	Lit. John	Thirdly, no yeoman, following Robin Hoode
		In Sherewod, shall use widowe, wife, or maid,
		But by true labour, lustfull thoughts expell.

Robin   How like yee this?

All   Master, we like it well.

Much   But I cry no to it. What shal I do with Jinny then?

Scarlet   Peace, Much; goe forwarde with the orders, fellowe John.

Lit. John   Fourthly, no passenger with whom ye meete
1350   Shall yee let passe till hee with Robin feast —
Except a Poast, a Carrier, or such folke,   *post (i.e., message carrier)*
As use with foode to serve the market townes.

All   An order which we gladly will observe.

Lit. John   Fiftly, you never shall the poore man wrong,
1355   Nor spare a priest, a usurer, or a clarke.

Much   Nor a faire wench, meete we her in the darke.

Lit. John   Lastly, you shall defend with all your power,
Maids, widowes, orphants, and distressed men.   *orphans*

All   All these wee vowe to keepe, as we are men.

1360   **Robin**   Then wend ye to the Greenewod merrily,
And let the light roes bootlesse from yee runne.   *deer*
Marian and I, as soveraigns of your toyles,   *toils*
Will wait, within our bower, your bent bowes spoiles.

Much   Ile among them master.

1365   *[Exeunt winding their hornes.*

Robin   Marian, thou seest though courtly pleasurs want,
Yet country sport in Sherewodde is not scant.

		For the soule-ravishing delicious sound	
		Of instrumentall musique, we have found	
1370		The winged quiristers, with divers notes,	*choristers*
		Sent from their quaint recording prettie throats,	
		On every branch that compasseth our bower,	
		Without commaund, contenting us each hower.	
1375		For Arras hangings, and rich Tapestrie,	
		We have sweete natures best imbrothery.	*embroidery*
		For thy steele glasse, wherein thou wontst to looke,	
		Thy christall eyes, gaze in a christall brooke.	
		At court, a flower or two did decke thy head:	
		Now with whole garlands is it circled.	
1380		For what in wealth we want, we have in flowers,	
		And what wee loose in halles, we finde in bowers.	
	Marian	Marian hath all, sweete Robert, having thee,	
		And guesses thee as rich, in having mee.	
	Robin	I am indeede,	
1385		For having thee, what comfort can I neede?	
	Marian	Goe in, goe in.	
		To part such true love, Robin, it were sinne.	[*Exeunt.*

[*Scene x*]

[*Enter Prior, Sir Doncaster, Frier Tucke.*

	Prior	To take his bodie, by the blessed Roode,	*Cross*
1390		Twold doe me more than any other good.	*It would*
	Doncaster	O tis an unthrift, still the Churchmens foe,	
		An ill end will betide him, that I knowe.	
		Twas hee that urg'd the king to sesse the clergie	*assess*
		When to the holy land he tooke his jorney;	
1395		And he it is that rescued those two theeves,	
		Scarlet and Scathlocke, that so manie grieves	
		To churchmen did. And now they say	
		Hee keepes in Sherewod, and himselfe doth play	
		The lawlesse rener; heare you, my Lord Prior;	*fugitive*
1400		He must be taken, or it will be wrong.	
	Prior	I, and he shall bee to.	*Aye*

343

	Tuck	I, I; soone sed. But ere he be, many wil lie deade —	*spoken*
		Except it be by sleight.	
	Doncaster	I there, there, Frier.	
1405	**Tuck**	Give mee, my Lord, your execution.	*writ*
		The widowe Scarlets daughter, lovely Jinny,	
		Loves and is belov'd of Much the millers sonne.	
		If I can get the girle to goe with mee,	
		Disguis'd in habit, like a pedlers mort,	*wench*
1410		Ile serve this execution, on my life,	
		And single out a time alone to take	
		Robin, that often carelesse walkes alone.	
		Why? Answere not. Remember what I saide.	
		Yonder I see comes Jinny, that faire maide;	
		If wee agree, then back me soone with aide.	

[Enter Jinny with a fardle.

bundle

	Prior	Tuck, if thou doe it . . .	
	Doncaster	Pray you doe not talke;	
		As we were strangers, let us carelesse walke.	
1420	**Jinny**	Now to the greene wodde wend I, God me speede.	
	Tuck	Amen, faire maid, and send thee, in thy neede,	
		Much, that is borne to doe thee much good deeds.	
	Jinny	Are you there, Frier? Nay, then yfaith we have it.	
	Tuck	What, wenche? My love?	
1425	**Jinny**	I, gee't mee when I crave it.	*Aye, give it to*
	Tuck	Unaskt I offer, pre thee, sweete girle, take it.	*pray you*
	Jinny	Gifts stinke with proffer; foh, Frier, I forsake it.	
	Tuck	I will be kinde.	
	Jinny	Will not your kindnesse kill her?	
1430	**Tuck**	With love?	
	Jinny	You cogge.	*flatterer (deceiver/mill wheel)*
	Tuck	Tut, girle, I am no miller; heare in your eare.	
	Doncaster	[*Aside*] The Frier courts her.	

	Prior	Tush, let him alone,	
1435		He is our Ladies Chaplaine, but serves Jone.	*a slut*
	Doncaster	Then, from the Friers fault, perchance, it may be	
		The proverbe grew, Jone's taken for my Ladie.	
	Prior	Peace, good Sir Doncaster, list to the end.	
	Jinny	But meane yee faith and troth, shall I go weye?	*with you*
1440	**Tuck**	Upon my faith, I doe intend good faith.	
	Jinny	And shall I have the pinnes and laces too,	
		If I beare a pedlers packe with you?	
	Tuck	As I am holy Frier, Jinny, thou shalt.	
	Jinny	Well, there's my hand; see, Frier, you do not halt.	
1445	**Tuck**	Goe but before into the miry mead,	
		And keepe the path that doth to Farnsfield lead.	
		Ile into Suthwell, and buy all the knacks,	
		That shall fit both of us for pedlers packes.	
	Jinny	Who be they two that yonder walke, I prey?	
1450	**Tuck**	Jinny, I knowe not; be they what they may,	
		I care not for them, pre thee doe not stay,	*pray you*
		But make some speede that we were gone away.	
	Jinny	Wel Frier, I trust you that we go to Sherewod.	
	Tuck	I, by my beads, and unto Robin Hoode.	*Aye*
1455	**Jinny**	Make speede, good Frier. [*Exit Jinny.*	
	Tuck	Jinny, doe not feare.	
		Lord Prior, now you heare	
		As much as I; get mee two pedlers packes,	
		Points, laces, looking glasses, pinnes and knackes:	
1460		And let Sir Doncaster with some wight lads,	*stalwart*
		Followe us close; and ere these fortie howers,	
		Upon my life, Earle Robert shall be ours.	
	Prior	Thou shalt have any thing, my dearest Frier,	
		And in amends, Ile make thee my subprior.	
1465		Come, good Sir Doncaster, and if wee thrive,	
		Weele frolicke with the Nunnes of Leeds belive.	*shortly*
		[*Exeunt.*	

[Scene xi]

[*Enter Fitzwater, like an olde man.*

Fitzwater	Well did he write, and mickle did he knowe,	*much*
1470	That said this worlds felicitie was woe,	
	Which greatest states can hardly undergoe.	
	Whilom Fitzwater in faire Englands court,	
	Possest felicitie and happie state;	
	And in his hall blithe fortune kept her sport,	
1475	Which glee, one howre of woe did ruinate.	
	Fitzwater once had castles, townes, and towers,	
	Faire gardens, orchards, and delightfull bowers;	
	But now nor garden, orchard, towne, nor tower	
	Hath poore Fitzwater left within his power.	
1480	Only wide walkes are left mee in the world,	
	Which these stiffe limmes wil hardly let me tread;	*limbs*
	And when I sleepe, heavens glorious canopy	
	Mee and my mossie coutch doth over-spreade.	
	Of this, injurious John can not bereave mee;	
1485	The aire and earth he (while I live) must leave mee.	
	But from the English aire and earth, poore man,	
	His tyranny hath ruthlesse thee exil'd.	
	Yet ere I leave it, Ile do what I can,	
	To see Matilda, my faire lucklesse childe.	

[*Curtaines open; Robin Hoode sleepes on a greene
banke, and Marian strewing flowers on him.*

	And in good time, see where my comfort stands,	
	And by her lyes dejected Huntington.	
	Looke how my flower holds flowers in her hands,	
1495	And flings those sweetes upon my sleeping sonne.	
	Ile close mine eyes as if I wanted sight,	
	That I may see the end of their delight.	

[*Goes knocking with his staffe.*   *feeling his way*

Marian	What aged man art thou? Or by what chance,	
1500	Cam'st thou thus farre into the wailesse wodde?	*pathless*
Fitzwater	Widowe or wife, or maiden if thou be,	
	Lend mee thy hand: thou seest I cannot see.	
	Blessing betide thee, little feel'st thou want.	

		With mee, good childe, foode is both hard and scant.	
1505		These smooth even vaines, assure mee he is kinde,	
		What ere he be, my girle, that thee doth finde.	
		I poore and olde am reft of all earths good	
		And desperately am crept into this wodde	
		To seeke the poore mans patron, Robin Hoode.	

1510	*Marian*	And thou art welcome, welcome aged man,	
		I, ten times welcome to Maid Marian.	*Indeed*
		Sit downe olde father, sit and call me daughter.	
		O God, how like he lookes to olde Fitzwater! [*Runs in.*	

1515	*Fitzwater*	Is my Matilda cald Maid Marian?	
		I wonder why her name is changed thus.	

[*Brings wine, meate.*

	Marian	Here's wine to cheere thy hart. Drink aged man.	
		There's venson and a knife, here's manchet fine.	*high quality bread*
		Drinke good old man, I pre you drinke more wine.	*pray*
1520		My Robin stirres, I must sing him a sleepe.	

	Robin	Nay, you have wak't me Marian with your talke.	
		What man is that, is come within our walke?	

	Marian	An aged man, a silly sightlesse man,	*innocent*
		Neere pin'd with hunger: see how fast he eates.	*destroyed*

1525	*Robin*	Much good may't doe him. Never is good meat	
		Ill spent on such a stomacke. Father, proface;	*welcome*
		To Robin Hood thou art a welcome man.	

| | *Fitzwater* | I thanke you master. Are you Robin Hood? | |

| | *Robin* | Father, I am. | |

1530	*Fitzwater*	God give your soule much good,	
		For this good meat Maid Marian hath given mee.	
		But heare you, master, can you tell mee newes,	
		Where faire Matilda is, Fitzwaters daughter?	

| | *Robin* | Why? Here she is, this Marian is shee. | |

| 1535 | *Fitzwater* | Why did she chaunge her name? | |

| | *Robin* | What's that to thee? | |

	Fitzwater	Yes, I could weepe for griefe that it is so,	
		But that my teares are all dryed up with woe.	

Robin	Why? Shee is cald Maid Marian, honest friend,	
1540	Because she lives a spotlesse maiden life,	
	And shall, till Robins outlawe life have ende,	
	That he may lawfully take her to wife;	
	Which, if King Richard come, will not be long;	
	For, in his hand is power to right our wrong.	

1545	**Fitzwater**	If it be thus, I joy in her names change.
		So pure love in these times is very strange.

Marian	Robin, I thinke it is my aged father.	
Robin	Tell mee old man, tell me in curtesie.	
	Are you no other than you seeme to be?	

1550	**Fitzwater**	I am a wretched aged man, you see.
		If you will doe mee ought for charitie,
		Further than this, sweete, doe not question mee.

Robin	You shall have your desire, but what be these?	

[*Enter Frier Tucke, and Jinny, like Pedlers,*
1555   *singing.*

Tuck	What lacke ye? What lacke yee? What ist ye wil buy?	
	Any points, pins, or laces, any laces, points or pins?	
	Fine gloves, fine glasses, any buskes, or maskes?	*stays*
	Or any other prettie things?	
1560	Come chuse for love, or buy for money.	
	Any cony cony skins,	*rabbit*
	For laces, points, or pins? Faire maids, come chuse or buy.	
	I have prettie poting sticks,	*(see note)*
	And many other tricks, come chuse for love, or buy	
1565	for money.	

Robin	Pedler, I pre thee set thy packe downe here.	
	Marian shall buy, if thou be not too deare.	

Tuck	Jinny, unto thy mistresse shewe thy packe;	
	Master, for you I have a pretty knacke.	
1570	From farre I brought it, please you see the same.	

[*Enter Sir Doncaster,*
and others weaponed.   *(see note)*

Frier	Sir Doncaster, are not we pedlerlike?	
Doncaster	Yes, passing fit, and yonder is the bower.	
1575	I doubt not wee shall have him in our power.	

Frier	You and your companie were best stand close.	

Doncaster	What shal the watchword be to bring us forth?	

Frier   Take it, I pray, though it be much more worth.
When I speake that aloude, be sure I serve
1580   The execution presently on him.

Doncaster   Frier, looke too't.

Frier   Now Jinny to your song.   [*Sings.*

       [*Enter Marian, Robin.*

Marian   Pedler, what prettie toyes have you to sell?

1585   *Frier*   Jinny, unto our mistresse shewe your ware.

Marian   Come in, good woman.   [*Exit.*

Frier   Master, looke here, and God give care,
So mote I thee, to her and mee, if ever wee,   *So might I thrive*
thee, that art so free, meane treachery.   Robin to

1590   *Robin*   On, Pedler, to thy packe;
If thou love mee, my love thou shalt not lacke.

Frier   Master, in briefe, there is a theefe, that seekes
your griefe, God send reliefe, to you in neede; for a foule
deede, if not with speede, you take good heede, there is
1595   decreede.
    In yonder brake, there lies a snake, that meanes to
take, out of this wodde, the yeoman good, calde Robin Hoode.

Robin   Pedler, I pre thee be more plaine: what brake?   *pray*
1600   What snake? What trappe? What traine?

Frier   Robin, I am a holy Frier, sent by the Prior, who
did mee hire, for to conspire thy endlesse woe, and over-
throwe; but thou shalt knowe, I am the man whome
Little John from Notingham desir'd to be a clarke to
thee; for hee to mee saide thou wert free, and I did see,
1605   thy honestie; from gallowe tree, when thou didst free
Scathlocke and Scarlet certainely.

Robin   Why then it seemes that thou art Frier Tucke.

Frier   Master, I am.

1610	**Robin**	I pray thee, frier, say
		What treachery is meant to mee this day?
	Frier	First winde your horne; then drawe your sworde.

[Hee windes his horne.

For I have given a friers worde
1615 To take your bodie prisoner
And yield you to Sir Doncaster,
The envious Priest of Hothersfield,
Whose power your bushie wodde doth shielde;
But I will die, ere you shall yield.

1620 *[Enter Little John, &c:*

And sith your yeomen doe appeare,
Ile give the watchword without feare.
Take it I pray thee, though it be more worth.

[Rushe in Doncaster with his crue.

1625	**Doncaster**	Smite down, lay hold on outlawed Huntington.
	Lit. John	Soft, hot spurd priest, tis not so quickly done.
	Doncaster	Now out alas, the frier and the maide
		Have, to false theeves, Sir Doncaster betraide.

[Exeunt omnes.

[Scene xii]

[Enter John crowned, Queene Elianor, Chester, Sals-
1630 *bury, Lord Prior. Sit down all. Warman stands.*

	Pr. John	As Gods Vicegerent, John ascends this throne,
		His head impal'd with Englands diademe,
		And in his hand the awfull rodde of rule,
		Giving the humble, place of excellence,
1635		And to the lowe earth, casting downe the proude.
	Queene	Such upright rule is in each realme allowed.
	Pr. John	Chester, you once were Elies open friend,
		And yet are doubtfull whether he deserve
		A publicke triall for his private wrongs.
1640	**Chester**	I still am doubtfull, whether it be fit
		To punish private faults with publicke shame

adorned (encircled)
scepter

350

In such a person as Lord Ely is.

Prior   Yes honorable Chester, more it fits
To make apparant sinnes of mightie men,

1645   And on their persons sharpely to correct
A little fault, a very small defect,
Than on the poore to practise chastisement.
For if a poore man die, or suffer shame,
Only the poore and vile respect the same;

1650   But if the mightie fall, feare then besets
The proud harts of the migtie ones, his mates.
They thinke the world is garnished with nets,
And trappes ordained to intrappe their states.
Which feare, in them, begets a feare of ill,

1655   And makes them good, contrary to their will.

Pr. John   Your Lordship hath said right. Lord Salsbury,
Is not your minde as ours, concerning Ely?

Salsbury   I judge him worthy of reproofe and shame.

Pr. John   Warman, bring forth your prisoner, Ely, the Chancellor,

1660   And with him, bring the seale that he detains.
Warman, why goest thou not?

Warman   Be good to mee, my Lord.

Pr. John   What hast thou done?

Warman   Speake for mee, my Lord Prior.

1665   All my good Lords, intreate his Grace for mee.
Ely, my Lord . . .

Pr. John   Why? Where is Ely, Warman?

Warman   Fled today, this mistie morning he is fled away.

Pr. John   O Judas, whom nor friend nor foe may trust,

1670   Thinkst thou with teares and plaints to answere this?
Doe I not knowe thy heart? Doe I not knowe
That bribes have purchast Ely this escape?
Never make anticke faces, never bende
With fained humblesse, thy still crouching knee;

1675   But with fixt eyes unto thy doome attend.
Villane, Ile plague thee for abusing mee.
Goe hence, and henceforth never set thy foote
In house or fielde, thou didst this day possesse.

		Marke what I say; advise thee to looke too't,
1680		Or else be sure thou diest remedilesse.
		Nor from those houses see that thou receive
		So much as shall sustaine thee for an hower;
		But as thou art, goe where thou canst get friends,
		And hee that feedes thee, be mine enemie.

| 1685 | *Warman* | O, my good Lord. |

| | *Pr. John* | Thou thy good Lord betrayedst, |
| | | And all the world for money thou wilt sell. |

| | *Warman* | What saies the Queene? |

| | *Queene* | Why thus I say: |
| 1690 | | Betray thy master, thou wilt all betray. |

| | *Warman* | My Lords, of Chester and of Salsbury? |

| | *Both* | Speake not to us, all traitors we defie. |

| | *Warman* | Good my Lord Prior. |

| | *Prior* | Alas, what can I doe? |

| 1695 | *Warman* | Then I defie the worlde; yet I desire |
| | | Your Grace would read this supplication. |

        [*John reades.*

	Pr. John	I thought as much; but Warman dost thou thinke
		There is one moving line to mercie here?
		I tell thee no; therefore away, away.
1700		A shamefull death followes thy longer stay.

| | *Warman* | O poore poore man! |
| | | Of miserable, miserablest wretch I am.   [*Exit.* |

	Pr. John	Confusion be thy guide; a baser slave
1705		Earth cannot beare. Plagues followe him, I crave.
		Can any tell mee if my Lord of Yorke
		Be able to sit up.

| | *Queene* | The Archbishoppes Grace |
| | | Was reasonable well even now, good sonne. |

1710	*Salsbury*	And he desir'd mee that I should desire
		Your Majestie to send unto his Grace,
		If any matter did import his presence.

Pr. John	Wee will ourselves steppe in and visit him.	
	Mother, and my good Lords, will you attend us?	
1715 **Prior**	I gladly will attend your Majestie.	
Pr. John	Now good Lord helpe us.	
	When I saide good Lords,	
	I meant not you Lord Prior. Lord I know you are;	
	But good, God knowes, you never meane to bee.	
1720	[*Exeunt John, Queene, Chester, Salsbury.*	
Prior	John is incenst, and very much I doubt	*fear*
	That villane Warman hath accused mee,	
	About the scape of Ely. Well, suppose he have.	
	Whats that to mee? I am a cleargie man,	
1725	And all his power, if hee all extend,	
	Cannot prevaile against my holy order;	
	But the Archbishoppes Grace is now his friend	
	And may perchance attempt to doe me ill.	
	[*Enter a serving man.*	
1730	What newes with you, sir?	
Servant	Even heavie news, my Lord; for the light fire	
	Falling, in manner of a fier drake,	*dragon*
	Upon a barne of yours, hath burnt six barnes,	*bushel*
	And not a strike of corne reserv'd from dust.	
1735	No hand could save it, yet ten thousand hands,	
	Labourd their best, though none for love of you.	
	For every tongue with bitter cursing band,	*cursing cursed*
	Your Lordshippe as the viper of the land.	
Prior	What meant the villanes?	
1740 **Servant**	Thus and thus they cride:	
	Upon this churle, this hoorder up of corne,	
	This spoyler of the Earle of Huntington,	
	This lust-defiled, mercilesse false Prior,	
	Heaven raigneth vengeance downe in shape of fier.	
1745	Old wives that scarce could with their crouches creep,	*crutches*
	And little babes, that newly learnde to speake,	
	Men masterlesse that thorough want did weepe,	*unemployed*
	All in one voice, with a confused cry,	
	In execrations band you bitterly,	*cursed*

1750		Plague followe plague, they cry, he hath undone
		The good Lord Robert, Earle of Huntington,
		And then . . .

| | *Prior* | What then, thou villane? Get thee from my sight. |
| | | They that wish plagues, plagues wil upon them light. |

| 1755 | | [*Enter another servant.* |

What are your tidings?

	Servant 2	The Covent of Saint Maries are agreed
		And have elected, in your Lordshippes place,
		Olde Father Jerome, who is stald Lord Prior,	*installed*
1760		By the newe Archbishoppe.

| | *Prior* | Of Yorke thou meanst. |
| | | A vengeance on him, he is my hopes foe. |

[*Enter a Herald.*

	Herald	Gilbert de Hood, late Prior of Saint Maries,
1765		Our Soveraigne John commandeth thee by mee,
		That presently thou leave this blessed land,
		Defiled with the burden of thy sinne.
		All thy goods temporall and spirituall,
		With free consent of Hubert Lorde Yorke,
1770		Primate of England and thy Ordinary,	*(see note); Diocesan Superior*
		He hath suspended, and vow'd by heaven,
		To hang thee up, if thou depart not hence,
		Without delaying or more question.
		And that he hath good reason for the same,
1775		He sends this writing firm'd with Warmans hand,
		And comes himselfe, whose presence if thou stay,
		I feare this sunne will see thy dying day.

| | *Prior* | O, Warman hath betraid mee. Woe is mee. |

[*Enter John, Queene, Chester, Salsbury.*

1780	*Pr. John*	Hence with that Prior, sirra do not speake,
		My eyes are full of wrath, my heart of wreake.	*vengeance*
		Let Lester come; his hault hart, I am sure,	*arrogant heart*
		Will checke the kingly course we undertake.

[*Exeunt cum Prior.*

| 1785 | | [*Enter Lester, drumme and Ancient.* | *standard-bearer* |

The Downfall of Robert, Earle of Huntington

Pr. John   Welcome from warre, thrice noble Earle of Lester;
Unto our court, welcome, most valiant Earle.

Leicester   Your court in England, and King Richard gone,
A king in England, and the king from home:
1790   This sight and salutations are so strange,
That what I should, I know not how to speake.

Pr. John   What would you say? Speake boldly, we intreat.

Leicester   It is not feare, but wonder barres my speach;
I muse to see a mother and a Queene,
1795   Two peeres, so great as Salsbury and Chester,
Sit and support proud usurpation,
And see King Richards crowne, worne by Earle John.

Queene   He sits as viceroy and a substitute.

Chester   He must and shal resigne when Richard comes.

1800 **Salsbury**   Chester, he will without your must and shall.

Leicester   Whether he will or no, he shall resigne.

Pr. John   You knowe your own will Lester, but not mine.

Leicester   Tell me among ye, where is reverent Ely,
Left by our dreade King, as his deputie?

1805 **Pr. John**   Banisht he is, as proud usurpers should.

Leicester   Pride then, belike, was enemy to pride:
Ambition in yourselfe, his state envied.
Where is Fitzwater, that old honoured Lord?

Pr. John   Dishonourd and exil'd, as Ely is.

1810 **Leicester**   Exil'd he may be, but dishonourd never.
He was a fearelesse souldier, and a vertuous scholler.
But where is Huntington, that noble youth?

Chester   Undoone by ryot.   *misrule*

Leicester   Ah, the greater ruth.

1815 **Pr. John**   Lester, you question more than doth become you.
On to the purpose, why you come to us.

Leicester   I came to Ely, and to all the State,
Sent by the King, who three times sent before,
To have his ransome brought to Austria;

1820   And if you be elected deputie,
Doe as you ought, and send the ransome money.

Pr. John   Lester, you see I am no deputie;
And Richards ransome if you doe require,
Thus wee make answere: Richard is a king,
1825   In Cyprus, Acon, Acres, and rich Palestine.
To get those kingdomes England lent him men,
And many a million of her substance spent,
The very entrals of her wombe was rent.
No plough but paid a share, no needy hand,
1830   But from his poore estate of penurie,
Unto his voyage offered more than mites,
And more, poore soules, than they had might to spare.
Yet were they joyfull. For still flying newes,
And lying I perceive them now to be,
1835   Came of King Richards glorious victories,
His conquest of the Souldans, and such tales
As blewe them up with hope, when he returnd
He would have scattered gold about the streetes.

Leicester   Doe Princes fight for gold? O leaden thought!
1840   Your father knewe that honour was the aime
Kings levell at. By sweete Saint John I sweare,
You urge mee so that I cannot forbeare.
What doe you tell of money lent the King,
When first he went into this holy warre?
1845   As if he had extorted from the poore,
When you, the Queene, and all that heare me speake,
Know with what zeale the people gave their goods:
Olde wives tooke silver buckles from their belts,
Young maids the gilt pins that tuckt up their traines,
1850   Children their prettie whistles from their neckes,
And every man what he did most esteeme,
Crying to souldiours, "Weare these gifts of ours."
This prooves that Richard had no neede to wrong
Or force the people that with willing hearts
1855   Gave more than was desir'd. And where you say,
You guesse Richards victories but lies,
I sweare he wan rich Cyprus with his sworde.
And thence, more glorious than the guide of Greece   *ruler*
That brought so huge a fleete to Tenedos,   *(see note)*

1860		He saild along the Mediterran sea,
		Where on a sunbright morning he did meete
		The warlike souldiours well prepared fleete.
		O still mee thinkes I see King Richard stand,
		In his guilt armour staind with Pagans blood,
1865		Upon a gallies prowe, like warres fierce god,
		And on his crest, a crucifix of golde.
		O that daies honour can be never tolde:

Six times six severall brigandines he boarded,   *war ships*
And in the greedie waves flung wounded Turkes,

1870   And three times thrice the winged gallies bankes,
(Wherin the Souldans sonne was Admirall)
In his owne person royall Richard smooth'd,   *rubbed out (eradicated)*
And left no heathen hand to be upheav'd
Against the Christian souldiers.

1875   **Pr. John**   Lester, so,
Did he all this?

Leicester   I, by God hee did,
And more than this; nay jeast not at it, John:
I sweare hee did, by Lesters faith hee did,
1880   And made the greene sea red with Pagan blood,
Leading to Joppa glorious victory,
And following feare that fled unto the foe.

Pr. John   All this hee did, perchance all this was so.

Leicester   Holy God helpe mee, souldiers come away:
1885   This carpet knight sits carping at our scarres,
And jeasts at those most glorious well fought warres.

Pr. John   Lester, you are too hot. Stay, goe not yet.
Me thinkes, if Richard wonne these victories,
The wealthie kingdomes he hath conquered
1890   May better than poore England pay his ransome.
He left this realme as a young orphant maid
To Ely, the stepfather of this state,
That stript the virgin to her very skinne.
And, Lester, had not John more carefull bin
1895   Than Richard, at this hower, England had not England bin.   *hour*
Therefore, good warlike Lord, take this in briefe:

We wish King Richard well,
But can send no reliefe.

Leicester   O, let not my heart breake with inward griefe.

1900   Pr. John   Yes let it, Lester, it is not amisse
That twenty such hearts breake, as your heart is.

Leicester   Are you a mother? Were you Englands Queene?
Were Henry, Richard, Gefferey (your sonnes)
All sonnes, but Richard, sunne of all those sonnes?   *i.e., supreme son*
1905   And can you let this little meteor,
This *ignis fatuus*, this same wandring fire,   *will-o-the-wisp*
This goblin of the night, this brand, this sparke,
Seeme through a lanthorne, greater than he is?
By heaven you doe not well, by earth you doe not.
1910   Chester, nor you, nor you, Earle Salsbury,
Ye doe not, no yee doe not what yee should.

Queene   Were this Beare loose, how he wold tear our mawes!   *throats (bellies)*

Chester   Pale death and vengeance dwel within his jawes.

Salsbury   But we can muzzle him and binde his pawes;
1915   If King John say we shall, wee will indeede.

Pr. John   Doe if you can.

Leicester   Its well thou hast some feare.
No curres, ye have no teethe to baite this Beare.
I will not bid mine ensigne bearer wave
1920   My tottered colours in this worthlesse aire   *tattered*
Which your vile breathes vilely contaminate.
Beare, thou hast bene my auncient bearer long,   *ensign*
And borne up Lesters Beare in forren lands.
Yet now resigne these colours to my hands.
1925   For I am full of griefe and full of rage.
John, looke upon mee: thus did Richard take
The coward Austrias colours in his hand,
And thus he cast them under Acon walles,
And thus he trod them underneath his feete.
1930   Rich colours, how I wrong ye by this wrong!
But I will right yee. Beare, take them againe,
And keepe them ever, ever them maintaine.
We shall have use for them I hope, ere long.

The Downfall of Robert, Earle of Huntington

	Pr. John	Darest thou attempt thus proudly in our sight?
1935	**Leicester**	What ist a subject dares, that I dare not?
	Salsbury	Dare subjects dare, their soveraigne being by?
	Leicester	O God, that my true soveraigne were ny.
	Queene	Lester, he is.
	Leicester	Madam, by God you ly.
1940	**Chester**	Unmannerd man.

Leicester
A plague of reverence,
Where no regard is had of excellence.   [*Sound drum.*
But you will quit mee nowe; I heare your drummes,
Your principalitie hath stird up men.
1945 And now ye thinke to muzzle up this Beare.
Still they come nearer, but are not the neare.

Pr. John What drums are these?

Salsbury I thinke some friends of yours
Prepare a power to resist this wrong.

1950 **Leicester** Let them prepare; for Lester is preparde,
And thus he wooes his willing men to fight;
Souldiers, yee see King Richards open wrong,
Richard that led yee to the glorious East,
And made yee treade upon the blessed land,
1955 Where He, that brought all Christians blessednesse,
Was borne, lived, wrought His miracles, and died,
From death arose, and then to heaven ascended;
Whose true religious faith ye have defended.
Yee fought, and Richard taught yee how to fight
1960 Against prophane men following Mahomet.
But if ye note, they did their kings their right,
These more than heathen, sacrilegious men,
Professing Christ, banish Christs champion hence,
Their lawfull Lord, their homeborne soveraigne,
1965 With pettie quarrels, and with slight pretence.

[*Enter Richmond, souldiers.*

O let me be as short as time is short,
For the arm'd foe is now within our sight.
Remember how gainst ten, one man did fight,

359

1970		So hundreds against thousands, have borne head.	*given battle*
		You are the men that ever conquered.	
		If multitudes oppresse ye that ye die,	
		Lets sell our lives and leave them valiantly.	
		Courage; upon them, till wee cannot stand.	

1975   **Pr. John**   Richmond is yonder.

         Queene   I, and sonne, I thinke,
                      The King is not farre off.

         Chester   Now heaven forfend.

         Leicester   Why smite ye not, but stand thus cowardly?

1980   **Richmond**   If Richmond hurt good Lester, let him die.

         Leicester   Richmond, O pardon mine offending eye,
                      That tooke thee for a foe; welcome deare friend;
                      Where is my Soveraigne Richard? Thou and he
                      Were both in Austria. Richmond, comfort mee,

1985   And tell mee where he is, and how he fares.
                      O, for his ransome, many thousand cares
                      Have mee afflicted.

         Richmond   Lester, he is come to London,
                      And will himselfe to faithlesse Austria,

1990   Like a true king, his promis'd ransome beare.

         Leicester   At London saist thou, Richmond, is he there?
                      Farewell, I will not stay to tell my wrongs,
                      To these pale coloured, hartlesse, guiltie Lords.
                      Richmond, you shall goe with mee, doe not stay,

1995   And I will tell you wonders by the way.

         Richmond   The King did doubt you had some injury,   *suspect*
                      And therefore sent this power to rescue yee.

         Leicester   I thanke his Grace. Madam adieu, adieu.
                      Ile to your sonne, and leave your shade with you.   *shadow*

2000   [*Exeunt.*

         Pr. John   Harke how he mocks mee, calling me your shade.
                      Chester and Salsbury, shall wee gather power,
                      And keepe what we have got?

         Chester   And in an hower,

2005   Be taken, judg'd, and headed with disgrace?

Salsbury, what say you?

Salsbury	My Lord, I bid your excellence adieu —
	I to King Richard will submit my knee,
	I have good hope his Grace will pardon mee.

2010 **Chester** And Salsbury, Ile goe along with thee.
Farewell, Queene mother; fare you well, Lord John.　　　*[Exeunt.*

Pr. John Mother, stay you.

Queene Not I sonne, by Saint Anne.

Pr. John Will you not stay?

2015 **Queene** Goe with me. I will doe the best I may,
To beg my sonnes forgivenesse of my sonne.　　　*[Exit.*

Pr. John Goe by yourselfe. By heaven twas long of you,　　*on account of*
I rose to fall so soone. Lester and Richmonds crue,　　*soldiers*
They come to take me. Now too late I rue
2020 My proud attempt. Like falling Phaeton,
I perish from my guiding of the sunne.　　*[Enter Lester and Richmond.*

Leicester I will goe backe yfaith once more and see,
Whether this mock-king and the mother Queene,
And, who! Heres neither Queene nor Lord.
2025 What, king of crickets, is there none but you?
Come off, off. This crowne, this scepter are King Richards right.
Beare thou them, Richmond, thou art his true knight.
You would not send his ransome, gentle John.
He's come to fetch it now. Come, wily Fox,
2030 Now you are stript out of the Lyons case,
What, dare you looke the Lyon in the face?
The English Lyon, that in Austria,
With his strong hand, puld out a lyons heart.
Good Richmond tell it mee; for Gods sake doe:
2035 Oh, it does mee good to heare his glories tolde.

Richmond Lester, I saw King Richard with his fist,
Strike deade the sonne of Austrian Leopold,
And then I sawe him, by the Dukes commaund,
Compast and taken by a troope of men,
2040 Who led King Richard to a lyons denne,
Opening the doore and in a paved court,
The cowards left King Richard weaponlesse.

Anone comes forthe the fier-eyde dreadfull beast,
And with a heart-amazing voice he roarde,
2045 Opening (like hell) his iron-toothed jawes,
And stretching out his fierce death-threatning pawes,
I tell thee Lester, and I smile thereat,
(Though then, God knowes, I had no power to smile)
I stoode by treacherous Austria all the while.
2050 Who in a gallery with iron grates,
Staid to beholde King Richard made a prey.

Leicester   What wast, thou smilest at in Austria?

Richmond   Lester, he shooke, so helpe me God, he shooke,
With very terrour, at the Lyons looke.

2055 Leicester   Ah coward; but goe on what Richard did.

Richmond   Richard about his right hand wound a scarfe
(God quit her for it) given him by a maide,   reward
With endlesse good may that good deede be paid,
And thrust that arme downe the devowring throat
2060 Of the fierce Lyon, and withdrawing it,
Drewe out the strong heart of the monstrous beast,
And left the senselesse bodie on the ground.

Leicester   O royall Richard! Richmond, looke on John.
Does he not quake in hearing this discourse?
2065 Come, we will leave him; Richmond, let us goe.
John, make sute for grace, that is your means you knowe.

[*Exeunt.*

Pr. John   A mischiefe on that Lester. Is he gone?
I were best goe too, lest in some mad fit
2070 He turne againe and leade me prisoner.
Southward I dare not flie; faine, faine I would
To Scotland bend my course; but all the woddes
Are full of outlawes that in Kendall greene
Followe the outlawed Earle of Huntington.
2075 Well, I will cloath myselfe in such a sute,
And by that meanes as well scape all pursuite,
As passe the daunger-threatning Huntington.
For having many outlawes theyl thinke mee,
By my attire, one of their mates to be.   [*Exit.*

[*Scene xiii*]

2080		[*Enter Scarlet, John, and Frier Tucke.*

Frier	Scarlet and John, so God me save,	
	No minde unto my beades I have.	
	I thinke it be a lucklesse day,	
	For I can neither sing, nor say,	
2085	Nor have I any power to looke,	
	On Portasse, or on Mattins booke.	*Breviary*

Scarlet	What is the reason, tell us Frier?	

Frier	And would yee have mee be no lyer.	

Lit. John	No: God defend that you should lie,	
2090	A Churchman be a lyer? Fie.	

Frier	Then by this hallowed Crucifixe,	
	The holy water, and the pixe,	*container for consecrated Host*
	It greatly at my stomacke stickes,	
	That all this day we had no guesse,	*guest*
2095	And have of meate so many a messe.	*food; serving*

[*Much brings out Ely, like a country man with a basket.*

Much	Well, and ye be but a market, ye are but a market man.	*if you*

2100	*Ely*	I am sure, sir; I doe you no hurt, doe I?

Scarlet	Wee shall have company, no doubt.	
	My fellowe Much hath founde one out.	

Frier	A fox, a fox! As I am Frier,	*deceiver*
	Much is well worthie of good hire.	

2105	*Lit. John*	Say, Frier, soothly knowest thou him?

Frier	It is a wolfe in a sheepes skinne.	
	Goe call our master, Little John,	
	A glad man will he be anone.	
	It's Ely man, the Chancelor.	

2110	*Lit. John*	Gods pittie looke unto him, Frier.	[*Exit John.*

Much	What, ha ye egges to sell, old fellowe?

Ely	I, sir, some fewe, and those my neede constraines	
	mee beare to Mansfield,	
	That I may sell them there, to buy me bread.	
2115	*Scarlet*	Alas good man: I pre the, where dost dwell?
	Ely	I dwell at Oxen sir.
	Scarlet	I knowe the towne.
	Much	Alas poore fellow, if thou dwell with Oxen,
		It's strange they doe not gore thee with their hornes.
2120	*Ely*	Masters, I tell yee truly where I dwell,
		And whether I am going; let mee goe:
		Your master would be much displeas'd I knowe,
		If he should heare, you hinder poore men thus.
	Frier	Father, one word with you before we part.
2125	*Much*	Scarlet, the Frier will make us have anger all.
		Farewell, and beare me witnesse, though I staid him,
		I staid him not.
		An olde fellowe, and a market man? [*Exit.*
	Frier	Whoop! In your riddles, Much? Then we shall ha't.

2130	*Scarlet*	What dost thou Frier? Pre thee, let him goe.	*Pray*

	Frier	I pre the, Scarlet, let us two alone.
	Ely	Frier, I see thou knowest me; let me goe,
		And many a good turne I to thee will owe.
	Frier	My masters service bids me answere no;
2135		Yet love of holy churchmen wils it so.
		Well, good my Lord, I will doe what I may
		To let your holinesse escape away.

[*Enter Robin and Little John.*

		Here comes my master, if he question you,
2140		Answere him like a plaine man, and you may passe.
	Ely	Thankes, Frier.
	Frier	[*Aside*] O, my Lord thinkes me an Asse.
	Robin	Frier, what honest man is there with thee?
	Frier	A silly man, good master. I will speake for you.
2145		[*Aside*] Stand you aloofe, for feare they note your face.

Master in plaine, it were but in vaine, long to detaine,
with toyes and with bables, with fond fained fables: but
him that you see, in so mean degree, is the Lord Ely, that
helpt to exile you, that oft did revile you. Though in his

2150   fall, his traine be but small, and no man at all, will give   *yield*
him the wall, nor Lord doth him call. Yet he did ride,   *right-of-way*
on Jennets pide, and knightes by his side, did foote it *pied Spanish horses*
each tide: O see the fall of pride.   *festival*

Robin   Frier, enough.

2155   **Frier**   I pray, sir, let him goe.
He is a very simple man in showe;
He dwelles at Oxen and to us doth say
To Mansfield market he doth take his way.

Lit. John   Frier, this is not Mansfields market day.

2160   **Robin**   What would hee sell?

Frier   Egges sir, as he saies.

Robin   Scarlet, goe thy waies, take in this olde man,
Fill his skinne with venson:
And after give him money for his egges.

2165   **Ely**   No, sir, I thanke you. I have promised them
To master Bailies wife of Mansfield, all.

Robin   Nay, sir, you doe me wrong.
No Baily, nor his wife, shall have an egge.
Scarlet, I say, take his egges and give him money.

2170   **Ely**   Pray, sir.

Frier   Tush, let him have your egges.

Ely   Faith, I have none.

Frier   Gods pittie, then he will finde you soone.

Scarlet   Here are no egges, nor any thing but hay.
2175   Yes, by the masse, here's somewhat like a seale.

Robin   O God, my Princes seale, faire Englands royall seale!
Tell mee, thou man of death, thou wicked man,
How cam'st thou by this seale? Wilt thou not speake?
Bring burning irons, I will make him speake.
2180   For I doe knowe the poore distressed Lord,

		The Kings Vicegerent, learned reverend Ely,	
		Flying the furie of ambitious John,	
		Is murdred by this peasant. Speake vile man,	
		Where thou hast done thrice honorable Ely?	*slain*
2185	*Ely*	Why dost thou grace Ely with stiles of Grace,	*rhetoric*
		Who thee with all his power sought to disgrace?	
	Robin	Belike his wisdome sawe some fault in mee.	
	Ely	No I assure thee honorable Earle:	
		It was his envie, no defect of thine,	
2190		And the perswasions of the Prior of Yorke,	
		Which Ely now repents; see, Huntington,	
		Ely himselfe, and pittie him, good sonne.	
	Robin	Alas for woe, alack that so greate state	
		The malice of this world should ruinate.	
2195		Come in, great Lord, sit downe and take thy ease,	
		Receive the seale and pardon my offence.	
		With me you shall be safe and if you please,	
		Till Richard come, from all mens violence.	
		Aged Fitzwater, banished by John,	
2200		And his faire daughter shall con verse with you;	*keep company*
		I and my men that me attend upon	
		Shall give you all that is to honour due.	
		Will you accept my service, noble Lord?	
	Ely	Thy kindnesse drives me to such inward shame,	
2205		That for my life I no reply can frame.	
		Goe, I will followe, blessed maist thou bee,	
		That thus releev'st thy foes in miserie.	*[Exeunt.*
	Lit. John	Skelton, a worde or two beside the play.	
	Frier	Now, Sir John Eltam, what ist you would say?	
2210	*Lit. John*	Me thinks I see no jeasts of Robin Hoode,	
		No merry morices of Frier Tuck,	*morris dances*
		No pleasant skippings up and downe the wodde,	
		No hunting songs, no coursing of the bucke.	*chasing*
		Pray God this Play of ours may have good lucke,	
2215		And the Kings Majestie mislike it not.	*If*
	Frier	And if he doe, what can we doe to that?	
		I promist him a Play of Robin Hoode,	

His honorable life, in merry Sherewod;
His Majestie himselfe survaid the plat,   *play*
2220 And bad me boldly write it, it was good,
For merry jeasts, they have bene showne before,
As how the Frier fell into the Well,
For love of Jinny that faire bonny bell:
How Greeneleafe robd the Shrieve of Notingham,
2225 And other mirthfull matter, full of game.
Our play expresses noble Roberts wrong,
His milde forgetting trecherous injurie;
The Abbots malice, rak't in cinders long,
Breakes out at last with Robins Tragedie.
2230 If these that heare the historie rehearst,
Condemne my Play when it begins to spring,
Ile let it wither while it is a budde,
And never shewe the flower to the King.

Lit. John One thing beside; you fall into your vaine,
2235 Of ribble rabble rimes, Skeltonicall,
So oft, and stand so long, that you offend.

Frier It is a fault I hardly can amend.   *scarcely*
O how I champe my tongue to talke these tearmes,
I doe forget oft times my Friers part;
2240 But pull mee by the sleeve when I exceede,
And you shall see mee mend that fault indeede.
Wherefore still sit you, doth Skelton intreat you,
While he facetè wil breefely repeate you, the history al,
And tale tragical, by whose treachery, and base injury,
2245 Robin the good, calde Robin Hood, died in Sherewodde:
Which till, you see, be rul'd by me, sit patiently, and give
a plaudite, if any thing please yee.   [*Exeunt.*   *applause*

[*Scene xiv*]

[*Enter Warman.*

Warman Banisht from all, of all I am bereft,
2250 No more than what I weare unto me left,
O wretched, wretched griefe, desertfull fall.
Striving to get all, I am reft of all;

367

Yet if I could a while myselfe relieve,
Till Ely be in some place settled,
2255 A double restitution should I get,
And these sharpe sorrowes that have joy supprest
Should turne to joy with double interest.

[*Enter a gentleman, Warmans cosin.*

And in good time, here comes my cosin Warman,
2260 Whome I have often pleasur'd in my time.
His house at Bingham I bestow'd on him;
And therefore doubt not, he will give me house-roome.
Good even, good cosin.

Cousin   O cousen Warman, what good newes with you?

2265 *Warman*   Whether so farre a foot walk you in Sherewod?

Cousin   I came from Rotheram, and by hither Farnsfield
My horse did tire, and I walkt home a foote.

Warman   I doe beseech you cousen at some friends,
Or at your owne house for a weeke or two,
2270   Give me some succour.

Cousin   Ha? Succour say you?
No, sir: I heard at Mansfield how the matter stands,
How you have justly lost your goods and lands,
And that the Princes indignation
2275   Will fall on any that relieves your state.
Away from mee; your trecheries I hate.
You when your noble master was undoone
(That honourable minded Huntington)
Who forwarder than you, all to distraine?
2280   And as a wolfe that chaseth on the plaine,
The harmelesse hinde, so wolfe-like you pursued   *doe*
Him and his servants: vile ingratitude,
Damnd Judaisme, false wrong, abhorred trechery,
Impious wickednesse, wicked impietie.
2285   Out, out upon thee, foh, I spit at thee.

Warman   Good cosen.

Cousin   Away, Ile spurne thee if thou followe me.   [*Exit.*

Warman   O just heaven, how thou plagu'st iniquitie!

		All that he has, my hand on him bestowed.	
2290		My master gave mee all I ever owed;	
		My master I abus'd in his distresse;	
		In mine, my kinsman leaves me comfortlesse.	

[*Enter Jayler of Notingham, leading a dog.*

		Here comes another, one that yesterday	
2295		Was at my service, came when I did call,	
		And him I made Jayler of Notingham.	
		Perchance some pittie dwelles within the man.	
		Jaylor, well met, dost thou not knowe me, man?	
	Jailer	Yes, thou art Warman; every knave knowes thee.	
2300	**Warman**	Thou knowest I was thy master yesterday.	
	Jailer	I, but tis not as it was, farewell, goe by.	*Indeed*
	Warman	Good George, relieve my bitter misery.	
	Jailer	By this fleshe and bloode I will not.	
		No if I do, the divell take me quicke.	*alive*
2305		I have no money; begger balk the way.	*pass by*
	Warman	I doe not aske thee money.	
	Jailer	Wouldst ha meate?	*have food*
	Warman	Would God I had a little breade to eate.	
	Jailer	Soft, let me feele my bagge. O heare is meate,	
2310		That I put up at Redford for my dogge,	
		I care not greatly if I give him this.	
	Warman	I pre thee doe?	
	Jailer	Yet let me search my conscience for it first.	
		My dogge's my servant, faithfull, trustie, true;	
2315		But Warman was a traitor to his Lord,	
		A reprobate, a rascall, and a Jewe,	
		Worser than dogges, of men to be abhorrd.	
		Starve therefore, Warman; dogge receive thy due;	
		Followe me not, least I belabour you,	
2320		You halfe-fac't groat, you thin-cheekt chittiface,	*pinch-faced*
		You Judas, villane, you that have undoone	
		The honourable, Robert, Earle of Huntington.	[*Exit.*

	Warman	Worse than a dogge, the villane me respects,	*regards*
		His dogge he feedes, mee in my neede rejects.	
2325		What shall I doe? Yonder I see a shed,	
		A little cottage, where a woman dwelles,	
		Whose husband I from death delivered.	
		If she denie mee, then I faint and die.	
		Ho, goodwife Tomson?	

| 2330 | **Woman** | What a noyse is there? |
| | | A foule shame on yee; is it you that knockt? |

| | **Warman** | What, doe you knowe mee then? |

	Woman	Whoop, who knowes not you?
		The beggerd banisht Shrieve of Notingham,
2335		You that betraid your master, ist not you?
		Yes, a shame on you; and forsooth ye come,
		To have some succour here, because you sav'd,
		My unthrift husband from the gallowe tree.
		A pox upon yee both. Would both for me
2340		Were hangd together; but soft, let mee see.
		The man lookes faint. Feelst thou indeede distresse?

| | **Warman** | O doe not mocke me in my heavinesse. |

| | **Woman** | Indeede I doe not; well I have within, | |
| | | A caudle made, I will goe fetch it him. | *(see note)* |

| 2345 | **Warman** | O blessed woman, comfortable word. |
| | | Be quiet intrals, you shall be releev'd. |

	Woman	Here, Warman, put this hempen caudle ore thy head.
		See downeward, yonder is thy masters walke,
		And like a Judas, on some rotten tree,
2350		Hang up this rotten trunke of miserie
		That goers by thy wretched end may see.
		Stirr'st thou not villane? Get thee from my doore.
		A plague upon thee, haste and hang thy selfe,
		Runne rogue away. Tis thou that hast undone
2355		Thy noble master, Earle of Huntington. [*Exit.*

	Warman	Good counsell, and good comfort by my faith.
		Three doctors are of one opinion,
		That Warman must make speede to hang himselfe.
		The last hath given a caudle comfortable,

2360		That to recure my griefes is strong and able.	*heal*
		Ile take her medcine, and Ile chuse this way,	
		Wherein she saith my master hath his walke.	
		There will I offer life for trechery,	
		And hang, a wonder to all goers by.	
2365		But soft what sound hermonious is this?	
		What birds are these, that sing so cheerefully,	
		As if they did salute the flowring spring?	
		Fitter it were, with tunes more dolefully	
		They shriekt out sorrowe than thus cheerely sing.	
2370		I will goe seeke sad desperations cell.	
		This is not it, for here are greene-leav'd trees.	
		Ah for one winter-bitten bared bough,	
		Whereon, a wretched life, a wretch would leese.	*release*
		O, here is one. Thrice blessed be this tree,	
2375		If a man cursed, may a blessing give.	

> [*Enter old Fitzwater.*

> But out alas, yonder comes one to me
> To hinder death, when I detest to live.

| | **Fitzwater** | What woefull voice heare I within this wod? | |
| 2380 | | What wretch is there complaines of wretchednesse? | |

| | **Warman** | A man, old man, bereav'd of all earths good, | |
| | | And desperately seekes death in this distresse. | |

	Fitzwater	Seeke not for that which will be here too soone,	
		At least if thou be guiltie of ill deedes.	
2385		Where art thou, sonne? Come and neerer sit;	
		Heare wholsome counsell gainst unhallowed thoughts.	

	Warman	The man is blinde. Muffle the eye of day	
		Ye gloomie clouds (and darker than my deedes,	
		That darker be than pitchie sable night),	
2390		Muster together on these high topt trees,	
		That not a sparke of light thorough their sprayes,	
		May hinder what I meane to execute.	

| | **Fitzwater** | What dost thou mutter? Heare mee wofull man. | |

> [*Enter Marian, with meate.*   *food*

| | **Marian** | God morrowe father. | |

	Fitzwater	Welcome, lovely maide,	
		And in good time, I trust you hither come.	
		Looke if you see not a distressefull man,	
		That to himselfe intendeth violence.	
2400		One such even now was here and is not farre;	
		Seeke, I beseech you, save him if you may.	

	Marian	Alas, here is, here is a man enrag'd,	
		Fastning a halter on a withered bough,	
		And stares upon mee, with such frighted lookes,	
2405		As I am fearefull of his sharpe aspect.	

	Fitzwater	What meanst thou, wretch? Say, what ist thou wilt doe?	

	Warman	As Judas did, so I intend to doe.	
		For I have done alreadie as he did:	
		His master he betraid: so I have mine.	
2410		Faire mistresse looke not on me with your blessed eyne.	*eyes*
		From them as from some excellence divine,	
		Sparkles sharpe judgement, and commaunds with speede.	
		Faire, fare you well. Foule fortune is my fate.	
		As all betraiers, I die desperate.	

2415	*Fitzwater*	Soft sir, goe Marian call in Robin Hoode.	
		Tis Warman, woman, that was once his steward.	

	Marian	Alas, although it be, yet save his life.	
		I will sende helpe unto you presently. *[Exit.*	

	Fitzwater	Nay, Warman, stay; thou shalt not have thy will.	

2420	*Warman*	Art thou a blinde man, and canst see my shame?	
		To hinder treachers, God restoreth sight,	*traitors*
		And giveth infants tongues to cry alowde,	
		A wofull woe against the trecherous.	

[Enter Much running.

2425	*Much*	Hold, hold, hold. I heare say, my fellowe Warman	
		is about to hang himselfe, and make I some speede	
		to save him a labour. O good master, Justice Shrive,	
		have you execution in hand, and is there such a murren	*plague*
		among theeves and hangmen, that you play two parts	
2430		in one? For old inquaintance, I wil play one part. The knot	
		under the eare, the knitting to the tree: Good master	
		Warman, leave that worke for mee.	

Warman	Dispatch me, Much, and I will pray for thee.	
Much	Nay, keepe your praiers; no bodie sees us.	

2435   [*He takes the rope, and offers to clime.*

| *Fitzwater* | Downe sirra, downe; whether a knaves name
clime you? | |

| *Much* | A plague on ye for a blinde sinksanker. Would I | *soothsayer* |
| | were your match. You are much blinde yfaith, can hit | |
2440   so right.

           [*Enter Little John.*

| *Lit. John* | What, master Warman, are yee come to yield
A true account for your false stewardshippe? | |

           [*Enter Scarlet and Scathlocke.*

2445   *Scathlock*   Much, if thou meanst to get a hundred pound,
                 Present us to the Shrieve of Notingham.

Much	Masse, I thinke there was such a purclamation.	*proclamation*
	Come, my small fellowe John,	
	You shall have halfe, and therefore bring in one.	

2450   *Lit. John*   No, my big fellow, honest master Much,
                 Take all unto yourselfe; Ile be no halfe.

Much	Then stand, you shall be the two theeves, and	
	I will be the presenter.	
	O master Shrieve of Notingham,	
2455   When eares unto my tidings came

(Ile speake in prose, I misse this verse vilely) that   *mismeter*
Scathlock and Scarlet were arrested by Robin Hood, my
master, and Little John, my fellowe, and I, Much his servant, and taken from you, master Shrieve, being well
2460   forward in the hanging way, wherein yee now are (and
God keepe yee in the same) and also that you, master Shrieve,
would give any man in towne, citie, or contrey, a hundred pound of lawfull arrant money of Englande, that   *current*
would bring the same two theeves, being these two. Now
2465   I, the said Much, chalenge of you, the saide Shrieve,
bringing them, the same money.

| *Scarlet* | Faith, he can not pay thee, Much. | |

	Much	I, but while this end is in my hand, and that about
		his necke, he is bound to it.
2470		[*Enter Robin, Ely, Marian.*
	Warman	Mock on, mock on; make me your jeasting game.
		I doe deserve much more than this small shame.
	Robin	Disconsolate and poore dejected man,
		Cast from thy necke that shamefull signe of death,
2475		And live for mee, if thou amende thy life,
		As much in favour as thou ever didst.
	Warman	O worse than any death,
		When a man, wrongd, his wronger pittieth.
	Ely	Warman, be comforted, rise and amend.
2480		On my word, Robin Hoode will be thy friend.
	Robin	I will indeede. Go in, heart-broken man,
		Father Fitzwater, pray you leade him in.
		Kinde Marian, with sweete comforts comfort him,
		And my tall yeomen, as you mee affect,
2485		Upbraide him not with his forepassed life.
		Warman, goe in, goe in and comfort thee.
	Warman	O God requite your honours curtesie.
	Marian	Scathlocke or Scarlet, helpe us some of yee.
2490		[*Exeunt Warman, Marian, Fitzwater, Scathlock, Scarlet, Much*
		Enter Frier Tucke in his trusse, without his weede.] *jacket; robe*
	Frier	Jesu benedicité, pittie on pittie, mercie on mercy,
		misery on misery. O such a sight, as by this light, doth
		mee affright.
	Robin	Tell us the matter, pre thee, holy Frier.
2495	**Frier**	Sir Doncaster the Priest, and the proud Prior
		Are stript and wounded in the way to Bawtrey,
		And if there goe not spedie remedie,
		Theyl die, theyl die in this extreamitie.
	Robin	Alas, direct us to that wretched place.
2500		I love mine uncle, though he hateth mee.
	Frier	My weede I cast to keepe them from the colde,
		And Jinny, gentle girle, tore all her smocke,

		The blodie issue of their wounds to stoppe.	
	Robin	Will you goe with us, my good Lord of Ely?	
2505	**Ely**	I will, and ever praise thy perfect charitie.	*[Exeunt.*

[*Scene xv*]

[*Enter Prince John, solus, in greene, bowe and arrowes.*   *alone*

	Pr. John	Why this is somewhat like, now may I sing,	
		As did the Wakefield Pinder in his note;	
		At Michaelmas commeth my covenant out,	
2510		My master gives me my fee.	
		Then, Robin, Ile weare thy Kendall greene,	
		And wend to the greenewodde with thee.	
		But for a name now, John, it must not bee,	
		Alreadie Little John on him attends.	
2515		Greeneleafe? Nay surely there's such a one alreadie.	
		Well, Ile be Wodnet, hap what happen may.	

     [*Enter Scathlocke.*

		Here comes a greene cote (good lucke be my guide).	
		Some sodaine shift might helpe me to provide.	*scheme*
2520	**Scathlock**	What, fellow William, did you meete our master?	
	Pr. John	I did not meete him yet my honest friend.	
	Scathlock	My honest friend? Why, what a terme is here?	
		My name is Scathlocke, man, and if thou be	
		No other than thy garments shewe to mee,	
2525		Thou art my fellowe, though I knowe thee not.	
		What is thy name? When wert thou entertaind?	
	Pr. John	My name is Woodnet, and this very day,	
		My noble master, Earle of Huntington,	
		Did give mee both my fee and liverie.	
2530	**Scathlock**	Your noble master, Earle of Huntington?	
		Ile lay a crowne you are a counterfait,	
		And that you knowe, lacks money of a noble.	
		Did you receive your livery and fee,	
		And never heared our orders read unto you?	
2535		What was the oath was given you by the Frier?	

375

	Pr. John	Who? Frier Tuck?	[*Enter Frier Tucke.*
	Scathlock	I doe not play the lyer;	
		For he comes here himselfe to shrive.	*hear confession*
	Pr. John	Scathlock, farewell, I will away.	
2540	Scathlock	See you this arrowe? It saies nay.	
		Through both your sides shall fly this feather,	
		If presently you come not hither.	
	Frier	Now heavens true liberalitie	
		Fall ever for his charitie	
2545		Upon the heade of Robin Hoode,	
		That to his very foes doth good.	
		Lord God, how he laments the Prior	
		And bathes his wounds against the fier!	
		Faire Marian, God requite it her,	
2550		Doth even as much for Doncaster,	
		Whome newly she hath laine in bed,	
		To rest his weary wounded head.	
	Scathlock	Ho, Frier Tuck, knowe you this mate?	
	Frier	Whats hee?	
2555	Scathlock	He saith my master late	
		Gave him his fee and livery.	
	Frier	It is a leasing, credit mee.	*falsehood*
		How chance, sir, then you were not sworne?	
	Pr. John	What meane this groome and lozell Frier,	*peasant, scoundrel*
2560		So strictly matters to inquire?	
		Had I a sword and buckler here,	
		You should aby these questions deare.	*pay penalty for*
	Frier	Saist thou me so lad? Lend him thine.	
		For in this bush here lyeth mine.	
2565		Now will I try this newcome guest.	
	Scathlock	I am his first man, Frier Tuck,	
		And if I faile and have no lucke,	
		Then thou with him shalt have a plucke.	
	Frier	Be it so Scathlock. Holde thee lad,	
2570		No better weapons can be had.	

376

The dewe doth them a little rust.
But heare yee, they are tooles of trust.

Pr. John Gramercy Frier for this gift,
And if thou come unto my shrift,
2575 Ile make thee call those fellowes fooles
That on their foes bestowe such tooles.

Scathlock Come let us too't.

[*Fight, and the Frier lookes on.*

Frier The youth is deliver and light,   *agile*
2580 He presseth Scathlocke with his might:
Now by my beades to doe him right,
—Ɖ I thinke he be some tryed knight.   *proven*

Scathlock Stay, let us breath.

Pr. John I will not stay.
2585 If you leave, Frier, come away.

Scathlock I pre the, Frier, holde him play.

Frier Frier Tuck will doe the best he may.

[*Fight. Enter Marian.*

Marian Why, what a noyse of swordes is here?
2590 Fellowes, and fight our bower so neere?

Scathlock Mistresse, he is no man of yours,
That fightes so fast with Frier Tucke;
But on my worde he is a man,
As good for strength as any can.

2595 **Marian** Indeede hee's more than common men can be,
In his high heart there dwels the bloode of kings.
Goe call my Robin, Scathlock: tis Prince John.

Scathlock Mistresse I will; I pray part the fray.   [*Exit.*

Marian I pre thee goe; I will doe what I may.
2600 Frier, I charge thee holde thy hand.

Frier Nay, yonker, to your tackling stand.   *youngster, hold your ground*
What all amort, wil you not fight?   *spiritless*

Pr. John I yield, unconquered by thy might,
But by Matildas glorious sight.

377

2605	*Frier*	Mistresse, he knowes you. What is hee?
	Pr. John	Like to amazing wonder she appeares,
		And from her eye, flies love unto my heart,
		Attended by suspicious thoughts and feares,
		That numme the vigor of each outward part.
2610		Only my sight hath all sacietie,
		And fulnesse of delight, viewing her deitie.

satisfaction

	Marian	But I have no delight in you, Prince John.
	Frier	Is this Prince John?
		Give me thy hand, thou art a proper man,
2615		And for this mornings worke, by Saints above,
		Be ever sure of Frier Tucks true love.
	Pr. John	Be not offended that I touch thy shrine;
		Make this hand happie, let it folde in thine.

[*Enter Robin Hoode, Fitzwater, Ely, Warman.*

2620	*Robin*	What sawcie wodman Marian stands so neere?
	Pr. John	A wodman, Robin, that would strike your deere,
		With all his heart. Nay never looke so strange,
		You see this fickle world is full of change.
		John is a ranger, man, compeld to range.

forester/wanderer

2625	*Fitzwater*	You are young, wilde Lord, and wel may travel bear.
	Pr. John	What, my olde friende Fitzwater, are you there?
		And you, Lord Ely? And old best betrust?
		Then I perceive that to this geere we must.
		A messe of my good friends, which of you foure
2630		Will purchase thanks by yielding to the King
		The bodie of the rash rebellious John?
		Will you, Fitzwater?

most reliable
business
group

	Fitzwater	No, John, I defie
		To stain my old hands in thy youthfull bloode.
2635	*Pr. John*	You will, Lord Ely, I am sure you will.
	Ely	Be sure, young man, my age means thee no ill.
	Pr. John	O you will have the praise, brave Robin Hood,
		The lustie outlawe, Lord of this large wodde.

2640 Hee'l lead a kings sonne, prisoner to a king,
And bid the brother smite the brother deade.

Robin   My purpose you have much misconstrued.
Prince John, I would not for the wide worlds wealth
Incense his Majestie, but doe my best,
To mitigate his wrath, if he be mov'd.

2645   **Pr. John**   Will none of you? Then here's one I dare say,
That from his childehoode knowes how to betray.
Warman, will not you helpe to hinder all you may.

Warman   With what I have beene, twit me not, my Lord.   *taunt*
My olde sins at my soule I doe detest.

2650   **Pr. John**   Then that he came this way, Prince John was blest.
Forgive me, Ely; pardon mee, Fitzwater.
And Robin, to thy hands myselfe I yield.

Robin   And as my heart, from hurt I will thee shield.

             [*Enter Much, running.*

2655   **Much**   Master, fly, hide ye mistresse, we al shall be taken.

Robin   Why, whats the matter?

Much   The King, the King, and twelve and twenty score of horses.

Robin   Peace, foole. We have no cause from him to fly.

             [*Enter Scarlet, Little John.*

2660   **Lit. John**   Scarlet and I were hunting on the plaine.
To us came royall Richard from his traine
(For a great traine of his is hard at hand)
And questiond us, if we serv'd Robin Hoode.
I saide wee did, and then his Majestie,
2665   Putting this massie chaine about my necke,
Said what I shame to say, but joyde to heare.
Let Scarlet tell it, it befits not mee.

Scarlet   Quoth our good King, "Thy name is Little John,
And thou hast long time serv'd Earle Huntington:
2670   Because thou leftst him not in miserie,
A hundred markes I give thee yearelie fee,
And from henceforth, thou shalt a squier bee."

Much	O Lord, what luck had I to runne away?	
	I should have bene made a knight, or a lady sure.	
2675 **Scarlet**	Goe, said the King, and to your master say,	
	Richard is come to call him to the court.	
	And with his kingly presence chase the clouds	
	Of griefe and sorrow, that in mistie shades,	
	Have vaild the honour of Earle Huntington.	
2680 **Robin**	Now God preserve him, hye you backe againe,	*hasten*
	And guide him, least in by-paths he mistake.	*lest*
	Much, fetch a richer garment for my father.	[*Exit Much.*
	Good Frier Tuck, I pre thee rouse thy wits.	
	Warman, visit myne uncle and Sir Doncaster,	
2685	See if they can come forth to grace our showe.	[*Exit Warman.*
	Gods pittie, Marian, let your Jinny waite.	*attend*
	Thankes, my Lord Chancellor. You are well prepar'd,	
	And good Prince John, since you are all in greene,	
	Disdaine not to attend on Robin Hoode.	
2690	Frolick I pray; I trust to doe yee good.	*Be happy*
	Welcome, good uncle, welcome Sir Doncaster. [*Enter Prior and Doncast.*	
	Say, will yee sit, I feare yee cannot stand.	
Prior	Yes, very well.	
Robin	Why, cheerely, cheerely then.	
2695	The trumpet, sounds, the King is now at hand.	
	Lords, yeomen, maids, in decent order stand.	
2700	[*The trumpets sound, the while Robin places them. Enter first, bare-heade, Little John and Scarlet; likewise Chester, and Lester, bearing the sword and scepter; the King follows crowned, clad in green; after him Queene Mother, after her Salsbury and Richmond, Scarlet and Scathlocke turne to Robin Hoode; who with all his company kneele downe and cry:*	
All	God save King Richard, Lord preserve your Grace.	
2705 **King**	Thanks all, but chiefely, Huntington, to thee.	
	Arise poore Earle, stand up, my late lost sonne,	
	And on thy shoulders let me rest my armes,	
	That have bene toyled long with heathen warres:	*wearied*
	True piller of my state, right Lord indeede,	
2710	Whose honour shineth in the denne of neede,	

I am even full of joy, and full of woe;
To see thee, glad; but sad to see thee so.

Robin O that I could powre out my soule in prayers,
And praises for this kingly curtesie.

2715 Doe not, dread Lord, grieve at my lowe estate.
Never so rich, never so fortunate,
Was Huntington as now himselfe he findes.
And to approve it, may it please your Grace,
But to accept such presents at the hand

2720 Of your poore servant, as he hath prepar'd.
You shall perceive, the Emperour of the East,
Whom you contended with at Babilon,
Had not such presents to present you with.

King Art thou so rich? Sweet, let me see thy gifts.

2725 **Robin** First take againe this jewell you had lost,
Aged Fitzwater, banished by John.

King A jemme indeede; no Prince hath such a one.
Good, good old man, as welcome unto mee,
As coole fresh ayre, in heats extreamitie.

2730 **Fitzwater** And I as glad to kisse my soveraignes hand,
As the wrackt swimmer, when he feeles the land. *shipwrecked*

Queene Welcome, Fitzwater, I am glad to see you.

Fitzwater I thanke your Grace; but let me hug these twain,
Lester and Richmond, Christes sworne champions,

2735 That follow'd Richard in his holy warre.

Richmond Noble Fitzwater, thanks, and welcome both.

Leicester O God, how glad I am to see this Lord!
I cannot speake; but welcome at a worde.

Robin Next take good Ely in your royall hands,

2740 Who fled from death, and most uncivill bands. *constraints*

King Robin, thy gifts exceede: Moorton my Chancellour!
In this man giv'st thou holinesse and honour.

Ely Indeede he gives me, and he gave me life,
Preserving me from fierce pursuing foes,

2745 When I too blame had wrought him many woes:

		With me he likewise did preserve this seale,	
		Which I surrender to your majestie.	
	King	Keepe it, good Ely, keepe it still for me.	
	Robin	The next faire jewell that I will presente	
2750		Is richer than both these, yet in the foyle,	*jewel setting*
		My gratious Lord, it hath a foule default,	
		Which if you pardon, boldly I protest,	
		It will in value farre exceede the rest.	
	Pr. John	[*Aside*] Thats me he meanes, yfaith my turne is next.	
2755		He calles me foile, ifaith, I feare a foile.	*overthrow*
		Well, tis a mad lord, this same Huntington.	
	Robin	Here is Prince John, your brother, whose revolt	
		And folly in your absence, let me crave,	
		With his submission may be buried.	
2760		For he is now no more the man he was,	
		But duetifull in all respects to you.	
	King	Pray God it proove so. Wel, good Huntington,	
		For thy sake pardon'd is our brother John,	
		And welcome to us in all heartie love.	
2765	**Robin**	This last I give, as tenants do their lands,	
		With a surrender, to receive againe,	
		The same into their owne possession:	
		No Marian, but Fitzwaters chast Matilda,	
		The precious jewell that poore Huntington	
2770		Doth in this world hold as his best esteeme.	
		Although with one hand I surrender her,	
		I holde the other, as one looking still,	*hoping*
		Richard returnes her: so I hope he will.	
	King	Els God forbid. Receive thy Marian backe,	
2775		And never may your love be separate,	
		But florish fairely to the utmost date.	
	Robin	Now please my King to enter Robins bower,	
		And take such homely welcome as he findes,	
		It shall be reckened as my happinesse.	
2780	**King**	With all my heart. Then as combined friends,	
		Goe we togither; here all quarrelles ends.	[*Exeunt.*

[*Manet Sir John Eltam and Skelton.*

	Eltham	Then Skelton here I see you will conclude.
	Skelton	And reason good: have we not held too long?
2785	**Eltham**	No in good sadnesse, I dare gage my life,
		His Highnesse will accept it very kindly.
		But I assure you, he expects withall,
		To see the other matters tragicall
		That followe in the processe of the storie,
2790		Wherein are many a sad accident,
		Able to make the strictest minde relent:
		I neede not name the points, you knowe them all.
		From Marians eye shall not one teare be shed?
		Skelton, yfaith tis not the fashion.
2795		The King must greeve, the Queene must take it ill;
		Ely must mourne, aged Fitzwater weepe,
		Prince John, the Lords his yeomen must lament,
		And wring their wofull hands, for Robins woe.
		Then must the sicke man fainting by degrees,
2800		Speake hollowe words, and yield his Marian,
		Chast Maid Matilda, to her fathers hands
		And give her, with King Richards full consent,
		His lands, his goods, late seazd on by the Prior,
		Now by the Priors treason made the Kings.
2805		Skelton, there are a many other things,
		That aske long time to tell them lineally.
		But ten times longer will the action be.
	Skelton	Sir John, yfaith I knowe not what to doe;
		And I confesse that all you say is true.
2810		Will you doe one thing for me, crave the King
		To see two parts. Say tis a prettie thing.
		I know you can doe much, if you excuse mee,
		While Skelton lives, Sir John, be bolde to use mee.
	Eltham	I will perswade the King; but how can you
2815		Perswade all these beholders to content?
	Skelton	Stay, Sir John Eltam; what to them I say,
		Deliver to the King, from mee, I pray.
		Well judging hearers, for a while suspence	*suspend*
		Your censures of this Plaies unfinisht end.
2820		And Skelton promises for this offence,

The second part shall presently be pend. *written*
There shall you see, as late my friend did note,
King Richards revels at Earle Roberts bower,
The purpos'd mirth, and the performed mone, *lament*
2825 The death of Robin, and his murderers.
For interest of your stay, this will I adde,
King Richards voyage backe to Austria,
The swift returned tydings of his death,
The manner of his royall funerall.
2830 Then John shall be a lawfull crowned king,
But to Matilda beare unlawfull love.
Aged Fitzwaters finall banishment,
His pitious end, of power teares to move
From marble pillers. The Catastrophe
2835 Shall shewe you faire Matildas Tragedie,
Who, shunning Johns pursute, became a nunne,
At Dunmowe Abbey, where she constantly
Chose death to save her spotlesse chastitie.
Take but my word, and if I faile in this,
2840 Then let my paines be baffled with a hisse. *disgraced*

FINIS.

Notes

This edition is based on John C. Meagher's edited facsimile collation of William Leake's black letter printing of 1601 (Malone Society, 1965). The full title in Leake's edition is *The Downfall of Robert, Earle of Huntington, Afterward Called Robin Hood of merrie Sherwodde: with his love to chaste Matilda, the Lord Fitzwaters daughter, afterwardes his faire Maide Marian*. Ten copies of Leake's printing survive. Meagher based his reprint on xerographs of the Harvard copy which he collated with the other nine copies. Line count in the present edition corresponds to the idiosyncracies of Meagher's edition. Leake printed the text in black letter with roman for speech-prefixes, stage directions, and names occuring within the text; and with italic for names occurring within stage directions. I have ignored such distinctions in this edition, using instead boldface for speech prefixes and italic for stage directions, with a smaller italic font on the right margin for glosses of hard words. In Leake speakers are identified in various ways. For the most part I have chosen uniform designations for characters — Lit. John, for Little John, Pr. John for Prince John — though I have maintained Leake's distinctions between Marian and Matilda which, though they are the same person, usually (though not always) refer to her in different contexts (Marian in the Greenwood, and Matilda at court). I occasionally have followed Leake's practices in capitalization but usually have followed modern usage. Except for the formation of genitives (where I have followed Leake's practices), I have converted all punctuation to modern usage. In some instances I have elided two word phrases to compound words according to modern practices (e.g., *to day* > *today, to morrowe* > *tomorrowe, my selfe* > *myselfe, your selfe* > *yourselfe*). I have noted significant emendations in the notes, and usually compared them with other modern editions.

Abbreviations: L = Leake's 1601 black-letter 4° edition. C = Collier's 1828 edition. H = Hazlitt's 1874 edition. F = Farmer's 1913 facsimile edition. M = Meagher, with date identifying appropriate edition.

[*Scene i*]. L does not specify scene divisions. But modern editions (C, H, F, and M) use them, so I have adopted them as well. They are not included in line count, however, as they are in *The Death*, where they are necessary if line count is to correspond to M's two editions, thus facilitating cross-reference.

385

1–39   The Induction, whereby the play leads the audience from familiar social banter between two men of letters into a theatrical representation of "history," or, at least, entertainment from a former time. By naming Skelton and Eltham as the protagonists, Munday implies that they are rehearsing a performance for Henry VII or Henry VIII ("his Majesty" — line 9; see also note to line 2741). M (1980, p. 465) suggests that the Induction perhaps imitates Shakespeare's *The Taming of the Shrew*, which was published twice with an induction (1594 and 1596), where revellers gather in a tavern before putting on their play. See also Greene's *James IV*, entered in the Stationer's Register in 1594, which likewise begins with an induction. Munday goes a step further by maintaining the illusion of actors rehearsing by placing an interlude between Skelton and Eltham in *The Death of Robert, Earle of Huntington* after Robert's death before moving on into the Tragedy of Matilda, and by having the Friar, played by Skelton, often interrupt the play to respond as "Skelton"; he then is usually reprimanded for his indulgence by Sir John Eltham, who is playing the part of Little John.

5   *Skelton*. John Skelton (c. 1460–1529) wrote court verse for three kings: Edward VI, Henry VII, and Henry VIII. He was designated poet laureate for the last two and served as tutor for Henry VIII in his youth, instructing the king-to-be in the performing arts. Noted for his satiric flair and witty short, rhymed verses (Skeltonics), he also wrote comedies, interludes, and morality plays, including the play *Magnificence*. He is thus a most suitable figure for Munday's theatrical device as he bustles about ordering up the play for his king. By setting the performance in the time of Henry VII or Henry VIII Munday evokes a time of exuberance when the Tudor dynasty was in its youth, a time when May festivals and Robin Hood theater flourished.

11–13   *Ferdinand* is king of Spain; *Sebastian*, king of Portugal. But, as M (1980) observes: "Since the former died in 1516 and the latter was born in 1557, the business of the negotiations is plainly the fanciful invention of the dramatist, designed merely to provide the equally fictitious Sir John Eltam with 'great affairs' " (p. 465).

28   *the boyes and Clowne*. These boys are the actors who will play the women's parts, once the play gets underway; the clown will become Much the Miller's son, from the Robin Hood ballads. As clown, he will speak in prose, despite

the fact that L's compositor occasionally breaks the prose up into irregular lines, as if it were verse. The list of characters and line 29 suggest that Marian is played by "little Tracy."

32   *Sir Thomas Mantle*. Mantle's identity is unknown, except that he seems to be the actor who will play Robin. L reads *mantle*; C capitalizes the word, which makes sense.

37   *dumbe scene*. A silent pantomime often used as prelude to a dramatic action in Elizabethan drama. Usually it anticipates the principal roles and plot of what follows. See, for example, the proleptic dumbshow at the outset of Norton and Sackville's *Gorboduc* (1562); or Lyly's *Endymion* (1588, 1591), where it foreshadows events about to unfold; or the dumbshow prior to the performance of The Mousetrap in *Hamlet* (1599–1601); or Bottom's confused exercise in *Midsummer Night's Dream* (1594–98). In Webster's *Duchess of Malfi* (1612–14) the dumbshow presents both events to come and events just passed. Here, in Munday, the dumbshow (lines 41–56) is repeated along with Skelton's commentary (lines 59–108) in a way similar to Peele's mingling of dumbshow and commentary in *The Battle of Alcazar* (1594). See also the dumbshows in *The Death of Robert, Earle of Huntington*, which establish the political environs of Matilda's tragedy.

73   *Now*. M (1980) silently emends to *No*. But *Now* makes good sense.

94   *Gilbert Hoode*. The name given to Robert's father in another Robin Hood play entitled *Look About You* (1600).

101   *troth-plight*. To engage a woman in a contract of marriage, i.e., engagement (OED). In line 208 Robin calls Marian his *spowse*, but as M (1980, p. 469) observes, the betrothal, which preceded the actual marriage by an indefinite period, made them man and wife.

116   *shot in his bowe*. A well-known proverb: "Many speak (talk) of Robin Hood that never shot his bow." See Morris Palmer Tilley, *A Dictionary of Proverbs in England in the Sixteenth and Seventeenth Centuries* (Ann Arbor: University of Michigan Press, 1950), R 148, who cites Haywood, Campion, Lyly, Puttenham, Harrington, etc.

118   Skeltonic verse is marked by short lines, irregular meter and rhymes, and

alliteration. M (1980), citing Puttenham, notes that Skelton was not often thought of as a serious writer but more as a jokester (pp. 469–70), though in the lines which follow the matter is serious indeed.

135 *catchpoles*. A catchpole is a barbed device on a pole that is attached to the neck of offenders being brought to justice. It was used originally by tax collectors but became a synecdoche of scorn for any apprehending officer or sheriff's man. See also *catchpole bribed groomes* in line 360.

139 *ribble rabble*. See also line 2235: an alliterative doublet of the sort common in popular verse (see *tit tattle* in line 432); perhaps a variant on *bibble babble*. See also *huckle duckle* in the play *Robin Hood and the Friar*, line 115.

141 *[Exit*. Not in L; C's emendation, followed by H and M (1980).

152 *[Exit Warman*. Not in L; C's emendation, followed by H and M (1980).

160 Robin's prodigality is offered as the reason for his being outlawed. The source, according to M (1980, p. 43), is probably Grafton's *Chronicle*: "But in an olde and auncient Pamphlet I finde this written of the Sayd Robert Hood. This man (sayeth he) discended of a noble parentage: or rather beyng of a base stocke and linage, was for his manhoode and chiualry aduanced to the noble dignitie of an Erle, excellyng principally in Archery, or shootyng, his manly courage agreeyng therevnto: But afterwardes he so prodically exceeded in charges and expences, that he fell into great debt, by reason whereof, so many actions and sutes were commenced against him, wherevnto he aunswered not, that by order of lawe he was outlawed."

167 *napkin on his shoulder*. M (1980, p. 471) notes that the shoulder is the usual place for napkins, citing *An Humerous Day's Mirth* (1599), where Verone enters with his napkin on his shoulder.

169 For discussion of outlawry, see the note to line 5 of the *Gest*.

173 In L the pre-speech signifier is *Iohn*. I have identified him as *Lit. John*, for the sake of clarity; later, Prince John, also called John sometimes in L, is here identified as *Pr. John*.

194 *Scene*. L frequently capitalizes terms for the theater, a practice I've adhered

to. E.g., lines 233, 238, etc.

275   *[Exit Marian*. Not in L; C's emendation, followed by H and M (1980).

284   The four locations identify Robert's country houses: *Rowford* = Rufford, Nottinghamshire; *Sowtham* = Southam, Warwickshire; *Wortley* is north of Sheffield; and *Hothersfield* = Hudderfield, Yorkshire.

290   *care will kill her*. Proverbial: see Tilley C84, for variations from "Sorrow hath killed many" to "care will kill a cat."

295   *Belsavage*. An inn that stood on Ludgate Hill, used to house Elizabethan plays. See M (1980, p. 475).

318   *must*. L: *mnst*: a compositor's error. Inverted letters are not uncommon in L. See also *hnmble* (line 536), *rnnne* (line 890), *Renenge* (line 959), *hane* (line 968), *aud* (lines 976, 1301, 1677, 1821, 2236), *turue* (line 1256), *thon* (lines 1605, 1680), *Yonr* (line 1656), *Bmt* (line 1675), *Scotlaud* (line 2072), *yon* (i.e., *you*, lines 1265, 1354, 2165, 2236).

347   *worshipt*. "honored your position with proper address." I.e., "I 'your-worshiped' you."

349   *buckram satchell*. A sachel of course linen rather than leather; hence, without class, as paltry as his pen-and-inkhorn status.

356–58 The trope of the sheep-killing mastiff epitomizes hypocrisy that is not easily recognized when found within one's own domain but which, once exposed, must be dealt with expeditiously.

360   See note to line 135.

370   *ran*. H emends to *run*.

417   *[Exit*. Not in L. C's emendation, followed by H and M (1980).

429   M (1980, p. 477) notes that *Prince* was used of male and female alike.

433   *and I say true*. In truth, he says false. M (1980) observes that good people lie

"with surprising freedom" in these plays (see also lines 227–56 and *Death*, lines 1770–81), but cites Guazzo, in Pettie's translation of *The Ciuile Conuersation* (1586): "I denie not, but that it is commendable to coine a lie at sometime, and in some place, so that it tend to some honest end."

457   *odly attyred.* Hazlitt conjuctures that Warman's wife, given her odd dialect in lines 460 ff., is French. But M (1980) doubts that that's the case. Perhaps her attire simply means she's eccentric and that her dialect is provincial, or that she is not well bred.

523   *Nich.* C emends to *Much.* M (1967) defends *Nich* as a characteristic distortion by Mistress Warman.

548   The sheriff's wife pretends to lofty speech now that she is a lofty woman, but seldom does she get things right. By *Paterne* she seems to mean *Patent* (i.e., the appointment of Warman to Sheriff). Compare the even more pretentious language of Ralph below (see note to line 939).

551–56   C suggests that lines 553–54 are spoken by Warman, with lines 555–56 again by Prince John. M (1980) acknowledges the possibility with bracketted speech prefixes.

558   *Earle John.* John bears both titles of earl and prince.

566   *receive.* L: *deceive.* H's emendation. M (1980) maintains *deceive.*

566   *[Enter John.* Not in L; C's emendation, followed by H and M (1980).

572–74   Proverbial paraphrase of Matthew 24.12.

594   *Marian.* L: *War.* Another instance of an inverted letter.

661   Rosamond was mistress to Henry II. She was supposedly killed by order of the jealous Queen Eleanor of Aquitaine, Richard and John's mother. Munday is having fun with "history."

662   *cankers.* H emends to *cank'rous*, or perhaps *cankred.*

676   *Zwouns.* God's wounds.

676   *after-arrant. Arrant* perhaps means "message"; an *after-arrant* could thus mean "subsequent message" such as the blow just given.

         [*Exit Messenger*. Not in L; supplied by C and all others.

679   *Simon*. M (1980, p. 482) notes that historically the reference should be to Robert de Beaumont, not Simon.

732   *Ely*. C suggests *Chester* could be the speaker.

782   As the stage direction here makes clear, Marian's name has been changed to Matilda. See note to line 1328. She is hereafter referred to as Matilda, except for a brief appearance in the greenwood (lines 1382 ff.), where she becomes Marian once again; Lord Lacy becomes Fitzwater; and the character hereafter called Salsbury was before called Leicester. A new Leicester appears later. M (1980) suggests that lines 1–781 were from early composition of the play which was later revised in the acted version (pp. 67–70); or, perhaps, the adjustments came after decisions were being made to write a two-part play which would center upon Matilda in the second part. See note to lines 871 ff. of *The Death of Robert, Earl of Huntington*, below.

786   *for and*. A common expression in the drama of the period, meaning "and also," "and moreover." Collier (cited by M [1980], p. 483) is wrong to suggest "for" to be useless. See, for example, Beaumont's *Knight of the Burning Pestle*, II.i.163–64: "Your Squire doth come and with him comes the Lady, / For and the Squire of Dames as I take it" (Cyrus Hoy, *Beaumont and Fletcher* [Cambridge: Cambridge University Press, 1980], Vol. I, 33); and the Gravedigger's song in *Hamlet*, V.i.82–83: "A pick-axe and a spade, a spade, / For and a shrouding sheet."

797   *cogge*. M suggests a "pun on *cog* (flattery, or an ingratiating speech of any kind) and *cog* (the cross-board on a mill wheel): cf. 1431–32" (1980, p. 485).

800   *his brother*. L: *brother*. C's emendation, which improves the meter; followed by all others.

843   *palliardize. Palliard* is a cant term for beggar.

890   *Skelton*. Skelton is playing the role of the Friar. He becomes so agitated with the vanity of the world that he falls from the Friar's character into his own "moral" voice and has to be reminded by John Eltham, who's playing Little John, to get back into his role. This gest on theatrical decorum proceeds from the Induction, where they assume their roles.

909   *[Exeunt*. Not in L; C's addition, followed by all others.

919   Will Scarlet, variously known in the ballads as "Scarlock," "Scathelocke," and "Scadlock," has been turned into two separate characters by Munday: *Scarlet*, in line 916, and *Scathlock* here.

921   "This is obviously a rationalization of traditions: the author has inserted Scarlet and Scathlock into the position otherwise held by three anonymous brethren, and must reconcile the diversity of names with their common sonship to the widow. The solution he chose gave him an extra father to employ, and it is with characteristic thoroughness that he insists on *both* fathers' kindness to Warman, throwing in Warman's father for symmetry and good measure" (M, 1980, p. 488).

939   By putting "inkhorn" terms (words borrowed from Latin, Greek, and French) into the mouth of Ralph, Warman's servant, Munday satirizes Ralph's pretension and positions himself with the numerous writers who ridiculed the use of obscure language when adequate English equivalents existed.

1001   *[Exit Frier*. Not in L; C's addition, followed by all.

1003   Friar Tuck is identified with St. Mary's Abbey, York, where, in the *Gest* (see lines 217, 337, and 930), Earl Robert's uncle is Prior.

1005–23 This passage is conceivably from an early version which Munday intended to cancel since it overlaps matter repeated in lines 1258–1387. But it cannot be deleted without adjustment of one passage or the other. Perhaps it was this kind of reworking that Chettle was paid to undertake on 25 November 1598, as the play was moved from the Rose Theatre to the Court. See *Henslowe's Diary (Part I: Text)* (London, 1904), fol. 52. M provides a thoughtful discussion of these problematic lines in his critical edition (1980, pp. 70–74).

1011   *[Exeunt Much, Scarlet, Scath*. C's addition, not followed by M.

1028   Salsbury is the name given now and henceforth to line 1785 for Leicester.

1203–04   The story of Cynthia and Endimion was well-known to theater-goers through Lyly's *Endimion* (1591).

1215   *Clepstowes*. C: *Chepstow's.*

1242   *[Exit Salsbury*. Not in L; C's addition, followed by all.

1282   *Barnsdale shrogs to Notinghams red cliffes*. In *Robin Hood and Guy of Gisborne* Robin is said to be from Barnsdale where mention is made of *shrogs*. See also the *Gest*, line 9 and note. M (1980, p. 498) suggests that Munday may be specifically alluding to the ballad here; and, given the fact that Nottingham does have red cliffs, no literary reference to which can M find, he speculates that Munday may have had first-hand knowledge of that region.

1283   *Blithe* is located on the Northumberland coast, north of Newcastle. *Tickhill* is in the West Riding of Yorkshire.

1284–85   *George a Greene at Bradford . . . Wakefields Pinner*. See M's long note on these lines (1980, pp. 499–500): Collier had thought Munday guilty of an error when he conflates George a Greene the pinner of Wakefield with the shoemaker of Bradford. But the text does not say that he is a shoemaker. M suggests that the source of the association of George a Greene with Bradford may be Robert Greene's 1592 play *George a Greene the Pinner of Wakefield*, which has a scene with both the Shoemaker of Bradford and George a Greene present along with Robin and Scarlet. The psalmic syntax of the two lines may simply mean that "George a Greene the pinner of Wakefield loved us well at Bradford." Wakefield, near Bradford, was an important weaving and dyeing center in the West Riding of Yorkshire.

1286   Barnsley, in the West Riding of Yorkshire, was known for its market.

1288   *Nunnes of Farnsfield*. Farnsfield is located near Sherwood Forest, though no convent is known to have been there.

1290   *Kendall greene*. Though Robin Hood and his men are often associated with Lincoln green, as in the *Gest* (line 1685), here, according to M (1980, p. 500)

Munday follows *A Mery Geste* where the May games are performed in Kendall green. Kendall, in Westmoreland, was noted for its green woollens since the Flemish weavers were established there in the reign of Edward III.

1291   Known for its manufacturing activities, Leeds was a center of coal and iron forging. As early as 1200, the monks of Kirkstall Abbey forged iron.

1292   *Rotheram* = Rotherham, West Riding, Yorkshire.

1295   *Mansfield*. In the heart of Sherwood Forest, in Nottinghamshire.

1296   *wrestling day*. See note to line 538 of the *Gest* on wrestling as a medieval sport.

1328   *Articles*. The six provisions constitute the outlaw code: 1) Earl Robert will henceforth be called Robin Hood; 2) Matilda will be called Maid Marian; 3) all yeoman swear to expel lustful thoughts about women; 4) all passers-by will be "invited" to feast with Robin Hood with the unstated condition that they pay for the privilege; 5) the outlaws swear never to wrong a poor man, but priests, usurers, and clerks are fair game; and 6) all yeoman swear to defend maids, widows, orphans, and distressed men. The last four items are drawn from the *Gest*.

1399   *rener*. C and H read *reaver*. Perhaps an archaic form of ME *renner*, a runner or fugitive. Or possibly a corruption of *renter*, "a farmer of tolls or taxes," which OED cites in Florio 1598 (sb.3); in which case a *lawlesse rener* would be one who doesn't pay his taxes. If C's emendation is sound, then the sense of *reaner* is "robber."

1427   *Gifts stinke with proffer*. Proverbial. See Tilley S252: "Proffered service (or ware) stinks."

1429   Proverbial. See Tilley K51.

1437   Proverbial. See Tilley J57: "Joan is as good as my lady in the dark."

1439   *weye*. C reads *wi'ye*, which is certainly the sense.

1446–47   Farnsfield and Southwell are near Sherwood Forest.

1526   *proface.* A formula of welcome at a meal; in frequent use from the early sixteenth century to mid-seventeenth century; literally "may it do you good." See C. T. Onions *A Shakespeare Glossary* (Oxford: Clarendon Press, 1919), p. 169. See, for example, Shakespeare 2 *Henry IV*, v.iii.28.

1554   *[Enter Frier Tucke . . .* Not in L. See note to lines 1571–72 below.

1556–65   More Skeltonics, which should be read in short, irregularly rhyming lines, as in lines 118–41, though here they are to be sung, perhaps in the manner of a street call, in a crude tetrameter. Keep in mind that the Friar is being played by Skelton, so perhaps he is simply being self indulgent. See note to lines 1587–1606 below.

1560   *chuse.* L: *cheape.* M's emendation, with note that *chuse* appears twice more in the song and functions as a refrain (1980, p. 505).

1563   *poting sticks.* A pote is a stick for poking, used for crimping linen to make ruffs.

1571–72   The stage direction in L reads: *[Enter Frier like a Pedlar, and Jinny, Sir Doncaster, and others weaponed.* But Tuck and Jinny have entered at lines 1554–55 and conversed with Robin. Now, as Doncaster enters, Tuck addresses him.

1582   [*Sings.* M (1980, p. 505) suggests that the song of lines 1556–65 be repeated here.

1587–1606 Clearly "Skelton" enjoys being the good guy as the Friar responds to Marian and then to Robin in Skeltonic verse. Earlier, lines 846 ff., the compositor printed the Skeltonics appropriately in short lines. Here, and in lines 1610–11, the lines are run together. In lines 2081–95 the lines are printed in tetrameter. Perhaps a different compositor is at work here, or the same one is short on space. I have maintained L's blocking of the lines so that the line count of this edition will correspond to M's critical edition and that of the Malone society.

1606   *certainely.* L: *certaine.* Emendation M's, for purposes of Skeltonic rhyme.

1628   *[Exeunt omnes.* Not in L; C's emendation, followed by all.

1737   *band*. Past tense of *ban*, "to curse."

1740   **Servant**. L: *Sor*. C emends to *Ser.*, followed by all.

1753   **Prior**. L omits speech prefix. But it is necessary and is added by C *et al.*

1754   C adds *[Exit Servant* after this line and after line 1760.

1764   **Herald**. No speech prefix in L.

1770   M (1980) notes that "Primate of England" is a title granted by the Pope to the Archbishop of York, while "Primate of All England" is the title granted the Archbishop of Canterbury (p. 508). Holinshed B3 gives the story.

1777   C adds: *Exit Herald.*

1782   *Let Lester come*. Presumably his drum (line 1785) is already being heard.

1825   *Acon, Acres*. One and the same place: a city in Asia Minor. Grafton's *Chronicle* uses the name *Acon*; Holinshed uses *Acre*. Munday uses both. Richard's title was "king of Jerusalem," which included all domains from the Holy City to Cyprus.

1831   *mites*. Perhaps an allusion to the widow's mite in Mark 12.41–44.

1856   *Richards*. C suggests *King Richards*, which improves the meter.

1858–59   *guide of Greece . . . to Tenedos*. Tenedos is the island off the coast of Troy which Agamemnon, the "guide," used as a mustering point against the Trojans. It is mentioned in *The Aeneid*: "Offshore lies Tenedos, famed and storied island, / rich and a power while Priam's throne held firm" (*Aeneid* II.21–22, Copley's translation). Its fame as a storied place continued into the Renaissance where the beauty of Marlowe's Helen "summoned Greece to arms, / and drew a thousand ships to Tenedos" (2 *Tamburlaine* II.iv.87–88).

1862   *souldiours*. C and H emend to *Soldan's*, which makes good sense.

1878   *not*. Omitted in L. Hazlitt's emendation, accepted by M (1980).

1881   *Joppa*. Haifa.

1885   *carpet knight*. One who earns glory not on the battle field but by sitting around at home; a term of derision.

1900–01   C speculates that these lines might better be spoken by the Queen.

1912   *Beare*. The "bear and ragged staff" denote the heraldry of Robert Dudley, Earl of Leicester. M (1980) points out that Munday used the emblem in his book *Two godly and learned Sermons, made by . . . Iohn Calvin*, which he dedicated to Leicester (pp. 512–13).

2011   *[Exeunt*. Not in L, but in all others.

2020   *Phaeton*. Son of Helios, who presumed to drive his father's chariot. When he veered too close to earth, thereby scorching it, Jove smote him with a thunderbolt (Ovid, *Metamorphoses* I.755 ff.).

2021   *[Enter Lester and Richmond*. Not in L. C/H place the entrance at line 2018; M (1980), at line 2021.

2032–61   See M (1980, pp. 514–16) on the popularity of the tale of Richard and the lion, which crops up in several sixteenth-century plays and romances. But probably Munday's source was a ballad such as that printed in Thomas Evans' *Old Ballads* (1784), I, 80–86.

2094   *guesse*. C/H's emendation to "guesste" is not followed by M (1980), who notes that *guesse* is a common Renaissance form of *guest*, whether singular or plural.

2118   *Oxen*. Probably Oxton, just north of Nottingham.

2128   *market man*. A man connected with the market: perhaps a vendor or a mercenary; or perhaps a pickpocket who haunts markets.

2138   L reads: *Enter Robin*. C adds: *and John*. John speaks at line 2159.

2147   *and*. L: *a*. A compositor's error for *&*.

2179   *burning irons.* Robin, known for his generosity, here threatens Ely, though all know that he will not carry out his threat, including Ely (see lines 2185–86).

2200   *con verse.* Robin thoughtfully gives Ely dignified company with which to *con verse.* The phrase carries several meanings: "tell tales," "make merry," "pass the time," as well as "keep company."

2221   *merry jeasts.* Apparently Robin Hood plays, perhaps from May festivals, that were especially popular in the late fifteenth and early sixteenth centuries. Skelton alludes to the story in *Colyn Cloute* (line 879). Or perhaps, as M (1980, p. 520) suggests, the allusion is to a specific play entered on the Stationers' Register in 1594 called a "pastorall plesant Commedie of Robin Hood and little John" in which Jinny was a prominent character and which included the friar-in-the-well story and an account of Greeneleafe's robbing the *Shrieve of Notingham* (line 2224). The ballad *The Friar in the Well* (Child V, no. 276) tells part of the story but does not name the maid. In the *Gest* (line 596) Little John assumes the identity of Reynolde Grenelef after winning the shooting match.

2229   This line must remain from an early version in which Robin's death was to conclude the play.

2248   The scene is set in Sherwood Forest.

2261   *Bingham.* In Nottinghamshire, about eight miles east of Nottingham.

2272   M (1980, p. 522) remarks on the precision of Munday's knowledge of Nottinghamshire's geography.

2310   *Redford.* Probably Retford, Nottinghamshire, north of Sherwood Forest.

2313   *Jailer.* L omits the pre-speech designation, though clearly it is necessary.

2318   L: *thererefore.*

2320   *thin-cheekt.* L: *thick-cheek't.* C changes to *thin-cheek'd*, followed by H and M (1980), to accord with *chittiface*, which means "thin-cheeked," or "pinch-face." But the Jailer is full of angry words and perhaps abuses the language, even as Mrs. Warman does, with his *thick-cheekt chittiface*, in which case the emendation spoils the joke. Or maybe *thick-cheekt chittiface* means something like "fat-faced skinflint."

2329   C adds *Enter woman*, then takes her off again at line 2344, has her reenter at line 2347, then exits her at line 2355.

2344   The woman cruelly tricks Warman with a pun: a *caudle* is "a warm drink consisting of thin gruel mixed with wine or ale, sweetened and spiced, given chiefly to aid people, especially women in childbed; also to their visitors" (OED, sb. 1). Thus the starving Warman thinks she means to provide him with nurture. But *caudle* also refers to the hangman's noose (*hempen caudle*) which is in fact what she brings him, thus dashing his hopes and providing the reality check of his villainy from which he cannot escape.

2355   The woman's exit is not marked in L.

2365   *sound hermonious.* M (1980) suggests that the moment was probably preceded by bird-sounds produced by the company's musicians.

2419   *not.* Not in L. M's emendation.

2438   *sinksanker.* Not in OED. Halliwell is certainly right in calling it a term of contempt; Hazlitt glosses it as a term applicable to a "card sharper." M (1980) suggests that it's nothing more than a malapropism for "blind soothsayer," used here "in reference to Fitzwater's ability to 'hit so right' despite his blindness" (p. 524).

2490   *trusse.* A close-fitting garment or jacket (OED). M (1980, p. 524) notes that Hensloe's inventory of 13 March 1597/8 included "the fryers trusse in Roben Hoode" (*Papers*, p. 121).

2496   *Bawtrey* = Bawtry, in southern Yorkshire.

2505   *[Exeunt.* Not in L; added by C *et al.*

2509–10   From *The Jolly Pinder of Wakefield*, lines 31–32.

2515   Another reference to the *Gest's* Reynolde Grenelef. See line 2224 and note to line 2221 above.

2531–32   *crowne . . . noble.* Pun on two English coins, as well as on political hierarchy. A *noble* was worth half a mark.

2671–72   Compare *Adam Bell*, where the king makes William a gentleman "of clothynge and of fee" (line 661).

2681   M adds: *[Exeunt Scarlet, John].*

2682   C adds: *Exit Much.* Not in L, but necessary for the sense.

2685   *[Exit Warman.* Not in L. C's addition.

2691   *[Enter Prior and Doncaster.* Not in L. C's addition followed by M (1980). C wonders if Warman might not enter here as well.

2706   *late lost sonne.* M (1980, p. 527) observes: "In *Look About You* (A2v), Robert, Earl of Huntington, is Richard's ward, which may have something to do with this line."

2721–23   Richard's apocryphal siege of Babylon is mentioned in Arnold's *Chronicle* and in romances of Richard and in some ballads. Wynkyn de Worde's *Kynge Rycharde cuer du lyon* (1528) includes the story. The title *Emperor of the East* occurs in *The Battle of Alcazar* (1594), A3. See M (1980, pp. 527–28).

2741   *Moorton my Chancellour.* John Morton, Bishop of Ely, was chancellor under Henry VII. Richard's chancellor was William Longchamp. Thus it would seem that Henry VII is the king Skelton is imagined to please in his production of this Robin Hood play. See above, "his Majesty" (line 9).

2787 ff.   M (1980, p. 529) notes: "The details predicted for the sequel play make it plain that if the opening section of the *Death* was not fully written at the time this epilogue was composed, it was at least clearly planned."

2827   M's note (1980, p. 529) on Richard's return to Austria is worth quoting in full: "This is, of course, an apocryphal journey, deriving from the romances; there, Richard's imprisonment takes place on the return journey from a pilgrimage (not a crusade), and part of the work of the subsequent crusade then becomes a trip to settle with his captor. But in all the extant romance versions, the imprisonment (and hence the return trip) is set in Almayn, not

Austria, with the villain being the Emperor of Almayn rather than the Duke of Austria. The ballad cited in 2032–6ln is the one exception; and it is possible that there was at one time a group of associated ballads dealing with the subject, or another version of the romance corresponding to the ballad."

2834   *The Catastrophe*. The sequel is *The Death of Robert, Earl of Huntington*, which presents *fair Matildas Tragedie* (line 2835) and her becoming a nun at *Dunmowe Abbey* (line 2837), a priory located in Essex.

2837   *Dunmowe*. L: *Dumwod*. Probably a compositor's error. The historical Fitzwater was patron of Dunmowe Priory in Essex. In *The Death*, Dunmowe is the Priory to which Matilda flees to escape the lewd advances of King John; there she is betrayed by the worldly prioress, poisoned, and, ultimately, buried.

Excerpts from *The Death of Robert, Earle of Huntington*

by Anthony Munday

List of Characters

in the order of their appearance

Friar Tuck.

King Richard.

The Bishop of Ely.

Lord Fitzwater.

Earl of Salisbury.

Earl of Chester.

Prince John (later, King John).

Little John.

Scathlock.

Much, a clown.

Sir Doncaster.

Prior of York, Uncle to Robin Hood.

Robin Hood, formerly Robert, Earl of Huntingdon.

Warman.

Eleanor, the Queen Mother.

Scarlet.

Matilda, Robin Hood's Maid Marian.

Jinny.

Chorus.

Characters of the dumbshow: Austria, Ambition, Constance, Arthur, Insurrection, King of France, Hugh le Brun (Earl of March), Queen Isabel, two children.

Hubert de Burgh (alias Bonville and possibly identical with Chorus).

Aubrey De Vere, Earl of Oxford (alias Salisbury).

Mowbray (alias Hugh).

Queen Isabel (anticipated in dumbshow).

Young Bruce (alias Young Fitzwater).

Old Bruce.

Earl of Leicester (perhaps having appeared earlier in play).

Earl of Richmond.

A Boy, messenger (no speeches).

Lady Bruce.

Winchester (alias Chester).

George, younger son of Old Bruce (no speeches).

A Messenger to Oxford on the battlefield.

Will Brand.

A Soldier, guide for Matilda (no speeches).

Abbess of Dunmow.

A Messenger to King John.

A Monk of Bury.

A Servant, messenger of Brand's death.

A Drummer.

Sir William Blunt (alias Sir Walter Blunt).

King John's masquers, ladies, soldiers, nuns.

Scene I

[Enter Frier Tucke.

Frier

olla, holla, holla: follow, follow,

followe.   *[Like noyse within.*

Now benedicité, what fowle absur-

ditie, follie and foolerie had like to fol-

lowed mee! I and my mates, are addle

pates, inviting great states, to see   *worthy dignitaries*

our last play, are hunting the hay,

with ho, that way, the goodly heart ranne, with followe   *deer*

Little John, Much play the man; and I, like a sot, have

wholly forgot the course of our plot; but crosse-bowe

lye downe, come on friers gowne, hoode cover my

crowne, and with a lowe becke, prevent a sharpe   *bow*

checke.   *reproof*

  Blithe sit yee all, and winke at our rude cry,

  Minde where wee left, in Sheerewod merrily,

  The king, his traine, Robin, his yeomen tall

  Gone to the wodde to see the fat deare fall.

  Wee left Maid Marian busie in the bower,

  And prettie Jinny looking, every hower,   *hour*

  For their returning from the hunting game,

  And therefore seeke to set each thing in frame.   *put things in order*

  Warman all wofull for his sinne we left.

  Sir Doncaster, whose villanies and theft

  You never heard of, but too soone yee shall,

  Hurt with the Prior; shame them both befall,   *Wounded (Aggrieved)*

  They two will make our mirth be short and small.

  But least I bring yee sorrowe ere the time,   *lest*

  Pardon I beg of your well judging eyne,   *eyes*

  And take in part bad prologue, and rude play:

  The hunters holloo, Tucke must needes away.

Therefore downe weede, howe doe the deede, to make

the Stagge bleede, and if my hand speede, hey for a cry,

with a throate strained hie, and a lowde yall, at the beasts   *high*
fall.   [*Exit, Holloo within.*

          [*Enter King, Ely, Fitzwater, Salsbury, Chester,*
          Prince John, Little John, Scathlocke.

40	**King**	Where is our mother?	
	Pr. John	Mounted in a stand.	
		Sir, fallowe deere have dyed by her hand.	
	Fitzwater	Three stags I slewe.	
	Ely	Two bucks by me fell downe.	
45	**Chester**	As many dyed by mee.	
	Salsbury	But I had three.	
	Prince	Scathlocke, wheres Much?	
	Scathlocke	When last I saw him, may it please your Grace,	
		He and the Frier footed it apace.	*were walking*
50	**Prince**	Scathlocke, no Grace, your fellowe and plaine John.	
	Lit. John	I warrant you, Much will be here anone.	
	Prince	Thinkst thou Little John, that he must Jinny wed?	
	Lit. John	No doubt he must.	
	Prince	Then to adorne his head, we shall have hornes	
55		good store.	
	King	God, for thy grace,	
		How could I misse the stagge I had in chase!	
		Twice did I hit him in the very necke,	
		When backe my arrowes flewe, as they had smit	
60		On some sure armour. Where is Robin Hood	
		And the wighte Scarlet? Seeke them Little John.	[*Exit John.* *clever*
		Ile have that stagge before I dine today.	

          [*Enter Much.*

	Much	O the Frier, the Frier, the Frier.	
65	**King**	Why, how now Much?	
	Much	Cry ye mercy, master King. Marry this is the matter;	
		Scarlet is following the stagge you hit, and has al-	
		most lodg'd him: now the Frier has the best bowe but	*except for*
		yours, in all the field, which and Scarlet had, he would	*if*

70		have him straight.	
	King	Where is thy master?	
	Much	Nay, I cannot tell, nor the Frier neither.	
	Scathlocke	I heare them holloo, farre off in the wod.	
	King	Come Much, canst lead us where as Scarlet is?	
75	*Much*	Never feare you; follow me.	[*Exeunt, hollooing.*

Scene II

[*Enter Sir Doncaster, Prior.*

	Doncaster	You were resolved to have him poysoned,	
		Or kild, or made away, you car'd not how.	
80		What divell makes you doubtfull to doo't?	*devil*
	Prior	Why, Doncaster, his kindnesse in our needes.	
	Doncaster	A plague upon his kindnesse, let him die.	
		I never temperd poyson in my life, but I imployd it.	*mixed*
		By th'masse and I loose this,	*if I lose*
85		For ever looke to loose my company.	
	Prior	But will you give it him?	
	Doncaster	That cannot bee.	
		The Queene, Earle Chester, and Earle Salsbury,	
		If they once see mee, I am a deade man.	
90		Or did they heare my name, Ile lay my life,	
		They all would hunt me, for my life.	
	Prior	What hast thou done to them?	
	Doncaster	Faith, some odde toyes,	*tricks*
		That made me fly the south. But passe wee them.	
95		Here is the poyson. Will you give it Robin?	
	Prior	Now by this gold I will.	
	Doncaster	Or as I said, for ever I defie your company.	
	Prior	Well, he shall die, and in his jollity;	
		And in my head I have a policy	
100		To make him die disgrac't.	

Doncaster	O tell it Prior.	
Prior	I will, but not as now.	[*Call the Frier within.*
	Weele seeke a place; the wods have many eares,	
	And some methinkes are calling for the Frier.	[*Exeunt.*

105
Scene III

[*Enter, calling the Frier, as afore.*

John	The Frier, the Frier?	
Scathlocke	Why, where's this Frier?	[*Enter Frier.*
Frier	Here, sir. What is your desire?	

110
[*Enter Robin Hoode.*

Robin	Why, Frier, what a murren dost thou meane?	pestilence
	The King cals for thee. For, a mightie stagge,	
	That hath a copper ring about his necke,	
	With letters on it, which hee would have read,	
115	Hath Scarlet kild, I pray thee goe thy way.	
Frier	Master, I will; no longer will I stay.	[*Exit.*
Robin	Good unkle, be more carefull of your health,	
	And you, Sir Doncaster, your wounds are greene.	
Both	Through your great kindnes, we are comforted.	
120 *Robin*	And, Warman, I advise you to more mirth.	
	Shun solitary walkes, keepe company,	
	Forget your fault: I have forgiven the fault.	
	Good Warman be more blithe, and at this time,	
	A little helpe my Marian and her maide.	
125	Much shall come to you straight. A little now,	
	We must al strive to doe the best we may.	[*Exit winding.*
Warman	On you and her Ile waite, untill my dying day.	

[*Exeunt, and as they are going out, Doncaster puls Warman.*

130 *Doncaster*	Warman, a word. My good Lord Prior and I
	Are full of griefe, to see thy misery.
Warman	My misery, Sir Doncaster? Why, I thanke God,

406

I never was in better state than now.

	Prior	Why, what a servile slavish minde hast thou?
135		Art thou a man, and canst be such a beast,
		Asse-like to beare the burthen of thy wrong?

| | *Warman* | What wrong have I? Ist wrong to be reliev'd? |

	Doncaster	Reliev'd saist thou?
		Why, shallow witted foole,
140		Dost thou not see Robins ambitious pride?
		And how he clymes by pittying, and aspires,
		By humble lookes, good deedes, and such fond toyes,
		To be a monarch, raigning over us,
		As if wee were the vassals to his will?

tricks (margin note at line 142)

| 145 | *Warman* | I am his vassall, and I will be still. |

	Prior	Warman, thou art a foole. I doe confesse,
		Were these good deedes done in sinceritie,
		Pittie of mine, thine or this knights distresse,
		Without vaine brags, it were true charitie;
150		But to relieve our fainting bodies wants,
		And grieve our soules with quippes, and bitter braids,
		Is good turnes overturnd. No thanks wee owe
		To any, whatsoever helps us so.

| | *Warman* | Neither himselfe, nor any that hee keepes, |
| 155 | | Ever upbraided mee, since I came last. |

	Doncaster	O God have mercie on thee, silly asse.
		Doth he not say to every gueste that comes:
		"This same is Warman, that was once my steward?"

| | *Warman* | And what of that? |

| 160 | *Prior* | Ist not as much to say: |
| | | "Why, here he stands that once did mee betray?" |

	Doncaster	Did hee not bring a troope to grace himselfe,
		Like captives waiting on a conquerours chaire,
		And calling of them out, by one and one,
165		Presented them, like fairings, to the king?

gifts from a fair (margin note at line 165)

	Prior	O, I; there was a rare invention.
		A plague upon the foole.
		I hate him worse for that than all the rest.

Oh, indeed (margin note at line 166)

407

	Warman	Why should you hate him? Why should you or you	
170		Envie this noble Lord, thus as you doe?	
	Doncaster	Nay rather, why dost thou not joyne in hate	
		With us, that lately liv'dst like us, in wealthy state?	
		Remember this, remember foolish man,	
		How thou hast bene the Shrieve of Notingham.	
175	**Prior**	Cry to thy thoughts, let this thought never cease,	
		I have bene Justice of my Soveraignes Peace,	
		Lord of faire livings; men with cap and knee,	
		In liveries waited howerly on mee.	*hourly*
	Doncaster	And when thou thinkst, thou hast bene such and such,	
180		Thinke then what tis to be a mate to Much,	
		To runne when Robin bids, come at his call,	
		Be mistresse Marians man.	
	Prior	Nay thinke withall.	
	Warman	What shall I thinke? but thinke upon my need,	
185		When men fed dogs, and me they would not feede,	
		When I despaird through want, and sought to die,	
		My pitious master, of his charitie,	
		Forgave my fault, reliev'd and saved mee.	
		This doe I thinke upon, and you should thinke,	
190		If you had hope of soules salvation,	
		First, Prior, that he is of thy flesh and bloode,	
		That thou art unkle unto Robin Hoode,	
		That by extortion thou didst his lands.	*possessed*
		God and I know how it came to thy hands,	
195		How thou pursu'dst him in his misery,	
		And how heaven plagu'd thy hearts extreamitie.	
		Thinke, Doncaster, when, hired by this Prior,	
		Thou cam'st to take my master with the Frier,	
		And wert thyselfe tane, how he set thee free,	*taken*
200		Gave thee an hundred pound to comfort thee,	
		And both bethinke yee how but yesterday,	
		Wounded and naked in the fielde you lay,	
		How with his owne hand he did raise your heads,	
		Powrd balme into your wounds, your bodies fed,	*Poured*
205		Watcht when yee slept, wept when he sawe your woe.	
	Doncaster	Stay Warman, stay. I grant that he did so,	

408

		And you, turnd honest, have forsworne the villainé?	*villainy*
	Warman	Even from my soule, I villany defie.	
	Prior	A blessed hower, a fit time now to die!	
210	*Doncaster*	And you shall, Conscience. [*Stab him, he fals.*	
	Warman	O forgive mee, God,	
		And save my master from their bloodie hands.	
	Prior	What, hast thou made him sure?	
	Doncaster	Its deade sure: he is dead, if that be sure.	
215	*Prior*	Then let us thrust the dagger in his hand,	
		And when the next comes, cry he kild himselfe.	
	Doncaster	That must be now. Yonder comes Robin Hood.	
		No life in him.	
	Prior	No, no, not any life. [*Enter Robin.*	
220		Three mortall wounds have let in piercing ayre,	
		And at their gaps, his life is cleane let out.	
	Robin	Who is it, uncle, that you so bemone?	
	Prior	Warman, good nephew, whom Sir Doncaster and I	
		Found freshly bleeding, as he now doth lye.	
225		You were scarce gone, when he did stab himselfe.	
	Robin	O God, he in his own hand houlds his own harts hurt;	
		I dreaded too much his distressed looke.	
		Belike the wretch despaird and slewe himselfe.	
	Doncaster	Nay, thats most sure, yet he had little reason,	
230		Considering how well you used him.	
	Robin	Well, I am sorie; but must not be sad,	
		Because the King is comming to my bower.	
		Helpe mee, I pray thee, to remoove his bodie,	
		Least he should come and see him murdered.	
235		Sometime anone he shall be buried. [*Exeunt Robin, Doncaster, with body.*	
	Prior	Good, all is good. This is as I desire.	
		Now for a face of pure hypocrisie.	
		Sweete murder, cloath thee in religious weedes,	
		Raigne in my bosome, that with helpe of thee,	
240		I may effect this Robins Tragedie.	

Robin Hood Plays

[*Enter Robin, Doncaster.*

Doncaster	Nay, nay, you must not take this thing so heavily.	
Robin	A bodies losse, Sir Doncaster, is much;	
	But a soules, too, is more to be bemon'd.	
245 **Prior**	Truly I wonder at your vertuous minde.	
	O God, to one so kinde, who'ud be unkinde!	
	Let goe this griefe, now must you put on joy,	
	And for the many favours I have found,	
	So much exceeding all conceipt of mine,	
250	Unto your cheere, Ile adde a pretious drinke,	*precious*
	Of colour rich, and red, sent mee from Rome.	
	There's in it Moly, Syrian Balsamum,	
	Golds rich Elixir — O tis pretious!	
Robin	Where it is uncle?	
255 **Prior**	As yesterday,	
	Sir Doncaster and I rid on our way,	
	Theeves did beset us, bound us as you saw;	
	And, among other things, did take from mee	
	This rich confection. But regardlesly,	*without regard*
260	As common drinke, they cast, into a bush,	
	The bottle, which this day Sir Doncaster	
	Fetcht, and hath left it in the inner lodging.	
	I tell you, cosin (I doe love you well),	
	A pint of this ransomde the Sophies sonne,	*ransomed*
265	When he was taken in Natolia.	
	I meant indeede to give it my liege lord,	
	In hope to have his favour; but to you	
	I put myselfe, be my good friend,	
	And, in your owne restoring, mee restore.	
270 **Robin**	Unkle, I will. You neede urge that no more.	
	But whats the vertues of this pretious drinke?	
Prior	It keepes fresh youth, restores diseased sight,	
	Helps natures weakenesse, smothes the scars of wounds,	
	And cooles the intrals with a balmie breath,	
275	When they by thirst or travell boyle with heate.	
Robin	Unkle, I thanke you, pray you let me have	
	A cuppe prepared, gainst the King comes in,	*before*

		To coole his heate. Myselfe will give it him.

	Prior	And when he drinkes, be bold to say he drinkes
280		A richer draught than that dissolved pearle
		Which Cleopatra dranke to Antonie.

	Robin	I have much businesse; let it be your charge
		To make this rich draught readie for the King,
		And I will quit it, pray yee doe not faile. [*Exit.*

285	**Prior**	I warrant you, good nephew.

	Doncaster	Better, and better still.
		We thought before but to have poysond him,
		And now shall Robin Hoode destroy the King.
		Even when the King, the Queen, the Prince, the Lords
290		Joy in his vertues, this supposed vice
		Will turne to sharpe hate their exceeding love.

	Prior	Ha, ha, ha, I cannot chuse but laugh,
		To see my cosin cosend in this sort.
		Faile him quoth you? Nay hang mee if I doe.
295		But, Doncaster, art sure the poysons are well mixt?

	Doncaster	Tut, tut, let me alone for poysoning. *you can rely on me*
		I have alreadie turnd ore foure or five *murdered*
		That angerd mee. But tell mee Prior,
		Wherefore so deadly dost thou hate thy cosin?

300	**Prior**	Shall I be plaine? Because if he were deade,
		I should be made the Earle of Huntington.

	Doncaster	A prettie cause. But thou a church-man art.

	Prior	Tut, man, if that would fall,
		Ile have a dispensation, and turne temporall. *secular*
305		But tell mee, Doncaster, why dost thou hate him?

	Doncaster	By the Masse, I cannot tel. O yes, now I ha't.
		I hate thy cousin, Earle of Huntington,
		Because so many love him as there doe,
		And I myselfe am loved of so fewe.
310		Nay, I have other reasons for my hate;
		Hee is a foole, and will be reconcilde
		To anie foe hee hath; he is too milde,
		Too honest for this world, fitter for heaven.
		Hee will not kill these greedie cormorants, *rapacious persons (see note)*

411

315		Nor strippe base pesants of the wealth they have;	
		He does abuse a thieves name and an outlawes,	
		And is indeede no outlawe, nor no theefe —	
		He is unworthy of such reverent names.	
		Besides, he keepes a paltry whinling girle,	*whining*
320		And will not bed, forsooth, before he bride.	
		Ile stand too't, he abuses maidenhead,	
		That will not take it, being offered,	
		Hinders the common wealth of able men.	
		Another thing I hate him for againe:	
325		He saies his prayers, fasts eves, gives alms, does good.	
		For these and such like crimes, sweares Doncaster	
		To worke the speedie death of Robin Hoode.	
	Prior	Well said, yfaith. Harke, hark, the King returns.	
		To doe this deede, my heart like fuel burns.	[*Exeunt.*

Scene IIII

330

[*Windehornes. Enter King, Queene, John, Fitzwater,
Ely, Chester, Salsbury, Lester, Little John, Frier Tuck, Scarlet, Scathlocke, and Much. Frier Tuck carrying a stags
head, dauncing.*

335	*King*	Gramercy, Frier, for thy glee,	*song*
		Thou greatly hast contented mee,	
		What with thy sporting and thy game,	
		I sweare I highly pleased am.	
	Frier	It was my masters whole desire	
340		That maiden, yeoman, swaine and frier	
		Their arts and wits should all apply,	
		For pleasure of your Majestie.	
	Queene	Sonne Richard, looke I pray you on the ring	
		That was about the necke of the last stagge.	
345	*Chester*	Was his name Scarlet, that shot off his necke?	
	John	Chester, it was this honest fellow Scarlet.	
		This is the fellowe, and a yeoman bold,	
		As ever courst the swift hart on the molde.	*pursued; earth*

	King	Frier, heres somewhat grav'd upon the ring,
350		I pray thee reade it. Meanewhile list to mee.

                                     [This while, most compassing the Frier about the ring.

Scarlet and Scathlock, you bold bretheren,
Twelve pence a day I give each for his fee,
And henceforth see yee live like honest men.

| 355 | *Both* | We will, my Liege, else let us dye the death. |

	Much	A boone, a boone, upon my knee,
		Good King Richard, I begge of thee.
		For indeede, sir, the troth is, Much is my father, and hee
		is one of your tenants in Kings Mill at Wakefield all on
360		a greene. O there dwelleth a jolly pinder, at Wake-
		field all on a greene. Now I would have you, if you wil
		doe so much for mee, to set mee forward in the way of
		marriage to Jinny: the mill would not be cast away upon
		us.

| 365 | *King* | Much, be thou ever master of that mill; |
| | | I give it thee for thin inheritance. |

| | *Much* | Thanks, pretious Prince of curtesie. |
| | | Ile to Jinny and tell her of my lands yfaith.   *[Exit.* |

| | *John* | Here, Frier, here, here it begins. |

| 370 | *Frier* [*reads*]: | "When Harold hare-foote raigned king, |
| | | About my necke he put this ring." |

	King	In Harolds time, more than a hundred yeare,
		Hath this ring bene about his newe slaine deere!
		I am sory now it dyde; but let the same
375		Head, ring and all be sent to Notingham,
		And in the castle kept for monuments.

	Fitzwater	My Leige, I heard an olde tale long agoe,
		That Harold being Goodwins sonne of Kent,
		When he had got faire Englands government,
380		Hunted for pleasure once within this wood,
		And singled out a faire and stately stagge,
		Which, foote to foote, the king in running caught.
		And sure this was the stagge.

| | *King* | It was no doubt. |

385	*Chester*	But some, my Lord, affirme
		That Julius Caesar, many yeares before,
		Tooke such a stag, and such a poesie writ.
	King	It should not be in Julius Caesars time:
		There was no English bred in this land,
390		Untill the Saxons came, and this is writ
		In Saxon characters.
	John	Well, 'twas a goodly beast.

[Enter Robin Hoode.

	King	How now Earle Robert?
395	*Frier*	A forfet, a forfet, my liege Lord.
		My masters lawes are on record;
		The Court-roll here your Grace may see.
	King	I pray thee, Frier, read them mee.
	Frier	One shall suffice, and this is hee.
400		No man that commeth in this wod
		To feast or dwell with Robin Hood
		Shall call him Earle, Lord, Knight, or Squire;
		He no such titles doth desire,
		But Robin Hood, plaine Robin Hoode,
405		That honest yeoman stout and good,
		On paine of forfetting a marke,
		That must be paid to me his clarke.

accountant

		My liege, my liege, this lawe you broke,
		Almost in the last word you spoke.
410		That crime may not acquited bee,
		Till Frier Tuck receive his fee.

[*Casts him purse.*

	King	Theres more than twenty marks, mad Frier.
	Frier	If thus you pay the clarke his hire,

wage

		Oft may you forfet, I desire.
415		You are a perfect penitent,
		And well you doe your wrong repent.
		For this your Highnesse liberall gift,
		I here absolve you without shrift.

confession

	King	Gramercies, Frier. Now, Robin Hood,
420		Sith Robin Hood it needes must bee,
		I was about to aske before

414

		If thou didst see the great stags fall.	
	Robin	I did my Lord, I sawe it all.	
		But missing this same prating Frier,	
425		And hearing you so much desire	
		To have the lozels companie,	*fool's*
		I went to seeke small honestie.	
	Frier	But you found much, when you found mee.	
	Robin	I, Much my man, but a jot	*only*
430		Of honestie in thee, God wot.	*knows*
	Queene	Robin, you doe abuse the Frier.	
	Frier	Madam, I dare not call him lyer;	
		He may be bold with mee, he knowes.	
		How now, Prince John, how goes, how goes	
435		This wod-mans life with you today?	
		My fellow Wodnet you would bee.	
	John	I am thy fellowe, thou dost see.	
		And to be plaine, as God me save,	
		So well I like thee, merry knave,	
440		That I thy company must have.	
		Nay, and I will.	
	Frier	Nay, and you shall.	
	Robin	My Lord, you neede not feare at all,	
		But you shall have his company,	
445		He will be bold I warrant yee.	
	King	Know you where ere a spring is nie?	
		Faine would I drink, I am right dry.	
	Robin	I have a drinke within my bower,	
		Of pleasing taste and soveraigne power.	
450		My reverend uncle gives it mee	
		To give unto your Majestie.	
	King	I would be loath indeede, being in heate,	
		To drinke cold water. Let us to thy bower.	
	Robin	Runne Frier before, and bid my unkle be in readines.	
455	**Frier**	Gon with a trice, on such good business. [*Exeunt omnes.*	

Scene V

[*Enter Marian, with a white apron.*

Marian	What, Much? What, Jinny? Much? I say.	[*Enter Much.*
Much	Whats the matter, mistresse?	

460   *Marian*   I pray thee see the fueller
Suffer the cooke to want no wodde.
Good Lord, where is this idle girle?
Why, Jinny?

Jinny [*within*]   I come, forsooth.

465   *Marian*   I pray thee bring the flowers forth.

Much   Ile goe send her mistres, and help the cookes, if
they have any neede.   [*Exit Much.*

Marian   Dispatch, good Much. What, Jin, I say?   *Hurry*

[*Enter Jinny.*

470   *Much*   Hie thee, hie thee: she cals for life.   *Hasten*

Marian   Indeede, indeede, you doe me wrong,
To let me cry and call so long.

Jinny   Forsooth, I strawed the dining bowers
And smoth'd the walkes with hearbes and flowers,
475   The yeomens tables I have I have spied,
Drest salts, laid trenchers, set on bread —
Nay all is well, I warrant you.

Marian   You are not well, I promise you,
Your forsleeves are not pind (fie, fie)
480   And all your hed-geere stands awry.
Give me the flowers. Goe in for shame,
And quickly see you mend the same.   [*Exit Jinny.*

[*Marian strewing flowers. Enter Sir Doncaster, Prior.*

Doncaster   How busie mistresse Marian is?
485   She thinkes this is her day of blisse.

Prior   But it shall be the wofull'st day
That ever chancst her, if I may.

	Marian	Why are you two thus in the ayre?	
		Your wounds are greene,	
490		Good cuz, have care.	

	Prior	Thanks for your kindnesse, gentle maid.	
		My cosin Robert us hath praid	
		To helpe him in this businesse.	

[*Enter Frier.*

495	Frier	Sir Doncaster, Sir Doncaster?	

	Doncaster	Holla.	

	Frier	I pray you, did you see the Prior?	

	Prior	Why, here I am. What wouldst thou, Frier?	

	Frier	The King is heated in the chace,	*chase*
500		And posteth hitherward apace.	
		He told my master he was dry,	
		And hee desires ye presently	
		To send the drinke whereof ye spake. [*Hornes blowe.*	

	Prior	Come, it is here; haste let us make.	

505

[*Exeunt Prior, Doncaster, and Frier.*

[*Enter King, John, Queene, Scarlet, Scathlocke, Ely, Fitzwater, Salsbury, Chester. Marian kneeles downe.*

	Marian	Most gratious Soveraigne, welcome once again.	
		Welcome to you and all your princely traine.	

510	King	Thanks, lovely hostesse; we are homely guests.	
		Wheres Robin Hood? He promised me some drinke.	

	Marian	Your handmaid. Robin will not then be long.	
		The Frier indeede came running to his unkle,	
		Who with Sir Doncaster were here with mee,	
515		And altogether went for such a drinke.	

	King	Well, in a better time it could not come,	
		For I am very hot and passing dry.	*exceedingly*

[*Enter Robin Hoode, a cuppe, a towell, leading Doncaster.
Tuck, and Much pulling the Prior.*]

520	Robin	Traitor, Ile draw thee out before the King.	*expose you*

	Frier	Come, murderous Prior.	

	Much	Come yee, dogges face.
	King	Why, how now Robin? Wheres the drink you bring?
525	**Robin**	Lay holde on these. Farre be it I should bring your Majestie, The drinke these two prepared for your taste.
	King	Why, Robin Hoode, be briefe and answere mee. I am amazed at thy troubled lookes.
530	**Robin**	Long will not my ill lookes amaze your Grace. I shortly looke, never to looke againe.
	Marian	Never to looke? What will it still be night? If thou looke never, day can never be. What ailes my Robin? Wherefore dost thou faint?
535	**Robin**	Because I cannot stand; yet now I can. [*King and Marian support him.* Thanks to my King, and thanks to Marian.
	King	Robin, be briefe, and tell us what hath chanst?
	Robin	I must be briefe, for I am sure of death, Before a long tale can be halfeway tolde.
540	**Fitzwater**	Of death, my sonne, bright sunne of all my joy? Death cannot have the power of vertuous life.
	Robin	Not of the vertues, but the life it can.
	King	What dost thou speak of death? How shouldst thou die?
	Robin	By poison and the Priors treachery.
545	**Queene**	Why, take this soveraigne pouder at my hands, Take it and live in spite of poysons power.

| 550 | **Doncaster** | I, set him forward. Powders, quoth ye? Hah, *Aye*
I am a foole then, if a little dust,
The shaving of a horne, a Bezars stone, *(see note)*
Or any antidote have power to stay
The execution of my hearts resolve.
Tut, tut, you labour, lovely Queene, in vaine,
And on a thanklesse groome your toyle bestowe.
Now hath your foe reveng'd you of your foe;
Robin shall die, if all the world sayd no. *even if* |
| 555 | **Marian** | How the wolfe howles! Fly like a tender kid
Into thy sheepeheards bosome. Shield mee love. |

		Canst thou not, Robin? Where shall I be hid?
		O God, these ravens will seaze upon thy dove.
	Robin	They cannot hurt thee, pray thee do not feare,
560		Base curres will couch, the Lyon being neare.
	Queene	How workes my powder?
	Robin	Very well, faire Queene.
	King	Dost thou feele any ease?
	Robin	I shall, I trust, anone:
565		Sleepe fals upon mine eyes.
		O I must sleepe, and they that love me, do not waken me.
	Marian	Sleepe in my lap, and I will sing to thee.
	John	He should not sleepe.
	Robin	I must, for I must die.
570		While I live therfore let me have some rest.
	Fitzwater	I, let him rest; the poyson urges sleepe.
		When he awakes, there is no hope of life.
	Doncaster	Of life? Now by the little time I have to live,
		He cannot live one hower for your lives.
575	**King**	Villaine, what art thou?
	Doncaster	Why, I am a knight.
	Chester	Thou wert indeede.
		If it so please your Grace,
		I will describe my knowledge of this wretch.
580	**King**	Doe, Chester.
	Chester	This Doncaster, for so the fellon hight,
		Was, by the king your father, made a knight,
		And well in armes he did himselfe behave.
		Many a bitter storme, the winde of rage
585		Blasted this realme with, in those woful daies,
		When the unnaturall fights continued,
		Betweene your kingly father and his sonnes.
		This cut-throat, knighted in that time of woe,
		Seaz'd on a beautious nunne at Barkhamsted
590		As wee were marching toward Winchester
		After proud Lincolne was compeld to yield;

Hee tooke this virgine straying in the field,
For all the nunnes and every covent fled
The daungers that attended on our troopes.
595 For those sad times too oft did testifie,
Wars rage hath no regard of pietie.
She humbly praid him, for the love of heaven,
To guid her to her fathers, two miles thence.
He swore he would, and very well he might,
600 For to the campe he was a forager.
Upon the way they came into a wood,
Wherein, in briefe, he stript this tender maid
Whose lust, when she in vaine had long withstood,
Being by strength and torments overlaid,
605 He did a sacrilegious deede of rape
And left her bath'd in her owne teares and blood.
When she reviv'd, she to her fathers got,
And got her father to make just complaint
Unto your mother, being then in campe.

610 **Queene** Is this the villaine Chester, that defilde
Sir Eustace Stutuiles chast and beautious childe?

Doncaster I, Madam, this is hee,
That made a wench daunce naked in a wood;
And for shee did denie what I desirde,
615 I scourg'd her for her pride till her faire skinne
With stripes was checkred like a vintners grate.
And what was this? A mighty matter sure.
I have a thousand more than she defilde,
And cut the squeaking throats of some of them:
620 I grieve I did not hirs.

Queene Punish him, Richard.
A fairer virgine never sawe the sunne.
A chaster maid was never sworne a nunne.

King How scap't the villaine punishment, that time?

625 **Fitzwater** I rent his spurres off, and disgraded him.

Chester And then he raild upon the Queene and mee.
Being committed, he his keeper slue,   *slew*
And to your father fled, who pardond him.

Richard God give his soule a pardon for that sinne.

420

630	**Salsbury**	O had I heard his name, or seene his face,
		I had defended Robin from this chance.
		Ah villaine, shut those gloomy lights of thine,
		Remembrest thou a little sonne of mine,
		Whose nurse at Wilton first thou ravishedst
635		And slew'st two maids that did attend on them?

	Doncaster	I grant, I dasht the braines out of a brat,
		Thine if he were, I care not; had he bin
		The first borne comfort of a royall king,
		And should have yald when Doncaster cried peace,
640		I would have done by him as then I did.

	King	Soone shall the world be rid of such a wretch.
		Let him be hangd alive, in the high way that joyneth to
		the bower.

	Doncaster	Alive or deade, I reck not how I die.
645		You, them, and these, I desperately defie.

	Ely	Repent, or never looke to be absolv'd,
		But die accurst as thou deservest well.

	Doncaster	Then give me my desert; curse one by one.

	Ely	First I accurse thee, and, if thou persist,
650		Unto damnation leave thee wretched man.

	Doncaster	What doe I care for your damnation?
		Am I not doom'd to death? What more damnation
		Can there insue your loud and yelling cryes?

	Prior	Yes divell. Heare thy fellowe spirit speake,	*devil*
655		Who would repent. O faine he would repent.	
		After this bodies bitter punishment,	
		There is an ever-during endlesse woe,	
		A quenchlesse fire, and unconsuming paine,	
		Which desperate soules and bodies must indure.	

660	**Doncaster**	Can you preach this, yet set me on, Sir Prior,
		To runne into this endlesse, quenchlesse fier?

	Prior	High heavens, shewe mercie to my many ils.	
		Never had this bene done, but like a fiend,	
		Thou temptedst me with ceaselesse divelish thoughts.	
665		Therefore I curse, with bitternesse of soule,	
		The hower wherein I saw thy balefull eyes.	*hour*

My eyes I curse, for looking on those eyes.
My eares I curse, for harkning to thy tongue.
I curse thy tongue for tempting of myne eares,
670   Each part I curse, that wee call thine or mine:
Thine for enticing mine, mine following thine.

Doncaster   A holy prayer. What collect have we next?   *offering*
           [*This time Robin stirres.*

Fitzwater   My Marian wanteth words, such is her woe;
675   But old Fitzwater for his girle and him
Begs nothing, but worlds plague for such a foe,
Which causelesse harmd a vertuous noble man,
A pitier of his griefes, when he felt griefe.
Therefore bethinke thee of thy hatefull deede,
680   Thou faithlesse Prior, and thou this ruthlesse theefe.

Prior   Will no man curse me, giving so much cause?
Then, Doncaster, ourselves ourselves accurse,
And let no good betide to thee or mee.

           [*All the yeomen, Frier, Much, Jinny cry.*

685   *All*   Amen, amen: accursed may ye bee,
For murdring Robin, flower of curtesie.

           [*Robin sits up.*

Robin   O ring not such a peale for Robins death;
Let sweete forgivenesse be my passing bell.
690   Art thou there, Marian? Then fly forth my breath.
To die within thy armes contents me well.

Prior   Keepe in, keepe in a little while thy soule,
Till I have powr'd my soule forth at thy feete.   *poured*

Robin   I slept not, unkle; I your griefe did hear.
695   Let Him forgive your soule that bought it deare.
Your bodies deede, I in my death forgive,
And humbly begge the King that you may live.
Stand to your cleargie, unkle, save your life,   *Claim benefit of clergy*
And lead a better life than you have done.

700   *Prior*   O gentle nephew, ah my brothers sonne,
Thou dying glory of old Huntington,
Wishest thou life to such a murdrous foe?
I will not live, sith thou must life forgoe.

		O happie Warman, blessed in thy end,
705		Now too too late thy truth I doe commend.
		O nephew, nephew, Doncaster and I
		Murdred poore Warman, for he did denie
		To joyne with us in this blacke tragedy.
	Robin	Alas, poore Warman. Frier, Little John,
710		I told ye both where Warmans bodie lay.
		And of his buriall Ile dispose anone.
	King	Is there no lawe, Lord Ely, to convict
		This Prior, that confesseth murders thus?
	Ely	He is a hallowed man and must be tried
715		And punisht by the censure of the Church.
	Prior	The Church therin doth erre: God doth allowe
		No canon to preserve a murderers life.
		Richard, King Richard, in thy grandsires daies,
		A law was made, the Cleargie sworne thereto,
720		That whatsoever Church-man did commit
		Treason, or murder, or false felonie,
		Should like a seculer be punished.
		Treason we did, for sure we did intend
		King Richards poisoning, soveraigne of this land.
725		Murder we did in working Warmans end,
		And my deare nephewes, by this fatall hand,
		And theft we did, for we have robd the King,
		The state, the nobles, commons, and his men,
		Of a true peere, firme piller, liberall lord.
730		Fitzwater we have robd of a kinde sonne,
		And Marians love-joyes we have quite undoone.
	Doncaster	Whoppe, what a coyle is here with your confession?
	Prior	I aske but judgement for my foule transgression.
	King	Thy own mouth hath condemned thee.
735		Hence with him.
		Hang this man dead, then see him buried;
		But let the other hang alive in chaines.
	Doncaster	I thank you, sir.

[*Exeunt yeomen, Frier, prisoners, Much.*

740	*John*	Myselfe will goe, my Lord,
		And see sharpe justice done upon these slaves.
	Robin	O goe not hence, Prince John. A word or two
		Before I die I faine would say to you.
	King	Robin, wee see what we are sad to see,
745		Death like a champion treading downe thy life.
		Yet in thy end somwhat to comfort thee,
		Wee freely give to thy betrothed wife,
		Beautious and chast Matilda, all those lands,
		Falne by thy folly, to the Priors hands,
750		And by his fault now forfetted to mee.
		Earle Huntington, she shall thy Countesse bee,
		And thy wight yeomen, they shall wend with mee,	*stout*
		Against the faithlesse enemies of Christ.
	Robin	Bring forth a beere, and cover it with greene,	*bier*

755
                              [A beere is brought in.

                     That on my death-bed I may here sit downe.

                              [Beere brought, he sits.

               At Robins buriall let no blacke be seene,
               Let no hand give for him a mourning gowne:
760   For in his death, his King hath given him life,
               By this large gift, given to his maiden wife.
               Chaist Maid Marilda, Countess of account,
               Chase, with thy bright eyes, all these clouds of woe
               From these faire cheekes, I pray thee sweete do so.
765   Thinke it is bootelesse folly to complaine,
               For that which never can be had againe.
               Queene Elianor, you once were Matilds foe;
               Prince John, you long sought her unlawfull love;
               Let dying Robin Hood intreat you both,
770   To change those passions: Madame, turne your hate,
               To princely love; Prince John, convert your love
               To vertuous passions, chast and moderate.
               O that your gratious right hands would infolde,
               Matildas right hand, prisoned in my palme,
775   And sweare to doe what Robin Hood desires.

	Queene	I sweare I will, I will a mother be,	
		To faire Matildas life and chastitie.	
	John	When John solicites chaste Matildaes eares	
		With lawlesse sutes, as he hath often done,	
780		Or offers to the altars of her eyes,	
		Lascivious poems, stuft with vanities,	*stuffed*
		He craves to see but short and sower daies,	*sour*
		His death be like to Robins he desires,	
		His perjur'd body prove a poysoned prey,	
785		For cowled monkes, and barefoote begging friers.	
	Robin	Inough, inough. Fitzwater, take your child.	
		My dying frost which no sunnes heat can thawe	
		Closes the powers of all my outward parts;	
		My freezing blood runnes backe unto my heart,	
790		Where it assists death, which it would resist.	
		Only my love a little hinders death.	
		For he beholds her eyes and cannot smite.	
		Then goe not yet, Matilda, stay a while.	
		Frier, make speede, and list my latest will.	
795	*Matilda*	O let mee looke forever in thy eyes,	
		And lay my warme breath to thy bloodlesse lips,	
		If my sight can restraine deaths tyrannies,	
		Or keepe lives breath within thy bosome lockt.	
	Robin	Away, away,	
800		Forbeare, my love; all this is but delay.	
	Fitzwater	Come, maiden daughter, from my maiden sonne,	
		And give him leave to doe what must be done.	
	Robin	First I bequeath my soule to all soules Saver,	*Saviour*
		And will my bodie to be buried	
805		At Wakefield, underneath the abbey wall.	
		And in this order make my funerall:	
		When I am dead, stretch me upon this beere,	
		My beades and primer shall my pillowe bee;	*rosary; prayer book*
		On this side lay my bowe, my good shafts here,	
810		Upon my brest the crosse, and underneath	
		My trustie sworde, thus fastned in the sheath.	
		Let Warmans bodie at my feete be laid,	
		Poore Warman, that in my defence did die;	

		For holy dirges, sing me wodmens songs	
815		As ye to Wakefield walke, with voices shrill.	
		This for myselfe. My goods and plate I give	
		Among my yeomen; them I doe bestowe	
		Upon my Soveraigne, Richard. This is all.	
		My liege farewell, my love, farewell, farewell.	
820		Farewell, faire Queene, Prince John and noble lords.	
		Father Fitzwater, heartily adieu,	
		Adieu, my yeomen tall.	
		Matilda, close mine eyes.	
		Frier farewell, farewell to all.	

| 825 | *Matilda* | O must my hands with envious death conspire, | |
| | | To shut the morning gates of my lives light? | |

| | *Fitzwater* | It is a duetie, and thy loves desire, | *duty* |
| | | Ile helpe thee girle to close up Robins sight. | |

	King	Laments are bootelesse, teares cannot restore	
830		Lost life. Matilda, therefore weepe no more.	
		And since our mirth is turned into mone,	*moan*
		Our merry sport, to tragick funerall,	
		Wee will prepare our power for Austria,	
		After Earle Roberts timelesse buriall.	*untimely*
835		Fall to your wod-songs therefore, yeoman bold,	*(see note)*
		And deck his herse with flowers, that lov'd you deare,	
		Dispose his goods as hee hath them dispos'd.	
		Fitzwater and Matilda, bide you here.	
		See you the bodie unto Wakefield borne,	
840		A little wee will beare yee company,	
		But all of us at London point to meete.	
		Thither, Fitzwater, bring Earle Robins men:	
		And Frier, see you come along with them.	

	Frier	Ah, my liege Lord, the Frier faints,	
845		And hath no words to make complaints;	
		But since he must forsake this place,	
		He will awaite, and thanks, your Grace.	

	Song:	Weepe, weepe, ye wod-men waile,	
		Your hands with sorrow wring:	
850		Your master Robin Hood lies deade,	
		Therefore sigh as you sing.	

		Here lies his primer and his beades,	*prayer book*
		His bent bowe and his arrowes keene,	
		His good sworde and his holy crosse,	
855		Now cast on flowers fresh and greene:	
		And as they fall, shed teares and say,	
		Wella, wella day, wella, wella day;	
		Thus cast yee flowers and sing,	
		And on to Wakefield take your way.	[*Exeunt all except Frier.*

860	**Frier**	Here dothe the Frier leave with grievance.
		Robin is deade, that grac't his entrance;
		And being dead he craves his audience,
		With this short play, they would have patience.

[*Enter Chester.*

865	**Chester**	Nay, Fryer, at request of thy kinde friend,
		Let not thy Play so soone be at an end.
		Though Robin Hoode be deade, his yeomen gone,
		And that thou thinkst there now remaines not one,
		To act an other Sceane or two for thee;
870		Yet knowe full well, to please this company,
		We meane to end Matildaes Tragedie.

	Frier	Off then, I with you, with your Kendall greene:
		Let not sad griefe in fresh aray be seene.
		Matildaes storie is repleat with teares,
875		Wrongs, desolations, ruins, deadly feares.
		In, and attire yee. Though I tired be,
		Yet will I tell my mistresse Tragedie.

[*As Friar Tuck announces the woes to follow, Chorus (played perhaps by Chester, who must have exited after line 872), appears in black. Tuck says we must "suppose king Richard now is deade, / And John, resistlesse [i.e., without resistence], is faire Englands Lord" (lines 903–04). Chorus introduces a dumb show which reveals three dreams of the sleeping King John:* **Austria** *appears, tempting him to add to his kingdom by conquest, but the king puts by* **Ambition**. **Constance** *(wife of Geoffrey, Henry II's third son, who was John's older brother) then appears (line 937) leading her young son Arthur, Duke of Brittany; both seek the crown but King John's foot "overturneth them" (line 938). Next,* **Insurrection**, *led by the French King and Lord Hugh le Brun, brings the child Arthur back to menace the king; this time when the king's foot overthrows Arthur he is taken up dead (line 943) and* **Insurrection** *flees. In the third dumb show/dream Queen Isabel (John's second wife), with her two children (the Princes Henry and Richard), wrings her hands while John turns his attention to chaste Matilda in mourning veil. Smitten by love, John resumes his "sutes,* *devices, practices and threats: / And when he sees all serveth to no end, / Of chaste Matilda let him make an end" (lines 891–93). During the next 2100 lines Matilda never yields to his pressure, takes refuge in a convent, but ultimately is poisoned by Brand, one of John's agents. The dying Matilda forgives her executioner, who, in remorse, confesses to having slain a hundred "with mine owne hands" (line 2621), including Lady Bruce and her young son George at Windsor Castle (lines 2622–23). Brand, stunned by Matilda's virtuous behavior at her death, escapes during the confusion and, Judas-like, hangs himself with his own garters in a tree. The branch breaks and his "bones and flesh / lie gasht together in a poole of bloode" (lines 2694–95). Bruce, who arrives too late to save his mother and brother, seizes Windsor Castle, and the barons confront King John, knowing that King Louis of France has landed in England to support their cause against the king. But they will not serve Louis: "can noble English hearts beare the French yoke?" (line 2998). When Queen Isabel, who sides with the rebel barons, allows that they know not the French king's nature — he may be worse than John — Bruce makes peace with John, who, having learned of Matilda's death, is now deeply repentent (lines 878–3033):]*

	Bruse	Of Windsor Castle here the keyes I yield.
3035	**King John**	Thanks, Bruse. Forgive mee, and I pray thee see Thy mother and thy brother buried.

            [Bruse offers to kisse [the dead] *Matilda.*

            In Windsor Castle Church, doe kisse her cheeke.
            Weepe thou on that, on this side I will weepe.

3040	**Queene**	Chaste virgine, thus I crowne thee with these flowers.
	King John	Let us goe on to Dunmow with this maid; Among the hallowed nunnes let her be laide. Unto her tombe, a monthly pilgrimage Doth King John vowe in penance for this wrong.
3045		Goe forward maids; on with Matildaes herse, And on her toombe see you ingrave this verse:

                Within this marble monument, doth lye
                Matilda martyrde for her chastitie.   *[Exeunt.*

                 Epilogus.

3050   Thus is Matildaes story showne in act.
            And rough heawen out by an uncunning hand,
            Being of the most materiall points compackt,
            That with the certainst state of truth doe stand.

                 FINIS.

Notes

The excerpts of *The Death of Robert, Earle of Huntington* are based on the Malone Society's edited text in facsimile type (1965 [1967]) of William Leake's 1601 quarto printing, prepared by John C. Meagher. The full title in Leake was *The Death of Robert, Earle of Huntington. Otherwise called Robin Hood of merrie Sherwodde: with the lamentable Tragedie of chaste Matilda, his faire maid Marian.* Imprinted at London, for William Leake, 1601. Line count corresponds to the idiosyncracies of Meagher's 1967 edition. Meagher based his reconstructed facsimile on the fourteen known copies of Leake's printing of the play, using xerographs of the Harvard copy as his base text against which he collated the two copies in the British Library, the two in the Bodleian, and the Lincoln College, Oxford, copy. He then checked variants against the other eight copies. Leake prints proper names in roman type, the text in black letter, and parentheticals in italics. I have ignored these distinctions in this edition. In the 4° version, speakers are identified in various ways: e.g., Prince John, later King John, may be *Pr. Iohn*, *Prin.*, *Ioh.*, and, at the end of the play, *King*. I have identified speakers in boldface type and, space permitting, expanded Leake's abbreviations to give the full name; I usually have followed his designations, however, so Marian, for example, appears as *Marian*, *Marilda*, and *Matilda*, and Prince John according to the designation printed in Leake. I have silently expanded all abbreviations of pronouns, prepositions, and conjunctions and followed the Middle English Texts Series policy of adjusting u/v and i/j to modern spelling. I have placed glosses of hard words in a smaller italic type at the right margin. I have not followed Leake's punctuation or idiosyncratic capitalizations, but have, rather, adhered to modern conventions, except where noted. I have not altered L's formations of genitive constructions, however; they remain as his compositor presented them. I have treated stage directions uniformly, marking them in italics at ends of lines, if that is where they appear in Leake, or between lines, but inset, if that is how they appear, since Meagher includes them, along with scene designations, in his line count in the edited facsimile edition.

Abbreviations: L = Leake's 1601 black-letter 4° edition. C = Collier's 1828 edition. H = Hazlitt's 1874 edition. F = Farmer's 1913 facsimile edition. M = Meagher, with date identifying appropriate edition.

1   *Scene I.* L: *Sceane I.* In this play L marks scene divisions, which are included in the line count. They were not so marked in *The Downfall.*

4–10   The irregular lines in this opening prose passage are headed by a large capital H in the 1601 edition, after which full length lines 11–16 complete the passage. I have maintained L's line division for the sake of reference to M's Malone Society edition.

4–16   Friar Tuck, with his rough Skeltonics, provides the play's Induction, somewhat as Skelton did in *The Downfall*. H suggests that the same actor played both roles (p. 219). In his bustle the Friar forgets even the plot (line 13) as Robin's Yeomen hunt for an audience ("the goodly heart") rather than deer; meanwhile, without missing a word, Tuck puts on his costume before our very eyes, then, in line 34, takes it off again to set the first scene. After Robin's death, the Friar takes his leave (lines 860 ff.) only to be interrupted by Chester, who objects that the play ends too soon, whereupon, Tuck provides a second Induction for the remainder of the play, serving as director and stage manager as the dumb show to *Matildaes Tragedie* (line 871) is introduced. Compare his role in *The Downfall*, where Skelton is also in and out of character for comic effect.

1–863   It seems likely that some version of these lines was originally the conclusion to *The Downfall*. M (1980) suggests that the reintroduction of Skelton may once have been part of the ending of *The Downfall*, rounding the play off by returning to the role he had in the Induction (p. 83); M also notes that no fewer than thirteen characters disappear permanently after Robin's death. Most had roles in *The Downfall*.

7–8   *followed*. C and H emend to *follow*. M (1980) accepts *to followed*, as ellipsis for "to have followed," but allows that the C/H emendation may be sound.

17   Now in his role, the Friar moves into verse to present his Prologue.

18   *where wee left*. The Friar alludes to *The Downfall*, or Part I, which has, presumably, preceded this production. Such lines must have been added to what was once the conclusion to *The Downfall* as it was converted to what Henslowe referred to as Part II.

28   *Hurt*. H emends to *Housed*, explaining that there are two inside plotting together (p. 220). But in line 202 we learn that both men have been wounded in the field *but yesterday*, thus explaining their *hurt* today. See *The Downfall*, lines 2495–98, where we learn of their wounding and Robin's rescue of their lives.

41   *Mounted in a stand.* Blinds were set up with bowmen in them toward which the game is driven with the hounds and hallooing. Queen Eleanor is herself presented as a bowman, as well she may have been. See Malory, Bk. XVIII, *The Great Tournament*, where ladies hunt with bow the "barayne hynde" but wound the resting Lancelot in the buttock by an accidental overshot.

43–44   According to Turbervile, *The Noble Arte of Venerie or Hunting* (1575), a stag is a five-year-old male and a buck a six-year-old. See M's notes (1980) on hunting details in the play.

49   *and.* L: *aud*; so too in lines 619, 714, 715, all compositor's errors.

54   To wear horns is to be cuckolded.

66   The speech prefix is omitted by L, but the lines are clearly spoken by Much in answer to the King. H's emendation, which I have followed.

82   *A plague upon his kindnesse, let him die.* Pairs of lurking villains who compete in villainy are common in Elizabethan and Jacobean drama. Robin's virtues are like goads to both Doncaster, a practiced murderer (see lines 83 and 297), and Robin's kinsman the Prior, who would destroy him simply because he is good. Together they embody the Machiavellian self-interest of the first two estates, the gentry and the church, against which the virtuous Robin so often competed and sought redress.

95   *Here is the poyson.* Both Sir Doncaster and the Prior are hypocrites who would rely on poison to accomplish their insidious evil while they practice their *policy* (line 99) and smilingly (line 247) profess to be helping Robin.

96   *by this gold.* Apparently Doncaster is bribing the Prior as well as playing upon his jealous hatred of Robin.

100   *To make him die disgrac't.* The jealous cousin's desire is not simply to murder Robin but to destroy his honor as well by having him unwittingly slay his friend the King through his acts of kindness.

104   C omits the *Exeunt*; M (1980) discusses the problem of taking the Prior and Doncaster off stage simply to bring them back on, observing: "it is never safe

to take exit-lines too seriously. It may be that the scene-heading and the *exeunt* were both added by another hand" (p. 533).

108   *[Enter Frier.* Not in L; C's emendation.

111   *murren.* "Hullabaloo" or "turmoil," but more literally "pestilence."

112   *The King cals for thee.* King Richard, desiring to have the letters upon the copper ring read, calls upon the Friar. Although the King is apparently unable to read himself, he is able to recognize the script as being English. See note to lines 388–91.

113–14   L places these lines in parentheses, which I have omitted.

148   *mine.* L: *minde.* C's emendation.

157   *not.* L: *uot*; a compositor's error.

165   *fairings.* Gifts brought from the fair. The implication is that Robin's presentations are tawdry and self-serving.

170   *Envie.* Warman sees through their "toyes" (line 142) and labels their villainy precisely.

210   *Conscience.* Envious Doncaster personifies Warman as Conscience, which he hates and has effectively slain in himself; he thus slays Warman as affirmation of his own dead conscience.

219   *[Enter Robin.* Not in L; C's emendation.

234   *murdered.* Suicide is self-murder, and thus a mortal sin. See line 244 where Robin grieves for Warman's presumably lost soul.

235   *[Exeunt Robin, Doncaster, with body.* L: *Exit.*

251   *Rome.* By claiming that the elixir came from Rome, the Prior insidiously suggests holy benefaction by papal endorsement.

252   *Moly* is the fabulous herb endowed with magical powers that protected Odysseus from Circe's charms and left him sexually superior. Precisely what plant it might be is unclear, though it is identified by some in Renaissance lore with mandrake root and by others with wild garlic, which was thought by some to have the power to ward off evil spirits.

      Syrian Balsamum. An aromatic resin thought to have soothing properties; sometimes called balm of Gilead or balsam of Mecca.

253   *Golds rich Elixir.* The elixer that would turn base metals into gold was sought by alchemists. Gold dust in liquid suspension was thought to have medicinal properties that could transform ill to good health. It was used into the eighteenth century in quack medicine. See Chaucer's Physician who, since "gold in phisik is a cordial, / Therefore he lovede gold in special" (CT I[A] 443–44).

263   *cosin.* In line 285 the Prior refers to Robin as his nephew and in line 700 as *gentle nephew . . . my brothers sonne.* Cousin here is a more general term for kinsman, frequently applied to nephew or niece, with a pun perhaps on "cousin" as victim, i.e., one who has been tricked, or "cousined." See also lines 293 and 307 where Robin is also identified as the Prior's cousin.

264   *Sophies sonne.* The Grand Sophy of Persia, a legendary ruler of fabulous wealth and power. See romances such as *The Sowdon of Babylon*, where his son is Firambras who betrays him, or *The Tragical Reign of Selimus* (1594) where the virtuous Sophy is poisoned by his villainous sons. M notes that *Sophies* "is here anachronistic, since the rulers of Persia were so styled only after ca. 1500" (1980, p. 535). *Sowdon* is the medieval equivalent. Perhaps the *Sophies sonne* is in this instance the *Souldans sonne*, admiral of the Turkish fleet, defeated by Richard in *The Downfall*, line 1871. There the source may be *Kynge Rycharde Coeur du Lyon.*

265   *Natolia.* See Marlowe's *Tamburlaine, Pt. II* (1590). According to Ethel Seaton "Natolia is much more than the modern Anatolia; it is the whole promontary of Asia Minor, with a boundary running approximately from the modern Bay of Iskenderun eastward toward Aleppo, and then north to Batum on the Black Sea" — "Marlowe's Map," *Essays and Studies by Members of the English Association*, 10 (1924), 20. It appears also in *The Tragical Reign of Selimus* (1594) as a walled city of the Turkish empire.

267–68   *to you / I put myselfe*. A characteristic device of the con-man is to put himself in his would-be victim's debt as a means of allaying suspicion.

280   *dissolved pearle*. Pliny, *Natural History,* IX, lines 119–21, tells how Cleopatra scorned Antony's sumptuous feasting and bet that she could spend ten million sesterces on a single banquet. When Anthony mocked her after the main course she took a glass of vinegar and dissolved in it one of the finest pearls seen by man and drank it, thus winning the bet. English Renaissance playwrights delighted in this image of luxury and often drew upon it: e.g., Ben Jonson, *Volpone* III.vii.192 (Herford and Simpson edn.); Hoy (*Dramatic Works of Thomas Dekker*, III, 292–93) cites other references: Dekker, *The Wonder of a Kingdom* III.i.50–51; and Nashe, *The Unfortunate Traveller*, II, 267), and Dekker in his commendatory verses to Brome's *The Northern Lasse* alludes to the marvel, as does *The Owles Almanacke* (1618) C2v. And, Thomas Rogers in "Leicester's Ghost" (c. 1598) writes: "What if I drinke nothing but liquid gold / Lactrina, christal, pearle resolv'd in wine, / Such as th' Egyptians full cups did hold, / When Cleopatra with her lord did dine; / A trifle, care not, for the cost was mine?" (lines 526–30). Pliny's modern editor, H. Rackham, in the Loeb Classic edition III, 244, is more sceptical and asserts that no such soluable vinegar exists and that Cleopatra "no doubt swallowed the pearl in vinegar knowing that it could be recovered later on."

306   *I cannot tel. O yes, now I ha't.* Like Iago, Doncaster has trouble explaining reasons for his hatred: he just hates. Bernard Spivack, *Shakespeare and the Allegory of Evil: The History of a Metaphor in Relation to His Major Villains* (New York: Columbia University Press, 1958), pp. 362–64, discusses Doncaster's villainous hatred in this passage at some length, stressing his professional pride in his villainy.

308–09   Doncaster provides a casebook definition of Envy in his hatred of Robin *Because so many love him as there doe, / And I myselfe am loved of so fewe.* See Gower's *Confessio Amantis*, Book II, where the first aspect of Envy is grief at another man's joy and the second joy at another man's grief.

310 ff.   Doncaster's litany of *reasons for my hate* defines the villain's practiced love of evil, in which he takes a kind of professional atheistic pride. In this regard he might be compared to Shakespeare's most envious villian, Iago, who begrimes all he looks upon.

314   *greedie cormorants*. A long-necked sea-bird of voracious appetite; in Renaissance figurative language "an insatiably greedy or rapacious person" (OED, sb. 2), with the idiom "money-cormorant" in popular usage. Elyot (*Gov.* III, xxii) speaks of such people as cormorants to which "neither lande, water, ne ayre mought be sufficient"; Shakespeare, *Richard II* II.i.38, speaks of the "insatiate cormorant," and Greene (1592), *Upstart Courtier* in the *Harliean Miscellany* II.21, speaks of "cormorants or usurers . . . gathered to fill their coffers." Sometimes spelled "corvorant," as in Holinshed II.704, with pun on L. *vorantem*, "devouring" (OED, sb. 3). That Doncaster specifies peasants to be greedy cormorants, along with the privileged, simply reflects his aristocratic view that he should have the wealth, the upstart lesser people nothing.

317   *no theefe*. Doncaster's point is that Robin was outlawed for financial reasons, not thievery, and thus abuses the good name of thief and outlaw that he (Doncaster) so villainously upholds.

356–57   *A boone, a boone . . . thee*. The phrasing often occurs in Robin Hood ballads. See, for example, *Robin Hood and the Curtal Friar*, lines 97–98.

360–61   *O there dwelleth a jolly pinder . . . on a greene*. H observes that the lines are taken, with slight change, from *The Jolly Pinder of Wakefield* (p. 232). Compare lines 1–2 of *The Jolly Pinder* in the present edition.

378–83   Ritson, *Notes and Illustrations of Robin Hood* (1828, I, 62), notes that Fitzwater confuses Harold Harefoot, the son and successor of Canute the Great, with Harold Godwin. M (1980) suggests that the confusion may be Fitzwater's rather than the dramatist's (pp. 537–38).

388–91   The King's sense of linguistics exceeds his wisdom in natural history. It does not seem to bother him that the deer would have to be some 1200 years old. His proof against Chester's suggestion that Julius Caesar may have banded the deer is that English is not written until after the establishment of the Saxons in the seventh century. Ritson (*Robin Hood* [London, 1832], p. lxxi) cites an inscription in *Rays Itineraries* (1760), p. 153, wherein a stag is found two miles from Leeds with a ring of brass about its neck with the inscription: "When Julius Caesar here was king, / About my neck he put this ring: / Whosoever doth me take, / Let me go for Caesar's sake." Perhaps Chester had been reading Pliny, *Nat. Hist.* VIII, 32, who mentions a deer over a hundred years old with a collar placed upon it by Alexander or Turbervile (v. 41n.), who says that

"Hartes and Hyndes may liue an hundreth yeres .... And wee finde in auncient hystoriographers, that an Harte was taken, a hauing [sic] coller about his necke full three hundreth yeares after the death of Cesar, in which coller *Caesars* armes were engraued, and a note written, saying, *Caesarus me fecit*." See M's excellent note (1980, p. 537).

445   *yee*. L: *you*. C/H's emendation for the sake of rhyme; followed by M (1980).

455   *with a trice*. H emends to *in a trice*, objecting that *with* lies outside Renaissance idiom and is "no doubt wrong" (p. 235). But the emendation is unnecessary.

458   *[Enter Much*. Not in L. C's emendation.

473   H identifies Jinny as "a country wench" whose language (*strawed*) is dialectical.

505   *[Exeunt Prior, Doncaster, and Frier*. L omits Doncaster. C's emendation.

518   *a cuppe, a towell*. M (1980) notes: "These may be brought on as instruments for bleeding Robin in attempt to counteract the poison, but nothing is done with them. It will be remembered that all extant versions of Robin Hood's death written before this play have him meet his end by being bled to death under the pretense of a medical bleeding" (p. 539).

534   H's stage direction.

535   *Thanks*. L: *Thans*. Certainly a compositor's error.

548   Shavings of animal horns were thought to be medicinal. Harts-horn shavings were said to be a preservative against poison, so perhaps that is the powder the Queen produces. M cites *Ioyfull News* (V.252n) on use of the unicorn's horn "for swilling in a drink as a precaution against poison (MM 2)" and identifies *Bezars stone* as a ruminant calcitrant, which "made into a pouder, in all kinde of venome ... is the most principal remedy that we know nowe, and that which hath wrought best effect in many that haue beene poysoned" (*Ioyfull News*, BB3v), noting that GG4v ff. has a separate treatise on the Bezar stone (1980, pp. 539–40). H cites Thomas Browne, *Vulgar Errors* (1658): "Lapis lasuli hath

in it a purgative faculty, we know: That *Bezoar* is *antidotal*, Lapis Judaicus diuretical, Coral antipilaptical, we will not deny." According to Browne, the bezoar nut has a "leguminous smell and taste, bitter like a lupine."

552–53   *thanklesse groome . . . foe.* M notes the reference to "the early part of the *Downfall*, where Eleanor becomes Robert's bitter enemy when he 'thanklessly' refuses her love (v. *Downfall*, lines 657–58). From this it may be inferred that the double-triangle shown in the opening part of the *Downfall* was retained when *Downfall* 1–781 was revised" (1980, p. 540).

555   *How the wolfe howles.* Marian recognizes that she is among wolves who would destroy her, were it not for Robin's protection. By the end of the play the *ravens will seaze upon thy dove* (line 558), but she will fly to heaven, unharmed, except by mortal poison.

560   *Lyon.* Robin knows that King Richard the Lion-Hearted will defend Marian, as long as he lives.

576   *I am a knight.* Doncaster audaciously claims the knighthood denied him earlier when his spurs were stripped. See note to line 625.

582   *your father.* I.e., Henry II, Queen Eleanor's husband, whose role as queen mother in *The Downfall* is prominent.

616   *vintners grate.* "The *grate* of a vintner was no doubt what is often-termed in old writers the red lattice, grate, or checkered pattern painted on the doors of vintners, and still preserved at almost every public house" (H, p. 241). See also John Brand, *Popular Antiquities of Great Britain, Comprising Notices of the Moveable and Immoveable Feasts. Customs, Superstitions, and Amusements Past and Present*, with large corrections and additions by W. Carew Hazlitt. 3 volumes (London: John Russell Smith, 1870), II, 277–78, where there are citations of the figure in several Renaissance plays.

625   *rent his spurres off.* To win one's spurs is to be knighted (OED, *spurs*, sb. 3). To remove the spurs is to degrade the knight, to un-knight him, so to speak, thus denying him participation in the honored roles of chivalry. Bradford B. Broughton, *Dictionary of Medieval Knighthood and Chivalry* (New York: Greenwood Press, 1986), cites instances of the degraded knight's spurs being thrown onto a dung heap (pp. 156–57); such disgrace might lead to hanging or

exile, but, at least, being cast out of privilege. Grant Uden, *A Dictionary of Chivalry* (New York: Thomas Crowell, 1968), cites the example of Sir Francis Mitchell's spurs being "hewn off his heels and thrown, one one way, the other the other" (p. 160). It is this degradation as much as the crimes themselves that prohibits Doncaster from being seen amongst certain aristocratic company, where, should he reappear, he would be pursued to his death. Thus he needs the Prior to do the poisoning for him. See lines 87–100, where the two plan that Robin himself die disgraced, and line 576 where Doncaster tenaciously proclaims his knighthood.

643   *bower*. L: *power*. C/H emendation, followed by M (1980).

689   *Let sweete forgivenesse be my passing bell*. M (1980, p. 30) suggests that this may be the play's principal theme, if it may be said to have one. Matilda, at the end, will likewise so overwhelm Brand, her murderer, with her forgiveness that he, smitten with remorse, hangs himself.

714   Ely identifies the Prior as churchman and thus not subject to secular law. But the Prior knows the law better than his fellow churchman or king and seals his own doom (lines 716 ff.).

737   *hang alive in chaines*. According to *The Common-Welthe of England* (1589) the most notable murderers were hanged in cords till they be dead and then "hanged with chaines while they rotte in the ayre." But before Elizabeth's reform the most villainous murderers were subject to the extraordinary torture of being hanged alive in chains. Henry Chettle, in *England's Mourning Garment* (1603), praises Elizabeth for her accepting of the death penalty as sufficient punishment in itself. See M (1980), p. 542.

753   *Against the faithlesse enemies of Christ*. King Richard announces his second crusade against the infidel on which he will take Robin's yeomen as his own. Thus they will not be available to help Marian against John as they were in *The Downfall*. The king's crusade figures prominently in subsequent Robin Hood adventures, where the king sets off not only prior to Robin's death but prior to there being a need for Robin and his yeomen.

762   *Chaist Maid Marilda*. The spelling seems intentional. Here we find the two titles blended as Maid Marian, assuming the role of Countess of Huntington, resumes her noble name. Henceforth, after this moment as *Marilda*, she is Matilda.

806–11 Robin's stylized composing of his bier reflects the ballad tradition as well as Renaissance stage conventions. See *Robin Hood's Death*, lines 133–42, in this volume.

835 *wod-songs*. This term does not appear in the OED, but evidently refers to the lament sung by Robin's *wod-men*, lines 848–59. Perhaps a pun is intended in *wod* (madness>grief); or perhaps *wod* simply alludes to the wood and its woodsmen, Robin's yeomen, that is, the common people who have joined him. The King exhorted Matilda and the nobility to cease their lamentation — *Laments are bootlesse, teares cannot restore / Lost life. Matilda, therefore weepe no more* (lines 829–30) — as if to suggest that the shrill keening be performed by the common folk, while the nobility piously reflect upon life's transience.

859 *all except Frier*. Added to *Exeunt* by C/H.

871ff. *Matildaes Tragedie*. In constructing this portion of the new play, for which the author(s) borrowed lines from the conclusion to an earlier version of *The Downfall* (see note to lines 1–863 above), Munday has drawn heavily for plot details upon Michael Drayton's *The Legend of Matilda* (1594; augmented, 1596), where King John lecherously pursues Lord Fitzwater's daughter, grieviously harming the nation's welfare. Drayton's poem was popular, which may account in part for the desire of theater impressario Philip Henslowe and the prolific playwright Henry Chettle to sponsor the new play as a sequel to *The Downfall*. Chettle may have assisted in the restructuring of the play into two parts to take advantage of the popularity of Drayton's poem by shifting the plot to the melodramatic hardships and death of the virtuous Matilda. The adaptation and continuation must have taken place rapidly, for Philip Henslowe purchased for the Admirals Men Munday's first Robin Hood play on 15 February 1597/98 and within five days made an initial payment for its sequel, which may not yet have been written. By the end of March the Master of the Revels licensed the two parts of "the downefall of earlle huntington surnamed Roben Hood," and the two plays were performed at the Rose Theatre.

872 *Kendall greene*. Perhaps referring to Chester, who at this point exits, though it seems odd that he would be dressed as a yeoman. Perhaps Chester put on green at Robin's dying request that none wear black. Or, perhaps, he's still in green from the previous play where Robin and the barons greet the returning King Richard, all dressed in green. See *The Downfall*, lines 2699–2700.

3034   *Bruse* is the younger of the play's two (or perhaps three) Bruces who, as kinsmen to the banished Fitzwater (Matilda's father), lead the opposition to John. See M's extended discussion of the confusions (1980, pp. 554–56).

3036   Bruce's mother and brother had been murdered earlier. Their bodies were displayed as Bruce drew back a curtain (line 2778) to reveal them in "this wide gappe" (line 2865) through some sort of stage arras designed as a discovery space. M's note on staging of the scene is useful (1980, pp. 575–76).

3040   The Queen is now Isabel. Earlier in the play she, misled by John, had attacked Matilda, tearing her hair and scratching her face. When Matilda subsequently defended the queen from having done so, putting the blame on the soldiers instead, Isabel honored her for her chastity and kindness and became her defender. At the end she reappears at Matilda's death, holding her in her arms to comfort her as Matilda forgives her enemies and dies, instructing her soul: *Fly forth my soule, heavens king be there thy friend* (line 2667).

3041   *Dunmow*. A Priory in Essex, historically under the patronage of Fitzwater.

3048   *Matilda martyrde for her chastitie*. Despite the sprawling structure of the play, the deaths of virtuous Robin and Marian/Matilda by poison provide a striking symmetry which Matilda, with gratitude to her executioner, emphatically recognized herself (lines 2589–2603).

Robin Hood and His Crew of Souldiers

Introduction

This play is preserved in a quarto pamphlet printed for James Davis in London in 1661 and, according to the title page, played in Nottingham on August 23rd of that year, the day of Charles II's coronation. Dobson and Taylor reprinted the text with a brief introduction (1976, pp. 237–42).

As a play, especially a Robin Hood play, this is unusual in that all genuine action takes place off stage. It begins with a distant shout and Little John goes off to discover what is happening, to return with news of the Restoration and the repression of all outlaws as rebels, including themselves. The king's messenger is resisted by the outlaws in argumentative mood, but when he invokes the king's royal authority Robin gives in at once, saying "I am quite another man; thaw'd into conscience of my Crime & Duty; melted into loyalty & respect to vertue" (lines 131–33).

Just as the play is less exciting than the usual vigorous action of a short Robin Hood drama, so are its politics new. This is a long way from the Robin who, while respecting the king, firmly resisted his authority, and the servile reception of the messenger is markedly different from the ruthless treatment of royal agents in earlier ballads.

However, neither the inactivity nor the royalism of this play are to be clearly sourced to the equally conservative gentrified tradition: this Robin is not seen as the noble dissident of Munday or Martin Parker, but simply presented as a criminal who becomes a post-war convert to the victorious cause. He is the social bandit rejected rather than the gentleman adapted. Nevertheless, the ideas of the play are not without context: the title may reflect Parker's use of "crew" in a somewhat negative sense (lines 38, 214, 466), just as the reading of Robin Hood as a revolutionary can be linked to a remark by Robert Cecil who in a letter of 1605 referred to the anti-parliament Gunpowder plotters as "the Robin Hoods in your part of the country" (Knight, 1994, p. 42). Closer yet in date, the arch-conservative jurist Edward Coke shared the messenger's view of Robin. Although he located him in Richard I's time, he described his actions in a contemporary criminal way as "robbery, burning of houses, felony, waste and spoile" (1634, p. 197).

The setting in Nottingham also relates to political events. This was where Charles raised his standard in 1642, but the city soon came under parliamentarian rule, and

441

towards the end of the war its leaders did not readily accept royal rule. Francis Harker was executed in 1660 for refusing to recant, and although Colonel John Hutchinson, a major local leader, was reprieved, he refused to conform fully and died in jail in 1664. There were clearly reasons why the anti-royal spirit of Nottingham, as represented by its most famous resistant hero, needed to be theatrically and publicly constrained on coronation day — a process in which the old communal character of the Robin Hood play-game was appropriated by the triumphant royalist state.

Unique though it is, and uniquely political in its thrust, *Robin Hood and his Crew of Souldiers* seems to belong to a renaissance of Robin Hood publication shortly after the Restoration. This may in part be caused by the general flood of cultural activity in newly relaxed conditions, but it is striking how many of the texts from this period effectively divert the resistant force of the hero into less radical modes. The gentrified life of 1662, the inherently pacific garland of 1663, the generalized blandness of *Robin Hood's Birth, Breeding, Valour, and Marriage* are other examples of a market-oriented and politically conservative recreation of what closer examination may show to be a Restoration Robin Hood, with this short play as the political cutting edge of that reformed figure.

A notable feature of the play in formal terms is its abandonment of sub-Shakespearean blank verse for prose after the opening scene. Originally it seems the stylistic change is for Little John to speak, but the dialogue remains in prose until the final song. This reduced stylistic grandeur matches the displacement of the outlaws as heroes. It also permits the play to lay out lucidly certain positions for rejection, and lets the messenger's determined king-worship have the appropriate modern form of a sermon.

It is noticeable that the outlaws represent a range of attitudes that are, post-Civil War, regarded as unacceptable. John at first sees their only values as enjoying "the sweets of theft and roguery," but a little later he takes a more principled position of dissent by speaking like one of the Levellers, that hard-core of revolutionaries:

> Every brave soule is born a King; rule and command o're the fearfull rabble, is natures stamp; courage and lofty thoughts are not ever confin'd to Thrones, nor still th' appendages of an illustrious birth, but the thatcht Hovell or the simple Wood oft times turns forth a mind as fully fraught with Gallantry and true worth as doth the marble Pallace . . . (lines 65–69)

Robin espouses a different rationale for resistance, and one that opposes royal rule from a quite different quarter. He asks "Why then should the severities of obedience, and the strait niceties of Law shackle this Noble soul, whom nature meant not onely free but soveraigne . . ." (lines 77–78). Stating that it is only "an easie fondnesse" (i.e., weak-mindedness) that allows men "to be manacled by Lawes" he, speaking as a "bold daring Spirit," sums up with a swashbuckling spirit, in a voice of curiously cavalier-sounding, yet actually anti-state, private interest:

> No we have Swords, and Arms, and Lives equally engaged in our past account, and whilest these Armes can wield our Swords, or our uncurdl'd blood give vigor to those Arms, hopes of submission are as vain as is the strange request. (lines 92–95)

Ill-matched as John's socialism and Robin's rampant — almost Hobbesian — individualism might seem, they are both in fact implicit in some of the earlier material: the social bandit tradition can be re-read in the highly charged politicized context of post-Civil War England as a "levelling" position, and Martin Parker represented Robin as something like a rogue Cavalier. Both positions are equally dangerous to the monarchist state and are explored and rejected in this intriguing play.

Opposite as it is to the spirit and the vigor of most of the Robin Hood material, *Robin Hood and his Crew of Souldiers* still focusses on recurrent features of the myth: Robin is the leader, but others have a powerful and somewhat dissenting voice; loyalty is the central value, though here it is constrained into being loyal to the king and his officers, not to the outlaw band; and the text ends with a festal celebration, but that too is reconstructed. Not a celebration of forest fraternity, it is a suddenly imposed and distinctly literary royalist song which, for all its musicality, offers by way of climax the "halters" of execution and the "perpetual brand" of ferocious law. The text finally explores those fierce threats of violence and constraint that actually underlay the allegedly glorious Restoration and are shown in their full propaganda form in this remarkable play, which, while being in itself quite untheatrical, is nevertheless the most dramatic of all the reversals in the Robin Hood tradition.

Select Bibliography

Text

Anon. *Robin Hood and His Crew of Souldiers.* London: Davis, 1661.

Commentary and Criticism

Coke, Edward, Sir. *The Third Part of the Institute of the Laws of England*. London: Hesler, 1634.

Dobson, R. B., and J. Taylor, eds. *Rymes of Robin Hood*. London: Heineman, 1976.

Knight, Stephen. "Robin Hood and the Royal Restoration." *Critical Survey* 5 (1993), 298–312.

———. *Robin Hood: A Complete Study of the English Outlaw*. Oxford: Blackwell, 1994.

ROBIN HOOD
AND HIS
Crew of SOULDIERS.

A
COMEDY
Acted at *Nottingham* on the day of His
faCRed Majeſties Corronation.
Vivat Rex.

The Actors names.

Robin Hood, Commander.

Little John.
Williams. } Souldiers.
Scadlocke.

Meſſenger from the Shieriffe.

LONDON,
Printed for *James Davis.* 1 6 6 1.

Robin Hood and His Crew of Souldiers

A COMEDY

Acted at Nottingham on the day of His
Sacred Majesties Corronation.

Vivat Rex.

The Actors names

Robin Hood, Commander.	Scadlocke.
Little John.	Soldiers.
William.	Messenger from the Sheriff.

London,
Printed for James Davis. 1661

[*A shout without the Bower.*]
[*Enter Robin Hood, Little John, William, Scadlocke, &c.*]

[Robin]   Whence springs this general joy?
What means this noise that makes Heavens
Arch'd vault eccho? and the neighb'ring woods
Return a dreadfull answer? With what uneven
5   Measures the amaz'd Birds cut through the
Trembling ayr? How the whole Forrest shakes,
As if with us 'twas sensible of wonder, and
Astonishment.   [*Shout again.*
Still the glad noise encreases
10   And with it our fear and wonder; Thus when
Unruly tempests force the weak banks,
Rolling the foamy billows o're the yielding
Strand, fear and amazement, confusion and
Distracting cares seize the neighbring villages,
15   And thus it is with us; the guilty breast
Still pants and throbs, when others are at rest.
Look out and learn the cause, and in the meanwhile
Each man betake himself to's armes.   [*Exit Little John.*

No danger unexpected to a mind
20   Prepar'd to meet the worst that it can finde.

[*Enter Little John and Shierifs Messenger.*]

Robin   Speak, what's the news?

Lit. John   Gives and Fetters, Hatchets and Halters, stincking prisons, and the death of dogs is all we can expect.

Robin   Why, what's the matter?

25   **Lit. John**   Tis the Kings Coronation; and now the Shieriffe with a band of armed men, are marching to reduce us to loyalty, and the miseries of an honest life; this Messenger here can tell you a rufull tale of obedience, that is expected.

Robin   Peace, and let him declare his errand.

Messenger   From my Master I am come to require and command your armes, and a
30   chearfull and ready submission to his Majesties Laws, with a promise of future obedience; and that forthwith you joyn with us to solemnize his happy Coronation, which is this day to be celebrated; this done, and the rest of your lives running in a smooth stream of loyalty and honest allegiance, I here bring pardon of all past misdemeanors; but otherwise, expect the miseries of a
35   sudden destruction: this told you, I wait your answer.

Lit. John   Did not I tell you this? he talks of submission to government, and good Laws, as if we were the sons of peace and idleness, or had bin such Whay-blooded fools to live thus long honestly. And hath thy Master so little braine to think that we who know the sweets of theft and rogery, to whom dangers are as
40   pleasant as dried suckets, who have been nurs'd & fed fat with blood and slaughter, can be content to bear part of your general joy, for that which takes from us the means of our beloved mirth.

Will   Shall I change Venison for salt Cats, and make a bounteous meal, with the reversion of a puddings skin? Or shall I bid adieu to Pheasant and Partrige,
45   and such pleasing Cates, and perswade my hungry maw to satisfaction with the bruis of an Egge-shell? Or shall it be said that thou O famous Little John becomes the Attendant of a Tripe-woman?

Lit. John   The very thought of it is dangerous, I have got the gout only with the apprehension, I was born for action, but yet I cannot plow nor thresh, except
50   it be mine enemy; and after all my fam'd exploits, to hang for stealing sheep 'twould grieve me. I hope our worthy Master will not credit the gingling words of pardon, and acts of grace, and sully all his former glories with a surviving repentance; for my part I had rather trust my self then any other with my life.

446

55 **Will**   If this geare takes then we may turn our Bows into Fiddle-sticks, or strangle
            our selves in the strings, for the daies of warre and wantonness will be done.
            Now must I whimper like a breecht School-boy, and make a face as soure as
            an Apes when he eates Crabs; and then learn manners, and to make legs with
            the patience of a setting-dog; and cry, I forsooth, and no forsooth, like a
60   Country wench at a Churching; Wakes and Bear-baitings, and a little Cudgel-
            play must be all our comfort, and then in some smoaky corner recount our
            past adventures, whilst the good wives blesse themselves at the relation. We
            must not dream of Venison, but be content like the Kings liege-people with
            crusts and mouldy Cheese.

65 **Lit. John** Every brave soule is born a King; rule and command o're the fearfull rabble,
            is natures stamp; courage and lofty thoughts are not ever confin'd to
            Thrones, nor still th' appendages of an illustrious birth, but the thatcht
            Hovell or the simple Wood oft times turns forth a mind as fully fraught with
            Gallantry and true worth as doth the marble Pallace; bounteous nature ties
70   not her selfe to rules of State, or the hard Laws that cruell men impose;
            shee's free in all her gifts, as the Suns generall light, which when it first
            peepes o're the Eastern hills, and glads the widdow'd earth with its fresh
            beams, is not straight stratcht into a Monarchs Court, and there imprisoned
            to guild his private luxurie, but spreads his welcome rayes, and cheares the
75   poor Orphan and dejected Widdow, with the same heat it doth the Persian
            Prince.

    Robin   Why then should the severities of obedience, and the strait niceties of Law
            shackle this Noble soul, whom nature meant not onely free but soveraigne,
            those ties that now by a boundless spreading force doe equally concern the
80   brave and base; first chiefly toucht the vulgar herd and throng of men, that
            masse of feare and folly, who therefore closed together, and with an easie
            fondnesse suffered themselves to be manacled by Lawes, because distrustful
            of their own free strength, and since being nur'st in idlenesse and soft
            intemperance, have grown inamoured of their Chaines, and caressed their
85   slavery, and doat upon their hateful Bondage. But the bold daring Spirit hath
            in all times disown'd this sneaking lownesse, and with a commendable brav'y
            challeng'd their darling Liberty; and from th'insulting Lawes rescu'd their
            enslaved honour: Those famous Heroes in this gallant attempt wee've boldly
            followed, and should we now sit down, and whine a vain repentance; or
90   tamely and coldly yield our hands and legs to fetters, and necks to the mercy
            of the haltar, the world might well esteem us rash and heady Men, but never
            bold or truly Valiant. No we have Swords, and Arms, and Lives equally

engaged in our past account, and whilest these Armes can wield our Swords, or our uncurdl'd blood give vigor to those Arms, hopes of submission are as
95   vain as is the strange request.

Messenger   Doubtless were the quality of actions the justice or injustice to be measured by the boldnesse or fear of the undertakers, what now is your shame, would be your greatest glory, and your Rebellion would be worthy of an honourable memory to eternal Ages; for none have begun and manag'd such wild designs
100   with more unshaken confidence, but since Laws were not made as you formerly imagine, to enslave the Generous, but Curb the Proud and Violent, th' ambitious and unruly nature, your disobedience betrayes aboundlesse pride, and desires unfix'd as mad-mens thoughts, and restless as the Seas watry motion. That by the Laws which careful Princes make, we are com-
105   manded to do well and live vertuously, free both from giving and receiving injuries, is not to be esteemed slav'ry but priviledge. And since we know the power of doing wrong is seldome ununcompanyed with a will someway answerable, it's our perfection to have that fairly chekt that so virtue and justice, the top and complement of our natures, may have their due
110   regard, which is the end of Lawes. Nor can a good or just Man, one who dares be virteous or honest (which is the truest gallantry) think it a loss of freedom to wait and obey the commands of his Prince, especially, when with his regality and Kingly power, are joyn'd the true embellishments of piety and real goodnesse. A Prince of such an influential sweetnesse, that every account
115   teaches a vertue and the meanest Subject by his great example grows up into an Heroe, as if his Princely Soul was grown his peoples Genious. A King so dear to Heaven as if he was it's onely care; His birth usher'd in by a bright Star, and each minute of his Life link'd to the former by a miracle, whose preservation was the amazement of his Enemies: and though the prayer, yet
120   scarce the hope of his most hearty Subjects; One who hath suffer'd injuries beyond example, yet of such an unparalleld charity, he pardons them beyond hope. Whose Virtue is as great as his Birth and his Goodness unlimitted as his Power, To whom the illustrious persons former Ages brag'd of were no more comparable then the Nights Glimmering to the Noon-dayes Splendor.

125   This Great, this Gracious Prince is this day Crown'd, and offers Life, and Peace, and Honour, if you will quit your wilde rebellions, and become what your birth challenges of you, nay what ever your boasted gallantry expects of you that is: loyall subjects.

Robin   Ha! whence is this sudden change? That resolution which but now was
130   remorseless as a Rock of Diamonds, and unyielding as the hardned Steel, is now soft and flexible as a weak womans passions. I am quite another man;

thaw'd into conscience of my Crime & Duty; melted into loyalty & respect to vertue. What an harsh savage beast I was before, not differing from the fiery Lyon or the cruell Bear, but in my knowledge to doe greater ill, my strength

135 and eager rashness was all my boast. How all my pride now is undermin'd? How am I dwarfd in mine own sight? remov'd from that advantage ground my fancy set me on, and shrunk to mine own low pitch? How am I torn now from my selfe? sure some power great and uncommon hath quite transform'd me, and consum'd all that was bad and vicious in me. Methinks these men,

140 companions in former ills, look like those Grecians, th' enchanted cup transform'd: they've shapes of beasts, rude, uncomely and very affrightfull; yet doe I see remorse bud in their blushing brows, as if with me they felt shame and true penitence for their fore-past Crimes. Let us all then joyne in the present sence of our duty, accept the profer'd pardon, ... and with one

145 voice sing, With hearty Wishes, health unto our King.

3 Voc.   Since Heaven with a liberal hand
Doth choicest blessings fling,
And hath (not only to our Land
Restor'd but) Crown'd our KING.

150   Let us to joy and generall mirth
This glad day set aside,
Let the Neighb'ring Woods now Eccho forth,
Our shouts and Loyal Pride.

    May Halters that Mans fate attend
155   That envies this dayes Glee
And's name meet a perpetual brand
For his Disloyalty.   [*Exeunt.*

FINIS

Notes

The opening stage direction refers to *the Bower*; this is an occasional Robin Hood place name, referring to some natural formation where the band can be imagined gathering. The name has a curiously pastoral ring in the context of rebellious outlaws.

The next direction reads *Enter Hobin Hood*, presumably an error for "Robin," which is read here. It continues *Little John, William, Scadlocke, &*. It is conceivable that other outlaws, indicated by *&*, are meant to be on the stage silent throughout the play, but this seems unlikely as the final song is for three voices, according to the direction *3 Voc*. Another peculiarity is that the punctuation seems also to suggest that William and Scadlocke are two separate characters. This could be viewed as a punctuation error except that the title page lists, beneath *Robin Hood, Commander*, three names one beneath each other, all followed by a full stop: *Little John. William. Scadlocke*. The three names are bracketed as *Souldiers*. Apart from John and Robin, only the character named *Will* speaks, and it seems that this apparent confusion must arise from the fact that the printer did not know that William Scadlock was an outlaw's full name and treated it as two.

In this edition I have maintained the capitalization and punctuation of the 1661 edition, except where noted.

1   The printed text does not assign a speaker to the opening lines, but it is Robin Hood who speaks.

22   *Gives and Fetters*. Handcuffs and chains worn by prisoners. *Hatchets*. A light ax. *Halters*. A noose used in hanging.

29–30   I have deleted periods after *armes* and *Laws* and have supplied, instead, commas.

33   *smooth. swooth*, a compositor's error.

37   *Whay-blooded*. Having the nature or quality of whey: watery, thin, pale.

40   *suckets*. Sweetmeats or candied fruit.

450

43   *salt Cats.* Item of choice foods, dainties or delicacies.

46   *bruis.* Breaking.

60   *Churching.* A purification rite for a mother after childbirth.

116   *his peoples Genious.* The guiding spirit of the nation.

130   The text reads *remoseless*, evidently a typesetter's error.

139   *these men.* Robin is alluding to the story of Circe whose potion transformed Odysseus' men into swine in Homer's *Odyssey*.

Later Ballads

Introduction

Robin Hood is one of the most popular topics in the broadside ballads of the seventeenth century, and as readerships and publishers grew more ambitious, the Robin Hood garland, a collection of ballads presented in booklet form, became a standard item of the bookseller's trade. Where the earlier ballads were in many cases chance survivals, these later ballads are often found in multiple copies.

The partially autonomous nature of the printed ballads is indicated by the fact that there is relatively little continuity between the late medieval Robin Hood ballads and the staple diet of the seventeenth and eighteenth centuries. Of the ballads presented in Early Ballads and Tales, none appeared in broadside or garland form. This is partly a matter of length: the *Gest* and *Adam Bell* are printed texts, but far too long to make into a one page broadside or to fit into a garland. *Robin Hood and the Monk*, *Robin Hood and Guy of Gisborne*, *Robin Hood and the Potter* would, at more than two hundred lines, have been too long. It may also be that their inherently medieval themes would not have suited the newly urbanized audience; the only one which does have printed connections is the town-focused *Robin Hood and the Potter*; in a shortened and adapted form as *Robin Hood and the Butcher* it was a typical broadside and regularly appeared in the garlands.

Though the form and topics of the broadside and garland ballads differ from the earliest group of Robin Hood texts, the themes of the later ballads show many connections with the medieval period. A number of them dramatize the process by which "Robin Hood meets his match," that is encounters a stranger, fights a draw and invites him — in one case her — to join the outlaw band. This process is implicit in the earliest materials and is here dramatized in *Robin Hood and the Curtal Friar*, *The Jolly Pinder of Wakefield*, *Robin Hood and Little John*, *Robin Hood and Will Scarlet* (formerly called *Robin Hood Newly Revived*), and, remarkably, *Robin Hood and Maid Marian*.

Augmenting the outlaw band is also a feature of *Robin Hood and Allin a Dale*, but this is a result of Robin's doing a good deed, another theme fully consistent with the medieval tradition, as found in the *Gest*, and also in *Robin Hood Rescues Three Young Men* (known to Child as *Robin Hood Rescuing Three Squires*). The latter ballad also maintains the hostility to the sheriff shown in the *Gest*, as does, in a somewhat

453

diluted form, *Robin Hood and the Golden Arrow*. The vendetta against regular clergy is pursued in *Robin Hood and the Bishop* and *Robin Hood's Golden Prize*, and is a subtext in *The Death of Robin Hood*, which gives full details of the story already known to the author of the *Gest*; *Little John a Begging* has a similar satirical thrust against religious-seeming pilgrims.

Two of the ballads in this section deal with issues not present in the earlier material. *Robin Hood's Progress to Nottingham* tells how he became an outlaw through the oppressive stupidity of Nottingham foresters. This fierce and popular ballad may well have been developed as a "prequel" like some of the "Robin Hood meets his match" ballads — that concerning Little John especially. The theme of *Robin Hood's Fishing* (also called *The Noble Fisherman*), in which Robin becomes a maritime hero in Scarborough, is certainly not known earlier, and it must be regarded as a hybrid ballad of a literary inspiration: its high relevance to a newly mercantile and nationally conscious context is indicated by its great popularity, shown in terms of the times it has survived.

That measure may not, of course, be fully accurate, because survival must to some degree depend on chance. It is hard to believe that *Robin Hood and Little John* and *Robin Hood Rescues Three Young Men*, which do not appear until quite late, but then in substantial numbers, were not distributed widely during the seventeenth century (and they were not as scarce as might seem: Child found two versions of *Robin Hood and Little John* that preceded the texts he lists in his main entry, and *Robin Hood Rescues Three Young Men* is in Percy's folio and was known to Munday). It is better to assume that those two were popular broadsides of the earlier seventeenth century that just did not survive. A more curious enigma of apparent unpopularity is that *The Death of Robin Hood*, a fine and long-known story, does not turn up in the printed versions until a late eighteenth-century garland. This may be no accident: it could be that although the garlands liked to shape a quasi-biography of the hero's career, they preferred to avoid its tragic ending.

Another source for a number of these ballads, and a sure sign of their being available by the mid seventeenth century at the latest, is Percy's folio manuscript. As is well known, this was torn in many places and most of the Robin Hood texts have suffered badly; it is also not a very accurate piece of scribal work. However, it provides texts of some value and also a link between the early and later texts: in addition to *Robin Hood and Guy of Gisborne* and a copy of *Adam Bell* which is taken from a printed text, it offers versions of *Robin Hood and the Curtal Friar*, *The Jolly Pinder of Wakefield*, *Robin Hood Rescues Three Young Men,* and *The Death of Robin Hood*. The recently discovered Forresters manuscript of c. 1670 has provided a better text than Child of *Robin Hood's Fishing* and the semi-gentrified archery contest story, *Robin Hood and Queen Catherin*.

Introduction

It is noticeable that the broadsides and garlands do not deal much with the gentrified Robin Hood, who basically belonged to higher genres — formal drama, ballad opera, and masque — but one of the texts in this section does aspire to such elevation, and ennobled the hero in a determined way. Martin Parker's *A True Tale of Robin Hood* belongs with the broadsides because of its date, technique, and sources, and also because it, like the other late ballads, reworks the tradition in terms of a new urban audience and their contemporary concerns. Parker names Robin as an Earl and then follows Grafton and Munday in making him fall from grace through a mixture of his own foolish generosity and the ferocious hostility of members of the Catholic Church. Yet although Robin is for Parker a hero, he was also visibly an enemy of the newly centralized state, and the final stanzas in particular show the problems an anti-authoritarian hero provides for a period where those who wish to keep popular with the ruling powers were wary of concepts of freedom and resistance.

Parker's stress on the viciousness of the unreformed church is a motif that in lighter form recurs through the broadside and garland ballads — abbots and bishops, rather than sheriffs, become Robin's direct enemies, though only Parker conceives of the outlaws' program of clerical castration. And literary, even modernized, as the thrust of the popular ballads clearly is, they are at the same time less politically conservative and austerely focused than Parker's somewhat inflexible epic. The ballads, like all popular forms, remain in many ways contradictory and so they are dynamic: Robin tricks the monks in *Robin Hood's Golden Prize*, but to do it he appears in full Catholic dress as a friar; he peacefully studies the considerations of honor in *Robin Hood and the Golden Arrow*, but he massacres the foresters in *Robin Hood's Progress to Nottingham*. A trickster par excellence in *Robin Hood and Allin a Dale*, in *Robin Hood's Fishing* he is a hero of national and mercantile progress.

Like the earliest ballads, these later narratives are imbued with the sense of an elusive, polymorphic hero, a noble outlaw whose very appeal lies in the mobile, spirited dynamism that still comes clearly through the ill-printed, clumsily-illustrated, street-level texts that, for the harassed citizens of London, York, Bristol, and other urbanized ballad locations, imagined into being a hero who was, as far as the forces of law and order were concerned, still a moving target.

Select Bibliography

Texts

A Collection of Old Ballads. 3 vols. London, 1723.

Later Ballads

Douce, Francis. Ballad collections II and III, Bodleian Library, Oxford.

The English Archer. Paisley, Neilson, 1786.

The English Archer. York: Nickson, n.d. (late eighteenth century).

Knight, Stephen, ed. *Robin Hood, The Forresters Manuscript, British Library Additional MS 71158*. Cambridge: D. S. Brewer, 1998.

Parker, Martin. *A True Tale of Robin Hood*. London: Cotes, 1632.

———. London: Clark, Thackeray and Passinger, 1686.

Percy's Folio Manuscript, British Library Additional Manuscripts 27879.

Robin Hood and Little John. London: Onley, 1680–85.

Robin Hood's Garland: Containing his merry Exploits, and the several Fights which he, Little John, and Will. Scarlet had, upon several occasions. London: Coles, Vere, Wright, 1670.

Robin Hood's Garland: or Delightful Songs, Shewing the noble Exploits of Robin Hood and his Yeomandrie. London: Gilbertson, 1663.

Wood, Anthony. Ballad collections 401 and 402, Bodleian Library, Oxford.

Commentary and Criticism

Child, F. J. *English and Scottish Popular Ballads*. 5 vols. Rpt. ed. New York: Dover, 1965.

Dobson, R. B., and J. Taylor, eds. *Rymes of Robin Hood*. London: Heinemann, 1976.

Hill, Christopher. "Robin Hood." In *Liberty Against the Law: Some Seventeenth Century Controversies*. London: Allen Lane, 1996. Pp. 71–82.

Holt, J. C. *Robin Hood*. Second ed. London: Thames and Hudson, 1989.

Knight, Stephen. *Robin Hood: A Complete Study of the English Outlaw*. Oxford: Blackwell, 1994.

——. " 'Quite Another Man': The Restoration Robin Hood." In Potter (1998), pp. 167–81.

Ritson, Joseph. *Robin Hood: A Collection of All the Ancient Poems, Songs and Ballads Now Extant Relative to the Celebrated English Outlaw*. 2 vols. London: Egerton and Johnson, 1795.

Sampson, George, ed. *The Cambridge Book of Prose and Verse in Illustration of English Literature: From the Beginning to the Cycles of Romance*. Cambridge: Cambridge University Press, 1924. Pp. 396–98.

Stallybrass, Peter. " 'Drunk with the Cup of Liberty': Robin Hood, the Carnivalesque and the Rhetoric of Violence in Early Modern England." *Semiotica* 54 (1985), 113–45.

Walker, J. W. *A True History of Robin Hood*. Wakefield: The West Yorkshire Printing Co., 1952.

Robin Hood and the Curtal Friar

Introduction

This ballad appears in the Percy folio manuscript but more than half has been torn away. It also appears, in a slightly expanded form, in a number of seventeenth-century versions, and the text from the garland of 1663 is used here to fill out the gaps. Lines 1–4, 35–67, 109–43 are from the Percy folio, while the garland text provides the remainder, with the insertion of one stanza from the garland at lines 125–28 where the Percy folio appears to have lost a few lines by scribal error; the two versions fit together well, with the change of one rhyme word needed at line 68.

Though this is not one of the earlier ballads in terms of its recording, it appears to have a late medieval origin. Friars themselves became outdated with the reformation, and there seems to be some relation between this fighting friar and the similar figure found in the play dated around 1475 and also in the more humorous play found at the end of Copland's *Gest* of c. 1560. Munday's *Downfall of Robert, Earle of Huntington* also presents a comic friar, played by a fictitious version of Skelton the poet. There remains a question whether this well-known figure should be identified with Friar Tuck. Percy's folio calls the ballad *Robin Hood and Fryer Tucke*, but the ballad itself does not use that name, unlike the plays. Child feels there is a separate tradition about the fighting hermit of Fountains Abbey (III, 122), but this may separate too much the elements of a single but varied tradition, especially as there are some early references to a rebellious Friar Tuck: a play of 1537 called *Thersites* refers to someone being "as tall a man as Frier Tuck" and, more remarkably, in 1417 a chaplain of Lindfield in Sussex took up a career of robbery under the alias Friar Tuck.

Although this ballad basically has a "Robin Hood meets his match" structure and the friar agrees at the end to join the outlaw band, few ballads, early or late, show the friar in action with the outlaws (*Robin Hood and Queen Catherin*, Child no. 145, a literary ballad, is an exception; while Robin impersonates a friar in *Robin Hood's Golden Prize*, there is no connection with Tuck). That absence might have been caused by reformation anti-church feeling, but as Child appears to have sensed, the friar-based material seems in some way extrinsic to the central narrative in the ballad genre, as distinct from its centrality in the performance versions of the outlaw myth.

Child nevertheless felt this "is in a genuinely popular strain and was made to sing, not print" (III, 121). Though the word *artillery* (line 10) seems thoroughly contemporary and literary, this is not a bookish ballad: the rhymes are occasionally weak as in many early texts, and it is notable how much of the lyrical ballad technique of "repetition with variation" is found. If that suggests considerable antiquity it is also worth noting that the theme of the dogs that could match fighting men also seems to have quite ancient roots; the story is reminiscent of the encounter between Arthur's men and the ferocious ravens belonging to Owein in the medieval Welsh story *Breuddwyd Ronabwy*, "The Dream of Rhonabwy," found in the Mabinogion collection. While it is in many ways a comic and festal text, *Robin Hood and the Curtal Friar* also, with a holy warrior, mysteriously powerful dogs, and a conflict at what seems to be a ford, touches some of the deeper resources in the Robin Hood myth.

Robin Hood and the Curtal Friar

But how many merry moones be in the yeere?
There are thirteen, I say;
The midsummer moone is the merryest of all,
Next to the merry month of May.

5   In summer time, when leaves grow green,
And flowers are fresh and gay,
Robin Hood and his merry men
Were disposed to play.

Then some would leap, and some would run,
10   And some would use artillery:
"Which of you can a good bow draw,
A good archer to be?

"Which of you can kill a buck?
Or who can kill a do?   *female deer*
15   Or who can kill a hart of greece,   *fat hart*
Five hundred foot him fro."

Will Scadlock he killd a buck
And Midge he killd a do,
And Little John killd a hart of greece,
20   Five hundred foot him fro.   *from him*

"God's blessing on thy heart," said Robin Hood,
"That hath such a shot for me;
I would ride my horse an hundred miles,
To finde one could match with thee."

25   That causd Will Scadlock to laugh,
He laughed full heartily:

Robin Hood and the Curtal Friar

"There lives a curtal frier in Fountains Abby   *(see note)*
Will beat both him and thee.

"That curtal frier in Fountains Abby
30   Well can a strong bow draw;
He will beat you and your yeomen,
Set them all on a row."

Robin Hood took a solemn oath,
It was by Mary free,   *generous (noble)*
35   That he would neither eat nor drink
Till the frier he did see.

Robin Hood put on his harness good,
And on his head a cap of steel,
Broad sword and buckler by his side,
40   And they became him weel.

He builded his men in a brake of fearne,   *stationed*
A litle from that nunery;
Sayes, "If you heare my litle horne blow,
Then looke you come to me."

45   When Robin came to Fontaines Abey,
Whereas that fryer lay,   *Where*
He was ware of the fryer where he stood,
And to him thus can he say:

"I am a wet weary man," said Robin Hood,
50   "Good fellow, as thou may see;
Wilt beare me over this wild water,
For sweete Saint Charity?"

The fryer bethought him of a good deed;   *remembered*
He had done none of long before;   *not long before*
55   He hent up Robin Hood on his backe,   *took*
And over he did him beare.

But when he came over that wild water,
A longe sword there he drew:
"Beare me backe againe, bold outlawe,
60   Or of this though shalt have enoughe."

Then Robin Hood hent the fryar on his back,   *took*
And neither sayd good nor ill,
Till he came ore that wild water,   *over*
The yeoman he walked still.

65   Then Robin Hood wett his fayre greene hoze   *stockings*
A span above his knee;
Says "Beare me ore againe, thou cutted fryer
Or it shall breed thy gree."   *cause you grief*

The frier took Robin Hood on's back again,   *on his*
70   And stept up to the knee;
Till he came at the middle stream,
Neither good nor bad spake he.

And coming to the middle stream,
There he threw Robin in:
75   "And chuse thee, chuse thee, fine fellow,
Whether thou wilt sink or swim."

Robin Hood swam to a bush of broom,
The frier to a wicker wand;   *willow tree*
Bold Robin Hood is gone to shore,
80   And took his bow in hand.

One of his best arrows under his belt
To the frier he let flye;
The curtal frier, with his steel buckler,   *small shield*
He put that arrow by.

85   "Shoot on, shoot on, thou fine fellow,
Shoot on as thou hast begun;
If thou shoot here a summers day,
Thy mark I will not shun."   *I will not hide from your shot*

Robin Hood and the Curtal Friar

Robin Hood shot passing well,
90   Till his arrows all were gone;
They took their swords and steel bucklers,
And fought with might and maine,

From ten o'th' clock that day,
Till four i'th' afternoon;
95   Then Robin Hood came to his knees,
Of the frier to beg a boon.

"A boon, a boon, thou curtal frier,
I beg it on my knee;
Give me leave to set my horn to my mouth,
100   And to blow blasts three."

"That I will do," said the curtal frier,   *fear*
"Of thy blasts I have no doubt;   *you will*
I hope thou'lt blow so passing well
Till both thy eyes fall out."

105   Robin Hood set his horn to his mouth,
He blew but blasts three;   *only*
Half a hundred yeoman, with bows bent,
Came raking over the lee.   *hurrying; open ground*

"I beshrew thy head," said the cutted friar,
110   "Thou thinkes I shall be shente;   *destroyed*
I thought thou had but a man or two,
And thou hast a whole convent.   *body of men*

"I lett thee have a blast on thy horne,
Now give me leave to whistle another;
115   I cold not bidd thee noe better play
And thou wert my owne borne brother."

"Now fate on, fute on, thou cutted fryar,   *play on, whistle away*
I pray God thou neere be still;   *never*
It is not the futing in a fryers fist   *whistling*
120   That can doe me any ill."

The fryar sett his neave to his mouth,   *fist*
A lowd blast he did blow;
Then halfe a hundred good bandoggs   *fierce dogs*
Came raking all on a rowe.   *hurrying*

125   "Here's for every man a dog,
And I myself for thee."
"Nay, by my faith," quoth Robin Hood,
"Frier, that may not be.

"Over God's forbott," said Robin Hood,   *May God forbid*
130   "That ever that soe shold bee;
I had rather be mached with three of the tikes   *dogs*
Ere I wold be matched on thee.

"But stay thy tikes, thou fryar," he said,
"And freindshipp I'le have with thee;
135   But stay thy tikes, thou fryar" he said,
"And save good yeomanry."

The fryar he sett his neave to his mouth,
A lowd blast he did blow;
The doggs the coucht downe every one,   *they lay*
140   They couched downe on a rowe.

"What is thy will, thou yeoman?" he said,
"Have done and tell it me."
"If that thou will goe to merry greenwood,
A noble shall be thy fee.   *coin worth six shillings and eightpence*

145   "And every holy day throughout the year,
Changed shall thy garment be,
If thou wilt go to fair Nottingham,
And there remain with me."

This curtal frier had kept Fountains Dale
150   Seven long years or more;
There was neither knight, lord, nor earl
Could make him yield before.

1–4   This stanza may well be meant as a chorus. The Percy MS reads *monthes* in line 1 and *thirteen in Mai* in line 2. Child emends *In May* to *I say* to make more sense but does not, unlike later versions of the ballad, change *monthe* in line 1 to *moone*, as is also required for sense. These changes are made here, though it is just conceivable that the manuscript is right and that the stanza (which is formulaic, and also used in *Robin Hood Rescues Three Young Men*, see p. 515, lines 1–4) is an element of nonsense song, a genre not unknown in the period.

5   This stanza begins a more familiar opening to a Robin Hood ballad, the "green wood setting" from which the action develops and to which (in line 143) it will return.

15   The Forresters manuscript, which has a version of the 1663 garland text, apparently transmitted by memory, and is less sharp, here has the more common idiom "a heart in grease."

17   The earliest printed text has *Sadlock*. Although the character is hostile to locks (his name is given as Scathelock and Scarlock, as well as the somewhat euphemized Scarlet), this must be an error.

18   This character's name remains the same in all the versions of this ballad, so can hardly be emended; he is obviously the figure elsewhere called Much, and in earlier dialectal forms some version of OE *mycel* might have been the base of the form. This may also lie behind the error *Nick* (see *Robin Hood and Allin a Dale*, line 22).

22   Child inserts *shot* after *hath*, but this seems unnecessary and does not appear until a much later version.

27   The term *curtal* has raised discussion. Most feel it refers to a shorter gown, worn for mobility: friars were associated with travel among the ordinary people, which was both a source of corruption and also, as in the Robin Hood tradition, popular acceptability. A "tucked friar" is another way of expressing this, which

has become the basis for the friar's usual name, Tuck. Child, however, feels that *curtal* goes back to *curtilarius* or "gardener" and that this had been the friar's role (III, 122).

Fountains Abby: This Cistercian monastery (never a friary) is, like a number of other locations connected with Robin Hood, in North Yorkshire, very close to Ripon.

29   The fact that other outlaws know the reputation of the man who will challenge Robin is also a feature in *Robin Hood and the Potter*; it seems as if Robin himself is being tested.

33–34   Mary is a special object of Robin's devotion elsewhere, see *Robin Hood and the Monk*, line 28, and the *Gest*, lines 36–37. Robin's oath to abstain from eating is also curiously like King Arthur's refusal to eat until he has seen a guest; see also *Gest*, lines 23–26.

42   It is not clear why Fountains, always a masculine foundation, is called a nunnery: the term may be being generally used like *convent*, line 112.

48   After this line the Percy folio has a stanza describing the friar as a "yeoman"; both the term and the stanza seem misplaced and should presumably apply to Robin. The stanza is omitted here.

51   The Percy folio lacks *me* in this line, which seems necessary, as Child suggests; the manuscript has a number of simple scribal omissions of this kind; see also line 112.

53–54   It is not clear what the friar's *good deed* done *none of long before* (that is, recently) might be: could it be an ironical reference to the encounter with Will implied in lines 27–28?

56   If *beare* were emended to past tense *bore* the rhyme would work properly, but this would not fit with the auxiliary *did*, needed for the meter. The rhyme is not particularly bad for an early ballad.

68   In the transition at lines 67–68 from the Percy folio to the garland text, the latter's rhyme in line 68, "pain," needs emending to *gree*.

76 The earliest printed text reads *sing or swim*, and could be taken as a droll variation of the cliché. But all the other broadside and Garland versions have *sink or swim* and that seems the most sensible reading; Child's emendation is accepted.

78 Forresters has the simpler *willow* for *wicker*.

79 Here Forresters preserves a line that seems sharper than the 1663 garland; "Robin Hood went dropping to the stone" (i.e., dripping).

95 The text actually reads *came ts knees*, but as the ellipsis is not needed for meter it seems best to treat it as a mistake.

99 As Child notes (III, 122), this is one of the many horn-blowing incidents in the myth, a feature which has frequent parallels in European folk-tale. This is the only instance, however, where his opponent has an answer to the assembly of the outlaws, which perhaps explains why the horn-blowing is stressed so much early in the ballad.

108 The text has *ranking* but, especially in the light of the dogs' *raking* in line 124, this seems an error. Later texts emend the second reference to "ranging," but Child's emendation to *raking* is accepted.

109 *cutted*. Referring to his shortened gown.

112 The Percy manuscript lacks *a* before *whole*, which seems necessary, as Child suggests.

The friar uses *convent* ironically; he is a religious hermit, but Robin brings a body of men against him.

117 Child reads the manuscript as *fate on, fate on* and emends both to *fute*, whistle, so fitting in with *futing* in line 119. In fact the MS reads *fate on, fute on*: this can be taken to mean "play on, whistle away" which makes good sense, and so the text is not emended here.

123 A *bandogg* is according to Child a hunting dog so fierce it needs to be kept in "bands" or chains. These dogs could be as big as Irish wolfhounds. In the expanded broadside versions they start to savage Robin and can catch arrows in

their mouths, but the Percy version does not envisage such an elaborate and improbable encounter.

125–28 This stanza is taken from the garland text as the Percy manuscript merely writes twice the lines: *"Every dogg to a man," said the cutted fryar, / "And I myself to Robin Hood."* Child inserts "of thine" before *a dog* in line 125, but this seems unnecessary.

146 Robin is offering the friar a "livery," that is, a new suit of clothing each year if he joins his service, as well as a joining fee of a noble, six and eightpence (line 144); Robin acts as a lord gathering a retinue.

147 As in the *Gest* and *Robin Hood and Guy of Gisborne*, the outlaw appears to operate in the well-separated areas of Nottingham and Yorkshire. In those cases it is suggested that separate traditions have come together; here there can be no cause other than a sense of geographical mobility.

The Jolly Pinder of Wakefield

Introduction

This ballad, like *Robin Hood and the Curtal Friar*, appears in Percy's folio manuscript and also in a number of seventeenth-century ballad and garland collections. It is, like other texts, damaged in the Percy MS: in this case too much is missing for that to be the basis of the text, but the Percy version provides some valuable corrections and extensions to the earliest complete broadside version, dated by Donald Wing to 1643 (*Short-Title Catalogue . . . 1641–1700*). There are two versions in the Forresters manuscript, one an independent version of the garland text (A), the other a larger text apparently related to the prose history of *George a Greene* (B). Forresters' A is close to the Wood version, Child's favored text, but as it seems edited or erroneous, though with some good readings, it is merely referred to in the notes and occasionally used for emendation.

The story of Robin Hood's encounter with the doughty pinder of Wakefield had clearly existed for at least a century when Percy's manuscript was compiled: a ballad with this title was recorded in the Stationers' Register in 1557–59, is quoted in Anthony Munday's play, and was used in the Sloane *Life of Robin Hood* which appears to have been compiled in the late sixteenth century. Child suggests the ballad is mentioned in several Shakespeare plays, but he is only referring to the linking of the names "Robin and Scarlet and John": this does occur in a number of other ballads (albeit later recorded and somewhat literary ones, *Robin Hood's Delight* and *Robin Hood and the Prince of Aragon*), and in any case this evidence is not needed to prove the widespread nature of the Wakefield saga. A prose life of *George a Greene*, the Pinder's name, existed from the early seventeenth century (by 1632) and, most striking of all, there was a five-act play of the same title, almost certainly by Robert Greene, written by 1594.

The pinder of Wakefield, like the friar of Fountains Abbey, and even like Gamelyn or Gamwell, was one of the local heroes who were drawn into the Robin Hood myth, whose aficionados no doubt enjoyed hearing of his achievements against the great man, and so the range of the tales how Robin met his match was expanded. In some sense the ballad has the simple structure of the "equal fight" ballads where Robin, or more usually Robin, John, and Will (sometimes Much as well or instead) have a good demanding fight with some opponents, and end either by calling a truce or by engaging the antagonist to join the outlaw band.

Stressing the fight as it does, *The Jolly Pinder of Wakefield* clearly belongs to that genre; yet it has resonances of a richer vein. The pinder is inherently a town official, controlling any stray animals and, as here, protecting the local crops from damage. Robin's conflict with the pinder and winning him over to the outlaws' side is not unlike his encounters with the sheriff and other urban forces. It is interesting to note that the play, *George a Greene*, incorporates Robin as a hero junior to the pinder, associating the outlaw to some extent with political rebellion and George with total loyalty to the crown (Knight, 1994, pp. 120–21).

These nuances are somewhat hidden in this "thoroughly lyrical" ballad (Child, III, 129) with its use of repeated lines and a number of imprecise rhymes and variation between a four- and six-line stanza. But popular as the ballad was, it does not delineate a central part of the myth so much as illustrate one of the difficult encounters between the hero and other cultural and social forces.

The Jolly Pinder of Wakefield

In Wakefield there lives a jolly pinder,   *impounder of stray animals*
In Wakefield, all on a green.

"There is neither knight nor squire," said the pinder,
"Nor barron that is so bold,
5   Dare make a trespasse to the town of Wakefield,
But his pledge goes to the pinfold."   *surety*

All this beheard three wight young men,   *strong*
'Twas Robin Hood, Scarlet, and John;
With that they spyed the jolly pinder,
10   As he sate under a thorn.   *thorn-bush*

"Now turn again, turn again," said the pinder,
"For a wrong way have you gone;
For you have forsaken the king his high way,
And made a path over the corn."   *through the field*

15   "O that were great shame," said jolly Robin,
"We being three, and thou but one."
The pinder leapt back then three good foot,
'Twas three good foot and one.

He leaned his back fast unto a thorn,
20   And his foot unto a stone,
And there he fought a long summer's day,
A summer's day so long.

Till that their swords, on their broad bucklers,
Were broken fast unto their hands.   *right up to*
25   "Hold thy hand, hold thy hand," said Robin Hood,
"And my merry men every one.

"For this is one of the best pinders
That ever I saw with eye.
And wilt thou forsake the pinder his craft,
30   And live in green wood with me?"

"At Michaelmas next my cov'nant comes out,   *contract*
When every man gathers his fee;
I'le take my blew blade all in my hand,
And plod to the green wood with thee."
35   "Hast thou either meat or drink," said Robin Hood
"For my merry men and me?"

"I have both bread and beef," said the pinder,
"And good ale of the best."
"And that is meat good enough," said Robin Hood,   *food*
40   "For such unbidden guest.

"O wilt thou forsake the pinder his craft,
And go to the green wood with me?
Thou shalt have a livery twice in the year,
The one green, the other brown."

45   "If Michaelmas day were once come and gone
And my master had paid me my fee,
Then would I set as little by him
As my master doth set by me.
I'le take my benbowe in my hand,   *long bow*
50   And come into the grenwode to thee."

Notes

1–2   This refrain is repeated after each stanza; the second and fourth lines of each stanza are also repeated, emphasizing the sung character of this ballad.

Wakefield, in West Yorkshire like a number of other places associated with Robin Hood, was thought by Joseph Hunter to be the home of the Robin Hood who served Edward II. More historically, it was a town of some importance in the wool trade and not far from the Yorkshire Barnsdale, so providing the tension between town and country that seems basic to much of the early Robin Hood material in the ballads.

A *pinder* is "an officer of a manor, having duty of impounding stray beasts" (OED). Also spelled "pinner." The *green* would be the *pinfold*, the place where the *pinder* will *pin* or pen the stray animals.

3   The text's reading *their* for *there* may be a variant version, but as the spelling of the two words is being distinguished at the time, it is better to treat it as an error and, with Child, emend.

4   The text has *barron,* though Child prints *baron* without explanation.

6   This suggests more than the mere impounding of stray animals: the Pinder is, it seems, a general defender of the town's liberties, which is how he appears in the play and in the undercurrent of this ballad.

7   The texts agree on the word *witty* except for Forresters' A version, which has *wight*. Child says in his notes that "witty" is "a corruption of wight," and Forresters justifies the emendation Child did not have the evidence to make.

13   The text retains *high way* as two words, though Child prints it as one.

17   Forresters agrees with *thirty* here but has *three* in the next line. Both are numerals, and emendation seems justified.

21   The day-long fight is an almost regular recurrence in these "Robin Hood meets his match" ballads, and is also found in many romances. Even major real battles were usually over in a few hours, so this must be a popular image of a grand and terrible conflict.

23   Child's lay-out of the ballad here departs from the four-line stanza, but to no good effect. He prints lines 19–24 as a six-line stanza with irregular rhyme (stone/king/hands) and then inserts a line of asterisks as if there were material missing. He also leaves a gap between lines 35–36. None of these responses seems necessary. As the ballad is laid out here there is a well-rhymed six-line stanza at lines 31–36, a weaker, but acceptably rhymed four-line stanza in lines 19–22, and a distinctly weaker one in lines 23–26. There may have been transmission damage to cause this bad rhyme, as there is another in the next stanza in Wood, but the Percy folio text, which is unavailable before this point, provides the proper rhyme there (see the next note).

28   Wood's earlier text does not rhyme here, since its line *That ever I try'd with sword* must rhyme either with line 26, *one*, or line 30, *me*. The Percy manuscript begins with this stanza and provides the line used here.

29   Wood's text has *thy pinder his craft,* which Child prints; this is clearly a double genitive. Hyper-correct usage expanded the genitive ending in -*s* to *his*, believing the *'s* was an abbreviation of the pronoun. Later texts abandon this, but emendation to *the pinder* is necessary, as found in line 41.

33   The blade is *blew* because it is made of good quality steel.

43   Robin offers *livery*, that is a new suit of clothes at regular intervals, as well no doubt as food and a fee for joining his band (like that offered the Curtal Friar). The Pinder will accept this when his present service contract runs out at Michaelmas, September 29th, which was a traditional "quarter day" for bills and agreements of this kind.

44   Child adds *shal be* for rhyme, though none of the printed texts, or Forresters, feel the need, and so their model is accepted. Percy's mysterious rhyme "Picklory" may suggest a lost original, but it would hardly have been corrupted to a bad rhyme on *brown*. It is conceivable that all colors have been reversed

and there was originally a weak rhyme with *green*, but stanzas without rhyme do occur in the ballads and there seems no good cause to emend as dramatically as Child.

49–50   Wood's version ends at line 48, but Percy concludes with this firm couplet, making a six-line stanza. Broadside ballads were often cut to fit the page, which may be the case in Wood.

Note that the Pinder, who has fought with a sword, is also able to use the long bow.

Robin Hood and Little John

Introduction

This ballad was printed by Child from a text in a 1723 London anthology, *A Collection of Old Ballads*; he later found a copy printed by W. Onley in London in 1680–85 (V, p. 297); this text is followed here. As with *Robin Hood and the Curtal Friar* and *The Jolly Pinder of Wakefield*, there is clear evidence of the much earlier existence of this story. A play called *Robin Hood and Little John* was registered in 1594 but has not survived, and there was another from 1640, though they may of course have been general dramas based on sources like the *Gest* or even *Robin Hood and the Monk*. A ballad with this title was registered in 1624, and that date is quite possible for an original version of this text. Dobson and Taylor (1976, p. 165) suggest that it has "every sign of having been produced by a professional ballad writer" with the intention of explaining how Little John came by his name and, long ago, joined the outlaw band: this would be one of the "prequels" like *Robin Hood's Progress to Nottingham* and *Robin Hood and Will Scarlet* which exploit and rationalize an existing tradition about a character.

Child describes the ballad as having "a rank seventeenth century style" (III, 133), and its language and technique suggest something rather later than the 1624 date when the title at least was in existence, having in particular the internal rhyme in the third line which is shared by most commercial Robin Hood ballads of the later seventeenth and eighteenth century. Child is convinced that all these ballads had the same tune, that of *Arthur a Bland* or *Robin Hood and the Tanner*. The rhymes and meter are, compared to earlier ballads, suspiciously smooth, and the language, which Dobson and Taylor found "very bathetic" (1976, p. 166), bears traces of the hackwriter's inkwell: *passionate fury and eyre*, line 71; *I prithee*, line 78; *accoutrements*, line 106; *And did in this manner proceed*, line 129; and, most remarkably, when the outlaws leave their entertainments it says *the whole train the grove did refrain*, line 152.

Nevertheless, this is a classic "Robin Hood meets his match" ballad, and bogus as some of it may be, there is a sign that the language and mannerisms grow more elaborate as the text proceeds, and there could be an earlier plainer ballad embedded in this one, signs of which may appear in lines 1–9, 26–33, 58–73 (except 71), 86–89, 94–113 (except 106), 118–27. Commercial as it may be, this ballad still outlines a focus of solidarity and tricksterism, presenting a central event in the myth which has

476

remained dear, even obsessive, in the hearts of theatrical and film redactors over the centuries. In Hollywood, the same actor (Alan Hale) played Little John in 1922, 1938 and 1946, with the same enduring portrayal of the ballad.

Robin Hood and Little John

When Robin Hood was about twenty years old,
With a hey down, down, and a down
He happen'd to meet Little John,
A jolly brisk blade, right fit for the trade,   *young man*
5   For he was a lusty young man.

Though he was call'd Little, his limbs they were large,
And his stature was seven foot high;
Whereever he came, they quak'd at his name,
For soon he wou'd make them to flie.

10   How they came acquainted, I'll tell you in brief,
If you will but listen a while;
For this very jest, amongst all the rest,   *(see note)*
I think it may cause you to smile.

Bold Robin Hood said to his jolly bowmen,
15   "Pray tarry you here in this grove;
And see that you all observe well my call,
While thorough the forest I rove.

"We have had no sport for these fourteen long days,
Therefore now abroad will I go;
20   Now should I be beat, and cannot retreat,
My horn I will presently blow."   *at once*

Then did he shake hands with his merry men all,
And bid them at present good by;   *God be with you (goodbye)*
Then, as near a brook his journey he took,
25   A stranger he chanc'd to espy.

They happen'd to meet on a long narrow bridge,
And neither of them wou'd give way;

478

Robin Hood and Little John

Quoth bold Robin Hood, and sturdily stood,
"I'll show you right Nottingham play."   *true*

30   With that from his quiver an arrow he drew,
A broad arrow with a goose-wing:
The stranger replyd, "I'll licker thy hide,   *tan (beat)*
If thou offer to touch the string."

Quoth bold Robin Hood, "Thou dost prate like an ass,
35   For were I to bend but my bow,
I could send a dart quite through thy proud heart,
Before thou couldst strike me one blow."

"You talk like a coward," the stranger reply'd;
"Well arm'd with a long bow you stand,
40   To shoot at my breast, while I, I protest,
Have naught but a staff in my hand."   *nothing*

"The name of a coward," quoth Robin, "I scorn,
Wherefore my long bow I'll lay by;
And now, for thy sake, a staff will I take,
45   The truth of thy manhood to try."

Then Robin Hood stept to a thicket of trees,
And chose him a staff of ground oak;   *oak sapling*
Now this being done, away he did run
To the stranger and merrily spoke:

50   "Lo! see my staff; it is lusty and tough,
Now here on the bridge we will play;
Whoever falls in, the other shall win
The battle, and so we'll away."

"With all my whole heart to thy humor I yield,
55   I scorn in the least to give out."
This said, they fell to't without more dispute,
And their staffs they did flourish about.

And first Robin he gave the stranger a bang,
So hard that it made his bones ring:
60   The stranger he said, "This must be repaid;
I'll give you as good as you bring.

"So long as I am able to handle my staff,
To die in your debt, friend, I scorn."
Then to it both goes, and follow'd their blows,
65   As if they'd been thrashing of corn.

The stranger gave Robin a crack on the crown,
Which caused the blood to appear;
Then Robin, enrag'd, more fiercely engag'd,
And follow'd his blows more severe.

70   So thick and so fast did he lay it on him,
With a passionate fury and eyre,   *ire*
At every stroke he made him to smoke,
As if he had been all on a fire.

O then into a fury the stranger he grew
75   And gave him a damnable look,
And with it a blow that laid him full low
And tumbl'd him into the brook.

"I prithee, good fellow, O where art thou now?"
The stranger in laughter he cry'd;
80   Quoth bold Robin Hood, "Good faith, in the flood,
And floting along with the tide.

"I needs must acknowledge thou art a brave soul;
With thee I'll no longer contend;
For needs must I say, thou hast got the day,
85   Our battle shall be at an end."

Then, then, to the bank he did presently wade,
And pull'd himself out by a thorn;
Which done, at the last, he blow'd a loud blast
Straitways on his fine bugle-horn.

Robin Hood and Little John

90 The eccho of which through the vallies did flie,
  At which his stout bowmen appear'd,
  All cloathed in green, most gay, to be seen;
  So up to their master they steer'd.

  "O what's the matter?" quoth William Stutely,
95 "Good master, you are wet to the skin."
  "No matter," quoth he, "the lad which you see,
  In fighting he tumbl'd me in."

  "He shall not go scot free," the others reply'd; [1]
  So straight they were seising him there,   *straightaway*
100 To duck him likewise, but Robin Hood cries,
  "He is a stout fellow, forbear.

  "There's no one shall wrong thee, friend, be not afraid;
  These bowmen upon me do wait;   *attend*
  There's threescore and nine; if thou wilt be mine,
105 Thou shalt have my livery strait.

  "And other accoutrements fit for my train,
  Speak up, jolly blade, ne'r fear;
  I'll teach thee also the use of the bow,
  To shoot at the fat fallow-deer."

110 "O here is my hand," the stranger reply'd,
  "I'll serve you with all my whole heart;
  My name is John Little, a man of good mettle;
  Ne'r doubt me, for I'll play my part."

  "His name shall be alter'd," quoth William Stutely,
115 "And I will his godfather be;
  Prepare then a feast, and none of the least,
  For we will be merry," quoth he.

---

[1] *scot free*: without paying his "scot" or shot, his bill

They presently fetch'd in a brace of fat does,
With humming strong liquor likewise;   *extremely*
120 They lov'd what was good, so in the greenwood,
This pritty sweet babe they baptize.

He was, I must tell you, but seven foot high,
And may be an ell in the waste;   *forty-five inches*
A pritty sweet lad, much feasting they had;
125 Bold Robin the christ'ning grac'd,

With all his bowmen, which stood in a ring,
And were of the Nottingham breed;
Brave Stutely comes then, with seven yeomen,
And did in this manner proceed:

130 "This infant was called John Little," quoth he,
"Which name shall be changed anon;
The words we'll transpose, so where-ever he goes,
His name shall be call'd Little John."

They all with a shout made the elements ring,
135 So soon as the office was o're;
To feasting they went, with true merriment,
And tipl'd strong liquor gallore.   *galore (in plenty)*

Then Robin he took the pritty sweet babe,
And cloath'd him from top to the toe
140 In garments of green, most gay to be seen,
And gave him a curious long bow.

"Thou shalt be an archer as well as the best,
And range in the green wood with us;
Where we'll not want gold nor silver, behold,
145 While bishops have ought in their purse.

"We live here like esquires, or lords of renown,
Without e're a foot of free land;   *ever*
We feast on good cheer, with wine, ale and beer,
And ev'ry thing at our command."

150   Then musick and dancing did finish the day
       At length when the sun waxed low,   *grew*
       Then all the whole train the grove did refrain,
       And unto their caves they did go.

       And so ever after, as long as he liv'd,
155   Although he was proper and tall,
       Yet nevertheless, the truth to express,
       Still Little John they did him call.   *Always*

Notes

3   *Little John*: the earliest references feature the two outlaws and do not clearly privilege Robin. Scottish play-games link the two on nearly equal terms, sometimes as equivalent to the Abbot and Prior of Bonacord. There is some connection between Little John and the Derbyshire Peak district (tradition places his huge grave at Hathersage), and there are two Little John (not Robin Hood) sites in Leicestershire in the Charnwood area, not far from Derbyshire. The surname Naylor, sometimes attached to him, derives from a confusion after a Colonel Naylor, in 1715, owned "Little John's bow" and wrote his name on it (Walker, 1952, p. 131). As a figure, Little John can be interpreted as the helpful giant of folklore, and it can be argued that as Robin is gentrified, John is steadily downgraded into the equivalent of a non-commissioned officer (Knight, 1994, pp. 83–84).

12   *jest*. Here would at first appear to mean "adventure" as in the title of the *Gest*, but the reference to a smile in the next line appears to redefine it as "humorous story."

25   The sudden meeting with the stranger is a normal part of a "Robin Hood meets his match" ballad.

50   Although the *r* and *t* are very similar, the Onley text clearly reads *tough*, Child's reading. Later texts read "rough."

54   Later texts read "the stranger reply'd" instead of *to thy humor I yield*.

64   Later texts read "both," like Onley's; Child reads *each*, perhaps for number agreement — *each goes*.

65   Onley's text reads *they'd*, which is metrically superior to Child's *they had*.

73   Onley's *all on a fire* is metrically superior to Child's version, which omits the article *a*.

86   *Then, then, to* seems acceptable: Child edits to *Then unto*.

108   *thee*: later texts have Robin using the polite plural *you* to John in this line.

114   *William Stutely* is a name that appears occasionally in the tradition; one seventeenth-century ballad describes the outlaw's rescue of him from the sheriff (Child, no. 141). Whether this is another form of Will Scathelock or Scarlet is not clear: in Munday there are two characters bearing those names, but not Stutely. Such name similarities and confusions are common in Arthurian romance as well.

125   Where Child ends the line with a full stop, the text has a comma and runs on into the next stanza — perhaps a sign of its somewhat bookish character; line 129 has a colon and is much the same in effect, but there also Child has a full stop against the syntax.

143   Though Child prints the word as *greenwood*, the sources have *green wood*, which is not quite the same. The concept of a single entity called greenwood is really a nineteenth-century concept influenced by Keats and Peacock (see Knight, 1996, ch. 5).

146   Later texts emend the meter by providing *'squires*; no doubt this was the pronunciation expected in Onley.

153   The mention of *caves* is a rare moment of realism: most ballads locate the outlaws simply in "the green wood," as if the weather was never hostile.

Robin Hood and Allin a Dale

Introduction

This ballad appears in seventeenth-century broadsides but did not find a place in the garland collections, perhaps because Allin a Dale (Allen in the later texts) was not a well-known member of the outlaw band. The basic story is told in the late sixteenth-century Sloane *Life of Robin Hood*, but there the lover is Scarlock and Robin enters the church disguised as a beggar (not unlike his actions in *Robin Hood Rescues Three Young Men*). The Forresters manuscript contains *Robin Hood and the Bride*, a reworked and diluted version of the text.

There is some sign that this is an "art" ballad in the fact that its plot structure is unusual: Allin a Dale joins the outlaw band, but this is not a "Robin Hood meets his match" story. Allin's joining is part of a "rescue" story as Robin and his men intervene to re-establish what he judges to be the "fit" situation (line 73). This involves elements of disguise, again in a composite mode, in this case both Robin as a harper and John as a priest. The latter sequence is more theatrical than trickster-like as John calls the banns seven times *Least three times should not be enough* (line 100), and the anti-clerical note is consistent with the tone of many of the ballads in this period. The frustration of the old knight on behalf of Allin and his love could be taken as consistent with Robin Hood's broad social mission, but is effectively derived from the genre of true love story, a stranger to the outlaw tradition.

Other "literary" features are the *Come listen to me* opening and the romantic song usage *finikin lass* (line 71, changed to *glittering* in later texts). Nevertheless, in spite of what Dobson and Taylor call the "mechanical obviousness of the language" (1976, p. 172), the text has some of the lively roughness, including uneven rhyme, found in relatively early Robin Hood ballads, and it lacks the jingling third line internal rhyme characteristic of the new popular ballads of the seventeenth century.

Allin a Dale ("of the dale") is unknown in other Robin Hood texts. The plot is used in a ballad opera of 1751, but the lovers have become Leander and Clorinda and the old knight is now Sir Humphrey Wealthy (Knight, 1994, pp. 149–50). The ballad was printed by Ritson, and then became a regular part of the tradition, especially in extended and stage versions, presumably because of its unusual love interest.

Robin Hood and Allin a Dale

Come listen to me, you gallants so free,
All you that love mirth for to hear,
And I will tell of a bold outlaw,
That lived in Nottinghamshire.

5   As Robin Hood in the forrest stood,
All under the green-wood tree,
There was he ware of a brave young man,
As fine as fine might be.

The youngster was clothed in scarlet red,
10   In scarlet fine and gay,
And he did frisk it over the plain,
And chanted a roundelay.   *lyrical love song*

As Robin Hood next morning stood,
Amongst the leaves so gay,
15   There did he espy the same young man,
Come drooping along the way.

The scarlet he wore the day before,
It was clean cast away;
And every step he fetcht a sigh,
20   "Alack and a well a day!"

Then stepped forth brave Little John,
And Nick the millers son,
Which made the young man bend his bow,
When as he see them come.

25   "Stand off, stand off," the young man said,
"What is your will with me?"

"You must come before our master straight,
Under yon green-wood tree."

And when he came bold Robin before,
30   Robin askt him courteously,
"O hast thou any money to spare
For my merry men and me?"

"I have no money," the young man said,
"But five shillings and a ring;
35   And that I have kept this seven long years,
To have it at my wedding.

"Yesterday I should have married a maid,
But she is now from me tane,
And chosen to be an old knights delight,
40   Whereby my poor heart is slain."

"What is thy name?" then said Robin Hood,
"Come tell me, without any fail."
"By the faith of my body," then said the young man,
"My name it is Allin a Dale."

45   "What wilt thou give me," said Robin Hood,
"In ready gold or fee,   *property*
To help thee to thy true love again,
And deliver her unto thee?"

"I have no money," then quoth the young man,
50   "No ready gold nor fee,
But I will swear upon a book
Thy true servant for to be."

"How many miles is it to thy true love?
Come tell me without any guile."
55   "By the faith of my body," then said the young man,
"It is but five little mile."

Then Robin he hasted over the plain,
He did neither stint nor lin,   *stop nor delay*
Until he came unto the church,
60   Where Allin should keep his wedding.

"What dost thou here?" the bishop he said,
"I prethee now tell to me."
"I am a bold harper," quoth Robin Hood,
"And the best in the north countrey."

65   "O welcome, O welcome," the bishop he said,
"That musick best pleaseth me."
"You shall have no musick," quoth Robin Hood,
"Till the bride and the bridegroom I see."

With that came in a wealthy knight,
70   Which was both grave and old,
And after him a finikin lass,   *fine*
Did shine like glistering gold.

"This is no fit match," quoth bold Robin Hood,
"That you do seem to make here;
75   For since we are come unto the church,
The bride she shall chuse her own dear."

Then Robin Hood put his horn to his mouth,
And blew blasts two or three;
When four and twenty bowmen bold
80   Came leaping over the lee.   *open ground*

And when they came into the church-yard,
Marching all on a row,
The first man was Allin a Dale,
To give bold Robin his bow.

85   "This is thy true love," Robin he said,
"Young Allin, as I hear say,
And you shall be married at this same time,
Before we depart away."

"That shall not be," the bishop he said,
90   "For thy word shall not stand;
They shall be three times askt in the church,
As the law is of our land."

Robin Hood pulld off the bishops coat,
And put it upon Little John;
95   "By the faith of my body," then Robin said,
"This cloath doth make thee a man."

When Little John went into the quire,
The people began for to laugh;
He askt them seven times in the church,
100   Least three times should not be enough.

"Who gives me this maid," then said Little John;
Quoth Robin, "That do I,
And he that doth take her from Allin a Dale
Full dearly he shall her buy."   *pay for*

105   And thus having ended this merry wedding,
The bride lookt as fresh as a queen,
And so they returnd to the merry green wood,
Amongst the leaves so green.

490

Notes

1   The "Come all ye" opening is only found in a few "commercial" Robin Hood ballads (*Robin Hood and Will Scarlet*, *Robin Hood and the Bishop* and, in restrained form, Parker's *A True Tale*). A more usual opening would be line 5; presumably this opening has been introduced in the process of production as a broadside.

9   Scarlet seems a suitable color for a lover, but there are early references to the outlaws wearing scarlet. Green as a color may itself be part of an early "green wood" consciousness. In the later development of the tradition, Allin a Dale and Will Scarlet often become confused, partly because they play the role of *ingenu*, perhaps also because of this shared color.

13   It is unusual to have this double opening; Robin usually stands still, sees something, and goes into action. This ballad seems structurally composite from the beginning.

22   Nick is presumably based on a misreading of Much, perhaps in a form closer to OE *mycel* (see Midge in *Robin Hood and the Curtal Friar*, line 18. Dobson and Taylor emend to Midge [p. 173]). See also Munday's *The Downfall*, line 523, where Warman's wife calls Much *Nich*.

27   The ballad begins as if Allin is a stranger, about to be robbed by the outlaw. But his honesty takes the outlaws off on another narrative track, and the sequence resembles the opening of the episode with Sir Richard in Fitt 1 of the *Gest*.

44   There are no other references to this character in the ballads. In the post-Ritson development of the myth, Allin is usually a minor figure, perhaps reaching his zenith as Alan A. Dale, played by Bing Crosby in *Robin and the Seven Hoods* (1964).

50   Like the knight in the *Gest*, Allin offers fidelity rather than money, and Robin accepts this as a basis for helping him.

63   Disguise as a harper is one of the most familiar versions of this motif; the reference to *the north countrey* (line 64) does not necessarily set this story in the north: harpers would be expected to come from the less urbanized parts of Britain.

83   The motif of the young hero who joins a band and at once becomes a leading figure because of his quality is common in folklore; another instance is in *Gamelyn*.

91   The bishop refers to the requirement to announce a forthcoming marriage three times — "calling the banns" — usually over a three-week period. John burlesques the tradition by asking the congregation seven times on the wedding day, a tricksterish feature.

96   The comment is both ironical and quite searching: in earlier culture clothes did in some sense establish the powers of the person. Hence the many "sumptuary" laws which regulated the clothing to be worn by specific grades of people. In this instance, a man of the cloth (the bishop) loses his cloth (clothes).

107–08   As with so many of these ballads, the final sequence is a festival in the forest, linking in some way with the nature rituals of the Robin Hood play-game.

Robin Hood and Maid Marian

Introduction

This ballad has only survived in a broadside ballad which, from its tone, may well be post-Restoration. Much about this ballad suggests that it was deliberately constructed to add an element to the Robin Hood tradition. It is the only ballad where Maid Marian plays a part; she is briefly mentioned in *Robin Hood and Queen Catherin* and *Robin Hood's Golden Prize*. The diction seems characteristic of popular literary style (*gallant dame*, line 5; *Perplexed and vexed*, line 30; *a shaded bower*, line 63), while also having a distinctly broadside element *(With finger in eye, shee often did cry,* line 28; *With kind imbraces, and jobbing of faces,* line 56). The internal rhyme in the third line indicates a late and popular production.

Commentators have been severe on the ballad. Child calls it "this foolish ditty" (III, 218), while Dobson and Taylor speak of its "complete lack of literary merit" and call it an "extreme and implausible attempt" to combine Robin the lover and fighter (1976, p. 176). The events of the ballad had already been foreshadowed in Munday's play, where Matilda Fitzwater goes to the forest, becoming Marian in the process, to meet the Earl of Huntington, alias Robin Hood. The popularity of Robin Hood ballads was so great that several of these "prequels" seem to have been produced, as in *Robin Hood's Progress to Nottingham* and *Robin Hood and Little John*. Structurally the interesting thing about *Robin Hood and Maid Marian* is that it shows the only credible way to join the outlaw band is to fight a draw with the leader: this is a "Robin Hood meets his match" ballad in a wider sense than usual. Foolish as commentators have found it, the notion of the hero's fight with his lover is a potent one, whether it testifies to the woman's possible martial skill, or the enormity of mistreating woman, or both at once. Found in the recent film *Robin Hood: Prince of Thieves* (1991), the motif is here taken quite seriously, down to the length of the fight and the sight of blood, however improbable it may be that Marian does not hear Robin's voice until he asks for respite (line 50).

Robin Hood and Maid Marian clearly shows the gentrification process finding its way into the popular genres, but it does not seem to have been very popular, never appearing in the garlands and very little referred to or reworked even after Ritson made it well known.

Robin Hood and Maid Marian

A bonny fine maid of a noble degree,
With a hey down down a down down
Maid Marian calld by name,
Did live in the North, of excellent worth,
5   For she was a gallant dame.

For favour and face, and beauty most rare,
Queen Hellen shee did excell;
For Marian then was praisd of all men
That did in the country dwell.

10   'Twas neither Rosamond nor Jane Shore,   *(see note)*
Whose beauty was clear and bright,
That could surpass this country lass,
Beloved of lord and knight.

The Earl of Huntington, nobly born,
15   That came of noble blood,
To Marian went, with a good intent,
By the name of Robin Hood.

With kisses sweet their red lips meet,
For shee and the earl did agree;
20   In every place, they kindly imbrace,
With love and sweet unity.

But fortune bearing these lovers a spight,   *dislike*
That soon they were forced to part;
To the merry green wood then went Robin Hood,
25   With a sad and sorrowfull heart.

And Marian, poor soul, was troubled in mind,
For the absence of her friend;

Robin Hood and Maid Marian

With finger in eye, shee often did cry,
And his person did much comend.

30 Perplexed and vexed, and troubled in mind,
Shee drest her self like a page,
And ranged the wood to find Robin Hood,
The bravest of men in that age.

With quiver and bow, sword, buckler, and all,
35 Thus armed was Marian most bold,
Still wandering about to find Robin out,
Whose person was better then gold.

But Robin Hood hee himself had disguis'd,
And Marian was strangly attir'd,
40 That they prov'd foes, and so fell to blowes,
Whose vallour bold Robin admir'd.

They drew out their swords, and to cutting they went,
At least an hour or more,
That the blood ran apace from bold Robins face,
45 And Marian was wounded sore.

"O hold thy hand, hold thy hand," said Robin Hood,
"And thou shalt be one of my string,
To range in the wood with bold Robin Hood,
To hear the sweet nightingall sing."

50 When Marian did hear the voice of her love,
Her self shee did quickly discover,   *reveal*
And with kisses sweet she did him greet,
Like to a most loyall lover.

When bold Robin Hood his Marian did see,
55 Good lord, what clipping was there!   *embracing*
With kind imbraces, and jobbing of faces,   *thrusting*
Providing of gallant cheer.

For Little John took his bow in his hand,
And wandring in the wood,
60   To kill the deer, and make good chear,
For Marian and Robin Hood.

A stately banquet they had full soon,
All in a shaded bower,
Where venison sweet they had to eat,
65   And were merry that present hour.

Great flaggons of wine were set on the board,
And merrily they drunk round
Their boules of sack, to strengthen the back,   *sack (dry white wine)*
Whilst their knees did touch the ground.

70   First Robin Hood began a health
To Marian his onely dear,
And his yeomen all, both comly and tall,
Did quickly bring up the rear.

For in a brave veine they tost off the bouls,   *manner*
75   Whilst thus they did remain,
And every cup, as they drunk up,
They filled with speed again.

At last they ended their merryment,
And went to walk in the wood,
80   Where Little John and Maid Marian
Attended on bold Robin Hood.

In sollid content together they livd,
With all their yeomen gay;
They livd by their hands, without any lands,
85   And so they did many a day.

But now to conclude, an end I will make
In time, as I think it good,
For the people that dwell in the North can tell
Of Marian and bold Robin Hood.

4   Marian's residence in the north is probably suggested more by Parker's *A True
         Tale* and its stress on the north than by any older connection with Yorkshire or
         even Scotland.

10   While Helen in line 7 is a familiar classical reference to beauty, Rosamond and
         Jane Shore are famous medieval English beauties: "Fair Rosamond" was Henry
         II's great love, and Jane Shore a mistress of Edward IV. Neither they, nor
         Helen, had particularly happy careers, but there seems no irony intended.

14   Robin is very rarely identified as the Earl in a ballad. The other instances are
         Parker's *True Tale* and, simply through attaching his epitaph, *Robin Hood and
         the Valiant Knight*, Child no. 153. The reference here is part of the unusual and
         unqualified gentrification of this ballad.

24   The green wood has, it seems, become conventionally *merry* even when the hero
         has *a sad and sorrowfull heart* (line 25).

34   The reason why Marian is so heavily armed while dressed as a page is, like her
         failure to identify Robin's voice until after the fight, one of the logical
         incoherences — and conventions — of this ballad.

38   The text places a comma after *hee* as well as before; Child only prints the first,
         and this changes the stress for the worse.

62   The text has *the had*, and while in early texts *the* is often used for *they*, in this
         case it seems to be a printer's error and should be emended, as Child does.

74   The text has *vente,* which could perhaps mean "vaunt" or "celebration." Percy's
         handwritten copy of this ballad here reads *venie*. Child speculates that *venie*,
         presumably a variant for *veine* is correct and was misread by the compositor as
         vente. Though *vente* is technically the harder reading and might therefore be
         preferred, the phrase *in a brave veine* has just the conventional character of this
         ballad, and is accepted here.

74   The text has only *the bouls*; Child's emendation to *their* seems unnecessary.

84   Robin and Marian, though lord and lady, do not live off their lands. They are
          in some form of exile, but there also seems to be a rapprochement here between
          the gentrified overlay of this ballad and the "yeoman" basis to the tradition.
          The ballad does not finally re-establish Robin as Earl, so perhaps indicating its
          hybrid status, but also suggesting Parker's influence: his version ends with
          Robin's death, and so is not a full gentrification narrative in that the dispos-
          sessed nobleman is not restored to his dignities.

Robin Hood and Will Scarlet

Introduction

This ballad is found in seventeenth-century broadsides and early garlands under the title *Robin Hood Newly Revived*. Child printed it under that title, which has been generally accepted. Ritson, however, decided this was *Robin Hood and the Stranger*, for which a tune was known (and other ballads were said to be sung to it) but no words. Ritson's title is not appropriate because other ballads are as well qualified for that title, but *Robin Hood Newly Revived* is itself a poor name as it has nothing to do with the content of the ballad and is basically a publicist's blurb. In this edition the ballad is named *Robin Hood and Will Scarlet* because it appears to be dedicated to explaining the arrival in the outlaw band of a well-known figure (like other ballads in this section) and so deserves a parallel name.

However, the outlaw who is introduced seems quite different from the hard-handed figure who began his career as Will Scathelock and stood with Little John beside his leader as Cai and Bedwyr support Arthur in early Welsh tradition. This ballad uses the "prequel" pattern as a way of absorbing into the tradition the materials surrounding Gamelyn, hero of a separate epic romance, and perhaps also as a way of using materials from the lyric ballad *Robin and Gandelyn*.

Robin Hood and Will Scarlet has a familiar set of opening moves, so familiar they may smack of a written rather than oral tradition: a "Come all ye" opening; the motif of adventure before food; Robin meets a stranger in the forest. This stranger is distinctly aggressive (as others have been, like the Beggar and the Tinker whom Robin meets in minor ballads, Child nos. 133 and 127). Robin's threat to shoot is matched by the stranger and it seems that the fatal situation of *Robin and Gandelyn* is developing. But instead a fierce sword fight follows.

So much is familiar in the "Robin Hood meets his match" tradition. But the stranger reveals he is "Young Gamwell," who is fleeing to seek his uncle, Robin Hood. This action is reminiscent of *Gamelyn*, where the hero flees to the forest having killed his brother's porter and is welcomed by the outlaw king. Gamwell, it transpires, is Robin's sister's son (an especially strong version of the uncle-nephew relationship) and he is welcomed, absorbed into the band and immediately becomes one of the inner group, with Little John and Robin (as seen in *The Jolly Pinder of Wakefield* and other ballads).

Later Ballads

In form the ballad seems relatively early and not too heavily marked as literary. It has some strong colloquial diction, as in *For we have no vittles to dine* (line 9) or *Go play the chiven* (line 30), and the ballad in general lacks the elaborate diction and internal third-line rhyme that tend to mark the commercial products of the period; the occasional weak rhyme also looks back to the earlier and orally oriented ballads.

However, unlike other seventeenth-century ballads, there are no other references to suggest that this story existed early, though the title *Robin Hood Newly Revived* might be taken to suggest that a previous text had been reshaped for publication. In its earliest form, as its final lines indicate, it has attached to it seven stanzas of *Robin Hood and the Scotchman*, and there is a second part to this ballad which exists separately as *Robin Hood and the Prince of Aragon*. In spite of the possibility that an earlier ballad existed connecting Gamwell directly to the Robin Hood tradition, there is nothing to suggest that this whole ballad was not itself produced in the commercial context by a writer particularly well attuned to the earlier style of ballad. Intriguing as the connections of this ballad may be, all that can be said certainly is, as Child sums up, that it appears to "have been built up on a portion of the ruins, so to speak, of the fine tale of Gamelyn" (III, 144).

Robin Hood and Will Scarlet

Come listen a while, you gentlemen all,
With a hey down, down, a down down,
That are in this bower within,   *chamber*
For a story of gallant bold Robin Hood
5   I purpose now to begin.

"What time of the day?" quoth Robin Hood then;
Quoth Little John, " 'Tis in the prime."   *early morning*
"Why then we will to the green wood gang,   *go*
For we have no vittles to dine."   *victuals (food)*

10   As Robin Hood walkt the forrest along —
It was in the mid of the day —
There was he met of a deft young man   *by a skilfull*
As ever walkt on the way.

His doublet it was of silk, he said,
15   His stockings like scarlet shone,
And he walkt on along the way,
To Robin Hood then unknown.

A herd of deer was in the bend,   *bent (grassy field)*
All feeding before his face:
20   "Now the best of ye I'le have to my dinner,
And that in a little space."   *time*

Now the stranger he made no mickle adoe,   *great fuss*
But he bends and a right good bow,
And the best buck in the herd he slew,
25   Forty good yards him full froe.   *from him*

"Well shot, well shot," quoth Robin Hood then,
"That shot it was shot in time,   *with good timing*

501

And if thou wilt accept of the place
Thou shalt be a bold yeoman of mine."

30   "Go play the chiven," the stranger said,   *Run away*
"Make haste and quickly go,
Or with my fist, be sure of this,
I'le give thee buffets store."   *aplenty*

"Thou hadst not best buffet me," quoth Robin Hood,
35   "For though I seem forlorn,   *lost (alone)*
Yet I can have those that will take my part,
If I but blow my horn."

"Thou wast not best wind thy horn," the stranger said,
"Beest thou never so much in hast,   *If you be*
40   For I can draw out a good broad sword,
And quickly cut the blast."   *stop the sound*

Then Robin Hood bent a very good bow,
To that shoot, and he wold fain;   *eagerly*
The stranger he bent a very good bow,
45   To shoot at bold Robin again.

"O hold thy hand, hold thy hand," qoth Robin Hood,
"To shoot it would be in vain;
For if we should shoot the one at the other,
The one of us may be slain.

50   "But let's take our swords and our broad bucklers,
And gang under yonder tree."
"As I hope to be savd," the stranger he said,
"One foot I will not flee."

Then Robin Hood lent the stranger a blow,   *dealt*
55   Most scar'd him out of his wit;   *Almost*
"Thou never felt blow," the stranger he said,
"That shalt be better quit."

Robin Hood and Will Scarlet

The stranger he drew out a good broad sword,
And hit Robin on the crown,
60   That from every haire of bold Robins head
The blood ran trickling down.

"God a mercy, good fellow!" quoth Robin Hood then,
"And for this that thou hast done,
Tell me, good fellow, what thou art,
65   Tell me where thou doest woon."   *dwell*

The stranger then answered bold Robin Hood,
"I'le tell thee where I did dwell;
In Maxfield was I bred and born,
My name is Young Gamwell.

70   "For killing of my own fathers steward,
I am forc'd to this English wood,
And for to seek an uncle of mine;
Some call him Robin Hood."

"But thou art a cousin of Robin Hoods then?   *relative*
75   The sooner we should have done."
"As I hope to be sav'd," the stranger then said,
"I am his own sisters son."

But Lord! what kissing and courting was there,
When these two cousins did greet!   *cousins or male relatives*
80   And they went all that summers day,
And Little John did meet.

But when they met with Little John,
He thereunto did say,
"O master, where have you been,
85   You have tarried so long away?"

"I met with a stranger," quoth Robin Hood then,
"Full sore he hath beaten me."
"Then I'le have a bout with him," quoth Little John,
"And try if he can beat me."

90   "Oh, oh, no," quoth Robin Hood then,
         "Little John, it may be so;
         For he's my own dear sisters son,
         And cousins I have no mo.

         "But he shal be a bold yeoman of mine,
95   My chief man next to thee,
         And I Robin Hood and thou Little John,
         And Scarlet he shall be,

         "And wee'l be three of the bravest outlaws
         That is in the North Country."
100   If you will have any more of bold Robin Hood,
         In his second part it will be.

9   This seems like a simple version of Robin's unwillingness, like that of King Arthur, to dine before an adventure is enjoyed; see the *Gest*, lines 21–24.

10   A characteristic "Robin Hood meets his match" beginning, with language not unlike the first meeting with Allin a Dale.

25   Forty yards, while perhaps realistic as a good hunting shot, is far shorter than the distances alleged to have been mastered by archers in the earlier texts: four hundred yards would be a commoner claim. It is conceivable that the Roman numerals for 400 yards have been misread as "iiiiti," a version of "forty."

30   Gamwell is not only brusque to Robin, but offers him a distinctly ungentlemanly form of violence with his fists — both are characteristics of Gamelyn.

     chiven. "A very shy fish that hides in holes" (OED). To "play the chiven" is to run away precipitately.

43   The text reads *To that shoot and he wold fain*. Child emends to *To shoot and that he wold fain*, which makes good sense and is a little smoother, but the existing reading is unlikely to have been a compositor's error and does make sense; so it is retained.

49   Robin refers to what is the actual outcome in this situation in *Robyn and Gandelyn*. Perhaps this is a euphemized version of that ballad.

52   The two earlier sources lack *he*, but both meter and the parallels with line 55 indicate it is necessary.

68   *Maxfield.* This place name recurs in *Robin Hood and the Prince of Aragon* when Will Scadlock's father is described as "Of Maxfield earl." There is a Maxfield in East Sussex, but this is a long way away from the ballad areas, though curiously a Gilbert Robynhood was recorded from this area in 1291 (Dobson and Taylor, 1976, p. 12). It may be that here, as in other obscure place names,

North Yorkshire is the best location, with Maxfield Plain. While it may seem tempting to link these references to Macclesfield in Derbyshire, which still has an Earl, that title was not established until 1721, well after both ballads were in printed form.

70   In the *Gest* the knight's son had killed a knight of Lancaster and a squire (lines 209–10), but it was not clear what happened to him afterwards; Gamelyn is forced to flee to the woods after he has, among other crimes, killed his brother's (and before that his father's) porter.

83   Child reads *there unto him*, but the text reads only *thereunto*: the stress falls on the initial *He*, and there is no need to insert *him* for meter.

88   In a "Robin Hood meets his match" ballad it is usual for the other outlaws to want to revenge Robin, or for Robin to intervene, as here.

90   The text reads *Oh, oh, no*. Child inserts another *no*, presumably for meter, but it is not needed.

91   The text lacks *not* in this line, which Child inserts, though there is no room for it in the meter. If Robin's words are taken to mean "It must be so," then the line makes sense in the original, which is retained.

97   The name Scarlet is introduced with very little fuss, and the next line seems to refer to the well-known opening of ballads which named the three outlaws Robin, John, and Will. This is the line which Child thought was taken from *The Jolly Pinder of Wakefield* to appear in Shakespeare's *Merry Wives of Windsor* and *Henry IV Part 2* and Beaumont and Fletcher's *Philaster* (III, 129).

99   The *North Country* is again the expected domain of the outlaw's activities; this ballad almost certainly post-dates Parker's *A True Tale*, which specified that as Robin Hood's area, and the idea is probably from there, not from the northern activities in the *Gest* or Andrew of Wyntoun's chronicle.

101   The *second part* is discussed in the Introduction to this ballad, p. 500.

Robin Hood's Progress To Nottingham

Introduction

This ballad appears in several seventeenth-century broadsides and the early garlands, and is the first to appear in the Forresters manuscript, under the title *Robin Hood and the Forresters*: that text seems a retelling, with some literary effect, of the Wood text dated by Wing in 1656. It represents a story that was certainly known by the time of the Sloane *Life of Robin Hood* in the late sixteenth century, so it is not clear why Child calls it "a comparatively late ballad" (III, 175) and prints it so late in his volume (no. 139), when, because of the earlier nature of the story, it should stand between *The Jolly Pinder* and *Robin Hood and Little John* (as no. 125).

The fierce tone of the ballad is very different from most that first appear in the seventeenth century: it tells how Robin, harassed by fifteen foresters, shoots them down in what seems an orgy of self-defence. Even the people of Nottingham are badly hurt as they chase the young hero, and there seems to be a *grand guignol* relish about the fact that in the process *Some lost legs, and some lost arms* (line 67). There is no sign that the ballad was meant to be read as grotesque or ironic, and it remained popular in the garlands. It harks back to the violent anti-forester spirit of *Johnie Cock* (which Child carefully placed just before the Robin Hood ballads) and has similarities in that way with the conflict between Robin and Guy of Gisborne.

The language and rhyme suggest this is a fairly old ballad, quite possibly of sixteenth-century origin as the Sloane *Life* would suggest, though it was presumably produced in prequel mode as a way of explaining how Robin became an outlaw, quite different from the gentrified explanations that he was over-generous (Grafton and Parker) or simply had clerical enemies (Munday). In this respect this ballad shows the multiple character of the tradition, and that the earlier severity of the outlaw survived in contrast to more sophisticated versions. The garlands of 1663 and 1670 print somewhat gentrified pieces like *Robin Hood and Queen Catherin* (Child no. 145) alongside this ballad's powerful assertion of how a social bandit can be created by the violent malice of the agents of law.

507

Robin Hood's Progress to Nottingham

Robin Hood hee was and a tall young man,   *fit (strong)*
Derry derry down
And fifteen winters old,
And Robin Hood he was a proper young man,
5   Of courage stout and bold.
Hey down derry derry down.

Robin Hood he would and to fair Nottingham,
With the general for to dine;   *To eat with the people*
There was he ware of fifteen forresters,
10   And a drinking bear, ale, and wine.   *beer*

"What news? What news?" said bold Robin Hood;
"What news, fain wouldest thou know?
Our king hath provided a shooting-match,
And I'm ready with my bow."

15   "We ho'd it in scorn," then said the forresters,   *hold*
"That ever a boy so young
Should bear a bow before our king,
That's not able to draw one string."

"I'le hold you twenty marks," said bold Robin Hood,   *bet*
20   "By the leave of Our Lady,
That I'le hit a mark a hundred rod,
And I'le cause a hart to dye."

"We'l hold you twenty mark," then said the forresters,
"By the leave of Our Lady,
25   Thou hitst not the marke a hundred rod,
Nor causest a hart to dye."

Robin Hood's Progress to Nottingham

Robin Hood he bent up a noble bow,
And a broad arrow he let flye,   *broad-headed*
He hit the mark a hundred rod,   *550 yards*
30   And he caused a hart to dy.

Some said hee brake ribs one or two,
And some said hee brake three;
The arrow within the hart would not abide,
But it glanced in two or three.

35   The hart did skip, and the hart did leap,
And the hart lay on the ground.
"The wager is mine," said bold Robin Hood,
"If't were for a thousand pound."

"The wager's none of thine," then said the forresters,
40   "Although thou beest in haste;
Take up thy bow, and get thee hence,
Lest wee thy sides do baste."   *beat*

Robin Hood hee took up his noble bow,
And his broad arrows all amain,   *strongly*
45   And Robin Hood he laught, and begun to smile,
As hee went over the plain.

Then Robin Hood hee bent his noble bow,
And his broad arrows he let flye,
Till fourteen of these fifteen forresters
50   Upon the ground did lye.

He that did this quarrel first begin,
Went tripping over the plain,   *hurrying*
But Robin Hood he bent his noble bow,
And hee fetcht him back again.

55   "You said I was no archer," said Robin Hood,
"But say so now again."
With that he sent another arrow
That split his head in twain.

509

"You have found mee an archer," saith Robin Hood,
60 "Which will make your wives for to wring,   *[their hands]*
And wish that you had never spoke the word,
That I could not draw one string."

The people that lived in fair Nottingham
Came runing out amain,   *quickly*
65 Supposing to have taken bold Robin Hood,
With the forresters that were slain.   *Because of*

Some lost legs, and some lost arms,
And some did lose their blood,
But Robin Hood hee took up his noble bow,
70 And is gone to the merry green wood.

They carryed these forresters into fair Nottingham,
As many there did know;
They digd them graves in their church-yard,
And they buried them all a row.

510

Notes

1   The Forresters text opens strangely with the line "Randolph kept Robin fifteen winters." It is hard to believe this is the Randolph, Earle of Chester, mentioned in *Piers Plowman* as appearing in "rhymes" with (or against) Robin, yet there seems no other link between the names. Perhaps the literary interests evident elsewhere in Forresters inspire a rationalization of the *Piers Plowman* reference, just as *Robin Hood and Will Scarlet* seems to rationalize the link between Gamelyn and the king of the outlaws.

7   It is not clear where Robin is coming from. The implication is that the end of the ballad is when he takes to the forest for the first time, so he must be coming to Nottingham from one of the surrounding villages, presumably those to the north, adjacent to or even within Sherwood forest.

11–14   The number of the speakers in this stanza is, according to Child, unclear. He feels that Robin speaks the first and last line, and the foresters the middle two lines, though he admits in his notes it is unlikely "in an older ballad" to have "three speeches in one stanza" (III, 177). But as he places this ballad fairly late, he presumably feels his punctuation is correct. In fact it seems quite improbable. There is no difficulty with Robin speaking the whole stanza, informing the foresters that there is news, and what it is.

15   The earliest text reads *ho'd*, a dialectal form of "hold."

21   A hundred rod, or five hundred and fifty yards, is about the limit of possible archery skills in the early ballads, especially for a fifteen year old. In the Forresters MS, no *mark* is mentioned, just the *hart*, which is clearer.

28   The broad-headed arrow is used for felling sizeable game, including men. Robin is heavily armed for a shooting-match.

39   Characteristic of Forresters' literary tone is "thou dost provoke us," the Forresters' response instead of the colloquial *The wager's none of thine*.

511

54   Presumably the text means that Robin stopped his flight with a near miss, made him run in the other direction back towards his dead colleagues, and then killed him.

Robin Hood Rescues Three Young Men

Introduction

This ballad has many slightly different versions, some of which show the influence of other Robin Hood ballads. Such a complex set of overlapping texts is common in the case of the "big" ballads like *Lady Isabel and the Elf-Knight* or *Clerk Saunders* but unusual in the Robin Hood tradition. As a result, the title of this ballad itself is not easy to fix: Child calls it *Robin Hood Rescuing Three Squires*, but only in some versions are the potential victims called squires. In others they are the widow's three sons or three brothers, and sometimes they are Robin's own men. The essence of the ballad is that Robin disguises himself as the hangman in order to rescue wrongfully condemned men, and a general title, *Robin Hood Rescues Three Young Men*, seems the best.

The ballad is found in a much damaged form in Percy's folio MS and the base text here is the earliest full version, found in an eighteenth-century garland; though the Percy version is a little different it only covers two incidents in a fairly long ballad, and while these are useful for collation and emendation, it would be inappropriate and require substantial editorial invention to link those episodes into the other text. The story clearly goes back some way; this is the only substantial borrowing from the ballad tradition to appear in Munday's *The Downfall of Robert, Earle of Huntington*, of 1598–99, where the rescue is of Scathelock and Scarlet, Robin's men and sons of Widow Scarlet. In that and in other versions of the ballad there seems some link between this old woman and the one who changes clothes with Robin for his protection in *Robin Hood and the Bishop*. On his way to rescue the young men Robin usually changes clothes with a beggar, in a scene that resembles one from *Robin Hood and the Beggar I* (Child, III, 157, see stanzas 16–18), though there the Beggar then becomes a worthy opponent in a "Robin Hood meets his match" structure.

The ballad, though recorded late in full form, appears to have a direct style likely to derive from the early seventeenth century at the latest: rhyme is reasonably accurate but not over-precise, diction is colloquial and direct with no sign of bookish invention. There is a good deal of repetition with change (lines 13–20, 37–48) as well as a good deal of rhetorical repetition (lines 73–74, 77–79, 89–92), both of which suggest an oral context of some kind. This is also a strong story of quick and decisive action, where Robin moves between the widow, the beggar, and the sheriff with speedy confidence. The ballad has the dramatic flavor of the earliest texts, and at least some of their sense of social conflict; the outlaws' real threat to bad authority is suggested when they move the gallows from the town to hang the sheriff in the glen, their own territory, where he has done his damage.

Unelaborate but highly effective, *Robin Hood Rescues Three Young Men* is clearly one of the more strongly popular of the mainstream outlaw ballads, and its multiplicity and manifold changes indicate how close it remained to the popular voice, rather than, like some others, becoming set in a literary form.

Robin Hood Rescues Three Young Men

There are twelve months in all the year,
As I hear many men say,
But the merriest month in all the year
Is the merry month of May.

5   Now Robin Hood is to Nottingham gone,
With a link a down and a day,
And there he met a silly old woman,   *(see note)*
Was weeping on the way.

"What news? what news, thou silly old woman?
10   What news hast thou for me?"
Said she, "There's three squires in Nottingham town
To-day is condemned to die."

"O have they parishes burnt?" he said,
"Or have they ministers slain?
15   Or have they robbed any virgin,
Or with other men's wives have lain?"

"They have no parishes burnt, good sir,
Nor yet have ministers slain,
Nor have they robbed any virgin,
20   Nor with other men's wives have lain."

"O what have they done?" said bold Robin Hood
"I pray thee tell to me."
"It's for slaying of the king's fallow deer,
Bearing their long bows with thee."

25   "Dost thou not mind, old woman," he said,   *remember*
"Since thou made me sup and dine?

By the truth of my body," quoth bold Robin Hood,
"You could not tell it in better time."   *remind me of it*

Now Robin Hood is to Nottingham gone,
30 With a link a down and a day,
And there he met with a silly old palmer,   *pilgrim*
Was walking along the highway.

"What news? what news, thou silly old man?
What news, I do thee pray?"
35 Said he, "Three squires in Nottingham town
Are condemnd to die this day."

"Come change thy apparel with me, old man,
Come change thy apparel for mine;
Here is forty shillings in good silver,
40 Go drink it in beer or wine."

"O thine apparel is good," he said,
"And mine is ragged and torn;
Wherever you go, wherever you ride,
Laugh neer an old man to scorn."   *Never laugh*

45 "Come change thy apparel with me, old churl,
Come change thy apparel with mine;
Here are twenty pieces of good broad gold,
Go feast thy brethren with wine."

Then he put on the old man's hat,
50 It stood full high on the crown:
"The first bold bargain that I come at,   *dispute (fight)*
It shall make thee come down."

Then he put on the old man's cloak,
Was patchd black, blew, and red;
55 He thought no shame all the day long
To bear the bags of bread.

Then he put on the old man's breeks,   *breeches*
Was patchd from ballup to side: *groin*
"By the truth of my body," bold Robin can say,
60 "This man lovd little pride."

Then he put on the old man's hose,
Were patchd from knee to waist:
"By the truth of my body," said bold Robin Hood,
"I'd laugh if I had any list."   *wish [to do so]*

65 Then he put on the old man's shoes,
Were patchd both beneath and aboon,   *on top*
Then Robin Hood swore a solemn oath,
"It's good habit that makes a man."

Now Robin Hood is to Nottingham gone,
70 With a link a down and a down,
And there he met with the proud sheriff,
Was walking along the town.

"O save, O save, O sherrif," he said,   *God save [you]*
"O save, and you may see!
75 And what will you give to a silly old man
To-day will your hangman be?"

"Some suits, some suits," the sheriff he said,
"Some suits I'll give to thee;
Some suits, some suits, and pence thirteen
80 To-day's a hangman's fee."

Then Robin he turns him round about,
And jumps from stock to stone.
"By the truth of my body," the sheriff he said,
"That's well jumpt, thou nimble old man."

85 "I was neer a hangman in all my life,   *never*
Nor yet intends to trade,
But curst be he," said bold Robin,
"That first a hangman was made.

517

"I've a bag for meal, and a bag for malt,
90   And a bag for barley and corn,
    A bag for bread, and a bag for beef,
    And a bag for my little small horn.

"I have a horn in my pocket,
    I got it from Robin Hood,
95   And still when I set it to my mouth,
    For thee it blows little good."

"O wind thy horn, thou proud fellow,
    Of thee I have no doubt;   *fear*
    I wish that thou give such a blast,
100 Till both thy eyes fly out."

The first loud blast that he did blow,
    He blew both loud and shrill;
    A hundred and fifty of Robin Hood's men
    Came riding over the hill.

105 The next loud blast that he did give,
    He blew both loud and amain,   *strongly*
    And quickly sixty of Robin Hood's men
    Came shining over the plain.   *shinning (hurrying)*

"O who are you," the sheriff he said,
110 "Come tripping over the lee?"
    "They're my attendants," brave Robin did say,
    "They'll pay a visit to thee."

They took the gallows from the slack,   *town common*
    They set it in the glen,   *valley*
115 They hangd the proud sheriff on that,
    Releasd their own three men.

1–4   This is very close to the stanza found at the beginning of *The Jolly Pinder of Wakefield*. It may have been a chorus in sung versions, referring to the late Maytime connections of Robin Hood activities.

7   The word *silly* here has resonances of its meaning as OE *saelig*, simple, blessed: modern British English "poor old" transmits the sense fairly accurately. See *Robin Hood and the Bishop* for another instance of Robin's alliance with an old widow.

24   In this version, as in a number of others, the young men, though called *squires* (line 35), are associates of Robin and his band.

31   A palmer is technically a pilgrim who has been to Jerusalem and so wears either a palm leaf or a badge representing a palm.

39   Forty shillings is a very substantial sum equivalent to many weeks' work; elsewhere Robin offers a noble (six shillings and eightpence) as a fee for joining his band.

56   The text reads *To wear the bags of bread*. One later text emphasizes the shame by adding the adjective *poor* before *bags*, and Child accepts *poor*: this seems unnecessary, partly because it is obviously an addition and also because it disrupts the meter. Child retains *wear*, but it seems hard to grasp how Robin, or the beggar, would actually "wear" the bags of bread, even if they are secreted in his old cloak. Later on it seems as if they are evident, lines 89–92. Emendation to *bear* seems sensible, better than imagining that *wear* means "carry."

68   This is similar to the remark made by Robin, equally ironically, when John plays the bishop in *Robin Hood and Allin a Dale*. Ideas about authenticity and pretence recur in the tradition and can be taken as the thematic version of disguise as a plot-motif.

76 This is the disguise motif, but here Robin is not just a harper or a potter — he is actually accepted as an agent of town authority, so the motif strengthens into one of infiltration.

77 It was traditional for the executioner to receive the clothes of the condemned person.

89–92 This stanza is very similar to stanza 18 of *Robin Hood and the Beggar I* (Child no. 133); Child thought that what he called *Robin Hood Rescuing Three Squires* was the source of the influence, which extends to plot in the later part of *Robin Hood and the Beggar I*, III, 156.

93–94 The statement is parallel to the claim of the pseudo-potter in *Robin Hood and the Potter* that he received his bow from Robin Hood. It seems that there is a kind of mythic presence of the outlaw before his real presence is revealed; this meshes with the common proverbial utterances about him, his mysterious strength and ubiquity.

96 The text reads *For me* which seems hard to understand; Child emends to *thee* and this is accepted.

100 Child emends *fly* to "fall," which seems unnecessary.

109 The text reads *O who are you?* Child emends to *who are yon*, feeling that Robin cannot really be part of the new arrivals. It is true that *yon* is the reading of the later texts and the two letters are often confused. Yet *who are yon* is a strange remark, and it is quite possible to make sense of the original reading, in that the sheriff suddenly realizes the supposed hangman has allies. The text is not emended here.

111 Child prints *The're my attendants* as in the source, but the substitution of *the* for *they* must at this late date be an error rather than a dialect variant; the text needs to be emended to *They're*.

113 This curious detail seems to relate to the common idea that criminals should be hanged at the site of their crimes, and so the sheriff is hanged on the outlaw's territory. More generally, taking away the gallows, like providing the hangman, is a blow at the whole system of oppressive law, expressing the elusive capacity of the outlaws, and their own form of justice.

Little John a Begging

Introduction

Little John a Begging appears in the Percy folio in a form too damaged by torn pages to be used as the basis for a text, but the earliest broadside is of a similar date as it was printed for William Gilbertson, who was active between 1640 and 1663. This text describes it as a "merry new song" (line 86) and while broadside publishers were not above claiming modernity for something borrowed, it does have the characteristics of a new creation. Both the internal rhyme in the third line and the stylistic fluency argue against antiquity, the refrain line "With a hey down down a down down" is common to many of the mid-century ballads, and the plot appears to be a composite of earlier narratives, focused for a change on Little John. This ballad appears towards the end of the Forresters manuscript and is one of the late texts apparently related, with some minor variations to the 1670 garland, so it has the curious status of apparently having been twice copied in manuscript from print.

The story opens with John being sent to beg for the outlaws in a palmer's clothes (reminiscent of *Robin Hood Rescues Three Young Men*, including the "bag" motif in lines 12–17). He meets beggars who claim poverty as do the monks met by outlaws in earlier ballads; he finds in their bags two lots of gold in hundreds of pounds, and the outlaws celebrate their new wealth. The plot is simple, and its only added complexity is the idea of false beggars who pretend to be dumb, blind, and crippled. The notion is found as early as Langland's *Piers Plowman* and its exposure of "faitours," but it has a contemporary ring in its critique of "sturdy beggars." A different formation lies in the idea that the hero can disguise himself as a beggar; this is central to the popular ballad "Hind Horn" (Child, no. 17, 1965, I, 202–07), Robin Hood does it in *Robin Hood Rescuing Three Squires*, and William Wallace does the same in a major episode in the late fifteenth-century epic that bears his name. A recurring structural feature is that the outlaws disguise themselves to expose the falsity of their enemies, with Robin appearing as a friar in *Robin Hood's Golden Prize*, and as a shepherd in *Robin Hood and the Bishop of Hereford*. In one sense John plays a tradesman (at the "begging-trade," line 66) with the same success as Robin had playing potter or butcher, or even sailor, and yet these beggars are morally corrupt in a way that the mercantile figures whom Robin imitated were not. In this case the polymorphic capacity of the hero is an instrument of his power of social evaluation: like Hamlet he pretends only to expose pretense.

521

Little John a Begging

All you that delight to spend some time
    With a hey down down a down down
A merry song for to sing,
Unto me draw neer, and you shall hear
5   How Little John went a begging.

As Robin Hood walked the forrest along,
And all his yeomandree,   *yeomanry (men)*
Sayes Robin, "Some of you must a begging go,
And Little John, it must be thee."

10   Sayes John, "If I must a begging go,
I will have a palmers weed,   *pilgrim's clothing*
With a staff and a coat, and bags of all sort,
The better then shall I speed.

"Come give me now a bag for my bread,
15   And another for my cheese,
And one for a peny, when as I get any,
That nothing I may leese."   *lose*

Now Little John he is a begging gone,
Seeking for some relief,
20   But of all the beggers he met on the way,
Little John he was the chief.

But as he was walking himself alone
Four beggers he chanced to spy,
Some deaf and some blind, and some came behind:
25   Says John, "Here's brave company!

Little John a Begging

"Good morrow," said John, "my brethren dear,
Good fortune I had you to see;
Which way do you go? Pray let me know,
For I want some company.

30 "O what is here to do?" then said Little John,
"Why rings all these bells?" said he,
"What dog is a-hanging? Come let us be ganging,   *let us go*
That we the truth may see."

"Here is no dog a-hanging," then one of them said,
35 "Good fellow, we tell unto thee;
But here is one dead wil give us cheese and bread,
And it may be one single peny."   *Even if*

"We have brethren in London," another he said,
"So have we in Coventry,
40 In Barwick and Dover, and all the world over,
But nere a crookt carril like thee.   *crooked churl*

"Therefore stand thee back, thou crooked carel,
And take that knock on the crown."   *head*
"Nay," said Little John, "I'le not yet be gone,
45 For a bout will I have with you round.

"Now have at you all," then said Little John,
"If you be so full of your blows;
Fight on all four, and nere give ore,   *never; over*
Whether you be friends or foes."

50 John nipped the dumb, and made him to rore,
And the blind that could not see,
And he that a cripple had been seven years,
He made him run faster then he.

And flinging them all against the wall,
55 With many a sturdie bang,
It made John sing, to hear the gold ring,
Which against the walls cryed "Twang."

523

Then he got out of the beggers cloak
Three hundred pound in gold.
60   "Good fortune had I," then said Little John.
"Such a good sight to behold."

But what found he in a beggers bag,
But three hundred pound and three?
"If I drink water while this doth last,
65   Then an ill death may I dye!

"And my begging-trade I will now give ore,   *over*
My fortune hath bin so good,   *been*
Therefore I'le not stay, but I will away,
To the forrest of merry Sherwood."

70   And when to the forrest of Sherwood he came,
He quickly there did see,
His master good, bold Robin Hood,
And all his company.

"What news? What news?" then said Robin Hood,
75   "Come, Little John, tell unto me,
How hast thou sped with thy beggers trade?
For that I fain would see."   *gladly*

"No news but good," then said Little John,
"With begging ful wel I have sped;   *prospered*
80   Six hundred and three I have here for thee,
In silver and gold so red."

Then Robin took Little John by the hand
And danced about the oak tree.
"If we drink water while this doth last,
85   Then an il death may we die!"

So to conclude my merry new song,
All you that delight it to sing,
'Tis of Robin Hood, that archer good,
And how Little John went a begging.

8	No other ballad shows the outlaws directly begging for money; in the *Gest* Robin orders his men off to seek money by robbery, but it seems unlikely that they would demean themselves by begging. The improbability of this opening is dictated by the later action in which John the false beggar exposes even falser beggars, but this forced quality is not found in the earlier ballads, which open with dramatic but inherently credible sequences.
11	The wording here closely resembles that of *Robin Hood Rescues Three Young Men*, 89–92; this is not so clearly the case in the version in the Percy Folio and some cross-influence in the London broadside industry appears to have occurred.
23	There are three beggars in the Percy version, not four; later in this ballad when Little John deals with them separately, only three are identified, see lines 50–53.
31	Little John pretends to hear bells ringing when, as becomes clear (and as he presumably has guessed), it is the coins he hears jingling in the coat pockets and bags.
38	In addition to London, the beggars mention two towns at opposite ends of England (Berwick in the north and Dover in the south) and Coventry in the midlands.
41	The "beggars" call John a crooked carril, or churl, because he is stooping in disguise; like them he is pretending to be physically disabled.
48	*nere*. The version in the 1663 garland has "never" in this line, which is perhaps metrically better, but this does not seem good enough reason to emend.
53	Wood's text reads "them," as if John makes all three beggars run, but the sense is sharper if "him," the reading of the 1663 and 1670 garlands and that of Child,

is accepted, as then John makes each of the beggars breach his previous pretence.

59   At a time when, it has been estimated, a craftsman earned three pounds a year, these are unimaginably large sums of money, perhaps equivalent to the astronomical "street value" quoted today for drugs impounded by police.

64   John's humorous oath, repeated by Robin at line 84, swears never to drink water until all the money is expended.

76   John's success at the "beggers trade" is reminiscent of Robin's as a potter or a butcher, and even John's as the sheriff's yeoman in the *Gest*. The outlaws expose the corrupt or improper nature of a trade and also make huge profits.

80   Both the 1663 and 1670 garlands read "Three hundred and three" but this must be an error as John collects two sums adding up to six hundred and three.

Robin Hood's Birth, Breeding, Valour, and Marriage

Introduction

This ballad was moderately well-known, with three versions surviving from the seventeenth century, that in the Roxburghe collection (dated by Wing at 1681–84) seeming earlier than the two collected by Pepys, and therefore the basis for this text. It appeared in three eighteenth-century collections before Ritson, but is not included in the early garlands, which may suggest it is less than fully popular in its distribution. That accords with its character: it is patently a literary confection, and unlike the author of *Robin Hood and Queen Catherin* the composer has wandered well outside the Robin Hood tradition for materials. The final reference to the King and the national hope for heirs appears to locate it soon after the Restoration in 1660 when there was a good deal of activity in constructing new forms of the Robin Hood tradition, as in *Robin Hood and His Crew of Souldiers*, the 1662 *Life,* and what appears to be the first of the garlands from 1663.

The title alone suggests an overview close to the gentrified tradition of heroic biography, but the ballad is actually less grand than its title might suggest. Robin has gentry connection, in that he is the nephew of Squire Gamwell of Gamwell Hall — a connection to be made much of in the lengthy development of the Victorian novel, especially Pierce Egan the Younger's *Robin Hood and Little John* (1840). Yet Squire George is a robust character, who could hardly be accused of gentrification, even though he comes from the gentry. He resembles Fielding's Squire Western in this, and another character projects a similar surprising rural directness. Robin has the good fortune to meet and instantly become engaged to a woman from the realms of pastoral, Clorinda the Queen of the Shepherdesses. But although she resembles Ben Jonson's Maid Marian (from *The Sad Shepherd*) in being a serious hunter, there is a direct quality to her instant agreement to marriage and her felling a buck, and also in her glee at the Tutbury Christmas fair — not to mention her shout to her forest lover as he has just killed five foresters:

> The bumpkins are beaten, put up thy sword, Bob,
> And now let's dance into the town. (179–80)

The same vigorous eclecticism infects the author's assemblage of material. After two

527

relatively familiar opening stanzas, Robin's father is introduced, to be instantly supplanted by a flood of characters from parallel traditions (the Pinder of Wakefield, already connected to Robin in a famous ballad), and the Cumberland outlaws Adam Bell, Clim of the Clough, and William of Cloudeslie, whose ballad was popular through the period. From further off he brings Robin's mother's uncle, Sir Guy of Warwick, from medieval romance and popular tradition. And then there is the question of the origin of the name Gamwell. As has been discussed in the context of *Robin Hood and Will Scarlet* (see p. 499) this may well have been another parallel outlaw story which simply becomes entangled in various ways with the Robin Hood story, much as that of Owein, Yvain, or Ywain did with the Arthur saga. After this improbably wide-ranging presentation of characters comes a brisk story in a highly competent style which celebrates the jovial squire and especially the bold, entrancing Clorinda, dark of hair and quick to shoot. But there is also rough action and comedy: Robin and John kill five of the eight foresters and then all involved enjoy the direct pleasures of the Tutbury Christmas fair, including the now defunct English market town sport of bull-running.

Tutbury, in Staffordshire, is in just the region of the Robin Hood riot that broke out in Walsall in 1497 (Knight, 1994, p. 108), and there are indications that this ballad is concocted with some local reference. The emphasis on specific personal names in lines 185–96 and at line 215 suggest that this ensemble of styles and stories is also locally connected, much as the nineteenth-century pantomimes, with just the same range of transgressiveness, also focus at times on local personalities and events.

Child found this ballad "jocular" (1965, III, 214), and while purists might frown at the mixed nature of its materials and tone, it has an undeniable vigor, not unlike some of the crass but energetic outlaw films of this century. It is particularly interesting that here, as in *Robin Hood and Queen Catherin*, some elements of gentrification are visible, yet the ballad as a whole lacks the constraint and the conservatism of that part of the tradition. While respectability was closing about some elements of the outlaw myth, the tricksterish and carnival forces that so often energize the material are seen, here at least, to be a good match for the forces of respectability: in later versions of this ballad the King offers Robin a place at court but, in the spirit of the *Gest*, he refuses.

Robin Hood's Birth, Breeding, Valour, and Marriage

Kind gentlemen, will you be patient awhile?
Ay, and then you shall hear anon   *at once*
A very good ballad of bold Robin Hood,
And of his man, brave Little John.

5   In Locksly town, in Nottinghamshire,
In merry sweet Locksly town,
There bold Robin Hood he was born and was bred,
Bold Robin of famous renown.

The father of Robin a forrester was,
10   And he shot in a lusty long bow,
Two north country miles and an inch at a shot,
As the Pinder of Wakefield does know.

For he brought Adam Bell, and Clim of the Clugh,
And William a Clowdeslé
15   To shoot with our forrester for forty mark,
And the forrester beat them all three.

His mother was neece to the Coventry knight,
Which Warwickshire men call Sir Guy,
For he slew the blue bore that hangs up at the gate,
20   Or mine host of The Bull tells a lye.

Her brother was Gamwel, of Great Gamwel Hall,
And a noble house-keeper was he,
Ay, as ever broke bread in sweet Nottinghamshire,
And a squire of famous degree.   *social status*

25   The mother of Robin said to her husband,
"My honey, my love, and my dear,

529

Let Robin and I ride this morning to Gamwel,
To taste of my brothers good cheer."

And he said, "I grant thee thy boon, gentle Joan,
30   Take one of my horses, I pray;
The sun is a rising, and therefore make haste,
For tomorrow is Christmas-day."

Then Robin Hoods fathers grey gelding was brought,
And sadled and bridled was he;
35   God wot, a blew bonnet, his new suit of cloaths,
And a cloak that did reach to his knee.

She got on her holiday kirtle and gown,
They were of a light Lincoln green.
The cloath was homespun, but for colour and make
40   It might a beseemed our queen.   *have suited*

And then Robin got on his basket-hilt sword,
And his dagger on his tother side,   *other*
And said, "My dear mother, let's haste to be gone,
We have forty long miles to ride."

45   When Robin had mounted his gelding so grey,
His father, without any trouble,
Set her up behind him, and bad her not fear,
For his gelding had oft carried double.

And when she was settled, they rode to their neighbours,
50   And drank and shook hands with them all,
And then Robin gallopt and never gave ore,
Til they lighted at Gamwell Hall.   *stopped*

And now you may think the right worshipful squire
Was joyful his sister to see,
55   For he kist her and kist her, and swore a great oath,
"Thou art welcome, kind sister, to me."

Robin Hood's Birth, Breeding, Valour, and Marriage

To-morrow, when mass had been said in the chapel,
Six tables were coverd in the hall,
And in comes the squire and makes a short speech,
60   It was "Neighbours, you're welcome all.

"But not a man here shall taste my March beer,
Till a Christmas carrol be sung."
Then all clapt their hands, and they shouted and sung,
Till the hall and the parlour did ring.

65   Now mustards, braun, roast beef and plumb pies   *boar flesh*
Were set upon every table,
And noble George Gamwell said, "Eat and be merry,
And drink, too, as long as you're able."

When dinner was ended, his chaplain said grace,
70   And "Be merry, my friends," said the squire,
"It rains and it blows, but call for more ale,
And lay some more wood on the fire.

"And now call ye Little John hither to me,
For Little John is a fine lad
75   At gambols and juggling and twenty such tricks
As shall make you merry and glad."

When Little John came, to gambols they went,
Both gentlemen, yeomen and clown;   *yokel*
And what do you think? Why as true as I live
80   Bold Robin Hood put them all down.

And now you may think the right worshipful squire
Was joyful this sight for to see,
For he said, "Cousin Robin, thou'st go no more home,
But tarry and dwell here with me.

85   "Thou shalt have my land when I dye and till then
Thou shalt be the staff of my age."
"Then grant me my boon, dear uncle," said Robin,
"That Little John may be my page."   *assistant*

531

And he said, "Kind cousin, I grant thee thy boon,
90   With all my heart, so let it be."
"Then come hither, Little John," said Robin Hood
"Come hither, my page unto me.

"Go fetch me my bow, my longest long bow,
And broad arrows, one, two, or three,
95   For when it is fair weather we'll into Sherwood,
Some merry pastime to see."

When Robin Hood came into merry Sherwood
He winded his bugle so clear,   *blew*
And twice five and twenty good yeomen and bold
100   Before Robin Hood did appear.

"Where are your companions all?" said Robin Hood,
"For still I want forty and three."
Then said a bold yeoman, "Lo, yonder they stand,
All under a green wood tree."

105   As that word was spoke, Clorinda came by,
The queen of the shepherds was she,
And her gown was of velvet as green as the grass,
And her buskin did reach to her knee.   *high boot*

Her gait it was graceful, her body was straight,
110   And her countenance free from pride;
A bow in her hand, and quiver and arrows
Hung dangling by her sweet side.

Her eye-brows were black, ay and so was her hair,
And her skin was as smooth as glass;
115   Her visage spoke wisdom, and modesty too:
Sets with Robin Hood such a lass.   *Suits*

Said Robin Hood, "Lady fair, whither away?
Oh whither, fair lady, away?"
And she made him answer, "To kill a fat buck,
120   For tomorrow is Titbury day."

Robin Hood's Birth, Breeding, Valour, and Marriage

Said Robin Hood "Lady fair, wander with me
A little to yonder green bower;
There sit down to rest you, and you shall be sure
Of a brace or a lease in an hour."   *two or three*

125   And as we were going towards the green bower
Two hundred good bucks we espy'd;
She chose out the fattest that was in the herd
And she shot him through side and side.

"By the faith of my body," said bold Robin Hood,
130   "I never saw woman like thee;
And comst thou from east, ay, or comst thou from west,
Thou needst not beg venison of me.

"However, along to my bower you shall go,
And taste of a forresters meat."
135   And when we come thither, we found as good cheer
As any man needs for to eat.

For there was hot venison and warden pies cold,
Cream-clouted with honey-combs plenty, [1]
And the sarvitors they were, beside Little John,
140   Good yeomen at least four and twenty.

Clorinda said, "Tell me your name, gentle sir."
And he said, "'Tis bold Robin Hood;
Squire Gamwel's my uncle, but all my delight
Is to dwell in the merry Sherwood.

145   "For 'tis a fine life, and 'tis void of all strife."
"So 'tis sir," Clorinda reply'd.
"But oh," said bold Robin, "how sweet would it be,
If Clorinda would be my bride!"

---

[1] *cold pear pies / With clotted cream and honey*

533

She blusht at the notion, yet after a pause
150 Said, "Yes, sir, and with all my heart."
"Then let's send for a priest," said Robin Hood
"And be married before we do part."

But she said, "It may not be so, gentle sir,
For I must be at Titbury feast;
155 And if Robin Hood will go thither with me,
I'll make him the most welcome guest."

Said Robin Hood, "Reach me that buck, Little John,
For I'll go along with my dear;
Bid my yeomen kill six brace of bucks,   *pairs*
160 And meet me tomorrow just here."

Before we had ridden five Staffordshire miles
Eight yeomen, that were too bold,
Bid Robin Hood stand and deliver his buck:
A truer tale never was told.

165 "I will not, faith," said bold Robin. "Come, John,
Stand to me and we'll beat 'em all."
Then both drew their swords, and so cut em and slasht em,
That five of them did fall.

The three that remaind calld to Robin for quarter,
170 And pitiful John beggd their lives;   *merciful*
When John's boon was granted, he gave them counsel,
And so sent them home to their wives.

This battle was fought near to Titbury town,
When the bagpipes bated the bull;   *teased*
175 I am king of the fidlers and sware't is a truth,
And I call him that doubts it a gull.   *fool*

For I saw them fighting, and fidld the while,
And Clorinda sung, "Hey derry down!
The bumpkins are beaten, put up thy sword, Bob,
180 And now let's dance into the town."

Before we came to it we heard a strange shouting,
And all that were in it lookd madly,
For some were a bull-back, some dancing a morris,
And some singing Arthur-a-Bradly.

185 And there we see Thomas, our justices clerk,
And Mary, to whom he was kind;
For Tom rode before her and calld Mary "Madam"
And kist her full sweetly behind.

And so may your worships. But we went to dinner,
190 With Thomas and Mary and Nan;
They all drank a health to Clorinda and told her
Bold Robin Hood was a fine man.

When dinner was ended, Sir Roger, the parson
Of Dubbridge, was sent for in haste;
195 He brought his mass-book and he bade them take hands,
And he joynd them in marriage full fast.

And then, as bold Robin Hood and his sweet bride
Went hand in hand to the green bower,
The birds sung with pleasure in merry Sherwood,
200 And 'twas a most joyful hour.

And when Robin came in the sight of the bower,
"Where are my yeoman?" said he.
And Little John answered "Lo, yonder they stand,
All under the green wood tree."

205 Then a garland they brought her, by two and by two,
And plac'd them at the bride's bed;
The music struck up, and we all fell to dance,
Til the bride and the groom were a-bed.

And what they did there must be counsel to me,   *kept secret by me*
210 Because they lay long the next day,
And I had haste home, but I got a good piece
Of the bride-cake, and so came away.

535

Now out, alas! I had forgotten to tell ye
That marryd they were with a ring;
215 And so will Nan Knight, or be buried a maiden,
And now let us pray for the king:

That he may get children, and they may get more,
To govern and do us some good;
And then I'll make ballads in Robin Hood's bower
220 And sing 'em in merry Sherwood.

Notes

5 *Locksly* is here located in Nottinghamshire, which does not seem historically to be an option. Near Sheffield in Yorkshire is the usual location for this place which the Sloane *Life*, c. 1600, is the first to link to the hero, but it does also mention other possible origins for the hero in Nottinghamshire which may have led to the error here.

11 Two miles and an inch is, according to Child, the longest of the feats of archery in the Robin Hood tradition: he comments on this in his "Index of Matters and Literature" (1965, V, 471), under the rubric "not to be taken seriously."

12 The Pinder did not in fact meet Robin's father in the ballad bearing his name. It is not clear if "he" in the next line refers to the Pinder or to Robin's father; it hardly seems important in this fast moving piece of name-juggling.

18 Sir Guy of Warwick is the hero of a major medieval romance, but he also became well-known in less elevated forms and continued to appear in chap-book stories into the nineteenth century.

21 For Gamwell see the discussion of *Robin Hood and Will Scarlet*; this family name came, through the mediation of Peacock in *Maid Marian*, into the mainstream of the Victorian novel. It plays a major part in Pierce Egan's 1840 *Robin Hood and Little John* and also in Alexandre Dumas's *Robin Hood, Prince des Voleurs* of 1872.

32 The fact that it is Christmas Eve marks a strong departure from the normal Robin Hood tradition; this is a festal Christmas ballad, not an early summer adventure.

35 Unusual and quite pantomime-like in effect is the fact that Robin wears light blue and his mother Lincoln green. The elements of the outlaw ballads are no longer understood, but are being deployed for merely theatrical effect.

41   *basket-hilt sword*. A sword with an openwork metal protection for the hand around the hilt.

61   *March beer*. According to the OED, a strong beer brewed in March; it would be especially strong by Christmas, as here.

62   Child emends *be sung* to "he sing," but this is in none of the texts and seems unnecessary.

65   The Roxburghe text reads *Mustards, braun*, but Child accepts the Pepys texts which read "Mustard and braun." This seems a false simplification, however, because the mustard would have been served with both the brawn (pork roast) and the roast beef and so should not be linked to the brawn by "and."

78   Child follows the Pepys texts with "gentleman, yeoman" but Roxburghe's plural makes good sense, and there seems no reason to emend.

97   There is no explanation of why Robin might have all these yeomen in Sherwood forest, since he is a respectable member of local gentry society.

105   Clorinda, or Clarinda, becomes a favorite name for Robin's partner in the moderately gentrified ballad operas of the eighteenth century.

108   The *buskin* is the chopine or high-heeled knee boot which was associated with tragic plays; it is a mark of Clorinda's dignity.

118   Child prefers "O" from the Pepys texts, but there seems no reason to emend Roxburghe's *Oh*.

119–20   The fierce skill Clorinda displays here is not unlike the dedicated hunting of Maid Marian in Ben Jonson's *The Sad Shepherd*.

120   *Titbury day*. The annual celebration and fair day at Titbury.

125   *we*. The ballad apparently is being sung by a local bard in the company of the foresters (an Allin a Dale type?), who joins in the feast (line 135). Later, in line 175, he claims to be *king of the fidlers*, who saw it all. The first-person device such as this is unusual in the ballads. See note to line 175.

149   All the existing texts have "motion" which Child retains. However, this reading seems most improbable, and the obvious emendation is *notion*.

152   Roxburghe reads "be merry," but the Pepys texts' *be married* seems to make much more sense in the context of the priest in the previous line.

159   Child prefers to start the line with "Go" as in the Pepys texts, but this seems both unnecessary and, with *go* in the previous line, clumsy.

161   The implication might be that Staffordshire miles, like Irish miles, might be unusually long, though this is not recorded elsewhere; when "Staffordshire" is used as a colloquial epithet it usually refers to blows with a club, or staff, as in "Staffordshire Law," martial or directly violent law. It is conceivable that the phrase here suggests "very dangerous miles."

171   Child prints "good" from the Pepys texts after *them*, but it seems unnecessary for sense or meter and is, as in the Roxburghe text, omitted here.

175   It is unusual in ballads for the narrator to be so visible (see note to line 125), but this feature appears to fit the eclectic and somewhat art-oriented character of this particular version.

184   Arthur-a-Bradly. A popular song about a young hero; may be the same as "Arthur a Bland," the tune of which is thought to have been used for several Robin Hood ballads. See Dobson and Taylor, 1976, p. 166.

194   Dubbridge is not a recorded place in Britain; the closest might seem to be Dudbridge in Gloucestershire, but the West Midlands have no real connection with the later Robin Hood tradition. North Yorkshire, on the other hand, is often represented in the myth, and the source here could be a number of Dub-place names in that area such as Dub Cote and Dub Garth. Apart from their credible location, these have the same unusual structure as Dubbridge: *dubh* is Gaelic for "black" or "dark" and these two names, like Dubbridge, combine the Celtic epithet with a non-Celtic location.

205   The Roxburghe text reads "the" which must at this stage be a compositor's error, not a dialect form of *they*.

206   The texts differ in this line: Roxburghe has the garlands placed at *the bride's*

bed, while Pepys has "on the bride's head." The choice is between the awkwardly repeated rhyme in Roxburghe and the rather bizarre idea of Clorinda wearing what seem to be thirty-four garlands on her head. Child prefers the latter, as in a number of other cases selecting Pepys for no good reason. It seems more likely that Pepys is edited for rhyme without remembering how many yeomen there are, rather than that Roxburghe is in error — its clumsiness does in fact make it the harder reading, and is retained here.

217   The reference to the king and his hope of heirs would seem to place this soon after the restoration in 1660 when a substantial number of Robin Hood texts of a non-radical character were produced; see the comments in the Introduction to *Robin Hood and his Crew of Souldiers*.

Robin Hood and the Golden Arrow

Introduction

This ballad is not recorded until an eighteenth-century garland, though it was known to the compiler of the Forresters manuscript and is used in *Robyn Hod and the Shyriff*. It describes the archery contest, a favorite episode in the outlaw tradition, found as early as the *Gest*. The question must be whether it is a literary reworking of that source, or a long preserved separate account. Child obviously thinks the former is the case as he says, "The first twenty-three stanzas are based upon the *Gest*, sts 282–95" (i.e., 1127–82, III, 223).

The description of the arrow (lines 26–27) and Robin's response (lines 32–33) certainly seem guided by the *Gest*, lines 1137–52, but the rest of the story is rather different. In the *Gest* Robin is identified and pursued, Little John is wounded, and the outlaws take refuge in Sir Richard's castle. Here Robin wins, but is not identified, and the outlaws think it is a matter of honor to inform the sheriff of Robin's victory with a message arrow, which makes the sheriff extremely angry. This resembles the way Arthurian romance carefully accords praise to combatants at a tournament, some of whom may have been incognito.

While honor is a fully medieval concept, it seems unlikely that such an actionless resolution to a Robin Hood ballad would have derived from the earlier period, and it seems most likely that this is a late reworking of the *Gest*'s episode of the archery contest rather like the Forresters ballads that derive from the *Gest* in combination with a broadside. Modern versions of the archery contest go back to the daring and danger of the earlier version (including even the Disney cartoon of 1973), rather than the somewhat smug contrivance of this later ballad.

The language and style of the text bespeak its late origin, with internal rhyme in the third line, rather precise rhyming and occasionally fussy language (*tricking game*, line 15; *whateer ensue*, line 57; *They thought no discretion*, line 65; *brave pastime*, line 101). In the same way, the idea that the sheriff is properly treated by being left *chafing in his grease*, line 130 — really annoyed to have missed Robin and also awarded him the honor — seems a far cry from the ferocity of *Robin Hood and Guy of Gisborne*, when an arrow through the head was thought an adequate response to the oppressions of royal law, rather than this distinctly unheroic outwitting.

541

Robin Hood and the Golden Arrow

When as the sheriff of Nottingham
Was come with mickle grief,   *much*
He talkd no good of Robin Hood,
That strong and sturdy thief.
5   Fal lal dal de

So unto London-road he past,
His losses to unfold
To King Richard, who did regard
The tale that he had told.

10   "Why," quoth the king, "what shall I do?
Art thou not sheriff for me?
The law is in force, go take thy course,
Of them that injure thee.

"Go get thee gone, and by thyself
15   Devise some tricking game
For to enthral yon rebels all;
Go take thy course with them."

So away the sheriff he returnd,
And by the way he thought
20   Of the words of the king, and how the thing
To pass might well be brought.

For within his mind he imagined
That when such matches were,
Those outlaws stout, without doubt,
25   Would be the bowmen there.

So an arrow with a golden head
And shaft of silver white,

Who won the day should bear away,
For his own proper right.

30   Tidings came to brave Robin Hood,
Under the green-wood tree.
"Come prepare you then, my merry men,
We'll go yon sport to see."

With that stept forth a brave young man,
35   David of Doncaster.
"Master," he said, "be ruld by me,
From the green-wood we'll not stir.

"To tell the truth, I'm well informed
Yon match is a wile;
40   The sheriff, I wiss, devises this   *know*
Us archers to beguile."

"O thou smells of a coward," said Robin Hood,
"Thy words does not please me;
Come on't what will, I'll try my skill   *of it*
45   At yon brave archery."

O then bespoke brave Little John:
"Come, let us hither gang,   *go*
Come listen to me, how it shall be
That we need not be kend.   *known*

50   "Our mantles, all of Lincoln green,
Behind us we will leave;
We'll dress us all so several   *differently*
They shall not us perceive.

"One shall wear white, another red,
55   One yellow, another blue;
Thus in disguise, to the exercise,
We'll gang, whateer ensue."

Forth from the green wood they are gone,
With hearts all firm and stout,
60 Resolving with the sheriffs men
To have a hearty bout.

So themselves they mixed with the rest,
To prevent all suspicion,
For if they should together hold
65 They thought no discretion.

So the sheriff looking round about,
Amongst eight hundred men,
But could not see the sight that he
Had long expected then.

70 Some said, "If Robin Hood was here,
And all his men to boot,
Sure none of them could pass these men,
So bravely they do shoot."

"Ay," quoth the sheriff, and scratchd his head,
75 "I thought he would have been here;
I thought he would, but, tho he's bold,
He durst not now appear."

O that word grieved Robin Hood to the heart;
He vexed in his blood;
80 "Eer long," thought he, "thou shalt well see
That here was Robin Hood."

Some cried, "Blue jacket!" Another cried, "Brown!"
And the third cried, "Brave Yellow!"
But the fourth man said, "Yon man in red
85 In this place has no fellow."

For that was Robin Hood himself,
For he was cloathd in red;
At every shot the prize he got,
For he was both sure and dead. *a dead shot*

90   So the arrow with the golden head
     And shaft of silver white
     Brave Robin Hood won, and bore with him
     For his own proper right.

     These outlaws there, that very day,
95   To shun all kind of doubt,
     By three or four, no less no more,
     As they went in, came out.

     Until they all assembled were
     Under the green wood shade,
100   Where they relate, in pleasant sport,
     What brave pastime they made.

     Says Robin Hood, "All my care is,
     How that yon sheriff may
     Know certainly that it was I
105   That bore his arrow away."

     Says Little John, "My counsel good
     Did take effect before,
     So therefore now, if you'll allow,
     I will advise once more."

110   "Speak on, speak on," said Robin Hood,
     "Thy wit's both quick and sound;
     I know no man amongst us can
     For wit like thee be found."

     "This I advise," said Little John;
115   "That a letter shall be pend,
     And when it is done, to Nottingham
     You to the sheriff shall send."

     "That is well advised," said Robin Hood,
     "But how must it be sent?"
120   "Pugh! when you please, it's done with ease,
     Master, be you content.

"I'll stick it on my arrow's head,
And shoot it into the town;
The mark shall show where it must go,
125   When ever it lights down."

The project it was full performd;
The sheriff that letter had;
Which when he read, he scratchd his head,
And rav'd like one that's mad.

130   So we'll leave him chafing in his grease,   *cooking; fat*
Which will do him no good;
Now, my friends, attend, and hear the end
Of honest Robin Hood.

24   Child inserts *all* before *doubt* with the later texts, but this is not necessary.

35   David of Doncaster is not mentioned elsewhere in the ballads. Though Roger of Doncaster is mentioned at the end of the *Gest* and a cleric called Doncaster appears in Munday's plays, they are both Robin's enemies, unlike David here, who plays the familiar role of the member of the outlaw band who advises Robin against his heroic rashness. Doncaster is in the area of the Yorkshire Barnsdale and the name may simply be constructed on the model of the Pinder of Wakefield, Robin of Loxley, John of Hathersage, and so on.

40–41   In some early ballads one of the outlaws tries to persuade Robin not to put himself in danger in this way; see *Robin Hood and the Monk* and *The Death of Robin Hood*.

47   In the text Little John says *hither*, and Child, following a later text, emends to *thither*. This does make a little more precise sense, but the context is general and the emendation seems unjustified.

60   Child inserts *then* after *Resolving* for the internal rhyme, but none of the texts have the word, and not all third lines have internal rhyme.

65   Child inserts *it* after *thought;* the later texts have this, but it seems more likely to be a compositor's fill-in than an error in the oldest text.

82–84   The colors do not quite match the outlaws' jackets described in lines 54–55 in that there is a brown jacket mentioned here and white there; otherwise it seems that the outlaws are the outstanding archers, with Robin as the champion.

100   The text has *relate*, and to obtain internal rhyme Child emends to *report*. But not all the third lines have internal rhyme, and the emendation, though not unlikely, is not adequately justified.

102   This discussion is curiously like the final sequence in an Arthurian romance when the public acknowledgement of the hero's honor seems even more important than his actual achievements.

112–13   The earliest text lacks these lines; they are printed by Child from a garland of 1811. The lines are not actually needed for sense but as the rhyming and stanza divisions in this ballad are very precise, it is not likely that the earliest version meant lines 110–11 to be part of a six-line stanza with the following four-line stanza, and so Child's emendation is accepted, even though lines 112–13 do read somewhat like an editorial fill-in.

122   In Parker's *A True Tale of Robin Hood* a message is sent on an arrow point to the king (lines 312–13), and this may well be the source of this sequence.

132   The reference is to the fact that this ballad is followed in the garlands by *The Death of Robin Hood*.

Robin Hood and the Bishop

Introduction

This ballad is found in seventeenth-century broadsides and early garland collections, and while there is no clear sign it existed before that, the incidents have an air of familiarity, being, as Child said (III, 191), "variations on a theme" of disguise found through many of the ballads (and in the story of Eustace); they also express the hostility to the established church found in the *Gest* and *Robin Hood and the Monk*. This story is told in the Forresters manuscript under the title *Robin Hood and the Old Wife*, with the sheriff playing the role of villain. While it is conceivable this was the original structure, and a hostile bishop introduced after the Reformation, this is probably a ballad originally starring the bishop, adapted by the highly inventive Forresters compiler, drawing here, as elsewhere, on the *Gest* as a source for the sheriff as villain.

The action contains some unusual features in that the bishop appears to be acting as the sheriff normally does, hunting the outlaws. This is not inherently unrealistic, as bishops were frequently of aristocratic class and perfectly capable of military actions, but the real source may be, as in Parker's *A True Tale of Robin Hood*, the post-Reformation tendency to make the church the major enemy of the outlaw. The final treatment of the bishop, tied back to front on his horse, has medieval carnival features but also serves a distinctly seventeenth-century anti-Catholic purpose.

In form this appears to be a characteristic commercial ballad, with the "Come all ye" opening, the internal rhyme in the third line and a distinctly literary feel to some of the language (lines 5–6, 39–40, 54). But it also has some clearly colloquial material (lines 33–36, 69–72), and the diction is fairly straightforward. By no means all of the third lines have internal rhyme, and this feature tends to grow rarer towards the end. That might suggest that an earlier ballad has been reworked for the commercial style — if the two opening stanzas and some stylistic titivation were removed this could be a plain ballad of the sixteenth century, though still literary in mode because it lacks the rhetorical repetition characteristic of the orally oriented early material. It is a swiftly told and tricksterish tale, reworking in basically comic form the aggressiveness of the early social bandit. Stallybrass has argued that the ending embodies a distinctly radical form of carnival (1985, p. 119), but while that might be the case if these events actually happened, as in a sense they did in Edinburgh in 1561, the tone of this enduringly popular ballad is basically comic.

Robin Hood and the Bishop

Come, gentlemen all, and listen a while,
Hey down down an a down
And a story I'le to you unfold:
I'le tell you how Robin Hood served the Bishop,
When he robbed him of his gold.

5   As it fell out on a sun-shining day,
When Phebus was in her prime,   *classical sun-god*
Then Robin Hood, that archer good,
In mirth would spend some time.

And as he walkd the forrest along,
10   Some pastime for to spy,
There was he aware of a proud bishop,
And all his company.

"O what shall I do?" said Robin Hood then,
"If the Bishop he doth take me;
15   No mercy he'l show unto me, I know,
But hanged I shall be."

Then Robin was stout, and turnd him about,   *brave*
And a little house there he did spy;
And to an old wife, for to save his life,
20   He loud began for to cry.

"Why, who art thou?" said the old woman,
"Come tel it to me for good."
"I am an out-law, as many do know,
My name it is Robin Hood.

25   "And yonder's the Bishop and all his men,
And if that I taken be,

Then day and night he'l work me spight,   *do me harm*
And hanged I shall be."

"If thou be Robin Hood," said the old wife,
30   "As thou doth seem to be,
I'le for thee provide, and thee I will hide,
From the Bishop and his company.

"For I well remember, on Saturday night
Thou bought me both shoos and hose;
35   Therefore I'le provide thy person to hide,
And keep thee from thy foes."

"Then give me soon thy coat of gray,   *at once*
And take thou my mantle of green;
Thy spindle and twine unto me resign,
40   And take thou my arrows so keen."

And when that Robin Hood was so araid,
He went straight to his company;
With his spindle and twine, he oft lookt behind
For the Bishop and his company.

45   "O who is yonder," quoth Little John,
"That now comes over the lee?
An arrow I will at her let flie,
So like an old witch looks she."

"O hold thy hand, hold thy hand," said Robin then,
50   "And shoot not thy arrows so keen;
I am Robin Hood, thy master good,
And quickly it shall be seen."

The Bishop he came to the old womans house,
And he called with furious mood,
55   "Come let me soon see, and bring unto me,
That traitor Robin Hood."

The old woman he set on a milk-white steed,
Himselfe on a dapple-gray,
And for joy he had got Robin Hood,
60   He went laughing all the way.

But as they were riding the forrest along,
The Bishop he chanc'd for to see
A hundred brave bow-men bold
Stand under the green-wood tree.

65   "O who is yonder," the Bishop then said,
"That's ranging within yonder wood?"
"Marry," says the old woman, "I think it to be
A man calld Robin Hood."

"Why, who art thou," the Bishop he said,
70   "Which I have here with me?"
"Why I am an old woman, thou cuckoldly bishop;
Lift up my leg and see."

"Then woe is me," the Bishop he said,
"That ever I saw this day!"
75   He turnd him about, but Robin so stout
Calld him and bid him stay.

Then Robin took hold of the Bishops horse,
And ty'd him fast to a tree;
Then Little John smil'd his master upon,
80   For joy of that company.

Robin Hood took his mantle from's back,   *from his*
And spread it upon the ground,
And out of the Bishops portmantle he   *travelling bag*
Soon told five hundred pound.   *At once counted*

85   "So now let him go," said Robin Hood;
Said Little John, "That may not be;
For I vow and protest he shall sing us a mass
Before that he goe from me."

Robin Hood and the Bishop

Then Robin Hood took the Bishop by the hand,
90   And bound him fast to a tree,
And made him sing a mass, God wot,
To him and his yeomandree.   *yeomanry (men)*

And then they brought him through the wood,
And set him on his dapple-gray,
95   And gave the tail within his hand,
And bade him for Robin Hood pray.

Notes

6   The text has *her,* corrected to *his* in later texts. Child emends, but the flavor of the broadsides is well communicated by this error.

16   The representation of the Bishop as a secular power capable of executing people is anachronistic, and no doubt part of post-reformation anti-Catholicism.

30   The earliest texts read *doth*, which is corrected to *dost* in all later texts, but like *her* in line 6, deserves to be left unemended as characteristic of the genre.

33   Child emends the text's *on Saturday night* to the more distant *one Saturday night*, but this reading does not appear until one of the later versions, and seems unnecessary: immediacy is often the essence of these stories.

39   The outlaw's disguise as a woman spinner is seen in *Eustache le Moine*; it also appears in Blind Hary's *William Wallace*.

47   The internal rhyme is awkward, requiring a caesura after *I*.

57   The horses come from a romance formula, sounding like suitable mounts for Sir Launfal and Dame Triamour.

62   The earliest text has *chance*. Although its peculiarities are accepted in lines 6 and 30, this would be a sudden change of tense as well as an erroneous form, and should be regarded as a compositor's error and emended, as Child has it.

71   Being unmarried, a Catholic bishop can hardly be a cuckold. The term seems generalized abuse, meaning something like "weakling" with, as the next line implies, a sense of sexual insult retained. Child records *cuckoldy* in the 1670 garland, but in fact it too has the full adverbial form *cuckoldly*.

72   *Lift up my leg and see*. The bawdy tone of this line is strongly reminiscent of the scene in *Eustache le Moine* in which the outlaw, disguised as a prostitute, mounts the sergeant's horse and offers to have sex with him.

81–84   Counting out the clerics' money seems a compulsive element in these stories, and the sums involved are usually enormous, as here.

83   The run-on line is rare, though the lack of internal rhyme suggests this line has not been rewritten by an editor. The final *he* which causes the run-on may well originally be a compositor's error, but remains in the later texts and should not be emended simply for being unusual.

87   The forced mass, mounting in reverse, and making the bishop pray for the outlaws are all elements of carnival which here seem to have burlesque rather than seriously radical force. On the practice of punishing venal ecclesiastics (especially summoners) by tying them backwards onto horses, then driving them from town, see Thomas Hahn and Richard W. Kaeuper, "Text and Context: Chaucer's *Friar's Tale*," *Studies in the Age of Chaucer* 5 (1983), 67–101. See also *A True Tale of Robin Hood*, lines 101–04.

Robin Hood's Golden Prize

Introduction

This is a mid-seventeenth-century ballad found in broadsides and garlands, and recorded in the Stationers' Register in 1656: Wing attributes it to Laurence Price, whose initials appear on an early copy, which Wing dates at 1650. The story, Child notes (III, 208), is one found in folklore, the essence being that the outlaw plays a trick on someone — usually a priest — by pretending that a miracle has occurred and money has emerged in return for prayer, when he knew quite well the money was there all the time. This robbery by cunning fits well with the trickster element of Robin Hood and also supports anti-clerical feeling, so strong a strain in the tradition in this period.

The ballad has a commercial ring in its opening, with elaborate language (*accoutered in his array*, line 12; *Come riding gallantly*, line 18). The first stanzas also advertize the Robin Hood connection and the special quality of this tale (line 8). But for the most part this is a fast-moving tale of Robin Hood's justified robbery, without the ferocity of the early ballads; as the verse introduction states, this is a "jest" of Robin Hood in both its senses, adventure and trick.

The image of a friar, fully realized in Catholic form (lines 11–13), does seem an odd choice in the protestant seventeenth century for Robin's disguise in which to humiliate the equally Catholic monks. This suggests either a remarkably tolerant audience or that the early idea that friars are more acceptable to the outlaw spirit than other regular clergy has somehow survived the reformation, and indeed lasted to the present. However, the somewhat pompous tone of the commercial ballad asserts itself finally as Robin returns to the green wood: *With great joy, mirth, and pride* (line 98).

Robin Hood's Golden Prize

I have heard talk of bold Robin Hood,
Derry derry down
And of brave Little John,
Of Fryer Tuck, and Will Scarlet,
5   Loxley, and Maid Marion.
Hey down derry derry down

But such a tale as this before
I think there was never none,
For Robin Hood disguised himself,
10   And to the wood is gone.

Like to a fryer, bold Robin Hood
Was accoutered in his array;
With hood, gown, beads and crucifix,
He past upon the way.

15   He had not gone miles two or three,
But it was his chance to spy
Two lusty priests, clad all in black,
Come riding gallantly.

"Benediceté," then said Robin Hood,   *Bless you*
20   "Some pitty on me take;
Cross you my hand with a silver groat,
For Our dear Ladies sake.

"For I have been wandring all this day,
And nothing could I get;
25   Not so much as one poor cup of drink,
Nor bit of bread to eat."

557

"Now, by my holydame," the priests repli'd,   *holy relic (sanctity)*
"We never a peny have;
For we this morning have been robd,
30   And could no mony save."

"I am much afraid," said bold Robin Hood,
"That you both do tell a lye,
And now before that you go hence,
I am resolvd to try."   *test (you)*

35   When as the priests heard him say so,
They rode away amain;   *quickly*
But Robin Hood betook him to his heels,
And soon overtook them again.

Then Robin Hood laid hold of them both,
40   And pulld them down from their horse:
"O spare us, fryer!" the priests cry'd out,
"On us have some remorse!"

"You said you had no mony," quoth he,
"Wherefore, without delay,
45   We three will fall down on our knees,
And for mony we will pray."

The priests they could not him gainsay,   *refuse*
But down they kneeled with speed.
"Send us, O send us," then quoth they,
50   "Some mony to serve our need."

The priests did pray with mournful chear,
Sometimes their hands did wring,
Sometimes they wept and cried aloud,
Whilst Robin did merrily sing.

55   When they had been praying an hours space,
The priests did still lament;   *ever (perpetually)*
Then quoth bold Robin, "Now let's see
What mony heaven hath us sent.

Robin Hood's Golden Prize

     "We will be sharers now all alike
60   Of the mony that we have,
     And there is never a one of us
     That his fellows shall deceive."

     The priests their hands in their pockets put,
     But mony would find none.   *refused to find*
65   "We'l search our selves," said Robin Hood,
     "Each other, one by one."

     Then Robin Hood took pains to search them both,
     And he found good store of gold;
     Five hundred peeces presently
70   Upon the grass was told.

     "Here is a brave show," said Robin Hood,
     "Such store of gold to see,
     And you shall each one have a part,
     Cause you prayed so heartily."

75   He gave them fifty pound a-peece,
     And the rest for himself did keep;
     The priests durst not speak one word,
     But they sighed wondrous deep.

     With that the priests rose up from their knees,
80   Thinking to have parted so;
     "Nay, stay," said Robin Hood, "one thing more
     I have to say ere you go.

     "You shall be sworn," said bold Robin Hood,
     "Upon this holy grass,
85   That you will never tell lies again,
     Which way soever you pass.

     "The second oath that you here must take,
     All the days of your lives
     You never shall tempt maids to sin,
90   Nor lye with other mens wives.

"The last oath you shall take, it is this,
Be charitable to the poor;
Say you have met with a holy fryer,
And I desire no more."

95   He set them upon their horses again,
And away then they did ride;
And hee returnd to the merry green-wood,
With great joy, mirth, and pride.

5   This is a unique reference to Loxley as a character who is apparently not Robin; the place (near Sheffield) is mentioned in the Sloane *Life*, which is presumably the source here, as the birthplace of the hero. Scott used the name in *Ivanhoe* as part of his downgrading of the hero's status.

13   The earliest text, unrecorded by Child, has a compositor's error in *kood*.

13–14   This very Catholic image would normally in this period be the basis for a character's humiliation like that of Archimago in Edmund Spenser's *The Faerie Queene*. In fact, in this guise Robin triumphs over the priests and finally insists on his status as a friar. This carries tricksterism to the point of pro-Catholicism, and is somewhat surprising if, as seems likely, the ballad was entered during the Commonwealth. The religious detail is so clear that there may be an earlier pro-friar song or ballad at the root of this one, but it would still be surprising that the detail is retained.

15   Child inserts *past* before *miles*, as in later texts, but this seems unnecessary.

27   *holydame*. Although the term *halidom*, a thing which one might swear by, refers to one's sanctity or holiness, the substitution of *dame* in this suffix was apparently due to popular etymology taking the word to mean "Our Lady." See OED for *halidom*. The sense of "holy relic" or "holy thing" was common in oaths and adjurations into the sixteenth century.

36   All the earlier texts lack *Then* at the start of the line; not needed for meter, it is not clear why Child inserts it.

84   The idea that the grass is holy is presumably part of the burlesque tone here.

89   The oath Robin makes the priests swear is one that, in late medieval tradition, is more appropriate to friars (see the remarks of the Wife of Bath on this topic at the beginning of her tale), which both suggests the anachronism of the ballad

and also makes more curious the purity of the friar's position in it. Perhaps that incongruity is part of Robin's jest.

Robin Hood and Queen Catherin

Introduction

Robin Hood and Queen Catherin was a popular ballad in the seventeenth century. It is in Percy's Folio, but too much of the text has been lost through ripped pages for this to be used as a basis for the text. A closely related version, entitled *Renowned Robin Hood*, exists in six separate broadsides and the two early garlands of 1663 and 1670. The earliest full text of this version in the Wood collection in the Bodleian Library, Oxford, must have been produced by 1655 when Grove, the printer, ceased operations. To judge from its royal content its publication is likely to have derived from before the Civil War began in earnest in 1642: Wing dates the earliest copy c. 1630. However, this ballad has always seemed somewhat incoherent in its opening section and quite unfollowable in its account of the archery contest: it was not clear how many of Robin's men shoot and what aliases they used — and was Clifton one of their disguises or the name of the king's leading archer? These problems were resolved with the discovery of the Forresters manuscript in 1993. This is one of the two ballads where Forresters is clearly superior to Child's versions, apparently because they represent a fuller text before it was cut down to fit a broadside page (the other is *Robin Hood's Fishing*). This is the text printed here.

The ballad seems to have been derived from a number of sources. The *Gest*, Parker's *A True Tale of Robin Hood*, *Robin Hood and the Bishop*, probably Munday's *Downfall* and perhaps *Adam Bell* were all known to the compiler of what is effectively a Robin Hood adventure within the framework of the court of Henry VIII. Although Robin is on good terms with the queen and becomes accepted by the king, this is not really a gentrified ballad, in that Robin is merely a highway robber and fine archer. The only truly gentrified touch is in the ending added to the ballad in the 1663 garland, where the king finally pardons Robin and makes him "Earle of fair Huntington." Both Wood and Forresters (the end of Percy is missing) conclude with a disagreement between Robin and John, rather unusual for this late date, and reminiscent of their earlier differences of opinion as in *Robin Hood and the Monk* or *Robin Hood and Guy of Gisborne*.

Even in its somewhat confused broadside form, this was an effective and popular ballad. Child found it "very pleasant" (1965, III, 197), but he also recognized its "exaggeration" and that it was a "piece of regular hack work." It clearly is a made-up ballad drawing on several popular elements. The idea that the queen sympathizes with outlaws is also found in the popular *Adam Bell*. *Robin Hood and Queen Catherin* is constructed for an audience in what the Percy version calls "lovely London," apart from Nottingham which is placed, perhaps in irony, far in the North, line 60. It is tempting to think the ballad may have been produced soon after Martin Parker's *A True Tale of Robin Hood*, which has royal connections, action in the north, and a sense of the conflict among the outlaws with which this full and, in the Forresters version, well-constructed ballad ends.

Robin Hood and Queen Catherin

Gold taken from the kings harbengers   *messengers*
As seldom hath been seen
And carryed by bold Robin Hood
A present to the queen.

5   "If that I live a year to an end,"
Thus gan Queen Catherin say,   *did*
"Bold Robin Hood, I'le be thy friend,
And all thy yeomen gay."

The king and queen to th' gardens gon,
10 To passe the time away,
And lovingly with one another
Till evening they did stay.

"What game, what game, my queen," he said
"For game or also for glee?"
15 "I'de have a shooting," she reply'd
"So please your majestie."

"Ile have a shooting for your sake,
The best in Christentie."
"Make lite the wager, sir," she said,
20 "And holden you shall bee."   *taken up*

"Ile make the wager light my queen,
For that you need not fear,
Three hundred tunn of Renish wine,   *barrels; Rhine*
Three hundred tunn of beer.

25 "Three hundred of the fattest harts   *deer*
That run on Dalum Lee."

565

"That's a princly wager," said our queen,
"Bravly holden you shall bee."

The queen is to her chamber gon
30 As fast as she can wend,   *go*
She calls to her her lovely page,
His name was Patrington.

"Com hether to me my lovely page,
Com hether unto me,
35 For thou must post to Notingham   *hurry*
As fast as thou canst dree.   *go*

"And when thou comst to Notingham
Search all that English wood;
Enquire of each good yeoman thou meetst
40 To finde out Robin Hood.

"And whan thou comst Robin Hood before
Deliver him this ringe,
And bid him post to London towne
And not fear any thing.

45 "I've made a shooting with the king
The best in Christentee,
And I have chosen bold Robin Hood
To be of my partie."

He tooke his leave of the royall queen
50 And fast away is gan,
Somtimes he rode, sometimes he rann,
Till he came to Nottingham.

And when he came to Nottingham
And there took up his inn,   *lodging*
55 He call'd for a pottle of Renish wine   *pot*
And dranck a health to his queen.

Then sate a yeoman by his side   *Then*
"Tell me, sweet page," said hee,
"What is thy businesse or thy cause
60   So farr in the North contrie?"

"This is my business and my cause
I tell it you for good;
I com from London," said the page,
"To seeke bold Robin Hood."

65   "Ile take my horse betimes i'th morn   *early*
Be it by break of day,   *Even at*
And Ile show thee bold Robin Hood
And all his yeomen gay."

He took his horse betimes i'th morne
70   As soon as he could see,
And had him to bold Robin Hood
And all his archerie.

When the page came to Robin Hood
He fell downe on his knee.
75   "Queen Catherin she doth greet you well
She greets you well by mee.

"Queen Catherin she dooth greet you well
And sends you here her ring,
She bids you post to London towne
80   And not fear any thing.

"She hath made a shooting with our king
The best in Christentee,
And desires you, bold Robin Hood,
To be of her partie."

85   Robin tooke his mantle from his back,   *cloak*
It was of Lincolne green;
"Here take my mantle," said Robin Hood,
"A present for the queen.

567

"And go thy way thou lovely page
90 And to Queen Catherin say
 'If Robin Hood doth loose the match
 He will the wager pay.'"

Fitt 2

 In summer time when leaves grow green
 'Twas a seemly sight to see
95 How Robin Hood himselfe had drest
 And all his yeomandrie.

 He clad himselfe in scarlett red
 His men in Lincoln green
 And so prepars for London towne,
100 To shoot before the lovly queen.

 They had bows of ewe and strings of silke   *yew*
 Arrows of silver chest,   *chased (engraved)*
 Black hats, white feathers all alike
 Full deftly they were drest.   *neatly*

105 "Com Little John, thou shalt be one,
 One Clifton thou shall bee,
 And so shall Midge the Millers son
 To bere us companie.

 "Will Scathlock to shall go alonge   *too*
110 For he will never faile,
 But Renett Browne shall stay behinde
 And look to Brensdale."   *guard*

 Robin came before the queen,
 He kneeld downe on his knee.
115 "Thou'rt welcome, Loxley," said our queen
 "And these thy yeomandrie.

"Thou'rt welcom," said the queen,
"And these thy archers good.
I hope ere this day be at an end   *before*
120   To call thee Robin Hood."

The queen's to the king's chamber gon,
As fast as she can dree,   *go*
"God save you lovly prince," she said,
"Welcom, my queen," quoth he.

125   "Our match goes ill and please your grace,
As far as I can ken,   *can tell*
Ther's not an archer in all my court,
Will shoot against your men."

"I knew it very well," said our king,
130   "My archers are so good,
That never a man durst shoott with them   *dared*
Except it were Robin Hood."

"Double the wager," said the queen,
"Brave holden you shall bee."
135   "No, by my truth," then said our king,
"Woman's full of subteltie."

Fitt 3

Our king is unto Finsbury gon
In all his best array,
The queen she follows after him,
140   With all her archers gay.

"Come hether, Tempest," said the king,
"Bow berer unto mee,
Ther's not in England, France, nor Spaine
An archer like to thee."

145   The queen took Loxly by the hand
       And gave him on his head tapps three,
       "Look wel to this man, my leig," she said,   *liege (lord)*
       "Hee'l prove as good as hee."

       "Com hether, Tempest," said the king,
150   "The best in Christentie,
       And measure out here with thy line
       How long the marks shall bee."

       With that bespoke bold Loxly then,
       Full quickly and full soon,
155   "Mesure no marks for us, my leige,
       Wee'l shoot at sun and moon."

       "Full fifteen score your marks shall bee,
       Full fifteen score shall stand.
       I'le lay my bow," quoth Clifton then,
160   "I'le cleave the willow wand."   *split*

       Then the king's archers led about
       Till it was three and none.
       With that the ladys began to pout,
       "Madam, the game is gon."

165   "A boon, a boon," then sais the queen,
       "Please your grace grant to mee.
       Two of your privy councellors
       To be of my partie."

       "Have I two in my privy councell,
170   This day will pleasure thee,
       If they bett any thing on thy side,
       Right welcom shall they bee."

       "Com hether then Sir Richard Lee,
       Thou art a knight right good,
175   Full well I know thy pedigree   *family*
       Thou'rt sprung from Gawain's blood.

"And come hether thou Bishop of Hereford,"
A noble preist was hee.
"By my silver myter," said the bishop,   *bishop's crown*
180 "I'le not bett one penny.

"Our king hath archers of his owne
Full redy and full light,
But these are strangers every one
I know not how they height."   *are named*

185 "What wilt thou bett," said Robin Hood,
"Thou seest our gam's the worse."
"By my silver myter," said the Bishop,
"All the money in my purse."

"What's in thy purse?" quoth Robin tho,   *then*
190 "Tell it downe on the ground."   *Count*
"Fifteen score of nobles," quoth the bishop,
"It's neer a hundred pounds."

Robin tooke his mantle from his back,
And threw it on the mould,   *ground*
195 Forth he pluck'd a velvett pouch,
It was well lin'd with gold.

Forth he pluck'd his velvet pouch
He told the gold on the green,   *counted*
Then cry'd Midge the Millers son,
200 "I know who the gold will win."

In came Will Scathlock to the rest
And to Little John did thrust,
"They shall not gett another shoot
And all their hearts would brust."   *If; burst*

205 Then the queen's archers led aboute
Till it was three and three,
And then the ladies gave a shoute,
"Woodcock, bewere thine eye."

"Tis three and three now," says our king,
210 "The next three pays for all."
Then Robin whisper'd to the queen
"The king's part will be but small."

Then shot Tempest for the king
He led it gallantly,
215 Then shott Loxly for our queen
And clove his arrow in three.   *split*

Then shott Midge the Millers son,
He was not far the worse,
Within a finger of the pegg,   *finger's breadth; bull's eye*
220 "Bishop, bewere thy purse."

The yeoman of the crowne who stod him by
Hee shott underhand,
But Clifton with a bearded arrow
He clove the willow wand.

225 "The upshott now," said Will Scathlock,   *result*
"For the honor o'th queen and mee,"
Hee tooke the prick on arrow poynt   *bull's eye*
The king and all did see.

Then spoke Tempest to our king,
230 "These archers are so good,
I'm sore affraid and like your grace,
They learn'd of Robin Hood."

"But fear not that," our king did say
For t'was told me of late
235 That Robin Hood and his wel wight men   *very strong*
Were slaine at pallas gate."   *killed; palace*

"A boon, a boon," Queen Catherin cry'd,
"I aske it on my knee,
Your grace will angry be with none
240 That are of my partie."

572

"They shal have forty days to come
And forty days to go
Twice forty days to sport and play
Then welcom friend or foe."

245   "Welcom Robin Hood," then said the queen,
"And so is Little John,
And so is Midge the Millers son,
Will Scathlock every one."

"Is this Robin Hood," then said the bishop,
250   "As it seems well to bee?
Had I knowne t'had bin that bold outlaw
I'de not bett one penny.

"Hee tooke me late one Satterday night,
And bound me to a tree,
255   And made me sing a masse, God wott,   *knows*
To him and's companie."   *and his*

"What if I did?" said Robin tho;   *then*
"Of that masse I was full faine.   *With; very pleased*
To recompence thee for that deed,
260   Heers halfe thy gold again."

"Now nay, now nay," sais Little John,
"Master, that may not bee.
Wee must give gifts to th' kings officers
'Twill serve both you and wee."

573

Notes

1   A sign that this ballad is a literary invention is that the robbing of the king's "receivers" occurs in Parker's *A True Tale of Robin Hood*, see lines 129–36; this ballad appears to have been developed using that event as the motive for an archery competition.

6   This is presumably one of the Queen Katherines to whom Henry VIII was married. Munday's play is set at his court, while the Robin Hood games in which he was involved, mentioned by Hall in his Chronicle (see Knight, 1994, p. 110), were dated in 1510 and 1515, that is Henry's younger days when he was married to Catherine of Aragon. The ballad appears to refer to a queen of her authority and activity, rather than the young Catherine Howard, who was executed after being queen in 1540–42, or Catherine Parr who tended the aged Henry from 1543–47.

23   These are very large quantities of wine, though they may be thought of as sums of money; a courtier like Chaucer — and like the Poet Laureate to the present day — was rewarded with stipulated amounts of wine, which could be commuted into cash at recognized rates.

26   Dalum Lee is not a known place name: the closest resemblance is Dalham, a small town about five miles east of Newmarket in East Anglia, but Dallow Moor, in North Yorkshire, may be a more probable original, as many Robin Hood connected place-names come from this area.

32   This does not appear to be a reference to a specific person, though like other elements in the Robin Hood tradition, the surname is associated with Yorkshire, as in Stephen Patrington, Bishop of Chichester, who died in 1417.

35   While to travel post is associated with eighteenth-century activities, the OED records usages from the early sixteenth century; it means to have fresh horses "posted" at intervals, so the traveller, or the mail, can keep moving at a fast pace.

41   Stanza 14, lines 53–56 is written here out of place in the manuscript before stanza 11, lines 41–44, but the stanza numbers in the left margin give it correctly as 14, a sign of careful editorial checking after the scribes had completed their work.

51   Presumably he was resting his horse when he ran. The line is also in the Wood versions.

57   The manuscript has *The*, which may well be a scribal error for *Then*, but the scribes make few simple errors of that kind and it is likely that the original might have read *Tho*, the older form for *Then*.

60   The London location of the ballad's creation is suggested by the idea that Nottingham is in the far North. The city was usually regarded as the beginning of the northern or highland zone of England, but is effectively a Midland town, so this seems a rather extreme idea, perhaps meant as a local joke by the yeoman.

      The manuscript reads *contie*, which is presumably an error for *contrie*, the form printed here, rather than a spelling for "county"; "the North county" is not a known phrase.

79   The earliest Wood version reads "London court" here which could be taken as a better, because harder, reading than "London towne," but, as it rhymes with "sport," that argument seems to have little force (though it is the first of the two rhyme-words).

86   Robin's sending of a Lincoln green mantle to the queen appears to be a conscious memory of the king's choice of such a robe in the *Gest*.

92   The manuscript reads *Heel will*, but there is a correction point below the second *e* of *Heel*. The scribe at first wrote a contracted form of "He will" and the editor presumably marked the error, as with the stanza misplacement at lines 53–56.

93   This stanza sounds like the traditional opening of a Robin Hood ballad; the action is beginning now after the explanatory preliminaries. It seems proper to mark this as a new fitt, though the manuscript has no such indication.

97   Robin's wearing of red both makes him stand out as leader in a way suitable to a generally gentrified context, but also links with a number of early references to red as the outlaw's color. To this day hunters often wear a bright color in order not to be shot themselves in the woods. The earliest texts do not mention the famous "Lincoln green" or its occasional variant "Kendal green." It could be that wearing green is a semi-pastoral reworking of an earlier tradition in which the outlaw's clothes were not described (unlike Chaucer's yeoman and his devil-forester in the Friar's Tale, who do wear green) or were a more probable bright color.

100   The word *lovly* is inserted above the line in the same scribal hand.

102   The manuscript reads *sugar*, an obvious error for silver. This suggests that the scribe is copying from an original written in a late gothic hand, when *v* was written somewhat like an elaborate *g*.

109   Scathlock is one of the older names of this outlaw; however, it is used in Munday and so is no sign of antiquity in this ballad.

111   *Renett Browne* is elsewhere unknown, though his Christian name is presumably a version of Reynold, a name which does occur at times as a minor figure or alias, including that of Little John in the *Gest*.

116   At this point the broadside texts begin to become confused about how many archers came with Robin and who they were. All but the last version of the Wood texts reads "yeomen three" here. Child felt that "yeomandry" as in the 1663 garland and the last Wood text must be right, and the Forresters' evidence supports his judgment. However, even Child (like all the versions except Forresters, and presumably except Percy, though it is too damaged to judge) appears to have misunderstood the outlaws' aliases, a confusion which seems based in thinking that Robin came with three archers, itself deriving from this misreading or mishearing of *yeomandrie* as "yeomen three."

137   As the action changes place here, it seems a natural break for a fitt. The manuscript has no sign of one, however. Finsbury Fields, as Child remarks, was an open area just north of the old City of London wall which was much used for archery practice (1965, III, 197–98).

141   In the Wood version, the name is given as *Tepus*; while this could well be seen as a harder reading, with priority over *Tempest*, the origins of both names seem obscure, and it seems best to use the Forresters version.

143   The manuscript reads *not* instead of the necessary *nor*.

157   Three hundred paces, or yards, is not one of the longer distances described as being within the range of a good longbowman, though it is improbable that targets could be hit with accuracy, let alone arrows or wands be split at that distance.

165   The Queen is seeking someone to lay a bet on her side, but without immediate success. However, when Robin asks the bishop to bet in line 185, he gives in at once — presumably a sign of Robin's innate force. The wager on the archery contest remains a basic feature of the scene in whatever version.

173   Sir Richard Lee is the name of the knight Robin helps in the *Gest*.

176   All the Wood texts have "Goweres blood," which Child retains, while the Percy folio reads "Gawiins blood." The fact that Forresters also reads "Gowers blood" suggests either that Percy has adapted the name in the context of its own romance orientation, or that the source of Forresters shared an error with the ballads. It seems likely that the creator of the ballad would have referred to King Arthur's heroic nephew rather than the late-fourteenth-century poet John Gower. Though he was of knightly family and had a coat of arms, Gower was entirely intellectual in his activities; he might have been known in the seventeenth century from his role as Prologue to Shakespeare's *Pericles*, but the reference to him seems a characteristic piece of ballad-mongering confusion, and should be emended to "Gawains."

177   The Bishop of Hereford is Robin's opponent in a ballad that names them both in its title (Child no. 144). In the Percy version, the bishop refers to this episode at this point in the plot, but all other versions give the reference later (see line 249). The other ballad also appears in Forresters, but under the name *Robin Hood and the Bishop*; Child's ballad by that title has been reworked into *Robin Hood and the Sheriff* in Forresters. The fact that the bishop refers to the action of the ballad at lines 253–56 suggests that it might have been a partial source for *Robin Hood and Queen Catherin*. Hereford, though in rich country-side and in the turbulent Welsh borders, is not a major see, and there may be

a particular bishop at the basis of the figure's role in the ballads. It is unlikely that William de Vere, courtier and bishop (1186–99) under Richard I, is the original, as this is the period used in gentrified texts which rarely retell robbery narratives. Peter de Aquabella, bishop from 1239–68, who was notoriously corrupt and whose money was in fact redistributed among the barons under Henry III, is a possible candidate, but most likely is Adam of Orleton, opponent of Edward II, who also became unpopular with Edward III; he seems the sort of mighty cleric who might have been lampooned in the ballads that were apparently in popular circulation by the mid-fourteenth century.

190   In making the bishop count out his purse, Robin's action is reminiscent of the ballads where he robs a wealthy churchman, and effectively the compiler of *Robin Hood and Queen Catherin* has added that motif to the "betting on the archery contest" structure.

192   The bishop's remark is unnecessarily vague: a noble was six shillings and eightpence, and three hundred of them are exactly one hundred pounds. The Wood version has precisely the same phrasing.

205   All the broadside versions of the ballad and Forresters here have "kings"; the Percy folio has *queens*, which must be correct (see line 161–62). The case is the same as with "Gawains" in line 176. It is surprising that no editor or compositor corrected this obvious error.

208   The later Wood versions here read *thy knee* and the earliest has *thy nee*. This is a possibly aural error for the reading on which Percy and Forresters agree, *thyn eye* (spelled in Percy as *ee*). Presumably this refers to a proverbial sign of a supreme archer — he could shoot out a woodcock's eye.

209   Only Forresters has a clear account of how the shooting match is resolved; the other texts omit entirely the king's archers, and also name Robin and Midge as such but leave Clifton in alias, so it sounds as if he (not in them known to be Little John) might be the king's archer. But the confusion does not seem to have been caused primarily by cutting: the Forresters sequence is only one stanza longer.

216   This appears to be the first instance of "splitting the arrow" in the Robin Hood myth; modern versions have all descended from the scene in Sir Walter Scott's *Ivanhoe* in Chapter 13 when Locksley splits the arrow of Hubert, the king's

archer. As there is no sign that Scott knew the Forresters manuscript, and the resemblance is so close between the two incidents, there would seem to have been a common source for the two, but it is not known.

222   In the Wood version it is Robin who shoots *underhand*, as a result of the text being condensed, but this appears to mean "below the target," and indicates a failure.

223   *Clifton* suddenly appears in the text in the Wood versions, to split the wand. The aliases are thoroughly confusing and the Percy folio is much too damaged to be of any help. Child thought he was Will Scarlett (1965, III, 197). Forresters has made things clear: Clifton is Little John (see line 105).

223   A "bearded" arrow carried longer feathers as flights and so could give more accuracy, though it required more power; it is appropriate for the giant archer Little John. Note that his achievement is the more traditional one of "splitting the wand"; in some of the very early ballads his archery skill seems greater than Robin's, but here "splitting the arrow" seems to give Robin precedence.

224   The manuscript reads *williow*.

225   Will appears to shoot fourth, score a bullseye, and clinch victory. Even Forresters does not have a very clear account of what happens here, though at least we know the order of shooting.

235–36 The king's notion that Robin has been killed in a gateway in the north sounds like a vague reference to the fighting in *Adam Bell*, lines 310–67. However, the manuscript reads "Pallarsgate" as if this were a place-name like Harrogate. If the original were "palace gate," as seems most likely (the Wood version), then the Forresters reading is probably an aural error, itself an interesting sign of the transmission of the text. But it is just conceivable that there was some other version of Robin's death occurring not at Kirklees (or its erroneous version Birklees) but somewhere sounding like "Pallarsgate" which was simplified in transmission into "palace gate." This is highly speculative, however, and the Wood reading is accepted. It is curious that the phrase "pallace gate" occurs in *Adam Bell* at line 449, but the context is different.

241   The king offers generous terms to the outlaws: they can travel freely for forty days in either direction without being taken, and have a parole of eighty days

(one hundred and twenty in the Wood versions) for their pleasure in between.

249   Although the bishop takes his name from the ballad *Robin Hood and the Bishop of Hereford*, he actually refers to an incident in the different ballad *Robin Hood and the Bishop*, which has an almost identical stanza, lines 89–92. The latter does not appear in Forresters, though the former does — under the title *Robin Hood and the Bishop*. In Forresters, Child's *Robin Hood and the Bishop*, no. 143, the one adapted in this stanza, has been reworked as *Robin Hood and the Sheriff* and does not use the "tying up" stanza.

252   The texts divide on tense here: Forresters and the two earliest versions of the Wood text omit "have" in this line. The others, including the Percy folio version, have the past tense; this is probably chance, as "have bet" is an easy change from the present tense, and there is no other sign of the later Wood texts having any access to Percy's version.

257   The Percy folio and the Wood texts read *and if* here (*an if*, the more correct form, in the second of Wood's versions). Forresters' simple "if" is one of its few signs of being smoother and possibly editorial compared with the Wood texts and must be taken as a free variation. There is no need to emend Forresters.

261   The manuscript reads *No nay, no nay* (possibly the second is *no-nay*), and while it is conceivable that the Wood reading *Now nay, now nay* is a simplification of this highly emphatic negative, it seems more likely that the Forresters' scribe, near the end of the long ballad, simply misremembered his source (if it was written in a late-Gothic hand as suggested above, he could hardly misread it, as in that script *w* was a very emphatic letter).

Robin Hood's Fishing

Introduction

This ballad is found in seventeenth-century broadsides and garlands and was entered in the Stationers' Register in 1631. The earliest of the Wood texts, which Child relied on (dated by Wing at 1650?), is quite unclear in the final action and appears to have been cut down to fit onto a broadside sheet. The version found in the Forresters manuscript has a fuller and more lucid sequence of final action, and, as its sense of completeness appears most unlikely to have been generated editorially from the broadside version, its text is used here.

Robin Hood's Fishing has Robin leaving the forest to make more money as a fisherman in Scarborough, Yorkshire. He is very poor at that trade, but proves his heroic quality with the bow and sword when a French pirate ship tries to steal the catch. Unique as this theme is, other connections of Robin with the sea are not completely absent — for example the remarkable occurrence of a ship named "Robin Hood" in Aberdeen as early as 1438, as well as the coastal village named Robin Hood's Bay (known as a smuggler's haven), south of Whitby and only twenty miles from Scarborough. The ballad itself has some connection with the north and probably with Yorkshire in what appears to be its underlying dialect, clearest in the Forresters version.

In its broadside versions the ballad is usually called *The Noble Fisherman*, with the subtitle *Robin Hood's Preferment*, which implies something like "professional advancement." It was entered in the Stationers' Register under the title *Robin Hood's Great Prize*, but this title was lost, perhaps confused with *Robin Hood's Golden Prize*, an archery contest ballad. Commentators have been severe on the ballad in general: Child thought it "may strike us as infantile" (III, 21), and Dobson and Taylor felt it was a "bizarre metamorphosis" for the hero (1976, p. 179). Yet the ballad was also extremely popular, appearing in "an exceptionally large number" of seventeenth-century broadsides (Dobson and Taylor, 1976, p. 179).

They attributed this to the "commercial attractions" of a song about Britain's most popular hero set in "the almost equally popular genre of a successful sea victory over the national enemy" (1976, p. 180). But it is not so clear that France was the only national enemy at the time, and it is an act of piracy, not national aggression, that Robin single-handedly frustrates. Dobson and Taylor do not follow up the interesting possibilities of their own term "metamorphosis": this ballad, for all its nautical setting is in many respects structured like *Robin Hood and the Potter*. In both, the hero goes from a greenwood setting to a mercantile trade, which he handles badly and so receives humiliation; yet his innate courage and skill bring him to both victory and wealth, which he shares generously. Curiously, both ballads involve Robin more or less platonically with a woman, here the widow and owner of the ship, there the Sheriff's wife.

In style the ballad has traces of a commercial author in the first attention-catching stanza, and some occasional Grub-Street-like usages — *most desperatly* (line 80), *most gallantly* (line 122). But otherwise it is straightforward in diction and technique, without the third-line internal rhyme of the commercial songsters. The name Robin chooses, Symon of the Lee, sounds like a reference to the *Gest*, which also seems in mind when the hero wishes to be back in Plumpton Park (line 71). In general *Robin Hood's Fishing* is a skilful reorientation of the outlaw tradition, certainly exploiting a range of national feeling against the French, but also more in tune with the spirit of the Robin Hood material than has been realized by those who have treated this ballad simply as an oddity.

Robin Hood's Fishing

In sumer time when leaves grow green,
When they do grow both green and long,
Robin Hood that bold outlaw
It is of him I sing my song.

5   "The thrassle cock and nightengaal   *thrush*
Do chaunt and sing with merry good cheer;
I am weary of the woods," said hee,
"And chasing of the fallow deer.

"The fisher-man more mony hath
10   Then any marchant two or three;
Therefore I will to Scarburough go
And there a fisher-man will bee."

Hee cald togeather his weight men all,   *strong*
To whom he gave or meat or fee,   *food or money*
15   Paid them their wage for halfe a year,
Well told in gold and good monie.

"If any of you lack mony to spend
If your occasions lie to speake with mee,   *If you need*
If ever you chance to Scarburrough com,
20   Aske for Symon of the Lee."

Hee tooke his leave there of them all,
It was upon a holy day;
Hee took up his inn at a widdows house,   *lodgings*
Which stood nigh to the waters gray.

25   "From whence came thou, thou fine fellow,
A gentleman thou seemist to bee."

"I'th contrey, dame, where I came from
They call me Symon of the Lee."

"Gen they call the Symon of the Lee,   *If; you*
30   I wish well may thou brook thy name."   *enjoy*
     The outlaw knew his courtisie,
     And so replyed "Gramercy, dame."

"Symon," quoth shee, "wilt bee my man,   *if you will be*
     I'le give to thee both meat and fee."
35   "By th'Masse, dame," bold Robin said,
     "I'le sarve yea well for years three."   *serve*

"I have a good shipp," then she said,
     "As any goes upon the sea.
     Ancors and plancks thou shalt want none
40   Nor masts nor ropes to furnish thee.

"Oars nor sayle thou shalt not want,   *lack*
     Nor hooks faile to thy lines so long."   *be lacking*
     "By my truth, dame," quoth Symon then,
     "I weat ther's nothing shall go wrang."   *know*

45   They hoyst up sayle and forth did hale   *set out*
     Merrylie they went to sea
     Till they came to th'appoynted place
     Where all the fish taken should bee.

Every man bayted his line
50   And in the sea they did him throw;
     Symon lobb'd in his lines twaine   *two*
     But neither gott great nor smaw.   *small*

Then bespake the companie,
     "Symon's part will bee but small."
55   "By my troth," quoth the master man,   *captain*
     "I thinke he will gett none at all.

"What dost thou heer thou long luske,   *lazy fellow*
What the fiend dost thou upon the sea.   *devil*
Thou hast begger'd the widdow of Scarburrough,
60 I weat for her and her children three."   *think*

Still every day they bayted their lines
And in the sea they did then lay,
But Symon he scrap'd his broad arrows,
I weat he suned them every day.   *sunned*

65 "Were I under Plumpton Parke," said hee,
"There among my fellows all,
Look so little you sett by mee,
I'd sett by yee twiyce as small.

"Heigh ho," quoth Symon then,
70 "Farwell to the green leaves on the tree,
Were I in Plumpton Parke againe,
A fisher-man I nare would bee."   *never*

Every man had fish enough,
The shipp was laden to passe home.   *travel*
75 "Fish as you will," quoth good Symon,
"I weat for fishes I have none."   *know*

They weyd up ankere, away did sayle,   *weighed (lifted)*
More of one day then two or three,   *than*
But they were awar of a French robber
80 Coming toward them most desperatly.

"Wo is me," said the master man,
"Alas, that ever I was borne,
For all the fish that wee have tane,   *taken*
Alas the day, 'tis all forlorne.   *lost*

85 "For all the gold that I have tane
For the losse of my fish I do not care,
For wee shall prisoners into France,   *shall go as*
Not a man of us that they will spare."

585

Symon staggerd to the hatches high,
90   Never a foot that he could stand.
"I would gladly give three hundred pounds
For one three hundred foot of land."

Quoth Symon, "Then do not them dread,
Neither master do you fear.
95   Give me my bent bow in my hand,
And not a Frenchman I will spare."

"Hold thy peace thou long lubber,   *clumsy landsman*
For thou canst nought but bragg and bost
If I should cast thee over boord,
100   There were nothing but a lubber lost."

Quoth Symon, "Ty me to the main mast
That at my marke I may stand fare,   *fairly, properly*
Give me my bent bow in my hand
And not a Frenchman I will spare."

105   They bound him fast to the main mast tree,
They bound Symon hard and seare,   *sorely (tightly)*
They gave him a bent bow into his hand,
And not a French man he would spare.

"Whom shall I shoot at, thou master man,
110   For God's love speake the man to mee."   *indicate*
"Shoot at the steersman of yon shippe,
Thou long luske now let me see."

Symon he took his noble bow,
An arrow that was both larg and long;
115   The neerest way to the steersmans heart,
The broad arrow it did gang.   *go*

He fell from the hatches high
From the hatches he fell downe below,
Another took him by the heels,
120   And into the sea he did him throw.

Robin Hood's Fishing

Then quickly took the helme in hand,
And steerd the shipp most gallantly,
"By my truth," quod good Symon then,
"The same fate shall follow thee."

125   Symon he took his noble bow
And arrow which was both streight and long,
The neerest way to the Frenchman's heart   *straight*
The swallow tayle he gard gang.   *caused to go*

He fell from the hatches high
130   From the hatches he fell downe below,
Another took him by the heele
And into the sea did him throw.

The shipp was tossed up and downe
Not one durst venture her to steer,   *dared*
135   The Scarburough men were very faine   *pleased*
When they saw that robber durst not com near.

"Com up master," Symon said,
"Two shoots have I shott for thee.
All the rest are for myselfe,
140   This day for Gods love merry be."

"Gods blessing on thy fingers, Symon," he said
"For weel I see thou hast good skill;
Gods blessing on thy noble heart,
Who hast employed thy bow so weele.

145   "I vow for fish thou shalt want none,
The best share, Symon, Ile give thee,
And I shall pray thee, good Symon,
Thou do not take thy marke by mee."   *aim at me*

"I had thirty arrows by my side,
150   I thinke I had thirty and three,
Thers not an arrow shall go waste,
But through a French heart it shall flee.

"Lose me from the mast," he said,
"The pitch ropes they do pinch me sare, *tarred ropes*
155   Give me a good sword in my hand,
Feind a French man I will spare." *Never a*

Together have the two shipps run
The fisher and the waryer free. *man of war (bold warrior)*
Symon borded the noble shipp
160   Found never a man alive but three.

He took a lampe unto his hand
The ship he searched by the light,
He found within that shipp of warr
Twelve hundred pounds in gold so bright.

165   "Com up, master," Symon said
"This day for God's love merry bee,
How shall we share this noble shipp,
I pray thee master, tell to me."

"By my troth," quoth the masterman,
170   "Symon, good councell Ile give thee:
Thou won'st the shipp with thine owne hands,
And master of it thou shalt bee."

"One half," quoth Symon, "of this shipp,
Ile deale among my fellows all; *share out*
175   The other halfe I freely give
Unto my dame and her children small.

"And if it chance to bee my lott,
That I shall gett but well to land,
Ile therefore build a chappell good,
180   And it shall stand on Whitby strand.

"And there Ile keep a preist to sing
The masse untill the day I dye.
If Robin Hood com once on shore,
Hee com no more upon the see."

1   The opening lines show familiarity with the "green wood" beginning common to a number of the outlaw ballads.

5   This unsurprising line replaces the highly unusual "lily leaf and elephant" in the Wood version ("lily-leaf and cowslip sweet" in the version printed by Dobson and Taylor [1976, p. 80]): although Forresters provides a structurally superior ballad, Wood's text may well have access to a different earlier tradition: its reading here seems unlikely to have been constructed by editorial processes. Forresters reading "nightengaal" seems unlikely to be a scribal error and may indicate that the source used here followed at least at times the practice of doubling vowels to indicate length.

7   In a number of ballads Robin separates from the outlaw band, but this is because of his sometimes rash adventurousness; the financial planning with which this ballad opens marks a major and mercantile-minded variation from the tone of earlier openings.

8   The manuscript reads *follow*.

17   The earliest Wood texts have *with Robin*; *with* is obviously a compositor's error for an abbreviated *quoth* (a sign of manuscript origin), and Child emends accordingly. Forresters here shows the quality of its detailed readings as well as its overall value.

19   The rapid leap from forest to Scarborough is in all the versions, and is not unlike the rapid transitions in some other ballads, which have at times led editors to think material is missing (e.g., see *Robin Hood and Guy of Gisborne*, lines 6–7).

24   The first letter of *gray* is not well written and appears to be corrected from, perhaps, the letter *b*, again indicating the possibility of a source in late gothic handwriting. It does not appear to be any other letter, certainly not *sp* from a notional "spray."

25   The *a* of *came* is overwritten, a sign of careful correction. The scribe first wrote the more familiar *From whence come thou*.

28   The locational surname "of the Lee" is very common, but it is used of the knight in the *Gest*, and recurs in *Robin Hood and Queen Catherin*, so it seems to be close to the outlaw in several ways. A "lee" was an open moor or untilled land, so just the place where an outlaw might be looking for game, animal or human; it is also, of course, a nautical term.

30   Presumably the widow is referring to the fisherman Simon in the New Testament, later known as Peter, as a model for Robin's behavior.

33   The widow has apparently inherited a fishing business from her husband; this was a common occurrence, and the techniques of business find their way into the outlaw myth here as they do in *Robin Hood and the Potter*.

36   Presumably *yea* is a variant spelling of "ye," not the idiom "yea well," meaning "very well," still heard in the USA.

44   *wrang*: the manuscript has a half-rhyme here; perhaps the source read *lang* (a northern form) in line 42. So too in lines 114 and 126.

49   The Wood versions, like Forresters, have *bare lines*, but Dobson and Taylor printed, from a garland of c. 1750, *bate lines* (1976, p. 181), though they state in a note it is a mistake in that garland. They feel that Robin throws in unbaited hooks in ignorance. Child proposes it was "wantonness" (1965, III, 211), suggesting a kind of tricksterish folly not unlike Robin's pricing policy in *Robin Hood and the Potter*.

57   The word in Forresters is clearly *luske*: "lubber" is what might be expected and appears in the Wood versions in about this position, though the narrative is a little different hereabouts.

60   The manuscript *I weat for* makes sense and is more metrical than the more grammatical *I weat*; it sounds like scribal padding, but should not be emended on that ground. The Wood versions have no parallel to this line.

64   *suned* is clearly the word in Forresters.

65   For Plumpton Park as a Robin Hood location, see the *Gest*, line 1427.

85   The manuscript has no noun after *the* in this line; it would seem that only "prize" or "gold" make sense, and the later is preferred because more familiar and so more easily dropped.

87   The phrase "go as" is understood after *shall*.

89   Wood's earliest text reads *ship-hatch*, which Child printed, but the plural as found in Forresters is more probable, even for a fairly small fishing boat.

126   The source's *And* might be thought an error for "an," which might fit better, but *And* makes sense and is retained.

128   *The swallow tayle* is an image of an arrow, with its feather flights having a shape at the rear not unlike a swallow's double-pointed tail.

136   MS: *now*. This does not make sense and might be an error for *not*.

148   MS: *Tho*. This needs emending to *Thou*.

155   In Wood Simon asks to be released and to have his "bent bow" in his hand. This is obviously a repetition from line 103, and makes no sense. The Wood version is heavily cut hereabouts, and the action quite lacks the lucid flow found in Forresters.

164   In Wood's version Robin finds twelve thousand pounds in gold, an improbably large sum.

173   Robin shares the spoils in the person of an outlaw leader. The Wood version shows him making this statement, but then has the ship's "master" say this "shall not be," but he must own it all himself. Robin seems to agree and merely says he will build "for the opprest . . . An habitation" — presumably an alms-house.

     But whereas Forresters allows *Robin Hood and Queen Catherin* to end in a somewhat argumentative mode, as Little John disagrees with the king and, it seems, Robin, the context here is much less strained than the Wood text.

184   The manuscript reads *not* with a correcting point under the *t*.

591

The Death of Robin Hood

Introduction

This ballad is not recorded until the Percy folio, a badly damaged copy, in the mid-seventeenth century; the first full text is from the late eighteenth-century garland *The English Archer* of 1786, though, as Child notes, it itself "is in the fine old strain" (III, 103). Child prints the ballad early in his collection, as no. 120. This early placement can be justified: the author of the *Gest* knew the tradition of Robin's death. It is presumably one of the "tragedies" which Bower mentions in the 1440s; Grafton in 1569 refers in some detail to the story, and the Sloane *Life* concludes with it. The details of these stories vary, though there is general agreement that a Prioress of Kirkley or Kirklees in Yorkshire, who may be related to Robin, is the main agent of his death, though Martin Parker blames a hostile friar, and both the *Gest* and Percy's version involve an enemy called Roger in the hero's death. In Munday's account, Robin is poisoned by his male clerical enemies, with no Prioress involved.

The text printed here combines the two earliest texts, using the structure of the garland to fill out the Percy version where the pages have been torn (see note to line 1 for details). The story opens with a variant of Robin going off alone against his comrades' advice. He wishes to be bled at Churchlees: in *Robin Hood and the Monk* he wanted to visit church and in *Robin Hood and Guy of Gisborne* he merely wanted to encounter Guy alone. Here it is Will who advises Robin to take men with him. He does take John, but in one version they appear to fall out.

A new motif is the old woman they meet who was *banning* Robin Hood (line 40). This has been taken to mean "curse" and the sequence has seemed mysterious, but it means "lament," and this woman is, like the washer at the ford, predicting the hero's death — a moment of some mythic force and antiquity. The Prioress overdoes the process of bleeding, and Robin has a somewhat obscure fight with Red Roger, in which the hero kills his opponent. In Percy's version John has been with Robin at Churchlees all the time, and Robin forbids him to take vengeance; in the garland version John arrives in response to his master's last call on his horn, but the effect is the same.

The motif in which Robin fires an arrow to locate his grave is not in the Percy version and is not mentioned in the earliest references, but it has become so potent it seems a proper part of the final frame, taken from the garland version. Both texts stress the natural burial place and the philosophical ending of the hero.

The Death of Robin Hood appears to be a fairly old ballad which develops the hero's end out of the familiar materials of the tradition and with some distinctly ancient and potent elements. There would seem to have been a ballad in existence by the mid-fifteenth century, and the Percy version may well have been in its present form before Grafton wrote. The text assumes a Catholic context, and the language and style are very much like that of *Robin Hood and Guy of Gisborne*, though the narrator's emotive interjections at lines 69–70 and 72 seem unlike the tone of the earliest texts.

It is curious that so important and well-remembered a part of the tradition should not have been preserved in earlier form, and especially surprising that no broadside or early garland version apparently appeared, even though the garlands are constructed partly on a biographical basis. Dobson and Taylor feel that the garland version was only produced in the mid-eighteenth century (1976, p. 134), but as it is substantially the same as the earlier text this seems improbable. It may be that, unlike the more somber patterns of high art, the busy commerce of the ballad market place did not place so high a value on tragedy as on tricksterish triumphs.

This ballad combines many of the central value-laden elements of the early tradition: the protective power of the band, the special bond with John, the treachery of the regular church, a rogue knight as a fearsome enemy, the closeness of Robin to the natural world, his determined retention of high values even in — or especially in — a crisis. To these it adds a special sense of the mysterious potential of the hero, and the appropriate nature of his final moments as he merges into both the forest and myth.

The Death of Robin Hood

When Robin Hood and Little John
Down a down a down a down
Went oer yon bank of broom,   *over; (see note)*
Said Robin Hood bold to Little John,
5 "We have shot for many a pound.
   Hey, etc.

"But I am not able to shoot one shot more,
My broad arrows will not fly;
But I have a cousin lives down below,
10 Please God, she will bleed me.

"I will never eate nor drinke," Robin Hood said,
"Nor meate will doo me noe good,
Till I have beene att merry Churchlees,
My vaines for to let blood."

15 "That I reade not," said Will Scarllett,   *advise*
    "Master, by the assente of me,
    Without halfe a hundred of your best bowmen
    You take to goe with yee.

"For there a good yeoman doth abide
20 Will be sure to quarrell with thee,
    And if thou have need of us, master,
    In faith we will not flee."

"And thou be feard, thou William Scarlett,   *If*
Att home I read thee bee."   *I advise you to stay at home*
25 "And you be wrothe, my deare master,   *If; angry*
    You shall never heare more of mee."

594

The Death of Robin Hood

"For there shall noe man with me goe,
Nor man with mee ryde,
And Litle John shall be my man,
30   And beare my benbow by my side."   *long bow*

"You'st beare your bowe, master, your selfe,   *you must*
And shoote for a peny with mee."
"To that I doe assent," Robin Hood sayd,
"And soe, John, lett it bee."

35   They two bolde children shotten together,   *young men*
All day theire selfe in ranke,   *order*
Until they came to blacke water,
And over it laid a planke.   *was lying*

Upon it there kneeled an old woman,
40   Was banning Robin Hoode;   *lamenting*
"Why dost thou bann Robin Hoode?" said Robin,
"Knowst thou of him no good?"

"We women have no benison   *blessing*
To give to Robin Hoode;
45   Wee weepen for his deare body,
That this day must be lett bloode."

"The dame prior is my aunts daughter,
And nie unto my kinne;
I know shee wold me noe harme this day,   *wishes me no harm*
50   For all the world to winne."

Forth then shotten these children two,   *went; young men*
And they did never lin,   *stop*
Until they came to merry Churchlees,
To merry Churchlees with-in.

55   And when they came to merry Churchlees,
They knoced upon a pin;   *knocked; door-latch*
Upp then rose dame prioresse,
And lett good Robin in.

Then Robin gave to dame prioresse
60   Twenty pound in gold,
And bad her spend while that wold last,
And shee shold have more when shee wold.   *desired it*

And downe then came dame prioresse,
Downe she came in that ilke,   *that same [place]*
65   With a pair of blood-irons in her hands,   *surgical knives*
Were wrapped all in silke.

"Sett a chaffing-dish to the fyer," said dame prioresse,
"And stripp thou up thy sleeve."
I hold him but an unwise man
70   That will noe warning leeve.   *believe*

She laid the blood-irons to Robin Hoods vaine,
Alacke, the more pitye!
And pearct the vaine, and let out the bloode,   *pierced*
That full red was to see.

75   And first it bled, the thicke, thicke bloode,
And afterwards the thinne,
And well then wist good Robin Hoode,   *knew*
Treason there was within.

He then bethought him of a casement there,
80   Thinking for to get down,
But was so weak he could not leap,
He could not get him down.

He then bethought him of his bugle-horn,
Which hung low down to his knee;
85   He set his horn unto his mouth,   *mouth*
And blew out weak blasts three.

Then Little John, when hearing him,
As he sat under a tree:
"I fear my master is now near dead,
90   He blows so wearily."

596

The Death of Robin Hood

Then Little John to fair Kirkly is gone,
As fast as he can dree;   *go*
But when he came to Kirkly-hall,
He broke locks two or three.

95   "What cheere my master?" said Little John;
"In faith, John, little goode.
My cousin and Red Roger,
Between them let my blood."

"I have upon a gowne of greene,
100   Is cut short by my knee,
And in my hand a bright browne brand   *sword*
That will well bite for thee."

But before then of a shot-windowe   *a shuttered window*
Good Robin Hood he could glide,
105 Red Roger, with a grounden glave,   *sharpened sword*
Thrust him through the milke-white side.

But Robin was light and nimble of foote,
And thought to abate his pride,
For betwixt his head and his shoulders
110 He made a wound full wide.

Says, "Ly there, ly there, Red Roger,
The doggs they must thee eate;
For I may have my houzle," he said,   *last rites*
"For I may both goe and speake."

115 "Now give me mood," Robin said to Little John,   *courage (see note)*
"Give me mood with thy hand;
I trust to God in heaven soe hye
My houzle will me bestand."   *confession; assist*

"Now give me leave, give me leave, master," he said,
120 "For Christs love give leave to me,
To set a fier within this hall,
And to burne up all Churchlee."

"That I reade not," said Robin Hoode then,   *advise*
"Litle John, for it may not be;
125   If I shold doe any widow hurt, at my latter end,
God," he said, "wold blame me.

"I never hurt fair maid in all my time,
Nor at mine end shall it be,
But give me my bent bow in my hand,
130   And a broad arrow I'll let flee;   *fly*
And where this arrow is taken up,
There shall my grave digged be.

"Lay me a green sod under my head,   *piece of turf*
And another at my feet;
135   And lay my bent bow by my side,
Which was my music sweet;
And make my grave of gravel and green,
Which is most right and meet.   *suitable*

"Let me have length and breadth enough,
140   With a green sod under my head;
That they may say, when I am dead
Here lies bold Robin Hood."

These words they readily granted him,
Which did bold Robin please:
145   And there they buried bold Robin Hood,
Within the fair Kirkleys.

598

Notes

1   This text is constructed from Percy's folio and, where the folio pages are torn, the 1786 *English Archer* version, as follows: Percy, lines 11–78, 95–126; *English Archer*, lines 1–10, 79–94, 127–46; editorial linking is provided in lines 42–43 and 97–98.

3   Broom is fairly often invoked in the refrains to lyrics and ballads. The flower that provided the badge of the Plantagenet kings, broom (genet) was thought to have special powers and seems to have been connected with springtime and magic.

5   Robin and John shoot for a wager in several early texts, such as *Robin Hood and the Monk* and *Robin Hood and Guy of Gisborne*.

6   *Hey, etc.* A nonsense refrain akin to line 2, to be sung at the end of each stanza. Compare *Hey nonny nonny* of "A lover and his lass" in Shakespeare's *As You Like It*. The refrains would bring each stanza to six lines.

8   The text reads *fly,* but Child emends to *flee* on the grounds of rhyme. (See line 130 where the form also appears.) Though the next issue of the garland corrects to *flee* the change is not necessary in the light of the many partial rhymes found in the less literary of the ballads.

13   The adjective *merry* seems odd for a priory, especially when it will be the location of a tragedy. The term is repeated in lines 53–55. The garland version merely calls the place *fair Kirklees*.

19   The MS reads *there is a good yeoman*, but this is clearly an error and *is* should be omitted, as it is by Child. The reference is presumably to Roger, who is involved with the Prioress as Robin's enemy in this and other versions of the story. There is a resemblance in the language to the presentation of Guy of Gisborne in the earlier ballad.

26   There is a reminiscence here, and in line 31, of the way in which Robin quarrels with his followers to his own disadvantage in *Robin Hood and the Monk* and, it seems, in *Robin Hood and Guy of Gisborne*. In the Percy version Little John seems to go with him nevertheless, but in the garland version Robin goes alone (without the preceding argument), and John hurries to help Robin when he hears his horn.

26–27   Child prints a row of asterisks here as if there is a gap in the text, but none appears in the Percy folio, and none seems implied in the dialogue and action; Dobson and Taylor do not indicate a break here. See the similar instance in *Robin Hood and Guy of Gisborne*, lines 6–7.

32   The MS reads *Nor shoote for a peny*. *Nor* is presumably a scribal error picked up from the beginning of line 28, and needs emending to *And*.

38   It sounds as if the outlaws laid a plank over the water, but *laid* means "was lying."

40   Commentators translate *banning* as "cursing"; this does not make sense. There is an earlier sense of *bann* as "call on" as in the marriage banns; line 45 makes it clear that the women are prescient of Robin's ending, and that the meaning of banning cannot be "curse," but "lament."

42–43   These lines are ripped out in Percy and are reconstructed as here.

69–70   The narrator's direct evaluative comment is unusual in a ballad.

97   Red Roger is presumably related to *Syr Roger of Donkesley* or *Donkestere*, who is involved in Robin's death in the *Gest* (lines 1806 and 1817).

97–98   The two versions of the ballad do not join neatly here. Lines 96–97 are provided editorially as Robin's answer to John, and the next stanza appears to be John's response, but see line 102.

99   This line is in Percy's hand in the manuscript, and is presumably a piece of editorial linking written by him.

102   The MS reads *bite of thee*, but if the speaker is John, then emendation to *for* is needed. It may be that preceding material has been lost which means Robin

speaks these lines in a threatening way to Roger. But with what text is available, the emendation is necessary to make sense.

103   The MS also has *forth then* as if Robin actually escapes, and Child prints this, but it is, from the following action, an impossible reading; to emend to *But before then of*, meaning "But before then from," makes sense.

The MS reads *shop-windowe* which must be a scribal error for *shot-windowe*. The action is obscure here; it seems that Robin, with John's help, is escaping, but Roger catches him at the window and stabs him; Robin is able to kill Roger. Robin knows he is badly wounded, but unlike Roger, who has died unabsolved, he will be able to receive his *houzle* before death.

105   The MS reads *grounding glave*, presumably an error for *grounden*, Child's emendation, which is accepted here.

115   Dobson and Taylor (1976, p. 136) suggest that *mood* here means "help" or "God" i.e., the sacraments; but this has been referred to in *houzle*, line 113. Child, in a late note (V, 240), feels that an emendation to "Give me my God" is "not perhaps too bold a suggestion." He returns to this still later (V, 297), arguing that communion bread was called "God." This seems unnecessary. The Old English word *mod* means courage, and that is the proper heroic thing to ask for at such a moment from a faithful attendant; this is effectively a secular and heroic redefinition of the Catholic deathbed practices, which a layman could not administer.

127   The garland version employs two six-line stanzas here.

136   The reference appears to be to placing a harp with a dead person.

146   Kirkleys is the only place where Robin is supposed to be buried, which is a little unusual for a hero with such a wide-ranging myth. Presumably this is because the *Gest*, Grafton, and Parker were all specific on this point. An epitaph and even an illustration of the alleged grave were in circulation by the seventeenth century.

A True Tale of Robin Hood

Introduction

Martin Parker, the best known professional ballad writer of the early seventeenth century, produced his lengthy compilation by early 1632. It was entered in the *Stationers' Register* in February; the copy in the Bodleian Library has been thought to have been produced late in 1631. Child printed his text from the copy in the British Library, but the Bodleian copy (here called Bod.) is used here as a base text, being both slightly more accurate (see lines 28, 80, 152, 263, 352, 374, 470) and perhaps an earlier edition. Both these early copies have been cropped for binding in a similar way, and at times the edition of 1686 needs to be consulted, including for some words in the highly elaborate subtitle:

> A brief Touch of the life and death of that Renowned Outlaw, Robert Earle of Huntington vulgarly called Robbin Hood, who lived and dyed in A.D. 1198, being the 9 yere of the reigne of King Richard the first, commonly called Richard Cuer de Lyon.

> Carefully collected out of the truest Writers of our English Chronicles. And published for the satisfaction of those who desire too see

> Truth purged from falsehood.

So scholarship and moralism arrive in what Parker suggests is the otherwise frail and fantastical realm of Robin Hood story. This is more a blurb than a commitment, however, because, as Child wryly points out, in his rejection of "fained tales" Parker uses plenty of the ballad fictions. He clearly is familiar with Grafton, and also is obviously aware of the *Gest* through the "Saint Maries" Abbey connection (line 33). And he follows fully Munday's gentrified representation of the hero (*Lord Robert Hood by name*, line 12). Incidents are drawn from *Robin Hood and the Bishop, Robin Hood and Queen Catherin*, Munday's *The Downfall of Robert, Earle of Huntington*, and probably the ending of *Robin Hood's Fishing*. Child suggested that the fight against the abbot (lines 173–220) and the Bishop of Ely (lines 221–56) came from "some lost broadside" (III, 227), but this Bishop figures in Munday, and the abbot story could easily be an assemblage of similar events.

Child finally remarks that Parker may have chosen his title *A True Tale* as a challenge to the popular proverb "Tales of Robin Hood are good for fools," but it

602

is clear from his sub-title and his final words that Parker is specifically associating himself with the popular scholarship that then, as now, sought to identify the real Robin Hood: he ends by quoting — probably composing — the alleged epitaph raised by the Prioress of Kirklees for her dead cousin.

Parker's business was to publish fluent and credible texts of some size on popular subjects of national interest, including King Arthur and St. George. His was, in a sense, the hardback trade parallel to the paperback world of broadsides. His *A True Tale* is in effect a new version of the *Gest*, a major compilation for a serious audience in a new context of readership. The *Gest* was suited to certain fifteenth-century tastes with its episodic narrative, its casual and sometimes humorous moralism, and its sturdy anti-authoritarianism. Parker's text bespeaks new values of biography and historicism, a hero not only named and placed, but also given a developed career with motives for his major deeds. It is also a text that thoroughly embraces central government and sees the old Catholic churchmen as the major enemy; insofar as Robin attacks them he is valued, but as an enemy of the modern state he is to be deplored. The readers are to be delighted that *in these latter dayes / Of civill government* there are *a hundred wayes / Such outlawes to prevent* (lines 433–36).

None of the humor of the earlier (and later) ballads survives, nor does their concern for the forest and natural values. Robin is worth discussing because he was a *man of fame* (line 10), generous and brave, fiercely anti-clerical — castrating monks and friars was a normal practice of *these sparkes* (lines 65–72). He only shed blood in self defence, and mostly that of the *crewell clergie* (line 274). Not only did he not resist the king seriously, he sued for his favor (via a message on an arrow) and the king would have agreed had not his advisers thought it a bad precedent (line 327). Robin's resistance faded away, as he did himself through the treacherous prioress and a *faithless fryer* (line 365).

Parker's need to negotiate what for his period were the rather complex politics of this outlaw is shown by the fact that some eighty lines follow the death of Robin, as the author works through a whole series of lessons to be drawn in a cautious, conservative way from this account. The events would now be *unpossible* (line 429), and in these days of guns, civil government, and of *plenty, truth and peace* (line 462), we can note the truth of this saga, but also confine it to the past.

Time, change, and politics have, it seems, overtaken the timeless present of the Robin Hood myth as it had been; later periods will take the same historicist viewpoint but re-interpret it in terms of heritage and good times passed. But that will not come directly from Parker's model. His solid, capable, and thoroughly controlled ballad epic — that is the only suitable generic name — was no doubt both too long and too unfanciful to be really popular. It has some unappealingly sheriff-like propensities in its attempt to imprison the outlaw hero in the anti-clerical status of its period, and even in the measured confidence of its orderly but somewhat lifeless stanzas. The extra rhyme of the *abab* scheme implies closure and authorial control rather than the more open and rough vigor of the older ballad meter.

Where Munday produced a sprawling dramatic rehash, and Ben Jonson a failed piece of forest fancy, where the later novelists were to find the Robin Hood materials too elusive for their best success, Parker did have the distinction of making a substantial genre fit firmly to the Robin Hood material — though in the process he misplaced the untidy dynamism and the elusive touches of myth that lay, and in some sense still do, behind the many tales, true or not, of Robin Hood.

A True Tale of Robin Hood

Both gentlemen, or yeomen bould,
Or whatsoever you are,
To have a stately story tould,
Attention now prepare.

5   It is a tale of Robbin Hood,
That I to you will tell,
Which being rightly understood,
I know will please you well.

This Robbin, so much talked on,
10   Was once a man of fame,
Instiled Earle of Huntington,   *Called (Styled)*
Lord Robert Hood by name.

In courtship and magnificence,
His carriage won him prayse,   *bearing*
15   And greater favour with his prince
Than any in his dayes.

In bounteous liberality
He too much did excell,
And loved men of quality
20   More than exceeding well.

His great revennues all he sould
For wine and costly cheere;
He kept three hundred bowmen bold,
He shooting loved so deare.

25   No archer living in his time
With him might well compare;

He practisd all his youthfull prime
That exercise most rare.

At last, by his profuse expence,
30   He had consumd his wealth,
And being outlawed by his prince,
In woods he livd by stealth.

The abbot of Saint Maries rich,
To whom he mony ought,   *owed*
35   His hatred to this earle was such
That he his downefall wrought.   *worked*

So being outlawed, as 'tis told,
He with a crew went forth   *gang*
Of lusty cutters, stout and bold, *swordsmen*
40   And robbed in the North.

Among the rest, one Little John,
A yeoman bold and free,
Who could, if it stood him upon,   *was necessary*
With ease encounter three.

45   One hundred men in all he got,
With whom the story sayes,
Three hundred common men durst not
Hold combate any wayes.

They Yorkshire woods frequented much,
50   And Lancashire also,
Wherein their practises were such
That they wrought mickle woe.   *great*

None rich durst travell to and fro,
Though nere so strongly armd,   *never*
55   But by these theeves, so strong in show,
They still were robd and harmd.

His chiefest spight to the clergie was,
That lived in monstrous pride;
No one of them he would let passe
60   Along the high-way side,

But first they must to dinner goe,
And afterwards to shrift;   *confession [of wealth]*
Full many a one he served so,
Thus while he livd by theft.

65   No monkes nor fryers he would let goe,
Without paying their fees;
If they thought much to be usd so,
Their stones he made them leese.   *testicles; lose*

For such as they the country filld
70   With bastards in those dayes;
Which to prevent, these sparkes did geld   *men (gallants); castrate*
All that came by their wayes.

But Robbin Hood so gentle was,
And bore so brave a minde,
75   If any in distresse did passe,
To them he was so kinde

That he would give and lend to them,
To helpe them at their neede:
This made all poore men pray for him,
80   And wish he well might speede.   *prosper*

The widdow and the fatherlesse
He would send meanes unto,   *money*
And those whom famine did oppresse
Found him a friendly foe.

85   Nor would he doe a woman wrong,
But see her safe conveid;
He would protect with power strong
All those who crav'd his ayde.

607

The abbot of Saint Maries then,
90   Who him undid before,
Was riding with two hundred men,
And gold and silver store.

But Robbin Hood upon him set
With his couragious sparkes,   *men (gallants)*
95   And all the coyne perforce did get,   *coin (money)*
Which was twelve thousand markes.

He bound the abbot to a tree,
And would not let him passe
Before that to his men and he
100 His lordship had sayd masse.

Which being done, upon his horse
He set him fast astride,
And with his face towards his arse
He forced him to ride.

105 His men were faine to be his guide,   *eager*
For he rode backward home;
The abbot, being thus vilified,
Did sorely chafe and fume.

Thus Robbin Hood did vindicate
110 His former wrongs receavd;
For twas this covetous prelate
That him of land bereavd.

The abbot he rode to the king
With all the haste he could,
115 And to his Grace he every thing
Exactly did unfold.

And sayd if that no course were tane,   *taken*
By force or statagem,
To take this rebell and his traine,
120 No man should passe for them.

The king protested by and by
Unto the abbot then
That Robbin Hood with speed should dye,
With all his merry men.

125   But ere the king did any send,
He did another feate,
Which did his Grace much more offend;
The fact indeed was great.   *deed*

For in a short time after that,
130   The kings receivers went
Towards London with the coyne they got,
For's Highnesse northerne rent.   *For his*

Bold Robbin Hood and Little John,
With the rest of their traine,   *following*
135   Not dreading law, set them upon,
And did their gold obtaine.

The king much moved at the same,
And the abbots talke also,
In this his anger did proclaime,
140   And sent word to and fro,

That whosoere, alive or dead,
Could bring him Robbin Hood,
Should have one thousand markes, well payd
In gold and silver good.

145   This promise of the king did make
Full many yeomen bold
Attempt stout Robbin Hood to take,
With all the force they could.

But still when any came to him,
150   Within the gay greene wood,
He entertainement gave to them,
With venson fat and good.

And shewd to them such martiall sport,
With his long bow and arrow,
155   That they of him did give report,
How that it was great sorow,

That such a worthy man as he
Should thus be put to shift,   *in difficulties*
Being late a lord of high degree,
160   Of living quite bereft.

The king, to take him, more and more
Sent men of mickle might: *great strength*
But he and his still beate them sore,
And conquered them in fight.

165   Or else, with love and courtesie,
To him he won their hearts:
Thus still he lived by robbery,
Throughout the northerne parts.

And all the country stood in dread
170   Of Robbin Hood and's men;   *and his*
For stouter lads nere livd by bread,   *never*
In those dayes nor since then.

The abbot which before I nam'd
Sought all the meanes he could
175   To have by force this rebell tane,
And his adherents bold.

Therefore he armd five hundred men,
With furniture compleate,   *equipment*
But the outlawes slew halfe of them,
180   And made the rest retreate.

The long bow and the arrow keene
They were so usd unto
That still they kept the forest greene,
In spight o'th' proudest foe.

A True Tale of Robin Hood

185 Twelve of the abbots men he tooke,
   Who came him to have tane;   *taken (seized)*
   When all the rest the field forsooke,
   These he did entertaine

   With banquetting and merriment,
190 And, having usd them well,
   He to their lord them safely sent,
   And willd them him to tell

   That if he would be pleasd at last
   To beg of our good king
195 That he might pardon what was past,
   And him to favour bring,

   He would surrender backe agen
   The money which before
   Was taken by him and his men,
200 From him and many more.

   Poore men might safely passe by him,
   And some that way would chuse,
   For well they knew that to helpe them
   He evermore did use.

205 But where he knew a miser rich,
   That did the poore oppresse,
   To feele his coyne his hand did itch;
   Hee'de have it, more or lesse.

   And sometimes, when the high-way fayld,
210 Then he his courage rouses;
   He and his men have oft assayld
   Such rich men in their houses.

   So that, through dread of Robbin then
   And his adventurous crew,
215 The mizers kept great store of men,
   Which else maintaynd but few.

611

King Richard, of that name the first,
Sirnamed Cuer de Lyon,   *Lionheart*
Went to defeate the Pagans curst,
220   Who kept the coasts of Syon.   *Zion (Palestine)*

The Bishop of Ely, chancelor,
Was left as vice-roy here,
Who like a potent emperor
Did proudly domminere.

225   Our chronicles of him report
That commonly he rode
With a thousand horse from court to court,
Where he would make abode.

He, riding downe towards the north,
230   With his aforesayd traine,
Robbin and his did issue forth,
Them all to entertaine.

And, with the gallant gray-goose wing,
They shewed to them such play,
235   That made their horses kicke and fling,
And downe their riders lay.

Full glad and faine the bishop was,
For all his thousand men,
To seeke what meanes he could to passe
240   From out of Robbins ken.   *knowledge (power)*

Two hundred of his men were kild,
And fourescore horses good;
Thirty, who did as captives yeeld,
Were carryed to the greene wood.

245   Which afterwards were ransomed,
For twenty markes a man;
The rest set spurres to horse, and fled
To th'town of Warrington.   *[in Lancashire]*

The bishop, sore enraged then,
250   Did, in King Richards name,
Muster a power of northerne men,
These outlawes bold to tame.

But Robbin, with his courtesie,
So wonne the meaner sort,
255   That they were loath on him to try
What rigor did import.

So that bold Robbin and his traine
Did live unhurt of them,
Untill King Richard came againe
260   From faire Jerusalem.

And then the talke of Robbin Hood
His royall eares did fill;
His Grace admir'd that i'th' greene wood
He thus continued still.

265   So that the country farre and neare
Did give him great applause;
For none of them neede stand in feare,
But such as broake the lawes.

He wished well unto the king,
270   And prayed still for his health,
And never practised any thing
Against the common wealth.

Onely, because he was undone
By th'crewell clergie then,
275   All meanes that he could thinke upon
To vex such kinde of men

He enterprized, with hatefull spleene;
In which he was to blame,
For fault of some, to wreeke his teene   *avenge his anger*
280   On all that by him came.

With wealth which he by robbery got
Eight almes-houses he built,
Thinking thereby to purge the blot
Of blood which he had spilt.

285   Such was their blinde devotion then,
Depending on their workes;
Which, if 'twere true, we Christian men
Inferiour were to Turkes.

But, to speake true of Robbin Hood,
290   And wrong him not a jot,
He never would shed any mans blood
That him invaded not.   *Who did not injure him*

Nor would he injure husbandmen,
That toyld at cart and plough;
295   For well he knew, were't not for them,
To live no man knew how.

The king in person, with some lords,
To Notingham did ride,
To try what strength and skill affords
300   To crush these outlawes pride.

And, as he once before had done,
He did againe proclaime,
What whosoere would take upon
To bring to Notingham,

305   Or any place within the land,
Rebellious Robbin Hood,
Should be prefered in place to stand   *ennobled*
With those of noble blood.

When Robbin Hood heard of the same,
310   Within a little space,
Into the towne of Nottingham
A letter to his Grace

614

He shot upon an arrow-head,
One evening cunningly;
315   Which was brought to the king, and read
Before his Majesty.

The tennour of this letter was
That Robbin would submit,
And be true leigeman to his Grace,
320   In any thing that's fit,

So that his Highnesse would forgive
Him and his merry men all;
If not, he must i'th' greene wood live,
And take what chance did fall.

325   The king would faine have pardoned him,
But that some lords did say,
"This president will much condemne   *precedent*
Your Grace another day."

While that the king and lords did stay
330   Debating on this thing,
Some of these outlawes fled away
Unto the Scottish king.

For they supposd, if he were tane,   *taken*
Or to the king did yeeld,
335   By th'commons all the rest on's traine   *of his following*
Full quickely would be quelld.   *killed*

Of more than full a hundred men
But forty tarryed still,   *only 40 remained*
Who were resolvd to sticke to him,
340   Let fortune worke her will.

If none had fled, all for his sake
Had got their pardon free;
The king to favour meant to take
His merry men and he.

345 But ere the pardon to him came,
   This famous archer dy'd.
   His death, and manner of the same,
   I'le presently describe.

   For, being vext to thinke upon
350 His followers revolt,
   In melancholly passion
   He did recount their fault.

   "Perfideous traytors!" sayd he then,
   "In all your dangers past
355 Have I you guarded as my men
   To leave me thus at last?"

   This sad perplexity did cause
   A fever, as some say,
   Which him unto confusion drawes,
360 Though by a stranger way.

   This deadly danger to prevent,
   He hide him with all speede   *hurried*
   Unto a nunnery, with intent
   For his healths sake to bleede.

365 A faithless fryer did pretend
   In love to let him blood;
   But he by falshood wrought the end
   Of famous Robbin Hood.

   The fryer, as some say, did this
370 To vindicate the wrong
   Which to the clergie he and his
   Had done by power strong.

   Thus dyed he by trechery,
   Who could not dye by force;
375 Had he livd longer, certainely,
   King Richard, in remorse,

Had unto favour him receavd;
He brave men elevated;
'Tis pitty he was of life bereavd
380 By one which he so hated.

A treacherous leech this fryer was,   *doctor*
To let him bleed to death;
And Robbin was, me thinkes, an asse,
To trust him with his breath.

385 His corpes the priores of the place,
The next day that he dy'd,
Caused to be buried, in mean case,   *in a poor state*
Close by the high-way side.

And over him she caused a stone
390 To be fixed on the ground;
An epitaph was set thereon,
Wherein his name was found.

The date o'th' yeare, and day also,
Shee made to be set there,
395 That all who by the way did goe
Might see it plaine appeare

That such a man as Robbin Hood
Was buried in that place;
And how he lived in the greene wood,
400 And robd there for a space.

It seems that though the clergy he
Had put to mickle woe,   *much*
He should not quite forgotten be,
Although he was their foe.

405 This woman, though she did him hate,
Yet loved his memory;
And thought it wondrous pitty that
His fame should with him dye.

This epitaph, as records tell,
410 Within this hundred yeares
By many was discerned well,
But time all things outweares.

His followers, when he was dead,
Were some received to grace;
415 The rest to forraigne countries fled,
And left their native place.

Although his funerall was but meane,
This woman had in minde
Least his fame should be buried cleane   *Lest; completely*
420 From those that came behind.

For certainely, before nor since,
No man ere understood,
Under the reigne of any prince,
Of one like Robbin Hood.

425 Full thirteene yeares, and something more,
These outlawes lived thus,
Feared of the rich, loved of the poore,
A thing most marvelous.

A thing unpossible to us
430 This story seemes to be;
None dares be now so venturous;   *adventurous*
But times are chang'd, we see.

We that live in these latter dayes
Of civill government,
435 If neede be, have a hundred wayes
Such outlawes to prevent.

In those dayes men more barbarous were,
And lived lesse in awe;
Now, God be thanked! people feare
440 More to offend the law.

No roaring guns were then in use,
They dreamt of no such thing;
Our English men in fight did chuse
The gallant gray-goose wing.

445   In which activity these men,
Through practise, were so good,
That in those dayes non equald them,
Specially Robbin Hood.

So that, it seems, keeping in caves,
450   In woods and forrests thicke,
Thei'd beate a multitude with staves,
Their arrowes did so pricke.

And none durst neare unto them come,
Unlesse in courtesie;
455   All such he bravely would send home,
With mirth and jollity.

Which courtesie won him such love,
As I before have told;
'Twas the cheefe cause that he did prove
460   More prosperous than he could.

Let us be thankefull for these times
Of plenty, truth and peace,
And leave our great and horrid crimes,
Least they cause this to cease.

465   I know there's many fained tales
Of Robbin Hood and's crew;
But chronicles, which seldome fayles,
Reports this to be true.

Let none then thinke this a lye,
470   For, if 'twere put to th' worst,
They may the truth of all discry
I th'raigne of Richard the first.

If any reader please to try,   *test*
As I direction show,
475 The truth of this brave history,
Hee'le finde it true I know.

And I shall thinke my labour well
Bestowed to purpose good,
When't shall be sayd that I did tell
480 True tales of Robbin Hood.

Notes

3 The adjective *stately* has interesting possibilities, both implying a formal style and also suggesting a concern with the state.

5 Both early texts read *Robbin* here, as later; it is not clear why Child emends to *Robin*; he does not do so in later instances.

6 Both of the earliest editions read *That* to begin this line; it makes a better variation with *Which* beginning line 7; the 1686 edition which Child consulted also reads *That*, and he does not explain the origin of what seems an inferior reading in *Which*.

9–12 Parker, like the gentrifying chroniclers, combines Robin's popularity with his elevated status, as if the two are intimately connected.

24 Bod. reads *loved* against BL *lov'd*.

27 Though the longbow was no longer a serious weapon of the battlefield, regular practice in archery was urged on all male town dwellers in the sixteenth and early seventeenth centuries.

28 BL spells *excercise* but Bod. is correct.

29 This reason for Robin's downfall is ultimately drawn from Grafton.

33 The abbot is in the *Gest,* but there he is antagonistic to the knight, not Robin. Here begins Parker's relentless portrayal of Catholic clerics as the real enemies of Robin Hood, a theme already outlined strongly in Munday's *Downfall.*

39 The noun *cutters* implies both swordsmen and robbers: purse-cutters.

49 The northern location of the outlaws is a consistent theme throughout this period. It presumably reflects difficulties London experienced in controlling the north throughout the sixteenth and seventeenth centuries.

68   A remarkable and unique assertion about Robin's anti-clerical ferocity, co-existing bizarrely with the outlaw's *gentle* and *kinde* qualities in the next few lines. In *Robin Hood's Golden Prize* he makes the priests swear celibacy, lines 87–90, but that is hardly a parallel.

80   BL reads *wisht* but Bod. has the correct *wish*, which Child also prints.

96   A mark was thirteen shillings and four pence; the sum taken was eight thousand pounds.

97–100   There is a clear resemblance to *Robin Hood and the Bishop*, which is not recorded until later than *A True Tale*, but was no doubt in circulation.

103   In the first editions the word is is spelt *ar—*; the 1686 edition spells the word out fully. On villains being forced to ride backwards, face-to-arse, see Thomas Hahn and Richard W. Kaeuper, "Text and Context: Chaucer's *Friar's Tale*," *Studies in the Age of Chaucer* 5 (1983), 67–101.

130   The fact that Robin here attacks the "king's receivers" complicates the politics of the ballad; this is a survival from the late medieval combination of king and abbot as forces ranged against the outlaws, and presumably this causes the withdrawal of sympathy from Robin at the end of the ballad. He is a hero for robbing and even castrating clerics, but tackling the king is another matter. It is interesting that Parker, however, did not completely emasculate his story in this respect, and the Robin Hood figure, *not dreading law* (line 135), finally poses the author with something of a challenge as well. This episode appears to have stimulated the start of *Robin Hood and Queen Catherin*.

152   Bod.'s *venson* is metrically a little better than BL's *venison*.

183   The 1686 edition has *he kept*, which appears to be a compositor's error.

211–12   Parker imagines the outlaw's crimes in vivid contemporary terms; for parallels see Richard Head, *The English Rogue* (1650).

229   It is more normal to say "up" if a journey is going north. The idea of a place's importance conveying height is still found in the idiom of "going down" from Oxford, whatever the direction.

233   Arrows often have goose-feather flights, so the term is used metonymically of the arrow itself.

250   The model being used here is the political disturbances of the late medieval period, like that led by "Robin of Redesdale" in 1469, when Sir John Conyers deliberately chose an outlaw-like name for his rising; another instance was led by "Robin of Holderness" in the same year.

253–54   Parker explains Robin's main support through his elite qualities — a sign of his reworking of the politics of the tradition.

263   Bod.'s *i'th'* is a little more precise than BL's *ith'*, as is also the case in line 323.

282   There is a general resemblance to the end of *Robin Hood's Fishing*, but a closer one perhaps, to the social self-reclamation attempted by donations to charity, especially founding alms-houses by many rich and violent men in the period — a particularly vivid and surviving set of examples are to be found in Stamford, Lincolnshire.

287–88   The statement apparently disavows the notion of penance through good works as in Catholic doctrine and moves towards the Reformation idea of those who were "elect" were the only true Christians.

293   An apparent reference back to the *Gest*, lines 51–52.

317–20   A curious prediction, and perhaps partial source, of the later play *Robin Hood and his Crew of Souldiers* in which Robin, in Nottingham in 1661, submits to the newly established king.

327   Renaissance, even Machiavellian, counseling finds its way into the myth; the political drama has become much less direct than it used to be.

329   Bod. has one of its rare compositor's errors here, reading *Kiug*.

333–36   Seventeenth-century politics are shaping here the course of the medieval outlaw's career. Robin no longer has the instinctive support of his men.

345–46   Robin's death is introduced almost as brusquely as in the *Gest* and with the same effect of resolving an impasse in the plot.

352   BL has *his* here, which must be an error picked up from line 350.

365   This is the first mention of another hostile cleric in the death sequence: the Prioress is sometimes helped by a yeoman who is hostile to Robin, rather like Guy of Gisborne. See the end of the *Gest*.

373   In spite of his modernization of the politics and his containment of the hero, Parker is still story-teller enough to underline the essential mythic elements of the story. Whether he is international hero or social bandit, the central figure only comes to death through treachery of someone very close to him, though as in line 383, the tone soon changes.

374   Bod. reads *Who*, which seems preferable to BL's *That*.

405   Parker attempts to resolve a contradiction in the story: Robin is betrayed at Kirklees yet also remembered there. Parker has some of the instincts of a scholar, or at least a rationalizer.

409   Parker clearly invokes the scholarly quest for Robin Hood as found in Grafton, Camden, and Leland.

419   Bod. has *cleare* which loses the rhyme and must be an error.

425   The *Gest* says Robin dwelled in the green wood after leaving the court *twenty yere and two*. Perhaps *thirteene* is meant as an unluckier period.

427   The resemblance to the theme song of the 1950s British television series starring Richard Greene —"Feared by the bad, loved by the good" — is presumably accidental.

429   Child reads *impossible* which he cites as the Bod. reading, and a correction to BL's *unpossible*. But Bod. actually also reads *unpossible*, which must be accepted.

431   There follows a curious passage, partly nostalgic for the heroic freedom of the past, partly anxious to assure readers of the security of the present. The Robin Hood tradition, it appears, has the power to test its transmitters.

442   BL and Child read *dreampt*, but Bod.'s *dreamt* is preferable.

448   The 1686 edition prints *Especially* but both early editions have the metrically slightly rougher *Specially*.

460   The meaning seems obscure. Does it imply that he "proved to be more prosperous than he ought to have done?" If so, then *should* might be a better reading, but the texts are unanimous for *could*. Or does it perhaps mean "he seemed more prosperous than he really was?" It is clear that Parker is here trying, as thoughout this passage, to moderate enthusiasm for the hero, and this seems to lead him into a lack of clarity.

463   It is not clear what Parker has in mind as *our great and horrid crimes*, but it adds to the sense of tension throughout this passage, and brings to a somewhat anxious climax the recurrent modernization of the Robin Hood story, as his actions hover between the anti-state violence and quasi-cavalier gentility.

470   Bod. has the slightly more accurate *if 'twere*, where BL reads *if't were*.

476   Child reads *Hee'l* but in fact both early editions have *Hee'le*.

478   BL has a comma after *Bestowed*, but Bod. does not; the latter seems the better reading.

480   To support his insistence on veracity, Parker appended the alleged epitaph from Kirklees: this was much copied, even translated into bogus Middle English and carved in stone. It appears to have been written by Parker on the basis of the remarks and hints given by Grafton and Camden; for a discussion, see Holt, 1989, pp. 41–42, and Knight, 1994, pp. 19–21:

> Robert Earle of Huntington
> Lies under this little stone.
> No archer was like him so good:
> His wildnesse named him Robbin Hood.
> Full thirteene years, and something more,
> These northerne parts he vexed sore.
> Such out-lawes as he and his men
> May England never know agen.

Robin Hood and the Pedlars

Introduction

According to Child the manuscript in which *Robin Hood and the Pedlars* occurs contains "a variety of matters, and, as the best authority [E. Maunde Thompson, Keeper of Manuscripts in the British Museum] has declared, may in part have been written as early as 1650, but all the ballads are in a nineteenth-century hand, and some of them are maintained to be forgeries" (III, 170). *Robin Hood and the Pedlars* is surely one of the "forgeries," a work composed most likely in the early nineteenth century by an antiquarian enthusiast who has read plenty of Robin Hood ballads and who has a good quotient of off-color wit. The verse is in rollicking ballad stanzas that mingle conventional devices (interrogatory opening with promises of smiles to come, stock phrases and situations, syntactic inversions, repetitions, action through dialogue, and archaisms) with bits and pieces of old plot. But there are surprises along the way, especially toward the end where the wounded Robin takes a "balsame" which, according to the decorous Child "operates unpleasantly" (III, 171) and which Gutch before him had labelled a "nasty incident" (II, 355). But what seemed obscene to nineteenth-century editors, namely, the once gentrified hero not only beheld vomiting, but vomiting in the faces of his buddies, is likely to seem crudely amusing to the more vulgar inclination of a late twentieth-century audience. Part of the amusement lies in the poet's blending of euphemism with specifics — no puking or even vomiting for the nineteenth-century writer but, rather "he gan to spewe, and up he threwe" (line 110); this he combined with a cute moral that warns against challenging people stronger than oneself (lines 117–20). Such ploys are sufficiently risqué and upright to reveal the anonymous author's playful delight in honoring his heroes by besmirching them. As in many a tale of Robin, the hero wins, then, over-confident in his rough and tumble way, loses only to win over his opponent through his fall, albeit here disgustingly.

Robin Hood and the Pedlars is part of popular representation of a carefree "former age" that early nineteenth-century England thrived upon under the penumbra of Scott's *Ivanhoe*. The matter is light, the imitations clever, and the effect primitively vulgar, a primitivism that enables a prim audience to titillate itself in a socially acceptable way, despite the unpleasantry and nastiness of what the "old ballad" said.

Robin Hood and the Pedlars

I have used Child's transcription as my base text, with some alterations in capitalization (Ff>F) and punctuation. I have not seen the nineteenth-century manuscript.

Select Bibliography

Robin Hood and the Peddlers. In *A Lytell Geste of Robin Hode with Other Ancient and Modern Ballads and Songs Relating to this Celebrated Yeoman, to which is prefixed his history and character, grounded upon other documents than those made use of by his former biographer, "Mister Ritson."* Ed. by John Mathew Gutch. London: Longman, Brown, Green, and Longmans, 1847. II, 351–55.

Robin Hood and the Pedlars. In *English and Scottish Popular Ballads.* Ed. F. J. Child. Boston: Houghton Mifflin, 1888. III, 170–72.

Robin Hood and the Pedlars

Will you heare a tale of Robin Hood,
   Will Scarlett, and Little John?
Now listen awhile, it will make you smile,
   As before it hath many done. [1]

5   They were archers three, of hie degree,   *high*
   As good as ever drewe bowe;
Their arrowes were long and their armes were strong,
   As most had cause to knowe.

But one sommers day, as they toke their way
10   Through the forrest of greene Sherwood,
To kill the kings deare, you shall presently heare   *deer*
   What befell these archers good.

They were ware on the roade of three peddlers with loade,
   For each had his packe.
15   Full of all wares for countrie faires,
   Trusst up upon his backe.

A good oke staffe, a yard and a halfe,
   Each one had in his hande,
And they were all bound to Nottingham towne,
20   As you shall understand.

"Yonder I see bold peddlers three,"
   Said Robin to Scarlett and John;
"We'le search their packes upon their backes
   Before that they be gone.

---

[1] Gutch reads *many a one.*

25 "Holla, good fellowes!" quod Robin Hood,
   "Whither is it ye doe goe?
  Now stay and rest, for that is the best,
   'Tis well ye should doe soe."

  "Noe rest we neede, on our roade we speede,
30   Till to Nottingham we get."
  "Thou tellst a lewde lye," said Robin, "for I   *stupid*
   Can see that ye swinke and swet."   *labor and sweat*

  The peddlers three crosst over the lee,
   They did not list to fight:
35 "I charge you tarrie," quod Robin, "for marry,   *wish*
   This is my owne land by right.

  "This is my mannor and this is my parke,
   I would have ye for to knowe;
  Ye are bolde outlawes, I see by cause
40   Ye are so prest to goe."   *eager*

  The peddlers three turned round to see
   Who it might be they herd;
  Then agen went on as they list to be gone,   *as they yearned*
   And never answered word.

45 Then toke Robin Hood an arrow so good,
   Which he did never lacke,
  And drew his bowe, and the swift arrowe
   Went through the last peddlers packe.

  For him it was well on the packe it fell,
50   Or his life had found an ende;
  And it pierst the skin of his backe within,
   Though the packe did stand his frend.

  Then downe they flung their packes eche one,
   And stayde till Robin came;
55 Quod Robin, "I saide ye had better stayde;
   Good sooth, ye were to blame.

629

"And who art thou? by S. Crispin, I vowe,   *Saint*
   I'le quickly cracke thy head!"
Cried Robin, "Come on, all three, or one;
60   It is not so soone done as said.   *more often boasted than done*

"My name, by the Roode, is Robin Hood,   *Cross*
   And this is Scarlett and John;
It is three to three, ye may plainelie see,
   Soe now, brave fellowes, laye on."

65   The first peddlars blowe brake Robins bowe
    That he had in his hand;
And Scarlett and John, they eche had one   *each took a blow*
    That they unneth could stand.   *scarcely*

"Now holde your handes," cride Robin Hood,
70   "For ye have got oken staves;
But tarie till wee can get but three,
    And a fig for all your braves."   *chutzpa*

Of the peddlers the first, his name Kit o Thirske,
   Said, "We are all content."
75   So eche tooke a stake for his weapon to make
    The peddlers to repent.

Soe to it they fell, and their blowes did ring well
   Uppon the others backes,
And gave the peddlers cause to wish
80   They had not cast their packes.   *taken off*

Yet the peddlers three of their blowes were so free
   That Robin began for to rue;
And Scarlett and John had such loade laide on
   It made the sunne looke blue.

85   At last Kits oke caught Robin a stroke
    That made his head to sound;
He staggerd and reelde, till he fell on the fielde,
    And the trees with him went round.

"Now holde your handes," cride Little John,
90   And soe said Scarlette eke;   *also*
"Our maister is slaine, I telle you plaine,
    He never more will speake."

"Now, heaven forefend he come to that ende,"   *forbid*
    Said Kit, "I love him well;
95 But lett him learne to be wise in turne,
    And not with pore peddlers mell.   *tangle*

"In my packe, God wot, I a balsame have got   *medicine*
    That soone his hurts will heale";
And into Robin Hoods gaping mouth
100   He presentlie powrde some deale.   *immediately poured; part*

"Nowe fare ye well, tis best not to tell
    How ye three peddlers met;
Or if ye doe, prithee tell alsoe
    How they made ye swinke and swett."   *labor and sweat*

105 Poore Robin in sound they left on the ground,   *unsound*
    And hied them to Nottingham,   *hastened themselves*
While Scarlett and John Robin tended on
    Till at length his senses came.

Noe sooner, in haste, did Robin Hood taste
    The balsame he had tane,   *taken*
110 Than he gan to spewe, and up he threwe
    The balsame all againe.

And Scarlett and John, who were looking on
    Their maister as he did lie,
Had their faces besmeard, both eies and beard,   *eyes*
115   Therwith most piteously. [2]

---

[2] Gutch suggests that "this nasty incident seems taken from *Don Quioxte*" (II, 355).

Thus ended that fray; soe beware alwaye
   How ye doe challenge foes;
Looke well aboute they are not to stoute,   *too strong*
120   Or you may have worst of the blowes.

From *Hereward the Wake*

Introduction

As Charles Plummer says, Hereward has a brief life in history and a long one in romance (*Two of the Saxon Chronicles Parallel* [1889], II, 265). The real Hereward (as recorded in *Domesday Book* and the *Anglo-Saxon Chronicle*) seems to have been a small south-Lincolnshire squire, holding lands from the abbeys of Crowland and Peterborough, and thus very much "the monk's man," although regularly in dispute as to tenancy agreements (*The Chronicle of Hugh Candidus*, ed. W. T. Mellows [1949] p. 79). The battle of Hastings which brought William of Normandy to power was not necessarily considered decisive in the more remote provinces, and Norman colonization was slow to reach this part of England. In the spring of 1070 the Danish king Swein Estrithson arrived in the mouth of the Humber, and was expected to make a bid for the crown. He despatched a body of housecarls under Jarl Asbjorn and Bishop Christian of Aarhus to secure a base on the Isle of Ely, a tract of fertile land capable of supporting six hundred households, some twelve by ten miles, in the middle of the swampy fenland of south Lincolnshire (Swanton, p. 188, note 18, and references there cited). Ely was admirably suited for defense; sea-going vessels could reach it via the Wash and River Ouse, but landwards it was cut off by swamps and a network of hidden waterways. Here the Danes were immediately joined by local people (many of whom were of Danish extraction), including Hereward. At Peterborough Abbey, on the western edge of the Fens two dozen miles away, the abbot Brand, perhaps Hereward's uncle, had recently died, and now the monks were warned that Hereward and his companions wanted to remove the monastery's valuables prior to the arrival of a Norman abbot, the tyrannical Turold, who was approaching with a band of 160 soldiers. The monks resisted Hereward and his men, who set fire to the town, forced the precinct gate and looted the monastery. Soon afterwards the Danes returned to Denmark, taking this loot with them. Hereward and his band remained behind, but were now *personae non gratae* with Turold and others who had taken up estates in the area.

Ely now became a notorious refuge for anti-Norman dissidents, including, among the better known, Earl Morcar of Northumbria, Bishop Æthelwine of Durham, and Siward Bearn, a substantial Midlands landowner. Popular rumor even suggested that Earl Eadwine, in fact now dead, and Archbishop Stigand, in fact now in prison, also sought shelter there (Freeman, IV, 9). At last William himself led an expedition against Ely. He bottled up the defenders, placing a naval blockade on the seaward side and then constructing a lengthy causeway to allow his land forces to advance through the swamps. Eventually the defenders surrendered to William who "did with them what he wanted." Florence of Worcester says that some he imprisoned, others he let go free, having cut off their hands or put out their eyes (*Chronicon ex Chronicis*, ed. B. Thorpe, II, 9). But Hereward slipped away with some of his followers and is heard of no more in any official record. Later, like some other resistance leaders, he may have been reconciled with the Conqueror. Gaimar suggests that he was in charge of an English contingent fighting on behalf of William in Maine, and was subsequently killed by a bunch of jealous Norman knights (*L'Estoire des Engleis*, ed. A. Bell, pp. 178–80). A man called Hereward held lands in Warwickshire at the time of William's death (*Domesday Book*, 23, *Warwickshire*, ed. J. Morris, 16: 26, 44, 48). The surname Hereward survived in Ely through the thirteenth century; thus, Robert Hereward, bailiff and seneschal of the Bishop of Ely *c*. 1296, and afterwards sheriff in Cambridgeshire and Norfolk (E. Miller, *The Abbey and Bishopric of Ely*, pp. 267–68).

The exploits of so notable a hero immediately captured the popular imagination. It is said that women and girls sang about him in their dances, and the author of the pseudo-Ingulf claimed to know ballads celebrating, and no doubt exaggerating, his deeds (*Gesta* III; *Rerum Anglicarum Scriptorum Veterum*, pp. 67–68). An extensive folk-literature was circulating within a few years of his death. Much of what was said seems to have been incorporated into the *Gesta*, from which extracts are printed here. He was soon ascribed fine family connections, and an elaborate pedigree by those keen to claim him as an ancestor. Of course, if he was actually related to one or another noble family, it would account for the prominence he is given in the record of resistance to William. The cognomen "the Wake" (i.e., the watchful one) is first recorded in a later chronicle attributed to one John of Peterborough (*Chronicon Angliae Petriburgense*) that acknowledges the necessary characteristics of the successful guerilla leader. Charles Kingsley's novel published in 1866, in which the story of this most famous of English freedom-fighters achieved its definitive modern form, is simply an engrossment of the *Gesta* material.

The origins of the *Gesta* are explained by the author in his introduction, addressed to an unnamed authority — perhaps Hervey, first bishop of Ely, 1107–31. It was compiled in two stages. The first developed out of the author's attempts to read a few decayed and mutilated pages which had apparently formed part of a collection of stories written in the vernacular, allegedly by Hereward's "well-remembered" chaplain Leofric, whose intention it had been to assemble all the doings of giants and warriors he could find in ancient fables as well as in "true reports." On the basis of this, perhaps half read, half invented, the author constructed a plainly fictional account of Hereward's youthful exile (corresponding to chapters III–XIII). Story rather than history, *geste* rather than *gesta*, most of the formulae are readily paralleled in contemporary saga and romance. It was conventional that a young man in exile should visit the courts of foreign princes, and there prove himself in deeds of valor and prowess. Hereward is made to follow the traditional route of the fictional exile through the peripheral regions of Britain combating a monstrous bear in Northumberland, rescuing a princess in distress in Cornwall, and fighting in Ireland, before passing on to Flanders, the common resort of refugees from England at this time. In the course of all this, the personality of the future guerrilla-fighter is anticipated: courageous, quick-witted, adept at disguise and watchful — sleeping not in but to one side of his bed for fear of night-time attacks. After a lengthy sojourn in Flanders, full of incident reminiscent of Harold Godwinson's period in Normandy, the hero is said to return to England.

At this point, apparently frustrated at finding no more adequate source, the author says he laid his work aside. But prompted by the original commissioner, he again takes up his pen and completes the book with the addition of a somewhat episodic account of Hereward's part in the defense of Ely, based on interviews with the hero's former associates in the anti-Norman campaign. Some of them are named, and one or two seem to have suffered retributive mutilation at the hands of the Normans. These chapters (chs. XIV–XXXVI *passim*) are entirely different in tone from the preceding farago. Albeit the reminiscences of now elderly veterans, and no doubt recalled "with advantages," these tales of guerrilla skirmishes have the air of reality. Even so, elements of romance creep in: the hero has a mysterious vision of St. Peter (ch. XXIX); a grey wolf guides his companions through the marsh, while will-o-the-wisp lights flicker around their spear-tips (ch. XXIX); one of his enemies begs for mercy with his head through a lavatory seat (ch. XXX); his eventual reconciliation with the king is brought about by the attentions of a beautiful and wealthy widow (ch. XXXI).

Author and Date

If we are to believe the author's claim that he drew on first-hand rather than second-hand accounts, the great likelihood is that the *Gesta* was composed in the first quarter of the twelfth century, at a time when Hereward himself was presumably dead, but a number of former companions, albeit elderly, were still alive and capable of remembering their old campaigns.

Some time in the mid-twelfth century an unnamed monk of Ely Abbey compiled an eclectic history of his institution, in the course of which he says he drew on a *Gesta Herewardi* made "not long since" by a respected and "most learned" fellow monk called Richard (*Liber Eliensis*, p. 188). There is a close verbal parallel with our text, and it is reasonable to suppose that this Richard was the author of the extant *Gesta* or an earlier version of them. By that time Richard was apparently dead ("of blessed memory"). His identity is uncertain, but he was clearly familiar with the locality and of sufficient status to be able to call on assistants; but his Latin is not of the clearest and scarcely fits the description *doctissimus* ("most learned").

Manuscript and Edition

The *Gesta* survives in a single manuscript copy, added to a thirteenth-century collection of Peterborough Abbey charters, legal documents, etc., belonging to Robert de Swaffham, pittancer and cellarer of the abbey, now Peterborough Cathedral Manuscript 1, ff. 320–39. A reliable text was printed by T. D. Hardy and C. T. Martin in their edition of Geoffrey Gaimar's *L'Estoire des Engles*, Rolls Series 91, London (1888–89), I, 339–404.

Select Bibliography

The Chronicle of Hugh Candidus. Ed. W. T. Mellows. London: Oxford University Press, 1949.

Chronicon Angliæ Petriburgense. Ed. J. A. Giles. London: David Nutt, 1845.

Chronicon ex Chronicis. Ed. Benjamin Thorpe. London: English Historical Society, 1848–49.

Domesday Book. Text and translation edited by John Morris. Chichester: Phillimore, 1975–92.

Freeman, Edward Augustus. *The History of the Norman Conquest of England*. 6 vols. Oxford: Clarendon Press, 1867–79.

Gaimar, Geoffrey. *L'Estoire des Engleis*. Ed. Alexander Bell. Anglo-Norman Text Society. Oxford: Basil Blackwell, 1960.

Hayward, John. "Hereward the Outlaw." *Journal of Medieval History* 14 (1988), 293–304.

Liber Eliensis. Ed. E. O. Blake. Camden Third Series XCII, London: Offices of the Royal Historical Society, 1962.

Miller, E. *The Abbey and Bishopric of Ely*. Cambridge: Cambridge University Press, 1951.

Swanton, Michael. *English Literature Before Chaucer*. London: Longman, 1987.

Two of the Saxon Chronicles Parallel. Ed. Charles Plummer, based on an edition by John Earle. 2 vols. Oxford: The Clarendon Press, 1889.

From *Hereward the Wake*

I

Here begins the preface of a certain work concerning the exploits of Hereward the renowned knight.

When some among us wanted to know about the deeds of the great Englishman Hereward and his famous men, and to hear with our ears his generous acts and exploits, your brethren eked out our sparse information by enquiring whether anyone had left anything in writing about such a man in the place where he used to live. For when I informed you that I had heard somewhere that a short account had been written about him in English, you were immediately kind enough to have it sought out; and soon it was translated into Latin, with the addition of things we happened to hear from our own people with whom he was familiar, living a distinguished life as a great warrior. So, wanting to satisfy your wishes, I took care to enquire in many places, yet found nothing complete — only a few loose pages, partly rotten with damp and decayed and partly damaged by tearing. However, having taken up the pen, I have with difficulty extracted from it a few details as to his origin, his parents and reputation — that is to say the early achievements of the most famous outlaw Hereward, written down in English by the deacon Leofric, his priest at Bourne. For it was the endeavor of this well-remembered priest to assemble all the doings of giants and warriors he could find in ancient fables as well as true reports, for the edification of his audience; and for their remembrance to commit them to writing in English. And although I'm not sufficiently expert at this, or rather, unable to decipher what is obliterated in the unfamiliar writing, nevertheless I gather that on his return to the place of his own ancestral home, he found his brother killed — and so on. I leave this raw material, written in a rough style, to your care and to the efforts of some trained person, to be arranged and set out in a less ornate and complex manner. For I have been able to decipher nothing further than this, always hoping for more but still finding nothing in full. For a long time my assistants were deluded by a vain hope, stimulated by those who said that there was a large book about his exploits in such and such a place. But although they sent to the place they found nothing of what was promised. So giving up the search altogether, I abandoned the work I had begun. It could not have remained secret from you for long; but unexpectedly, you were kind enough to direct that at least the opening should not be denied you. Whereupon I took care, although not confident of any great ability, that your eyes might

638

see the complete work. I took up the pen once more to unfold to you a little book in the style of a history, dealing with things I heard from our own people and from some of those who were familiar with him from the beginning and who were associated with him in many exploits. I have frequently seen some of these men — tall in stature, well-built and exceptionally courageous. And you yourself, I hear, have also seen two of these men — that is to say his knights Brother Siward of Bury St. Edmunds and Leofric Black, men of distinguished appearance, although having lost the beauty of their limbs due to the trickery of enemies, being deprived of certain members through envy. And from these and others whom I have seen and tested in many matters if on no other grounds, here is sufficient for you to understand how valorous their lord was, and how much greater his deeds were than those reported of him. For truly to know who Hereward was and to hear about his magnanimity and his exploits is conducive to magnanimous acts and generosity, especially in those wishing to undertake the warrior's life. So I urge you to pay attention, especially you who are concerned to hear of the exploits of brave men; listen carefully to this account of so great a man who, trusting in himself rather than rampart or garrison, alone with his men waged war against kings and kingdoms and fought against princes and tyrants, some of whom he conquered. Concerning these matters, beginning with his parents, everything has been arranged in due order, so that what is clearly set down here may be easily remembered.

II

Of what parents Hereward was born, and how from his boyhood he increased in the splendor of his deeds, and why he was driven forth by his father and country; whence he was surnamed "The Outlaw."

Many very mighty men are recorded from among the English people, and the outlaw Hereward is reckoned the most distinguished of all — a notable warrior among the most notable. Of very noble descent from both parents, his father was Leofric of Bourne, nephew of Earl Ralph the Staller; and his mother was Eadgyth, the great-great-niece of Duke Oslac. As a boy he was remarkable for his figure and handsome in his features, very fine with his long blond hair, open face and large gray eyes — the right one slightly different from the left. However, he was formidable in appearance and rather stout because of the great sturdiness of his limbs; but despite his moderate stature he was very agile and there was great strength in all his limbs. From his childhood he exhibited such grace and vigor of body; and from practice when a youth the quality of his courage proved him a perfect man. He was excellently endowed in every way with the grace of courage and strength of spirit. And so far as generosity is concerned, he was particularly liberal with his own and his father's possessions, giving relief to all in need. Although tough in work and rough in play, readily provoking fights among those of his own age and often stirring up strife among his elders in town and village, he had no equal in acts of daring and bravery, not even among his elders. So when young, and as he grew older, he advanced in boldness day by day, and while still a youth excelled in manly deeds. In the meantime he spared nobody whom he thought to be in any way a rival in courage or in fighting. In consequence he often caused strife among the populace and commotion among the common people. As a result of this he made his parents hostile towards him; for because of his deeds of courage and boldness they found themselves quarreling with their friends and neighbors every day, and almost daily having to protect their son with drawn swords and weapons when he returned from sport or from fighting, from the local inhabitants who acted like enemies and tyrants because of him. Unable to stand this, eventually his father drove him out of his sight. He didn't keep quiet even then; but when his father went visiting his estates, Hereward and his gang often got there first, distributing his father's goods amongst his own friends and supporters. And on some of his father's properties he even appointed stewards and servants of his own to see to provisions for his men. And so his father ensured that he was banished from his homeland by King Edward, disclosing everything that he had perpetrated against his parents and against the inhabitants of the locality. And this being done, he at once acquired the name of "Outlaw," being driven away from his father and his native land when he was eighteen years old.

[*During his exile, Hereward engages in various adventures. III: He slays a monstrous bear in Northumberland, and IV: a braggart in Cornwall, suitor for the hand of the princess; and V: the leader of an invading army in Ireland. VI: He returns to the Cornish princess and attends her nuptials in disguise, rescues the girl and ensures her marriage to an Irish prince. VII: Now determined to return home, Hereward is shipwrecked in Orkney, and again in Flanders where he is honorably detained by the count, changing his name to Harold. VIII–IX: Hereward fights on behalf of the Count of Flanders against the neighboring Count of Guines, and his true name is revealed. X: During the course of his sojourn, the skilled and enterprising girl Turfrida falls in love with him, and he with her, despite the violent opposition of another knight. XI–XII: Hereward takes the central role in two campaigns against rebellious Frisian armies. XIII: While in Frisia he acquires a particularly swift mare he names Swallow, and her colt Lightfoot.*]

Hereward the Wake

XIV

How he returned to his country and to his father's house, where he found that his brother had been slain the day before, and of the grand vengeance he took the same night.

After Hereward had spent a few days in idleness [in Flanders], thinking this disgraceful he left and immediately set out for England. He wished to visit his father's house and his homeland, now subject to the rule of foreigners and almost ruined by the exactions of many men, wanting to help any friends or neighbors who perhaps might still be alive in the place. He returned from foreign parts with his personal attendant Martin Lightfoot as his sole companion, leaving his two nephews, Siward the Blond and Siward the Red together with the wife he had just taken. He arrived back at his father's manor called Bourne one evening time, and was entertained on the outskirts of the village by a certain soldier of his father's called Osred. There he found the head of the household and his neighbors very gloomy, all full of grief and in great fear, having been given over to the subjection of foreigners. And what was worse for them, they were bewailing the fact that they were subject to those who the previous day had slain the innocent younger son of their lord. Immediately therefore Hereward, who appeared as if a stranger, asked who their lord now was, who was responsible for the death of their former lord's son, and the reason for it. And they answered him: "Although it is a help and a comfort in sadness to share one's grief, we shouldn't involve you in our misfortune, for we see that you're a great man with whom we ought to be joyful for the sake of hospitality. Nevertheless, because you appear to be in every way a great and famous man, we might look to you for some remedy for our sorrow, so we will readily explain the business to you. There was among us a certain younger son of our lord whom his father, when dying, commended to his people, together with his mother; and he was to be his heir if his brother, called Hereward, shouldn't return — a man most vigorous and conspicuous in all courage, whom while still a lad his father had driven away from his presence by way of punishment. And now, three days ago, certain men seized his inheritance with the consent of the king and took it for themselves, destroying our light, the son and heir of our lord, while he was protecting his widowed mother from them as they were demanding from her his father's riches and treasures — and because he slew two of those who had dishonorably abused her. By way of revenge because he had killed two Frenchmen, they cut off his head and set it up over the gate of the house — here it still is. Alas, wretched men that we are, we have no power of vengeance! Would that his brother Hereward, a very great man so we've often heard, were here now; for then truly before the moon set and the sun sent forth its rays of light, every one of them would be lying dead like our lord's son!" Hearing this, Hereward lamented greatly, sighing inwardly. At length, being drowsy after their conversation, they all retired to rest. After lying on his bed for a while, Hereward heard

641

some way away the voices of people singing, the sound of harp and viol and the merriment of those applauding. Summoning a lad, Hereward enquired what the sound was that echoed in his ears. He immediately declared it to be the merriment of those joining in the party given on the occasion of their entering into the inheritance of his lord's son, who had been killed by them the previous day.

After a little while Hereward called his servant and, taking a mail-coat and helmet from beneath a black cloth — a maidservant's cloak — put on his tunic and took a sword. And thus, with his servant protected by light armor, he approached the party-goers who were now overcome with drunkenness, intending to pledge them for his brother's death with a draught of bitterness and wine of sorrow. Then he came near; he found his brother's head over the gate. Taking it, he kissed it and concealed it, wrapped in a cloth. This done, he advanced through the entrance of the building to search out the guests. He saw them all by the fireside overcome with drunkenness, the soldiers reclining in the women's laps. Among them was a jester playing a lute, abusing the English race and performing antics in the middle of the hall meant in imitation of English dancing, who eventually demanded in payment from their lord something which had belonged to the parents of the remarkable lad killed the previous day. At this one of the girls at the banquet, unable to tolerate these words, replied: "There still survives a distinguished soldier by the name of Hereward, brother to the lad killed yesterday and well-known in our country (that is to say, in Flanders); and if he were here, none of these would be left alive when the sun spread abroad its rays of light!" Indignant at these words, the lord of the household answered thus: "Well, I happen to know the man, and a great scoundrel he is, for he stole the gifts which were sent to the prince of our country from Frisia and distributed them unfairly after the prince had appointed him leader of the soldiers. Now he would have suffered death on the gallows, if he hadn't ensured his safety by running away, not daring to stay in any land this side of the Alps!" On hearing this, the jester continued repeatedly to abuse him as he sang to the lute. Eventually unable to tolerate this any longer, Hereward leapt out and struck him through with a single blow of his sword, and then turned to attack the guests. Some were incapable of rising because they were drunk, and others unable to go to their help because they were unarmed. So he laid low fourteen of them together with their lord, with the aid of the single attendant whom he set at the entrance of the hall so that whoever escaped the hands of one might fall to the other. And that same night he set their heads over the gate where his brother's head had been, giving thanks to the Bestower of all grace that his brother's blood was now avenged.

XV

For what reason some fled from him in alarm; and whence he chose for himself men of war.

In the morning, however, the neighbors and those living round about were filled with astonishment at what was done. And almost all the Frenchmen in the district were frightened, abandoning the lands assigned to them and fleeing, lest the same thing should happen to them at the hands of such a man should they have him for a neighbor. But having heard about him, the inhabitants of the country and his kinsfolk flocked to him, congratulating him on his return to his native land and to his father's inheritance, and advising him to guard it carefully in the meantime, dreading the anger of the king when he came to learn of the affair. In fact not unmindful of such matters, he lodged there forty-nine of the bravest men from his father's estate and among his kinsfolk, equipped and defended with all necessary military accouterments. Meanwhile he wanted to carry on for a few days taking vengeance on those of his enemies in the neighborhood who still remained on their manors.

XVI

For what reason he wished to be made knight in the English manner, and where he was made knight.

When Hereward realized that he was the leader and lord of such men, and day by day saw his force growing larger with fugitives, the condemned and disinherited, he remembered that he had never been girt with the belt and sword of knighthood according to the tradition of his race. And so with two of the most eminent of his men, one named Winter and the other Gænoch, he went to the abbot of Peterborough called Brand, a man of very noble birth, in order that he might gird him with the sword and belt of knighthood in the English tradition, lest after becoming the chief and leader of so many men, the inhabitants of the country should disparage him for not being knighted. He received the accolade of knighthood from the abbot on the Feast of the Nativity of the Apostles Peter and Paul. And in his honor a monk of Ely named Wulfwine, who was both a faithful brother and prior and also a friend of Hereward's father, made his comrades knights. Hereward wanted himself and his men to be knighted in this way because he heard that it had been ruled by the French that if anyone were knighted by a monk, cleric or any ordained minister, it ought not to be reckoned the equal of true knighthood, but invalid and anachronistic. Opposing this regulation, therefore, Hereward wished almost all those serving him and under his rule to be knighted by monks. So if anyone wanted to serve under him he had to receive the sword in the manner the knight's tradition demands, from a monk at least, if from no one else. Often he would point out: "I know from common experience that if anyone should receive the knightly sword from a servant of God, a knight of the kingdom of heaven, such a man will pursue valor most excellently in every kind of military service." And hence arose the custom among those at Ely that if anyone there wished to be made a knight, he ought always to offer his naked sword upon the altar at high mass and the same day receive it back again after the gospel reading from the monk who was singing mass, the sword being placed on his bare neck with a blessing; and by making over the sword to the recruit in that way, he was made a full knight. This was the custom of abbots in those times. Later Hereward was to go to the Isle of Ely and, together with its inhabitants, defend it against King William who by that time had subjected almost the entire country to himself.

XVII

How he was sought out by a certain man who desired to kill him, and how Hereward slew him.

Having returned to his own people, Hereward learned that a certain Frederick, who was the brother of the old Earl William de Warenne, had been making frequent enquiries for him in many places, in order that he might either take him personally into the king's presence and hand him over to punishment for what was mentioned a little earlier; or alternatively cut off his head and set it up for a sign at a cross-roads on the public highway, in the same way as he had exhibited over the gate of his house the heads of those who had stolen his inheritance and slain his brother; and further, that he might drive into exile or mutilate all those who continued to support Hereward or rendered him any assistance. But Hereward and his men immediately set about preempting him, intending to treat him in the same way if by chance they should meet with him. For Hereward had learned that Frederick was in Norfolk together with a military force, so that as soon as anything was heard of Hereward, Frederick might make his way there protected by a troop of soldiers. But what Frederick intended should happen to Hereward happened to himself instead. One evening time while he was plotting the death of Hereward, the outlaw himself arrived and slew him.

XVIII

Why Hereward departed again into Flanders, where he soon performed some noteworthy deeds.

To allow the situation to cool down after this, Hereward went into Flanders to see the

644

wife he had recently taken, promising those whom he left in England that he would return within the year. And there at St. Omer he came to his wife and the two nephews whom he had left with her. He had not been there a fortnight before he was invited by Baldwin, a certain highly celebrated knight of that province, to join a campaign he had undertaken against the Viscount de Pynkenni. The lord of Brabant with his nobles was also to be present at this encounter. And on this expedition Hereward and his two aforementioned nephews Siward the Blond and Siward the Red, together with the aforesaid noble knight Baldwin who led them there, acted in such a way that even the opposing party did not withhold their commendation but greatly praised them, picking out Hereward especially as an object of admiration. Once when his boldness had carried him too far among the enemy, they killed his horse beneath him, and thus being alone and on foot they surrounded him on all sides. Not that this did them any good, for it proved the speedy destruction of his attackers, since he slew seven of those who rushed to seize him. At length when he was surrounded by a wall of enemies on all sides, several of the leaders of the opposing party, perceiving his spirit and courage, helped him by calling off his attackers. They said it was shameful for so many to be attacking a single man the whole day long, and scarcely finish the business in the end. "And even if he were to be eventually overcome, what sort of victory would that be for us, for one man to be overcome by so many? There would certainly be a slur on our reputation. And even though he may fall in the end, he deserves to be esteemed above everyone else." While Hereward was duly recovering a little from these attackers, unharmed by any weapon, a mounted comrade showed great enterprise, coming to his aid and snatching him up so that he was reunited with his men. Then from horseback he told everybody what had happened to him and recounted with what generosity the enemy had acted despite the fact that he had killed seven of their men who had inadvisedly attacked him. This event resulted in such good-will on both sides that, out of respect for such a knight, all those who were formerly at odds were reconciled; and they honored him with gifts.

XIX

How on his return to England his men gathered themselves together to him, on his giving the signal which he had arranged at his departure.

But as he had promised his men, Hereward, now eminent in all military matters, returned to England together with his two nephews and his loving wife Turfrida who was already superior to the usual feminine weaknesses and regularly proved capable in every exigency which befell her celebrated husband. There also came with him a certain chaplain of his, Hugo the Breton by name, who although a priest, was no less trained in arms than endued with virtue, and Wivhard his brother, a splendid knight of soldierly courage. He obviously also brought with him those in his service. Some of these Hereward immediately sent to explore his own area and his father's house, so as to make careful enquiries as to what had been decided about him by the king's majesty, and with the utmost caution to find out from friends in his father's territory where those men whom he had left in England now were. When they eventually got there, they found his inheritance entirely undisturbed, no one having dared to enter it. Some of his men they found in hiding, thus ensuring their safety. And these, instantly delighted at his return, hastened to join him, namely: a certain Winter, a distinguished knight who was short in stature but particularly robust and strong; and Wenoth and Ælfric Grugan notable in all courage and bravery for they were as powerful in action as they were big and tall. In addition to these were three of Hereward's nephews: Godwine Gille, who was called Godwine because not dissimilar to Godwine the son of Guthlac who is so celebrated in stories of olden days; and Duti and Outi, two twin brothers similar in character and appearance and both praiseworthy soldiers. The remainder of his band of followers, however, was scattered over the entire kingdom. At his departure he had arranged a signal for them — to set in flames three villages on Brunneswold near to Bourne; and so he set fire to them and retired into the forest until his men were gathered around him.

And when they were all assembled, they were all the most eminent men, not one among them being counted of knightly rank without first having achieved some notable deeds. These are their names (with those mentioned above making up the number): Wulfric the Black, who got his name because he had once daubed his face with charcoal and gone unrecognized into a garrison, laying low ten of them with a single spear. And his friend was a certain Wulfric Rahere, or "The Heron," so-called because he once happened to be at Wroxham Bridge where four brothers were brought who, although innocent, were to be executed; and terrifying the hangmen who had called him "heron" in mockery, he manfully caused the innocent men to be released and killed some of their enemies. Others too were numbered among the more distinguished of Hereward's knights: Godric of Corby, a nephew of the Earl of Warwick; and Tostig of Daveness, kinsman of the same earl and whose name he received at baptism; and Acca Hardy, the son of a gentleman from the outskirts of Lincoln who was personally responsible for one of the towers of the city; and Leofwine Mowe, that is "The Sickle," who got his name because, chancing to be alone in a meadow cutting grass, he had been set upon by a score of local peasants with iron pitchforks and spears in their hands, whereupon quite alone with only his sickle he wounded many and killed some, charging among them like a reaper, and finally putting them all to flight.

In company with these was also a certain Tunbeorht, a great nephew of Earl Edwin, and Leofwine Prat, that is "the Dodger," who was called this because although often captured by enemies he had astutely escaped, frequently killing his guards. And in addition to these must be numbered others also very experienced in warfare: Leofric the

Deacon, the Bailiff of Drayton; Thurcytel Utlamhe — that is to say, "the Outlaw"; Hereward's cook Hogor; Hereward's kinsmen Winter and Leofred, two distinguished men; and Rapenald, steward of Ramsey. These were leaders; so also: Wulfric the Black and Wulfric the Blond, Ælfric Grugan, Yiardus, Godwine Gille, Outi — and the other Outi I mentioned before — and those two splendid men, Siward and the other Siward the Red, who were Hereward's nephews. Then with these there were other most eminent knights: Godric of Corby, the Norman priest Hugo and his brother Yiardus, Leofric the Deacon, Tostig of Rothwell, Leofwine Prat, Thurcytel, and the Bailiff of Drayton. All of these were among the most distinguished and splendid knights in the whole kingdom; and there were not a few others, whom it would take too long to name and describe separately.

XX

How the men in the Isle of Ely sent for Hereward; and how on the road he discovered an ambush by the Earl of Warenne.

Now when those who lived in the Isle of Ely, then beginning to hold out against King William who had gained England in battle, heard of the return of such a man as Hereward, they directly sent to him and negotiated through messengers for him to join them with all his men, to take part together with them in the defense of the homeland and their fathers' liberties, assuring him that such a knight as he was would have the foremost position among them. This message was delivered especially in the name and on behalf of Thurstan, abbot of the church at Ely, and his monks, who had lordship of the Isle, and by whom it was put in a state of defense against the king, in particular because William intended to set a certain foreign monk over them — one of those monks for whom he had already sent from the French nation, to set as deans and priors in all the churches of the English.

However, having previous knowledge of this, a certain well-known knight and seaman, Brunman by name, being familiar with the coast, intercepted them at sea, ducked them in the ocean in a large sack that he had tied to the prow of his ship, and sent them back, thus freeing the English monasteries from foreign domination for the time being. Hereward was delighted to receive this envoy and finally directed his men to make preparations for the journey, boarding ship at Bardney. Hearing of this, the Earl de Warenne, whose brother Hereward himself had recently slain, prepared many ambushes along his road in secret hiding-places near the routes out from the Isle through the swamp, cautiously placing a guard round the waters on the land-side and hoping to capture him without serious loss to his own men. In the event, however, this was not hidden from Hereward. Certain of the guards stumbled across some stragglers from his force and assailed them with missiles. Coming to their aid and capturing their attackers, he ascertained from these that the ambush was laid by the Earl de Warenne who was himself coming to Earith the following day. Whereupon, hastening with his ships, Hereward assembled his men there. Concealing his troops near the river bank, Hereward himself with three knights and four archers well equipped with arms drew close to the edge of the river opposite to where the earl and his men had just arrived. Upon seeing them, one of the earl's men approached and said this to them: "Are you from the company of that great scoundrel Hereward who has ruined so much by trickery and has drawn so many to help him in his nefarious deeds? Would that the villain could be betrayed to our lord the earl. Anyone who agreed to do so would be well worth payment and honors. For this hostile band, although not dangerous, may eventually force us to live in this detestable swamp, and to chase them unarmed through muddy marsh, swirling water, and sharp reeds. Every one of them is destined to an early death, for the king has already surrounded the whole island on all sides with his army, and has closed off the area so that he may destroy its inhabitants." At these words, one of them retorted: "You good-for-nothing! How much longer are you going to incite us to betray our lord and desert our leader? Run off back; shift your feet, before you go down under fierce javelins. And tell your lord that the man he's asking for is here on this side of the water." Learning this, the earl immediately approached and, catching sight of Hereward, urged all his men to swim across the water with him to avenge the blood and death of his brother. But they insisted that it wasn't possible, saying that Hereward had come there just to trap them in that very way. Whereupon, snarling, he railed against those lying across the water: "Oh, would that your master, that limb of Satan, were in my grasp now; he should truly taste punishment and death!" Understanding these words, Hereward declared: "But if by good luck we two happened to be by ourselves anywhere, you wouldn't be so keen to have me in your feeble grasp nor be glad that we met!" And leaning forward a little, Hereward stretched his bow and shot an arrow with force against the earl's breast. Although it rebounded from the protecting mailcoat, the earl was rendered almost lifeless by the blow. Whereupon his men, very anxious on their lord's account because he had fallen from his horse at the blow, quickly carried him away in their arms. Meanwhile Hereward went away and that very day withdrew his men into the Isle of Ely, where he was now received with the greatest respect by the abbot and monks of the place. And he was honored by the important men in the Isle, that is to say by the former Earl of Leicester, Edwin, and his brother Morcar Earl of Warwick, and by another earl called Tostig, all of whom had fled to join those in the Isle having suffered many wrongs at the hands of the aforesaid king and being harassed by many demands. Not a few of the country's distinguished men had fled and were led to the place for the same reason.

XXI

How the king attempted to take the Isle, where he nearly lost his entire army; while no man, except one brave knight, entered it.

Consequently when the king heard about this he was moved to enormous anger and, goaded by deep indignation, furiously applied himself to taking the Isle by storm. In fact, he moved his whole army to Aldreth where the surrounding water and swamp was narrower, the breadth there extending only four furlongs. Having brought there tools and fitments of timber and stone, and heaps of all kinds of things, they built a causeway through the swamp, although it was narrow and quite useless to them. Moreover, close to the big river near this place, that is to say Aldreth, they assembled in the water large tree-trunks joined together with beams, and underneath tied whole sheep-skins, flayed and reversed and fully inflated so that the weight of those going over it might be better borne. When this was finished such a multitude rushed onto it all at once, greedy for the gold and silver and other things, not a little of which was thought to be hidden in the Isle, that those who went hurrying in front were drowned together with the road itself they had made. Those who were in the middle of the company were swallowed up in the watery and deep swamp as well. A few of those who were following at the rear got away with difficulty, flinging down their weapons, wallowing in the water and making their way through the mud. Thus in this way, with hardly anybody pursuing them, great numbers perished in the swamp and waters. And to this day many of them are dragged out of the depths of those waters in rotting armor. I've sometimes seen this myself. And out of this entire company I've talked of, not one got into the Isle, except by chance a single eminent knight called Deda who went on in front of everybody. But in any case, nobody from the Isle was caught in the trap. For some of them had made a heap of turves on the bank of the aforesaid river in front of the bulwarks and ramparts, laying ambushes to both right and left. The king, observing all these things from a distance, evidently saw where his men in front were swallowed up in the swamp and water; wherefore, groaning with deep, heartfelt sorrow, he left together with those of his men who still survived — very few compared with the number of those who were drowned — setting aside all hope of making any further attack on the Isle. Nevertheless, he set a guard there and positioned soldiers round about lest the islanders should have free passage to lay waste the district.

XXII

Of a soldier who went into the Isle, and resolved to be the first to give information to the king about the Isle and its inhabitants.

Now the cunning soldier whom I mentioned a little while ago as having got into the

Isle, was captured and led before the chief men and dignitaries in the Isle of Ely. When he was asked his name and the reason for his coming, they found out from him that he went by the name Deda, and the reason was this. The king, in the presence of his men, had made a bargain that whoever was first to make his way into the Isle and inflict injury there, might ask him for any property in the Isle, and the king promised he should have it for sure. When they heard this, the islanders praised his boldness and courage and had him stay with them for a few days so that he might get to know their valor from personal experience and realize what a secure position they held, being provided with the protection of a strongly fortified location and strengthened in no small way by companies of distinguished soldiers. For, as he often declared in their presence, he had heard many times that they were less proficient in war and less skilled in military affairs than other races. But before he left he recognized that they were quite excellent in all matters, and proficient in the art of warfare. And so he was given permission to leave on these terms: that he should report about them nothing other than what he had seen and heard — and this he had to affirm with an oath. Enriched with a gift, he eventually got to the court of the king. On his arrival everyone together there heartily congratulated him, and indeed the king himself was delighted, for he was the most renowned among the more distinguished of the king's knights. When questioned before the whole court, Deda explained how by some lucky chance he had entered the Isle unharmed. As related above, great numbers perished while going along the road which they had made. He said that out of all of them he alone had been brought alive into the Isle by Hereward, the leader of the soldiers in the island. He affirmed that through Hereward he had been given an honorable place amongst the more distinguished of the troop of soldiers. Then at Hereward's enquiry he had told them of the reason for his coming — explaining to him the king's promise that the first man to enter the Isle and inflict injury there should be rewarded with a very great honor. On the king's closely questioning Deda still further, he went through the ranks of the chief men in the island and their names, and recounted the splendid nature of their activities in defense of the Isle, and how well strengthened they were by troops of distinguished soldiers, and in no small measure protected by groups of the toughest men. Those he ascribed to the first rank were: the three earls mentioned earlier, namely Edwin, Morcar and Tostig, and the two noblemen Ordgar and Thurcytel "the Lad."

And in talking about them he extolled Hereward and his men more highly than themselves and above all the knights he had seen among the French, or in the German Empire, or at Byzantium for valor and courage in all matters; and although some might be equal to Hereward, none, he said, could surpass him. At this the Earl de Warenne, whose brother Hereward had recently killed as I explained above, moved to anger and goaded by deep indignation declared: "Well, it's quite evident from what you say that you're not a little deceived, in that you would induce our lord king to show kindness by extolling his enemies with false praise and arguments of this sort. Besides are you going to set up that great scoundrel Hereward for courage and bravery? Now leave off burdening his respected majesty the king with such frivolous talk!" To whom the aforesaid soldier replied, saying that he had not been seduced by a bribe or gift, nor was he persuaded by any consideration; he had only to tell the truth about them without fear or favor, and having taken an oath to this effect he had been allowed to leave. And in replying, he asked how he could keep silent about such things when they demanded to know what he had seen with his own eyes and had himself experienced, without either offending the lord king or violating his oath by falsely reporting other than the truth. So the king directed that he should tell them, but that he should be considered without offence in this, declaring that he had long known him to be a truthful soldier, and reckoned that he was not exaggerating in this now. Once more, therefore, the aforesaid soldier was closely questioned, not only by the king but by many others, asking if the enemy were in need of provisions or any other necessaries, or if there were any further experienced men than those he had previously related, so as to find him out in any contradiction in his account, or rather that they might learn something to assist them in the siege. To this he made just one reply: "Well, if you are still anxious to hear their cause it is, as I understand it, as follows: It is because his respected majesty the king had given instructions that monks from overseas should be appointed deans and priors in all the churches of the English — and for whom your eminence had just recently sent, that is to say those whom a certain distinguished English knight called Brunman intercepted at sea because of this, ducking them in the ocean in a big sack and sending them back, thus freeing his kindred from foreign domination for the time being. For this cause, fearing subjection to foreigners, the monks of that place risked endangering themselves rather than be reduced to servitude, and gathering to themselves outlaws, the condemned, the disinherited, those who had lost their parents, and such like, they put their place and the island in something of a state of defense. There's no pressure on account of the numbers of the army over there, and they aren't oppressed by the enemy. For although besieged by four kings and their subjects, the ploughman doesn't take his hand from the plough, nor does the right hand of the reaper hesitate in reaping; the hunter doesn't neglect his hunting spears, nor does the fowler stop lying in wait for birds by the banks of rivers and in woods, so those in the Isle are well and plentifully supplied with almost all living things. At the time when the water-fowl are molting and changing their appearance, I've commonly seen trappers there bringing in lots of small birds: very often a hundred, sometimes two hundred or more, and occasionally not far off a thousand from one stretch of water. Similarly from the woods that are in the Isle there is at one time of the year a good supply of heron, quite apart from the abundance of wild and domesticated animals. And certainly the waters which surround the Isle abound with all kinds of fish. What more need I say? Indeed, every day during the time I spent there we made ourselves sick with the sumptuous English-style feasts in the monks' refectory — soldier and monk always going to dinner and supper together, at the high table the abbot with the three earls mentioned earlier, seated side by side with the two most distinguished men, Hereward and Thurcytel the Lad. Above each and every knight and monk there hung against the wall a shield and lance; and down the middle of the hall from top to bottom on the bench were placed mailcoats, helmets, and other arms, for the monks as well as the soldiers never scorned to take their turn and go out on a military patrol. Indeed, in what I noticed there, this one thing above all others struck me as remarkable, that almost all the monks of that place are so well-versed in warfare — a thing I've certainly never heard of before, nor have I come across such anywhere else. Certainly I don't know that they are in need of anything as regards defense, let alone in spirit, when they have a fruitful island, so productive of every kind of grain and growing things, and so well fortified by waters and swamp, much stronger than any castle surrounded by walls. Nevertheless, I hope that my lord king will not cease attacking them, and then he will find that I haven't deviated from the truth, and will realize that in the end it would be better to make peace with them than be continually attacking them and getting absolutely nowhere."

XXIII

What they did when they were disheartened about the Isle, and how the king was disposed to make peace with them, unless some of his own men had dissuaded him.

Well, just then while he was relating this, one of those soldiers the king had sent to effect the blockade at Reach Dyke came in, and as soon as the story was finished, expostulated: "Don't you believe it? Does it seem so unlikely? Only yesterday I saw several men coming out of the Isle — not many — only seven, but dressed for battle and girt with proper war-equipment — all but two of whom were manifestly monks, and like the others well-versed in warfare. And exercising the rights of the military, they set fire to the village of Burwell and did damage everywhere — and not only these men but often others as well, rushing in all directions. Some of our men, ten in number who were engaged in the blockade, dashed in front of us all without consideration for themselves, thinking to capture them because they were fewer in number than us. Anyway, they finally intercepted them opposite the aforesaid dyke, within mutual lance-throwing distance. And after a long struggle all our men finally succumbed except for one distinguished soldier called Richard, who took his surname from his uncle Sheriff Osbeorht. One of the outlaws called Wennoth, leaving the main body, had stuck closely to Richard in order to take him. While these two continued to struggle, those who had come out from the Isle stood by for a long time and could see neither of them prevailing. And observing us approaching from a distance with a force of soldiers, the leader of their soldiers, Hereward, had them separated and allowed no one to offer violence against Richard, saying that it was shameful for two or three to fight against one man, and would in no way allow such a thing to be done by his men; and this we learnt from the mouth of Richard himself. However, we finally pursued them right up to their ships, killing one of their boatmen with a javelin and capturing another who told us their ranks and described who they were, adding their names: the leader of the soldiers Hereward, Wennoth, young Thurstan who was afterwards named prior, Brother Siward of St. Edmunds, Leofric, and Acca Hardy, so named because he was hardy in enduring pain. Although monks, these were certainly most highly distinguished in all military matters and had frequently undertaken deeds of valor with Hereward and were well-tried in their experience of battle.

However, the king made no reference to this, no word either good or bad, saying to himself that it was unworthy to abuse men who had acted generously, and equally so to favor his enemies with praise in front of his own men. He contemplated making peace with them, knowing the Isle to be strongly defended both by nature and by the finest of men, and realizing that he could in no way prevent their coming and going there. So summoning the magnates and counsellors, he explained to them what was in his mind, to make peace with those in the Isle, declaring that it would be very serious to leave such men in the middle of the land at his rear, when they ought already to be marching against the Danish army and after that to go directly to Normandy. Whereupon several of the leaders who were present and were most intimate with him, hearing this, hastily dissuaded the king from doing it, because the islanders had invaded many of their estates and taken their property, sharing it all out among themselves. They said: "If you let them off with impunity — those who have rebelled against your sovereignty so forcibly and for so long — and are persuaded to make peace with them without their humbly begging and pleading for it, and even concede them privileges, then everyone will laugh at your supremacy and no one will be afraid to act likewise in your kingdom." To this the king angrily replied that he could not take the Isle or any place so naturally fortified by the power of God. To which one of those present, Ivo de Taillebois by name, indignantly answered: "Well, for a long time now I've known a certain old woman who could by her art alone, if she were present, crush all their courage and defense and drive them all out of the island in terror." And moreover he declared that he was willing to send for her, if the king agreed. On hearing this, all those who were present earnestly urged this on the king, saying that they should not oppose but rather assist such a work, and enrich with the greatest rewards anyone who could by art, invention, or any way whatever, crush the enemies of the lord king. And so the king, complying with their words and arguments, ordered the hag to be brought directly; but it was to be done in secret though, not openly. Afterwards he had his army again gather to surround the Isle, guarding it closely on all sides, personally appointing sentries here and there and arranging a blockade, lest anyone should come out from the island and discover what action they were taking towards assaulting it, whereby they might contrive some opposing art or invention.

XXIV

How Hereward dressed up as a potter and went to the king's court to spy out what they meant to do; and how he cheated them, and slew some in the king's court, and returned unharmed.

These matters being put in hand by the king therefore, the entrances to the Isle were so blocked up that it was quite impossible to enter or leave it. This was an unexpected cause for despondency and alarm to them, not knowing what action was to be taken against them, or what kind of attack, inasmuch as they heard that the king had learned of some new method of making war. So they decided that they ought, somehow or other, to send a man out to reconnoitre. Finding no one quite suitable however, at length it seemed best to Hereward to go out himself to reconnoitre in disguise, although everyone objected strongly, resisting his inclination. But in the end he set off, taking with him his mare called Swallow, who was perpetually drooping and awkward in appearance but whose great speed and willing endurance I have mentioned before. As he left he changed his clothes, cut his hair and beard and donned a greasy cloak. Coming across a potter, he took his jars and, pretending to be a potter, made his way to the king's court at Brandon. Arriving there the same evening, he happened to spend the night at the house of a widow where there lodged the witch whom I mentioned earlier had been brought in to destroy those who were in the Isle. There that same night Hereward heard them discussing in French how they were going to bring about the downfall of the Isle. (They supposed him to be a peasant and unfamiliar with the language.) Then in the middle of the night Hereward saw them go out silently to a spring of water which flowed to the east near the garden of the house. So he promptly followed them, and at a distance heard them talking, questioning some unknown guardian of the spring and awaiting replies. In the end he decided to deal with them on their return, but their lengthy delay prevented this plan, although leading to even greater and more daring adventures.

Early next morning Hereward took up his pots and left. Wandering all round the king's court, he called out in the manner of a potter: "Pots, pots, good pots and jars! All first-class earthenware!" Now in the course of this he was led into the king's kitchen by some servants so that they might buy some pots. And one of the town bailiffs coming in by chance immediately exclaimed on catching sight of him that he had never seen a man so much like Hereward in his appearance, nor so much like him in his bearing — insofar as a poor man could resemble a man of noble birth, or a peasant a knight. Hearing this, some people came to look at one who so resembled Hereward; and thus he was led into the king's hall among the knights and squires so they could see him. And looking at him closely, some of them declared that a man of such moderate height could scarcely boast so much bravery and valor as popular rumor attributed to him. And others asked him if he knew or had ever seen the scoundrel Hereward. To which he replied: "Would that I had that limb of Satan here among us now; then I'd get my own back! He's more detested by me than anybody, for he stole a cow of mine, four sheep, and everything I had, except for my pots and my nag, which up to now have been the livelihood of me and my two boys!"

Now in the meantime orders were given for the king's dinner to be prepared, and Hereward returned to the kitchen. Then after dinner the servers, cooks, and kitchen-boys together plied themselves with wine and strong drink, with the result that they got drunk and made great fun of Hereward. In the end, sodden with wine, they tried to shave his head and pluck out his beard; and they blindfolded him and put his pots down on the ground all around so that he broke them. When he refused to submit to their buffoonery, one of them came up and hit him hard. But Hereward hit him back under the ear so that he fell to the ground insensible, as if he were dead. Seeing this, the man's friends all rose up and attacked Hereward with two- and three-pronged forks. So snatching a piece of wood from the fireplace, he defended himself against them all, killing one of them and wounding many. This was immediately made known throughout the palace, with the result that he was seized and taken prisoner.

Then while he was in custody, the king having gone out hunting with his retinue, one of the guards approached, carrying in one hand iron shackles with which he intended to load Hereward, and in the other an unsheathed sword. Hereward promptly seized him and attacked him with his own sword, so that he tasted death; and after him he dealt out destruction to several others. And so, setting himself free, he went down over fences and ditches into the lower courtyard of the house, where he found his horse. As he mounted, one of the king's pages caught sight of him and accosted him with foul language, warning his friends and the king's servants to give chase to him; but the pursuit of one and all was so slow, and Hereward's flight so effective that, crossing the island of Somersham and travelling throughout that evening and at night by the light of the moon, he came secretly to the Isle in the early hours of the dawn. Out of all those who had given chase, none heard any word of him, or saw any sign, except for one man who chanced to go deeper into the forest, where his horse unexpectedly succumbed to fatigue and he himself could hardly stand on his feet. Coming across him by chance, Hereward immediately asked him who he was, and he replied: "One of the servants from the king's retinue who have been pursuing a fugitive peasant who by guile today killed his guard and one of the king's pages. So if you've seen or heard anything, for God's sake, and of your kindness, tell me!" "Well," said Hereward, "since you ask for God's sake, and appeal to my kindness, let me tell you that I am myself the man you're looking for. And now, so that you'll know me better, and will the more truthfully declare to your lord the king that you've spoken with me, you can leave behind your sword and lance as a token and, if you want to keep your life, promise me that you'll tell them the way it was!" And so this aforesaid servant eventually got back and, as he had promised, told the king about Hereward. Everybody listened in amazement; and the king declared that Hereward was a generous and most remarkable knight.

XXV

How Hereward disguised himself as a fisherman, and cheated the king a second time; and how the king attacked the Isle, and about their means of defense.

Then when the war-engines were prepared as he had arranged, and in furtherance of which he had travelled there, the king began the attack, leading his entire army to Aldreth. He had also brought heaps of wood and stone and all materials for building ramparts there. And he ordered all the fishermen in the district to come with their boats to Cottenham so that they could ferry across what had been brought there, and with it construct mounds and hillocks at Aldreth from the top of which they might fight. Among these came Hereward, like a fisherman with a boat along with the rest. They diligently ferried across everything that had been brought there. Finally on the same day — the sun not going down without some damage done — Hereward finished his work and before he left set fire to it. As a result it was entirely burnt, and several men killed and swallowed up in the swamp. He had shaved his beard and head so as not to be recognized, employing various disguises to encompass the death of enemies and the destruction of foes, preferring to look bald for a while and forego his finely-styled locks, rather than spare his opponents. When it was learned that Hereward had again escaped with impunity, the king declared that it was shameful to be so frequently ridiculed by him. However, the revered king, among other things, gave instructions commanding his men that above all Hereward should be brought to him alive, and that they should keep him unharmed. And taking warning from the damage done on this occasion, they set a day-and-night guard over all their property and operations.

Thus struggling for a week they just about completed one mound and set up four wooden bastions on which to site the war-engines. But those in the Isle resisted vigorously, building outworks and ramparts to oppose them. And then on the eighth day they all advanced to attack the island with their entire force, placing the witch I mentioned earlier, in an elevated position in their midst, so that being sufficiently protected on all sides, she might have space in which to practice her art. Once mounted, she harangued the Isle and its inhabitants for a long time, denouncing saboteurs and suchlike, and casting spells for their overthrow; and at the end of her chattering and incantations she bared her arse at them. Well, when she had performed her disgusting act three times as she wished, those who had been concealed in the swamp all around to right and left among the sharp reeds and brambles of the marshland, set fire to part of it so that, driven by the wind, the smoke and flames surged up against the king's camp. Spreading for as far as two furlongs, the fire ran hither and thither among them, making a horrible sight in the swamp, and the roar of the flames and crackling of twigs in the brushwood and willows making a terrible noise. As a result, stupefied and greatly alarmed, the king's men fled, each man for himself. But they could not go far along those watery paths through the wastes of the swamp, and they could not keep to the track easily. In consequence very many of them were suddenly swallowed up, and others, overwhelmed with arrows, drowned in the same waters, for in the fire and in their flight they were unable to use their lances against the bands of those who came cautiously and secretly out from the Isle to repel them. Among them the aforesaid woman who practiced her abominable art, fell down in the greatest terror head-first from her exalted position and broke her neck.

And among the few who escaped — compared with the number of the fallen — the celebrated king himself carried right back to his men's camp an arrow stuck deep in his shield. Seeing which, his men were alarmed, thinking him wounded and bewailing the fact. To banish their hesitancy and fear, the king declared: "I've no wound to complain of, but I am pained that I didn't adopt a sounder plan from all those that were suggested to me; for which reason almost all our men have fallen, deceived by the cunning of an abominable woman and encouraged by our ignorance as to her detestable art — even to listen to whom ought to be damnable! In fact, we've deserved what's happened to us."

About this time Earl Ralph Guader, having secretly assembled a very large army, invited certain persons from among the English people to his wedding and by force and trickery compelled them to bind themselves to him by an oath. And he laid waste and subjected to himself the entire country between Norwich, Thetford, and Sudbury. Wherefore, thinking he was making a bid for the kingdom and nation, the three well-known earls and all those of high birth who were in the Isle now went off to join him, leaving Hereward and his men to guard the Isle alone.

XXVI

How and wherefore the men of Ely made an agreement with the king; upon which Hereward wanted to burn the church and town.

At length the king recognized that despite all these preparations, his efforts to take the island by war or by force were to no avail. And considering how many of his men he had just lost on this one occasion, and also what great numbers he had lost previously, he decreed that the external lands of the church and the property of the monks should be divided among his more eminent followers, who only had to guard the island from outside. In consequence therefore, several people appropriated the church lands in the vicinity, claiming them for themselves. Hearing this, the monks of the church in question adopted a more prudent plan in their activities; and upon the return of the abbot, who together with the aforesaid earls had fled in disguise to Bottisham with the ornaments and treasures of the church, asked the king for peace-terms, on condition that he would freely and honorably restore to them all the lands of the church. This was done one day in secret though, so that Hereward should not know of it They were received graciously by the king; and they arranged for the king to come to the Isle rapidly and secretly at a certain time when Hereward was out foraging with his men, in order that it might be managed without bloodshed and serious slaughter. However, one of the monks, Eadwine son of Ordgar, went to tell him that they had already been received by the king and had struck a bargain with him. He met Hereward already en route, marching with his men from the river bank, carrying brands to set fire to the church and town as a result of what they had heard. The monk with many prayers and entreaties stood out against him, warning him rather to look to his safety by flight, if he was unwilling to join them in securing peace, adding that the king with all his army was within a furlong at Witchford. Eventually he yielded to his words and arguments because he had been a friend to him and a good comrade in war and of practical help in many of his needs. Thus he was persuaded. He decided upon immediate action and, with his boats which he had well defended with arms to guard the waters surrounding the Isle, withdrew to a certain mere called Wide near Upwell, a large expanse of water with ample channels and having an easy way out. And because he had dispatched some of his men to inflict damage at Soham and lay waste the land with fire there, he intended to wait there until the scouts that he secretly sent should lead them to him quickly to prevent their being captured. When at length they were found in a little island called Stuntney, they thought Hereward's messengers were chasing them, and hid themselves among the reeds some distance away in the swamp. In fact, two of them lurking together, a certain Starcwulf and Broga, reckoned it might give them a better chance of safety if they had a tonsure like monks. And so they gave each other a tonsure as best they could with their swords. But in the end a shouted exchange brought mutual recognition, and assembled together they made their way back to their leader.

XXVII

How Hereward was reduced to such straits that he slew with his own hands his excellent horse; and how next he overcame the army of five provinces.

After some respite from serious pursuit in the aforesaid mere, Hereward was more severely besieged by those in the region and by the king's men, and so hard-pressed that in despair he slew with his own hands his splendid horse, so that no lesser man should boast that he had got Hereward's horse. But at length he escaped from this danger with his men, passed over Brunneswold and went to live in the great forests of Northampton-shire, laying waste the land with fire and sword. Eventually therefore at the king's command an army was assembled from the counties of Northampton, Cambridge, Lincoln, Holland, Leicester, Huntingdon and Warwick, which all came together on a pre-arranged day and with a host of soldiers tried to capture Hereward and his men, searching for him everywhere in the forests near Peterborough where he was staying at the time. And there, when surrounded by enemies and unable to avoid their hands, he moved about from place to place in the more remote parts of the forests in the district, waiting for his men and friends whom he had summoned to help him. Meanwhile he had the shoes on his horses' feet put on back-to-front, so that it could not be discovered from their tracks where they were or where they were going. He gave instructions that the friends and fellow-soldiers for whom he had just sent were to do the same. These arrived one by one as best they could. Now that Hereward knew that there was no place to turn to, because warfare closed in on him on all sides, it seemed best to him to make an attack on his pursuers with a small number from the rear, front or flank, before they were prepared for battle, since he now had a hundred picked soldiers with him, and among them some of the toughest men, besides a few archers and slingmen. For in those days Hereward happened to have many men, both from that region and further afield, who came to him for military training and who, in order to be instructed in this, left their lords and friends and joined Hereward, having heard of the fame of his men. Several even came from the king's court to find out whether what they had heard of him could possibly be true. Hereward received these with caution, however, and with an oath of fidelity. For there was a very great number of knights and foot-soldiers from the regions there, and Turold, abbot of Peterborough, and Ivo de Taillebois were leading the king's army to deal death to them all. Then Hereward and his men, not frightened by their numbers although they were seriously beset on all sides, made preparations. They concealed all their archers and slingmen positioned in the trees, standing unseen among the branches to discharge their missiles from above, so that when fighting they might be shielded from below and defended in this way lest they were unable to endure the force of a charge in any way. And thus they advanced from beneath the woodland trees under cover of their archers, Hereward always leading the way in everything. Immediately following him came

Regenweald, steward of Ramsey, who always acted as standard-bearer to his army. And other celebrated soldiers shared positions given them to right and left, the names and valor of which most distinguished men in so famous a battle it would be proper to record, in memory of what the few achieved against so many. And the most famous of them, and rightly held foremost both for warfare and courageous spirit, one Winter by name, was on the left flank. These had advanced on horseback, not without due consideration, to take the brunt of the attack. And becoming separated from the rest in the foray, these daring men charged the enemy, broke through their front line and killed many. And having inflicted some damage thus, they retired to the forest for protection, lest they should be unable to withstand the host of the enemy if they attacked in force. Finding their feet however, they retraced their steps again — and again and again, all day long, advancing and retreating, attacking great numbers, their friends continually covering them with missiles hurled from above and ensuring their safety in retreat. As they strove in this way into the afternoon, the horses of their adversaries as well as the heavily-clad soldiers were greatly irritated, pursuing them in their flight, and waiting in armor all day long for them to come out again. Eventually they left off besieging the camp. And then Hereward with all his men immediately came on them from the rear in a single rush, engaging in a significant encounter, capturing and taking prisoner several men including five of some importance. Among these the aforesaid abbot of Peterborough was captured, as well as others of great distinction. Then, learning of this, the enemy ceased fighting, although they were at close quarters, lest they should ill-treat or kill those whom they had taken. I have recounted the remarkable course of their battle up to this point. This last engagement proved a great blow and no little destruction to the enemy, who were completely worn down with fatigue; and being cut off from their camp, they now began to retreat.

XXVIII

How Hereward took vengeance upon the abbot of Burgh.

Afterwards the aforesaid abbot of Peterborough was released from captivity by Hereward for a ransom of thirty thousand pounds. And one of Hereward's kinsmen called Siward the Blond set free the abbot's nephew and others whom they had captured, all of whom he had treated with honorable hospitality out of respect for the abbot. But remembering neither their kindness nor their agreement, they repaid Hereward by once more making war on him and his men. To this purpose, the aforesaid abbot distributed many of the estates of his church to knights on condition that they gave military assistance to subdue Hereward, on account of the trouble he had given the abbot. He arranged that they should attack Hereward as a duty in return for their lands. However, when Hereward heard reports of this, and that a punishment hung over him in return for his kindness, he did not long delay, but the same night went with his men to Peterborough to avenge themselves. And laying waste the whole town with fire, they plundered all the treasures of the church and chased the abbot, although he and his men managed to escape by hiding themselves.

XXIX

Of a vision and a marvelous occurrence seen by Hereward.

In his sleep the following night, Hereward saw standing before him a man of indescribable appearance, in old age, fearsome of countenance, and more remarkable in all his clothing than anything he had ever seen or imagined in his mind, now menacing him with a great key which he brandished in his hand, and with a fearful injunction that if he wished to ensure his safety and avoid a miserable death the next day, he should restore in their entirety all those possessions of his church which Hereward had taken the previous night. Indeed, on waking he was seized with holy dread, and that very hour carried back everything he had taken away, and then moved on with all his men. On their journey they unexpectedly went astray, losing the right path. A marvelous thing happened to them while they were astray thus — a miracle, if such things can reasonably be said to happen to flesh and blood. For while in the stormy night and gloom they were wandering hither and thither through the forests, not knowing where they were going, a huge wolf came in front of them, fawning on them like a tame dog and walking along in front of them down the path. In the obscuring gloom they mistook it for a white dog because of its grey coat, and urged one another to follow the dog closely, declaring that it must have come from some village. This they did. And in the midst of the night, while they discovered that they had succeeded in getting out of the by-way and recognizing the road, suddenly there appeared burning lights clinging to the soldiers' lances — not very bright, but like those popularly called will-o-the-wisps. No one could get rid of them, or extinguish them, or throw them away. Whereupon, greatly marvelling amongst themselves, although they were stupefied they could see their way, and went on led by the wolf. And then with dawning day they all eventually found to their astonishment that their guide had been a wolf. And while they were at a loss to know what had happened to them, the wolf disappeared, the lights vanished, and they had got to where they wanted, beyond Stamford. And realizing that their journey had been successful, they gave thanks to God, marvelling at what had happened to them.

XXX

How Hereward pursued an enemy and granted him mercy.

Hereward had not been there more than three days when he heard that an enemy of his would be in the aforesaid town, a man who had often tried to ruin him and hand him over to those enemies who had lately broken faith with him. Whereupon to see if what he had heard was true, he set out with just two men. And when the fellow realized that Hereward was on his way, he immediately resorted to flight. Hereward hastily followed his track from house to house, from garden to garden, with a naked sword and a small shield in his hand, right into the great hall where many men from the man's own district were assembled at a club dinner. But having nowhere to turn, Hereward being so close on his heels, he left, fleeing into the interior of the house where, putting his head through the hole in a lavatory seat, he begged for mercy. And moved by a generous spirit, for he was always most gracious in all his ways, Hereward did not touch him there, nor inflict any injury in word or deed, but returned the way he had come, passing rapidly through the middle of the house. And being astonished, none of those feasting there ventured to grumble or upbraid him about what had happened, since they had nothing in their hands but just drinking-horns and wine-cups.

XXXI

How Hereward's wife assumed the habit of a nun at Crowland.

In the interval, however, Turfrida, the aforesaid wife of Hereward, had already begun to turn away from him because at the time he was receiving frequent envoys from a woman asking him to marry her. She was the widow of Earl Dolfin and particularly powerful on account of her wealth. She should obtain a license from the king which, as she had heard from the king's mouth, she could have for the asking if Hereward were peaceable and willing to pledge faith with him. For this reason, therefore, charmed with the beauty of the woman, Hereward gave his consent, for there was nobody more lovely nor more beautiful in the realm, and scarcely anybody more eminent in their wealth. Consequently, he sent messengers to the king and asked for the aforesaid woman, saying that he was willing to be reconciled with the king's majesty. He received Hereward's messengers graciously and, accepting what he proposed, appointed a day to meet him, adding that he had for a long time been wishing to receive him into his favor. In consequence Hereward's own wife, about whom I spoke a little earlier, went to Crowland and chose the better life, taking the holy veil. As a result of this many unfortunate things happened to him later on, because she had been very wise and good with advice in an emergency. For subsequently, as he himself often admitted, much happened to him which would not have done in his rise to success.

XXXII

How Hereward overcame a certain very eminent knight in single combat.

Once when Hereward was off on a journey across Brunneswold, he met with a certain Saxon soldier, a man of great courage and tall stature called Letold, who was well-known and highly praised in many regions for his skill and valor in war. Highly courteous as usual, Hereward promptly first wished him well, and then enquired his name, rank and family. Not taking his words and questions in good part, Letold answered haughtily, calling him a simpleton and peasant. So finally moved to anger, they came to blows. And not only they but their soldiers grappled at the same time — five on the side of the aforesaid knight and three on Hereward's side, namely: Gærwig, Wennoth, and Mæthelgar. As they fought, Gærwig soon laid low one soldier and turned to attack one of his comrades. Soon afterwards the other two also overcame their adversaries. Meanwhile, however, the aforesaid famous knight did not cease fighting with Hereward although his men were overcome. Nevertheless, Hereward would not allow any of his men to assist him, saying then as always when anyone was fighting with one of his men or with himself, that it was shameful for two to fight against one, and that a man ought to fight alone or else surrender. While these two continued to fight, the result of the combat between them being in doubt for some time, Hereward's sword unexpectedly broke off at the hilt, whereupon hesitating for a moment he stumbled over a helmet, the other standing thunderstruck. Immediately one of his soldiers, Gærwig, speaking in a friendly manner, asked him if he had forgotten what he had close by his side for such an emergency, adding that he wished Hereward would let him take over his place in the fight. Greatly encouraged by this, Hereward drew from its sheath a second sword which he had forgotten, and attacked his opponent more vigorously. And at the first blow, while feigning an attack on the head, he struck the man in the middle of his thigh. Still the soldier defended himself for some time on his knees, declaring that for as long as there was life in him he would never be willing to surrender or look beaten. Admiring which, Hereward praised his bravery and courage and stopped attacking him, leaving him and going on his way. And talking further about him to his men, he said: "I've never found such a man, nor did I ever meet with his equal in courage! Nor have I ever been in such danger when fighting anybody, nor had so much difficulty in conquering anyone."

XXXIII

How Hereward went to the king's court with his soldiers.

He was making his way to the king's court with these three men, but when at length he approached, he reflected that it would not be a distinguished way to meet the king, and immediately retraced his steps. And on his return he brought with him forty other most distinguished soldiers, all very big and tall in stature and proficient in warfare, and remarkable for their mere appearance and equipment in arms, if nothing else. He and his men were received by the king with great kindness and honor. However, the king would not allow Hereward's band to stay along with his courtiers, but gave instructions for them to be entertained at the next town, lest by chance any disturbance should break out between them and his own men. Nevertheless he took Hereward with just three soldiers into the palace, so as to deal the next day with his proposal. On the following day, however, the revered king himself went to see Hereward's soldiers and had them stand and march before him, both armed and unarmed. And he was greatly delighted with them and praised them, complimenting their handsome appearance and stature, and added that they ought all to be really very distinguished in warfare. After this, however, Hereward allowed them all to go home, except for two soldiers in addition to those already with him. And after having paid homage to the king, Hereward waited to receive his father's estate undiminished.

XXXIV

How he fought with a soldier of the king's court, and overcame him.

Now some of the king's soldiers at court, indignant at this, felt aggrieved that strangers and enemies should suddenly have come into favor with the king's majesty like this, and attempted to do him some harm. In fact they had a discussion in secret with a certain very eminent soldier of their company called Ogga, and arranged that he should challenge Hereward to single combat, knowing that he could not keep his hands off anyone if impudently or haughtily provoked to a fight or test of courage. They were afraid to raise a hand against him in the presence of the king, but reckoned to get some remedy for their jealousy even if he refused, for they were optimistic that he would be beaten by such a soldier, since he was taller than Hereward and seemed very much stronger just from the look in his eyes. And so they incited this man against Hereward, as though he had been insulted. And he was to do it secretly, lest it should become known to the king before the combat took place. After being repeatedly abused, Hereward eventually consented. So they directly went some distance away to a woodland, together with just three companions on either side under agreement on oath that nobody should assist either of them but just stand by in case they wished for a truce or should prefer to fight it out. Thus they grappled and fought for a long time. Meanwhile, Hereward repeatedly urged him to desist from the attempt, pointing out that it was a very stupid thing to do to go on fighting the whole day long for nothing. The soldier paid no attention to his words, but instead became more confident of himself, assuming that Hereward kept harping on this out of fear or feebleness of body, and resolving rather to see him defeated. And so he attacked him increasingly; at which Hereward over and over again gave way, so that the vain hope constantly deceived him. But finally unwilling to put up with this, Hereward made a stand. And as it was his custom in tournament and battle always to fight to a finish like a man, he stood bravely against him and did not stop until he had conquered him, his own right arm being seriously wounded.

XXXV

How Hereward was accused by Robert de Horepol and put into prison.

When therefore these things came to the notice of certain of his enemies, jealous of his success, they came to court and made many false reports about him to the king, and deceitfully urged him not to have near him such men any longer, traitors and enemies of his realm; just so they ought neither to be received at his court nor afforded a truce, but ought rather to be handed over to punishment or else be kept in perpetual imprisonment. The revered king did not take much notice of these words; nevertheless, in order to satisfy them, he gave orders for him to be taken into custody within the hour, making him over to a certain respected man, Robert de Horepol, at Bedford, where he remained for nearly a whole year, merely bound with fetters. But the Earl de Warenne and Robert Malet and Ivo de Taillebois remained hostile to him, dissuading the king from setting him free from custody, declaring that it was because of him that the country was not pacified. When they heard about this, Hereward's men dispersed. Nevertheless, they often sent in disguise to their lord a certain clerk of his called Leofric the Deacon, who was always astute in all his doings, and able to feign foolishness in place of learning — and cleverly so. On one occasion there went with him Utlah the cook, a man who was cautious at all points yet very witty at the expense of the foreigners. In the presence of these men one day, Hereward's aforementioned warder, pitying him together with the rest, exclaimed: "Alas, alas! Soon now, through the machinations of Ivo de Taillebois, this man once renowned for hosts of soldiers and the leader and lord of so many very eminent men, is to be taken from here and delivered into the hands of a detestable man and sent to the castle of Rockingham. Would that those whom he formerly enriched with gifts and raised with honors, or who were on the Isle, would follow the tracks of their master and intercept us en route, so as to set their lord and master free!" Hearing this, and after receiving signs from their lord, Hereward's two men described what they had heard to his soldiers and all his men. So having secretly reconnoitered a forest through which the convoy would have to pass, they picked out a place and all assembled there on the day it was due to arrive. Upon their arrival, Hereward's men immediately rushed on them by surprise, overthrowing many of them before they could even take up their light arms. When they had recovered their arms, however, they resisted bravely, for there were a lot of them — in fact all of the soldiers from the castles round about. In the end it nearly proved the death of all of these; for when they could escape they wouldn't, and yet in the end they couldn't be seized. And then from the midst of several of them who still survived, Hereward shouted out that they should be careful not to injure the troops of his respected warder, and that Robert himself with his men should be allowed to go unharmed. Being set free from ten chains, Hereward moved here and there among those of his men who were still fighting, declaring that Robert had saved his life, so they immediately ceased from the pursuit. On the march Robert's men had come last, forming a rearguard, while Hereward was led in chains in the midst of those in front. At last his aforesaid warder wished to leave together with those of his comrades who survived, and Hereward returned him repeated thanks, for he had kept him in custody with courtesy and carefully treated him with honor. And Hereward asked Robert to make representations on his behalf to the lord king.

XXXVI

How Robert of Horepol made a good report of Hereward to the king.

After this the aforesaid Robert de Horepol immediately went to the court of the king, informing him of everything that had taken place, and how Hereward's men had set him free. Finally, he added the request he had carried: that Hereward might avail himself of the king's clemency, remembering how he had come to his court under his protection and safe-conduct, and has thus been unjustly put in prison and under custody. However, if the king would even now carry out what he had then promised him, Hereward would in every way serve his most dear lord, knowing that this injury had not been perpetrated by him but through the persuasion and machinations of enemies. After reflecting on these words a little, the revered king replied that Hereward had not been justly treated. And when Robert realized that the king had taken his words well, he promptly recounted to the king many commendable things about Hereward and his men, adding that such a warrior in whom there might be found great sincerity and fidelity, ought not to be lightly banished from him and from his realm for so trivial a reason. And he declared that if there was any new disturbance in the country, Hereward would certainly prefer to rely on his former resources unless he could find favor rather than servitude in the king's eyes, and should in the king's kindness receive back his father's estates. At this the king instantly said that he ought by rights to have it, giving a document addressed to Hereward and the men of the district stating that he was to receive his father's estate and enjoy quiet possession of it; but if he wished to retain the king's friendship hereafter, he must henceforth be willing to pursue peace rather than folly.

And so Hereward, the famous knight, tried and known in many places, was received into favor by the king. And with his father's land and possessions he lived on for many years faithfully serving King William and devotedly reconciled to his compatriots and friends. And thus in the end rested in peace, upon whose soul may God have mercy.

From *Eustache the Monk*

Introduction

Written in Old French, with traces of the Picard dialect, *Eustache the Monk* survives in a unique text, now Bibliothèque Nationale fonds française 1553 (fols. 325v–338v), dated 1284. The anonymous poet, who composed the 2307 verses in rhymed couplets, wrote the work between 1223 and 1284 (Conlon, pp. 10–11).

Both *Eustache the Monk* and *Fouke le Fitz Waryn*, the final selections in this section, are set in the historical time of King Richard I, King John, and King Philip Augustus of France. Because an awareness of the historical background is vital to an understanding of both works, we have included the following brief summary of the important events.

1199   Richard I dies leaving no male heir. Contenders for the succession are Arthur, son of Richard's eldest brother Geoffrey, and Prince John. John's claim is supported by Hubert Walter, Archbishop of Canterbury, the English barons, and his mother, the powerful Eleanor of Aquitaine. Arthur's claim is supported by King Philip Augustus of France, who sees an opportunity to expand the Capetian empire into Angevin territory in France.

When John is crowned in Westminster on 27 May 1199, he faces three major conflicts during his seventeen-year reign: war with France, excommunication by the Pope, and rebellion of the English barons.

1200   John divorces his childless first wife, Isabel of Gloucester, and marries Isabel, daughter of the Count of Angouleme, then twelve years old and already betrothed to Hugh Lusignan, a baron of Aquitaine. When Lusignan lodges a complaint with Philip Augustus, the king issues a formal summons ordering John to appear before his court. When John refuses to appear, Philip seizes the opportunity to declare John's fiefs — Normandy, Anjou, Maine, and Touraine — forfeit. To add insult to injury, Philip gives Arthur all of the Angevin fiefs except Normandy and betroths him to his daughter Mary.

1204   John withdraws from France after the disappearance and murder of his nephew Arthur in 1203.

1207   John invades and captures Poitou. A truce is made.

1208   Pope Innocent III declares an interdict against John for disobeying his order to install Stephen of Langton as Archbishop of Canterbury and for imposing a new tax on the clergy. John responded by confiscating the property of the clergy who obeyed the interdict.

1212   King John forms an alliance with the Count of Boulogne, Otto IV of Germany, and Ferdinand of Portugal with the aim of fighting Philip Augustus, but the plan is abandoned due to lack of baronial support and rebellion in Wales.

1213   Pope Innocent III authorizes Philip to invade England, and Philip assembles a large army and fleet of 1500 ships. John responds by calling out the feudal levies and all ships capable of carrying six horses. The invasion is averted when John agreed to the Pope's conditions — Stephen Langton is accepted as the Archbishop of Canterbury and all the exiled clergy are reinstated. In addition, John cedes overlordship of England to the Pope in order to win his protection from his disaffected barons. King Philip, disgusted at the outcome, burns his own fleet.

1214   King John invades France with a large army, recaptures Poitou and Angouleme, defeats the Lusignans, and occupies Angers, capital of Anjou. The victories are short-lived as John's coalition of forces — Otto IV, the Counts of Flanders, Boulogne, Holland, Brabant, and Limburg, and the Duke of Lorraine — are soundly defeated at the battle of Bouvines. John returns to England with ruined schemes to face his unpopularity among the northern barons.

1215   Although John accepts the articles of Magna Carta on June 15, he has no intention of honoring them. Instead, he prepares for war against the barons.

1216   The barons successfully negotiate with Louis of France, Philip's son, promising him the English throne if he will help depose John. Louis lands in England and advances to London, while John, ill from dysentery, retreats to the west. When John dies, the barons choose young Henry III, and Louis returns to France.

Like *Hereward the Wake* and *Fouke le Fitz Waryn*, *Eustache the Monk* is based on the life of an actual person, Eustache Busket, who lived from c. 1170 to 1217. But the poet transformed Busket's life into the stuff of legend and folklore. While it may be impossible to separate fact from fancy, the following summary, drawn from Conlon's French introduction, pp. 14–19, represents a brief biography of Eustache.

c. 1170   Born at Courset in the district of Boulogne, he entered the Abbey of Saint Samer as a monk.

1190   After his father, Baudoin Busket, peer of the Boulonnais province, was ambushed and killed, Eustache left religious orders to demand justice from the Count of Boulogne, Renaud of Dammartin. To settle the dispute, a judicial duel was arranged and Eustache's champion was killed.

1200   Eustache is appointed seneschal of the Count of Boulogne during his expedition with King Philip Augustus to reclaim territories held by King John of England. Upon his return in 1203, Eustache was accused of mismanaging the Count's financial affairs. Suspecting treachery, Eustache fled into the forest surrounding Boulogne, and the Count retaliated by confiscating his properties.

1205   King John orders the port bailiffs to help a William Little recover his ship captured by Eustache, who has been roving the English Channel as a pirate. As a mercenary mariner, he enters the service of King John, who gave him ships to wage war against King Philip.

1209   Still in the service of King John, Eustache witnesses the signing of a charter in Boulogne as an English ambassador to the Count of Boulogne. When the Count learns of his visit, he outlaws him.

1212   Now in London, Eustache witnesses a charter of allegiance between Count Renaud and King John. Again suspecting foul play, Eustache switches sides and joins forces with King Philip.

1213   In support of the northern English barons attempting to depose King John, King Philip prepares for the invasion of England on May 10, but when the Pope lifts the excommunication of John, he hesitates, and his ships are attacked and destroyed by John's navy at Damne. Eustache loses the *nef de Boulogne*, a huge ship in the shape of a castle.

1214   Eustache supplies arms to the northern barons rebelling against King John.

1215   Eustache and his navy control the English Channel. King Philip warns a papal legate not to cross the Channel.

1216   In May, 800 ships of Louis, Philip's son, leave for England in order to help the barons depose John. When Louis disembarks from Eustache's ship on the Isle of Thanet, he learns of the death of King John and the barons' decision to choose young Henry III as king. On August 24, Eustache's ship is surrounded by four English ships, and he is captured and beheaded on the spot. Louis eventually withdraws from England and a peace treaty is signed on September 11.

To this substratum of bare historical fact, the poet has added a rich layer of fantastic exploits and adventures, derived from the popular romances, *chanson de geste*, and fabliaux of the day. Among these works, the influence of the *Romance of Reynard the Fox* or *Roman de Renart* is, as we will see, particularly strong. After completing his apprenticeship as a sorcerer in Toledo, Spain, Eustache sets out for the monastery of Saint Samer with his companions. While in Monferrant he gets into a fight in a tavern and casts a magic spell, causing the tavern-keeper and her customers to strip off their clothing, straddle the wine casts, and engage in a bawdy feast. Next, Eustache casts a spell on a cart-driver, making the cart and horse go backwards rather than forwards. Once he arrives at the monastery, he creates mayhem by casting more spells: the monks fast when they should eat; they go barefoot when they should wear shoes; and they swear when they should remain silent. He then turns a side of bacon into an ugly old woman, terrifying the cook. Finally, he gambles away in a tavern the crucifixes, statues, and books of the monastery.

Upon learning of his father's death, Eustache leaves the monastery to demand justice from the Count. When his champion is killed in the judicial duel, Eustache burns the Count's windmills and is outlawed. Fleeing into the forest of Hardelot, he begins a career as a trickster outlaw. In a series of adventures designed to revenge himself on the Count, Eustache uses various disguises in order to harass, embarrass, and rob the Count: a monk, a shepherd, a pilgrim, a coal-man, a potter, a prostitute, a *villein*, a leper, a fish-merchant, and a baker. In this second set of episodes, Eustache no longer resorts to magic spells but to trickery and deception instead. These "slapstick" adventures owe much to the spirit if not the substance of the popular Reynard the Fox stories. To avoid execution by hanging in Branch I, for instance, Reynard promises to go on a pilgrimage across the sea, and he dons the pilgrim's scrip and staff (Owen, p. 25). In Branch Ib, after Reynard is outlawed by King Noble, he prays to God to provide him "with such a disguise that no beast who sees me may be able to tell who I am." His prayer is answered when he falls into a tub of yellow dye at a dyer's house: "it's made me a shining yellow," he says, and "I'll never again be recognized wherever I've been seen before" (Owen, pp. 38–39). Other impersonations include a fiddler (p. 41), a monk (pp. 128–29), and a physician (p. 199). Another compelling link is found in Branch XI, *Renart Empereur*, which was composed between 1196 and 1200 — the precise historical time depicted in *Eustache the Monk*. In this story Reynard plays the role of a "baron, féodal, grand seigneur, hardi, ambitieux, brutal et sans scruples, qui conspire à usurper la place de son monarque absent" (Flinn, p. 99). Ernest Martin, cited in Flinn, opines that the poem was inspired by the conduct of Prince John during the absence of King Richard and King Philip Augustus on the Third Crusade. The Reynard role is thus played by Prince John. It seems reasonable to conclude that the *Eustache* poet, recognizing the political allegory in Branch XI, adapted it as well as the trickster motifs for use in his poem.

Relation to Robin Hood Legends

In assessing the relationships between *Eustache the Monk* and the Robin Hood legend, we need to consider their similarities and differences, their dates, and their opportunities for contact. Beyond the obvious shared features — both are outlaws living in the forest, venturing out to punish and humiliate the Count of Boulogne and the Sheriff of Nottingham — there are also a number of episodes too similar to be accounted for by coincidence or common tradition. In the first pair of scenes, the count and the sheriff come face to face with the outlaw leader in the forest. In lines 776–853, Eustache, disguised as a pilgrim, tricks the count into the woods where he captures him. Eustache offers to make peace with his adversary, but the count refuses and is released unharmed. In the *Gest*, lines 722–817, Little John, disguised as Reynolde Grenelef, meets the sheriff in the forest and lures him into Robin's camp by promising him a "ryght fayre harte," who of course turns out to be Robin "the mayster-herte." Once he is fed, the sheriff asks to be released, and after swearing an oath that he will not harm Robin or his men, he is let go. In the next pair of episodes, the waylaid victims who tell the truth are allowed to keep their money. In lines 930–54, Eustache meets a merchant from Boulogne and asks him how much money he has. The merchant answers truthfully that he has forty pounds and fifteen sous. Upon counting the money and discovering that he is telling the truth, Eustache returns the full amount and lets the merchant go unharmed. In the *Gest*, lines 145 ff., after the impoverished knight dines with Robin in the forest, he is asked to pay for the meal, and when the knight truthfully replies that he has only ten shillings, he is rewarded many times over. However, in another pair of scenes, when the victims — both ecclesiastics — lie about the money they are carrying, they are severely dealt with. For example, in lines 1746–77, Eustache confronts the Abbot of Jumièges on the road and asks how much money he has; the abbot replies untruthfully that he has only four silver marks. When Eustache discovers thirty marks on his person, he keeps twenty-six marks and returns four. As we have already seen, Eustache and Robin Hood are masters of trickery and disguise. In order to fool the count, Eustache, in lines 996–1141, disguises himself first as a coal-man and then a potter. When the count meets the potter, he is crying "Pots for sale!" and tricks the count into believing that the coal-man, with whom he has switched identities, is really Eustache the Monk. Similarly, in *Robin Hood and the Potter*, Robin assumes the identity of the potter when he goes into Nottingham to spy on the sheriff.

Although J. C. Holt admits that "some of the analogous material must have been transmitted, by confusion of memory or literary borrowing, from one tale to the other," he concludes that "the ballads are not bred in simple fashion from the romances" (Holt, 1989, pp. 64–66). Maurice Keen, after detailing the parallel passages described above, asserts that the romances "cannot be said to be much of an anticipation of the ballads of Robin Hood, except as regards isolated incidents" (Keen, 1987, p. 59). In stressing the differences between *Eustache the Monk* and the Robin Hood ballads, Holt and Keen seem to deny the ability of the English poets to adapt creatively characters and plot situations from their sources. It should be recalled too that the Anglo-Norman community in England was bilingual, and, consequently, stories could be easily translated from one language to another. Finally, when Holt (p. 65) claims that the restoration of a lost inheritance plays a fundamental role in *Hereward the Wake, Fouke le Fitz Waryn*, and *Eustache the Monk*, he neglects to mention that this too is a central theme in *Gamelyn*, an early outlaw tale in Middle English, and in later Tudor dramas, such as Munday's *The Downfall of Robert, Earle of Huntington*.

The following excerpts from *Eustache the Monk* were translated from Denis Conlon's French edition, *Li Romans de Witasse le Moine*, by Thomas E. Kelly especially for this volume.

Other Outlaw Tales in Prose Translation

Translator's Note

As for the title character of the romance, it should be noted that the Monk's name has been normalized in English to the spelling "Eustache." The manuscript used for the translation has a number of variant spellings in Old French: *Witasse/Wistace/-Wistasces*, and *Uistasces/Uistasses*.

The original text is composed in octosyllabic rhymed couplets, the same verse form used by Chrétien de Troyes in his romances. The form lends itself to a fast-paced narrative style which is difficult to render into modern English prose. Also lost in translation is the sharp wit of a storyteller who never lets up on his word play, especially puns and double-entendre. The word *conte,* for example, lends itself to frequent semantic shifts from the *tale* itself to the *Count* of Boulogne, to the settling of Eustache's ac*counts* with the Count. In the passage where Eustache disguises himself as a leper (lines 1366-1422), the author delights in frequent puns on the various meanings of *tour/retour*: "retraced tracks," "turn," "turn about," "turn"= trick/disguise — which are impossible to convey in an English prose translation. The present translation has the modest objective of rendering as accurately as possible only the content of the narrative details, without attempting to focus the reader's attention on stylistic or linguistic nuances: *traduttore = traditorre*!

Select Bibliography

Editions and Translations

Burgess, Glyn S., trans. *Two Medieval Outlaws: Eustace the Monk and Fouke Fitz Waryn*. Cambridge: D. S. Brewer, 1997. Pp. 3–87.

Conlon, Denis Joseph, ed. *Li Romans de Witasse Le Moine: Roman de treizième siècle*. Édité d'après le manuscrit, Fonds Français 1553, de la Bibliothèque Nationale, Paris. University of North Carolina Studies in Romance Languages and Literatures, Number 126. Chapel Hill: The University of North Carolina Press, 1972.

Dufournet, Jean, ed. *Le Roman de Renard*. Paris: Garnier-Flammarion, 1970.

Kelly, Thomas E., trans. *Eustache the Monk*. In *Medieval Outlaws: Ten Tales in Modern English*. Ed. Thomas H. Ohlgren. Stroud: Sutton Publishing, 1998. Pp. 61–98, 299–302.

Eustache the Monk

Owen, D. D., trans. *The Romance of Reynard the Fox*. Oxford: Oxford University Press, 1994.

Commentary and Criticism

Flinn, John. *Le Roman de Renart dans la littérature Française et dans les littératures étrangères au Moyen Age*. Toronto: University of Toronto Press, 1963.

Holt, J. C. *Robin Hood: Revised and Enlarged Edition*. London: Thames and Hudson, 1989.

Keen, Maurice. *The Outlaws of Medieval Legend*. Revised paperback edition. London: Routledge & Kegan Paul, 1987.

From *Eustache the Monk*

1. How Eustace becomes an outlaw

Summary: Hainfrois de Hersinguehans plots with the Count and sets him against his Seneschal (Eustache). When he is summoned to give an account of his bailliage Eustache takes flight. When he learns that the Count has confiscated all his possessions the Seneschal sets fire to two mills in Boulogne. In spite of all the Count's efforts to capture him, Eustache succeeds in escaping.

Translation (lines 373–429):

The Monk was in the service of the Count of Boulogne and rendered to him an accounting in all matters. He was Seneschal of the Boulonnais, peer and bailiff — that was his duty and rank. Hainfrois [of Hersinguehans] spoke ill of him to the Count and plotted against him. As a result, the Count quickly lost confidence in his Seneschal. The Count sent for Eustache immediately and asked him for an accounting of his stewardship as bailiff. Without delay Eustache said: "I stand ready to give an accounting, because you have summoned me here in the presence of your lords and barons. For I too am one of the peers of the Boulonnais." And the Count replied: "You are hereby summoned to Hardelot, where you will give a formal accounting of your service. For there you will be unable to deceive me." Eustache answered: "That is treason! You merely want an excuse to have me put me into prison."

The Monk took flight immediately and with great difficulty escaped from the Count. Many times since then he had cause to lament his having to flee thus. The Count seized all of Eustache's possessions and burned his fields. Eustache the Monk swore that the Count would live to regret burning his fields; it would cost him 990 gold marks. One day Eustache came upon two mills which the Count had built just outside the city of Boulogne and which were unguarded. In one of the mills, Eustache found a miller and threatened to cut off his head unless he accepted to go to the city where they were celebrating Simon of Boulogne's wedding feast.

The miller was instructed thus: "When you get there you shall say that Eustache the Monk has come to enlighten them, for they lack enough light to see what they are eating. I will set fire to the Count's two mills which will be like two candles to light up the festivities." The miller sets off and, as instructed, gives the message to the Count.

Eustache the Monk

Without delay the Count leaps up from the table where he was sitting, and has great difficulty shouting instructions: "Eustache the Monk . . . , everyone . . . , after him!" The mayor and the provost come forth and immediately have the bell sounded to signal Eustache's banishment as an outlaw. When Eustache hears the bell ring he begins his flight. The Count's men begin the chase but can't catch him. On the wedding feast of Simon of Boulogne Eustache set fire to the two mills you heard about earlier. And that's the honest truth!

2. How Eustache is betrayed by one of his men.

Summary: The Count pursues Eustache throughout the forest of Hardelot. One of Eustache's watchmen offers to deliver his master into the Count's hands. Unfortunately for him, a second watchman witnesses the treason and reports it to Eustache. When the traitor arrives Eustache kills him on the spot. Shortly thereafter the Count arrives, again too late to capture Eustache, but two of his sergeants are seized. In a fit of anger the Count puts out the two men's eyes.

Translation (lines 660–741):

The Count continued his relentless pursuit of Eustache. He followed him into the forest of Hardelot, pursing in all directions. Eustache had two watchmen posted in the forest. Day and night the two men were on watch, never taking any rest. The two young men had been well taken care of by the Monk, who had raised them since childhood. One day, as the Count continued his hunt for Eustache, one of the two young men came before him. "Sire," said he, "how much will you give me if I deliver my lord to you? For I am Eustache the Monk's man." "In truth," said the Count of Boulogne, "if you deliver him to me you will do well, and I will make you a young gentleman at my court." "Sire, at this moment he is sitting at table eating his meal. If you follow me I will show you where you can capture him." "Go," said the Count, "I will follow you at a safe distance, but be careful he does not suspect anything. I fear lest he deceive you." The second watchman overheard the first and immediately sensed treason. His comrade had betrayed his lord, biting the very hand that had fed him. In due haste he came to Eustache and told him that the other had sold out to the Count. Eustache said: "You may take your leave, but as soon as my other watchman arrives to betray and deceive me I will give him the garrote, for he has served me ill." The young watchman left Eustache just as his former companion arrived to hear Eustache say: "It would do you well to cut this willow branch for me." "Willingly, Sire," said the boy as he cut the sapling. "Twist it well and make a cord out of it." The young man very fearfully twisted the strip of willow, after

677

which Eustache put it around his neck and pulled it tight. "God have mercy," said the boy. "Sire, why do you want me hanged? Could you not wait until I have had chance to go to confession?" Eustache replied: "You have taken great pleasure in doing evil, but you see I am well informed about that. You have fallen into evil hands, thinking you could have me wait here long enough for the Count to capture me. I have little time to spare for your confession of sins. Up there on the tree you will have time enough to talk to God. In fact, when you climb high up on that tree you'll be closer to God for your chat. So go ahead, climb up there and tell me how you sold me out to the Count." "Sire," said he, "by Saint Remi I did in fact sell you out and betrayed you. But tell me first, who in the devil told you I did it? Now there will be no man to kill you, but you would do well to leave immediately and not tarry here any longer." Eustache answered: "I will not delay seeing you hanged, so climb up there and we'll get the job done." The young traitor climbed up quickly into the tree and was hanged with the rope he had himself prepared. Soon after, the Count arrived, spurring on his horse. As he remounted Moriel, his own horse, Eustache saw the Count coming after him and declared: "Sire, since I have no one else to watch over him, I will depart, leaving this hanged man, my former watchman, in your care." The Count, like a mad man, along with his troops quickly chased after Eustache. They succeeded only in stopping two of the Monk's sergeants. Their first reaction, in a fit of anger, was to gouge out the two men's eyes. When Eustache received news of the deed, he swore an oath by the Holy Virgin that in retaliation for the four eyes put out, he in turn would maim four of the Count's men by cutting off their feet.

3. Capture and release of Sheriff / Count of Boulogne

Summary: Eustache leads the Count of Boulogne and seven of his knights into an ambush set by thirty of Eustache's men. Eustache seeks a reconciliation; but the Count, after contemptuously rejecting the offer of a settlement, is given a safe-conduct.

Translation (lines 776–853):

One day as he went wandering through the forest Eustache the Monk put on a hair-shirt and a rough homespun pilgrim's cloak. Thus woefully dressed, he came upon twenty knights along the way. He greeted them simply, and they in turn responded joyfully: "Say, where are you coming from, and where are you going?" "My Lords, I'm coming from Boulogne and am on my way at this very moment to see Count Dammartin to lodge a claim against a bad monk. He says he has a feud with the Count and has stolen a hundred marks from me in this very country. The man is a scurrilous mendicant who refuses to give me even a piece of his bread in the morning or at supper. My Lords, tell me without delay where I might find the Count." One of the knights replied: "At Hardelot. Go there, on my advice." Eustache set off for Hardelot and, arriving at mealtime, exclaimed to one of the Count's men: "In God's name I seek justice against this devil! My good sir, which one is the Count of Boulogne?" The man answered: "There he is." Forthwith the Monk went up to the Count. "Sir," he said, "may God have mercy! I am a bourgeois from Les Andelys. On my way from Bruges in Flanders I was carrying fine woollen breeches and a sum of money, some thirty pounds, when a drunken dim-wit (he was tonsured like a priest, but looked too much like a monk to be truly one; he also said he was your sworn enemy), robbed me of all my gold and silver, my furs; he even took my horse and cloak. I beg you. Do me justice against this mad monk. He is nearby, not far from where we are standing." (He was telling the truth, since it was in fact he who was talking to the Count.) "This false monk, son of a bitch, had me put on this pilgrim's cloak and made me swear that I would come to speak with you. You should know he is not far from here. As a matter of fact, I saw the spot where he went into the woods." The Count asked: "What does the man look like? Is he black or white, tall or short?" "About my height," said Eustache. The Count leaped forward immediately, shouting: "Quick, take me to the spot, and you will have your revenge." Eustache said: "Come on. I'll turn him over to you, and you can take him prisoner." The Count, accompanied by seven of his men, followed Eustache, who had thirty of his own men with him. As Eustache led the Count off, the latter became wary, surrounded as he was by Eustache's band. The Count became frightened. "Don't be scared," said Eustache. "I seek only reconciliation. By God's mercy, my sweet lord, let's talk peace." But the Count replied sarcastically: "Leave me alone in peace! It's all for naught, the die is cast. Our differences can never be reconciled." Eustache responded: "Go then, since things cannot be otherwise. You came here in my safe-conduct, and no harm will come to you." The Count returned home, and Eustache went off on another path.

4. Those who "tell the truth" allowed to keep their money.

Summary: Eustache meets a merchant from Boulogne and demands his money. The merchant swears that he has only forty pounds and fifteen sous. Eustache notes that the man is telling the truth, so he gives him back his purse.

Translation (lines 930–54):

One day as Eustache was wandering through the forest he met a merchant who was carrying forty pounds on his way home from Bruges in Flanders. The merchant was himself from Boulogne, so he recognized Eustache the Monk immediately. Knowing the

Monk's reputation he was obviously worried about the money he had on him. Eustache promptly asked: "Tell me, how much money do you have?" To which the merchant replied: "Sir, I tell you truthfully without a lie I have forty pounds in a belt and I also have fifteen sous in my purse." Eustache quickly took it from him and led the man into a thicket where he proceeded to Count all the money. He immediately gave the merchant back his money, saying: "Go! May God be with you! If you had in any way lied to me you would have left here without a cent. You would have lost all you have, keeping not even a penny." The merchant thanked him for his generosity.

5. Eustace entertains the Count for dinner and, disguised as a leper, steals his horse.

Summary: Eustache and his men are preparing a meal in the forest. Inadvertently Hainfrois of Heresinguehains arrives in the enemy camp and is invited to dinner. Eustache forgives him for causing his father's death and sends him back to Count Renaut. The Count does an about turn and immediately comes upon a leper to whom he gives twenty-eight deniers. The leper returns the favor by stealing one of the horses.

Translation (lines 1366–1422):

Eustache and his men fled into the woods where they found a safe hiding place. One day, just as they were sitting down to eat, Hainfrois, Eustache's mortal enemy, inadvertently came upon their meal. He had gone into the woods to seek relief (piss/shit), but once there he thought he would never get out alive. As he sat there on his horse, frightened to death, Eustache stood up and said: "Well then, do dismount and join us for a meal." Hainfrois dismounted, fearing for his very life. Little did he trust Eustache. When the meal was over Hainfrois began to plead great mercy of Eustache. In reply the Monk said: "Get out of here! You killed my father and my cousin, bringing both to their end, not to mention the mess you have gotten me into with Count Renaut. But should anyone give me all of France I would not seek reconciliation with him. The same is not the case between you and me. Because you and I have eaten together, from this day forth you will have nothing to fear from me. For you and I take leave quits. As for the Count, you can tell him on my behalf that when — just a short time ago, while you and I were quenching our thirst together — you asked what direction he was planning to take, the Monk told you that he would stay put, in the forest right where he was." Hainfrois took leave of Eustache and ran to tell the Count what had happened. When the Count learned all that had been said, he immediately retraced his tracks, only to find that Eustache had taken still another turn.

Eustache next turned up in the guise of a leper carrying his bowl, along with a crutch and a wooden rattle. As soon as he saw the Count approaching he began to shake the rattle, with the result that the Count and his knights put twenty-eight deniers into the poor beggar's bowl. The troop passed by, but one of the men riding a fine battle horse had the misfortune to remain alone in the rear. Eustache the leper tripped the animal, knocked the rider out of his saddle, and rode away. The horseless rider came to the Count and cried: "Sire, upon my word, a leper stole your horse from me." Furious, the Count cursed: "By bowels, belly and legs . . . the damn Monk tricked us once again. He was the leper that shook his rattle at us. Yet, upon my word," so says Count Renaut, "he really did look like a leper, with his fingers all bent over like claws and his face all pustulous." And so the Count continued his relentless pursuit of Eustache the Monk.

6. Robs those who fail to "tell the truth."

Summary: Eustache comes upon the Abbot of Jumièges, threatens him and demands his purse. The Abbot says he only has four marks; but, when he opens the purse, Eustache finds thirty marks. He keeps twenty six and gives the Abbot back the four marks he said he had.

Translation (lines 1746–77):

Eustache spotted the Abbot of Jumièges as he was coming down the road. "Sir Abbot," he said, "stop where you are! What are you carrying? Come now, don't hide it." The Abbot answered: "What's it to you?" At this, Eustache was ready to hit him, but instead replied: "What's it to me, fat-ass [couillon = balls]? Upon my word, Ill make it my business. Get down, fast, and not another word out of you, or I'll let you have it. You'll be beaten up so badly you won't be worth a hundred pounds." The Abbot thought the man was drunk, and said, more politely this time: "Go away. You won't find what you are looking for here." Eustache responded: "Cut the bullshit and get off your horse fast, or you'll be in for a lot of trouble." The Abbot got down, frightened now. Eustache asked how much money he had with him. "Four marks," said the Abbot, "in truth I only have four marks silver." Eustache searched him immediately and found thirty marks or more. He gave back to the Abbot the four marks he claimed to have. The Abbot became duly furious; for, had he told the truth, he would have got back all his money. The Abbot lost his money only because he told a lie.

7. Disguise as a Potter.

Summary: One of the Count of Boulogne's spies finds Eustache's hideout; he informs the Count who then sets an ambush in a ditch. When Eustache learns of the ambush from a watchman, he disguises himself as a coal-man. Shortly thereafter, Eustache comes face to face with the Count, telling him he is looking for the Count of Boulogne for the purpose of filing a grievance for damages against Eustache. The Count asks where he might find Eustache and goes after him. Eustache again changes identity, this time becoming a potter. The Count returns and inquires of the potter where he might now find the coalman. Eustache sends him down the road toward Boulogne, and the Count comes upon the real potter who had the misfortune to exchange his pottery for the donkey and coal of Eustache. This individual is seized and mistreated until finally recognized by one of the Count's men-at-arms. The Count retraces his steps, Eustache by this time having thrown off his disguise as a potter.

Translation (lines 996–1141):

One day the Count was out hunting. A spy came and told him that Eustache was in the forest. The Count put on his heavy brown cloak, and he and his men followed the spy on foot. They set up an ambush in a ditch. One of Eustache's watchmen approached the group and recognized the Count. He found Eustache and told him of the ambush. Eustache then approached a coal-man and his donkey. The coal-man's donkey was used to carry the coal to market. Without further ado, Eustache put on the coal-man's clothes and black hat. He smeared coal dust on his face and hands, as well as around his neck. As a result, he was marvelously blackened. The donkey's back was loaded with sacks of coal. Goad in hand, Eustache set off with the donkey toward Boulogne. Not recognizing his foe, the Count paid him no attention and didn't even deign to speak to him as he passed by. So Eustache shouted to them: "My lords," he said, "what are you doing there?" The Count was the first to answer: "What's it to you, you scurvy fellow?" Eustache replied: "By Saint Omer! I'll go lodge a formal complaint with the Count telling him how shamefully we are treated by Eustache the Monk. I dared not bring my draft horse to carry my coal to market for fear that Eustache might steal it. Right now he is lying comfortably next to a good coal fire eating meat and venison. He has burned all my coal and has already cost me plenty." "Is he nearby?" asked the Count. Eustache replied: "He is in this very forest. Go straight down this road if you want to talk to him." Eustache struck Romer (the donkey) with the goad as the Count and his men began to enter the forest. In the meantime, the real coal-man had found it appropriate to put on the monk's clothes. As a result, the poor man was mistaken for Eustache, beaten and mistreated. The Count's men had thought, without any doubt, that he was Eustache the

Eustache the Monk

Monk. "My lords," said he, "why are you beating me so? You can have these clothes. Be advised I have no money; this is the robe of Eustache the Monk who at this moment is on his way toward Boulogne with my coal and my donkey. His hands, face and neck are well blackened with coal dust. He is also wearing my black cap. He made me take off my clothes and put on his." And the Count said: "Listen, my lords! Catch him if you can. By God's teeth, I have been burned by this living devil so many times! He was disguised as the coal-man who spoke to us just a short while ago on this very spot." The Count added: "Quick, after him!" The horses were nearby, so they mounted and rode off in haste after Eustache. Eustache had by that time washed his face before meeting a potter. The potter was shouting: "Pots for sale! Pots for sale!" And Eustache, who was no fool, knew he was being chased. So he immediately struck a deal with the potter; in exchange for his donkey and coal, he got pitchers, pots, and vases. The swap was made and so Eustache became a potter and the potter became a coal-man. The latter was a fool for giving up his own trade. Eustache went off shouting: "Pots for sale! Pots for sale!" Just at that moment the Count came out of the woods and asked the potter if he had seen a coal-man. "Sir," said Eustache the Monk, "he went down this road straight toward Boulogne, leading his donkey loaded with coal sacks." The Count dug in his spurs, and he, his servants, and knights caught up with the coal-man. They proceeded to beat and mistreat the poor man. Sorely did they strike him with their fists, while tying him up hands and feet. They then threw him over the back of a horse, with his head dangling over the animal's rump. The poor fellow screamed, shouted, and cried: "My Lords," said he, "in God's name, I beg you, have pity on me. Tell me why you have taken me thus; and, if I have done you any ill, I will willingly make amends." "Aha! Aha! sir scoundrel," said the Count, "you thought you could escape? I will soon have you hanged." One of the Count's knights looked closely at the man and recognized him as the potter whom he knew well. This wise knight, who knew where the man was born, said: "What devils have turned you into a coal-man? You used to be a potter; no man will ever stay healthy who takes on so many different trades." "My Lord, have mercy," said the man, "for this donkey and this coal I gave my pots to the coal-man. May God strike him down, the one by whose doing I am so sorely tried. I think he probably stole the goods; by God's name I can truly say I didn't steal anything. I gave him my pots in exchange for the donkey. He rode off in haste into the woods, shouting: 'Pots for sale! Pots for sale!'" The knight spoke to the Count in these words: "Eustache is a shameful fellow! Just a short while ago he was dressed as a coal-man, now he has become a potter." "So I see," said the Count, "by the pluck! Quick, after the man, let's go! Bring to me everyone you meet today and tomorrow. I'll never catch the Monk unless I take all of them." So they left the poor coal-man and set off into the forest, once again on the chase. By this time Eustache had gotten rid of all his pots, having thrown them into a swamp.

8. Disguise as a Prostitute.

Summary: The Count sets up his court in Neuchatel. Eustache disguises himself as a prostitute. One of the Count's men (a sergeant) burns with passion for this slut in the forest, but he is quickly disabused of his desire after he loses his two horses. Eustache orders him back to tell the Count what happened, but the sergeant's shame is so great that he does not dare return to his master. Instead he prefers flight from the Boulonnais region.

Translation (lines 1186-1283):

The Count goes to Neuchatel where he sets up his new court. Eustache, who had many tricks up his sleeve, entered after him into the city. He dressed up in a woman's clothing, and his disguise was so good he did in fact look just like a woman. He put on a linen dress, covered his face with a veil, and carried a distaff by his side. As he sat there spinning, a sergeant arrived almost immediately, riding one of the Count's horses and leading another. Eustache exclaimed: "Let me mount your horse and in return I will let you fuck me." "Quite willingly," said the sergeant. "Climb up, then, on this good ambling palfrey, and I'll give you four-pence if you let me fuck you. I will also teach you how to ass-play." In reply Eustache said: "Here and now, I declare, never has any man screwed thus." Eustache lifts a leg to the horseman; and, as he does so, lets off a loud fart. "Hah, damsel, you fart!" Eustache responds: "You are mistaken, sweet handsome friend, don't let it bother you, but it's only the noise of the saddle cracking." Eustache the Monk climbs up on the second horse, and he and the sergeant ride off in haste into the forest side by side. "Let's not go any farther. I am riding my master's horse, and you have his best palfrey." The sergeant added: "I will have great shame if this affair of ours is not quickly finished." "Sergeant," said Eustache the Monk, "I too am all desirous to fuck. So let's get to our ass-playing quickly. Come a little closer so that no one can spy on us." "Damsel," said the sergeant, "be careful there is no trickery. Should there be such, I swear by Saint Mary's bowels I would take your life." In reply Eustache said: "My dear friend, no need to get so upset, my lodge is just ahead. Come, just a bit farther now." The sergeant foolishly follows along as Eustache comes upon his own band of men. He seizes the poor wretch by the scruff of the neck as if he were mad. Here you have a good illustration of the truth in the popular saying: "Thus scratches a trapped goat when ill befalls it." Eustache ordered: "Get down off the good horse. You won't ride it any farther. The palfrey too will stay here quite well. The Count will never again mount it." Both riders dismount there amid great bursts of laughter. "My lords," said Eustache the Monk, "this sergeant will do his duty, for I have his word." He leads the poor man forward a bit, and takes him to a mud-pit. "Sergeant," he says, "don't let it trouble you.

Quick, strip off all your clothes. I know how anxious you are to have a fuck." The sergeant enters the mud-pit for he dares not contradict Eustache. The latter exclaims: "Now, about that ass-play! You can fuck at your leisure, all stretched out for some good ass-play, or you will be beaten so badly you'll never be able to leave. You thought you would fuck me. Aren't you ashamed for wanting to bugger a black monk?" The sergeant replied: "May God have mercy, do not put me to such shame here. Sire, by Our Lady, I thought you were a woman!" Eustache (who was neither heretic nor bugger, nor sodomite), answered: "Well then, come forward before you leave. You are to tell the Count on my behalf how I used you." "I will tell him straight away on your behalf," so says the sergeant as he sets off immediately. In fact, his shame was such that he dared not return to tell the Count anything of what had happened to him. Instead, he left the Boulonnais for a foreign land, never to return. Following this episode, the war between Eustache the Monk and the Count lasted a long time. Eustache continued to put his adversary to even greater shame.

9. Eustace invades England.

Summary: Eustache serves the King of France well, accompanying Prince Louis to England. Yet he is suspected of complicity in the defeat of the combat fleet assembled at Damme by Louis-Philippe. There is, however, none courageous enough to charge him with responsibility for the defeat.

Translation (lines 2250–65):

The Monk was a fine warrior; he was bold and proud, and on the other hand did many devilish things on the islands. He led King Louis and his large fleet across the sea, personally capturing the Nef de Boulogne. He took the French King with him to the port of Damme. That was the year [1213 A.D.] the King lost his ships! They blamed Eustache for having betrayed the King's fleet. Eustache justified himself by claiming there was no man bold enough to furnish proof of such treason. And so they left him alone after that.

10. The Death of Eustace.

Summary: Eustache sets out to sea again to wage battle against twenty English ships. A violent combat ensues during which the English set up a curtain of smoke before boarding Eustache's vessel. They cut off Eustache's head and the battle is lost (2266–2305). The romance ends with a moralizing comment of the life of Eustache (2306–07).

Translation (lines 2266–2307):

Once again he set out to sea in a great fleet of ships. With him there was Robert de Tornelle, along with Varles de Montagui. When Eustache, the courageous warrior, got out on the high seas he soon encountered more than twenty English ships bearing down on him. The enemy set out in skiffs and attacked the ships with long bows and cross bows. The Monk's men guard themselves against everything thrown at them in the chase. They kill many Englishmen and defend themselves nobly. Eustache himself crushed many with the oar he wielded, breaking arms and legs with every swing. This one he killed, another one he threw overboard. This one he knocks down, another he tramples under foot, and a third one has his wind-pipe crushed. But Eustache is assailed from all directions. Battle axes strike his ship on all sides. On the first wave the defenders were able to ward off the attack, preventing the enemy from coming on board. Then the English started hurling big pots of finely ground lime on board, with the result that great clouds of dust covered the decks. That was what caused the most damage, against which Eustache's men could not defend themselves. To their misfortune the wind was against them, which caused further torment, for their eyes became filled with ash. In the confusion the English leaped onto Eustache's ship and mistreated his men badly, taking all the nobles prisoner. As for Eustache the Monk, he was slain, his head cut off. Thus ended the battle.

"No man can live long who spends his days doing ill."

From *Fouke le Fitz Waryn*

Introduction

The story, written in Old French prose, survives in a miscellany of works in Latin, French, and English, dating from c. 1325–40. The manuscript, now British Library, Royal 12.C.XII, contains some sixty pieces, ranging from liturgical texts in honor of Thomas of Lancaster, parodies of church offices, hymns to the Virgin, prophecies, satirical verses, mathematical puzzles, cooking recipes, a metrical chronicle, and treatises on a variety of pseudo-scientific subjects (Hathaway, pp. xlvii–li). The text of *Fouke le Fitz Waryn*, occupying folios 33–61, is based on a lost late-thirteenth-century verse romance, remnants of which can be detected in two verse prophesies and in numerous verse fragments embedded in the prose (Hathaway, pp. xix–xx).

Author

The creator of the prose version, whose identity is unknown, is usually called the compiler or *remanieur* ("adapter"): "it is highly likely that he inherited, or had easy access to, the manuscript of the couplet romance, and that he was himself the author of the prose *remanieur* which he copied" (Hathaway, p. xxxvii). E. J. Hathaway surmises that he might have been a tutor in a baronial household in Ludlow before seeking ecclesiastical preferment (p. xliv).

Genre

As M. Dominica Legge suggests, *Fouke le Fitz Waryn* is an ancestral romance that focuses on the fortunes of a single family from the Norman Conquest to the thirteenth century. Invented in England and Scotland, the family chronicle was popular as a genre from the twelfth to the fourteenth centuries. Other examples include: *Guillaume d'Angleterre* (late twelfth), *Waldef* (late twelfth), *Boeve de Haumtone* (late twelfth), *Fergus* (thirteenth), and *Gui de Warewic* (thirteenth). These romances were composed by clerics, members of religious houses patronized by the parvenue families celebrated in the stories. Such stories have several elements in common: 1) the hero is the founder of the family; 2) he is exiled to foreign lands; 3) he undertakes fantastic adventures, such as fighting a dragon; 4) he is reconciled to the king in the end and reclaims his inheritance; 5) since genealogy is important, his marriage and relations are carefully recounted; and 6) he is buried in a monastery that he founded (Legge, pp. 139–75).

Historical Background

The romance "is a weird mixture of accurate information, plausible stories that lack confirmation, and magnificent flights of pure imagination" (Sidney Painter, quoted by Hathaway, p. ix) that recounts the Norman settlement, begun by William the Conqueror, on the Welsh border, the feudal rivalries among the Marcher barons, their allies, and the native Welsh rulers, and the complex dynastic relations achieved through marriage and conquest among all these groups. On this historical continuum, which sweeps from the Norman Conquest to the mid-thirteenth century, is super-imposed the changing fortunes of one Norman family—the Fitz Waryns. The first third of the story traces the history of the family from Warin de Metz to the birth of Fouke Fitz Waryn III, who is the hero of the last two-thirds of the romance. In the first part, which is omitted in the translation that follows, Warin de Metz marries the Peverel heiress, Melette, and thus gains the lordship of Whittington. Their son, Fouke le Brun, marries another heiress, Hawyse, daughter of Joce de Dynan, and thereby gains the castle and town of Ludlow. Through the treachery of the Norman Ernalt de Lyls, the Dynan holdings are lost, and Fouke le Brun, Warin de Metz, and Joce de Dynan are defeated by the Welsh prince Yervard and his Norman ally Walter de Lacy. Severely wounded, Fouke seeks refuge with King Henry I, who commands Lacy to release his prisoners, but refuses to return Whittington to Fouke, granting release instead to Morys fitz Roger. Thus, the first part ends as the Fitz Warins are dispossessed of their lands and titles. The reclaiming of Whittington will be the principal challenge of Fouke le Brun's eldest son, Fouke III, in the second part of the romance.

The second part (translated here) contains a mixture of largely accurate local history and what Hathaway calls "traditional folklore" (p. xxxiii). Among the known historical elements are "the revolt of Fouke in 1200–01 after Whittington castle had been adjudged to the Welsh castellan, Morys fitz Roger; the outlawry, terminated on 15 November 1203 by the pardon of Fouke himself and of more than forty other men who had been associated with him in his outlawry; and the marriage of Fouke III to Matilda of Caus, the widow of the Irish baron Theobald Walter" (p. xxvii). The folklore elements in the second part consist mainly of the outlaw narrative, which, as we will see, has a number of striking parallels to the later Robin Hood tradition, though there are some encounters with giants and dragons.

Relation to Robin Hood tradition

With *Hereward the Wake, Eustache the Monk,* and *Fouke le Fitz Waryn*, we come to the end of an early form of the outlaw romance in which the heroes' adventures represent a mixture of history, legend, and myth. As Maurice Keen observes, the romantic hero, who travels the world, slays dragons, and rescues princesses, and the forest outlaw, who fights against more local evil and corruption, part ways. In the later stories of Robin Hood, Gamelyn, and Adam Bell, "chivalrous adventures in a world of enchantment find no place" (p. 39). While Keen is certainly correct, there remains a continuity of plot elements and character types linking the later outlaw stories to the earlier materials. Although there are significant differences between *Fouke le Fitz Waryn* and the later Robin Hood legend, the works share at least three major episodes, which suggest to us that we are dealing with sources rather than analogues.

In *Fouke* the outlaw's brother, John, confronts a caravan of ten merchants transporting "expensive cloths, furs, spices, and dresses for the personal use of the king and queen of England" (p. 694). Likewise, in the *Gest* Little John and Much stop the caravan of two monks, fifty-two yeomen, and seven pack-horses transporting the goods of the abbot of St. Mary's Abbey in York. In both works, the two groups are abducted into the forest, where they are questioned about the amount and ownership of their property. The truthfulness of their answers determines whether or not they can keep their goods. Fouke asks, "Are you speaking the truth" (p. 695), while Robin queries, "What is in your cofers? . . . Trewe than tell thou me" (lines 970–71). In both works, the "guests" dine with the outlaws, and, after the meal, they are allowed to leave without their property and money.

In another pair of episodes, disguise and deception are used to lure the victims into the outlaw's lair. Hiding in the forest of Windsor, Fouke observes that King John is hunting deer (p. 711). Disguising himself as a collier, Fouke greets the king and kneels before him. Upon being asked if he has seen any deer, Fouke, lying, replies that he has seen "One with long horns" and offers to guide the king to it. Going into the thicket, the king is captured by Fouke's men. Fearing that he will be killed, King John begs for mercy, and, after swearing an oath that he will restore Fouke's inheritance and grant him love and peace, he is released unharmed. Returning to the court, the king breaks his oath and plots to capture Fouke. In the parallel episode in the *Gest*, Little John, disguised as Reynolde Grenlefe, greets the sheriff who is hunting in the forest and "knelyd hym beforne" (line 729). When Little John tells the sheriff that he has just seen "a ryght fayre harte" (line 738) and a herd of deer, he foolishly asks to be taken to the spot where Robin, "the mayster-herte" (line 753), awaits him. After dining with the outlaw band, the sheriff is stripped of his clothing and forced to sleep on the ground. Begging to be released the next morning, he swears an oath that he will not harm Robin or his men in the future. Upon being released, he, humiliated but unharmed, returns to Nottingham where he breaks his oath by plotting to capture Robin at the archery tournament.

In the final pair of similar episodes, one of the gang members is wounded in a fight and begs the leader to kill him. Fouke's brother, William, is severely wounded by a Norman soldier and, rather than be captured, he begs Fouke to kill him by cutting off his head. Fouke replies that he would not do this for the world (p. 713). In the *Gest* (lines 1206 ff.), Little John is wounded in the sheriff's ambush after the archery tournament, and he begs Robin to kill him by cutting off his head. Robin refuses and carries him to safety.

Previous critics have been reluctant to assert a direct connection between the French outlaw genre and the later English Robin Hood. While Maurice Keen admits that some of the episodes are "almost identical" and "substantially the same," he is largely quiet about the "French connection." J. C. Holt also comments upon the shared themes, but, like Keen, he largely dismisses any direct linkage because the Robin Hood tradition lacks an emphasis on the restitution of inheritance which "plays a fundamental role" in *Hereward, Eustace,* and *Fouke.* He asserts that "there is nothing of this in Robin Hood," who "moves in a different world from that of the dispossessed feudal landowner" (p. 65). While the assertion may hold true for the *early* cycle of tales, it applies neither to *Gamelyn*, the earliest outlaw tale in Middle English, nor to the later Tudor Robert Hood, the disinherited and dispossessed Earl of Huntington. By stressing the differences, rather than the similarities — some strikingly close, both Keen and Holt have fostered the illusion of a native English outlaw tradition immune from outside influences.

Note on the Thomas E. Kelly's Translation

The translation is based on the Anglo-Norman Texts edition, edited by Hathaway, Ricketts, Robson, and Wilshere. The starting point occurs on p. 22, line 23, of that edition. Bracketted material marks either the Norman French form or material added for clarificattion. I have usually translated names as they appear in the Anglo Norman, but in some instances have regularized them. For instance, *Blauncheville* I have transcibed as *Whittington*; *Bretaigne le Menour* (Little Britain) as *Brittany*.

Fouke le Fitz Waryn

Fouke's wife *Mahaud* (Maud) or *Mahaud de Caus* I have translated as *Matilda*, since
Robert Eyton's *Antiquities of Shropshire* (1861) VII 73, n. 28, identifies Fouke's wife
as Matilde le Vavasour. It is perhaps coincidence that Marian, Robin Hood's finacée,
is referred to as Matilda Fitzwater in Munday's two plays, *The Downfall of Robert,
Earle of Huntington* and *The Death of Robert, Earle of Huntington*.

Select Bibliography

Text

British Library, Royal 12 C. XII, folios 33–61.

Editions and Translations

Burgess, Glyn S., trans. *Two Medieval Outlaws: Eustace the Monk and Fouke Fitz
Waryn*. Cambridge: D. S. Brewer, 1997. Pp. 3–87.

Hathaway, E. J., P. T. Ricketts, C. A. Robson, and A. D. Wilshere, eds. *Fouke Le Fitz
Waryn*. Anglo-Norman Text Society. Oxford: Basil Blackwell, 1975. [Base text for
Kelly's translation.]

Kelly, Thomas E., trans. *Eustache the Monk*. In *Medieval Outlaws: Ten Tales in
Modern English*. Ed. Thomas H. Ohlgren. Stroud: Sutton Publishing, 1998. Pp. 61–98,
299–302.

Stevenson, Joseph, ed. and trans. *The Legend of Fulk Fitz-Warin*. In *Rerum Britanni-
carum Medii Aevi Scriptores*, or *Chronicles and Memorials of Great Britain and Ireland
during the Middle Ages*. Rolls Series. Vol. 66. London: Longman and Co., 1857, 1875;
rpt. Kraus Reprint, 1965. Pp. 275–415. [The selection included here occurs on pp.
323–415. Stevenson's translation is, according to Hathaway, creditable and service-
able but "not impeccable" (p. cxxi).]

Commentary and Criticism

Brandlin, Louis. "Nouvelles recherches sur *Fouke Fitz Warin*." *Romania* 55 (1929),
17–44.

Francis, E. A. "The Background to *Fulk Fitzwarin*." In *Studies in Medieval French Presented to Alfred Ewert in Honour of his Seventieth Birthday*. Oxford: Clarendon, 1961. Pp. 322–27.

Hathaway, E. J., *et al*. See above.

Holt, J. C. *Robin Hood*. Revised and enlarged edition. London: Thames and Hudson, 1989.

Jones, Timothy Scott. "Redemptive Fictions: The Contexts of Outlawry in Medieval English Chronicle and Romance." Ph.D. diss. University of Illinois at Urbana-Champaign, 1994. [Section on *Fouke le Fitz Waryn*.]

Keen, Maurice. *The Outlaws of Medieval Legend*. Revised paperback edition. London and New York: Routledge and Kegan Paul, 1987.

Legge, M. Dominica. *Anglo-Norman Literature and Its Background*. Oxford: Clarendon Press, 1963.

Painter, Sidney. *The Reign of King John*. Baltimore: John Hopkins Press, 1949.

From *Fouke le Fitz Waryn*

Fouke and [his wife] Hawyse remained for some time with the King, long enough in fact to have five sons: Fouke, William, Philip the Red, John, and Alan. During the same period King Henry had four sons: Henry, Richard the Lion-hearted, John, and Geoffrey, who later became Duke of Brittany. Henry was crowned during his father's lifetime, but died before his father. Richard then reigned after his father's death, followed in turn by his brother John who, all his life, was wicked, contrary, and spiteful. Fouke the younger [also called Foket] was brought up with King Henry's four sons, and he was much loved by all of them except John, with whom he quarreled frequently.

It so happened that one day John and Fouke were sitting all alone in a room playing chess. John picked up the chess board and struck Fouke a great blow with it. Feeling the pain, Fouke raised his foot and delivered John a swift kick to the chest. John's head struck the wall so hard that he became dizzy and fainted. Fouke's immediate reaction was fright, but he was glad there was no one else in the room with them. He rubbed John's ears, and he regained consciousness. John immediately went to the King, his father, and lodged a complaint. "Be quiet, you good-for-nothing," said the King, "you are always squabbling. If Fouke did all you said he did, you most likely deserved all you got." He called the boy's master and had the Prince soundly whipped for his complaint. John was very angry with Fouke, and from that day forward never again had any true affection for him.

When King Henry, the father, died his son Richard became King. Richard held Fouke le Brun, the son of Waryn, in very high esteem because of his loyalty. At Winchester the King summoned before him the five sons of Fouke le Brun — Foket, Philip the Red, William, John, and Alan — and their cousin, Baldwin de Hodenet. With great pomp all six men were dubbed and raised to knighthood. Sir Fouke the younger, along with his brothers and their troops, crossed the sea to seek honor and distinction. There was not a single tourney or joust at which they did not wish to be present. And so highly were they esteemed everywhere that it became a common saying that they were without equals in strength, bounty, and bravery. For they had such good fortune that they came into every combat being considered and praised as the best.

Following the death of Fouke le Brun, King Richard sent letters to Sir Fouke to come to England to receive his father's lands. Fouke and his brothers were deeply saddened to learn that Fouke le Brun, their good father, was dead, and they all returned to London. King Richard was very glad to see them, and he restored to them all the feudal holdings

693

which Fouke le Brun possessed at his death. The King was preparing for his journey to the Holy Land, so he entrusted all the March to the keeping of Sir Fouke. The King loved and favored him much for his loyalty and great reputation. Fouke stood well with the King during the whole of the life of King Richard.

After Richard's death, his brother John was crowned King of England. Soon thereafter, John sent for Sir Fouke to come and talk with him about various matters concerning the March, and said that he was coming there himself on a visit. He went first to Baldwin, now called Castle Montgomery. When Moris, the son of Roger de Powys, lord of Whittington (Shropshire), perceived that King John was approaching the March, he sent to the King a handsome steed and all white molted gyrfalcon.[1] After John thanked him for the gifts, Moris came to speak to the King who asked him to stay and to be of his council, making him warden of the entire March.

When Moris saw the time was ripe he asked the King, if it were his pleasure, to confirm by royal charter the honor of Whittington [Blauncheville] to him and his heirs, as King Henry his father had formerly confirmed it to his own father, Roger de Powys. The King knew full well that Whittington belonged to Sir Fouke by right, but he also remembered the blow that Fouke had given him when they were young. He delighted that he now had an excellent opportunity for revenge. So he granted that whatever Moris should put into writing, he would seal it; and, for the favor, Moris also promised John one hundred pounds cash.

There was a knight nearby who had overheard all that the King and Moris had said. He came in haste and told Sir Fouke how the King had confirmed by his charter to Sir Moris the lands which of right belonged to Fouke. With his four brothers Fouke came before the King and asked him that they might have the benefit of common law, whereby these lands were theirs by right and reason as Fouke's inheritance. And they pleaded with the King that he would have the goodness to accept one hundred pounds, on condition that he would grant them the award of his court for gain or for loss. The King told them that he would maintain the grant which he had already made to Sir Moris, whether Fouke was angry or not. Then Sir Moris spoke out saying to Sir Fouke: "Sir Knight, you are very foolish to challenge my lands. If you say that you have right to Whittington you lie. Were it not for the King's presence, I would prove it upon your body." Before any further words were spoken Sir William, Fouke's brother, stepped forward, and with his fist gave Sir Moris such a blow on the face that it was covered with blood. The knights came between them so that no more damage was done. Then Sir Fouke said to the King: "Sire, you are my liege lord, and I have become bound to you by fealty since I have been in your service, and because I hold lands from you. In return you ought to afford me reasonable

---

[1] Stevenson translates the adjective *muer*, "molted," as "for his mews."

support, but you fail me both in reason and in common law. Never has a good King denied law in his court to his free tenants; therefore, I renounce my allegiance to you." Having said this, he departed from the court and went to his house.

Fouke and his brothers armed themselves immediately, and Baldwin de Hodenet did the same. When they had gone half a league from the city they encountered fifteen well-armed knights, the strongest and bravest of all the King's retainers, who ordered them to return. The knights said they had promised the King that he should have their heads. Sir Fouke turned round and exclaimed: "Fair sirs, you were very foolish when you promised to give what you could not get." Then they attacked each other with lances and swords, and four of the King's most valiant knights were soon killed. All the others were wounded to the point of death, save one, who seeing the peril took to flight. When he came to the city the King inquired of him whether Fitz Waren had been taken prisoner. "Not at all," he replied, "nor was he even injured. He and all his companions have escaped, and all of our men, excepting myself, were slain. I alone escaped with great difficulty." "Where," said the King, "are Gyrart de France, Pierre of Avignon, and Sir Amys le Marchys?" "Slain, sire." Then ten knights arrived, all on foot, for Sir Fouke had made off with their chargers. Some of these knights had lost their noses, some their chins. All ten were a piteous sight. The King swore a great oath that he would take revenge on them and all their lineage.

Fouke next went to Alberbury [in Shropshire] and told dame Hawyse, his mother, how he had traveled to Winchester. Fouke took a great sum of money from his mother and left with his brothers and his cousins for Brittany [Bretaygne le Menur], where he remained for some time. King John seized all the lands which Fouke had in England and did much harm to all his relatives.

Fouke and his four brothers, along with two cousins, Audulph de Bracy and Baldwin de Hodenet, bid adieu to their friends in Brittany, and returned to England. In the day time they rested in woods and moors and traveled on only at night, for they dared not face an attack in daylight. They did not have sufficient manpower to engage the King's troops. At length they came to Higford [in Shropshire], to Sir Walter de Higford, who had married dame Vyleyne, the daughter of Waryn de Metz. Her true name was Emelyne, and she was Sir Fouke's aunt. When he arrived at Alberbury, the next stop on his journey, the local people told him that his mother had recently been buried. On her tomb Fouke deeply grieved his mother's death and prayed compassionately for her soul.

That same night Sir Fouke and his people went into a forest called Babbins Wood [Babbyng], near Whittington, to watch for Moris Fitz Roger. A valet passing nearby spotted them and ran to tell Moris what he had seen. Moris armed himself in regalia, taking his shield — green, with two wild boars of beaten gold, and the border of argent, with fleurs-de-lys of azure. He had in his company the nine sons of Guy de la Montaigne and the three sons of Aaron de Clerfountaygne, so that there were thirty men well-mounted and five hundred foot soldiers.

When Fouke saw Moris he raced out of the forest. A sharp fight was begun between them, with Moris being wounded in the shoulder. After many knights and foot soldiers had been killed, Moris finally fled towards his castle with Fouke in pursuit. Fouke thought to have struck Moris on the helmet as he was escaping, but the stroke fell on the saddle of his charger. Then Morgan the son of Aaron shot forth from the castle, and with a crossbow bolt he struck Fouke through the leg. Fouke was angry that he could not thus finish the battle and avenge himself upon Sir Moris. As for the wound in his leg, he took no heed of it.

Sir Moris made his complaint to the King that Sir Fouke had returned to England and had wounded him in the shoulder. The King became wondrously enraged, and appointed one hundred knights with their retinue to go through all England to search for Fouke, to capture him, and bring him to the King — alive or dead. The King was to pay all their expenses, and in addition he promised to give them lands and rich fees if their search were successful. The knights went throughout the whole of England in search of Sir Fouke. But wherever they heard that Sir Fouke might be located, they avoided going to that place; for they feared him beyond measure. Some loved him, but many feared his noble chivalry, apprehending the danger that might happen to them should they test his strength and daring.

Sir Fouke and his company came to the Forest of Braydon [in Wiltshire] where they remained in hiding. They dared not venture forth openly, for fear of the King. One day, more than ten burgesses arrived carrying through the forest expensive cloths, furs, spices, and dresses for the personal use of the King and Queen of England. The men were merchants who had purchased these rich goods with the money of the King of England, and were traveling to deliver their purchases to the King. They were followed by twenty-four foot-soldiers charged with guarding the King's treasure.

When Fouke saw the merchants he called his brother John and told him to go and speak with these people and find out what country they were from. John spurred on his horse and rode off to speak with the merchants. When he inquired from what land they might be, a spokesman for the group, a haughty and proud person, came forward and asked what business it was of his to have such information. John replied politely by inviting them to come and speak with his master in the forest. If they would not go willingly, he said, he would have to use force. A man-at-arms came forward and struck John a great blow with his sword. In return John gave him such a stroke on his head that he fell senseless to the ground. Then Sir Fouke and his company arrived on the scene and attacked the merchants. They defended themselves very vigorously, but at length they surrendered, for they could not do otherwise.

Fouke took them into the forest, where they told him that they were the King's merchants. When Fouke heard this he was delighted, and said: "Sir merchants, if you lose this property, on whom will the loss fall? Tell me the truth." "Sir," they said, "if we lose it through our cowardice, or by our own carelessness, we ourselves are responsible; but if we lose it otherwise, by danger of the sea, or by force, the loss will fall upon the King." "Are you speaking the truth?" "Assuredly, sir," they replied. When Fouke understood that the loss would be the King's, he then measured out the rich cloth and the expensive furs with his lance. He clothed all who were with him, tall and short, in this rich cloth. To each he gave according to his degree. Everyone of his followers received a liberal share, and of the other goods, each took what he liked.

When evening came and the merchants had dined heartily, he bid them Godspeed, and asked them to salute the King in the name of Fouke Fitz Waryn, who thanked him heartily for all this fine clothing. During the entire time that he was a banished man neither Fouke nor any of his followers did damage at any time to any one, save the King and his knights.

At last the merchants and their foot-soldiers arrived before the King. Wounded and maimed, they repeated to him all that Fouke had charged them to convey, describing how Fouke had taken the King's property. He became enraged, and in his fury sent out a proclamation throughout the realm. Any person who would bring Fouke to him, dead or alive, would receive a thousand pounds. The King would, moreover, add to this cash reward all the lands that belonged to Fouke in England.

Fouke next journeyed into the forest of Kent. Leaving his knights in the thick of the forest, he went riding alone along the highway. There he met a messenger, wearing a wreath of red roses around his head, who was singing merrily. Fouke asked him politely for the chaplet of flowers, and if he would be so kind would pay him double for it. "Sir," said the messenger, "He is very niggardly of his property who will not give a chaplet of roses at the request of a knight." And he gave the wreath to Fouke, who, in return, gave him twenty shillings. The messenger recognized Fouke, for he had seen him often.

When the messenger later arrived in Canterbury, he met the hundred knights who had been searching for Fouke through all of England. "Sirs," he said to them, "where have you come from? Have you yet found the man you have been seeking by the order of our lord the King and for your own advancement?" "No," they replied. "Then what will you give me," he said, "if I take you to the place where I have seen and spoken with him today?" The knights' reply, in both goods and promises, was so generous that the messenger told them where he had seen Fouke. He also described how he had received twenty shillings in exchange for the chaplet of roses which he had graciously given.

The hundred knights immediately sent out a summons through the countryside. They hastily rounded up knights, squires, and foot-soldiers, in sufficient numbers to encircle the whole forest. As if this were an animal hunt, beaters and receivers were placed at strategic points. Others were positioned throughout the countryside with horns to give warning the moment Fouke and his companions came out of the forest. Fouke, however, remained in the forest, unaware of all this activity. At length he heard a horn sounded by one of the attacking knights. He became suspicious and ordered his brothers to mount their horses. William, Philip, John, and Alan immediately mounted, as did Audulph de Bracy, Baldwin de Hodnet, and John Malveysyn. The three Cosham brothers, Thomas, Pieres, and William, who were good cross-bowmen, and all the rest of Fouke's followers were soon ready for the assault.

With his companions Fouke came out of the forest and saw, before all the others, the hundred knights who had been hunting him throughout England. In the first rush of battle Fouke's men killed Gilbert de Mountferrant, Jordan de Colchester, and many other knights. They made several passes back and forth through the hundred knights, knocking them down in great numbers. At length, however, many knights, squires, burgesses, foot-soldiers, and people in great numbers joined in the battle. Fouke wisely perceived that he and his men could not continue thus. Finally, after his brother John received a bad head wound, he decided to return into the forest. Fouke and his companions spurred their horses. But before they left, many a good knight, squire, and foot-soldier were slain. People from all over then began to sound the cry, and they were pursued by the populace everywhere they went. At length they entered into a wood and saw a man raising his horn, about to sound the warning. In an instant, one of Fouke's men shot him through the body with a cross-bow bolt. That put a quick end to the warning blast.

Fouke and his companions were soon forced to leave their horses and fled on foot towards a nearby abbey. When the porter saw them coming he ran to shut the gates. Alan, being very tall, quickly got over the wall, and the porter began to run away. "Stop," said Alan, and ran after him. He took the porter's keys from him and gave him a blow with the chain from which the keys hung. The porter thus had good reason to regret his attempted flight. Alan then let all his brothers enter the abbey. Once inside, Fouke grabbed the habit of an old monk and speedily dressed himself in it. Taking a large staff in his hand, he went out of the gate. After he had shut the gate he walked on, as if lame of one foot, supporting his whole body on his big stick. Shortly thereafter the knights and foot-soldiers arrived followed by a great mob. One of the knights shouted: "Old monk, have you seen any armed knights pass here?" "Indeed, sir, and may God repay them for all the mischief that they have done!" "Just what have they done to you?" "Sir," he replied, "I am old, and I cannot help myself, so worn out am I. Seven came on horseback, and with them fifteen others on foot. Because I could not get out of their way quickly enough, they did not spare me. They had their horses trample over me, and took little account of my protest." "Say no more," replied the knight "you shall be well avenged this very day." The knights and all the others rode off in such haste to pursue Fouke that they quickly left the abbey a full league behind them. Meanwhile, Sir Fouke was left there in peace to see what would happen next.

Sir Gyrard de Malfee soon arrived accompanied by ten well mounted knights. They had come from a distance and were riding horses of great value. Gyrard said mockingly, "Well, here is a fat and burly monk. He has a belly big enough to hold two gallons of cabbage." Fouke's brothers were still inside the gate, from where they could see and hear all of Fouke's proceedings. Without a word, Fouke raised his big staff and struck Sir Gyrard such a blow beneath the ear that he fell senseless to the ground. Fouke's brothers, when they saw this, immediately rushed out of the gate and subdued Sir Gyrard and the ten knights. After tying up their prisoners very tightly in the porter's lodge, they took all the harnesses and the good horses and rode off non-stop until they came to Higford [in Shropshire]. Once there, John's wounds were able to be healed at last.

During their stay at Higford a messenger arrived who had been seeking Sir Fouke for some time. He greeted him on behalf of Hubert, Archbishop of Canterbury. The Archbishop wanted to speak with Fouke as soon as possible. So Fouke led his men to a place near Canterbury, in the forest where he had been before. There he left all his company, except his brother William. The two dressed themselves like merchants and went into Canterbury to meet with the Archbishop, Hubert Walter.

"Gentlemen," said the Bishop, "you are very welcome. You no doubt know that Sir Thebaud le Botiler [Theobald Walter, Butler of Ireland], my brother, is now deceased. Before his death he married dame Matilda de Caus, a very rich lady, and the fairest in all England. King John himself desires her for her beauty, and it is with great difficulty that she guards herself from him. She is here in Canterbury under my protection, but you shall see her presently. My dear friend Fouke, it is with some urgency that I pray and command you to take her for your wife, with my blessing." Fouke soon met with the lady, seeing for himself how good, as well as beautiful she was, not to mention her excellent reputation. As for her possessions in Ireland, she had fortresses, cities, and lands, plus rents and great fiefs. So with the assent of his brother William and on the counsel of Archbishop Hubert, he married dame Matilda de Caus.

Fouke remained two days in Canterbury, and then bid his farewell. He left his new wife there in the care of the Archbishop before returning to join his companions again in the forest. When he told them all that he had done, they made fun of him, laughed at him, and called him "husband." They also asked him just where he would put the fair lady, in a castle or in the forest. Yet, while they often joked together in this way, they also did more serious mischief to the King everywhere the opportunity presented itself. But they did such to none other than the King, excepting those persons who were openly their enemies.

A knight named Robert Fitz-Sampson was residing in the march of Scotland. The knight frequently received Sir Fouke and his company, and he entertained them with great honor. He was a man of great wealth whose wife's name was dame Anable. She was a very courteous lady. At that time also there was a knight in the country named Pieres de Bruvyle. This Pieres was in the habit of gathering together all the gentlemen's sons of

699

the country who were addicted to thieving, along with ribalds. It was their custom to go through the country, killing and robbing decent people, merchants and others. Whenever this Pieres led his company out to rob people, he assumed the name of Fouke Fitz-Waryn. As a result, the real Fouke and his companions had acquired a very bad reputation for matters in which they were blameless.

Fouke's fear of King John was such that he dared not tarry too long in one place. So it was by night that he came into the march of Scotland, very near the court of Robert Fitz-Sampson. As he approached he saw a light within the court and could hear people talking. He heard his own name mentioned often in the conversations. After telling his companions to remain outside, Fouke himself boldly entered the courtyard from where he made his way into the great hall. Once inside he could see Pieres de Brubyle and some other knights sitting at supper. Robert Fitz-Sampson and his good lady and all their household were bound with ropes, laid out on the floor off to one side of the hall. Sir Pieres and his men were all wearing masks. Those who were serving the meal, when they knelt before Sir Pieres, called him their lord Sir Fouke. The lady, who lay bound near her husband in the hall, said very pitifully, "Oh, Sir Fouke, for God's sake have mercy. I never did you any harm, but have loved you as best I might."

To this point Sir Fouke had kept quiet, listening to everything that had been said. But when he heard the lady speak, she who had done him much kindness, he could bear it no longer. Alone, without any of his companions, he stepped forward with his sword drawn and said: "Silence! I order you, stay where you are. Let no one move hand or foot." And he swore that, if any one were so bold as to move, he would cut him into small pieces. Pieres and his companions felt trapped. "Now," said Fouke, "which of you here calls himself Fouke?" "Sir," said Pieres, "I am a knight; I am called Fouke." "Well, Sir Fouke," he shouted, "by God, you had better move quickly. Tie up all your companions tightly. If you do not, you shall be the first to lose your head." Pieres, terrified by the threat, got up and unbound the lord and the lady and all the others of the household. He then tied all his companions well and firmly. Next, Fouke made him cut off the heads of all those whom he had bound. After he had beheaded all his companions [Fouke said]: "You recreant knight, you who called yourself Fouke, you are a cowardly liar. I am Fouke, and you will now pay dearly for having falsely caused me to be charged with theft." Forthwith he cut off Pieres' head, after which he called his companions inside to join him in supper. All made themselves very comfortable. Thus did Sir Fouke save Sir Robert and all his treasure, so that nothing was lost.

Very often King John did great harm to Sir Fouke, but Sir Fouke was no less wise and crafty than he was strong and bold. The King and his people very frequently pursued Sir Fouke by tracking the footprints of his horses. Fouke countered on many occasions by having his horses shod with the shoes put on backwards. In that way the King was deceived in his pursuit. Sir Fouke was to suffer many a hard fight before he finally regained his inheritance.

Sir Fouke took leave of Sir Robert Fitz-Sampson and went to Alberbury where he set up camp in a forest near the river. Fouke called on John de Rampaigne, saying to him: "John, you know a lot about minstrelsy and juggling. Do you have the courage to go to Whittington and perform before Moris Fitz-Roger to discover just what they are up to?" John agreed to do it. He prepared himself by first crushing an herb and putting it into his mouth. As a result, his face began to swell so badly that it puffed out. His whole face became so discolored that his own companions scarcely knew him. John dressed himself in poor clothes, and he took his box with his juggling equipment and carried a great staff in his hand. When he arrived in Whittington he told the porter that he was a juggler. The porter brought him before Sir Moris Fitz-Roger, who asked him where he was born. "Sir," he replied, "in the march of Scotland." "And what news do you have from there?" "Sir, I know none, other than the recent death of Sir Fouke Fitz-Waryn. He was killed in a robbery which he was committing in the house of Sir Robert Fitz-Sampson." "Are you speaking the truth?" "Yes, certainly," he said, "people from all over the countryside say it is so." "Minstrel," said he, "I will give you this cup of pure silver for your news." The minstrel took the cup, and thanked Sir Moris for his generosity.

John de Rampaigne was very ugly of face and body, and consequently the scoundrels of the household mocked him. They treated him like a fool, and pulled him by his hair and his feet. He raised his staff and gave one of the scoundrels such a blow on the head that his brains flew into the middle of the room. "Wicked rascal," said the lord, "what have you done?" "Sir," said he, "by God's mercy, I cannot help myself. I have a malady which is very grievous, as you may judge by my face, which is so swollen. This malady takes entire possession of me for certain hours of the day every week. It is not within my own power to contain myself." Moris swore that were it not for the good news which John had brought him he would have him beheaded forthwith. The juggler thus hastened his departure, for he had no desire to tarry further. So he returned to see Fouke and described word for word what he had heard and done at the court in Whittington. One important item of news was the fact that Sir Moris, in his function as keeper of the march, was planning a trip. Along with fifteen knights and his entire household, he was to leave the very next day for the castle of Shrewsbury. Sir Fouke was delighted to learn this news, and so were his companions.

The next morning Fouke was up early. He and his men armed themselves well for the events to follow. Moris and his fifteen knights set out towards Shrewsbury. Also in the company were the four sons of Guy Fitz Candelou of Porkington [now Brogyntyn in Shropshire], and the rest of the household. When Fouke caught sight of his enemy, he was very pleased. At the same time, he was also much incensed, because Guy was unlawfully keeping his heritage from him by force. Moris looked off in the direction of Great Ness, where he quickly recognized the heraldic markings on a shield: quartered with gules and argent dancetté [a silver fesse (two horizontal lines defining the middle third) marked by three indentations]. By this coat of arms he immediately knew that it was Fouke. "Now I am certain," said Moris, "that jugglers are liars. For there stands Fouke, very much alive." Moris and his knights fought bravely. Boldly they attacked Fouke and his companions and called them thieves. They said that before evening many heads would be placed on the high tower of Shrewsbury. Fouke and his brothers defended themselves with such vigor, however, that Sir Moris, his fifteen knights, and the four sons of Guy Fitz-Candelou of Porkington were all quickly slain. Fouke had that many fewer enemies!

From there Fouke and his companions went towards Rhuddlan [in Flintshire] to speak to Sir Lewys [Llewelyn the Great, Prince of Gwynned 1199–1240], the Prince of Wales who had married Joan, the daughter of King Henry and the sister of King John.[1] The visit was prompted by the fact that Sir Lewys had been brought up together with Sir Fouke and his brothers in the court of King Henry. The Prince was very glad at the coming of Sir Fouke and asked him what agreement there was between the King and him. "Sir," said Fouke, "None, for I cannot have peace with the King no matter what I do. Sir I have, therefore, come to you and to your good lady to make peace with you." "Truly," said the Prince, "I grant and give you my peace, and you shall have a good reception from me. The King of England doesn't know how to have peace with you, or me, or any other." "Sir," said Fouke, "many thanks, for I trust much in you and in your great loyalty. But since you have granted me your peace, I must tell you something else. Moris Fitz-Roger is dead, for I have killed him." When the Prince learned that Moris was dead he became very angry. He exclaimed that had he not just given his peace to Fouke he would have had him drawn and hanged, for Moris was his cousin. At that moment Princess Joan stepped forward to confirm the peace made between her husband and Sir Fouke. They embraced each other and all ill-will was pardoned.

At this time there was great discord between Prince Lewys and Gwenwynwyn, son of Owen Cyfeiliog, to whom a great part of the country of Powys belonged. Gwenwynwyn was very proud, haughty, and fierce. He refused to submit himself to the Prince for any reason. Instead, he brought great destruction to his land. By force the Prince had totally beaten down the castle of Metheyn and had taken possession of Mochnant [in Montgomeryshire], Llannerch Hudol [in Montgomeryshire], and other lands which belonged to Gwenwynwyn. The Pince assigned Fouke to act as overseer of all his land holdings, commanding him further to attack Gwenwynwyn and destroy all his lands.

Fouke, however, was prudent and very wary, for he knew that the Pince was in the wrong. So he told him very courteously: "Sir, for God's sake, you should pardon

---

[1] See the Hathaway edition, note 22.9, for a discussion of these alliances.

Gwenwynwyn. If you do what you have planned, you will be much blamed in foreign countries by all people. And please do not be annoyed with me for what I am telling you. Everyone says, in fact, that you have sinned against him. Sir, for God's sake, therefore, have mercy on him. He will most surely reform himself in his dealings with you, and will serve you to your satisfaction. Do not lose sight of the fact that you don't know when you will need your barons." Fouke preached and talked to the Prince at length and so convinced him to change his strategy. Shortly thereafter, Lewys and Gwenwynwyn were reconciled with each other when the Prince gave back all the lands which he had previously taken.

King John was at Winchester when the news came to him that Fouke had killed Moris, Roger's son. He learned further that Fouke was staying with Prince Lewys, the husband of his [John's] own sister. His immediate reaction was a moment of thoughtful reflection. For a good while he did not utter a word. Then he shouted: "Hey! By Saint Mary, I am the King. I rule England. I am duke of Anjou and Normandy, and the whole of Ireland is under my lordship. Yet I cannot find a single man in all my jurisdiction who, no matter how much I offer to give, will avenge me for the damage and the disgrace which Fouke has done me. But you can be certain that I will not desist until I avenge myself upon this Prince." He then sent forth a summons to all his earls and barons and his other knights that they should on a certain day be at Shrewsbury with all their people.

When all those summoned got to Shrewsbury, Lewys was warned by his friends that King John was planning to wage war against him. At that he called Fouke and told him the bad news. Fouke in turn assembled thirty thousand trusted men at castle Bala in Pennlyn [in Merionethshire]. Gwenwynwyn, the son of Owen, also came with his troops, all strong and bold men. Fouke was a very crafty strategist in war and was familiar with the terrain over which King John must travel, including all the narrow passes. One in particular, called the ford of Gymele,[1] was a very tight passage. It was very narrow, enclosed with woods and marshes, so that the only way to pass was by the highway. Fouke and Gwenwynwyn, when they reached the ford with their troops, dug out beyond the highway a long, deep, and broad ditch. They filled the ditch with water, so that no one could pass, partly because of the marsh on one side, and partly because of the ditch. Beyond the ditch they built a well fortified palisade. To this day that ditch is still to be seen.

King John with his army finally reached the ford, which he expected to pass safely. Then he noticed just beyond it more than ten thousand armed knights, who were guarding the passage. Fouke and his companions had passed the ford by a hidden path that they had made and found themselves on the same side as the King. Gwenwynwyn and

---

[1] Fr. "le Gue Gymele." See Hathaway, note 35.9, for a discussion of this location.

many other knights were also with them. The King immediately recognized Fouke and ordered his knights to attack from all sides. Fouke and his companions defended themselves like lions. They were often knocked off their horses, but quickly remounted, killing many of the King's knights in the process. Gwenwynwyn, however, took a bad blow to his helmet and received a serious head wound. When Fouke saw that neither he nor his men could long remain on the outside of their ditch, they returned by their hidden path to defend their palisade and the ditch. From that position they were able to shoot crossbow bolts and light spears against the King's troops, killing many and wounding an immense number in that manner. This fierce struggle lasted till the evening. When the King saw so many of his people killed and wounded, he was so sorrowful that he did not know what to do. He finally returned to Shrewsbury.

As for King John's character, he was a man without conscience, wicked, cross, and hated by all good people. In addition he was lustful. Whenever he heard described any fair lady or damsel, he wished to have her at once, either to entrap her by promise or gift, or to ravish her by force. It mattered little whether she was the wife or daughter of an earl or a baron, or of any other for that matter. That was why he was the most hated. For this reason too many great lords of England had renounced their allegiance to the King, which in turn led to his being less feared by many.

John Lestrange, lord of Knokin and of Ruyton-of-the-Eleven-Towns [in Shropshire], remained faithful to the King and continued to bring harm to Prince Lewys and his people. For this reason the Prince had the castle of Ruyton overthrown. When King John learned that this entire garrison was captured and imprisoned, he was very upset. Soon thereafter, Prince Lewys summoned Sir Fouke to castle Bala for the purpose of restoring to him not only Whittington, his heritage, but also Ystrat Marchell [in Montgomeryshire] and Dinorben [in Denbighshire]. After first expressing his thanks to the Prince, Fouke went to Whittington with his own people and had the castle restored and thoroughly repaired.

John Lestrange came to the King and told him that Fouke had done great harm to his people by taking the castle of Ruyton. Since he was in very good standing with the King, he took the liberty to request royal troops in order to avenge himself upon Sir Fouke. To that end the King summoned Sir Henry de Audley [of Staffordshire], who was lord and first conqueror of the Red Castle. He commanded Sir Henry to take ten thousand knights, the most valiant of England, and ordered that the lord and his knights should be obedient to Sir John Lestrange in all matters. Sir Henry and Sir John and their knights set out for Whittington. Along their way, they slew whatever men and women they found and pillaged the countryside. A cry of panic was raised everywhere.

Fouke remained in Whittington, where he had assembled a large contingent of men to defend his newly acquired lands. The company included seven hundred Welsh knights and many foot soldiers. When the news came that Sir John and Sir Henry were coming towards Whittington, Sir Fouke and his men armed themselves forthwith, going secretly to Middle Pass. The moment Sir John saw Sir Fouke he spurred on his war horse with lance down. He gave Sir Fouke such a blow with his lance that it flew into splinters. Sir Fouke in turn repaid Sir John by a blow to the face that sliced through his helmet and knocked him to the ground. The scar left by this blow was to be visible for the rest of John's life. In an extraordinary act of valor, however, John quickly leaped up from the ground and cried out: "Now, my lords, all of you attack Fouke." Fouke proudly answered: "By all means, and here comes Fouke to meet you all." Then the knights from both camps struck out at each other. Fouke, Sir Thomas Corbet, and their other companions slew many; but, Alan the son of Waryn, and Philip his brother, were wounded. When Fouke saw his brothers wounded, he became so enraged that he slashed out at all around him. Whomsoever his sword hit had no chance to escape from death. Unfortunately, Sir Fouke's troops were vastly outnumbered. In the battle he had only seven hundred knights, while the others were ten thousand or more. Seeing that he could not win this skirmish, Fouke returned towards Whittington. In the press Sir Audulph de Bracy was knocked from his horse. Although he had boldly defended himself, at the last he was taken prisoner and carried off to Shrewsbury.

Sir Henry and Sir John were much delighted with the capture. They came to Shrewsbury before the king, where they delivered up Sir Audulph. The King argued heatedly with his prisoner, swearing boastfully that he would have him drawn and hanged, because he was both a traitor and a thief. He had killed his knights, burnt his cities, and overthrown his castles. Audulph in reply answered the King boldly, saying that neither he nor any of his kindred had ever been traitors.

Back in Whittington, Fouke saw first to the care of his brothers and his other troops. When their wounds had been cleaned and their injuries attended to, it came to his attention that Sir Audulph was missing. He searched everywhere, but when he realized Audulph was nowhere to be found he thought he would never see him again. No one ever expressed sorrow at the loss of a friend more movingly than did Sir Fouke on this occasion. At length John de Rampaygne, seeing the depth of Fouke's grief, came forward and said: "Sir, have done with this lamentation. If it please God, before tomorrow at prime, you shall have good news of Sir Audulph de Bracy. For I myself shall go to speak to the King."

John de Rampaygne was a fairly skillful musician and juggler. He could play the harp and vielle, as well as the psaltery. He dressed himself in fine clothes worthy of any earl or baron and stained his hair and the whole of his body jet black. In fact, there was nothing left white except his teeth. Around his neck he hung a beautiful tabor, before mounting a handsome palfrey. Once inside the town of Shrewsbury he rode through, as far as the gate of the castle and was stared at by many as he rode along. John presented himself to the King by kneeling before him and saluting very courteously. The King

705

saluted him in return and asked him whence he came.

"Sire," said he, "I am an Ethiopian minstrel, having been born in that country." In reply the King inquired further. "Are all the men of your land the same color as you?" "Yes, my lord, men and women alike." "What do they say of me in foreign realms?" "Sire," said he, "you are the most renowned King in the whole of Christendom. It is your great renown that explains my visit to your court." "Sir," said the King, "you are very welcome." John thanked him briefly, then added quietly that the King was renowned more for his wickedness than his goodness. Of course the King did not hear the last remark. So John spent the remainder of the day just playing his tabor and other instruments. When the King had gone to bed, Sir Henry de Audley sent for the black minstrel to be brought to his chamber. All present joined in the singing, and when Sir Henry had drunk a great deal he said he to a valet: "Go get Sir Audulph de Bracy, whom the King intends to put to death tomorrow. He shall at least have a pleasant night before his death." The valet quickly brought Sir Audulph into the chamber, where all were talking while the music continued. John began playing a song which Sir Audulph was accustomed to singing. Sir Audulph raised his head and looked the minstrel straight in the face. With some difficulty he finally recognized John. Then, when Sir Henry asked for drink, John obligingly leaped to his feet and served the cup to everyone in the room. John acted very cunningly, sprinkling a powder into the cup in such manner that no one perceived him. He was, after all, an excellent juggler. All those who drank became so drowsy that very soon afterward they lay down to go to sleep. When they were all asleep, John dragged one of the King's fools over and placed him between the two knights who had been assigned to guard the condemned prisoner. John and Sir Audulph then found some towels and sheets which were in the chamber, and escaped by a window facing the Severn River. They immediately headed towards Whittington, which was twelve leagues from Shrewsbury.

The matter could not long be hidden. Early the next morning, when he was told the details of the escape, the King was furious. That same morning Fouke had risen early, for he had slept little the preceding night. As he looked in the direction of Shrewsbury he saw Sir Audulph and John approaching. No need to ask whether he was glad when he saw them. He ran out to embrace and kiss them both. Sir Audulph told him all that John had done and how they escaped. Fouke, who until shortly before had been sad, rejoiced greatly at this good news.

Now let us return for a moment to speak of Fouke's wife, dame Matilda de Caus. When the King, who had lusted after Matilda, learned for certain that she was married to Sir Fouke, his enemy, by the counsel of Archbishop Hubert, he did great harm to both the Archbishop and the lady. He wished to have her carried off by violence, but she was able to find refuge in the church. There she gave birth to a daughter, Hawyse. who was later to become Lady of Wem. The Archbishop himself baptized the baby.

Fouke le Fitz Waryn

Somewhat later Fouke and his companions came to Canterbury under cover of night. From there they took his wife to Higford, where she remained for some time. It then came to pass that the lady was again with child. During this pregnancy she remained in hiding in Alberbury. She soon discovered, however, that she was under surveillance by the King's men, so she fled secretly to Shrewsbury. At that point, she was so big with child, that she could travel no farther. So she took refuge in the church of Our Lady at Shrewsbury, and there she gave birth to another daughter. At her baptism this baby was given the name Joan, and later in life she was married to Sir Henry de Pembridge. Subsequently, Matilda had still another child, this time a son. He was born in Wales, up in the mountains, and was baptized in a stream which flowed from the Maiden's Well [Fontaine des Puceles]. The mother and child were very weak, for the child was born two months before term. In their weakened condition both had to be carried down from the mountain to a farmhouse, nearby Carreg-y-nant ['stone by the stream' — a common Welsh name] . When the child was later healthy enough to be confirmed by the Bishop, he was called Fouke.[1]

When the King saw he could in no way avenge himself upon Fouke, nor disgrace or take his wife, he sent a letter to his own brother-in-law, Prince Lewys. In the letter he begged Lewys to remove from his household his mortal enemy, the felonious Sir Fouke. Should he comply, John promised in return that he would restore all the lands which the King's ancestors had ever taken from his lordship. The single condition was that he must deliver Sir Fouke's body. The Prince called his wife Joan into his chamber and showed her the letter which the King, her brother, had sent him. When the lady had heard the letter, she immediately sent a full report of it to Sir Fouke, thereby informing him that the King wished to come to terms with her husband. Fouke was distressed at this news and feared treason. His first reaction was to protect his wife, dame Matilda. In the company of Baldwin de Hodenet she was sent secretly to the Bishop of Canterbury. Following that mission, Baldwin was to meet him again at Dover.

Fouke and his four brothers, along with Audulph and John de Rampaygne, armed themselves fully and set out with all their men for Castle Bala to speak to Prince Lewys. Fouke said to him: "Sir, I have served you loyally to the best of my ability, but these days a man does not know whom to trust. For, on the mere promise made by the King, you wish to abandon me. I am all the more fearful, sir, since I know that the King has sent that promise in a letter which you have concealed from me." "Fouke," the Prince replied, "stay with me; for assuredly I plan to do you no treason." "Indeed, sir," said Fouke, "even though I can believe your word full well, I will not remain on any account." At that he and all of his companions took leave of the Prince. From Castle Bala he journeyed

---

[1] I have reversed the order of the last two sentences in this paragraph for the sake of clarity.

night and day until he arrived in Dover. There he met up with Baldwin, who had taken his wife Matilda to stay in safety with the Archbishop. They put to sea and arrived in France at Whitsuntide.

When they got near to Paris, Fouke and his men saw a tournament underway. King Philip of France had come into the fields to watch his French knights in action. Fouke himself was still disguised, as were his companions. When they saw such a fair assembly, they tarried to see the jousts. Noting the presence of some English knights, the Frenchmen exerted themselves much the more to do well. Then Sir Druz de Montbener, a very proud Frenchman, sent word to Sir Fouke asking that he come joust with him. Fouke immediately accepted the invitation. Fouke and his brothers armed themselves and mounted their war-horses. John de Rampaigne was richly attired, mounted on a fine charger. At the entrance to the tilting fields John gave a drum-beat on the tabor he was carrying. The tabor beat was so loud that the hills and the valleys resounded, causing the horses to caper. Then, when the King saw Sir Fouke in full battle dress, he said to Sir Druz de Montbener: "Take heed, sir, for it is quite obvious that this English knight is very valiant." "Sire," he replied, "there is not a knight in all the world whom I would not dare to take on man-to-man, either on horse or on foot." "May God be with you!" said the King.

Fouke and Sir Druz spurred their horses and engaged the combat. Fouke pierced his opponent's shield with his lance, which also sliced through the knight's hauberk and into his shoulder. The blow hit with such force that the lance flew into pieces. Sir Druz ended up flat on the ground. Fouke then led the riderless horse back to Sir Druz and offered it to him as a present. For Sir Fouke had no desire to keep the horse as a prize of battle. A second French knight immediately came forward ready to avenge Sir Druz. He struck such a blow with his lance that it went clear through Fouke's shield. Fouke struck back, hitting his attacker on the helmet with such a blow that his lance broke up into fragments. The knight also lost his balance and fell from his saddle. Fouke's brothers and companions stood ready to joust, but the King would not permit it. Instead, he spurred his horse in Fouke's direction. "English knight," he said, "a blessing upon you, for you have done exceedingly well." The King then graciously requested that Fouke remain with him. He was very thankful for the offer and consented to stay at the King's pleasure. Fouke had such grace that he was held to be the finest of knights and without peer. From that day forward the English knight was held in highest esteem by many in France and was praised everywhere he went for his courage, chivalry, and prowess.

Fouke remained for some time in France and was loved and honored by the King and Queen and all the gentry. When the King asked him what his name was, Fouke told him that he was called Amys del Boys. "Sir Amys," said the King, "do you know Fouke Fitz-Waryn, of whom so much good is spoken everywhere?" "Yes, sire, I have seen him quite often." "And what is his stature?" "Sire, in my opinion, he is about the same height as

I am." "That he may well be, for you are both valiant men." Fouke traveled all over France to jousts and tourneys. Everywhere he went he was praised, loved, and honored for his prowess.

The King of England finally learned that Fouke was residing with King Philip of France. He sent a letter to the King respectfully requesting that Sir Fouke Fitz-Waryn, his mortal enemy, be expelled from Philip's household. When the King of France heard the letter read, he swore by Saint Denys that no such knight was in his retinue. This was in effect the answer he sent back to the King of England. Sir Fouke in turn heard the news and went directly to see the King of France to announce his imminent departure. "Tell me what prompts your sudden decision," said the King. "I will make full amends for any failing on my part which might have occasioned your desire to leave me." Fouke replied simply: "Sire I have heard news that compels me to set out with all due haste." At these words the King understood immediately his real identity. "Sir Amys de Boys," said the King, "I believe that you are in fact Fouke Fitz-Waryn." "Yes, my lord, I am indeed." The King then pleaded: "Stay here with me, and I will give you richer lands than any you have ever had in England." "With due respect, my lord" he responded, "a man who cannot reasonably hold those which are his own by right heritage is unworthy to receive lands as a gift from someone else."

Fouke took leave of the King and headed toward the coast. As he approached he saw some ships afloat on the sea, but there was no wind in the direction of England, although the weather was fair. Fouke saw a mariner, who appeared to be bold and hardy. He called out to him: "Sir, is that your ship?" "Yes, indeed, sir," came the reply. When asked his name the mariner answered: "Sir, I am Mador of Mont de Russie, where I was born." "Mador," said Fouke, "how well have you mastered your trade? Are you able to take passengers by sea into various regions?" "Frankly sir, there is no known land within Christendom to which I do not know how to take a ship safely." "Assuredly," said Fouke, "yours is a very perilous trade. Tell me, brother Mador, of what death did your father die?" Mador answered that he had drowned at sea. "How did your grandfather go?" "In the same way." "How about your great-grandfather?" "In like manner, as did all my relations, to the fourth generation, as far as I know." "Truly," said Fouke, "it is very foolhardy of you to venture out to sea." "Why indeed, sir? Every creature shall have the death that is destined for him," said Mador. "Now then, if you please, answer my question. Where did your father die?" "In his bed, of course." "Where did your grandfather die?" "In the same place." "And your great-grandfather?" "Certainly, all of my lineage, as far as I know, died in their beds." "Assuredly, sir," said Mador, "since all your kindred have died in their beds, I am much astonished that you dare go near any bed." At that Fouke was forced to concede that the mariner had told him a simple truth. Every man shall have such a death as is appointed him; and he does not know whether it shall be on land or on sea.

Judging that Mador well understood the business of ships, he contracted with him to have a ship planned and built, and promised to meet all the expense involved. Mador agreed and the ship was made in a forest near the sea, according to the mariner's own specifications. All the ropes and other tackle with which Mador outfitted the vessel were of exceptional quality. It was an exceedingly well-provisioned ship.

Fouke, his brothers, and all his retinue put out to sea and drew near the coast of England. Mador saw a well-manned ship coming towards them. When the ships drew near each other a knight on board called out to Mador: "Mariner, who owns the ship which you are steering, and what is her provenance? For it is an unfamiliar vessel in these waters." "The ship is my very own, sir," said Mador. "'By my faith!" the knight retorted, "In no way is that so. You are thieves, and I know it by the quartered sail, which bears the arms of Fouke Fitz-Waryn. He must be on board the ship, and this very day I will deliver his body up to King John." "Well indeed," said Fouke, "you will do no such thing. Should you, however, want some of our provisions, you are welcome to them gladly." "I prefer instead to take all of you," he said, "and whatever belongs to you, with or without your consent." "On that account you are sadly mistaken," said Fouke. Mador, who was an excellent mariner, let out his sails and steered his ship directly into the path of the other vessel. He cut the other ship cleanly in two, so that the sea poured into its hold. Fouke and his companions immediately boarded the ship after it was struck. They plundered the contents, including all the food, and carried the booty back onto their own ship. The enemy vessel was destroyed, but many a hard blow was struck first. The other ship then disintegrated and sank to the bottom.

For an entire year Fouke continued sailing just off the coast of England. He sought to bring harm to no one other than to King John. On many occasions he seized the King's property and whatever else of his he could find. Finally, the ship set sail for Scotland, but a strong west wind forced them to continue on for three additional days' journey, well beyond their intended destination. A very beautiful island appeared in the distance, and as they drew near it they found a good port. Fouke and his four brothers, along with Audulph and Baldwin, went ashore to see the country and find food for their ship. Their first encounter was with a young shepherd, who came forward to greet them in very bad Latin. Fouke asked him if he knew whether there might be any provisions for sale in the country. "Truly sir, none at all," he said. "For this is an island inhabited by very few people, and those who do reside here live only off their animals. But if you will please come with me, such food as I have, I am willing to share with you." Fouke thanked the lad and followed along as he led them down into an underground cavern, which was very beautiful. The shepherd asked them to be seated and otherwise received them graciously. He then told them he had a servant on a nearby hill. "Please, do not be annoyed," he said, "if I blow my horn to summon him. That way we will be able to dine more quickly." "Please do so, in God's name!" said Fouke. The young man went outside the cavern and blew six blasts before returning into the cavern.

Forthwith six tall and fierce peasants arrived, dressed in coarse and dirty tabards. Each one was carrying a strong, hard club. When Fouke saw them he immediately suspected mischief. The six peasants went into a chamber, took off their dirty tabards and replaced them with much richer cloth of a fine green color. Their shoes were ornamented with gold, and in all their attire they were as richly dressed as any King might be. Returning to the hall, all six respectfully greeted Sir Fouke and his companions. Their first request was that rich chessboards with pieces made of fine gold and silver be brought to them. The guests were all invited to play. Sir William played a game, but he lost it immediately. Sir John played another, and in no time he too lost. Philip, Alan, Baldwin, and Audulph, one after the other played, and each in turn lost the game. Then one of the haughtiest shepherds said to Fouke, "Will you play?" "No," he answered. "Indeed, sir," said the shepherd, "you shall either play chess or you will have to wrestle with me. You have no other choice." "By my faith," said Fouke, "you are a villainous shepherd and a liar. Since I am forced either to wrestle or play chess despite myself, I choose instead to play the game I know best." So he leaped up, drew his sword, and struck such a blow that the shepherd's head flew into the middle of the room. A second, then a third one met a similar fate. Fouke and his companions ended up killing all those peasant scoundrels.

Fouke then entered a chamber where he found an old woman sitting. She was holding a horn which she tried repeatedly to put up to her mouth, but she had not the strength to blow it. When she saw Fouke she begged for mercy. He asked her of what use the horn might be if she could blow it. The old woman answered that if the horn were blown, help would come immediately. Fouke took the horn from her and went into another chamber. There he found seven beautiful damsels, dressed very richly, who were doing fine hand work. When they saw Fouke they threw themselves on their knees and cried for mercy from him. Fouke asked them where they were from, and one of them said: "Sir, I am the daughter of Aunflor of Orkney. My father is resident in one of his castles in Orkney, called Castle Bagot, which is in a very beautiful forest near the sea. One day I and my maidens, with four knights among others, took a boat and went for a pleasure ride on the sea near my father's castle. As we were sailing, the seven sons of the old woman, whom you just saw with her horn, attacked us from a well-manned ship. They killed all our people and brought the survivors here. Against our consent they have repeatedly ravished our bodies, and heaven is our witness! Wherefore we pray, in the name of the God in whom you believe, to save us from this misery. Please, help us to escape from here, if you can. Judging by your appearance, I perceive that you are not from this country." Fouke comforted the damsels, assuring them that he would help them to the best of his ability.

During their search for provisions Fouke and his men also found great treasure, including armor. Fouke kept for himself a rich haubergeon which he came to love so much that he often wore it secretly. During the rest of his life he would neither give it away nor sell it at any price.

Fouke first provisioned his ship liberally and placed the damsels on board, comforting them as best he could. Then he commanded all his men to arm themselves quickly. When all were ready, Fouke sounded the little horn that he had taken from the old woman. More than two hundred robbers from all over the countryside came running through the fields. There were no other inhabitants on the whole island except robbers and thieves. They lived there as pirates venturing forth from their haven to kill whomsoever they could reach upon the sea. Although they defended themselves vigorously Fouke and his company immediately fell upon these robbers and killed more than two hundred of them.

[Fouke travels to the Orkneys to return the damsels to their homes. He then sails to the seven islands of the ocean, including Ireland, Gotland, Norway, Denmark, and Sweden, where none dwell but horned serpents and venemous beasts with mastif heads, driven from Ireland by St. Patrick. Caught in a tempest, he's driven through ice-filled waters to Carthage, where Fouke rescues a duke's daughter from a dragon. The duke offers the daughter in marriage, a gift which Fouke would gladly have received were he not already married and a Christian (Hathaway, p. 45, line 7, to p. 48, line 34.)]

Fouke and his companions at last sailed towards England. When they came to Dover they went inland, but first making certain that Mador remained with the ship at a safe location where they could find him whenever they might need him again.

Fouke and his companions had learned from the peasants that King John was presently at Windsor, so they made their way secretly in that direction. During the day they slept and rested themselves, while during the night they went on until they came to the forest. Since they were already very familiar with the area, they easily found a place to hide, for Fouke knew well every part of Windsor Forest. When they heard a horn sounding, Fouke and his companions armed themselves for a skirmish, for they realized immediately that the King's hunters and beaters were getting ready for a hunt. Fouke swore an oath that fear of death would not deter him from taking revenge on the King, who by force had wrongfully disinherited him. He would thus challenge the King to restore his rights and his heritage. Fouke decided to act on his own, so he told his companions to remain where they were. Having said this, he set out alone to seek adventure.

Fouke's first encounter was with an old charcoal-burner carrying a shovel, dressed all in black, as becomes a collier. Fouke kindly asked him to give him his clothes and his shovel. "Willingly, sir," he said. In exchange, Fouke gave him ten besants [Byzantine gold coins], and asked him to tell this to no one. The charcoal-burner went his way; Fouke stayed there and immediately put on the clothes which the collier had given him. He then saw to his coals and began to stir the fire. There was a large iron fork that he used to arrange the logs on one side and the other.

Fouke le Fitz Waryn

King John soon arrived on foot accompanied by three knights and saw Fouke tending the fire. Fouke immediately recognized the King; and, throwing down his fork, saluted his lord by falling humbly to his knees before him. The King and his three knights laughed and made great sport over the politeness and demeanor of the charcoal burner. After standing there for a long time, the King said: "My good peasant, have you seen a stag or doe pass this way?" "Yes, my lord, some time ago." "What kind of an animal did you see?" "One with long horns, my lord." "Where is it now?" "Sire, I can very easily lead you where I saw it, but I ask your permission to allow me to take my fork. For if it were stolen it would be a great loss to me?" "Yes, peasant, if you like, go on and we will follow you."

Carrying his big iron fork, Fouke conducted the King to an excellent place from which to shoot. The King was a very good bowman. "My lord," said Fouke, "would you like me to go into the thicket and direct the animal to come this way?" "Yes, indeed," said the King. Fouke leaped into the thick of the forest, and summoned his band hastily to take King John. "Be quick, for I have led him here with only three knights. Come while all of his retinue is still on the other side of the forest." Fouke and his band rushed out of the thicket and quickly captured the King. "Now, sire," said Fouke, "I have you at last in my power. Shall I pass such a sentence upon you as you would upon me if you had taken me?" The King trembled in fear, for he greatly dreaded Fouke. Fouke swore that he should die for the great damage and the disinheritance that he had inflicted upon him and upon many a good man in England. The King cried for mercy, and in God's name, begged for his life. He promised that he would restore to Fouke his entire inheritance and whatsoever he had taken from him and all his friends. Moreover, he would grant him his friendship and peace for ever. To that end, John pledged to abide by whatever guarantees of security Fouke himself might decide appropriate. Fouke accepted the King's offer on one condition. In the presence of all the knights here present, he would have to give his solemn word to keep this covenant. The King pledged solemnly that he would keep faith with Fouke. He was overjoyed to be able thus to escape so easily.

Upon his return to the palace, King John assembled his knights and his retinue and told them in detail how Sir Fouke had deceived him. Since his solemn oath was made under duress, he had no intention whatever to keep it. He therefore commanded all to arm themselves in haste and capture these felons while they were still in Windsor Forest. Sir James of Normandy, who was the King's cousin, requested that he be placed in the vanguard. He claimed that the English, at least all the nobles, were cousins to Sir Fouke, hence they were most probably traitors to the King and would not help take these felons. Randolph, the Earl of Chester, protested vehemently. "In faith, sir, with due respect to the King, but not to you, that is a bold lie." He would have punched him in the face, had the Earl Marshal not restrained him. He claimed that they were not now nor ever had been traitors to the King or to anyone else. Furthermore, he reminded Sir James firmly that many nobles here present, including the King himself, were cousins to Sir Fouke. The Earl Marshal interrupted, saying: "Let us go after Sir Fouke. Then the King will see for himself who might be holding back for reasons of family ties." Sir James of Normandy and his fifteen knights armed themselves splendidly all in white armor and nobly mounted on white steeds. This nobleman hastened forward with his company in quest of fame.

John de Rampaigne had overheard all these proceedings and reported them back to Sir Fouke, who concluded that there was no means of escape open to him other than to fight. Sir Fouke and his companions thus armed themselves well and boldly took on Sir James in battle. They defended themselves vigorously and killed all their opponents except four, who were seriously wounded. Sir James himself was taken prisoner. Sir Fouke and his men immediately put on the arms of Sir James and the other Normans. They also mounted the healthier white horses, for their own horses were tired and lean. Tying his mouth so that he could not speak, they dressed Sir James in the arms of Sir Fouke, including the helmet. and rode towards the King. When the King saw them approaching he immediately recognized them by the arms. He believed that Sir James and his men were bringing back Sir Fouke.

Sir James was delivered to the King, with the prisoner being identified as Sir Fouke. At this news, both the Earl of Chester and the Earl Marshal were deeply saddened. Assuming that he was in fact addressing Sir James, the King presently commanded him to kiss him. Sir Fouke replied that, because he was in such haste to follow the other Fitz-Waryns, he had not time enough even to take off his helmet. So the King dismounted from his good horse and ordered James (i.e., Fouke) to mount it, for it was a swifter one for pursuing his enemies. Sir Fouke got down from his own horse and mounted the King's steed. When he finally rejoined his companions, they all fled to a spot some six leagues farther away. Safe at last, they disarmed themselves in a thicket and tended to their injuries. They bound up the wounds of William Fitz-Waryn, whom they considered as dead, for he had been severely wounded by one of the Normans. All his companions shared Fouke's deep grief over his brother's fate.

Meanwhile, the King proceeded to order that Sir Fouke be hanged. Sir Emery de Pyn, a Gascon who was a relative of Sir James, stepped forward and said that he would see to the hanging himself. He took charge of the prisoner and, leading him off a short distance, made him take off his helmet. He saw immediately that it was not Fouke. With his mouth unbound, Sir James was at last able to explain what had happened. Emery brought Sir James back to the King and reported what Sir Fouke had done. When the King realized that he had been thus deceived he was furious. He swore an oath that he would stay armed in his hauberk until such time as he had taken these traitors. Fouke knew nothing of the King's oath.

The King and his nobles pursued Fouke's band by following the tracks left by their horses until they reached the wood where Fouke was hiding. When Fouke saw them coming, he stood disconsolate, lamenting for his wounded brother, William. He felt that all was lost. William begged them to cut off his head and take it with them. That way, when the King arrived, he would not be able to identify William's body. Fouke refused the request. With warm tears streaming down his face, he prayed for God's mercy and help. No one has ever seen greater sorrow than that shared between these two brothers.

Randolph, the Earl of Chester, led the assault. Upon seeing the Fitz-Waryns, he commanded his troops to halt. He went on alone to beg Fouke, for the love of God, to surrender himself to the King. If he did so, Randolph gave his word of guarantee for safe passage, assuring him further that he would be reconciled with the King. Fouke replied that he could not do so for all the gold in the world. "My dear cousin," said Fouke, "for the love of God I beg your help for my brother lying here near death. Promise me that after he dies you will make certain that his body is buried, so that wild beasts do not devour it. Please do likewise for the rest of us when we too are dead. For now, go back to your lord the King, and do his service without hesitation or regard for us who are related to you by blood. We will stay to face the destiny which awaits us here." Very sadly, the earl returned to join his companions. Fouke remained there weeping greatly, out of pity for his brother, whom of necessity he would be compelled to leave there to die. He could do little more than pray that God come to their aid.

The earl ordered the assault, and his men attacked in full force. Randolph himself fell upon Sir Fouke, but lost his horse in the attack, during which most of his retinue was killed. Fouke and his brothers defended themselves doggedly. Sir Berard de Blois came up behind Fouke and struck him with his sword on the side, thinking that he had killed him. Fouke, however, turned on his assailant and struck back, hitting him on the left shoulder with his sword grasped in both hands. Cut through to the heart and lungs, Berard fell dead from his horse. Fouke had bled so much, however, that he slid down upon the neck of his horse, and the sword fell from his hand. Saddened by this turn of events, the Fitz-Waryns rushed to the aid of their wounded brother. John leaped behind Fouke on the horse and held him up so that he could not fall. They all then took to flight, for their forces were overwhelmed. The King and his men rode in pursuit, but were unable to overtake them. All that night they went on thus, till in the morning they came to the spot on the coast where they had left Mador the mariner. When Fouke revived, he asked where he was and whether he had been taken prisoner. His brothers comforted him as best they could, and put him to bed in the ship. John de Rampaigne tended his wounds.

After the fighting, the Earl of Chester looked out on the field of battle. He saw that he had lost many of his own people, but he also remembered Fouke's earlier request. So, when he came upon William Fitz-Waryn nearly dead, he had the body sent to a nearby abbey to be nursed. At length William was discovered there. Forthwith the King had him transported in a litter to Windsor Castle, where he was promptly thrown into a dungeon.

715

King John was exceedingly angry with the Earl of Chester for having concealed his charitable action. "Fouke too is mortally wounded," said the King, "but at least I have one of his family here now. The other Fitz-Waryns will be my prisoners too before they know it. To be sure, pride is at the heart of the matter, for had not it been for his excessive pride Fouke would still be alive. While he lived, there was no better knight in the whole world, hence his death is an even greater loss."

In the sea near the coast of Spain there is an island called Beteloye. It is closed in with high rocks, and there is only one entrance. Neither man nor beast dwells on this island, which measures half a league in length and an equal distance in breadth. On the seventh day of their voyage Fouke and his companions arrived at this island. Fouke was at last able to find rest. For the six days of the sea voyage he had been unable to sleep. While his brothers and the others went off to explore the land, he himself remained alone asleep on the ship. Suddenly, a terrible wind came up and broke the cords of the ship, even though it was firmly anchored to a rock. The ship was carried out onto the high sea. When Fouke finally awoke he saw the stars in the night sky. He called his brother John and his other companions, but no one answered. Slowly he became aware that he was alone on the sea and began to curse his cruel destiny. As he wept for his lost brothers, sleep overcame him at last. Soon afterwards his ship arrived in the land of Barbary at the city of Tunis.

At that time Messobrin was the King of Barbary. In the company of four other Kings and six emirs, who were all Saracens, he was standing in a tower overlooking the sea. When he saw this amazing galley approaching his land, the King ordered two soldiers to go and see what it was. The soldiers boarded the ship, finding nothing except one knight asleep. One of them kicked Fouke and ordered him to awake. The frightened knight leaped up and struck the soldier such a blow with his fist that he fell overboard into the sea. The other one fled to report to the King what had happened. A hundred knights were promptly dispatched by the King to take this ship and bring the knight to him. Well armed, the hundred knights surrounded the ship and assailed it from all sides. Fouke, even though badly outnumbered, defended himself bravely, but at last was forced to surrender. This, however, he did under very favorable conditions. For, when he was brought to the palace, Fouke was taken to one of the royal chambers. There, by order of the King, he was to be well attended.

Isorie, the King's sister, was a very beautiful and gentle damsel. She often came to visit Fouke and bring him comfort, because she had noticed that he had a bad wound in his side. She graciously asked him to tell her his name and where he was from, as well as how he had come to be wounded. He told her his name was Maryn le Perdu [Lost Sailor] of France. He was deeply in love with the daughter of an earl in his home country. The lady seemed to return his affection, but she apparently loved another even more. "And it happened that one day she and I met for an amorous tryst. As she was holding me in her arms very closely, the other man whom she loved more arrived. He struck me with his sword here, in my side, and put me onto a galley for dead. The ship set out to sea and brought me to these parts." "This damsel was certainly not very courteous," Isorie remarked, as she picked up a richly ornamented harp. Her songs and melodies were her way of bringing solace to this handsome knight, whom she could see was of truly courtly bearing.

Fouke asked lovely Isorie what was all the commotion before the King in the great hall. "I will tell you, indeed," she said. "In the province of Murcia in Iberia there lived a nobleman, the Duke of Cartagena, who had a very beautiful daughter, Ydoyne. While her father was alive, she dwelt with him in his castle in Cartagena. One day a dragon came and carried her to a high mountain in the sea. There he kept her for more than seven years, until a knight of England, called Fouke the son of Waryn de Metz [Mees], came to the mountain and slew the dragon, thereby restoring the maiden to her father. Shortly afterwards the duke died and his daughter ruled over the duchy. My brother, the King of Barbary, sent messengers to her, offering to take her as his wife, but she refused him. Feeling shame at the refusal, the King reacted by assembling an army which destroyed Ydoyne's cities and overthrew her castles. The damsel fled abroad to seek reinforcements. She has now returned with her own large contingent of troops and has begun fiercely to wage war upon my brother. To end this struggle she proposes rules of battle whereby two champions, to be chosen from the two armies now set against each other, will square off against one another. If her chosen knight is conquered, she accepts to give up her duchy and go with Messobrin to Barbary. If ours is beaten, however, my brother the King must entirely restore to her all the land he has taken.

That was the context of the deliberations you overheard earlier today in the great hall, upon the arrival of some messengers sent by Ydoyne. Would that it pleased the God Mahomet that you were such a one as dared undertake the battle on the part of my brother the King! For you would earn great honor in doing so." "My lady, I am greatly indebted to my lord the King, and especially to you; but I could never undertake battle for a Saracen against Christians. I would rather die first. But if the King would renounce his law, be baptized and become a Christian, on such conditions I would, however, accept to undertake the battle as his champion. If I succeed, this land and its people will be saved. The King will, moreover, finally have this damsel of whom you have spoken." Isorie ran immediately to report to her brother Messobrin, the King of Barbary, all that Fouke, who called himself Maryn le Perdu of France, had told her. The King accepted the generous offer unconditionally, promising to follow any orders Fouke might give, if he could but accomplish all that he had promised!

The day of the battle was appointed. The King and his emirs, along with the Berbers and all his other people, came forward, very well armed to face Ydoyne and her troops. Sir Fouke had been provided with rich arms, and Isorie herself graciously attended him.

717

When all was ready, the King put forward his champion knight (Fouke) to do battle, and the duchess put forward hers. The two bold knights spurred on their horses and exchanged lance blows such that the splinters flew all over the field. Then they drew their swords and had go at each other bravely. Fouke struck his opponent's horse such a blow that it fell dead, although he would have preferred to hit the knight instead. When the knight hit the ground he shouted: "Wicked heathen, evil Saracen of pagan faith, may the God of Heaven curse you. Why have you killed my horse?" Fouke dismounted, and the two knights continued their fierce combat well into the evening.

At last the knight asked Fouke: "You, sir, may be a pagan, yet you are strong and noble. Please tell me where you were born." "If you want to know my country of birth I will not tell you, unless you tell me first about yours. Only then will I reply to your question." The knight said that he was a Christian born in England, the son of Waryn de Metz. His name was Philip the Red. He recounted his whole life and that of his brothers in great detail, telling how the duchess had come in a ship to the island of Beteloye and had rescued them. They had been stranded on that island half a year or more. Almost to the point of starvation, they were even forced to eat their own horses. "And when the countess saw us, she knew immediately who we were, and provided us with all the food we needed. She told us that she had just come from England, where she had gone in search of us to help her carry on her war against the King of Barbary. So, there you have a full account of the hard life we have led." At that point Fouke interrupted: "Dear brother, Philip the Red, do not you know me? I am your brother Fouke." "You, sir, are a Saracen; you cannot be my brother. You are trying to deceive me; by God you shall not do so!" Then Fouke showed him something, saying: "Here is a sign." Philip recognized it at once. There was great joy all around, and the battle was adjourned till the following day. Philip explained to the duchess that it was his brother Fouke with whom he had been fighting. Then Fouke, Philip, and their other brothers took counsel with Messobrin. He and all his household were baptized, and the King married the duchess with great honor.

Fouke, his brothers and their men stayed for some time with the King in order to make proper preparations for their return voyage to England. The King gave them gold, silver, horses, arms, and all the luxury goods which they might desire. They filled their ship with such riches that it was a wonder to behold. When they arrived secretly in England, Fouke arranged to have John de Rampaigne go disguised as a merchant to locate King John and find out whether his brother William were alive or not. John dressed himself in the clothes of a rich merchant and went to London. There he made the acquaintance of the mayor and all his household. He gave them such rich gifts that he was even invited to live in the mayor's house, where he was attended to as a wealthy guest. Taking advantage of this privileged status, John asked the mayor to arrange an audience with the King so that he might seek royal favor in allowing his ship's cargo to be unloaded in England. Although he spoke bad Latin, the mayor understood him very well.

Fouke le Fitz Waryn

So the mayor brought the merchant before King John at Westminster. He greeted the King very courteously in his own language. The King understood his words and asked him who he was and his country of origin. "Sire, I am a merchant from Greece. I have been in Babylon [i.e., the medieval city of Old Cairo], Alexandria, and Greater India. I have a ship laden with heavy merchandise, including rich cloths, jewels, horses, and other valuables, which might be of great value in your realm." "It is my pleasure," said the King, "that you and your people should be free to land in my country. I grant you my surety." The merchant, together with the mayor, was invited to remain and eat at the King's table.

Two sergeants-at-mace soon entered, bringing into the hall a tall knight with a long black beard and poorly clothed. They led him to the middle of the room and gave him some food. When the merchant asked the mayor who this was, he was told that it was a knight named Sir William Fitz Waryn, and was given the poor man's full story and that of his brothers. Upon hearing the man's name, John was overjoyed to see him still alive, yet very troubled at heart by the poor man's wretched condition. As soon as it was feasible for him, the merchant hastened to Sir Fouke to report on William's plight. Later he had his ship brought as near to the city as he could.

The following day the merchant took a palfrey, the like of which there was none so handsome in all the kingdom, and presented it to King John, who gladly received this gift so marvelous for its beauty. In fact, the merchant gave so liberally that he won his way into everyone's graces. As a result, he was allowed to do whatever pleased him at the King's court.

One day John went to the court at Westminster accompanied by his men, who had first put on sailors' tunics and armed themselves well. After they were nobly received, they noticed William Fitz Waryn being led by his keepers to the prison. The merchant and his companions took William by force from the guards and carried him toward their boat, which was moored very near the palace. The keepers immediately sounded the alarm and followed in pursuit. But the merchants were well armed and defended themselves bravely. They escaped to their galley, placed William on board, and headed out to sea. No need to ask whether Fouke was delighted to see his brother William and John de Rampaigne, still dressed in his merchant garb. The brothers embraced, and each one told the other a tale of adventures and misfortunes. When the King heard that he had been deceived by the merchant, he thought himself ill used.

Fouke and his companions arrived in Brittany, where they remained with relatives more than six months. At last he made up his mind that nothing would deter him from returning to England. When he got to England, he went straight to New Forest [in Hampshire], where he had often spent time. There he met the King, who was hunting a wild boar. Fouke and his men captured him, along with six of his knights, and brought them back to their galley. The King and all his followers were very frightened by all this.

Many heated words were exchanged, but at length the King pardoned them his ill will, and restored all their inheritance. He also promised them that he would proclaim a truce through all England. As a token of good faith that he would indeed fulfill his promise, he left his six knights as hostages until the peace could be proclaimed.

The King returned forthwith to Westminster, where he assembled earls, barons, and the clergy, and told them openly that he had willingly granted his peace to Fouke Fitz Waryn and his brothers, and to all their followers. He ordered that henceforth the Fitz Waryns should be honorably received throughout the realm, since he had decided to grant them once again their entire heritage.

Hubert the Archbishop was delighted at this news. He promptly sent letters to Fouke, to the Earl of Gloucester, to Randolph Earl of Chester, and to Hugh Bigod, Earl Marshal, to come immediately to Canterbury. When they were all assembled, it was appointed that Fouke and his companions should surrender themselves to the King in London.

Fouke with his brothers and the three earls, along with all their forces, equipped themselves as richly as they could and set out for London in noble apparel. They knelt before the King at Westminster, and surrendered themselves to him, upon which the King returned to them all their rightful possessions in England. They were given a royal reception and were invited by the King to stay awhile with him at court, which they did for an entire month.

Then Fouke took his leave and went for a visit with the Earl Marshal, who surrendered to him Ashdown and Wantage in Berkshire and other lands as well. Fouke and his brothers put on full armor and next went to Abingdon [in Oxfordshire], where they removed whatever they could find. These possessions were then taken on to Wantage, which was later to become a market town. The fair that Fouke set up in the town has been held there ever since.

Fouke took leave of the Earl Marshal and went to see Earl Randolph of Chester, who was assembling an army to go to Ireland to defend his rights there. When they got there a great troop of their enemies was waiting for them. The earl commanded his men to take up their arms. Fouke himself set off with three young brothers whom the earl had brought with him. The three young men were of great valor and strength, well armed and mounted on fine horses. Among the enemies facing them stood a hideous giant. He was well armed, black and horrible, twelve feet taller than any other. The giant stepped forward and shouted out: "Earl of Chester, send me the most valiant knight whom you have, to defend your rights." The three youths heard the shout and rushed to engage the giant. He killed them swiftly, one after the other, with the hatchet which he was wielding.

Then Fouke charged forward on his steed and tried to pierce him with his lance; but the giant dodged the blow, striking Fouke instead, such that he almost disabled him. Fearful now, Fouke became very cautious, until he was finally able to smite his opponent through the body with his lance. As he was falling down, the giant struck Fouke's horse, severing its two legs. Fouke himself fell to the ground, but quickly leaped up again. He drew his sword and cut off his enemy's head. After the battle, Fouke was later to take this giant's hatchet to his castle at Whittington. For now he helped the Earl of Chester in his conquest of all these lands and castles in Ireland. Sir Randolph stayed long enough in that country to restore his lands, after which he returned to England.

At long last Fouke came to his stronghold at Whittington, the beautiful castle he had built on marshy ground. There once again he found Matilda, his wife, and his children, who greeted him with great joy. Fouke proceeded to have all his treasures brought to Whittington. He gave lands and horses to his servants and friends very liberally, and maintained his land in great honor.

Fouke reflected on the fact that he had sinned greatly against God by killing many men, not to mention his other great misdeeds. So, in order to gain remission for his sins, he founded a priory in honor of Our Lady, of the order of Saint Mary of Grandmont, near Alberbury, in a forest on the River Severn. It is called the New Abbey [Alberbury Priory]. Shortly thereafter, Fouke's wife, Dame Matilda de Caus, died and was buried in this priory. A good while after the death of this lady, Fouke married another very noble woman, Dame Clarice d'Auberville. Both of his wives bore him fair and healthy children.

Fouke's reputation for prowess and goodness was such that his children benefitted greatly from their father's renown. The hand of his daughter Eve, for one, was granted upon formal request of the Prince of Wales [Llewelyn the Great]. She was married with great honor and solemnity to the Prince after the death of his first wife, Dame Joan, who was herself the daughter of King Henry of England. But Llewelyn lived only a year and a half after the wedding. He died and was buried at the Cistercian abbey of Conway [Caernarvonshire]. Eve, who had no children from Llewelyn, was afterwards married to a worthy knight, the Lord of Blancmostiers [either Oswestry or Whitchurch in Shropshire].

One night Fouke and his wife, Dame Clarice, were lying in bed in their chamber. The lady was asleep, but Fouke kept awake reflecting upon his youth, and he repented deeply in his heart for his misdeeds. Suddenly, he saw a wonderful brightness in the room. He wondered what it could be. Then he heard a thundering voice in the air say to him: "God has granted to you, His vassal, a penance which is of greater worth to you here than elsewhere." At these words the lady awoke and saw the great brightness. She covered her face for fear. Then this brightness vanished, after which Fouke never saw anything again. He was to remain blind for the rest of his life.

This Fouke was a good and generous host. He had the path of the royal road changed so that it passed nearby the hall at his manor in Alveston. That way, no stranger should travel by without being offered food, lodging, or other honors which were his to give. Merlin says that:

Other Outlaw Tales in Prose Translation

In Great Britain
A wolf shall come from the Blaunche Launde [i.e., Whittington];
Twelve sharp teeth shall he have,
Six below and six above.
He shall have such a fierce look,
Such strength and power,
That he shall chase the Leopard
From the Blaunche Launde.

But now we know that Merlin
Said this about Fouke Fitz Waryn;
For each of you must know well
That in the time of King Arthur
The place called Blaunche Launde
Is now named Whittington [Blauncheville].

For in this country was located the beautiful chapel of
Saint Augustine [of Canterbury],
Where Cahuz the son of Yvain dreamed
That he stole the candlestick,
And that he met a man
Who wounded him with a knife,
And wounded him in the side.
While asleep Cahuz cried so loud
That King Arthur heard him.
And when Cahuz awoke from his sleep
He put his hand to his side;
There he found the knife
Which [in his dream] had wounded him.

This is all recounted in the Grail story,
The book of the Holy Vessel.
We also learn therein how King Arthur
Recovered his health and his valor,
When he had lost all
His chivalry and his power.

From this very country came the wolf,
As the sage Merlin said,
And by his shield
We have known the twelve sharp teeth.

Fouke le Fitz Waryn

He bore a shield dancetté,
As the heralds have devised:
On the shield there are twelve teeth
Of gules and of argent.
It is well understood that King John
May be known as the Leopard,
For he bore on his shield
Leopards of beaten gold.

Fouke remained blind for seven years, suffering his penance gladly. Dame Clarice died and was buried at the New Abbey. After her death Fouke lived only one more year. He died at Whittington, and he too was buried with great honor at the New Abbey. His body lies near the altar. May God have mercy on his soul!

And may God have mercy upon all, the living and the dead! AMEN.

Volumes in the Middle English Texts Series

The Floure and the Leafe, *The Assembly of Ladies*, and *The Isle of Ladies*, ed. Derek Pearsall (1990)

Three Middle English Charlemagne Romances, ed. Alan Lupack (1990)

Six Ecclesiastical Satires, ed. James M. Dean (1991)

Heroic Women from the Old Testament in Middle English Verse, ed. Russell A. Peck (1991)

The Canterbury Tales: Fifteenth-Century Continuations and Additions, ed. John M. Bowers (1992)

Gavin Douglas, *The Palis of Honoure*, ed. David Parkinson (1992)

Wynnere and Wastoure and The Parlement of the Thre Ages, ed. Warren Ginsberg (1992)

The Shewings of Julian of Norwich, ed. Georgia Ronan Crampton (1993)

King Arthur's Death: The Middle English Stanzaic Morte Arthur and Alliterative Morte Arthure, ed. Larry D. Benson and Edward E. Foster (1994)

Lancelot of the Laik and Sir Tristrem, ed. Alan Lupack (1994)

Sir Gawain: Eleven Romances and Tales, ed. Thomas Hahn (1995)

The Middle English Breton Lays, ed. Anne Laskaya and Eve Salisbury (1995)

Sir Perceval of Galles and Ywain and Gawain, ed. Mary Flowers Braswell (1995)

Four Middle English Romances: Sir Isumbras, Octavian, Sir Eglamour of Artois, Sir Tryamour, ed. Harriet Hudson (1996)

The Poems of Laurence Minot (1333–1352), ed. Richard H. Osberg (1996)

Medieval English Political Writings, ed. James M. Dean (1996)

The Book of Margery Kempe, ed. Lynn Staley (1996)

Amis and Amiloun, Robert of Cisyle, and Sir Amadace, ed. Edward E. Foster (1997)

The Cloud of Unknowing, ed. Patrick J. Gallacher (1997)

Robin Hood and Other Outlaw Tales, ed. Stephen Knight and Thomas Ohlgren (1997)

The Poems of Robert Henryson, ed. Robert L. Kindrick (1997)

Moral Love Songs and Laments, ed. Susanna Greer Fein (1998)

John Lydgate, *Troy Book: Selections*, ed. Robert R. Edwards (1998)

Thomas Usk, *The Testament of Love*, ed. R. Allen Shoaf (1998)

Prose Merlin, ed. John Conlee (1998)

Middle English Marian Lyrics, ed. Karen Saupe (1998)

John Metham, *Amoryus and Cleopes*, ed. Stephen F. Page (1999)

Four Romances of England: King Horn, Havelok the Dane, Bevis of Hampton, Athelston, ed. Ronald B. Herzman, Graham Drake, Eve Salisbury (1999)

The Assembly of Gods: Le Assemble de Dyeus, or Banquet of Gods and Goddesses, with the Discourse of Reason and Sensuality, ed. Jane Chance (1999)

Thomas Hoccleve, *The Regiment of Princes*, ed. Charles R. Blyth (1999)

John Capgrave, *The Life of St. Katherine*, ed. Karen Winstead (1999)

John Gower, *Confessio Amantis*, vol. 1, ed. Russell A. Peck (2000)

Other TEAMS Publications

Documents of Practice Series:

Love and Marriage in Late Medieval London, by Shannon McSheffrey (1995)

A Slice of Life: Selected Documents of Medieval English Peasant Experience, edited, translated, and with an introduction by Edwin Brezette DeWindt (1996)

Sources for the History of Medicine in Late Medieval England, by Carole Rawcliffe (1996)

Regular Life: Monastic, Canonical, and Mendicant Rules, selected with an introduction by Douglas J. McMillan and Kathryn Smith Fladenmuller (1997)

Commentary Series:

Commentary and Notes on the Book of Jonah, Haimo of Auxerre, translated with an introduction by Deborah Everhart (1993)

Medieval Exegesis in Translation: Commentaries on the Book of Ruth, translated with an introduction by Lesley Smith (1996)

Nicholas of Lyra's Apocalypse Commentary, translated with an introduction and notes by Philip D. W. Krey (1997)

Rabbi Ezra Ben Solomon of Gerona: Commentary on the Song of Songs and Other Kabbalistic Commentaries, selected, translated, and annotated by Seth Brody (1998)

To order please contact:

MEDIEVAL INSTITUTE PUBLICATIONS
Western Michigan University
Kalamazoo, MI 49008–3801
Phone (616) 387–8755
FAX (616) 387–8750

http://www.wmich.edu/medieval/mip/index.html